Why Do You Need This New Edition?

If you're wondering why you should buy the third edition of *How English Works*, here are 5 great reasons!

- New and updated material on electronically-mediated communication such as texting and the etiquette of Instant Messaging.

- A major new section on literature and speech with tools for reading and analyzing literary works and speech acts.

- A new explanation of where (some) contractions, like *ain't*, fit into English word formation.

- An extended discussion of attitudes about language focusing on the debate between those who believe English is decaying and those who feel language change is natural and should be accepted.

- An improved section on "what makes good writing."

How English Works

A LINGUISTIC INTRODUCTION

Third Edition

Anne Curzan

University of Michigan

Michael Adams

Indiana University

Longman

Boston   Columbus   Indianapolis   New York   San Francisco   Upper Saddle River
Amsterdam   Cape Town   Dubai   London   Madrid   Milan   Munich   Paris   Montreal
Toronto   Delhi   Mexico City   São Paulo   Sydney   Hong Kong   Seoul   Singapore   Taipei   Tokyo

Senior Acquisitions Editor: Vivian Garcia
Executive Marketing Manager: Joyce Nilsen
Senior Supplements Editor: Donna Campion
Production Manager: Denise Phillip
Project Coordination, Text Design, and Electronic Page Makeup: Laserwords
Cover Design Manager: John Callahan
Cover Designer: Nancy Sacks
Photo Researcher: Rona Tuccillo
Senior Manufacturing Buyer: Dennis J. Para
Printer and Binder: R. R. Donnelley & Sons/Harrisonburg
Cover Printer: R. R. Donnelley & Sons/Harrisonburg

For permission to use copyrighted material, grateful acknowledgment is made to the copyright holders on pp. 526-528, which are hereby made part of this copyright page.

Library of Congress Cataloging-in-Publication Data

Curzan, Anne.
    How English works : a linguistic introduction / Anne Curzan, Michael P. Adams. — 3rd ed.
        p. cm.
    Includes bibliographical references and index.
    Previous ed.: 2009.
    ISBN-13: 978-0-205-03228-0
    ISBN-10: 0-205-03228-1
  1. English language—Grammar.   I. Adams, Michael   II. Title.
    PE1106.C876 2011
    420—dc22

                                                                2010050688

1 2 3 4 5 6 7 8 9 10—DOH—14 13 12 11

Longman
is an imprint of

www.pearsonhighered.com

ISBN-13: 978-0-205-03228-0
ISBN-10:   0-205-03228-1

Brief Contents

Detailed Contents

Chapter **5**   **English Syntax: The Grammar of Words   128**

Chapter **6**   # English Syntax: Phrases, Clauses, and Sentences   163

Chapter **11**   # Language Variation   346

Chapter **13**
History of English: Old to Early Modern English   417

List of Symbols, Linguistic Conventions, and Common Abbreviations

Symbols and Conventions[†]

/ /	Phonemic transcription
[ ]	Phonetic transcription
*	In historical linguistics, a reconstructed form for which linguists have no record
*	In syntax, a grammatically unacceptable sentence (in the descriptive sense)
?	In syntax, a grammatically questionable sentence (in the descriptive sense)
+	In syntax, one or more of this constituent can appear
word	Italics are used to refer to a word as a word
'meaning'	Single quotes are used to refer to a word's meaning

[†]For the transcription conventions for spoken conversation, see Exercise 8.7.

Common Abbreviations

AAE	African American English
ADJ	adjective
ADJP	adjective phrase
ADV	adverb
ADVP	adverb phrase
ASL	American Sign Language
C	consonant (in phonology)
C	complement (in syntax)
COCA	Corpus of Contemporary American English
CONJ	conjunction
DET	determiner
EMdE	Early Modern English
ESL	English as a Second Language
IPA	International Phonetic Alphabet
ME	Middle English
MICASE	Michigan Corpus of Academic Spoken English
N	noun
NP	noun phrase
O	object
OE	Old English
OED	*Oxford English Dictionary*
P	preposition
PDE	Present-Day English
PP	prepositional phrase
PRED	predicative
PRO	pronoun
RP	Received Pronunciation
S	sentence (in syntax)
S	subject (in syntax)
V	vowel (in phonology)
V	verb (in syntax)
VP	verb phrase

Preface to Instructors

How English Works: A Linguistic Introduction has proven to be a highly successful introductory language/linguistics textbook designed specially for English and education majors. This engaging, accessible textbook provides extensive coverage of issues of particular interest to English majors and future English instructors, and it invites all students to connect academic linguistics to the everyday use of the English language.

One of the principal challenges of an introductory course in English linguistics is helping students see the material as relevant to their professional and personal lives. Linguistics textbooks often present technical linguistics as if it were disconnected from what students already know about language. Our goal with this book is to encourage students to connect academic linguistics to the everyday use of the English language around them, as well as to relevant social and educational questions. We provide students with the tools to make these connections to explore their own questions about English, to understand more fully the language they see and hear every day. The book also shows students how English and the study of English are dynamic: it engages students with ongoing changes in English, new insights in linguistics, and problems that remain to be solved. Students thereby become active participants in the construction of linguistic knowledge. And the book emphasizes for students why the study of English matters—not only for them as students but also for them as parents, teachers, and citizens.

For example, students take a narrative walk among dialect areas in order to discover how subtle shifts in vocabulary and pronunciation—and attitudes about them—are related to isoglosses on maps. They see how the world of computer technology has employed natural word-formation processes to create most of the needed high-tech vocabulary (e.g., *blog, cyberspace, to google*). They encounter the origins of prescriptive usage rules and see their relationship to descriptive grammar. They explore the integral role of indirect speech acts in dating rituals. They learn why some speakers are more fluently bilingual than others and have the opportunity to consider the implications for educational policy.

Thus, in *How English Works* we apply the premise that by moving away from a more esoteric study of language and by making connections between the study of linguistics and the everyday use of language, students will:

- be more interested in and care more about the material because it is relevant to their lives outside the classroom;
- learn the material more effectively because they can integrate it with what they already know; and
- apply and use the information beyond the class, and talk about the material with others.

Organization

How English Works: A Linguistic Introduction covers topics at the core of linguistics (e.g., syntax, phonology, discourse analysis, language variation), complemented by related topics particularly relevant to English majors and future English teachers (e.g., language attitudes and authority, bilingual and bidialectal education, the history of English spelling and prescriptive usage rules). You might visualize the book's organizational structure as a progression inside a frame.

The first two chapters frame the book by introducing the foundations of systematic language study and addressing some of the prior understandings that students may have, both about the nature of language and about sources of language authority.

The central ten chapters (Chapters 3–12) progress "up" through the levels of language structure, and the units of analysis at each level serve as building blocks for the next. For example, sounds combine to make words, which combine to make sentences. Sentences in combination can be analyzed as text or discourse. All of this information can be analyzed as the linguistic and communicative competence of a speaker; speakers together create speech communities, which generate language variation.

The final two chapters focus on language change. Chapters 13 and 14 provide an historical context in which to consider the preceding ten chapters on the structure of Modern English. These two chapters describe the history of English: how English looked before and how it may look after this particular historical moment.

The third edition continues to create strong connections among chapters. For example, it employs the distinction between form and function to explain syntax at the level of the word (Chapter 5) and at the level of the clause/sentence (Chapter 6); it integrates more explicitly the discussion of semantics (Chapter 7) with syntax (Chapters 5 and 6) and pragmatics (Chapter 8); it shows how speech acts (Chapter 8) help us understand and analyze literature (Chapter 9).

The chapters can be reordered and some might be omitted, depending on how instructors choose to organize the course.

New to This Edition

The third edition of *How English Works* includes new material on recent research findings, for example on the effects of texting on written English, on the origins of the "rule" about splitting infinitives, on differences between expert and novice academic writing, and on the relationship of language and thought. The examples of language change in progress and current slang have also been updated throughout the text—although we know that, especially with slang, the language will always be ahead of any book, and we forever risk being unhip in describing any slang as "current." But such is the nature of language!

Below are some of the key features of each chapter and the most significant revisions in the third edition:

- What makes human language unique? Chapter 1 ("A Language Like English") situates English with respect to the definition of language and the development of languages to capture what makes English, as a human language, unique and worthy of detailed study. It includes detailed material on animal communication and a more extended discussion of attitudes about language change. The new edition includes an opportunity for students to reframe their own pet peeves about language in the context of new information about language variation and change.

- Why did the punctuation guide *Eats, Shoots & Leaves* become a best seller? Chapter 2 ("Language and Authority") tackles the concept of "rules" and language authority, providing students with critical background on traditional sources of language authority such as dictionaries and grammar books. The third edition contains a nuanced treatment of the definition of Standard English that addresses the relationship of dialect and register, particularly formality.

- How does a stream of continuous sounds become words in our brains? Chapter 3 ("English Phonology") not only explains the fundamental concepts of the English sound system but also connects this material to dialect variation, sound change, and English spelling. The new edition includes an additional exercise on reading phonetic transcription.

- How do we make up new slang? Chapter 4 ("English Morphology") covers important morphological categories, and it explains how frequency, systematicity, and creativity play into the stability of parts of the lexicon and the striking creativity that accounts for slang, new technical terms, and the annual Words of the Year (all updated in the third edition). The third edition features a new box on clitics in English.

- What does it mean that all speakers "know grammar"? Chapters 5 ("English Syntax: The Grammar of Words") and 6 ("English Syntax: Phrases, Clauses, and Sentences"), in recognition of the challenge grammar poses to many students, provide extended coverage to parts of speech before discussing the structure of phrases and clauses; the chapters also discuss the origins of prescriptive usage rules in relation to descriptive grammar. Examples in both chapters include both standard and nonstandard varieties of English.

- How do we all agree on what *dog* means? Chapter 7 ("Semantics") connects technical semantics to more philosophical approaches to meaning and to issues such as politically correct language, the relationship of language and thought, and the sensical nonsense of "Jabberwocky."

- Dude, what is going on with *dude*? Chapter 8 ("Spoken Discourse") explains how conversations work, from implied meanings to turn-taking to those "meaningless" words like *like*, *you know*, and *dude*; it also provides students the tools to pursue their own (critical) discourse analysis of spoken text. The third edition provides an improved discussion of performative speech acts and felicity conditions.

- Can linguistics really help us "close read" better? Chapter 9 ("Stylistics") provides students with an extensive set of tools and frameworks for detailed linguistic analysis of written text, both literary and nonliterary. The third edition includes new sections on speech acts and literature, which show students how they can exploit what they learned in Chapter 8 to analyze literature. The special focus on what makes good writing has also been significantly revised to include corpus-based studies that compare expert and novice academic writing.

- How do kids learn language so easily while their parents struggle? Chapter 10 ("Language Acquisition") covers not only the stages of children's language acquisition but also the implications of cognitive linguistic research for language education. In addition, the chapter includes recent research on language learning for speakers in isolation and speakers with brain damage.

- Why don't all speakers of English sound the same? Chapter 11 ("Language Variation") gives students a general framework for thinking about a range of sociolinguistic factors (e.g., gender, age, race and ethnicity, class, region) in the study of language variation. The third edition provides a more streamlined discussion of sociolinguistic methodologies. Chapter 12 ("American Dialects") then focuses specifically on the history and present status of dialect variation in the United States, including the implications for language attitudes and education. Case studies of regional and social variation in the United States include Appalachian English, California English, African American English, and Chicano English.

- Just how much has English changed? Chapters 13 ("History of English: Old to Early Modern English") and 14 ("History of English: Modern and Future English") provide an overview of major linguistic events in the history of the English language, with a final section that examines the future status of English as a world language and the implications of electronically mediated communication, from e-mail to Instant Messenger to texting. Will emoticons and acronyms take over the written language? What will English of the twenty-fifth century look like? A new exercise allows students to investigate the etiquette of Instant Messaging.

Pedagogical Approach

The pedagogical approach used in *How English Works* reflects our respect for students' ability to contribute new knowledge to ongoing conversations about language, which involves acknowledging where linguistic knowledge comes from and posing questions for students that will help them participate in the conversation. Throughout the text we use the following pedagogical tools to help students see English linguistics as relevant to their lives, concerns, and curiosities:

- *Chapter Opener Vignettes*: Each chapter begins with an engaging scenario that opens the door for students to make the material relevant to their own experience.

- *Special Interest Boxes*: In the special interest boxes, we use questions and facts about English as a way to make connections to students' experience with actual language in use and to introduce more technical material.

Discussion boxes pose provocative questions that instructors can use as prompts for in-class discussion or for short written assignments.

Language Change at Work and Language Variation at Work boxes show students how the technical material connects to diversity and change in English.

Language Acquisition at Work boxes provide students with insights about the relationship between language acquisition and, for example, facial imitation and hand gestures.

Scholar profile boxes introduce students to major figures in the field and help students put faces and histories to theories and facts.

- *End-of-Chapter Exercises*: Exercises at the end of each chapter cover the range of the material, sometimes asking students to apply this information to discrete problems and sometimes asking students to go out into the world, collect information (e.g., from observation or interviews), and analyze it in relation to the information presented in the chapter.

- *Figures and Photos*: Throughout the book, figures and photos liven the text, providing not only visual representations of information presented in the prose but also memorable images, from Panbanisha communicating with her keyboard to Andrew Meltzoff's imitation experiments to a T-shirt advertising /r/-less pronunciations in Boston.

- *Tone*: The book presents a host of current examples, from modern slang to current popular culture, and is written in a narrative, colloquial style that draws students into the interest of the material without simplifying it.

- *Glossary*: The extensive glossary provides not only clear, concise definitions, but also examples whenever possible and critical cross-references to other terms, so that students can use it to study material as well as to look up terms about which they are unsure.

Instructor's Manual

The Instructor's Manual (0-205-03231-1/978-0-205-03231-0) provides practical, tried-and-true advice and class activities for the material in each chapter. For each chapter, we provide learning objectives and an explicit statement of where students may find challenges with the material and where they will be particularly engaged. We then detail specific in-class and out-of-class activities that instructors can use to review and complement material provided in the book with related exercises and information (e.g., events from the news, data collected by students, material on the Web). We specify for each chapter which discussion boxes and which homework problems can be used effectively for classroom activities. We also provide additional resources, such as helpful Web sites and reference books.

The manual provides full answer keys for the relevant exercises in each chapter in a form that instructors can copy should they want to provide answer keys to students.

Acknowledgments

We cannot possibly thank here all the many people who have helped and supported us at every step of the process of writing this book and then revising it for this third edition, but to all of you, please know that we are grateful beyond words. We would like to start by acknowledging our students, who have taught us much of what we know about how to teach this material successfully and who have shown us how to hone the book for the third edition. We are especially grateful to Bethany Davila, James Beitler, Katie Glupker, Jessica Grieser, Stephanie LaGrasso, Zak Lancaster, Lauren Puccio, Joseph Ruple, and Amber Shewalter for their notable contributions. In addition, we have had many wonderful colleagues who have generously shared their material, experiences, and advice over the years and who, we hope, will be pleased to see all the ways that it has shaped this book. We would like to thank specifically: Richard W. Bailey, Alicia Beckford Wassink, George Dillon, Kimberly Emmons, Robin Queen, Gail Stygall, Thomas E. Toon, and Walt Wolfram.

To the many instructors from around the United States and around the world who have shared their feedback on the first and second editions, we want to extend our appreciation; we hope our revisions respond effectively to your very helpful questions and suggestions.

This book has also benefited enormously from the detailed, constructive critiques and suggestions from numerous reviewers, including:

Rebecca Day Babcock, University of Texas–Permian Basin

Richard W. Bailey, University of Michigan

Dennis Baron, University of Illinois–Urbana

Naomi S. Baron, American University

Rusty Barrett, University of Kentucky

Mary Bucholtz, University of California–Santa Barbara

Neal Bruss, University of Massachusetts at Boston

Mark Canada, University of North Carolina–Pembroke

Andrew Carnie, University of Arizona

Sarah K. Crowder, University of North Texas

Deborah Crusan, Wright State University

Anthony DeFazio, New York University

Dorothy Disterheft, University of South Carolina

Andrew Elfenbein, University of Minnesota

Carmen Fought, Pitzer College, Claremont Colleges

Therese Gallegos, University of Texas at Brownsville

Joseph Galasso, California State University–Fullerton

Shadi Ganjavi, Mount Saint Mary's College

Barbara Gleason, City College of New York, City University of New York

Arthur Wayne Glowka, Georgia College and State University

Matthew Gordon, University of Missouri–Columbia

Michael Hancher, University of Minnesota–Twin Cities

Karon Harden, University of Kentucky

Kirk Hazen, West Virginia University

Michael Hegarty, Louisiana State University

Eric Hyman, Fayetteville State University

Paul A. Johnston Jr., Western Michigan University

Barbara Johnstone, Carnegie Mellon University

Susan Major, Croft Institute, University of Mississippi

Alice Moorehead, University of Minnesota–St. Paul

Karen Mullen, University of Louisville

Dana Nichols, Gainesville State College

Iyabo F. Osiapem, The College of William and Mary

Christen M. Pearson, Grand Valley State University

Alison Rukeyser, University of California–Davis; California State
University–Sacramento

Aaron Huey Sonnenschein, California State University–Northridge; California
State University–Los Angeles

William Spruiell, Central Michigan University

Glenn A. Steinberg, College of New Jersey

Erik Thomas, North Carolina State University

Rachelle Waksler, San Francisco State University

Anja Wanner, University of Wisconsin–Madison

Kathleen Martha Ward, University of California–Davis

Rebecca Wheeler, Christopher Newport University

Many thanks for the time and thoughtfulness that these reviewers put into their responses.

For their endless encouragement, support, and patience throughout our writing process, we send heaps of gratitude and love to our families, and in particular to Jennifer Westerhaus Adams and Mary Curzan, who now know the prose of the book inside and out. And, finally, our heartfelt thanks to Erika Berg, our editor for the first edition, Matthew Wright, the editor who successfully guided the second edition, and Vivian Garcia who led us through the third; Barbara Conover, who edited our prose carefully for the first and second editions; Haley Pero, who so effectively kept the entire process of making the first and second editions coordinated and efficient; and Heather N. Vomero, who has been equally effective in coordinating the third. Any errors that remain in the text are our own.

Anne Curzan

Michael Adams

Letter to Students

Dear Students:

Do you use *friend* as a verb? Can you use *Coke* to refer to all pop/soda? Did you realize these are questions we legitimately ask in English linguistics? As you read *How English Works,* you will have the chance to connect more technical linguistic information to your own daily experience with language, whether it is slang or American dialects or blogging or writing a formal essay or watching a child learn language.

Please join in …

The linguistic study of the English language continues to evolve from conversations among scholars. There remain complex questions to be answered. And you can be an active participant in the conversation about the English language. You have the ability to make new and interesting observations about the English language that inform the questions raised throughout the book, and we hope you will do so.

But first …

In this book, we question and probe every part of language. Along the way, the book is going to ask you to question some of your commonsense beliefs about language. As native speakers of language, we all come to the study of language with strong prior understandings, some of which are accurate and some of which are not. Sometimes it can be difficult to accept the findings of linguists, particularly if these findings, presented as "facts" about language, run counter to what we think we already know about language.

For example, here are a few questions about English that may or may not challenge what you've heard or thought about the language: Did you know the English language is always changing? This does not mean (no matter what you have been told!) that it is being ruined by "lazy" or "sloppy" speakers. Nor does it mean that it is improving as speakers become ever more technologically sophisticated. But how could the rules of "standard written English" have changed so much over time that, for example, the double negative (e.g., *I can't give no more*) used to be standard? And if the contraction *ain't* is just as old and logical and grammatical as other English contractions such as *won't* and *can't*, then why do some speakers consider it "wrong"? As you'll discover, "right" and "wrong" are very complicated concepts when it comes to language use.

We encourage you to think about, question, argue, and try to make sense of these and similar concepts that you will meet throughout the book. After you finish reading *How English Works*, we hope that you may exclaim, as have some of our past students: "It's so distracting: I just can't stop noticing language everywhere I go!"

We have enjoyed writing this book. We hope you enjoy reading it.

Anne Curzan and Michael Adams

Chapter 1

A Language Like English

The sixth line of this excerpt from "The Physician's Tale" illustrates Chaucer's occasional use of *axe* for *ask* in *The Canterbury Tales*. Surprised? Turn the page to read more about the history of *ask/aks*.

Every day we use things whose inner workings we do not fully understand: the toaster, the washing machine, the laptop computer, the gas pump, a lightbulb, the English language.

Wait a minute, you might say: *the English language* is not a machine like the others.

True. English is clearly not a machine. And English, like any other language, was not "invented," like these other everyday objects. But the English language is systematically structured, much like these other everyday objects. It follows predictable rules and patterns. There may even be a blueprint, but that's a complicated question that we'll return to later in the text. The point is that English is a complex, rule-governed system that we use every day without having to think about its intricacies. For example, do we consciously group sounds together to make a word or methodically think through word order to make a grammatical sentence? Do we wonder how the words *I am sorry* uttered together function as an apology? And when do we ever reflect on how we learned to use language in the first place?

This book provides you with the tools to think about how English works. If you were to take apart your watch, you would need the appropriate tools to pull out each part. If you ever wanted to reassemble the watch, you would need not only these tools but also an understanding of how each part functions. You would need to understand the broader framework of how each part relates to the whole. Here, we will open up English like a machine to be taken apart, and we will provide you with the analytical tools and the conceptual framework with which to understand it.

Each chapter of this text equips you to poke around, explore, and analyze an aspect of the English language. As you see how each aspect of English works, you will increase your understanding of how the language as a whole works. You will also understand how the English language got to be the way it is.

If you are reading this book, English is clearly one of the languages you control. For many of you, it is probably your native language and the language in which you work, live, and play. We use the language so much, we hardly notice it—like a light-bulb, we tend to take it for granted. Language can seem mundane because we learn it as children and use it every day without having to think consciously about it. In fact, one of the fundamental properties of spoken (or signed) human language is that we learn it without explicit instruction as long as we are exposed to it. Like a lightbulb, language can seem simple. But also like a lightbulb, there is much more to language than meets the eye, or the ear, as the case may be. Language is an enormously complex system, and it enables humans to communicate about everything under and including the sun.

Every chapter of this book begins with a story about the English language at work around you. Often the examples come from everyday experiences with language that you may have noticed but not thought too much about. Once you do start thinking about these examples, they will open up questions about how we use language, how a language changes, and how our attitudes about language are shaped. Each chapter then provides you with answers to many of these questions, as well as tools to pursue further questions of your own. So here's our first story.

The Story of Aks

In January 2007, an anonymous employee in New York wrote to Randy Cohen, the ethicist for the *New York Times*, with a question about *aks*. The employee was to screen candidates for a job that required extensive phone interaction with high-end, "snobbish" clients, and the employee's boss had instructed, "Don't bring in anyone who wants to 'ax' you a question." The employee worried that the boss, normally supportive of equal opportunity, was being racist in this prejudice against *aks*.

What is it about this word? This one word alone, as the boss's instructions make clear, seems to be enough for many Americans to judge a speaker as igno-rant, unintelligent, uneducated, or in some other way not worthy of an oppor-tunity. The people who complain about *aks* often assume that it would be both easy and appropriate to substitute *ask* for *aks*. At this moment in history, a lot of negative social attitudes about speakers are heaped on one little word, but this has not always been the case.

The pronunciation of *ask* as *aks* is an example of **metathesis**, a systematic process of sound change that you will read more about in Chapter 3. Metathe-sis involves the reversal, or switching places, of two sounds. For example, the

Modern English word *bird* used to be *brid*. The Modern English verb *ask* can be traced back to the Old English verb *ācsian*, the form used throughout England through the eighth century. So in the early Old English verb, the sound /k/ occurs before /s/. During the ninth century, the metathetic form *āscian* (with the sounds reversed) appeared, the sound /s/ moving before /k/. This new form is the ancestor of Modern English *ask*, and it gradually replaced the earlier form for most speakers, although this process took several centuries. In other words, *ācsian* is the older form; *āscian* is the newer form. And back in Anglo-Saxon England, many who witnessed the variation may have wondered why some people "just couldn't learn to speak correctly."

The English poet Chaucer, writing in the last quarter of the fourteenth century, used *ask* and *aks* (or *axe*) interchangeably. And though Standard English, as it developed, codified *ask* as the "standard," folks throughout England employed the archaic form well into the twentieth century. Noah Webster, in *Dissertations on the English Language* (1789), reported that *ax* was common in New England—brought to America by English settlers. By 1953, E. Bagby Atwood noted in *A Survey of Verb Forms in the Eastern United States* that *aks/ax* no longer occurred north of the Mason-Dixon line. Once widely spoken in America, *aks* had become regarded as a Southernism—even though speakers throughout the United States can be heard using it. As African Americans migrated from the South, they carried *aks* with them, and today enough African Americans employ it, regardless of where they live, that it also counts as a feature of African American English.

All living languages change over time, and all show variation, such as *ask* and *aks*. Just because a current form was common in English 1,500 years ago doesn't mean that we should use it today or think it is somehow better—and clearly in the case of *aks*, age has not given this form authority. But given these details about the history of *aks*, it is difficult to insist that *aks* is somehow wrong or inferior. It is a systematic variant of *ask*. From one perspective, the present is merely a continuation of the past, and much nonstandard American English is older than the innovations now considered "standard."

This story may shake up some things that you thought you knew about language, such as that *aks* is just wrong or bad English. Clearly, many English speakers do not think of the words *ask* and *aks* as equals. But in the structural system of the English language, *ask* and *aks* are linguistically equal ways to refer to the act of posing a question, and they are related historically to each other.

This chapter explores how sets of sounds, such as *ask* and *aks*, are associated with particular meanings that we all agree on. It is arbitrary that the string of sounds in *ask* or *aks* refers to posing a question, but it is critical to the system of language that we all accept this arbitrary relationship and use the words accordingly. After all, if you were to use *ask* to mean 'to pose a question' and we were to use it to mean 'porcupine', then arbitrariness would have gotten the better of the system. In this chapter, we also discuss what makes this kind of language system uniquely human—why porcupines and bees and dolphins and even chimpanzees don't use words like *ask* or *aks*, let alone use words to debate correct and incorrect usage.

Language, Language Everywhere

Language inundates us, and every one of us is not only inundated but an inundator. Few of us wake up to silence; most of us groan out of our sleep to the jarring noise of the morning radio blaring from our alarm clocks. Whether in our kitchens at home or in the cafeteria at school, many of us eat a rushed breakfast (if we eat breakfast at all!) between sleepy conversations about the day ahead and a rushed glance through the morning paper. Sometimes the television drones in the background. Once at school, the flood of language continues: lectures, classroom discussions, campus meetings— during all of which we may not only listen but also have much to say. Who doesn't also steal snatches of the day to send text messages or surf the Internet? Even a serious workout at the gym can entail language, for example, if we're flirting with someone on the next machine—although, in this case, body language may matter even more than speech. On top of racking up cell minutes talking and texting, there's always homework: reading, reading, reading . . . writing, writing, writing. And then you sleep, so that your body and mind are sufficiently rested to survive another arduous linguistic day.

Where in life doesn't language act its part? In what human medium do we gain more, learn more, express more, play more, or live more? Language composes, though not exclusively, what we are as a species and who we are as individuals in society. Birds sing and bees dance to communicate, but they don't use language creatively in the way that humans do. Animals (other than humans) don't argue about meaning and look words up in dictionaries. Most animal communication is unambiguous. When an oriole calls out an alarm, for example, all the orioles in the neighborhood, and a number of other animals as well, flee, whether or not they are actually threatened by a predator. So if a nearsighted oriole mistakenly warns of a predator day after day, the other orioles will fly away nonetheless. Animals are not held accountable for their communication, but humans are—another reason for us to study and use language carefully.

Language is a kind of work by which we accomplish things. Language is also a kind of social link: we use it to establish and maintain our networks of friends and acquaintances. Language is also, importantly, play. We read novels and poetry, attend performances of Shakespeare, or sing along with fellow groupies at a rock concert. We play with language itself, for example by making bad puns and laughing at them despite ourselves (e.g., "The show *Queer Eye for the Straight Guy* is driving straight men into their closets"). Maybe we do the daily crossword puzzle or play along with reruns of *Wheel of Fortune*. Sometimes, language serves a concrete purpose; sometimes, it defines us as social beings; sometimes, it elevates the spirit or provokes thought; sometimes, it's just plain fun. Most of the time, it's a combination of purposes, sociability, learning, and play. Can you imagine anything that deserves our careful consideration more than language?

The Power of Language

The common saying "Sticks and stones may break my bones, but words will never hurt me" is not, in fact, true. Words can, and do, hurt—not only those we speak to, but also ourselves, as we are judged by the language we use. Words have the power to hurt and heal, inform and misinform, reveal and hide. Words can create and destroy the social connections critical to our lives.

Name Calling

We all recognize names as powerful. For example, many of us feel we own the words in our names in a way different from other words, and we grant only certain people permission to use some versions. If your name is Katherine, it may feel disrespectful or off-putting if people other than your friends and family call you Kate, let alone Katie. If they rename you without your permission, they may be asserting a *right* to do so: sometimes nicknaming is a matter of affection; sometimes it is all about power. Yet, in other circumstances, you may well say "Call me Kate," to create a more intimate social connection. Names alone have the power to do that.

Sometimes words have such religious or mystical power that speakers will not utter them. Judaism, for example, prohibits the use of God's real name (substituting *Yahweh, Adonai,* or *Eloim,* instead). Even today, many Jews who write English prefer *G-d* to *God* for this reason. And Judaism is not alone in fearing the power of God's name: *by golly* (originally African American) is a euphemism for *by God,* and *gosh* is a similar evasion. Use God's name, the theory goes, and you will call down God's wrath. The characters in the Harry Potter books refrain from uttering Voldemort's name and refer to him as "he who must not be named." As the Harry Potter stories remind us, magic, too, endows words with power, in spells, charms, and curses, and these words eventually become taboo: utter certain words and you can animate the forces of nature to create (as in a love charm) or destroy (as in a curse).

Speakers hesitate to utter other words because they have the power to offend. Some speakers don't use "bad words," and from a very young age, children raised in no-bad-words households quickly figure out that there is something powerful about these words—they still try out the words, but they do so knowing that they are putting themselves at risk. Some speakers refer to the "F-word," the "C-word," or the "N-word" because these words seem too offensive or too risky to utter aloud, even though the audience knows exactly which words the speaker means. Some of these words are banned from (or bleeped out of) network television and radio, and their use by public figures can be considered news in and of itself, as when a live microphone caught Vice President Joe Biden say to President Obama "This is a big fucking deal" after the passage of the health care reform bill in 2010.

Although some of our beliefs about the magic of language may have shifted, our sense of its power remains. For example, superstitions persist that make us "knock on wood" when we say things, for fear that the words will affect future events. Our sense of linguistic appropriateness means that we avoid some words for others in order to respect, for example, the deceased (rather than "the dead") or women (rather than "girls" or "chicks"). In all these ways, we recognize the power of words; we recognize that it is not "just language," because the consequences of language use are very real.

Judging by Ear

As soon as you begin speaking to another person, that person, often without even being aware of it, starts to judge you based on your speech—not only what you say, but how you say it. Where are you from originally? Are you a native speaker of English? How educated are you? With what social groups do you identify?

In any given speech situation, each of us makes choices, usually subconsciously, about how we present ourselves linguistically. For example, do you want to sound like a well-educated applicant in a job interview? If so, you may decide to speak more formally than you would if you were with your friends. If you control more than one dialect of English, you may use primarily features of one of those dialects to express your affiliation with that speech community. Do you want, for instance, to mark your membership in the Southern speech community or the New York speech community? We shape our identities and how others perceive us through our speech—it is an important part of how we negotiate our social worlds.

Is it fair to judge others based on how they speak? We can often legitimately tell many things about people from how they talk—often things that they want us to know. But we can also make very unfair judgments about people based on their speech, and it is important to be aware of those leaps from linguistic features to stereotypes or unjustified beliefs associated with those features. For example, it is not fair to judge speakers of nonstandard dialects as less intelligent or less educated. Schools may teach Standard English, but many bidialectal speakers who control Standard English do not choose to use it in all situations. So it is unfair to judge a speaker who uses *aks* as inferior in some way. It is equally unfair to assume that a speaker who uses Standard English is inherently more qualified for a given job.

In her book *English with an Accent* (1997), Rosina Lippi-Green describes language as the last back door to discrimination in the United States. She argues that we make judgments about people and discriminate for or against them based on their language. We know we should not judge people based on their race, ethnicity, or gender, but we often do judge others by their speech. Yet Lippi-Green notes that the language we learn as children is a fundamental part of our identity and not something that we can, or necessarily want to, give up to conform to the Standard-English-speaking world in all situations. We cannot change our language like we change our clothes. It's not an equivalent demand to insist that speakers should "just" substitute *ask* for *aks* or "put on" Standard English as they should put on a suit for a job interview.

Humans size each other up whenever they meet, evaluating each other's clothes, haircut, demeanor, language, and much more. The power of language to express identity is critical to its effective functioning in a speech community. At the same time, we must be aware of unwarranted leaps we may be making when a linguistic feature leads us to judge a speaker's character or competence.

A Question to Discuss

What Makes Us Hear an Accent?

Our brains are tricky when it comes to accents. If we hear someone speaking differently from us, perhaps in a way that we can identify with a particular social group or geographic region, we can jump to conclusions about that person. On the flip side of the coin: if we already know something about someone (e.g., where the person is from or the person's race or ethnicity), we can sometimes hear an accent in ways we otherwise might not.

One study examined the relationship between undergraduate students' expectations and what they "heard" in an instructor's lecture (Rubin 1992, described in Lippi-Green 1997). Sixty-two undergraduates listened to one of two prerecorded, four-minute lectures, on a topic either in the sciences or in the humanities. The voice on the tapes was of a native speaker of English from central Ohio. Before listening to a tape, students were shown one of two pictures of "the lecturer": one of a Caucasian woman and one of an Asian woman, who were photographed in similar settings with similar hairstyles, clothes, and other aspects of outward appearance. All of the students listened to the same voice, but students who believed the Asian woman was the speaker were more likely to rate the speaker as having an accent. These students also scored lower on the comprehension test given after the mini-lecture than those who believed that they were listening to a Caucasian woman. So students' expectations or preconceptions of how a lecturer might talk, given the person's appearance, seem to have the power not only to create "imaginary accents" but also to set up learning obstacles. In this case, the students convinced themselves that the lecturer's accent was confusing.

If you have taken courses from instructors who spoke with unfamiliar accents, does this study make you reflect differently on that experience? How much responsibility do you think that students should take for understanding an instructor who is highly trained in his or her academic field and may speak English with an unfamiliar accent? In other words, how do you think the "communicative burden" should be split between the instructor and the students?

The System of Language

"Birds do it, bees do it," sang Cole Porter, and certainly human beings do it. We all communicate (and perhaps fall in love, but that is a different matter—although definitely related to communication). But just how far do the similarities among animal species go? In the most general sense of the term *language*, we could argue that many animal species—birds, bees, dolphins, and chimps, as well as humans—communicate by means of sound or patterned movement. The oriole's alarm call can warn other birds of danger, and bee dances can communicate important information about the location of pollen. Human language differs significantly from bird song and bee dance, however. Human language is, in fact, one of the defining features of being human. So we need a more specific definition.

With the caveat that defining human language is a very difficult task, and with the knowledge that defining language is clearly central to this book, we start with a basic definition of human language:

> Human language is a conventional system of signs that allows for the creative communication of meaning.

Now let's unpack that definition:

- *Conventional:* There is, for the most part, no direct relationship between linguistic elements such as words and the meanings they represent. Instead, the meaning of linguistic signs rests on conventional understandings—that is, the understandings that are shared by a community of speakers (see the discussion of the linguistic sign below). For example, English speakers all use the string of sounds in "English" to refer to the language in which we are writing this book—although if we all agreed to it, the string could just as well be "Lisheng" instead.

- *System:* The organization of language is rule governed. These rules apply to the way linguistic elements are related to each other and the way they combine to create meaning. In other words, we cannot combine words any which way in a sentence (e.g., *which a any in sentence way*) but must instead follow specific word-order rules. And if, for example, we want to make a noun plural, we follow a systematic rule for doing so.

- *Creative communication of meaning:* Language allows speakers to create new utterances to convey new meanings as needed, both about the world around them and about abstract ideas, including about language itself.

Some scholars argue that human language is an evolutionary adaptation, like opposable thumbs and upright locomotion, and other scholars disagree. It is certainly an intellectual and expressive faculty that leads to art and to e-mail, even to our capacity for self-reflection. Human cultural history is thus partly linguistic history, and current culture is inextricably tied to language. We cannot fully understand human behavior or human achievement without understanding language. (Throughout the rest of the book, we often use the term *language* as shorthand for 'human language'.)

Arbitrariness and Systematicity

Most Americans recognize the "thumbs up" sign as an indication of approval. There is, of course, nothing inherent in that gesture that means 'good job'. In fact, putting up your third finger, rather than your thumb, means something radically different. The key point here is that these gestures carry meaning through social convention.

Human language also depends on convention. A set of sounds (or hand gestures in the case of signed languages) carries a particular meaning because a community of speakers agrees that it does. The relationship of those sounds to a given meaning depends on that agreement—not on any meaning inherent to those sounds. This definition of language can be traced back to Ferdinand de Saussure, a Swiss linguist working at the beginning of the twentieth century, who proposed the following formulation:

$$\text{Signifier} + \text{Signified} = \text{Sign}$$

The **signifier** is the linguistic form (the string of sounds), and the **signified** is the concept to which the signifier refers (be that a real-world object or an abstract idea). Together, the relationship of the signifier and the signified create the **linguistic sign**—what we might think of as a meaningful word. So, for example, the sequence of sounds in "dog" and the concept of the four-legged canine creature together create the linguistic sign we think of as *dog*. Or the sequence of sounds in "ask" or "aks" and the concept of requesting information or posing a question together create the linguistic sign *ask* or *aks*.

Saussure made the critical observation that, with a few exceptions, the relationship between the signifier and the signified is arbitrary. There is no direct relationship between the sound of the word (e.g., the sounds in *dog*) and its meaning (e.g., 'four-legged canine creature'). One of the clearest pieces of evidence for the arbitrariness of the linguistic sign is that different languages employ different strings of sound to refer to the same concept—or, in the case of *ask/aks*, two different strings of sound in the same language refer to the same concept. The obvious exception to the arbitrariness principle is onomatopoetic words, such as *slush* or *plop*, but these words are a very small subset of the lexicon. Sounds we conventionally ascribe to animals do not correspond exactly to real-world sounds animals make: for instance, dogs say "woof" or "bow wow" in English but "woah-woah" in French and "wang-wang" in Chinese.

Although the relationship of the signifier and signified is arbitrary, the relationship of linguistic signs to each other, Saussure argued, is systematic. The meaning of a linguistic sign is related to and in some ways determined by the meaning of the other signs in the system. Saussure drew an analogy to chess: the role of each piece and its movement has meaning only in relation to the other pieces. This system of interrelated signs, which makes up language, is what Saussure called *langue*. He proposed a fundamental distinction between **langue** and **parole**, concepts that we refer to with their French

A Scholar to Know

Ferdinand de Saussure (1857–1913)

Ferdinand de Saussure, a Swiss linguist whose ideas have shaped modern linguistics, didn't actually write his best-known work, *Course in General Linguistics*, which details the material summarized here. Former students at the University of Geneva compiled his lecture notes after his death. The lectures span three courses on general linguistics between 1907 and 1911 and capture Saussure's theories about language and his proposed direction for the field now called linguistics. Saussure broke from traditional historical approaches to language (and, therefore, his own training), and his own approach was therefore radical.

He did not publish this important work before he died, though he was clearly preparing to publish a book somewhat different from the one for which he is famous. In 1996, unpublished manuscripts in his hand were discovered, and a new edition of Saussure's great work has since been published (Saussure 2006). We are glad, though, that we didn't have to wait until the twenty-first century for his basic argument. So take good notes in class, because you never know if your instructor might turn out to be the next Ferdinand de Saussure.

terms because there are no perfect English translations. *Langue* refers to the underlying abstract system of a language—the signs and their relationships to one another both in the lexicon and combined into sentences; *parole* refers to the actual speech that speakers produce, based on this system. Saussure was interested in studying the abstract system, not in documenting speech.

Noam Chomsky, probably the most influential linguist of the twentieth century, has proposed a different way to understand "the systematicity of language." He argues that linguists should focus on the systematic knowledge of language in the mind of the ideal, native speaker. Chomsky's approach distinguishes between **linguistic competence** and **linguistic performance**. Linguistic competence refers to a speaker's knowledge of the grammatical rules that govern his or her language; linguistic performance is a speaker's realization of these rules in his or her speech. As we all know, performance can be imperfect: we stumble over words, make speech errors, and speak in incomplete sentences. Performance also varies: speakers in various parts of America use different words for the same thing or pronounce the same word differently. But our competence is stable; it is an innate human faculty. Chomsky and the school of "generative linguistics" that he founded are interested in examining linguistic competence—the mental rules that explain our ability to construct grammatical utterances. One core principle of this approach is that a language's grammar allows the creation of an infinite number of grammatical utterances from a finite number of elements. Linguists try to describe the underlying rules that make such creativity possible. (You will read more about Chomsky and generative grammar in Chapter 6.)

Sociolinguists, who study the use of language in society, argue that language variation within speech communities is also systematic or structured. One fundamental principle of sociolinguistics is that language variation, far from being random, corresponds to relevant social variables such as socioeconomic status, race and ethnicity, gender, and other components of speakers' social identities. Speakers use language to perform identity and create discourse communities in systematic ways. If linguists consider social factors, they can account for many patterns of language variation. In other words, the performance of language in speech communities is patterned, and performance can and should be, sociolinguists argue, a central focus of linguistic study.

Linguistic competence can also be understood to encompass speakers' knowledge about discourse conventions: how to negotiate conversations and other discursive situations and how to select (consciously or unconsciously) among linguistic variants in a specific linguistic context. Sociolinguists argue that every language is actually a bundle of dialects that share many features but also vary from one another.

Creativity

The grammar of human language allows speakers to create (and process/understand) an infinite number of utterances from a finite set of linguistic resources (sounds, words, grammatical rules). You may ask incredulously, "Infinite?" The answer is "Yes, infinite." First of all, consider that you have never before encountered the exact sequence of words that you have read so far in this chapter, and yet you have been processing this "creative input" with no linguistic difficulty (we hope). But we know this fact alone may not convince you of the infinitely creative potential of language. Instead, we turn to an example you may not think of as creative, but which allows for an infinite number of "new utterances":

> The experts said that the newscaster said that some random people on the street said that we said that they said that her friend Lola said . . . (ad infinitum) that the near-sighted oriole went to get her eyes checked.

Every time we embed a new "X said" clause into this sentence, the meaning changes, and we can embed an infinite number of these clauses into such a structure (although the sentence will quickly surpass the human brain's ability to unpack all of the clauses). The capacity of language to embed an infinite number of elements into its grammatical structures is known as **recursion**. The infinite creativity of human language is one feature distinguishing it from other animals' communication systems.

We can also be creative in the ways we combine and recombine grammatical elements: the lexical items in a sentence, for instance, can often be arranged in several different ways, and new meanings result from the new arrangements. The items in the straightforward question "What exactly do you think you mean?" can be resorted into the slightly accusing "Exactly what do you think you mean?" as well as the even more skeptical "What do you think you mean, exactly?" But wait, there's more! For instance, if you doubt that your friend is as thoughtful as she claims, you can say, "What exactly do you mean, you think?" And if you want to drive the conversation to a certain level of precision, you might ask, "Do you mean what you think exactly?" These permutations are not infinite, in the nature of recursion, but the rule-governed rearrangement of elements within grammatical structure allows for yet another dimension of creativity.

Grammar

The terms **grammar** and **grammatical** merit more explanation here. Many speakers use the word *grammatical* to refer to sentences that conform to rules in grammar or usage books for how we should write (e.g., some usage guides tell you not to use *impact* as a verb: that the "grammatically correct" form is *to have an impact*, not *to impact*). Linguists use the term *grammatical* much more broadly, to refer to all language constructions that conform to the systematic rules of a language and are, therefore, comprehensible to another speaker of the language. Under this definition, *to impact* is grammatical: it is a new verb that English speakers use systematically like any other verb. For our native languages, we learn this kind of grammar as children through interaction with other speakers—without explicit instruction. Thus, the definition of *grammar* in linguistics is clearly not the same as the everyday definition of *grammar* captured in the student's lament "My grammar isn't very good," or the teacherly recommendation "You need to work on your grammar."

To take a specific example, suppose you walk into a bakery and ask for a low-fat blueberry muffin. The clerk responds, "I don't have none of those today," indicating that you are out of luck. A school grammar or usage book may state that using two negatives in this way is "illogical" or "incorrect," but the sentence "I don't have none of those today" is perfectly grammatical in a dialect of English that employs two or more negatives to create negation. Many languages, and many dialects of English, use multiple negatives as systematically as other languages use only one. As you can see, the linguist's definition of grammaticality requires a reexamination of notions like "right" and "wrong" in describing linguistic constructions. A construction may not conform to a grammar book's rules about Standard English, but it may still be grammatically legitimate and "right" according to the grammatical rules of a particular variety of English. (You will be reading more about Standard English and questions of language and authority in Chapter 2.)

The word *grammar* is also used more broadly by linguists to encompass the structure and rules governing a language at the level of sound, word formation, syntax, and semantics. So the linguist's understanding of *grammar* includes many rules so basic and natural to native speakers that they would never be found in a usage book.

Linguistics

Linguistics can be defined as the principled study of language as a system. Linguists employ specific methodologies and theoretical frameworks for investigating the system of language. Linguistics incorporates both scientific approaches to language as a system and a focus on language as a social phenomenon.

The field of linguistics typically is highly comparative, examining many languages and comparing the structure of one language to others. In fact, if you ever tell someone you are a linguist, the first question he or she may ask is "How many languages do you speak?" This book, designed for an English linguistics course, focuses almost exclusively on the English language—both its structure and its use. In the process, we compare English to other languages. We also often compare Modern English to earlier stages of English to demonstrate some fundamental changes English has undergone and to show how these changes explain features of Modern English.

Linguistics comprises many subdisciplines, some of which correspond to the levels on which language is organized. **Phonology** is the study of sound systems and sound change, usually within a particular language, and is accompanied by **phonetics**, the description and classification of sounds more generally and the study of their production and perception. **Morphology** is the study of how words form. **Syntax** considers the structure of phrases, clauses, and sentences. **Semantics** is the study of meaning, the relationship between linguistic signs and the things or ideas they represent. Many linguists study language as a system or web of systems independent of use; their approach is formal rather than functional.

Pragmatics and **discourse analysis**, attempt to explain how we manage to communicate with language. In order to understand what language means in context (e.g., how *dude* functions as both a signal of approval and a warning), we must consider language as it is used by real people in real social situations. **Stylistics** is the study of language as it is used in written contexts, usually literary, but including courtroom rhetoric, political speeches, and journalism, as well as poetry, novels, and graffiti. **Sociolinguistics** is the study of language in use more generally, including the study of language variation by region (sometimes specifically called **dialectology**) or by socioeconomic status, gender, race, age, or other category. **Applied linguistics** encompasses all applications of linguistic theory to real-world problems, including areas such as language policy, language education, language acquisition and loss, speech pathology, lexicography, and discourse analysis.

Any aspect of language can be considered historically (or **diachronically**) and is then a branch of **historical linguistics**, which studies processes of language change and their results. Any aspect can also be considered in terms of the present, or **synchronically**. The ways in which we acquire and understand language fall under **psycholinguistics**. As this term indicates, language is studied in disciplines other than linguistics, including psychology, anthropology, communications, and most specific language disciplines (e.g., Romance or Near East languages and literatures).

Because this book is an introduction to the field, we dip into each subfield to give you the broadest sense of the field as a whole. We also show how these subfields overlap: phonology and morphology are often interconnected, as are syntax, semantics, and discourse. Language acquisition and loss are central to a theory of linguistic competence, but they are also matters of applied linguistics. The boundaries between subfields of linguistics are permeable, and we must cross them in order to understand how language works.

Human Language versus Animal Communication

We can assert with a very high degree of confidence that humans are the only living animal species on Earth capable of either speech or language as defined earlier. As we move into the details of what makes human language unique, however, we enter more contested territory. What exactly makes human language distinctive? How related is human language to our other cognitive skills, or is there a separate "language gene" or "language organ" in the brain? How related is human language to the communicative abilities we find in animals?

Many people think their pets can understand human language. Dogs, for example, certainly do associate strings of sound with meaning (or with requested behavior), but odds are that a well-trained dog would hit the floor in response to both "I want you to lie down" and "I want to give you the low down" if the last two words were spoken to it with the same intonation and pitch. Apes may understand much more, as we discuss later in this chapter, but they still cannot match a ten-year-old human. Other species vocalize and communicate with one another, but vocalization and speech are not the same, and neither are communication and language. Other species do not talk about language itself, as we are doing right now. Nor do they seem to have abstract verbs to describe particular linguistic and nonlinguistic acts, such as imagining, wondering, or asking. Unlike humans, other animals do not have an infinitely creative grammar.

Our ability to speak depends partly on the position of the human larynx, which is lower in the throat than in other primates (e.g., chimpanzees and other apes), and thus can express a greater variety of sounds. Scientists used to believe that the descended larynx was uniquely human, but it turns out that, for example, lions and koalas have a descended larynx, and some other animals, including dogs, pigs, and monkeys, lower their larynx when they vocalize. In some species, the descended larynx may have been an evolutionary adaptation that allowed male animals to exaggerate their body size through deeper calls (that is, they would seem more threatening to potential competitors). In humans, however, the larynx descends in both male and female infants at about three months. Scientists are still debating whether the descended larynx in humans was an adaptation for speech or for size exaggeration and then speech. In either case, from an evolutionary point of view, one suspects that speech must have constituted a significant evolutionary advantage, an advantage that outweighed the risk of suffocation. The descended larynx places it unusually close to the esophagus and entry into the digestive tract. It never hurts to swallow your words, but you have probably swallowed food that has "gone down the wrong pipe." Without the Heimlich maneuver, the relative position of the larynx constitutes a risk: swallowing food into the "windpipe" or larynx can be lethal.

Speech also depends partly on our muscular tongue and uniquely shaped jaw, which together assist in the production of the distinctive sounds of human language. Unlike other animals, we have fine motor control over the tongue and jaw, which allows us to produce the various distinctive sounds of human language.

None of these human advantages challenges the miracle of animal communication. It is no small thing that orioles can warn one another of predators vocally—that is, without direct physical or visual contact among themselves, such as a nudge or a wink. Vervet monkeys' calls distinguish different kinds of predators (e.g., a predatory bird versus a snake) so that other monkeys know whether to scurry up or down the tree, for example. But the parable of the nearsighted oriole is nonetheless instructive. Bird calls—indeed, the calls of most animals—are holistic (to be interpreted as a whole) and unambiguous. Most animals neither analyze nor interpret the messages they hear. For animals other than humans, messages cannot be parsed into elements and then freely recombined to make new sentences, and words with multiple possible meanings do not exist. First we discuss research on the communicative systems of birds, bees, and apes, and then we outline some of the features that make human language distinctive.

Birds and Bees

Birds sing as spring approaches because the increased light stimulates hormones that trigger the parts of the brain that control song. Birds sing by instinct. A young bird taken from its species will start singing that species' songs at a given age, although it will do so imperfectly (it needs the input from adults to get the songs exactly right). If an abandoned oriole chick were raised among a family of starlings, the oriole would sing imperfect oriole songs, not starling songs.

A young child, on the other hand, needs language input in order to produce language. Infants laugh and cry by instinct, but language is different. Abandoned children who have lived in the wild, and abused children kept in isolation, have a chance of learning language more or less naturally, if they are discovered and socialized before adolescence. If they are discovered and socialized *after* adolescence, though, they never learn to produce language as adult speakers do. And a child born to Russian parents but raised by Swahili-speaking parents will speak Swahili, not Russian. This linguistic flexibility among humans isn't analogous to animal inflexibility, however, because Russian speakers and Swahili speakers are members of the same species, whereas orioles and starlings are not.

Bees have a relatively sophisticated means of communication. When a bee finds a lush, pollen-rich field of flowers, it returns to the hive and performs a dance. The dance is specific to the pollen's location, so bee dances differ according to facts, according to the bee's experience. But in this case, too, communication is not language: the bee apparently inserts distance and direction into the equivalent of a function or algorithm (not to say that bees are doing complex math in their heads) and comes up with a dance—yet

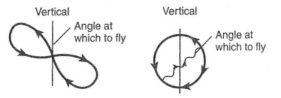

FIGURE 1.1 The sickle dance (on the left) looks much like a figure-eight, and the waggle dance (on the right) involves two semicircle arcs.

there's no thinking or real creativity involved. As far as we know, bees do not dance for reasons other than mapping the hunt for pollen.

Karl von Frisch (1886–1982) conducted landmark studies of honeybee dances starting in the 1940s, training blue-dyed bees to feed close to the hive and red-dyed bees to feed much farther from the hive, and then watching their movements—or dances—when they returned to the glass-fronted hives that he constructed. He discovered that there are three bee dances (see Figure 1.1):

- The *round dance* indicates that the food source is very nearby—usually within 20 feet—although the dance does not show direction. The more intense the movements, the richer the source.

- The sickle dance (which looks much like a figure-eight) indicates that the food source is relatively close—within 20–60 feet—and the angle of the dance shows the direction of the nectar in relation to the sun. How? The dancing bee, on the vertical wall of the hive, orients the dance straight up if the source is in exactly the direction of the sun from the hive and straight down if it is in exactly the opposite direction. Otherwise, the angle of the dance indicates the angle between the source and the sun. Like the round dance, more intense movements describe a richer source.

- The *waggle dance*, performed with serpentine tail wagging in a straight line followed by a semicircle arc, indicates that the food source is farther than 60 feet. The speed and number of repetitions of the dance per minute—slower means farther—specify how far beyond 60 feet the source is.

Amazingly, honeybees, therefore, have a highly effective system of communication, but as far as we know, they cannot add information such as, "Beware of the lawn mower" or "I was feeling sluggish in flight today so the pollen may not be as far as I'm saying it is." New studies show that other bees communicate by leaving scent trails without the more complex dances at the hive. Some researchers hypothesize that the honeybees dance in the hive to thwart competitors for the food sources. The dances provide an evolutionary advantage.

Chimps and Bonobos

It's only natural to wonder whether animals more similar to humans than birds or bees, like chimpanzees, have language or something resembling it. Certainly, not all primates have language. Vervet monkeys, for instance, use alarm calls—the presence of a leopard elicits one call, the presence of a vulture another—but they cannot form sentences any more than orioles can.

Chimpanzees cannot speak, but they have been taught to recognize a limited human vocabulary and to communicate with words, though never more than 300 or so. Chimpanzees are semantically more advanced than most other species, because it is clear that they can use words to represent concepts, rather than just objects. They can generalize a term to cover more than the original object to which it referred—in other words, *banana* is not the name of the banana for which the chimp first learns the word, but instead refers to all bananas. But chimps, as far as current research suggests, do not possess syntax. (See also Gill 1997, Cattell 2000, and Kenneally 2007 for good detailed summaries of chimp and other ape research.)

Two early experiments in the 1930s and 1940s involved baby female chimps adopted into human families to test whether they could acquire language like young children. The Kelloggs raised the chimp Gua with their son Donald, and although she could respond to about one hundred words by a year and a half old, Donald soon surpassed her. Gua never moved much beyond that one-hundred-word point. The Hayes had a similar experience with the chimp Vicki, but Vicki, unlike Gua, is supposed to have mouthed some words, although it's not clear that anyone other than her human parents could understand her. Most researchers today assert with confidence that chimps cannot be taught to speak.

The bonobo Panbanisha learned to communicate using the symbols on a keyboard.

In the 1960s, Alan and Beatrice Gardner decided to try to teach American Sign Language to Washoe, the young chimp they raised. Washoe learned close to one hundred signs in her first four years and could produce sequences of signs, but researchers have raised concerns about whether she really understood grammar. If Washoe used a series of signs in a different sequence, was she really signaling a different meaning, or was the sequencing more haphazard? It is clear, however, that Washoe, who died in 2007 at the age of about 42, understood quite a lot of sign language, and she was capable of the abstract extension of meaning. For example, she knew the sign for 'open' in relation to a door, and she then used it to request the opening of a briefcase. Washoe also taught some sign language to her adopted chimp son.

A decade later, a chimp named Sarah, owned by Ann and David Premack, learned how to use colored plastic shapes to communicate. The shapes were all in arbitrary relation to the referent, like any human language. For example, a pink square meant 'banana' and a blue triangle 'apple'. Through exercises involving trial and error, Sarah learned which sequences would get her what she wanted. For example, 'give apple Sarah' would get her the apple, whereas 'apple Sarah give' would not. She learned a good number of symbols for objects and actions, but serious questions remained about her language learning. How fundamentally different is using plastic symbols from using language? And to what extent was she learning grammar versus learning which sequences would lead to a successful outcome (e.g., getting the apple she wanted)? In other words, it was unclear whether Sarah was being creative with these symbols the way that humans are with words.

The fundamental question underlying much of this research with chimps has been whether the difference between animal communication and human language is a matter of degree along a scale, with humans representing a much more advanced level, or whether human language is qualitatively different—a sort of quantum leap in communication. Right now, most researchers seem to agree that human language is qualitatively different. But work over the past two decades by Sue Savage-Rumbaugh and her colleagues with the bonobos Kanzi and Panbanisha has at least some scholars questioning their confidence in this assertion.

Bonobos, a species of ape, may be more like humans than other apes. They are less aggressive than chimps, and some researchers argue that bonobos can empathize emotionally with others, much like humans. The bonobo Kanzi learned to communicate by watching researchers try to teach his mother, Matata, how to use the symbols on a computer keyboard to express meaning. He looked like he was just playing and trying to distract his mother, but what his mother could not seem to learn, he began to do as soon as his mother was taken away for breeding. Apparently, he decided to please the adult humans in his life once his bonobo mother was no longer there, and using these symbols to communicate with the human researchers clearly made them very happy.

Kanzi was able to express what he wanted and what he planned to do, including where he planned to go in the woods on his walks. In other words, he could engage in purposeful communication. His comprehension of language reached the level of a two- or three-year-old human, at which point he probably struggled more with the limits of his memory than with his ability to comprehend complex grammatical structures. In one test, when Kanzi was nine, he responded correctly 72 percent of the time to 660 different commands, ranging from "Put the raisins in the shoe" to "Use the toothbrush and brush Liz's teeth" to "Go get the noodles that are in the bedroom" (Savage-Rumbaugh et al. 1998, 68–69). Kanzi was able to use signs from the keyboard in combination, as well as combinations of symbols and gestures, but there is some question about how grammatical those utterances were. His comprehension, even more than his production, has raised challenging questions.

Bonobos, although relatively advanced in their ability to understand human language and to use linguistic signs for purposeful communication, still fall far short of humans in terms of language abilities. But do they blur any distinct line between human language and animal communication? Savage-Rumbaugh presents us this challenge:

> Kanzi had learned to comprehend and use printed symbols on his own without special training. He had also learned to understand many spoken words, even though he himself could not speak. He knew that words could be used to communicate about things he wanted or intended to do, even though those actions were not happening at the time of the communication. He could also purposefully combine symbols to tell us something . . . we would have had no way of knowing otherwise. He recognized that two symbols could be combined to form meanings that neither symbol in isolation could ever convey. He used this skill to communicate completely novel ideas that were his own and had never been talked about with him. Consequently, whether or not he could be shown to possess a formal grammar, the conclusion remained inescapable that Kanzi had a simple language.
>
> Nonetheless, many scientists continued to insist that until the use of grammatical rules could be shown in his language, the rest of what Kanzi had done was of little interest. Such an extreme view is taken, I believe, because many scientists are hesitant to conclude that apes are capable of rational thought, foresight, or purposeful communication—behaviors formerly held to be exclusively human. If we allow that apes such as Kanzi are indeed attempting to tell us what is on their minds, and that their minds are shaped by their experiences just as the minds of young children are, we lose our claim to being drastically different from all other creatures on the planet. (63–64)

Let the discussion continue. But while it does, let us outline some fundamental differences between human language and all other observed, naturally occurring animal communication systems.

Distinctive Characteristics of Human Language

Drawing hard and fast lines between human cognitive abilities and those of other animals has proven tricky: many other animal species share cognitive abilities with humans. For example, a range of other animals also seem to have a reasonably rich inner (mental) life. The African gray parrot understands conceptual categories like shape and number. Chimps and elephants seem to have self-awareness (e.g., they recognize themselves in mirrors). Dolphins and chimps can generalize, learning patterns and applying them to new situations. Bonobos and orangutans seem to have a sense of the future. (See Kenneally 2007 for further examples.) In other words, if these animals had words and syntax, they might have something to say. But other conceptual systems seem to be more human specific: Theory of Mind (understanding of our own and others' full range of mental states, including beliefs, desires, and intentions), ownership, essences, multipart tools, fatherhood, romantic love, and most moral concepts (Pinker and Jackendoff 2005, 205).

We summarize here four significant ways that human language differs from other animal communication. But it's important to note that this is a lively field of debate right now, including a rapid-fire exchange of papers in 2005 in the journal *Cognition*, between coauthors Steven Pinker and Ray Jackendoff and coauthors Marc Hauser, Noam Chomsky, and W. Tecumseh Fitch, about what exactly is special about the human language faculty.

First, humans acquire language in speech communities. A human baby learns whatever human language is spoken in the community in which it is raised; it does not matter what language the baby's biological parents spoke if it is raised in a different speech community. Communicative systems are inborn in other animals. In humans, the capacity for language may be biological, but the specific linguistic signs that we acquire are determined by what we hear after we are born.

Second, human words are unique compared to other animal signs (Pinker and Jackendoff 2005). The sheer number of words that an average human uses (about 50,000) has no rival in the rest of the animal kingdom, by at least one-hundred-fold. The size of the human vocabulary suggests a phenomenal ability by children to use vocal imitation to learn, to decipher the proper meanings of words—from the very concrete (*diaper*) to the highly abstract (*love*) to the grammatical (*of*)—and to remember all these words. With this rich vocabulary, humans talk far beyond the "here and now" and the physical stimuli around us. We reminisce about last year, we make plans for summer vacation, and we debate the possibility of a perfect love. Humans exhibit **displacement**, or the ability to project forward and backward in time, as well as to discuss the abstract. We express the notion that something "could" or "might" happen, which allows us to use language to form hypotheses and to question the hypotheses of others. Language may even allow humans to

Bird calls, like that of the oriole, are unambiguous and respond to particular stimuli, such as danger. Birds do not possess the creativity in their communicative system to discuss, for example, the near-sighted oriole's false alarms.

conceptualize things they couldn't without language, from the idea of a "week" to the supernatural to, arguably, higher numbers. Language labels things, classifies them according to properties, and helps us conceptualize entities such as time and space. Language organizes much of our world.

Third, human language can be ambiguous. Many of our words carry multiple meanings, and sentences can have more than one interpretation. The oriole's alarm call and the bee's tail-wagging dance are unambiguous. But if you say "You lost me," there are at least three possible interpretations: (a) a description of a past event in which you got lost; (b) a request for someone to repeat information because you are confused; and (c) a sarcastic jab at someone who just said something ridiculously obvious. As this third interpretation demonstrates, we can also imbue our utterances with emotional content that is separate from the words themselves. In "Human and Animal Languages," Jacob Bronowski (1977) explains that human language entails separation of affect: it distinguishes between the emotional and factual contents of a message. Animals cannot compartmentalize emotional response from informational stimulus in the way that humans do.

Fourth, and most remarkably, human language is infinitely creative. Given the powers of syntax, we understand our sentences as made of combinable (in fact, infinitely combinable) parts. With a closed inventory of linguistic signs (although we certainly do introduce new ones on a regular basis as a community), we can use the rules of grammar to say anything that we think needs to be said, both about what we experience physically and about what we think. Syntactic recursion, as described earlier, is fundamental to human language's creativity, and the crux of the debate in 2005 in the *Cognition* papers was whether recursion alone is both uniquely human and uniquely linguistic. Are other features of human language unique? In 2004, linguist Dan Everett, after thirty years of fieldwork, made the highly controversial argument that the Amazonian language Pirahã shows no evidence of recursion. If this claim holds up, it would be a first among human languages.

No animal communication other than human language exhibits all the properties just described. And all these properties mean that human language changes from generation to generation in ways that far surpass any other animal communication system. Because other animal sign systems are inborn, they rarely change from one generation to the next, and when they do, it is very gradual change. In a similar way, human laughter and crying remain very stable from generation to generation. Human language, on the other hand, in all its creativity and ambiguity, changes rapidly as each new generation of speakers learns, modifies, adds to, and subtracts from the language of its speech community.

The Process of Language Change

All living languages change all the time. Do you struggle to understand Chaucer and Shakespeare? Your teachers insist that both authors wrote in English, but sometimes it's Greek to you. The distance between you and Chaucer (who wrote at the end of the fourteenth century) or Shakespeare (who wrote at the end of the sixteenth century), or indeed between Chaucer and Shakespeare themselves, can be measured in terms of language change: sound change, grammatical change, semantic change. What results is not quite a foreign language but at least a language that can only be interpreted with help from footnotes or a historical dictionary like the *Oxford English Dictionary (OED)*—until you become familiar with it, of course. Still, if you and Shakespeare met on the street and began to speak to each other, your respective versions of English would be mutually intelligible: you would understand each other, though not effortlessly. You could not engage the poet who wrote down *Beowulf* (in the tenth century, scholars think) in conversation, however. Old English and Present-Day English are not mutually intelligible. The difference between them is 1,000 years—an eyeblink in evolutionary terms, but more like an eternity on the time-scale of language change.

Language Genealogies

Old English did not fall to earth with a meteorite or hatch from an egg or in any other way magically appear. It developed from the Germanic dialects brought to England in the fifth century. Many English speakers think English is a Romance language (descended from Latin) because English has so many Latinate words. But these words are borrowings into English, not signs of its genealogy. As shown in Figure 1.2, English is a member of the

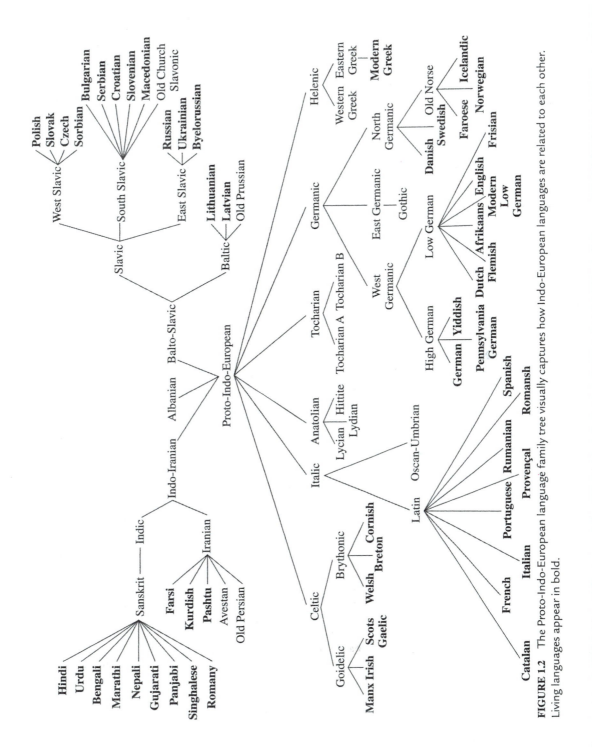

FIGURE 1.2 The Proto-Indo-European language family tree visually captures how Indo-European languages are related to each other. Living languages appear in bold.

21

Germanic family of languages, "cousins" with language like German, Dutch, and Icelandic. You can tell that these languages are related. English *father*, for example, closely resembles Dutch *vader* and German *vater*.

The job of the historical linguist is to explain just what the relationships are and how differences among related languages came to be. *Father, vader,* and *vater,* for example, all have a common ancestor word in a shared early Germanic ancestor language. These words are **reflexes** of that ancestor and **cognates** to one another; the ancestor is their **etymon.**

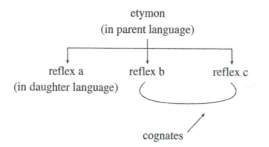

Cognate words or languages are, therefore, related to each other through a shared ancestor word or language.

In 1786, Sir William Jones, known as "Oriental" Jones, a justice of India's Supreme Court when India was under British rule, proposed that similarities among Greek (*patēr*), Latin (*pater*), and Sanskrit (*pitar-*) suggested that they had all developed from a common ancestor. In 1822, Jacob Grimm (one of the brothers of fairy-tale fame) took the argument a step further, specifically explaining sound changes that happened to make the sounds in Germanic words different from their Romance cognates—and different in systematic ways. For example, Indo-European *k* remains the sound /k/ in Latin but becomes /h/ in Germanic, which explains why in Modern English our *hearts* (an English word) are cared for by *cardiologists* (a Latin borrowing). This system of sound correspondences, known as Grimm's Law, explained the relationship between English *father* and Sanskrit *pitar-* and initiated the reconstruction of Indo-European, the common source for most current and historical languages of Europe and the Indian subcontinent.

Indo-European is a **proto-language**, one for which we have no written evidence, but which we can infer from comparison of its descendents and development of the laws according to which its sounds and word-forms changed. In other words, historical linguists must reconstruct Indo-European forms from evidence in its daughter languages and the rules of change that they have hypothesized. Linguists always put an asterisk (*) next to a hypothesized form in a proto-language to indicate that it is hypothesized—that we have no written evidence for it.

Linguists have traditionally dated Proto-Indo-European back about 6,000 years. Recent work by biologist Russell D. Gray, which applies mathematical tools for genes and species family trees to language family trees, proposes a much earlier date: 8,700 years ago, give or take 1,200 years. These conflicting dates add fuel to an ongoing debate based in part on archeological evidence about whether these Proto-Indo-European speakers were warriors who spread from the steppes of Russia or farmers who spread from ancient Turkey.

We can draw similar trees for other language families, such as Uralic and Altaic. The larger unresolved question is how all of these family trees are related to each other. Is there one proto-language from which they all descend, which can be traced back to our first ancestors in Africa? You may have heard of Nostratic, which some linguists propose as a parent language of several language families, but it is not widely accepted as such.

Mechanics of Language Change

Looking at the Indo-European language family tree, you can grasp the big picture of language change. But you might naturally wonder how exactly dialects develop and then change within themselves so dramatically over time. Part of the answer goes back to the creativity inherent in human language. Every day, perhaps several times a day, each of us speaks or writes in ways that challenge conventional uses of English. When enough people do so often enough (or continually enough) for a long enough time, then a change is generalized (especially as children learn it as part of the system of English) and becomes a feature of the language. And those changes add up over time.

All fundamental aspects of a language change over time: sound, word forms, syntax, and vocabulary. William Labov, a leading American linguist who has completed two volumes in a proposed three-volume study of linguistic change, describes three factors that motivate change:

- *Internal factors*—those inherent to the structure, especially the sound structure of the language.
- *Social factors*—those that depend on the behavior of speech communities.
- *Cognitive factors*—those that depend on our comprehension of the language and on our mind's language processes.

Sociolinguists continue to learn how language change starts and spreads. You will read more about this in Chapter 11.

There is no decisive moment at which a daughter language splits from a parent language and gets its own name. Historical linguists make language family trees in retrospect. One could argue that French is Latin spoken in France, but because it has changed so dramatically from Latin and from other daughter languages such as Italian and Spanish, French is described as a distinct language with its own name. The Germanic tribes brought their Germanic dialects to England in 449 CE. "English" is said to begin around this time because the Germanic dialects spoken in England began to diverge and develop independently from the other Germanic dialects spoken in continental Europe. But in 449, the Germanic speakers in England did not think of themselves as speaking a new language. And subsequent generations of speakers in England were not aware of the larger implications of the small changes occurring in their language—that it was splitting further from German, Swedish, and other Germanic cousins and would one day get its own name.

Progress or Decay?

Because human language is infinitely creative, speakers are constantly using words in new combinations and with slightly—if not radically—new meanings. If other speakers start to use the words in this new way, they can create new conventional meanings or uses. In other words, if enough speakers adopt a new meaning or construction, it becomes a conventional, accepted part of the day-to-day language. For example, after the noun *google* entered the language, some speakers began using it as a verb to describe the act of searching for something on the Internet. As more and more speakers have adopted the word as a verb, this use has become a conventional part of the language.

In a book about language change, Jean Aitchison (2001) raises a question that many people want answered: Is all this change progress or decay? Aitchison provides an answer but does not choose one side over the other. Language change, she asserts, is not decay or progress. While languages sometimes become more regular, they also sometimes introduce new exceptions that disrupt existing patterns. As Aitchison puts it:

> even if all agreed that a perfectly regular language was the "best," there is no evidence that languages are progressing towards this ultimate goal. Instead, there is a continuous pull between the disruption and restoration of patterns. In this perpetual ebb and flow, it would be a mistake to regard pattern neatening and regularization as a step forwards. Such an occurrence may be no more progressive than the tidying up of a cluttered office. Reorganization simply restores the room to a workable state. Similarly, it would be misleading to assume that pattern disruption was necessarily a backward step. Structural dislocation may be the result of extending the language in some useful way. We must conclude therefore that language is ebbing and flowing like the tide, but neither progressing nor decaying, as far as we can tell. (253)

Some linguists argue that languages maintain equilibrium over time in terms of grammatical complexity: a language may lose complexity in one feature while gaining it elsewhere.

All languages, and every historical stage of any given language, are equally capable of expressing anything that the speakers need to express. Languages often express similar things differently, but not because some are more "evolved" than others. For example, some varieties of Modern English use multiple negation (e.g., *I won't have none of that*) and some do not (e.g., *I won't have any of that*) because some varieties lost multiple negation over the centuries since Old English, while others retained this historical feature. Moving from multiple to single negation in the history of some varieties of English is not the result of laziness, sloppiness, or decay; it is also not the result of streamlining, efficiency, or improvement. Both structures are equally capable of expressing negation. It is all part of ongoing language change.

A Question to Discuss

Can Your Language Peeves Be Rethought?

All of us have our language peeves: the words or grammatical constructions that grate on our ears, that we just don't like. Maybe it's *BRB* pronounced "burb" or the road sign "Drive Slow" that uses a flat adverb (*slow* rather than *slowly*) or the notice at the grocery store that reads "Ten Items or Less." Often, our peeves focus on parts of the English language that are undergoing change. And as we discuss in the Special Focus section, sometimes usage that people don't like at one historical moment becomes standard at a later historical moment. What are your language peeves? Then for each one, try reframing it so that it is a positive rather than a negative development in the language.

Special Focus: Attitudes about Language Change

Near the end of the eighteenth century, Benjamin Franklin wrote to Noah Webster to complain about the new verbs *notice*, *advocate*, and *progress* (all created from nouns), in hopes that Webster might use his authority as a dictionary maker to obstruct these changes in the language. Franklin also conceded in a letter to David Hume that the words *colonize* and *unshakeable* were bad and low (qtd. in Safire 2003). From our current perspective, these concerns about language change can seem quaint, as all of these words have become standard.

These are only the tip of the iceberg in terms of new words that commentators have worried are signs of the decay of English. Do you have a problem with the adjective *talented*? Probably not, but Samuel Coleridge and other nineteenth-century writers did; the problem, as they saw it, was that there is no verb *to talent*. Ambrose Bierce, in *Write It Right: A Little Blacklist of Literary Faults* (1909), included *talented* along with *run a business* ("vulgar") and *electrocution* ("disgusting") (Freeman 2009).

But similar complaints still abound today. For example, Edward Rothstein describes the verb *incentivize* as "boorish bureaucratic misspeak" in an article in *The New York Times* in 2000, and laments its inclusion in the fourth edition of the *American Heritage Dictionary*. In a 2008 column in *The Ann Arbor News* entitled "Country Rife with Sloppy English," an English department head cites innovations such as *invite* as a noun and the abbreviation *EVOO* for extra virgin olive oil as examples of language change that "eviscerates the language." And while one can now run a business without condemnation of the verb, in 2002, 80 percent of the American Heritage Usage Panel rejected the relatively new transitive use of *grow* in *grow our business*.

New grammatical constructions can also create anxiety. In the nineteenth century, the new use of the passive progressive, in a clause such as *the house is being built*, was singled out for vicious criticism. The clause should correctly be *the house is building*, critics argued; to use the passive progressive was not just awkward but an outrage, according to some. Now what seems outrageous to us is the criticism itself. How else could you say the house is being built? (As a side note: while *the house is building* sounds archaic, expressions such as *dinner is cooking* may be remnants of this earlier passive.)

The point is that we have several centuries of evidence of commentators lamenting changes in the English language. What seemed like a terrible change in the nineteenth century now often seems to us unremarkable, and this is an important perspective to keep on changes that we notice—and that some people denounce—in current English usage. At the beginning of the twenty-first century, some commentators will look back to the eighteenth and nineteenth centuries as times when "good English" was spoken and written. As the examples show, commentators in the eighteenth and nineteenth centuries did not necessarily hold up their language as "good English."

But, you might ask, are some language changes better than others? American writer David Foster Wallace raised exactly this question in a 2001 article in *Harper's Magazine*, which challenged some of the descriptions of language change that linguists may see as givens. Linguistics books such as this one assert that "Language changes constantly." Foster Wallace replies: "OK, but how much and how fast?" Descriptive linguistics asserts that "Change is normal." Foster Wallace responds: "Same thing. Is Heraclitean flux [everything flows and nothing abides] as normal or desirable as gradual change? Do some changes actually serve the language's overall pizzazz better than others?" (45). You will be able to frame detailed answers to his questions, complete with examples, by the time you have finished this book. Let's address briefly the issues here.

The speed of language change varies. Communities that experience a lot of contact with speakers of other dialects or languages may undergo more rapid change than isolated communities. For example, after the Norman Conquest in 1066, which involved extensive language contact, English seems to have undergone more dramatic changes than its cognate languages at the time. More oral cultures may experience more rapid change than more literate ones, especially if these literate communities have more rigid prescriptive practices (e.g., widespread education in writing and "correct grammar"). But literacy and prescriptivism certainly do not stop language change, and linguists are not sure how much they slow it down.

Are some language changes better than others? Beauty (or pizzazz) is in the eye of the beholder. Our judgment to embrace or to reject a language change that we notice is usually more socially motivated than linguistically motivated. The metathesis of *aks* to *ask* is neither good nor bad in and of itself.

Many English speakers object to language change, and this is natural: most of us prefer stability to change. Some resistance is generational. How often do your parents ask you to turn down the volume of the sweet, optimistic lyrics (okay, maybe not) sung by Eminem? You may see generational resistance to language change as you speak with your parents and grandparents. Perhaps your parents object when you say "This sucks!" Or they nag you about using an interruptive like *like*, as in "It's, like, not fair! This sucks!" Or they shake their heads at how you quote when you tell them about your best friend's bad day: "And then he goes, 'That test was hella hard!' and I'm like, 'Dude, don't go ballistic.'"

Some change is temporary: it doesn't stick. For example, *jiggy* was hot, but now it's not. Some changes do stick and alter English beyond the span of our lifetimes (e.g., *go* meaning 'say', and probably *like* meaning 'say'). As one of the authors of this book has written, we should admire the linguistic engine's formidable power: "Language stops for no one, not even an Oxbridge or an Ivy League grammarian: when one hears the engine whistle, one may pull a switch and temporarily divert the language's course, but one might as well just jump out of the way." Some people pull and pull and refuse to jump—their resistance is just one among many social factors in linguistic change.

☑ Summary

- Language is the primary means by which humans communicate. It is how we express complex ideas and emotions. It is how we negotiate our social relationships. The discipline of linguistics systematically investigates the structure and use of language.

- Human language involves a conventional system of signs, in which the relationship between the linguistic form (signifier) and the meaning or referent (signified) is arbitrary.

- The grammar of human languages allows the creation of an infinite number of creative utterances from a finite set of linguistic resources. This aspect of human linguistic competence distinguishes human language from all other animal communication systems.

- All living languages change all the time, and historical linguists can trace language histories to create language genealogies or family trees. English is one of the Germanic languages, which make up one branch of the Indo-European language family tree.

- Linguists continue to search for more definitive answers about how language change starts and spreads. What they know definitively is that all languages will continue to change, no matter whether we try to stop them from doing so or not.

Suggested Reading

The First Word: The Search for the Origins of Language (2007), by linguist and journalist Christine Kenneally, provides a highly readable and informative account of research on language evolution. We encourage all interested in the theoretical debate about what makes human language unique to read the original papers in *Cognition*, as well as the 2002 paper in *Science* by Hauser, Chomsky, and Fitch to which they respond. *Apes, Language, and the Human Mind* (1998), by Sue Savage-Rumbaugh et al., describes the bonobo Kanzi's language learning in detail and devotes several chapters to a more philosophical discussion of the distinction between human and animal communication. For more on curses and taboo words, see Geoffrey Hughes's *Swearing: A Social History of Foul Language, Oaths and Profanity in English* (1991), Edwin Battistella's *Bad Language* (2005), and Keith Allan and Kate Burridge's *Forbidden Words: Taboo and the Censoring of Language* (2006). Rosina Lippi-Green's *English with an Accent* (1997) provides further case studies of the link between language and discrimination. April McMahon's *Understanding Language Change* (1994) provides an excellent technical overview of historical linguistics, as well as a fascinating discussion of the question of linguistic evolution; for a lively, more generally accessible account of language change and attitudes, see Jean Aitchison's *Language Change: Progress or Decay* (2001). All who study English linguistics seriously should read these major works of William Labov, *Principles of Linguistic Change: Internal Factors* (1994) and *Principles of Linguistic Change: Social Factors* (2001). Two of the standard introductory linguistics textbooks are Victoria Fromkin, Robert Rodman, and Nina Hyams's *An Introduction to Language* (8th ed., 2007), which is informative, highly readable, and full of entertaining cartoons about language, and the denser, perhaps more upper-level text by Edward Finegan, *Language: Its Structure and Use* (5th ed., 2008), which covers an impressive amount of material about the many subfields of linguistics. For a more general history of linguistics, consider the more comprehensive *A Short History of Linguistics* by R. H. Robins (1997), as well as Randy Allen Harris's lively account of the Chomskyan revolution and twentieth-century linguistics in the United States in *The Linguistics Wars* (1993).

Exercises

Exercise 1.1   Sense and Nonsense

As a thought experiment, consider the following poem from Lewis Carroll's *Alice's Adventures through the Looking-Glass* (2003 [1871]):

Jabberwocky

'Twas brillig and the slithy toves
Did gyre and gimble in the wabe:
All mimsy were the borogoves,
And the mome raths outgrabe.

"Beware the Jabberwock, my son!
The jaws that bite, the claws that catch!
Beware the Jubjub bird, and shun
The frumious Bandersnatch!"

He took his vorpal sword in hand:
Long time the manxome foe he sought—
So rested he by the Tumtum tree,
And stood awhile in thought.

And, as in uffish thought he stood,
The Jabberwock, with eyes of flame,
Came whiffling through the tulgey wood,
And burbled as it came!

One, two! One, two! And through and through
The vorpal blade went snicker-snack!
He left it dead, and with its head
He went galumphing back.

"And hast thou slain the Jabberwock?
Come to my arms, my beamish boy!
O frabjous day! Calloo! Callay!"
He chortled in his joy.

"Jabberwocky" is considered nonsense verse, but the first thing one notices about the poem is that it makes at least as much sense as it doesn't. True, a number of words are unfamiliar, and one can't find most of them in a dictionary, but even these words are formed from parts meaningful in English. For instance, *jabber* (in *Jabberwock*), *snatch* (in *Bandersnatch*), and *out* (in *outgrabe*) make sense to English speakers, as do the plural suffix -*s* in three of the nouns and the various adjective suffixes, -*y*, -*ous*, -*al*, -*(s)ome*, and -*ish*. In fact, *beamish*, though used infrequently, has been an item of English vocabulary since the sixteenth century.

Some other elements in these words, though obscured, look like English because they are. According to Carroll, -*wock* in *Jabberwock* is a form of Old English *wocor* 'offspring, fruit'; *slithy* combines *slimy* and *lithe* and means 'smooth and active'; *outgrabe* is past tense of *outgribe*, supposedly related to the archaic English verb *grike* or *shrike*, from which Modern English developed *shriek* and *creak*, and means 'squeaked' (see Carroll 2003, 328–33, for these explanations and more commentary on the language of "Jabberwocky").

So the supposedly nonsense words are archaic English words, derived from archaic English words, or formed like English words.. Two other features contribute to our general feeling that the poem almost makes sense. First, the words sound like English words (*frabjous/fabulous*) and are often onomatopoetic (*uffish, galumphing*). Second, the sentences are unmistakably structured as English sentences, so that, even if a word's lexical meaning isn't clear, its grammatical function is. Thus we grasp the relations among words and infer a general meaning for a word that in isolation would be meaningless. Finally, the poem makes some sense to us because a few of the words (*galumphing* and *chortle*, for instance) have been assigned meanings because of the poem itself and entered in dictionaries. *Jabberwocky* itself has come to mean 'nonsense'—you can look it up!

If the poem were really nonsense, that is, if it made no sense, we wouldn't read it. Instead, from our intuitive knowledge of English and the overwhelming, human need to understand, we supply meanings, even if only imagined meanings, to the words in front of us. The imagining is what makes the poem fun: "Jabberwocky" is a puzzle that draws on our linguistic experience and exercises our linguistic ingenuity.

Now it's your turn. Try your hand at writing two additional stanzas for "Jabberwocky," parallel to stanzas 4 and 5, about the boy's subsequent encounter with the Jubjub bird or the Bandersnatch (or both). Include 8–10 made-up words that, like those in the original poem, generally sound and function like English words.

Then exchange your stanzas with another member of your class and attempt to translate each other's work. Share your translations and find out how close you came to what, as authors, you had in mind.

Exercise 1.2   Linguistic Creativity

Wilhelm von Humboldt (1767–1835), a German philosopher and linguist, once asserted that the grammar of human language can "make infinite use of finite means." Using your own words, explain what he is saying. Direct your explanation to a skeptical audience. Be sure to explain both parts: "infinite use" and "finite means." And provide at least one concrete example.

Exercise 1.3   Language Judgments

Imagine that you, instead of Randy Cohen, are "The Ethicist" who responds to the question about the ethics of evaluating job applicants on the basis of their preferences for *aks* or *ask*. How would you answer the question from the anonymous employee in New York on p. 2? You can find Cohen's published answer at the *New York Times* Archive (www.nytimes.com), in the January 28, 2007, column.

Exercise 1.4   Language Change

English has changed dramatically over the past millennium, and it has even changed recognizably during your lifetime. The following questions focus on language changes both in the more and less distant past. These are designed as puzzles: you may not *know* the answers to these questions, but you can figure out many of them with a little stretching of linguistic muscles and sometimes a good dictionary. Take your best shot at explaining the "why" and "how" behind each change.

1. President George W. Bush, like many Americans, says the word *nuclear* "noo-kyuh-luhr." Compare this pronunciation with the spelling. What has happened? (Hint: consider the history of *ask/aks*.)

2. Many speakers of English now say "heighth" for "height." How would you account for this change in pronunciation?

3. When Americans first began using the Russian word *Sputnik* in the late 1950s, they did not pronounce it "correctly" with the Russian vowel "oo" as in "boot." Why might Americans pronounce *Sputnik* the way they do, so that *Sput* rhymes with *putt*?

4. The word *mouse* has taken on a new meaning to refer to the small clicker device attached to many computers. Why is it called a mouse?

5. The word *gay*, which for much of the twentieth century was used as an insulting reference when applied to men, has been reappropriated by the homosexual community as the preferred term for referring to homosexual men. The word *gay* meaning 'happy' still appears in Christmas carols and other conventionalized contexts, but many speakers no longer use the word *gay* to mean 'happy'. Suggest a reason for this shift.

6. In the Old English version of Genesis, Eve is tempted to eat the forbidden fruit by a *nædre*, meaning 'snake'. This word for the evil tempter has come down to us in Modern English as an *adder*. What reason can you give for the disappearance of the initial *n* in *adder*?

7. The word *another* comes from *an* + *other*. What has happened that allows the insertion of *whole* into the middle to create *a whole nother*? (Hint: consider the adder from question 6.)

8. When the phrase *a moot point* was first used in English in the sixteenth century, it referred to a point that was open to debate, uncertain, or doubtful. In the United States, it now usually refers to a point of no practical significance or relevance. Suggest a reason for this shift.

9. Some speakers of American English now say "mute point" instead of "moot point." Why might they do this?

10. The noun *burglar* (from Anglo-French and Anglo-Latin) appears in English by the Renaissance. The English verb *burgle* (which does not appear in French or Latin) is relatively recent, first appearing in the late nineteenth century. Suggest an explanation of its origins.

11. In March 2003, the cafeteria in the U.S. House of Representatives replaced "French fries" on the menu with "freedom fries." Why? (The House quietly changed the name back to "French fries" in July 2006.)

12. The plural of the noun *syllabus* in English has historically been *syllabi*. These days, however, many instructors might say, "Are there any extra syllabuses?" Why has *syllabus* developed this new plural form? Bonus question: Should one of these two plurals be considered "right" or "wrong"? Why or why not?

Chapter 2

Language and Authority

The game of Scrabble begs the question of what counts as a real word and who has the authority to decide.

Imagine that you are playing Scrabble with your grandmother. You need all of the points that you can get—you're not letting her win. You lay down the tiles for *blog*. She challenges you. She doesn't know the word. Even worse, *blog* isn't in the dictionary that you have on hand—some dictionaries are more up-to-date than others. Should you be denied points for playing a word just because your opponent doesn't recognize it and your dictionary is behind the times? Who wrote the dictionary we choose to settle the dispute, and why does it have the authority to tell us what is a word and what is not? The assumptions that underlie our reliance on dictionaries are suspect from a linguistic point of view.

For instance, how did we get comfortable with the phrase *"the* dictionary" when, in fact, there are many different types of dictionaries? And within each type, dictionaries vary considerably. You may not find the word you lay out on the Scrabble board in a pocket dictionary or a college dictionary, but it may be registered in an unabridged dictionary. Perhaps the word was used 700 years ago but not today, and you could find it if you had a copy of the multivolume *Middle English Dictionary* in your living room. And you might be able to defend your score if you consulted *Merriam-Webster's Third New International Dictionary,* which includes more words than any other dictionary of its type. But, in fact, competitive Scrabble players are bound to the *Official Scrabble Players Dictionary,* published by Merriam-Webster. If a word can't be found there, tournaments check Funk and Wagnall's *Standard College Dictionary,* but if the word isn't registered there either, then the player who proposed it is out of luck. The only words that count in the game are those included in the dictionaries declared "authoritative" by the Scrabble tournament officials.

Most speakers assume that there are centers of authority for the English language, but they rarely step back to analyze this assumption critically. Who makes decisions about what is "standard"? Throughout our schooling, we have been sent to dictionaries, grammar books, and style guides in order to learn "the rules" for the written language, but who are the people empowered to write these books? Why do they assume authority over English, and why do we cede authority to them?

This chapter explores the relationship between language and authority in broad historical and social terms. It provides information about traditional sources of language authority, as well as a framework in which to think critically about notions of "right" and "wrong" in language. In Chapters 5 and 6, you will read about some of the specific grammatical rules you may have learned (e.g., don't split infinitives), in order to examine where these rules originated and how they correspond to actual usage. But before we look at such details, let's consider the big picture.

Who Is in Control?

We start by addressing the "who" behind the rules of Standard English.

Language Academies

In France, the Forty Immortals of the Académie Française, founded in 1635, have the power to legislate acceptable and unacceptable change in the French language. In recent years, the Académie's efforts to ban or replace English borrowings such as *e-mail* (to be replaced by the Québécois word *courriel*) and *software* (to be replaced by *logiciel*) have received some press coverage, even in the United States—and met with little success as English words continue to proliferate, especially in Paris. Language change is very hard to control by decree. And the Académie now includes, for example, *les bluejeans* in the recently published ninth edition of its dictionary.

There has never been a successful academy to govern the English language, either in Britain or in the United States, although it has certainly been suggested. John Dryden proposed one in the 1660s. Jonathan Swift floated the concept in 1712. In "A Proposal for Correcting, Improving and Ascertaining the English Tongue," Swift wrote:

My Lord; I do here, in the name of all the Learned and Polite Persons of the Nation, complain to Your lordship, as *First Minister,* that our Language is extremely imperfect;

that its daily Improvements are by no means in proportion to its daily Corruptions; and, that in many Instances, it offends against every Part of Grammar. . . . [A] free judicious Choice should be made of such Persons, as are generally allowed to be best qualified for such a Work, without any regard to Quality, Party, or Profession. These, to a certain Number at least, should assemble at some appointed Time and Place, and fix on Rules by which they design to proceed. . . . [W]hat I have most at Heart is, that some Method should be thought on for *ascertaining* and *fixing* our Language for ever, after such Alterations are made in it as shall be thought requisite.

This desire to "fix" the language—that is, to secure it in a stable form—motivated many eighteenth-century grammarians and lexicographers (or dictionary makers), including famous man of letters Samuel Johnson. By the time Johnson published his dictionary in 1755, however, he seems to have realized that English would change despite efforts to keep it stable. In the preface to his dictionary, Johnson wrote:

> Those who have been persuaded to think well of my design, require that it should fix our language, and put a stop to those alterations which time and chance have hitherto been suffered to make in it without opposition. With this consequence I will confess that I flattered myself for a while; but now begin to fear that I have indulged expectation which neither reason nor experience can justify. . . . [T]he lexicographer [may] be derided, who being able to produce no example of a nation that has preserved their words and phrases from mutability, shall imagine that his dictionary can embalm his language, and secure it from corruption and decay. (Johnson 1974/1755, 9)

Johnson, like Swift, saw most language change as corruption. Whether language change seems like progress or decay, however, is in the eye of the beholder, and who receives the blame for linguistic "corruption" often reflects social prejudice. As we discussed in Chapter 1, there is no reason to believe that the English language is getting necessarily worse or better over time.

Nonetheless, there have been attempts in the United States to establish an academy to monitor the language. In 1774 there was a proposal for an American Society of Language, and in 1806 a bill for such an academy was introduced in Congress. In 1820 the American Academy of Language and Belles Lettres was established under President John Quincy Adams, with the task of maintaining purity and uniformity in the language, but it broke up after two years, in part because of lack of funding.

Language Mavens

Today, English is governed by a loose network of "language authorities," sometimes called "language mavens": English teachers, editors, journalists, columnists on language, and authors/editors of dictionaries, grammar and usage books, and style guides. We invest in these people the authority to tell us what constitutes proper and improper usage, especially in the written language. Many of these people are highly educated, qualified experts on language, and not all of them attempt to legislate usage. For example, lexicographers (who create dictionaries) often see their goal as describing usage rather than legislating it, even though we turn to dictionaries for "answers" about correct usage.

Language columnists, however, often attempt to distinguish between good and bad usage. William Safire, who wrote the weekly column "On Language" for the *New York Times Sunday Magazine* until he died in 2009, was probably the best-known language pundit in America, and many readers of the *Times* enjoyed his observations about current usage and relied on his judgments about acceptability. To take a good example, in a December 2006 column subtitled "Incorrections" (a correction that is itself incorrect), Safire reverses his position and accepts one change that has happened in American English (the use of *raise* rather than *rear* in reference to children) but holds the line on the distinction between *disinterested* and *uninterested* (unlike the majority of speakers of American English!). He writes that although he usually holds the prescriptive line, he's now decided "that to tut-tut at 'I'm raising my kid to be a billionaire' is to commit an incorrection." But he goes on to say that *disinterested,* no matter how people may be using it in speech and in the blogosphere, does not, in his opinion, mean 'uninterested'. Safire concludes: "Rear up and rage, rage against the dying of an enlightening distinction."

Sometimes language mavens go too far: they attempt to exercise an authority over language they do not and cannot have and can foster unpleasant language attitudes. For instance, Barbara Wallraff, who writes columns on language titled "Word Court" and "Word Fugitives" for the *Atlantic Monthly,* has established what she calls the "Word Police" (she is the Police Commissioner): "As a certified word police officer," she writes, "you will be entitled to issue Grammar Citations when you see or hear crimes against the language." Needless to say, such crimes are metaphorical, but the tone is very authoritarian. The Word Police can't actually arrest you, but they may well feel "entitled" to judge you based on their own language pet peeves.

A surprising number of people feel this entitlement, feel licensed to punish language offenders. One of the most prominent recently is Lynne Truss, whose award-winning book *Eats, Shoots & Leaves: The Zero Tolerance Approach to Punctuation* (2003) has sold several million copies worldwide. Truss's book appeals especially to those she calls "sticklers," people who want punctuation to be solid, undeniable fact, even though it's really a matter of convention and varies remarkably across the universe of punctuation use. The message of the book seems to be (or is taken to be by many readers) that either we adhere to strict rules of punctuation or we face punctuation anarchy. But this may be a false dichotomy.

A Question to Discuss

Does the SAT Know Good Grammar from Bad?

In 2003, the SAT included a question about the following sentence: "Toni Morrison's genius enables her to create novels that arise from and express the injustices African Americans have endured." Is it grammatical? The College Board, the organization that designs, administers, and evaluates the SAT, originally expected those taking the test to respond "E" or "no error." But Kevin Keegan, from Silver Springs, Maryland, objected: *her,* he pointed out, refers not to *Toni Morrison* but to *Toni Morrison's,* so the phrase "enables her to create" is grammatically incorrect because the sentence lacks a referent for *her.* In fact, judgments about grammaticality are often more open to interpretation than we expect (see Mark Liberman's detailed entry on Language Log, January 31, 2005, for a longer discussion). In other words, the SAT's version of "good" grammar is continually problematic, but no one can deny the high stakes involved in good SAT verbal scores. Do you think the SAT should have the grammatical authority to legislate linguistic "correctness"?

Some would argue that Truss's appeal is as much about good manners, maybe even morality, as it is about rescuing punctuation. As James Boylan put it in the *Columbia Journalism Review* (2003), Truss is "a kind of madcap Martha Stewart of punctuation." She promises to restore written order and civility to a language—if not a world—overwhelmed by the unruliness of e-mail and text messages. But is that really enough for Truss to appeal to so many millions of readers? Why do we rely on any language mavens for advice about language use, besides the fact that they have considerable experience and insight into certain types of usage? American culture is a culture of aspiration, of getting ahead and keeping up with the Joneses. We know that others judge our use of language—different others judge us differently on the basis of what we say and how we write. So it stands to reason that we should look for the rules that guide us to "better" language, with the belief that once we master the rules, greater educational, social, economic, and political success will follow. And once we have mastered the rules, it can be hard to resist imposing them on others. As long as language is intimately involved in our social identities, we will attempt to use it to advantage. The question is: to what extent do we trust language mavens to point us in the direction of best language use?

Many local papers publish language columns or articles on a regular basis, such as the following:

"What to Do with 'Myself'? Bury It and Resurrect Oldies" (*Denver Rocky Mountain Post,* June 18, 1995)

"Having a Problem with 'No Problem'" (*Milwaukee Journal Sentinel,* February 8, 1998)

"Musical Grammar Tips: Word Gal and Music Guy Weigh in on Songs That Are Grammatically Challenged" (*Jackson Citizen Patriot,* January 21, 2007)

Headlines like the first two suggest conservative reactions to new usage, and the accompanying articles often disparage the linguistic behavior or confusion of "young people" and clarify "right" from "wrong," rather than searching for the source of change or confusion. The third article is almost a full two-page spread, with photos, devoted to the grammar of songs such as "Lay Down Sally," by Eric Clapton, "Between You and I," by Jessica Simpson, and "If You Love Somebody Set Them Free," by Sting. Grammar Girl (aka Mignon Fogarty) argues for the importance of good grammar in popular songs as well as everywhere else. For example, she responds to "21 Questions," by 50 Cent, with "50 Cent is talking about a hypothetical future situation (becoming poor) that is contrary to his current situation (he's rich), so the lyrics should be in the subjunctive case: 'Would you love me if I were down and out?'" (She also believes that Bo Diddly's "Who Do You Love?" should be "Whom Do You Love?") DJ Steve (aka Steve Seel) takes a more accepting approach, without challenging "the rules," but just their relevance to pop lyrics: "It doesn't bother me, coming from a song, because pop songs are a vernacular art. Pop music uses colloquial language—an understood language that's separate from formal English."

Some newspaper columns or articles do record language change, often reflecting the fascination of older generations with the language of younger ones:

"Radi-oh: He's Fly (and Jiggy, Too)" (*Seattle Times,* February 28, 1999)

"*Duh:* Today's Kids Are, Like, Killing the English Language. Yeah, Right" (*New York Times,* August 9, 1998)

"Kanye West: 'Bling' Is Out" (*Toronto Sun,* August 9, 2007)

Sometimes a newspaper column will "okay" a change in written guidelines, often to bring them more in line with actual usage, as when a column in the *Seattle Times* (May 13, 2001) stated that "it isn't always sensible not to split infinitives."

Language change and questions of usage are thus considered "newsworthy," and many columnists who write about language assert public authority about how the rest of us should view these issues. Of course, there are lots of changes going on in the language all the time, but only a handful of them make headlines. The use of *hopefully* as a sentence adverb ("Hopefully you are finding this reading interesting") has attracted a great deal of attention and condemnation, for example. Traditionally, *hopefully* meant 'in a manner full of hope', as in "Jack opened the envelope from Wisconsin hopefully, because he wanted to be admitted there more than to any other university." Those conservative about usage objected when the adverb came to mean 'I hope' or 'it is to be hoped that', as in "Hopefully, he'll get into Wisconsin." Yet very few people seem to have noticed that the verb *peruse* has undergone an almost perfect reversal in meaning, from 'read carefully' to 'skim'—probably because we use *hopefully* much more than we use *peruse,* at least in everyday speech. Change tends to occur first in the spoken language. Change then attracts the pundits' attention as it infiltrates the written standard. What counts as acceptable or "standard" can be remarkably arbitrary.

Defining Standard English

Most definitions of Standard English are fuzzy. First, Standard English is not associated with any particular locality. Second, the network of authorities that assumes responsibility for prescribing the standards for the English language is an informal one, and not all authorities are "on the same page." Linguist Rosina Lippi-Green describes Standard English as a "myth." There are, however, some features that are generally ascribed to Standard English. The *Oxford Companion to the English Language* provides a useful starting point:

> In everyday usage, *standard English* is taken to be the variety most widely accepted and understood within an English-speaking country or throughout the English-speaking world. It is more or less free of regional, class, and other shibboleths, although the issue of a "standard accent" often causes trouble and tension. It is sometimes presented as the "common core" (what is left when all regional and other distinctions are stripped away), a view that remains controversial because of the difficulty of deciding where core ends and peripheries begin. Linguists generally agree on three things: (1) The standard is most easily identified in print, whose conventions are more or less uniform throughout the world, and some use the term print standard for that medium. (2) Standard forms are used by most presenters of news on most English-language radio and television networks, but with regional and other variations, particularly in accent. (3) Use of standard English relates to social class and level of education, often considered (explicitly or implicitly) to match the average level of attainment of students who have finished secondary-level schooling. (McArthur 1992, 983)

As this definition suggests, Standard English could be generally described as the "prestige social dialect" in the wider speech community—that is, the dialect that most speakers assume isn't a dialect and the one they accept as authoritative, for whatever social reason. There are several key distinctions in this definition that merit more discussion: written versus spoken Standard English; formal versus informal usage; and accent versus grammar versus vocabulary.

Standard English is often associated primarily with formal speech and writing, but like any dialect, it encompasses both formal and informal language. Formal Standard English could be called Edited Standard English (whether it is written or spoken in formal settings), as it tends to be edited to adhere to the prescriptions in usage guides about what is standard or "correct." The process of standardization, which seeks to suppress language variation, can more effectively control formal language, making it more homogeneous in public social settings where "correctness" is valued.

Informal Standard English is harder to pinpoint, although speakers are able to judge informal speech as being more and less standard. In their book *American English,* Walt Wolfram and Natalie Schilling-Estes (2006, 12–13) point out that speech samples of American English that are rated as standard typically exclude socially stigmatized grammatical structures (such as multiple negation) but often allow what would traditionally be incorrect pronouns (as in "It is a great honor for my good friend, the honorable senator from Utah, and I to cosponsor this bill"). Informal Standard English may show more variation in accent and some regionally distinctive vocabulary (like *y'all,* which isn't excluded from professional speech in the South, though it would be counted nonstandard in the North). That said, there are shibboleths in terms of pronunciation (like *aks*— see Chapter 1) and vocabulary (e.g., *poke* 'bag'—see Chapter 12). Sometimes Standard English can most easily be described by what it is not.

So while Standard English, particularly the formal varieties, is a surprisingly homogeneous entity, it demonstrates some variation. Sometimes the variation spans the informal/formal style distinction. For example, many speakers do not hear the use of *hopefully* as a sentence adverb as nonstandard, but it is not yet universally acceptable in the written standard. Sometimes two or more variants coexist in accepted written standards without one being stigmatized (e.g., *I have proved* versus *I have proven*). And as mentioned earlier, spoken Standard English seems to allow some variation in accent and vocabulary.

There is a spectrum of language use, on which Standard English is a band, like red or orange in the color spectrum. There is a spectrum of use *within* Standard English, too, though variation within that variety is less marked than variation between it and other varieties. But it's hard to know just where red ends and orange begins: varieties of English overlap and speakers position themselves on the spectrum depending on what varieties they control and how well a variety or level of formality serves their social or stylistic goals.

The *Oxford Companion to the English Language* notes that, while for some speakers Standard English has negative connotations (it seems stuck up, or fussy, or it represents privilege to the less privileged), it appears to be positive or neutral for most speakers. Commentators on language are split: "Some commentators regard standard English as a convenient fiction, like the law; others see it as a thoroughly inconvenient fiction built on social elitism and educational privilege" (982).

The terms used to describe the standard variety of English vary. *Standard English* is the most general term. The old term *General American* has been replaced by *Standard American English, Mainstream United States English* (MUSE), and the *Language of Wider Communication* (LWC). The term *Received Pronunciation* (RP) is used for British English. No matter which term you use, remember that Standard English is a dialect of English elevated to the status of "standard" for social and political reasons, as well as utilitarian ones. And as many speakers are well aware, Standard English is not always the best or most appropriate choice in a given context: nonstandard varieties carry more localized prestige and important cultural capital within particular speech communities. For instance, if you run for political office, you'd better not sound like a newscaster or an English professor, at least not all of the time. Many voters respond to whatever American English they hear as "down home." They prefer leaders who are well spoken but not *so* well spoken that their audiences feel like they're back in school. "Perfect" English "talks down" to every other variety, and this fact leads to a paradox at the heart of controversy over usage: almost everyone acknowledges a standard; almost no one learns or uses it absolutely.

Educated and respected writers regularly violate many of the rules for the standard written language as a *stylistic choice*. **Style** generally refers to the use of "good English"—language used effectively for clarity, appropriateness, and aesthetic appeal. English constructions can be stylistically awkward without being ungrammatical (for instance, "I and my competitor both strive better to serve the people"). English constructions can also be stylistically accepted, or even admired, while being relatively ungrammatical. For instance, most of us will accept (in speech, at least, if not in writing) "No one likes their writing style criticized," and some would prefer it to "No one likes others to criticize his or her style." Even though the first sentence mixes technically singular and plural forms, leaves out grammatically significant phrases, and uses the passive voice without any good reason, it sounds more straightforward, and few of us would find it confusing.

Style emphasizes questions of choice, dependent on how a writer wishes his or her audience to respond. And respected writers have the power to define accepted style. If enough educated writers make the same stylistic choice (e.g., using contractions, using *hopefully* as a sentence adverb, preferring "If I was to go with you" to the historically correct subjunctive "Were I to go with you"), then it is difficult to see it as a grammatical error or a violation of "good English." Indeed, most of us don't.

Descriptive versus Prescriptive Grammar Rules

The distinction between prescriptive and descriptive grammatical rules is fundamental. The stems of the two words signal the difference: to *prescribe* is to establish rules, often as an authoritative guide; to *describe* is to give an account that characterizes something. Language pundits are usually (but not always) **prescriptivists**; linguists and lexicographers are usually (but not always) **descriptivists**. With the rise of language blogs, like Language Log and Mr. Verb, more linguists and lexicographers have become pundits, and current arguments over language are better balanced than they once were, though not necessarily tending toward agreement between the extremes.

Prescriptive rules establish and enforce what we should say or write according to established notions of "good" and "bad," "right" and "wrong." These rules judge the correctness of utterances and try to enforce one formal norm. Examples of prescriptive rules are:

Do not end a sentence with a preposition.

Do not use *hopefully* as a sentence adverb.

Use singular inclusive pronouns to refer back to indefinite pronouns such as *everyone* (e.g., "Everyone should mind his or her manners").

Descriptive rules attempt to model speakers' linguistic competence and performance, what speakers know about a language and how they actually use it. Such rules describe what we do say or write in any given language. These rules assume knowledge, most of it unconscious, of phonetics, phonology, morphology, syntax, and semantics, and they evaluate the structural well-formedness of an utterance, not its appropriateness or stylistic correctness. Such rules are generally associated with the spoken language. Examples of descriptive rules are:

> Adjectives precede the nouns they modify.
>
> Regular nouns form the plural by adding -*s*.
>
> Indefinite pronouns such as *everyone* are often referred back to with plural pro-
> nouns because they seem semantically plural (e.g., "Everyone should mind
> their manners").

Descriptive rules typically do not appear in grammar books and style guides. There is little need to include them, since most of them are so basic to the spoken language that we learned them as children, and we rarely "make mistakes" that violate these rules. Prescriptive grammar books tend to focus on points of usage where there is variation, often because the spoken and written forms of language diverge, either because the grammatical construction is in flux as the language changes (e.g., the use of *who* and *whom*), or because a prescriptive rule imposed on the written language never corresponded to spoken language (e.g., the rule not to split infinitives). When there are multiple possibilities for a construction, language pundits may state that one is better, preferable, or more appropriate than the others, or, in the most extreme cases, that one is right and the others are wrong, but we should assess the basis of any such prescriptive judgment.

In order to clarify the distinction, here are three case studies of how actual usage corresponds (or doesn't correspond) to prescriptive rules.

Case Study One: Multiple Negatives

The term *multiple negative* refers to grammatical constructions that use two or more grammatical elements to express negation (e.g., *I didn't give her none*). The term does not refer to speakers' intentional use of two negatives in opposition to each other (e.g., *I couldn't not do it*).

Multiple negatives used to be standard in most varieties of English—as they are in many other languages, such as French. Double negatives appear in *Beowulf* and throughout the works of Chaucer. In the Renaissance, some varieties of English, including the variety that became Standard English, came to favor constructions with single negation, but many varieties continued to employ multiple negation. Consider the following examples from French, Middle English, Early Modern English, and Modern English:

> "*Rien ne vit qu'en details*" 'Nothing exists but in things' (the negative *nothing* is
> composed of *rien* and *ne*);
>
> "For ther nys no creature so good that hym ne wanteth somewhat of the perfec-
> cioun of God" For there is not no creature so good but he lacks to some degree
> the perfection of God (Chaucer, *The Canterbury Tales*);
>
> "I cannot goe no further" (Shakespeare, *As You Like It*);
>
> "He ain't nothing no more—never was nothing" (Marvin X, "Take Care of Business,"
> published in *TDR*, 1968).

In his *Short Introduction to English Grammar* (1762), Robert Lowth asserted that double negatives cancel each other, as they do in some mathematical operations. Of course, in most instances, this is absurd: no one would interpret "I can't give you no money" as a speaker's willingness to fork over cash. But the notion that multiple negatives were somehow illogical and therefore wrong slowly took hold, to the point that multiple negatives in nonstandard dialects came to be condemned.

There is nothing wrong with multiple negatives according to descriptive rules of grammar. In fact, their loss was even lamented by some language commentators through the nineteenth century. Richard W. Bailey (1991, 241) quotes the following excerpt about the double negative from Fitzedward Hall's *Modern English* (1873): "If we examine the history of the language, we perceive, that, since the date of the authorized translation of the Bible,—the finest example of English,—the alterations that have taken place have been, generally, for the worse. The double negative has been abandoned, to the great injury of strength of expression." Viewed from a historical perspective, all prescriptive rules are suspect.

Case Study Two: *Ain't*

The much maligned word *ain't* has taken more criticism and condemnation than any other contraction in English, to the point where language authorities now regularly condemn the word as "vulgar," "ignorant," "uneducated," or worse. Some warn that any speaker who uses the word will risk being judged with similar adjectives. Of course, many speakers of English use *ain't* naturally as part of their dialects, and many other speakers, whose dialects do not regularly employ *ain't,* still exploit the word for expressive purposes. Why is *ain't* considered so much worse than, say, *don't* or *can't?*

The word first appeared at the end of the seventeenth century as *an't,* a contracted form of *am not* and *are not*. Use later expanded to cover *is not* as well as *has not* and *have not*. In 1781, the Reverend John Witherspoon condemned a whole list of "vulgar abbreviations," including "an't, can't, han't, don't, should'nt, would'nt, could'nt, &c." (quoted in Gilman 1994, 61). As you can see, most of these contractions (with the apostrophe occasionally in a different place) have redeemed themselves, except for *ain't*. One reason *ain't* may have been so criticized is that its form does not clearly correspond to all of the forms for which it is a contraction (*am, is, are, has, have,* and in some dialects *does* and *do*); however, one could make a similar point about the contraction *won't*. Although *ain't* has been condemned in prescriptive resources, and many speakers believe the word is somehow fundamentally corrupt, there is nothing grammatically wrong with *ain't* according to descriptive rules, and many speakers use the word productively in their speech in many contexts.

Case Study Three: *Who* and *Whom*

As grammar books explain, the distinction between *who* and *whom* is relatively straightforward: *who* is the subject form and should be used when it functions as the subject of a clause; *whom* is the object form and should be used when it functions as an object, direct or indirect.

"*Who* came?" (subject)

"*Whom* did you invite?" (direct object)

"I know the student *who* thinks linguistics is fascinating." (subject)

"I know the student *whom* the linguistics instructor recommended." (direct object)

Why do speakers confuse these forms? The answer seems to be "language change in progress." In Modern English, we rarely differentiate between subjects and objects in terms of a noun's form, though speakers of Old and Middle English did (see Chapter 13). A rose is a rose, as they say, whether it is the subject or the object. Word order distinguishes subject from object in Modern English: subjects come before verbs and objects after them, or after prepositions. Only in pronouns does English still distinguish between subjects and objects in terms of form (e.g., *I/me, he/him, who/whom,* etc.), and some of these distinctions are becoming confused. *Who/whom* is especially difficult because these words, whether interrogative pronouns marking questions or relative pronouns heading relative clauses, tend to occur at the beginning of sentences or clauses. They often look like subjects, regardless of their grammatical functions. As a result, many speakers are tempted to use *who* in almost all grammatical contexts. For many speakers, *whom* sounds more formal, so sometimes they will use it to sound correct, even when it isn't. For example, you may hear "Whom shall I say is calling?" when "Who shall I say is calling?" is technically correct. Historians of English note that we have evidence for *who/whom* confusion as far back as the fifteenth century.

The Status of Prescriptive Rules

As these case studies suggest, there is often a gap between prescriptive rules and speakers' documented usage. Grammarians may create prescriptive rules at particular points in time based on their personal preferences, rather than actual language usage. Many prescriptive rules are conservative: they attempt to preserve older forms of the language in the face of language change, though others may dismiss older aspects of English preserved in contemporary speech as incorrect. For example, no current prescriptivist recommends multiple negation, even though double and multiple negatives are as old as Old English and have been used throughout the history of English.

At this point you may be thinking either "Great! I can use *ain't* in my college papers, and my instructors will be wrong to grade me down!" or "No, this book must be wrong, because no college professor would ever let me write a paper full of double negatives." Here's the linguistic scoop. You are typically not allowed to use *ain't* in college papers, but not because there is anything grammatically wrong (in the descriptive sense) with *ain't*. It is prescriptive rules that disallow *ain't* in formal writing. That said, your college professor has lots of legitimate justifications for trying to ensure that you control prescriptive grammar rules in your writing. For instance, your level of education—and perhaps your qualifications more generally—will be judged in some contexts by your control of Standard English and of a set of formal, written, stylistic conventions.

What we are saying here is that the prescriptive rules speakers and writers of English have come to accept (more or less) are socially constructed and (to a great extent) arbitrary. They are not more logical than other possible rules of speech. They are not always justified by actual use of the language over time or even at the present moment. "Correct" speech is not necessarily better aesthetically than other speech: beauty is in the ear of the listener, if not also of the speaker or writer.

The prescriptive/descriptive distinction is fundamental to much of linguistics. Linguistic texts often characterize prescriptive rules as "unnatural" impositions on language use. But in the book *Verbal Hygiene* (1995), Deborah Cameron complicates this characterization. She argues that the desire to regulate, improve, and clean up the speech of other speakers is a natural behavior in speech communities. Within any community of speakers, some speakers will try to tell other speakers how to speak. In this sense, prescriptive tendencies, while they may be imposed, are not unnatural to language use; instead, they are one of many social factors that affect speakers' linguistic behavior. After all, descriptive linguists prescribe when they tell speakers that descriptive approaches are a better way to think about language. Cameron argues that we need to shift the debate away from the question "should we prescribe?" and instead ask questions about "who prescribes for whom, what they prescribe, how, and for what purposes" (11).

In other words, prescription has its place in the history of English, in its development and use, from Old English to the present day. But authority over language use is a social rather than a purely linguistic matter.

Spoken versus Written Language

It is much easier to control the written language than the spoken language, and almost all of us adhere to the grammatical rules of formal, Standard English more in our written language than in our speech. Written, formal Standard English is a social construction: it's not natural speech but a refined code reflecting language authorities' preferences for certain linguistic features and patterns. The standard is closely tied to educational and professional success, and we are all strongly encouraged to adopt its conventions in formal writing, if not in more formal speech. Most of us, though, most of

A Question to Discuss

Are We Losing Our Memories?

Plato worried in the fourth century BCE that, with the invention of writing, we would lose our memories. It is hard to argue that he was wrong. When we want to remember things, we write them down, and memorizing even a short poem can be taxing for many speakers. To be the *scop* (singer) who sang *Beowulf* from memory, all 3,000 lines or so, is almost incomprehensible to many modern English speakers—although many hip hop performers still spontaneously create and re-create long oral poems using some comparable poetic devices. Today, actors who memorize enormous amounts of material are now the exception—acting on film or recorded television is not the same as standing on stage, night after night, repeating the same speech.

None of this means that we cannot learn great amounts of material. But the fact is that we do not have to, so this cognitive capacity is not regularly exercised. As a result, television networks like NBC and FOX can make lots of money from shows like *The Singing Bee* and *Don't Forget the Lyrics,* respectively, because even those who think they know song lyrics verbatim actually don't. On *The Singing Bee,* contestants are expected, for example, to sing along with a song and then sing the next line unprompted, fill in blanks in the lyrics, or sing complete choruses of songs without prompting. Nowadays, even short bursts of prompted memory prove challenging—at least to those who lose *The Singing Bee* or similar contests.

the time, speak on the fly, and we don't edit our speech to suppress variation. And most of us speak varieties of English that differ from Standard English, at least in some features, even though we have been taught to avoid them in formal settings.

Most linguists view spoken language as primary for a couple of reasons:

1. Speakers acquire the spoken language naturally as children, without explicit instruction, whereas writing is a consciously acquired skill.
2. Many spoken languages exist without written forms (many Native American languages, for instance).

Of course, there are written languages without spoken forms, either because the spoken form has died (e.g., Latin) or because the language was created for a specific communicative purpose (for instance, though some advocates of Esperanto do learn to speak it, it is no one's native language, and much more written and read than spoken). But these languages are never the natural or first languages of their users. Signed languages are equivalent to spoken languages, as children acquire them naturally, without explicit instruction, if they grow up in a community of sign language users.

There are many general differences between spoken and written language. Spoken language allows significantly more variation than written language, although both vary depending on the level of formality. With the spoken language, we typically have a clearer sense of audience. When we talk to those physically present or present aurally (as on the telephone), we can tailor our utterances more specifically and clear up misunderstandings if we sense confusion. In these spoken situations, we also usually have a clearer understanding of shared context, whether physical surroundings or shared knowledge, on which we can rely within the communicative event. Written language also has context, defined by the physical location of the text and information about its production. Internet texts are written and received in a context different from that of a novel, for instance. Writers, however, often have less knowledge of—and control over—their audiences and typically have no opportunity to clarify meaning if it is not understood (other than to rely on readers to reread the passage or keep reading for clarification). Spoken language tends to be more immediate; written language can involve a delay between production and reception.

You may challenge the distinction between spoken and written language, however, and with good reason. E-mails, texting, and instant messaging blur conventional distinctions between writing and speech. Electronic communication, which is discussed in Chapter 14, is motivating significant changes in the current phase of Modern English and promises to propel change in future English, too.

We process language differently as listeners than we do as readers, which accounts for some of the grammatical differences between spoken and written English. On a page, we can retrace our steps through a sentence if the syntax becomes complicated and confusing, or if we've forgotten the referent for a pronoun. This kind of retracing is difficult and usually not necessary in conversation, which tends toward repetition and simpler clause and sentence structures. We often speak (or write online) in run-on sentences and sentence fragments. And, in conversation, whether spoken or Web-based, we can ask for clarification.

We are taught, however, to create more sophisticated prose when we write, for example, by using subordinate clauses with conjunctions such as *because, although, while, when.* Or we might use devices such as ellipsis, leaving out "understood" words in parallel constructions ("I took linguistics as my optional class, and Joe astrophysics").

The emphasis on subordination in the written language can be traced back to the Renaissance, when scholars advocated imitating the highly subordinated syntax of Latin as a way of making English more eloquent. Old and Middle English texts, in contrast, contain many more sentences strung together with coordinating conjunctions (see Chapter 13). Current speech and electronic communication may extend the habits of Old and Middle English grammar and in part reverse the sentence patterns favored from the Renaissance into the twentieth century.

If you ask a room full of English majors and faculty members whether they feel more comfortable with the written or spoken language, a surprising number will say that the written language feels more basic and more comfortable. They feel that they can express themselves better in writing than they can in speech. This response reflects the overwhelmingly literate world in which we live. Many English speakers read and write as part of their daily lives. Written English has become our most trusted source of knowledge and authority. In order to guarantee things, we sign them; a handshake is fine, but we trust the agreement only when it is signed. In order to remember things, we write them down. In order to verify factual information, we turn to written sources; an authoritative speaker is fine, but we usually feel more comfortable when information is confirmed by a written source. We confirm marriage vows with a marriage certificate. Perhaps one of the only places where we still rely solely on the oral is in the courtroom, where witnesses swear orally to tell the truth and nothing but the truth, without signing a similar statement.

English was spoken in a primarily oral culture before the advent of printing in the late fifteenth century. Historians of literacy such as Michael T. Clanchy note that when writing is introduced into oral cultures, it is often mistrusted. Why should speakers believe the authority of a written text when the author is not present to be questioned or to defend his or her words? Human interaction—an oral pact or promise—can be a greater source of trust and authority. Authenticity, in other words, is judged in cultural terms.

Dictionaries of English

We are brought up to think of the dictionary as an ultimate language authority: fussy (or fastidious) people, for example, may check to see which pronunciation of a word is listed first, insisting that, for some reason, it's more legitimate than others listed (or not listed). The notion that dictionaries are especially authoritative is relatively new, first conceived only about 250 years ago. Given the advanced age of English, dictionaries are a relatively new invention.

The Earliest Dictionaries of English

Old English manuscripts sometimes include interlinear or marginal glosses, or brief translational definitions, as do Middle English manuscripts. And medieval writers occasionally compiled glossaries, usually providing English definitions of Latin words. William Caxton, who introduced printing to England in 1476, published an untitled French-English glossary in 1480, and in 1499, he printed an English-Latin glossary, the *Promptorium Parvulorum sive Clericorum,* or 'storehouse [of words] for boys, especially [those training to be] priests'. Thomas Elyot's *Dictionarie* (1538), a Latin-English glossary, is the first *dictionary* reference work to use the word for such a book that we use today.

Printing and literacy walked hand in hand into the sixteenth century, a time when an enormous number of borrowed words from classical languages was being introduced into

English. As a result, readers increasingly felt the need for an English dictionary, and Robert Cawdrey finally supplied one in 1604, with a long title that begins *A Table Alphabeticall*. This slim, "hard word" dictionary—that is, a dictionary of words that most people wouldn't know—is fundamentally different from the modern dictionary. Today, we expect general dictionaries to describe the English vocabulary, or at least the bulk of it, but early lexicographers didn't see the need for such extensive treatment of the vocabulary. Surely, people would use a dictionary only to discover the meanings of words they did not know!

The seventeenth century saw the publication of several more "hard word" dictionaries, most notably Henry Cockeram's *The English Dictionarie: Or, an Interpreter of Hard English Words* (1623) and Thomas Blount's *Glossographia: Or, A Dictionary Interpreting all such Hard Words . . . as are now used in our refined English Tongue* (1656). Modern unabridged dictionaries include, on average, around 500,000 entries. Cawdrey's *A Table Alphabeticall* lists around 2,500 and Cockeram's dictionary a mere 1,600. Some of these hard words did not survive to Modern English (such as *periclitation* 'jeopardy'), and others (such as *ocean*) no longer seem hard at all.

The Beginnings of Modern Lexicography

The eighteenth century witnessed the birth of the kind of dictionary with which we are most familiar today. John Kersey's *A New English Dictionary* (1702) was the first to include not only hard but also common words, and Nathan Bailey's *An Universal Etymological English Dictionary* (1721), though far from comprehensive in modern terms, included nearly 40,000 words and first gave serious attention to etymology, a feature of dictionary entries we now take for granted (even if we rarely consult them). The landmark lexicographic event of the century, though, was the publication of Samuel Johnson's *Dictionary of the English Language* (1755).

Johnson's *Dictionary* was not particularly innovative, but it was a better general dictionary than any of its predecessors. It included about the same number of entries as Bailey's. It was not the first to analyze the meaning of words into numbered senses, nor the first to illustrate the use of entered words with quotations from literature. Yet, where the best earlier dictionaries had been adept at one or another aspect of understanding English words, Johnson's was better justified, better organized, more consistently analytical, more systematic in its presentation, more informative about pronunciation (though in a limited way), and, in its definitions, not only precise but often eloquent. It was the first English dictionary one might consult as much for pleasure as for mere reference. Some of the entries are notoriously quirky: for example, *oats* 'a grain which in England is generally given to horses, but in Scotland supports the people'; and *lexicographer* 'a writer of dictionaries; a harmless drudge, that busies himself in tracing the original, and detailing the signification of words'.

Johnson's dictionary, like all modern dictionaries of any significance, did not assume the meanings of words, their pronunciations, or their grammatical functions. Like modern lexicographers, Johnson and his six assistants relied on a vast collection of texts for evidence of word use from which they could draw their conclusions. They pored over literature from the preceding 150 years (sometimes earlier) to collect illustrative quotations for all of the more than 40,000 words they included in the great dictionary. Amazingly, these seven men accomplished all of this work, by hand, in only six years.

Johnson, as noted earlier, had expressed in the preface of his dictionary his initial intention to "fix" the language, not to 'repair' so much as to 'establish permanently'. As modern as Johnson's method was, his dictionary was motivated more or less equally by descriptive and prescriptive inclinations. Johnson aimed to create an authoritative volume, and he succeeded in raising the expectations of users that dictionaries would exercise such authority.

Historical Lexicography

Soon after Johnson's dictionary was published, the very nature of the study of linguistics changed irrevocably. Sir William Jones, followed by Rasmus Rask (a Danish linguist) and Franz Bopp and Jacob Grimm (two Germans), established historical linguistics and the comparative study of Indo-European languages. By the early nineteenth century, comparative philology laid the foundation for a new species of dictionary, one achieved by historical lexicography. The brothers Grimm were the first to attempt a historical dictionary (of German) on the basis of the "new philology," but the English were not far behind. By 1859, the Philological Society in London had organized a project to produce *A New English Dictionary on Historical Principles* (now known as the *Oxford English Dictionary*). The goal was to tell the history of every word in English, going back to 1100 CE. It would take seventy years to complete, although no one knew this at the time. This Herculean task required an editor of exceptional talent and persistence.

The Philological Society found such an editor almost twenty years later in James A. H. Murray, a descriptivist at heart. Murray, with Henry Bradley, William A. Craigie, and C. T. Onions, the *NED/OED*'s other chief editors over its seventy years, and a slew of assistants (including Murray's children), relied heavily on a host of volunteer readers, who excerpted citations from English of all periods and sent these citation slips to the editors. These citation slips formed the body of material from which the language would be analyzed and illustrated, word by word. The slips were filed in cubbyholes in the Scriptorium, a shedlike building where the compilers all worked, and then sorted by hand, often on the floor, into the different meanings under a given headword.

In 1928, the completed *OED* filled nearly 16,000 pages, with three columns of text on each page. It contained more than 400,000 entries illustrated by almost 2 million quotations, drawn from a file of nearly 5 million citations excerpted in the dictionary's reading program. The *OED* was expanded, not only by the 1933 supplement, but by four volumes that extended the *OED*'s coverage well into the twentieth century, edited by Robert W. Burchfield (1972–1986). There was also a second edition, incorporating the supplements and additional material, compiled by J. A. Simpson and E. S. C. Weiner (1989). A completely reedited third edition, under Simpson's editorship, is in progress.

From every vantage, the *OED* is incalculably an advance over earlier English dictionaries. It registers many more words and illustrates them more fully and systematically than any previous (or subsequent) general dictionary of English. Its etymologies benefit from historical linguistics, and its sense analysis benefits from the exceptional volume of citations considered by the editors and subeditors when writing definitions. But it is also a dictionary different in kind from any previous dictionary of English: it traces the history of each word entered, from the end of Old English to (close to) the present day. In other words, it is a diachronic rather than a synchronic dictionary.

American Lexicography

After American independence near the end of the eighteenth century, the first dictionary of American English may have been motivated as much by the desire for linguistic independence from Britain as by actual linguistic divergence of American English. Noah Webster, a patriotic lexicographer from Connecticut, wrote his *American Dictionary of the English Language* (1828), according to the preface, "for the continued increase of the wealth, the learning, the moral and religious elevation of character, and the glory of my country."

Whatever it did for young America's economy or morality, Webster's dictionary did promote American English and contribute to the nation's glory. In many respects, it was an excellent dictionary. It included 70,000 words, outdistancing contemporary revisions of Johnson's dictionary. And Webster was one of the best definers in the history of lexicography. However, the dictionary also has its faults. For one thing, it lacks any illustrative quotations (Webster had actually attacked Johnson's dictionary for including too many). And the etymologies are atrociously bad because Webster ignored the discoveries of historical linguistics and exercised his imagination instead. The *American Dictionary of the English Language* was the first great American dictionary, but it left plenty of room for improvement.

Improvements came throughout the nineteenth and twentieth centuries. After Webster died, in 1843, his family sold rights to the dictionary to the G. & C. Merriam Company, who revised it continually and promoted it aggressively until it became the standard American dictionary. The pressure to revise was great, because, from 1830 forward, Joseph Worcester published a series of dictionaries to great critical acclaim and threatened the Webster dictionary's dominant position in the market. Worcester had

A Question to Discuss

Should Dictionaries Ever Prescribe?

In 1997, Delphine Abraham looked up the word *nigger* in the *Merriam-Webster Collegiate Dictionary* and was dismayed at what she found there. The first definition read "a black person—usu. taken to be offensive," and the second was similar: "a member of any dark-skinned race—usu. taken to be offensive." Randall Kennedy, a professor at Harvard Law School, in *Nigger: The Strange Career of a Troublesome Word* (2002, 135), quotes Abraham's reaction: "Most people believe, as I do, that the N-word needs a more accurate first definition reflecting that it is a derogatory term used to dehumanize or oppress a group or race of people." Abraham mobilized a boycott of the dictionary if it refused to review the definitions. Kweisi Mfume, the president of the National Association for the Advancement of Colored People (NAACP), called on Merriam-Webster to revise the definitions.

Merriam-Webster stood by its definition and usage comments, arguing that these were the definitions supported by the material illustrating *nigger* in their citation files. In other words, Merriam-Webster held that the entry was describing the language as it is used, whereas Abraham wanted them to prescribe certain uses of the term.

Kennedy defends Merriam-Webster: "The question is, should Abrahams [sic], Mfume, or anyone else have felt insulted by Merriam-Webster's definition? No. The definition notes that the term is usually taken to be offensive and then states, for good measure, that the N-word 'now ranks as perhaps the most offensive and inflammatory racial slur in English'" (135).

What do you think? Should a dictionary describe a word like *nigger,* or should it prescribe, or even proscribe, its use?

ain't \'änt\ [contr. of *are not*] (1749) **1** : am not : are not : is not **2** : have not : has not **3** : do not : does not : did not — used in some varieties of Black English

usage Although widely disapproved as nonstandard and more common in the habitual speech of the less educated, *ain't* in senses 1 and 2 is flourishing in American English. It is used in both speech and writing to catch attention and to gain emphasis 〈the wackiness of movies, once so deliciously amusing, *ain't* funny anymore —Richard Schickel〉 〈I am telling you—there *ain't* going to be any blackmail —R. M. Nixon〉. It is used esp. in journalistic prose as part of a consistently informal style 〈the creative process *ain't* easy —Mike Royko〉. This informal *ain't* is commonly distinguished from habitual *ain't* by its frequent occurrence in fixed constructions and phrases 〈well—class it *ain't* —Cleveland Amory〉 〈for money? say it *ain't* so, Jimmy! —Andy Rooney〉 〈you *ain't* seen nothing yet〉 〈that *ain't* hay〉 〈two out of three *ain't* bad〉 〈if it *ain't* broke, don't fix it〉. In fiction *ain't* is used for purposes of characterization; in familiar correspondence it tends to be the mark of a warm personal friendship. It is also used for metrical reasons in popular songs 〈*Ain't* She Sweet〉 〈It *Ain't* Necessarily So〉. Our evidence shows British use to be much the same as American.

The entry for *ain't* in Webster's *Third* created a firestorm of criticism because it lacked a usage note or label. In its *Collegiate Dictionary* (11th ed., 2005), Merriam-Webster has modified the *ain't* entry, as shown here.

worked at one time with Webster, and Webster believed that Worcester's dictionaries plagiarized his own. The charge was unfair. Dictionaries have always drawn on one another rather freely (sometimes scandalously so), but Worcester's work was independent and in some respects better than Webster's. It included illustrative quotations and sound etymologies, devoted more space to synonyms, and provided a more general or "standard" treatment of pronunciation. (If Noah Webster had had his way, all Americans would have sounded like Connecticut Yankees.)

Competition between the Webster and Worcester dictionaries was so fierce that it became known as the "war of the dictionaries." The war ended in the early 1860s. Worcester's last and greatest dictionary, *A Comprehensive Dictionary of the English Language,* appeared in 1860. In 1864, the Merriams published a new edition of Webster's dictionary, with completely new etymologies and many features adopted from Worcester's dictionaries. By imitating the enemy, and taking much of the Webster out of the Webster dictionary, the Merriams won the war. The 1864 Webster is generally considered the first "unabridged" dictionary, the model for all those published later.

Merriam-Webster published its *New International Dictionary of the English Language* in 1890. It was followed by a *Second New International Dictionary* (1934) and a *Third New International Dictionary* (1961). The public and conservative literary establishment had some difficulty accepting the first two editions, but Webster's *Third* met with a firestorm of criticism. Philip Babcock Gove, the chief editor of Webster's *Third,* was very self-consciously a descriptivist. He included many words people thought did not belong in a dictionary, and he labeled them less critically. Few words in Gove's version were labeled "vulgar" or "obscene," and he rarely allowed commentary on the appropriateness of a word. For example, he included the word *ain't* with no usage note or condemnatory label. The dictionary's strengths were overlooked by those angry at what they thought was its abnegation of its responsibility as a language authority. Over the centuries, speakers had learned to assume that the dictionary would evaluate as well as describe the English language.

Other publishers saw the Merriam-Webster dictionaries as vulnerable, and they produced "unabridged" dictionaries of their own. For instance, the *Random House Dictionary of the English Language* appeared in 1966; Houghton Mifflin's *The American Heritage Dictionary of the English Language* appeared in 1969. Publishers also produced "college dictionaries," the progenitor of which was Clarence Barnhart's *American College Dictionary* (1947), published by Random House. Desk dictionaries, school dictionaries, pocket dictionaries, and crossword puzzle dictionaries also appeared. A century after winning the "war of the dictionaries," Merriam-Webster was embattled again, but dictionary users are the winners this time. In order to compete, each new dictionary had to distinguish itself: this dictionary comments on usage to satisfy the prescriptivist public, and that dictionary avoids such comments to appeal to those users descriptively inclined, and so on. One wonderful thing about studying the English language at the beginning of the twenty-first century is our easy access to so many outstanding dictionaries, each one of them representing the language in ways sometimes slightly, sometimes profoundly, different from the others. It makes you think.

English Grammar, Usage, and Style

Until at least the late fourteenth century, the period in which Chaucer wrote, English was not a prestige language in England. The church conducted its affairs, from diplomacy to the mass, in Latin. The schools and universities depended on Latin as well. After the Norman Conquest, in 1066, most official business was conducted in Anglo-French; no law was presented to the English in English until 1258. No one could make a speech in the parliament or plead in the law courts in English until 1362. Certainly, no one saw the need to write a grammar of English in the Middle Ages—English, as a vernacular language, just wasn't important enough.

The Earliest Usage Books

The history of grammars of English roughly parallels that of dictionaries. The very fact that they were written at all signaled the growing status of English as a language that deserved consideration in itself, on a par with Latin. The first grammar of English, William Bullokar's *Short Introduction to Guiding,* was published in 1580. Amusingly, Paul Greaves's *Grammatica Anglica* (1594), though a grammar of English, was written in Latin. From the sixteenth century until very recently, grammars of English were much more strenuously prescriptive than dictionaries: they have, for the most part, deliberately attempted to regulate the language.

Writing a prescriptive grammar assumes a standard English. No one saw the need to write a grammar that accounted for all of the regional and social varieties of English. The influence of Latin is partly responsible for this. English authorities, educated primarily in Latin, took it as a model for what English should be. Scholars studied literary Latin, the language of the classical texts that constituted the foundation of Renaissance learning, and, as a result, they considered Latin a "pure" language, one of great formal consistency. Yet Latin also had dialects. All of the Romance languages began as dialects of Vulgar Latin, the Latin that plain folk used. As a language in use, Latin thus showed great variation, just like English.

In the eighteenth century, so many newly literate people populated literate professions that nearly a million grammars were sold across the English-speaking world. Some of this multitude of grammars were ambitious and influential. In America, Thomas Dilworth produced a *New Guide to the English Tongue* (1751); in Britain, Joseph Priestley, the chemist who isolated oxygen, published *Rudiments of English Grammar* (1761), which was almost immediately superseded by Robert Lowth's *A Short Introduction to English Grammar* (1762). Many academics preferred William Ward's *Essay on Grammar* (1765). Lowth's was the most influential, with the American lawyer Lindley Murray's textbook *English Grammar* (1795) a worthy competitor. But George Campbell's *The Philosophy of Rhetoric* (1776) is perhaps the most significant, a linguistic manifesto as important to the discipline as Adam Smith's *The Wealth of Nations* (published in the same year) to political economy.

Prescriptive versus Descriptive Tendencies in Grammars of English

Robert Lowth was a great proponent of Standard English, and he was willing, sometimes aggressively, to argue the "correctness" of the standard and the inferiority of the nonstandard. He is known as one of English's arch-prescriptivists. As he wrote in the preface to his grammar,

> The Principal design of a grammar of any Language is to teach us to express ourselves with propriety in that Language; and to enable us to judge of every phrase and form of construction, whether it is right or not. The plain way of doing this is to lay down rules, and to illustrate them by examples. But, besides showing what is right, the matter may be further explained by pointing out what is wrong.

The emphasis on rules and what is wrong has plagued students (and their teachers) ever since.

George Campbell's views on grammar, though significantly different from Lowth's, were ultimately equally influential. Much like Samuel Johnson's dictionary, Campbell's grammar, *The Philosophy of Rhetoric* (1776), accommodated prescriptive and descriptive tendencies. Campbell argued that the study of grammar should be descriptive, but he was not a descriptivist in the current sense. Rather, he believed that correctness was the province of rhetoric: while grammar described use, rhetoric would determine which usage was better than the rest. In other words, Campbell drew the line between grammar and style, an innovation to which relatively few people paid much attention at the time. But Campbell's grammar established another genre of language reference, the usage or style guide, which eventually became both popular and powerful.

Lowth's view of correctness still dominates most instruction on the English language. We hope that those who read this book—among whom are undoubtedly future teachers and other authorities on the English language—will understand the linguistic ideology and fallacies that underlie automatic acceptance and promotion of a standard dialect's superiority. Standardization is a sociolinguistic fact, but our attitudes about the relationship of the standard to other dialects are learned. It doesn't mean that we don't teach Standard English and prescriptive grammar, but it can mean that we provide a context for Standard English and teach descriptive grammar, too.

As descriptivism became the norm among linguists, descriptive grammars followed. In 1951, George L. Trager and Henry Lee Smith published *An Outline of English Structure;* a year later, Charles Carpenter Fries published *The Structure of English.* Many books supporting the descriptivist tendency appeared subsequently, but none of them has yet had much effect on primary and secondary school grammatical instruction. In 1985, Randolph Quirk, Sidney Greenbaum, Geoffrey Leech, and Jan Svartvik published *A Comprehensive Grammar of the English Language,* the title of which should be taken seriously; published in 1999, the *Longman Grammar of Spoken and Written English* (Biber et al.), weighing in at over 1,150 pages, uses corpora to capture variation and frequency in its grammatical descriptions. Taking "comprehensive" to new heights is *The Cambridge Grammar of the English Language* (Huddleston and Puilum 2002) at 1,842 pages. After 250 years, Campbell's ideal grammar was finally achieved.

Modern Approaches to English Usage

In America, where self-improvement has always sold well, Henry Watson Fowler's *A Dictionary of Modern English Usage* (1926) became the authoritative guide for the early twentieth century—so much so that, though the book discussed the parameters of standard British English, many Americans deferred to it as well. Fowler discussed issues as diverse as the proper use of metaphor (and the impropriety of mixed metaphors) and why *gypsy* and *pygmy* should be spelled thus, rather than *gipsy* and *pigmy.*

Fowler sometimes reads like a schoolmaster (which, for a time, he was), and sometimes his judgments are irascible or cranky. According to Fowler, for example, "The use of *equally as* instead of either *equally* or *as* by itself is an illiterate tautology, but one of which it is necessary to demonstrate the frequency, & therefore the danger, by abundant quotations" (which Fowler did, indeed, provide; see Fowler 1926, 143). Lots of literate speakers and writers succumb to *equally as,* and we have yet to suffer great "danger" from its use. But Fowler's love of language is evident and appealing, and his views are always informative and interesting. He tells us, for example, that the *y* in *gypsy* reflects the word's origin in *Egyptian,* and the *y* in *pygmy* reflects an origin in the Greek word *pygmê,* meaning 'elbow to knuckles' or 'short'.

Overall, *Modern English Usage* promoted thoughtful use of the language. In the discussion of the distinction between *that* and *which,* Fowler noted,

> What grammarians say should be has perhaps less influence on what shall be than even the more modest of them realize: usage evolves itself little disturbed by their likes and dislikes. And yet the temptation to show how better use might have been made of the material to hand is sometimes irresistible. (634)

That many considered Fowler's book an infallible authority was less Fowler's fault than an expression of the public's desire for rules and regulations. In 1996. Robert W. Burchfield updated Fowler's classic significantly to reflect advances in linguistics and a more consistently relaxed approach to the right and the wrong.

Of course, Fowler's success led to other usage books, some of them much less genial. Wilson Follett's *Modern American Usage: A Guide* (1966) begins with a prescriptivist manifesto:

> Despite the modern desire to be easy and casual, Americans from time to time give thought to the language they use—to grammar, vocabulary, and gobbledygook. And as on other issues they divide into two parties. The larger, which includes everybody from the proverbial plain man to the professional writer, takes it for granted that there is a

right way to use words and construct sentences, and many wrong ways. The right way is believed to be clearer, simpler, more logical, and hence more likely to prevent error and confusion. Good writing is easier to read; it offers a pleasant combination of sound and sense.

Against this majority view is the doctrine of an embattled minority, who make up for their small number by their great learning and their place of authority in the school system and the world of scholarship. They are the professional linguists, who deny that there is such a thing as correctness. The language, they say, is what anybody and everybody speaks. Hence there must be no interference with what they regard as a product of nature; they denounce all attempts at guiding choice; their governing principle is epitomized in the title of a speech by a distinguished member of the profession: "Can Native Speakers of a Language Make Mistakes?"

The "distinguished member of the profession" was Allen Walker Read, who was addressing a 1964 meeting of the Linguistic Society of America. But Follett shouldn't be so quick to dismiss the professional linguists. After all, Read's question is actually a very interesting one. In Old and early Middle English, *bird* was *bridde* and *third* was *thridde*. They were altered by the process of sound change called metathesis (which we discussed in Chapter 1 and return to in Chapter 3). Undoubtedly, the first few speakers of the later forms were, in their own context, in error, or at least their neighbors probably thought so.

But at what point did error metamorphose into correctness? How many people around you say sentences like "My parents gave their old car to my brother and I"? According to prescriptive rules, it should be "my brother and me"—*I* is the subject pronoun, and *me* the object pronoun. Prescriptivists might find the sentence a grammatical sin and evidence of the speaker's disordered thought. But most descriptivists, indeed most speakers of English, would disagree. Have you ever really been confused by such a sentence? Many linguists would consider such usage **hypercorrection,** an attempt to speak correctly that results in a supposed "error." When insecure about grammatical rules, speakers may overcompensate by using words and phrases that sound more formal—even when such usage might actually be incorrect according to prescriptive rules. This insecurity developed in school, from oral correction and red marks on papers, and from the general attitude that there is only one right way to use a word or construct a sentence. But at what point does hypercorrection simply present us with a new grammatical possibility?

In fact, despite Follett's charge, linguists generally do not "denounce all attempts at guiding choice." The question is, to repeat Deborah Cameron, "who prescribes for whom, what they prescribe, how, and for what purposes." The power to label constructions "right" and "wrong" can discriminate rather than simply guide. Users can and should feel empowered to think critically about the guidance they are given. At the same time, no one's use of English ever became less effective from knowing more about the language and considering others' opinions about it.

Special Focus: Corpus Linguistics

While we may think we know exactly how we use language, computers can usefully test our intuitions and give us an even better sense of how language actually works. For example, when speakers use the double *is* in *The thing is is* . . . , does it have to be followed by *that? The thing is is that it's a lot of money* versus *The thing is is it's a lot of money.* Or let's imagine someone tells you that *data* is plural and you "can't" say *the data is,* yet you are sure that *the data is* represents common usage. Where would you turn? There are now large electronic text databases available, usually described as **corpora** (singular: **corpus**), which students and scholars of language can search systematically in order to examine language in use. And we can learn surprising things.

For example, did you know that we *migrate* south twice as often as north? That we *chide* ourselves more than we *chide* others? Erin McKean, chief editor of the second edition of *The New Oxford American Dictionary,* uses these examples to show how the 1.8-million-word Oxford English Corpus (which includes both spoken and written English) can help lexicographers write more accurate dictionaries, capturing what words mean and how they are really used at whatever time the corpus represents (McKean 2007). In the case of *chide,* for example, the definition might reflect the fact that chiding is usually self-directed.

Corpus linguistics involves the systematic, empirical study of language based on "real life" examples of language use, written and spoken. It typically exploits computer-searchable corpora in order to uncover patterns of language use and to explore what contextual factors influence these patterns (e.g., the genre/register of the text, the gender of the speaker/writer, the grammatical context of the phrase or sentence). Corpus linguistics is descriptive to its core.

Brief History of Corpus Linguistics

One can find the origins of corpus linguistics in modern lexicography. Dictionary projects collect many citations of actual use in order to justify the information they present in entries (as you may recall, Samuel Johnson and his assistants did this by hand; Erin McKean can now use a huge computerized corpus).

In the 1960s Nelson Francis and Henry Kučera assembled "corpus-wise" linguists at Brown University in Rhode Island and began the Brown Corpus, a groundbreaking corpus of about 1 million running words of printed American English. The London-Oslo/Bergen Corpus (LOB), a similarly sized parallel corpus of written British English from about 1960 to 1961, was published in the 1970s.

In the years since, the number of corpora and corpus-based studies has exploded. The British National Corpus (BNC), first released in 1995 with 100 million words of written and spoken British English from the later part of the twentieth century, set a new bar for how big a standard corpus could be. In 2001, the Michigan Corpus of Academic Spoken English (MICASE) was published, with almost 2 million words of spoken English from lectures, office hours, seminars, and other academic interactions. Setting an entirely new bar in terms of scale is the recent Corpus of Contemporary American English (COCA), which is over 400 million words of spoken and written American English from 1990–2011 (and it continues to grow). Both MICASE and COCA are freely available online.

Important historical corpora include the Helsinki Corpus (1.5 million words of written text from 850–1710), the Corpus of Early English Correspondence or CEEC (2.5 million words of private letters by writers selected for a range of sociolinguistic variables), and several others. The International Corpus of English is made up of multiple corpora of various national varieties of English (e.g., Jamaica, India, Singapore, New Zealand). International varieties of English are also captured in independent corpora such as two 1-million-word Wellington corpora, one of spoken and one of written New Zealand English.

In principle, any collection of texts can be called a corpus (from Latin *corpus* 'body'). In corpus linguistics, the term tends to be used in a more specialized sense, to refer to a systematically compiled, finite electronic text database that aims to be representative of a particular language variety (McEnery and Wilson 1996, 21–24).

Often language scholars turn to less systematically compiled corpora, such as collections of literary texts from a particular time period—for example, the entire Shakespeare corpus is now available electronically. And one can search all of the electronic *OED* for evidence of an author's use of language, linguistic features of a literary work, or evidence of a linguistic form across periods, authors, and text types. Corpus linguists sometimes use the Web as a source of linguistic data, but the Web's status as a reliable resource is hotly contested.

Computers provide many advantages for linguistic analysis. They allow the identification and analysis of complex patterns of language use, with larger databases than could be parsed by the human eye and hand. They also provide consistent and reliable data collection. As one corpus linguistic textbook notes, computers don't "change their mind or become tired during an analysis" (Biber, Conrad, and Reppen 1998, 4). Corpus data keep linguists "honest": purely intuitive or introspective approaches, what researchers "think" they know, can be unreliable. For example, you might think that no one says or writes "there're," but a corpus would prove you wrong.

Noam Chomsky, a harsh critic of corpus linguistics given its focus on linguistic performance, faulted the early assumption that the full array of sentences in a language could ever be collected and analyzed. Modern corpus linguists emphasize the representativeness—rather than comprehensiveness—of corpora, and they often combine corpus data and introspection; in other words, corpus-based studies often allow us to follow up on hypotheses derived from intuition, and it is necessary to use native-speaker-like intuition to analyze corpus results.

Applications of Corpus Linguistics in the Twenty-first Century

Here's a question for you: Is the form *corpora,* the form that we have used throughout this section of the text, really the most used plural form of *corpus,* or is *corpora* losing ground to *corpuses?* According to COCA, *corpora* outpaces *corpuses* 81 instances to six (neither form occurs in the spoken part of COCA), so no need for us to revise this yet. If we return to our earlier question about *data,* COCA pulls up 1,625 instances of *these data,* compared with 537 of *this data,* which starts to give us a sense of plural versus singular usage; but if we restrict the search to spoken usage only, there are more than twice as many instances of *this data* than *these data.* Some of the health of *data* as a plural seems to be the result of editors following a prescriptive rule that *data* should be considered plural, despite spoken usage. You could examine all the ways that *like* is used in a spoken corpus (e.g., COCA or MICASE; see Figure 2.1)—although we have to warn you that this task, given the popularity of *like,* could quickly become overwhelming! In a historical corpus, you could track the slow demise of *thou/thee,* from a second-person singular pronoun (as in *Beowulf* and *The Canterbury Tales*), to an informal second-person pronoun (as Shakespeare often used it), to an archaic, rarely used (unless we are quoting Shakespeare) pronoun today.

Scholars such as Geoffrey Leech have used corpora from the early, mid, and late twentieth century to track current changes in the language. For example, corpora show

File #		Key Word in Context		Sp. ID
Total matches:	46			
OFC300JU149	1	sure alright. it's actual has	like a bunch of different parts	S4
OFC300JU149	2	it's just really nice to	like hear what everybody has to	S4
OFC300JU149	3	to think, right right about	like what you write. okay, reality	S4
OFC300JU149	4	two thousand and i felt	like, it was the end how	S4
OFC300JU149	5	the hum museum, it was	like uh, this last weekend and	S4
OFC300JU149	6	was actually a part of	like my performance oh okay that	S4
OFC300JU149	7	that i put on. okay	like i didn't really go through	S4
OFC300JU149	8	this was just kind of	like um, like helping my thought	S4
OFC300JU149	9	just kind of like, um,	like helping my thought process of	S4
OFC300JU149	10	my thought process of uhuh	like maybe what i wanted to	S4

FIGURE 2.1   This search of the Michigan Corpus of Academic Spoken English (MICASE) for the word *like* shows the word in context. Different links will take you to the full text of the conversation or lecture as well as to information about the speakers and academic situation.

the decline of the preposition *upon* and the increase in negative contractions (e.g., *don't*) in British English. There appears to be an ongoing decline in the "core modals" (e.g., *will, would, may, might, should*), led by American English. The modal *must* seems to be dropping in use especially quickly, and the semimodal *have to* is gaining ground in written English (as is *need to*). American and British English speakers also are using the present progressive more and more, including as interpretive statements (e.g., "she is talking out her ear").

Have you noticed how speakers now use *absolutely* as a free-standing affirmative response to another speaker? One speaker asks, "Would you be up for some Scrabble tonight?" and the other responds, "Absolutely!" Or a speaker asserts, "I think performance on multiple-choice tests doesn't always accurately reflect a student's understanding of the material," and someone else responds, "Oh, absolutely. This has been my experience." How did absolutely come to mean 'absolutely yes' and not 'absolutely no'? Hongyin Tao (2007) used four corpora of spoken American English to look at the ratio of dependent uses of *absolutely* (e.g., *absolutely perfect*), the original use of the adverb, and these independent uses, which he argues are derivative. All four corpora show that the dependent use is still the most common, but the independent use is widespread (see Table 2.1). The corpus evidence also shows how dependent *absolutely* occurs more than twice as often with a positive adjective (e.g., *absolutely right*) than with a negative one (e.g., *absolutely impossible*), which may be an important factor in the emergence of *absolutely* as an affirmative, free-standing discourse marker that speakers can use at the beginning of a turn to indicate agreement.

Searches that could have taken scholars a lifetime can now sometimes be performed in a matter of minutes. Imagine trying to discover how speakers use *must* or the present progressive today by reading hundreds of books, magazines, and newspapers; by lurking in chat rooms and visiting Web sites; and by recording speech from sermons, lectures, television and radio programs, films, song lyrics, and casual conversation. Corpora allow any one of you to come up with an interesting linguistic question, to design a systematic methodology for collecting data, to analyze those data (or *that data,* depending on what the corpora tell you about this usage question), and to add to

TABLE 2.1   **The Frequency of Different Uses of *Absolutely* in Four Corpora**

	Michigan Corpus of Academic Spoken English (approx. 1.7 million words)	*Cup-Cornell Corpus (628,939 words)*	*Corpus of Spoken Professional American-English (subset: 878,817 words)*	*Santa Barbara Corpus of Spoken American English (subset: 170,000 words)*	*Total*	*(%)*
Dependent *absolutely*	90	45	64	10	209	65%
Independent *absolutely*	40	29	43	1	113	35%
Total	130	74	107	11	322	100%

Source: From Tao (2007).

all of our understanding of how the English language works as spoken and written by real people in real time.

☑ Summary

- Although no one organization officially has the authority to legislate "correct usage" in English, a loose network of language authorities—including English teachers, editors, language pundits, and grammar book and dictionary writers/editors—unofficially govern what is regarded as proper, Standard English.

- Standard English is the prestige social dialect in the wider speech community. It is generally accepted as neutral, if not good English, and it is not associated with any particular geographic region.

- Prescriptive grammar rules tell speakers what they should say or write to be "correct." Descriptive grammar rules model what speakers do say, following the systematic grammatical rules that make up their linguistic competence. Many constructions condemned by prescriptive grammarians are perfectly logical and systematic according to the descriptive rules of that variety of English.

- Prescriptive rules are more easily enforced in the written language. Language change typically happens first in spoken language, which linguists tend to view as the primary or basic form of language.

- Grammar and style are two distinct concepts in the use of a language.

- Most dictionaries are created as descriptive resources, but many speakers turn to dictionaries to prescribe correct usage. The "comprehensive dictionary" is a relatively new concept in the history of English.

- Most grammar books and style guides are created as prescriptive resources, and they typically provide strict guidelines for what constitutes "proper English." Some new comprehensive grammars draw on corpus linguistic approaches to provide a more descriptive account of English grammar.

- Standard English is elevated as a dialect for social reasons, and prescriptive grammar rules are socially constructed. At the same time, Standard English provides a useful means of shared communication, and mastering Standard English is critical to many forms of professional mobility in the United States. Critically examining the status of Standard English and of prescriptive rules does not mean that we should not also master them.

Suggested Reading

Several recent books address the question of "proper English" and "language myths," including Ronald Wardhaugh's *Proper English: Myths and Misunderstandings about Language* (1999), Edward Finegan's *Attitudes toward English Usage: The History of a War of Words* (1980), and John McWhorter's *Word on the Street: Debunking the Myth of a "Pure" Standard English* (1998). For details on the history of Standard English, John H. Fisher's work is "the standard," and his most cited essays are compiled in *The Emergence of Standard English* (1996). Two recent collections of essays also provide important perspectives on the development and status of Standard English: *The Development of Standard English, 1300–1800* (2000) edited by Laura Wright, and *Standard English: The Widening Debate* (1999) edited by Tony Bex and Richard J. Watts. One of the most valuable resources available for learning more about the history of prescriptive grammar rules and of sticky points of usage is the *Merriam-Webster Dictionary of English Usage* (1994) edited by E. Ward Gilman.

Sidney I. Landau's *Dictionaries: The Art and Craft of Lexicography* (2001) is essential reading for anyone interested in lexicography. Henry Hitchings's *Defining the World: The Extraordinary Story of Dr. Johnson's Dictionary* (2005) is an engaging account of its subject. You may already know about Simon Winchester's account of William Chester Minor, *The Professor and the Madman* (1998), a gripping and somewhat sensational story of the *OED*'s principal contributor, and also an astute and informative account not only of the *OED* but also of modern lexicographical method. Recently, Winchester published *The Meaning of Everything: The Story of the* Oxford English Dictionary (2003), but you should also read K. M. Elisabeth Murray's *Caught in the Web of Words: James Murray and the* Oxford English Dictionary (1977), Lynda Mugglestone's *Lost for Words: The Hidden History of the* Oxford English Dictionary (2005), and Charlotte Brewer's *Treasure-House of the Language: The Living OED* (2007). Herbert C. Morton's *The Story of* Webster's Third: *Philip Gove's Controversial Dictionary and Its Critics* (1994) is essential to an understanding of the prescriptivist/descriptivist debate, as is *Dictionaries and* That *Dictionary* (1962), James Sledd and Wilma R. Ebbitt's anthology of articles involved in the controversy over *Webster's Third*. For an interesting life of H. W. Fowler, turn to *The Warden of English* (2001) by Jenny McMorris.

Three textbooks provide helpful introductions to corpus linguistics: Charles Meyer's *English Corpus Linguistics* (2002), Douglas Biber, Susan Conrad, and Randi Reppen's *Corpus Linguistics: Investigating Language Structure and Use* (1998), and Tony McEnery and Andrew Wilson's *Corpus Linguistics* (1996).

Exercises

Exercise 2.1   Standard English

Make five copies of the map of the United States provided below and ask five speakers of American English to identify (by circling or shading areas) where they believe Standard English is spoken. Be sure to record what they would identify as their original home region in the United States. How do your results compare to American dialectologist Dennis Preston's map created by Michigan speakers?

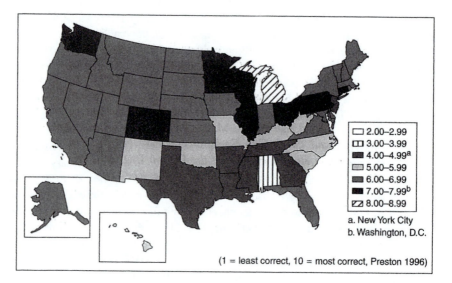

☐	2.00–2.99
⊞	3.00–3.99
■	4.00–4.99[a]
▨	5.00–5.99
▧	6.00–6.99
■	7.00–7.99[b]
▨	8.00–8.99

a. New York City
b. Washington, D.C.

(1 = least correct, 10 = most correct, Preston 1996)

This map illustrates the means of Michigan speakers' ratings of the linguistic correctness of the English spoken in all fifty states (1 = least correct, 10 = most correct).
Source: Courtesy of Dennis Preston.

Exercise 2.2   Prescriptive versus Descriptive Rules

1. Locate at least two usage guides, perhaps those by Fowler, Burchfield, and Follett, and at least two dictionaries. Find a word or subject treated in all or most of these sources (for instance, *ain't*) and compare the entries. Do the authorities agree? In what matters do they disagree? Which of the entries seems most useful to you and whose advice would you take? Why?

2. Ask ten speakers of various ages to complete the following sentences with either the word *who* or *whom*. First, give five speakers these sentences in written form; then ask another five speakers to complete the sentences when you read them aloud. Record all the responses along with the age and gender of the speaker. When you finish, tally the results and see if you can find any patterns to the use of *who* and *whom* based on grammatical constructions, on the form in which the question was asked, or on the age or gender of the speakers.

   a. _____ are you talking to?

   b. _____ gave you that book?

   c. _____ shall I say is calling?

   d. To _____ are you giving the book?

   e. I like the man _____ I gave the book to.

   f. I don't particularly like the man to _____ I gave the magazine.

   g. I really like the woman _____ gave me the book.

3. Ask these same ten speakers of various ages to define the word *peruse*. Record their answers and ages. Now look up the word in a good dictionary. Can you find any pattern to the speakers' responses and how they compared to the dictionary definition?

Exercise 2.3   Dictionaries

1. Choose two relatively recent college dictionaries (preferably from 2000 or after) from two different publishing houses and provide the title, edition, and year of publication of both dictionaries. Then address the following questions.

   a. Who is the editor in chief of each dictionary? How many editors are there? Why do you think the editors' names don't appear on the cover or title page? (Or do they?)

   b. Examine the introductory material in the front of each dictionary. For words with multiple definitions, how are the definitions ordered? Does the dictionary provide etymologies? Pronunciations? How are these ordered?

   c. Look again at the introductory material in the front of each dictionary. What usage labels does each dictionary employ? Also note anything that seems of interest in the explanation of these labels.

   d. Open each dictionary to a random page. How many words do you not recognize on each page? Provide a couple of examples.

e. Look up the word *text* in each dictionary. How does each dictionary arrange the different parts of speech for this word? Is there anything you would add to the definitions?

f. Look up two slang or taboo words of your choosing. How are they labeled in each dictionary? What do you think of the definitions?

2. Access one electronic dictionary. What information is provided about how definitions are ordered and what usage labels are employed? What do you think of the online dictionary's design? What do you think are the benefits of the electronic dictionary format? What are the drawbacks?

Exercise 2.4   Corpus Linguistics

1. Before pursuing these questions, read the background information about the Michigan Corpus of Academic Spoken English (MICASE) and its transcription conventions, all available at the MICASE Web site: http://www.hti.umich.edu/m/micase/index.html.

a. How many times do you find *could care less* compared with *couldn't care less?* In these examples, how is *could care less* used? (You can see the full transcript of the conversation.)

b. How many times do speakers use *different from* compared with *different than?* Of the uses of *different than,* how many are by speakers age 17–23? 24–30? (Some pundits blame "young speakers" for *different than,* which they see as a corruption of the language.)

c. Of the uses of the word *cute,* how many are by men and how many by women? What about *lovely?*

2. Now let's explore the Corpus of Contemporary American English (COCA): www.americancorpus.org. Before you get started, take the "Brief Tour," which will acquaint you with the various search capabilities.

a. Which is more common in COCA, *reason why* or *reason that?* Provide the exact numbers.

b. Which is more common in spoken English: *on accident* or *by accident?* What about in magazines? Newspapers? Provide the counts for each.

c. Which is more common in COCA, *sneaked* or *snuck?* If you select List and then "yes" under Sections in Display, the results will give you the breakdown by register (spoken, newspapers, etc.). What do you notice about the use of each form in spoken versus newspapers/academic prose?

d. Sometimes writing instructors will say to a student, "Just write it down like you would say it." But as you all know, written academic prose is different from speech in many respects, from word choice to grammatical structures. Let's do a comparison of speech to academic registers using the "chart" function under display. See what you discover about the differences in use for the following conjunctions, stance adverbs, and conjunctive adverbs: *however, but, thus, therefore, so, because, due to, regardless, probably, likely.* What do you make of these differences?

e. Let's try one wild card search. According to COCA, determine which words tend to occur in this construction: ____*ing the rules.* (Did this match your intuition?)

f. And finally, let's do one search with a part-of-speech (POS) tag. What prepositions tend to occur right after *go.* (If you click on "POS List" under Search, it will let you select what part of speech you want. So you don't have to know all the technical symbols—the system will insert them for you.)

g. Think of a question that interests you concerning patterns of language used in spoken and written English. Devise a strategy for how to search COCA to come up with useful results. Once you have a strategy, proceed to searching! Then write up your results, both in the form of a quantified analysis (e.g., a chart with the overall numbers) and a qualitative analysis (i.e., prose explaining what you make of these results).

3. All of *Time* magazine, from 1923 to the present, is now available as an electronic corpus at http://corpus.byu.edu/time/. Let's test Geoffrey Leech's finding that the modal *must* is on the decline while *have to* is on the rise. Do a search of both forms, using the "chart" feature to display the results. What do you find about their frequency over the decades?

Chapter 3

English Phonology

The word *sandwich* sometimes gets spelled *samwich*, as it is on this sign. What happens phonologically with this word to cause the *samwich* spelling?

A child learning to write, or any inexperienced writer, often writes words the way that he or she says them. So a child might write *samwich* for *sandwich* or *snift* for *sniffed*. The first pronunciation, "samwich," is common for many speakers of English, not just kids. If you are honest with yourself, do you really say the "d" when you say *sandwich* fast in natural speech? You would be in good company if you do not. Even if you do pronounce the "d," where did that "d" go for many speakers of English? The answer is that speakers delete the "d" to simplify what would otherwise be a string of three consonants.

That said, there remains another question: with the "d" deleted, why does the "n" turn into an "m" for some speakers? What happens is that the sound /n/ becomes more like the sound /w/ that follows it, and when /n/ becomes more like /w/, it turns into /m/. The study of the English sound system, or English phonology, explains how /m/ is more like /w/ than /n/ is. (As a side note, sometimes it's hard to grasp how sounds work in relation to one another without sounding them out. We encourage you to do so—you'll discover, for example, the similar position of your lips in making /m/ and /w/ much more efficiently by sounding them out than purely by reading paragraphs about the details of their pronunciation.)

What about *snift* and *sniffed*? We all pronounce *sniffed* with a final "t." We learn that for most verbs the past-tense ending is spelled *-ed*, and many of us stop paying attention to the fact that this past-tense ending does not always sound like a "d." There are, in fact, three different pronunciations of the *-ed* ending: one with /t/ (e.g., *sniffed*), one with /d/ (e.g., *snored*), and one with a full extra syllable ending in /d/ (e.g., *snorted*). And it is entirely predictable, based on the last sound of the verb, which ending will be added, as we will discuss in this chapter.

In every variety of every language, sounds are arranged according to a complex set of rules. We begin the study of the structure of the English language with the sound system for two main reasons: (1) sounds are the fundamental building blocks of language; and (2) sounds perhaps most clearly demonstrate the "systematicity" of language, that is, the ways in which language is rule governed and the elements of a language are interrelated. The study of phonetics and phonology may be one of the most unfamiliar units in a course on the English language, as this is a way of thinking about sound that you may never have encountered before.

Phonetics and Phonology

When you listen to another English speaker talk, you probably think that you are hearing separate words that string together to make sentences. On a page, words are separated by white spaces. But when you listen to another person talk, you don't hear white spaces. In fact, you hear a nearly continuous stream of sound. How does your brain separate this stream of sound into meaningful segments?

Within the continuous stream of sound that we usually think of as "speech" or even "language," our brains distinguish individual sound units or segments, which linguists call **phonemes**. A phoneme is what native speakers hear as a distinctive sound of a language, a sound different from all other sounds in the language. The "p" in *puck* and *cup* is a phoneme distinct from any of the other sounds in those words—those other sounds are phonemes, too. To be absolutely precise, when we say the "p" in *cup*, we are representing the phoneme in speech—the phoneme is an abstraction.

Many phonemes have subtle variants, which linguists call **allophones**. A sound may be produced differently in different "environments," that is, depending on the position of the sound in a word (e.g., initial or final) or the other sounds that appear next to the sound. For instance, the "p" in *puck* isn't exactly the same as the "p" in *cup*. If you say *puck*, you'll hear (or feel) the aspiration, the puff of air, as "p" moves into the vowel that follows it. But the "p" in *cup*, which is in the word-final position (that is, it occurs at the end of the word), stops the airflow—there's no aspiration. Native speakers of a language hear all of the allophones, the variants of a sound, as the same sound or phoneme. We return to this concept below.

Phonology is the study of the sound system of any given language: the organization of a language's sounds and their relationships to one another. Phonology examines which sounds make up the distinctive consonants and vowels of a language, which sounds would be considered by speakers just to be variants of those distinctive sounds, and which sounds or sound combinations do not occur in that language. Every language differs from others in at least one of these categories. Some languages contain sounds that other languages do not (the African language Xhosa has clicks and English does not). Some languages distinguish between two sounds that other languages do not (English distinguishes between /l/ and /r/ and Japanese does not). Some languages allow consonant clusters that others do not (German allows the cluster /ʃp/ and English does not, except in Yiddish borrowings). When we study English phonology, we are attempting to describe the system of English sounds.

When we talk about "English phonology," we are simplifying the situation enormously. As discussed in the preceding chapter, "English" encompasses many dialects of the language, all of which have slightly different sound systems. Most of the charts in this chapter will describe one variety of English, often called "Standard American English" (SAE) or "Mainstream United States English" (MUSE), and it is important to remember that the sounds of your dialect may not correspond exactly to these charts: the charts represent only one variety of English. What we think of as "accents" are, in fact, perceptible phonological variations among dialects. (And remember: we all have accents.) Interestingly, speakers sometimes associate a set of phonological features with a particular social or regional group, but other, equally noticeable phonological differences go unnoticed, at least at the conscious level. It is impossible to discuss phonological variation among dialects much in this chapter, or even completely in a textbook like this one. Chapters 11 and 12, however, unravel this thread of inquiry into English phonology a little further.

Phonetics is the study of speech sounds more generally, how they are produced and how they are perceived. Phonetics can be divided into three types:

- **Articulatory phonetics** focuses on how speech sounds are produced (i.e., what **articulators**, like the tongue, teeth, lips, hard and soft palate, and so forth, in the mouth and elsewhere do to create sounds).

- **Acoustic phonetics** focuses on how speech sounds are transmitted (i.e., the characteristics of sound waves created and perceived as part of "speech").

- **Auditory phonetics** focuses on how the ear translates sound waves into electrical impulses to the brain and how the brain perceives these as speech sounds (i.e., how the brain translates sound waves into speech sounds).

As this description of phonetics makes clear, the transmission of speech from speaker to hearer is a highly complex process. In general, the speaker expels air from the lungs through the mouth and/or nose and simultaneously manipulates his or her tongue, lips, and other parts of the mouth in order to create a particular set of vibrations in the stream of air. We call these vibrations sound waves, and they move through the air from the speaker's mouth to the hearer's ears, where they strike the eardrum. The hearer's brain then reinterprets the electrical impulses stimulated by these sound waves into a concept of the sound. Our brains are more highly adept at handling human language than any other kind of noise: we can process about thirty distinct language sounds per second, but only about fifteen distinct nonlanguage sounds.

Some linguists do not agree that phonemes are the most basic unit of sound. Peter Ladefoged (2001b, 170) argues that phonemes are "largely figments of our good scientific imaginations" and that speech movements are organized in terms of larger units more like syllables. In addition, many speech errors occur at syllable boundaries, rather than at phoneme boundaries, which might also suggest that syllables are more basic than phonemes. In this chapter, however, we follow the conventional view of phonemes as the basic units of sound, relying on the charts of American English vowels and phonemes that Peter Ladefoged created for the *Handbook of the International Phonetic Association* (1999). (The International Phonetic Alphabet is discussed below.)

In this chapter, we are interested primarily in English phonology and discuss phonetics only so far as it is useful in that context. Phonology allows us to describe the inventory of available sounds in English, how they are related to and form combinations with one another, and how they vary systematically from dialect to dialect. Within phonetics, our focus is articulatory phonetics—how we manipulate our speech organs to produce sounds—though we do consider the perception of sound some near the end of the chapter. Phonetics constitutes an important branch of linguistics in its own right, and the more subtle and advanced one's study of phonology, the more useful phonetics, including acoustic and auditory phonetics, becomes. The section on "Suggested Reading" at the end of this chapter includes several books about phonetics.

The Anatomy of Speech

Before we get to the description of sounds in terms of their articulatory characteristics, you should become more familiar with the inside of your mouth, as well as the terms linguists use to describe the characteristics of the speech organs. As you will notice, many of the terms we use in phonetics and phonology to describe sounds are Latinate (or Greek in origin but borrowed from Latin into English). Throughout this chapter, we gloss most of these Latinate terms with corresponding English descriptions to make the derivation of the Latin description more transparent.

In English, as in many of the world's languages, sounds are created by pushing air up from the lungs out through the mouth and nose with an exhalation slightly longer than normal breathing. These sounds are, therefore, technically called pulmonic egressive ('lung-related outgoing') sounds. (Some languages also have ingressive sounds, created by sucking air back into the lungs.) Air flows from the lungs up through the **trachea** (sometimes called the windpipe) to the **larynx**. The larynx is protected by the **epiglottis** (cartilage at the root of the tongue), which directs food and other foreign objects to the stomach rather than to the lungs. The **vocal cords** (note the spelling) are elastic muscles that stretch over the larynx. When viewed from above, they look somewhat like lips. Air coming up from the lungs forces the vocal cords apart, after which they snap back together to create vibrations (called **voicing**, when we talk about linguistic sounds). Vocal cords can vibrate several hundred times per second when we speak.

The especially important parts of the mouth with respect to English phonology include the lips, teeth, and tongue, as well as various sections of the top of the mouth, where the tongue can be placed in order to create distinctive sounds (see Figure 3.1). If you put the tip of your tongue on the back of your teeth and then move it slightly up and back, you will feel a ridge behind your teeth, called the **alveolar ridge**. If you continue

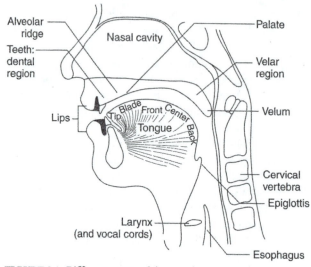

FIGURE 3.1 Different parts of the vocal tract are involved in the production of different sounds.

to move the tip of your tongue back along the top of your mouth, you will feel the hard flat surface called the **hard palate**. If you continue to move your tongue back along the top of your mouth (and be careful here not to make yourself gag), you will feel the surface become soft in the back; this area is called the **soft palate** or **velum**. In order to allow air to flow from the lungs out to the mouth, the velum raises and moves to the back of the oral cavity. It can also lower to block the mouth, in which case the air flows from the lungs out the nose (as it does when we sound "nasal").

The tongue is a surprisingly big muscle, and it has, as Peter Ladefoged (2001b, 169) describes it, "enormous athletic ability." During speech, the tongue is moving with great rapidity around the mouth, with different parts of the tongue often striking different areas of the mouth, such as the teeth, alveolar ridge, and hard palate. Typically, we describe sounds by the "articulators" involved: an active articulator (usually the tongue or another speech organ near the bottom of the oral cavity) moves toward or touches a passive articulator (usually along the top of the oral cavity, toward which the active articulator moves). If the tongue is the active articulator, different parts of the tongue (the tip, the blade, the back) may come in contact with the passive articulator. It helps to experiment with this. Say the letter "l": the tip of your tongue, the active articulator, presses against the alveolar ridge, the passive articulator. Now say "k": the base of your tongue, the active articulator, presses against the velum, the passive articulator.

The fundamental distinction between consonants and vowels is familiar to most speakers of English, but you may not be able to come up with a better description of the difference than "Vowels are a, e, i, o, u." Such a description is highly unsatisfactory, however, both because it lacks details about the nature of vowels and consonants and because there are many more than those five vowels in English. Phonetics provides a more technical distinction between consonants and vowels. **Consonants** generally involve stopping or impeding the airflow from the lungs as the articulators near or touch each other. Consonants also appear at the margins of syllables (e.g., *bad* /bæd/). **Vowels** are characterized by unimpeded airflow, during which speakers change the shape of the oral cavity and the relative position and shape of the tongue to create different sounds. Vowels also serve as the center or nucleus of syllables (e.g., *bad* /bæd/). Some sounds share features of both consonants and vowels, and in English they are considered consonants for reasons described below.

The International Phonetic Alphabet

The **International Phonetic Alphabet** (IPA) provides an established, consistent set of symbols for representing the sounds of all the world's known languages. With the IPA, scholars and students of language do not need to know or depend on a particular language's spelling system in order to know what the language sounds like. The IPA also facilitates comparison across languages. The IPA accurately represents even those languages for which the written form of the language does not directly represent sound. For example, Chinese characters represent syllables, and there is no direct relationship between the shape of the character and its sound. Languages with alphabetic written forms may have a more direct relationship between sound and spelling, but spelling still often does not capture the subtleties of a language's sounds, and there are often spelling irregularities, so the IPA provides a useful representation.

English spelling is notoriously unreliable when it comes to the relationship between a word's spelling and its sound. The final section of this chapter addresses the question of how the English spelling system became so divorced from sound in many instances. Mario Pei (1967, 337) has described English spelling as "the world's most awesome mess." Other scholars, though, argue that spelling and punctuation have a predictable relationship in over 80 percent of English words—the exceptions are many and well known. Inconsistencies of English spelling are a source of humor, as in this excerpt from "English Is Tough Stuff" (which has been circulating on the Internet for several years):

Just compare heart, beard, and heard,
Dies and diet, lord and word,
Sword and sward, retain and Britain.
(Mind the latter, how it's written.)
Now I surely will not plague you
With such words as plaque and ague.
But be careful how you speak:
Say break and steak, but bleak and streak;
Cloven, oven, how and low,
Script, receipt, show, poem, and toe.

As a second example, we have come up with ten different ways to spell the sound /k/ in English (and you may well be able to come up with a few more!): *kick, cow, khaki, queen, quay, choir, clique, accomplish, McLaughlin.*

Given the irregularities of any language's spelling system, the IPA provides a way to transcribe words with a one-to-one correspondence between sound and symbol, so that we write /kɪk/ for *kick*, /kaʊ/ for *cow*, and /klik/ or /klɪk/ for *clique*. If you look in most dictionaries, you will find different systems for representing pronunciation. Some use double letters and **diacritics**, the marks that modify letters in order to represent different sounds: *á, ă, ä*, for instance. The *Oxford English Dictionary* employs the IPA, our focus here.

The IPA was originally developed between 1886 and 1888 in Paris by the International Phonetic Association, known at the time as Dhi Fonétik Ticerz´ Asóciécon (FTA), a group that grew from eleven members in 1886 to 1,751 members (in forty countries) by 1914. Because the early members of the association were primarily teachers of European languages, the roman alphabet served as the basis for the IPA, supplemented by other characters and diacritics. The IPA has been revised several times since 1888 (most recently in 1996), and the association regularly discusses how to improve symbolic representation of sound and how to handle newly discovered sounds in the world's languages.

As the *Handbook of the International Phonetic Association* explains, the IPA rests on some fundamental assumptions about sound systems:

- Some distinctions in speech are linguistically relevant (e.g., the difference between consonants and vowels, allophonic variation in the production of a phoneme, intonation), and others are not (e.g., personal voice quality).

- Speech can be represented as a sequence of distinct sounds or "segments," and those segments can be usefully divided into two categories: consonants and vowels.

- Phonetic descriptions of sounds can be made with reference to how the sounds are produced (their articulation) and how they sound (their auditory characteristics).

This chapter first examines how we can describe sounds. It then examines which phonetic characteristics are relevant and distinctive for English consonants and vowels.

You will notice that we employ a specific format in discussions of spelling and sound. When we refer to a word as a word (as opposed to using the word to refer to something), the word is italicized. Transcriptions of sounds and words (i.e., representations of what words sound like) appear in slashes (/ /) for phonemic transcriptions (transcriptions of sounds considered in the abstract) and brackets ([ ]) for phonetic transcriptions (transcriptions of sounds actually produced in speech).

English Consonants

Linguists have proposed multiple systems for how best to describe the characteristic features of consonants and how best to categorize them. We employ here one of the most common approaches, although we also mention features of other systems. According to this very common description, English consonants can be distinguished and categorized by three **distinctive features**:

- **Place** (or **point**) **of articulation**: identifies the location of the passive and active articulators.

- **Manner of articulation**: describes how close the articulators get and how that affects the airflow.

- **Voicing**: indicates whether the vocal cords are pulled back (voiceless or unvoiced) or vibrate (voiced) when a consonant sound is produced.

TABLE 3.1   **Consonants of English**

Manner of Articulation	Bilabial	Labiodental	Interdental	Alveolar	(Alveo-) Palatal	Velar	Glottal
Stops	p			t		k	
	b			d		g	
Fricatives		f	θ	s	ʃ (š)		h
		v	ð	z	ʒ (ž)		
Affricates					tʃ (č)		
					dʒ (ǰ)		
Nasals (voiced)	m			n		ŋ	
Liquids (voiced)				l (lateral)			
				r (bunched)			
Glides	w (ʍ)					j	

/p/ = pat, lap
/b/ = bat, lab
/t/ = tap, cot
/d/ = dam, cod
/k/ = kong, car
/g/ = gong, dog
/f/ = fan, cliff
/v/ = van, swivet

/θ/ = thigh, path *unvoiced*
/ð/ = thy, the *voiced*
/s/ = sap, cats
/z/ = zap, jazz
/ʃ/ = shine, posh
/ʒ/ = measure, treasure
/h/ = happy, hill
/tʃ/ = chill, touch

/dʒ/ = jill, judge
/m/ = mull, skim
/n/ = null, skin
/ŋ/ = ring, rank
/l/ = lava, hill
/r/ = ring, mar
/w/ = will, tower
/j/ = yes, yard

Through the combination of these three features, every consonant in English can be distinguished from every other consonant. See Table 3.1 for a chart of English consonants and the three distinctive features. The column headings across the top of the table indicate the various places of articulation. The headings on the left indicate the various manners of articulation. Voiced/voiceless pairs of sounds appear together in a cell, with the voiceless sound in the shaded area.

Stops

Stops completely obstruct the airflow from the lungs through the mouth followed by a release of the air. There are six stop phonemes in English; three are voiceless and three are voiced.

- To create a bilabial ('two-lip') stop, purse your lips to stop the airflow and then release the air. If your vocal cords are pulled back so there is no voicing, you will produce and hear the voiceless bilabial stop **/p/**. If the vocal cords vibrate to create a voiced sound, you will produce and hear the voiced bilabial stop **/b/**. You can actually feel voicing. Put your index and middle finger on the front of your throat, over your vocal cords, and make the sound /b/. You should feel vibration under your fingers. If you then make the sound /p/ (be sure not to make a vowel with it), you should feel no vibration.

- To create an alveolar stop, put the tip of your tongue on the alveolar ridge as you cut off and release the airflow. Without voicing, you will produce the voiceless alveolar stop **/t/**. With voicing, you will produce the voiced alveolar stop **/d/**.

■ To create a velar stop, move your tongue all the way back to the velum (the back of your tongue will touch the velum) as you cut off and release the airflow. Without voicing, you will produce the voiceless velar stop /k/. With voicing, you will produce the voiced velar stop /g/.

The **glottal stop** ([ʔ]), which we refer to later, involves the complete stoppage of airflow and then release (as in the stop in the middle of *uh-oh*). The glottal stop is not included in the chart of English phonemes because it is a variant of /t/ and /d/ in specific positions, thus an allophone rather than a phoneme.

Fricatives

Fricatives occur when the passive and active articulators are brought very close together and create friction as the air passes through the mouth.

■ To create a labiodental ('lip-teeth') fricative, put your top teeth on your lower lip and push the air through. Without voicing, you will produce the voiceless labiodental fricative /f/. With voicing, you will produce the voiced labiodental fricative /v/.

■ To create an interdental ('between-teeth') fricative, put your tongue between your teeth and push the air through. Without voicing, you will produce the voiceless interdental fricative /θ/. With voicing, you will produce the voiced interdental fricative /ð/. English speakers typically think of both these sounds as "th." Many American English speakers produce both of these sounds with the tongue pressed up against the back of the teeth rather than between them.

■ To create an alveolar fricative, put the tip or blade of your tongue on the alveolar ridge and push the air through. Without voicing, you will produce the voiceless alveolar fricative /s/. With voicing, you will produce the voiced alveolar fricative /z/.

■ To create an alveopalatal or palatal fricative, move the blade or front of your tongue back toward the hard palate and push the air through. Without voicing, you will produce the voiceless alveopalatal fricative /ʃ/—what English speakers

Language Change at Work

Is /h/ Disappearing from English?

The fricative /h/, some linguists argue, may be slowly disappearing from English. Some dialects have already lost /h/ and are referred to as "h-dropping" varieties. Speakers of some British varieties say, for example, "ouse" (/aʊs/) for *house*. In dialects that still have /h/, /h/ typically only appears in one position: at the beginning of a stressed syllable. So the sound /h/ almost never appears in English at the end of a syllable or at the beginning of an unstressed syllable. April McMahon (2002, 54) provides the useful example of /h/ appearing for many speakers when the stress shifts from the first syllable in *'vehicle* to the second syllable in *ve'hicular*.

A Question to Discuss

Does English Have Initial or Final /ʒ/?

The fricative /ʒ/ is relatively rare in English and appears primarily in the middle of words (e.g., *treasure, leisure*). Most words with /ʒ/ have been borrowed into English from French, where /ʒ/ is a much more common sound. In another set of words, the /ʒ/ results from a sound change several centuries ago in English in which the combination of sounds /zj/ became /ʒ/ (e.g., *usual, seizure*).

The distributional pattern of /ʒ/ (i.e., that it almost always appears in the middle of words) seems to encourage some

borrowed words in English to change their sound. Because /ʒ/ so rarely occurs at the beginning or end of a word, if English speakers borrow a word with /ʒ/ at the beginning or end, English speakers often turn the /ʒ/ into the sound /dʒ/ in that position. For many speakers this has happened with the final sound in the word *garage* and the initial sound of the word *genre*. In other words, many English speakers make the word conform to English phonological patterns—they "Englishify" it.

think of as "sh." With voicing, you will produce the voiced alveopalatal fricative /ʒ/—a fairly rare sound in English that occurs primarily in the middle of words such as *measure*. A common American variation of the IPA uses the symbols /š/ and /ž/ to represent these sounds, in part because they are typographically easier.

- The sound /h/ is usually described as a glottal fricative. In fact, /h/ can be described as a puff of air preceding a vowel. Some linguists describe /h/ as a voiceless vowel, but as it cannot serve as the nucleus of a syllable, others categorize it as a consonant.

Affricates

Affricates combine a stop and a fricative. There are only two affricates in English.

- To create an alveopalatal or palatal affricate, start by making an alveolar stop and then create an alveopalatal or palatal fricative. Without voicing in either sound (i.e., /t/ and /ʃ/), you will produce the voiceless alveopalatal affricate /tʃ/—what English speakers typically think of as "ch." With voicing in both sounds (i.e., /d/ and /ʒ/), you will produce the voiced alveopalatal affricate /dʒ/—what English speakers may think of as "j." The American variation of the IPA mentioned earlier uses the symbols /č/ and /ǰ/ to represent these sounds.

Stops, fricatives, and affricates can all be described as **oral sounds** because the airflow is funneled through the mouth. Oral stops, fricatives, and affricates can all be described as **obstruents**, as they all involve an obstruction of the airflow from the lungs through the mouth. The rest of the consonants in English can be described as **sonorants** because they are sonorous, making what are sometimes described as "humming sounds."

Nasals

Nasals involve the flow of air from the lungs through the nose. Nasals are considered a kind of stop because the airflow in the mouth is cut off. In English, all nasals are voiced.

- To create a bilabial nasal stop, purse your lips and as the air flows through your nose, make a humming noise. You will produce **/m/**.

- To create an alveolar nasal stop, put the tip or blade of your tongue on the alveolar ridge and create noise as the air flows through the nose. You will produce **/n/**.

- To create a velar nasal stop, move the back of your tongue all the way back to touch the velum (be careful not to gag!) and create noise as the air flows through the nose. You will produce **/ŋ/**—what English speakers think of as "ng." But for most English speakers, there is no stop (/g/) at the end of words spelled with a final -ng.

Liquids and Glides

Liquids and **glides** are categorized as **approximants** because the articulators are near each other but not enough to impede airflow entirely. The distinctions among these sounds are created by the shape and placement of the tongue.

The two liquids in English are distinguished by the position of the tongue and the way in which the airflow is directed around the tongue. The sound **/l/** is described as a **lateral liquid** because the tongue touches the roof of the mouth and the air flows around the sides of the tongue. The liquid **/r/** is called **bunched in** standard American English because most speakers "simply bunch the body of the tongue up" (Ladefoged 2001b, 103), and the exact place of articulation is hard to determine. There is simultaneous constriction in the pharyngeal and palatal areas. The sound /r/ is referred to as a **retroflex liquid** in standard British English because the tip of the tongue is curled up toward the top of the mouth and the air is funneled up and over the tongue. As just these two examples from standard American and British English demonstrate, different varieties of English have different types of "r," all of which we are representing here with /r/. And exactly where /r/ is pronounced in the mouth is often hard to tell, although it is usually categorized as alveolar. In using the symbol /r/ for English, we are also straying a bit from the IPA, where /r/ technically represents a trilled *r* (as in Spanish) and /ɹ/ represents a retroflex *r*. But almost all treatments of English phonology use the symbol /r/ for this liquid in English, so we will follow that convention here.

The two glides in English are distinguished by their place of articulation. The sound **/w/** is typically considered a bilabial glide, because the lips come close together as they round, but it also has a velar component based on the position of the tongue; /w/ is sometimes referred to as labiovelar. The sound **/j/** is a palatal glide, as the tongue moves up near the hard palate. English speakers typically think of the palatal glide as "y." Some speakers have a voiceless bilabial glide: **/ʍ/**. If you say *witch* and *which* identically, you probably do not have this voiceless glide; if you say *which* with a puff of air as you round your lips (what you might think of as "h"), then you have /ʍ/ in your phonological repertoire.

From these descriptions, you can see that liquids and glides are more like vowels than the other consonants are. We categorize them as consonants because they behave like other consonants in the formation of consonant clusters and because glides cannot function as the center of syllables.

Syllabic Consonants

Four consonants (all sonorants) can behave as **syllabic consonants** in English. The nasals /m/ and /n/ and the liquids /l/ and /r/ can act as a syllable nucleus. Syllabic consonants often occur word finally in unstressed syllables (as in *bottom, button, bottle, butter*), but they can also occur in stressed syllables (as in *first*). The IPA represents syllabic consonants by adding a short vertical line below these consonant symbols: /m̩, n̩, l̩, r̩/. Some linguists argue these final unstressed syllables are better represented by schwa (see the next section) plus the consonant (e.g., /əm, ər/); others state that the two representations capture a phonetic difference.

According to a study cited by Peter Ladefoged (2001b, 87–88), the most frequent consonants in English, starting with the most common of them, are /n, r, t, l, s, d/. These are the letters that smart contestants on *Wheel of Fortune* lead with, because they are the ones most likely to occur in any word or phrase. You will notice that all of these sounds are alveolar sounds, produced relatively near the center of the mouth. These are not, however, the first sounds that children seem to acquire; most children first acquire bilabial sounds (e.g., /b, p, m/), probably because sounds that involve stopping the airflow with the lips may be the easiest to imitate and to articulate. So it is not a coincidence that words like *mama, baba, dada,* and *papa* are used around the world to refer to parents.

English Vowels

All vowels in English are voiced and involve a continuous stream of air through the oral cavity—there are no active or passive articulators involved, no stopping of air, so we need a different system for categorizing these sounds. English vowels can be distinguished and categorized by three distinctive features, all related to the placement and form of the tongue:

- **Height** indicates whether the tongue is high in the mouth, low, or in between, closer to its "resting position" (mid).
- **Frontness** (or **backness**) indicates whether the front of the tongue is nearer the front of the mouth, toward the hard palate, or the back of the tongue is nearer the back of the mouth, toward the velum.
- **Tenseness** (or **laxness**) indicates whether the tongue muscle is tense (and nearer the periphery of the mouth) or lax (and more centralized).

Through the combination of these three features, every vowel in English can be distinguished from every other vowel. Sometimes "rounding" (whether the lips are rounded when the vowel is produced) is added as a fourth distinctive feature for English vowels. But in Modern English, rounding is predictable: back vowels (except ɑ) are more rounded and front vowels are unrounded.

The diagram in Table 3.2 represents the two-dimensional profile of the mouth (imagine that the speaker is turned to the left). The oddly nonparallel shape of the chart reflects that, in the front of your mouth, if you move your tongue from high to low, it must also move back, given the shape of the jaw. The chart has not always looked exactly this way, as linguists have debated what angles of the quadrilateral are most appropriate. And not all linguists agree that the vowel chart should try to represent a

TABLE 3.2   **Vowels of English**

/i/ = b<u>ea</u>t, <u>ea</u>ten	/ə/ = <u>a</u>bout, ph<u>o</u>netic
/ɪ/ = b<u>i</u>t, <u>i</u>nnocent	/ʌ/ = w<u>a</u>s, t<u>u</u>b
/e/ = b<u>ai</u>t, <u>a</u>te	
/ɛ/ = b<u>e</u>t, <u>e</u>nd	
/æ/ = b<u>a</u>t, <u>a</u>sh	/u/ = b<u>oo</u>t, red<u>u</u>ce
	/ʊ/ = g<u>oo</u>d, s<u>oo</u>t
	/o/ = b<u>oa</u>t, <u>o</u>pen
	/ɔ/ = b<u>ou</u>ght, c<u>o</u>ffee
	/ɑ/ = c<u>o</u>t, b<u>o</u>ther

Diphthongs

ɑɪ = b<u>uy</u>

ɑʊ = b<u>ough</u>

ɔɪ = b<u>oy</u>

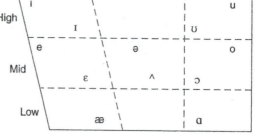

The vowel phonemes of American English drawn according to their distinctive features.

physical mapping of tongue position. We follow the IPA in reproducing the chart this way. (This version of the chart also corresponds to a reversed, inverted graph of the F1 and F2 formants of the vowels. That sentence probably doesn't make sense to you now, but the section below on the perception of sound provides more information about formants—it should clarify the issue.)

You will discover that the English spelling of vowels and the IPA symbols shown in Table 3.2 often do not correspond. For example, we pronounce the IPA symbol written with an *e* as /i/ and the IPA symbol written with an *i* as /ɑɪ/, as in the pronoun *I*. A historical vowel change, called the Great Vowel Shift, accounts for much of this discrepancy, as described in the section on spelling at the end of this chapter.

Front Vowels

Front vowels, from high to low, move from /i/ to /æ/ (from the vowel in *beat* to the vowel in *bat*). As you move from pronouncing /i/ to /æ/, you will feel your jaw drop in order to widen the oral cavity to produce the low front vowel. If you produce the high front vowel /i/ (as in *beat*) and then /ɪ/ (as in *bit*), you should feel your tongue lower slightly and become more central. The same is true for the mid front vowels /e/ (as in *bait*) and /ɛ/ (as in *bet*). We typically describe /ɪ/, /ɛ/, and /æ/ (the name for the last symbol is pronounced "ash" /æʃ/) as lax vowels, because the tongue is less tensed. The vowels /i/ (as in *beat*) and /e/ (as in *bait*) are tense vowels, and the tongue is more tensed and at the periphery of the oral cavity. For most speakers of American English, the vowel /e/ actually has an offglide and can be written /eɪ/ to indicate that it is not a "pure vowel."

An **offglide** is a sound made when a vowel moves into a glide (/j/ or /w/). An **onglide** moves from the glide into a vowel—for instance, some speakers pronounce *Tuesday* /tjuzdeɪ/. When an English vowel such as /e/ ends in an offglide, the diphthongized vowel moves toward the periphery. For this reason, some linguists argue that it would be more accurate to represent the diphthongized vowel as /ei/ rather than /eɪ/ (and as /ou/ rather than /oʊ/). In this book, we use the more traditional form with the lax vowel.

Back Vowels

Back vowels, from high to low, move from /u/ (as in *boot*) to /ɑ/ (as in *bother*). Again, as you move from pronouncing /u/ to /ɑ/, you will feel your jaw drop. Like the front vowels, the high vowels /u/ (as in *boot*) and /o/ (as in *boat*) are considered tense vowels and are articulated more at the periphery of the oral cavity. The high vowel /ʊ/ (as in *put*), the mid vowel /ɔ/ ("open o," as in *bought*), and the low vowel /ɑ/ (as in *pot*) are considered lax vowels. For most speakers of American English, the vowel /o/ is also slightly diphthongized—that is, it has an offglide—and can be written /oʊ/.

Most speakers of American English no longer distinguish between /ɔ/ and /ɑ/ (see the Language Change at Work box on the *cot/caught* merger). If this is the case for you, you probably produce a vowel closer to /ɑ/. When you transcribe words, do so as you say them, and don't worry if some other speakers have /ɔ/. One other note: many textbooks represent the low back vowel /ɑ/ with the symbol /a/, but in the IPA, the symbol /a/ technically represents a front low vowel.

Central Vowels

The **central vowel** is the most common in English and is represented with two different symbols: /ʌ/ ("wedge") when the vowel appears in a stressed syllable (as in *but*), and /ə/ ("schwa") when the vowel appears in an unstressed syllable (as in the first syllable in *about*). Many unstressed vowels in English words become /ə/. Not all charts of IPA vowels provide both symbols—some show only /ə/—because while the two vowels are phonetically different (/ʌ/ is lower and more back), the difference between /ə/ and /ʌ/ is not contrastive (in other words, there are not two distinctive words in English that are exactly the same except that one has /ə/ and the other /ʌ/). Here, we adhere to the following distinction: we use /ə/ in unstressed syllables and /ʌ/ in stressed syllables (except for syllables that can be represented by a syllabic consonant, discussed in more detail below).

In this description, we have talked about the front vowels together and then the back vowels, but we could have divided the vowels by other natural classes. For example, we could have talked first about the high vowels (/i, ɪ, u, ʊ/), then the mid vowels (/e, ɛ, ʌ, ə, o, ɔ/), and then the low vowels (/æ, ɑ/). As you pronounce these vowels, you will hear that the tense vowels /i, e, u, o/ have a slightly longer duration than the lax vowels, because they were historically long vowels, while lax vowels were short vowels. Vowel length is now predictable in Modern English: vowels are shortest before a voiceless sound (*seat* /sit/), longer before a voiced sound (*seed* /sid/), and at their longest when they appear at the end of a syllable/word (*sea* /si/).

Diphthongs

The vowels described earlier (with the possible exception of /e/ and /o/) are all typically categorized as monophthongs or "pure vowels." In English, there are also three diphthongs. (The word *diphthong* is traditionally pronounced /dɪfθɔŋ/, although you will hear many speakers—one of the authors included—say /dɪpθɔŋ/). **Diphthongs** begin at the point of articulation of one vowel and end at the point of articulation of another. Some linguists also describe diphthongs as the combination of a vowel and a glide

Language Change at Work

The *cot*/*caught* and *pin*/*pen* Mergers

Many speakers of American English have merged the vowels /ɑ/ and /ɔ/, so that they pronounce the two words *cot* (/ɑ/) and *caught* (pronounced before the merger with /ɔ/) the same way, usually with a vowel close to /ɑ/. This merger seems to have first taken hold in regions around western Pennsylvania and spread westward (see Figure 3.2). It also appeared relatively early in parts of Canada and eastern New England.

Interestingly, most speakers do not notice this merger until it is brought to their attention. Another vowel merger in American English, however, commonly known as the *pin*/*pen* merger (see Figure 3.3), is one that speakers do tend to notice and identify as "Southern." The *pin*/*pen* merger describes the merger of the vowels /ɪ/ and /ɛ/ into /ɪ/ before nasals.

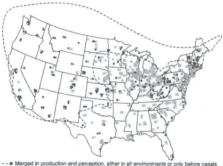

– – ● Merged in production and perception, either in all environments or only before nasals
○ Unmerged in production and perception

FIGURE 3.2 This dialect map shows where speakers of American English have merged the vowels in *cot* and *caught* and where speakers retain distinct vowels in the two words. (From the TELSUR project.)

Source: Atlas of North American English, 2005.

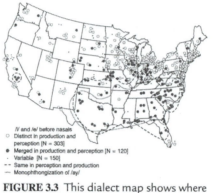

/ɪ/ and /e/ before nasals
○ Distinct in production and perception [N = 303]
● Merged in production and perception [N = 120]
· Variable [N = 150]
– – Same in perception and production
— Monophthongization of /ay/

FIGURE 3.3 This dialect map shows where speakers of American English have merged the vowels in *pin* and *pen* and where speakers retain distinct vowels in the two words. (From the TELSUR project.)

Source: Atlas of North American English, 2005.

(either /j/ or /w/). We follow IPA conventions here and use the notation based on two vowels:

/aɪ/	as in *buy* and *I*
/aʊ/	as in *bough* and *ow*/*ouch*
/ɔɪ/	as in *boy* and *oy* (as in *oy vay!*)

There is ongoing discussion about how the second vowel in the diphthongs should be represented. Some linguists argue that it would be more accurate to represent the sounds as /ɑi/, /ɑu/, and /ɔi/. Another common transcription device is to include a diacritic under the second vowel (e.g., /ɪ̯/) to indicate that it is not syllabic—that is, that the two vowels are articulated together to produce a diphthong rather than separately as the centers of two different syllables (so /aɪ̯/, /aʊ̯/, and /ɔɪ̯/).

In reality, many spoken vowels are not pure vowels—it is hard to find monophthongs in natural English speech. As we mentioned earlier, for example, /e/ and /o/ are often pronounced with an offglide (/eɪ/ and /oʊ/).

Natural Classes

Consonants and vowels as described so far help us to identify **natural classes** of sounds. A natural class is a set of sounds that can be described by their shared features so as to include all those sounds and exclude all others. So /p, b, t, d, k, g/ is the natural class of oral stops in English (they are stops because they stop airflow). The set of sounds /p, b/ is the natural class of bilabial oral stops. And /p, t, k/ is the natural class of voiceless stops. The set of sounds /p, t/ is not a natural class because while these sounds are both voiceless stops, that description would also include /k/, so /p, t/ is incomplete as it stands. As another example, the natural class /i, ɪ, u, ʊ/ captures all the high vowels in English. The set of sounds /ɪ, ɛ/ is not a complete natural class because the set of front, lax vowels in English must include /æ/ to be complete.

Linguists have set up the consonant and vowel charts in rows and columns to capture some of the major natural classes of sounds. Another natural class of sounds relevant to an exercise below is the **sibilants** (or "hissing" sounds): /s, z, ʃ, ʒ, tʃ, dʒ/.

Why do we care about natural classes? Because natural classes of sounds all tend to behave in similar ways phonologically, as we see in the next sections. Natural classes provide us a shorthand for descriptions: rather than saying /p/, /t/, and /k/ all behave in a specific way, we can say that voiceless stops behave in a specific way.

Phonemes and Allophones

As noted, both consonants and vowels often have phonetic variants called allophones: variations of a sound that are phonetically distinct, but that native speakers of a language typically hear as "the same sound." Importantly, allophones are predictable in terms of which variant will occur in a particular phonological environment. To explain this fairly complicated concept, let's begin with an analogy. (Bear with us. The analogy really does help!)

Stoats, small mammals that look something like big weasels, have reddish-brown coats most of the year (except for a black tip on the tail). In winter, they develop white coats (except for the same black tip) and they (as well as their fur) are called ermine. Clearly, stoats and ermines are the same animal—two variants of the same animal—and the variants appear depending on the season. We could say that the stoat is the "more basic" of the two because most of the time the animal is brown and called a stoat. We could represent the situation as follows:

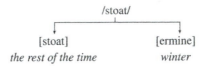

/stoat/

[stoat]   [ermine]
the rest of the time   *winter*

In this diagram, you can think of /stoat/ as being like the phoneme: the basic sound in the phonological system. The predictable variants [stoat] and [ermine] are like the allophones of a phoneme: they represent variants of one animal/sound, and we know

Stoat

Ermine

when one or the other will appear (and both could never occur in one season/environment). The distribution of the variants [stoat] and [ermine] is predictable, just like the distribution of allophones. So now back to sounds.

Sample Allophones

One of the most commonly cited examples of consonant allophones in English involves the aspiration of voiceless consonants. An aspirated consonant is produced with a small puff of air accompanying the sound, while an unaspirated consonant has no such puff. You can feel the difference if you put your hand in front of your mouth and say *pit* (/pɪt/) then *spit* (/spɪt/). You should feel a puff of air with the /p/ in *pit*. We represent this sound phonetically [pʰ]. Or try holding the corner of a piece of paper in front of your mouth and saying *pit* and *spit*. You'll see a difference in how much the paper flutters with the aspirated [pʰ]. The aspiration of a voiceless stop is completely predictable in English. Aspirated voiceless stops appear at the beginning of a word or at the beginning of a stressed syllable, when the sound appears without a preceding consonant (e.g., *pit*). When a voiceless stop appears after /s/ or as the second element of any consonant cluster, it will be unaspirated (e.g., *spit*).

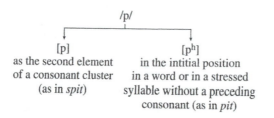

/p/

[p]
as the second element
of a consonant cluster
(as in *spit*)

[pʰ]
in the intitial position
in a word or in a stressed
syllable without a preceding
consonant (as in *pit*)

Most English speakers will not hear the difference between aspirated and unaspirated /p/ in words, but they are phonetically distinct. Speakers of Thai, though, will absolutely hear the difference, because aspirated /pʰ/ and unaspirated /p/ are phonemes or distinctive sounds in Thai. In other words, aspiration is a distinctive feature of Thai consonants, but not of English consonants.

Other allophones of a voiceless consonant also appear in predictable environments. If we add up all of these environments, we will cover every possible position of the consonant. This organization of a sound's allophones is called **complementary distribution** because the environments complement each other (i.e., they do not overlap), and together they comprise all possible environments for the sound. Let's take the sound /t/ in English as an example.

We already know that /t/ will be aspirated when it occurs word initially (at the beginning of a word) or at the beginning of a stressed syllable without a preceding consonant, and /t/ will be unaspirated when it occurs as the second element of a consonant cluster. The consonant /t/ will typically be "unreleased" when it occurs as the final sound in a syllable (you hold onto the /t/ in words like *spot* and *spat*).

In many dialects of English, /t/ will become either an alveolar **flap** ([ɾ]) (sometimes known as a tap) or a glottal stop ([ʔ]) when it occurs medially (i.e., in the middle of a word) after a stressed syllable and before an unstressed syllable. Think of a word like *bottle*. If you are a speaker of American English and you say this word aloud, you probably don't actually produce a /t/ in the middle; you probably produce a flap—a voiced sound produced when the tongue taps or bounces off the alveolar ridge on its way to the production of another sound. If you are a speaker of American English and you say the word *mitten*, you probably don't actually produce a /t/ in the middle; instead, you probably stop the airflow and then release it, which we represent as a glottal stop. (You may find, however, that you have a flap in this word as well.)

American English speakers tend to produce the glottal stop medially after a stressed syllable before /n/ (as in *patent*) but not before other consonants. Speakers of some varieties of British English produce the glottal stop for /t/ in this position before consonants such as /l/, /r/, and /m/ as well (as in *bottle*, *butter*, and *bottom*). In American English, the sound /d/ also becomes a flap or a glottal stop medially after a stressed syllable (as in *pudding*).

Table 3.3 shows the allophones of the phoneme /t/ and their environments. As Table 3.3 makes clear, allophones typically occur in complementary distribution. That is, the environments in which the allophones occur do not overlap, and together they account for all the environments in which the sound can occur. There are exceptions, and linguists say

TABLE 3.3   **Allophones of the Phoneme /t/**

Allophones of /t/	Environment
[tʰ]	Word initially and at the beginning of a stressed syllable without a preceding consonant (*tip, atop*)
[t̚]	Unreleased, syllable finally (*pat, pet, pit, pot, put*)
[ɾ] or [ʔ]	Medially, after a stressed syllable and before an unstressed syllable (*pitter patter*)
[t̪]	Dental, before an interdental fricative (*at the, eighth*)
[t]	Elsewhere (*print, cleft*)

that these allophones occur in free variation in these environments (although there may be nonphonetic factors that explain their distribution).

As another example of allophones, the liquid /l/ has two allophonic variants—clear and dark—which you can hear if you say the words *let* and *hull*. In *let*, we have clear [l], which is more front than the velarized, dark, more back [ɫ]. Clear [l] occurs in the onset of syllables (i.e., at the beginning) and dark [ɫ] occurs in the coda after a vowel. So the word *lull* has a clear [l] at the beginning and a dark [ɫ] at the end: [lʌɫ].

All vowels have nasalized allophones when they occur before a nasal consonant (indicated by a [~] over the vowel). In preparation for producing the nasal consonant, the velum is lowered, often a little early, while the vowel is being produced, so that the vowel is produced with air escaping through the oral and nasal cavity. You can feel these effects when you say words like *some* or *grin* or *ping-pong*.

Minimal Pairs

Another way to describe phonemes is as sounds that when substituted for another create meaningful differences (i.e., different words). For example, in the sequence of sounds /__æt/, we get *bat* if we use /b/ in initial position and *pat* if we substitute /p/. That is, /b/ and /p/ are two different phonemes, and the distinction between /b/ and /p/ (voicing) is significant in English (it can distinguish between words). The pair of words /pæt/ and /bæt/ is called a **minimal pair**: a pair of words differentiated by only one feature of one sound, which proves that the feature in question is phonemic in that language.

If we take the same sequence /__æt/, it would be impossible in English to create a minimal pair for aspiration because, for example, if /p/ were to begin the word, it would have to be aspirated. Say the word *pat* while holding your hand in front of your mouth and feel the air escape after the unvoiced, word initial /p/. Then say *bat* with voiced, word initial /b/. This time, there is no aspiration. So, in this feature, the two words do not constitute a minimal pair, and aspiration is not phonemic in English. In a language like Thai, however, it would be possible to create a minimal pair demonstrating aspiration as a phonemic or contrastive difference, in the same way that we created a pair for voicing in English.

To take another example, the minimal pair *mean* /min/ and *main* /men/ prove that /i/ and /e/ are two distinct phonemes and that vowel height (the difference between a high and mid front tense vowel) is a distinctive feature. Note that /min/ and /men/ are exactly the same except for the vowel, and the two vowels in question share all the same features except for height, which allows us to isolate height as the distinctive feature between the two vowels.

Phonological Rules

The consonant and vowel charts in Tables 3.1 and 3.2 capture the systematicity of English sounds. The sounds distribute in systematic ways—that is, according to phonological rules. Phonological rules express the ways in which sounds change predictably in certain environments and describe patterns or types of sound changes. The word *rule* in this context means "what happens" rather than "what should/must happen"—phonological rules are descriptive rather than prescriptive rules. The following types of phonological rules and types of sound change capture only some of the many categories of sound change. They are in no way comprehensive.

Assimilation

Assimilation rules describe the ways in which a sound becomes more similar to surrounding sounds. In English, most examples of assimilation involve consonants. The primary motivation of assimilation is ease of articulation: it is easier to articulate two consecutive sounds if they share features such as place/manner of articulation or voicing. Assimilation can occur both forward (in a sequence of sounds AB, B becomes more like A) or backward (in a sequence of sounds AB, A becomes more like B).

An example of assimilation involves the prefix in- meaning 'not' in English, which sometimes appears as *in-* and sometimes as *im-*. If you make a brief list of some of the words in English that employ this prefix, you will start to see the pattern:

insufficient	*impractical*
intolerant	*impossible*
inhospitable	*immature*
innumerable	*immeasurable*
inevitable	*imbalance*
inglorious	*improper*

In the second column, the root words all begin with a bilabial sound, so the prefix *in-* becomes *im-* (with the bilabial sound /m/) preceding bilabial sounds. If you were to articulate this observation as a rule for the prefix, it would look like this:

$$\text{In} \longrightarrow \text{Im} / \underline{\quad} [+ \text{ bilabial}]$$

You would read this rule as follows: /ɪn/ becomes /ɪm/ when it precedes a bilabial sound. In rapid speech, this kind of assimilation can occur across word boundaries. So *in between* can be pronounced /ɪmbətwin/.

Another example of assimilation is the change of [n] to [ŋ] before /k, g/ in Old English (see Exercise 3.3), as [n] came to be articulated as a *velar* nasal before the *velar* consonants /k, g/. In Modern English, vowels become nasalized before nasal consonants, which is also assimilation.

Deletion

Deletion is a process through which sounds come to be omitted from words. American and British English are stress-timed languages, which means that stressed syllables tend to occur at fairly regular intervals in naturally occurring speech. As a result, unstressed syllables can get shortened and occasionally deleted. For example, in American English, the primary stress on the word ´labora`tory is on the first syllable, with secondary stress on the (third or) fourth syllable (-*to*-). In rapid speech, the vowel in the second syllable can be deleted to create the cluster /br/, and the word becomes four syllables long. In some varieties of English, the first vowel in a word like *police* can be deleted to create a one-syllable word with the initial /pl/ cluster: /plis/. In other varieties of English, final consonant clusters that share voicing (i.e., both consonants are voiced or both are unvoiced) are simplified by the deletion of the second consonant: /hænd/ ⟶ /hæn/ and /lɪft/ ⟶ /lɪf/.

Language Change at Work

Is *larynx* Undergoing Metathesis?

How do you say the word *larynx*? Traditionally, this word has been pronounced /lærɪŋks/. In current usage, some young speakers seem to say /lærnɪks/, reversing the order of the nasal and the vowel. If you want to see how pervasive this new pronunciation is among the young speakers at your school, have each person in the class create a word list of five words with *larynx* as one of them (you don't want the interviewees to know what you are looking for). Then, each of you should interview five speakers, asking them to read your list. Record the results for *larynx* and tally them as a class.

Insertion

Insertion is a process in which sounds are added to words, most obviously when an affix (e.g., a prefix or suffix) is added. Take, for example, the noun *length*, where the suffix *-th* (/θ/) is added to a word ending in *-ng* (/ŋ/). If you listen to yourself say *length*, you may hear an inserted /k/: /lɛŋkθ/. As speakers move from the voiced velar nasal to the voiceless interdental/dental fricative, they may produce /k/ as a transitional sound: /k/ is voiceless (like /θ/) and a velar stop (like /ŋ/). The insertion of /p/ in "sumpthing" (/sʌmpθɪŋ/) is similar. The intrusive /r/ in some dialects in pronunciations such as "warsh" and "idear" is yet another example of insertion.

Metathesis

Metathesis describes the process of sounds reversing their order. Historical examples include Old English /brid/ and /θrid/ becoming Modern English *bird* and *third*. You can now see how the initial consonant cluster *thr-* (as in *three* and *thrice*) is related to *third*. Also recall the story of *aks*, another notable example of metathesis, recounted at the beginning of Chapter 1.

There are many other phonological rules, of course, such as those that govern schwa insertion, vowel lengthening, voicing, flapping, and so on. And there are contrastive rules as well, not rules that describe phonological characteristics within a single variety of English, but those that describe the variation in characteristics among dialects and account for the differences among English accents. One contrastive rule, for example, is that intrusive /r/ occurs in some dialects and not in others.

Syllables and Phonotactic Constraints

A **syllable** is a unit of speech consisting of uninterrupted sound, composed of one or more phonemes, that generally includes a vowel **nucleus** (or center) and may include a consonant **onset** or **coda** or both. Except when the syllable is composed of a syllabic consonant, the nucleus is always a vowel and in English is the only required component of a syllable. Not all languages work this way. In some languages, for example, the onset is also required; some languages have no codas.

The most common syllable type is CV (that is, consonant/vowel). Whenever possible, words break into CV syllables. In other words, in a string of phonemes CVCV, the syllables will break as CV / CV (not, for example, CVC / V). So the word *relent* breaks as /rə lɛnt/, and *retreat* breaks as /rə trit/. This second example demonstrates the principle of "onset maximalism." As April McMahon (2002, 111) describes it: "Where there is a choice, always assign as many consonants as possible to the onset, and as few as possible to the coda. However, remember that every word must also consist of a sequence of well-formed syllables."

Phonotactic constraints refer to the parameters for what sounds can appear in onsets and codas in a particular language. In English, for example, /ŋ/ cannot appear in syllable onsets and /h/ cannot appear in syllable codas. For instance, English cannot have the word *ngash or the word *smah, where the *h* is pronounced as /h/. (Remember, the * symbol indicates a hypothetical word or phrase.) In other words, not all sounds can occur next to all other sounds in the construction of a syllable. If you try reading words backward, you quickly discover which "backward words" are still allowable English strings of sound, even though they are not English words (e.g., *brubus, yalp*), and which are not (e.g., *hsilgne, dnuos*).

Perception of Sound

Acoustic phonetics examines the characteristics of the sound waves of speech, and auditory phonetics examines how our brains perceive sound. We cannot do justice to these complex fields here and will try instead simply to provide some basic information about sound waves and a few quite interesting findings related to auditory phonetics. We encourage any of you who find this material intriguing to take a full course in phonetics.

Machines called spectrographs can produce **spectrograms** or images of the shape of sound waves—often called waveforms (see Figure 3.4). The resonances in the vocal tract are described as **formants**. The first formant (F1) indicates the air vibration behind the tongue (in the throat); auditorily, it is involved in our perception of height. The second formant (F2) indicates the air vibration in the mouth; auditorily, it is involved in our perception of backness or frontness. The third formant (F3) plays a role in the production of rounded sounds and is key to our perception of /l/ and /r/.

American linguist Erik Thomas provides a useful analogy for understanding the nature of resonance in the vocal tract and how that is related to formants:

> The cavities in the vocal tract work much like a woodwind instrument—the longer the cavity, the lower its resonance. Thus, an oboe produces lower frequency sounds than a flute because it is longer. In the mouth, there are two cavities for most of the vowels, one in front of the tongue and one behind it. They each produce a resonance, and the resonances are termed the first and second formants, or F1 and F2 for short. For [i], the front cavity is short and the back cavity is long, with the result that there is a high-frequency resonance and a low-frequency resonance. For [ɑ], on the other hand, the two cavities are nearly the same length, so that the two resonances show nearly the same frequencies. There is one important difference between a vocal tract and a woodwind instrument, though. In a woodwind instrument, the sound is produced by air rushing through the cavity. In a vocal tract, however, the sound is produced by the vibration of the vocal folds and is simply "shaped" by the cavities in the mouth. Whistling is like a woodwind instrument in this regard. In whistling, the sound is produced by air rushing through the cavity between the tongue and the lips.

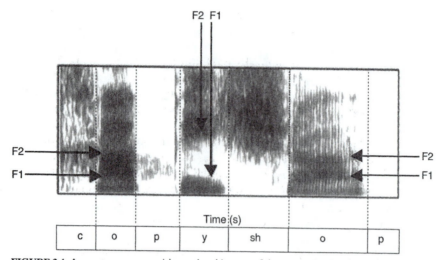

FIGURE 3.4 A spectrogram provides a visual image of the acoustic signal when we speak. On a spectrogram, the vertical axis represents the frequency of the waveforms and the horizontal axis represents time (moving positively toward the right). The dark horizontal bands represent different formants. This spectrogram captures an adult woman saying "copy shop." You'll notice that the vowels, which are technically the same phoneme, look slightly different because their articulation is affected by the neighboring sounds.
Source: Spectrogram provided by Robin Queen.

Various other details are left out of the above explanation. . . . [F]or high vowels (and to some extent for mid vowels), the first formant, or F1, isn't, strictly speaking, the resonance of the back cavity, but instead is the resonance of the back cavity and the constriction between the tongue and the roof of the mouth together, which form a bottle-shaped cavity called a Helmholz resonator. In fact, any narrow-mouthed bottle forms a Helmholz resonator, which is why you can blow on the top of a bottle to make a sound. Yet another detail is that for [ə] and [æ], there is no constriction at all, and all of the resonances are resonances of the resulting single long cavity between the larynx and the opening of the mouth. If the lips are rounded, the lip rounding will affect the resonances by lowering them. Nasality is even more complicated!

The vowel chart in Table 3.2 (page 74) represents a graph (inverted and reversed) of the average values of the F1 and F2 formants of the vowels (for a given group of speakers) mapped against each other.

Pitch refers to the rate of repetition or vibration of the vocal cords and, therefore, the air pressure. **Tone** languages are languages in which the pitch of a word can change *the meaning of a word.* For example, in Chinese, the same syllable with rising pitch and falling pitch will constitute two different words. **Intonation** refers to differences in pitch that can change *the meaning of a sentence.* In Standard English, pitch usually falls at the end of clauses and sentences. Rising intonation is usually associated with questions, although, as you will discover in the next chapter, "uptalk" has changed that. Some dialects of British English (Scots, for instance) have rising intonation in declarative sentences, both now and historically. In any case, in most dialects of English, "You are going to the store" with rising intonation at the end would typically be interpreted as a question. With falling intonation at the end, the same sentence would be perceived as a command or a statement of fact.

We still have much to learn about how the brain perceives and interprets sound waves. Research on how children acquire language indicates that by about the age of six months, babies have learned to perceive the phonemes specific to the language around them and disregard allophonic differences. How could one possibly determine this with children too young to speak? In brief, linguists have created a "suck test" (carried out with a pacifier that is electronically attached to a monitor) to help them gauge babies' responses. The premise is that if babies hear the same sound repeated over and over, their sucking on a pacifier will slow down until they hear a different sound, at which point their sucking will speed up.

Up until six months, babies can hear all the sounds relevant to all the world's languages—which makes sense, given that they may have to learn any of the world's languages, depending on their environment. So up to six months, babies growing up in an English-speaking environment will hear [p] and [pʰ] as distinct sounds and speed up their sucking if the soundtrack switches from one to the other. Around six months, these babies will have figured out that this contrast, based on aspiration, is not phonemically relevant in English. They seem to begin to perceive [p] and [pʰ] as the same sound—their sucking will not speed up if the aspiration on the soundtrack is switched. As speakers then grow older, they find it harder and harder to overcome these early learned categories, so that for adult English speakers, aspiration can be very difficult to perceive.

Another experiment in auditory phonetics indicates that there is a visual component to hearing. What we see can have an effect on what we "hear." This phenomenon is often called the **McGurk Effect**, after the Australian psychologist Harry McGurk, whose 1976 paper "Hearing Lips and Seeing Voices" (published with John MacDonald) described this discovery. The phenomenon is observable when the visual input given to a subject does not correspond to the auditory input. The classic example involves a tape that plays the repeated sound /bɑ/ spliced to a video in which a speaker is visually producing the sound /gɑ/ repeatedly. If speakers listen to the tape without looking at the speaker's mouth, they will hear /bɑ/; when they look at the speaker, they will usually hear either /dɑ/ or /ðɑ/. What is happening? It would appear that the brain is making a compromise between auditory input (a bilabial voiced stop) and visual input (a velar voiced stop) and perceiving an alveolar voiced stop or interdental fricative.

McGurk Effect

auditory input		visual input		perception
/bɑ/	+	/gɑ/	=	/dɑ/ or /ðɑ/
[bilabial]		[velar]		[alveolar voiced stop/interdental fricative]

One could argue that speakers frequently lip-read to some extent as part of speech perception.

Linguist Dennis Preston argues that speakers' knowledge of dialectal variation also affects perception. For example, Detroit speakers tend to front the vowel /ɑ/ (as in *bother*) so that it is closer to /æ/ (as in *bat*); speakers from the Upper Peninsula of Michigan usually do not. Preston has demonstrated that if Detroit speakers hear a slightly fronted /ɑ/ spoken by another Detroit speaker, they will interpret it as /ɑ/, but if they hear the same fronted vowel spoken by a "Yooper" (someone from the Upper Peninsula, who would not front /ɑ/), they will interpret it as /æ/. As Preston sums up the results: "The ear hears phonetics but the brain hears phonemes."

Special Focus: History of English Spelling

Mark Twain once wrote, "I don't give a damn for a man that can spell a word only one way." Is it *catalogue* or *catalog*? *Centre* or *center*? And where did the *u* in *forty* go? The answer to the first two questions is: It depends whether you live in Britain or in the United States. The answer to the third question is: Historians of English don't know. Chaucer could still write *fourty*, but sometime in the following two centuries, the *u* disappeared. The following very brief history of spelling touches on only a few reasons for some of the patterns and irregularities in English spelling; we hope it answers some of your questions about English spelling and piques your curiosity to learn more.

English was first written with the Latin alphabet after the introduction of Christianity to England, beginning in 597 CE with the mission of Saint Augustine. (See Chapter 13 for more details.) The Latin alphabet has only twenty-three letters for about thirty-five sounds in English. So, in Old English (449–1066 CE), we have letters doing "double time": for example, *t* for /t/ as well as /θ/; and *h* not only for /h/ but as part of representing /θ/, /ʃ/, and /tʃ/.

The English were invaded and conquered by the Norman French in 1066. French scribes began writing down English, and, as they did so, introduced some French spellings into English. For example, the French word *cité* uses the letter *c* for the sound /s/, and French scribes introduced this use of *c* into English in words like *city* and *cellar.* And French *qu*, in which the *u* doesn't represent a glide, substituted for the sound /kw/, which was spelled *kw* or *cw* in Old English. This explains why, to this day, no one knows how to pronounce the word *quay.* Some pronounce it with /k/ followed by the glide /w/; others pronounce it like *key*, as in *Key West.*

Scribes also tried to deal with the fact that long and short vowels had the same letter form. They tended to double a consonant that followed a vowel if the vowel was short. But they did not do this consistently. They tended to add an extra vowel if the vowel was long. But there was no universal agreement about what the extra vowel should be (*ee, ea, ei*).

In many cases, the spelling of English words does not correspond to their sounds because the spelling preserves an older pronunciation of the words: English spelling is a museum of older pronunciations. For example, initial /k/ and /g/ were pronounced in the clusters /kn/ and /gn/ in words such as *knight* and *gnat*. These initial sounds were lost in the Early Modern English period (1476–1776) but are preserved in the spelling. The final *-e* in English words such as *name* used to be pronounced; it isn't pronounced today, but spelling preserves the historical sound.

The Great Vowel Shift (GVS), which didn't happen all at once but gradually (and variously) from as early as the fourteenth century and well into the seventeenth century, affected the historically long vowels (many of which we would now label as tense vowels), and they "moved up" in their articulation. Low long vowels became mid vowels, mid long vowels became high vowels, and high long vowels (with nowhere else to go) became diphthongs. Figure 3.5 provides a simplified schema of the effects of the Great Vowel Shift.

The Great Vowel Shift happened just as and after spelling was becoming more standardized with the invention of printing and mass production of texts, so many of our spellings still reflect pre-GVS pronunciation. Examples are *mouse* (formerly /uː/ which became /aʊ/), *mice* (formerly /iː/ which became /aɪ/), *boot* and *goose* (formerly /oː/ which

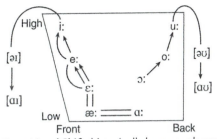

FIGURE 3.5 During the Great Vowel Shift, historically long vowels were raised and the high vowels became diphthongs. Long /æ/ eventually was raised all the way to /e/ and long /ɛ/ to /i/ (except for a few words like *great, break,* and *steak*). Many English spellings reflect pronunciations before the Great Vowel Shift.

became /u/), *see* and *meet* (formerly /e:/ which became /i/), *mate* (formerly /a:/ which became /e/). Note: in phonetic transcriptions, a colon after a vowel indicates a long vowel sound.

Revived interest in classical Greece and Rome, a chief characteristic of the Renaissance, affected the written form of English, as scholars sometimes changed English spelling to conform to Latin spelling. English spellings often reflected French forms—Latin words were often borrowed into English not directly but through French. Some Renaissance scholars, however, traced forms back to Latin and inserted letters that had been lost, both in French and English. Often, such respelling had no effect on pronunciation but gave us silent letters in words such as *debt, doubt,* and *indict*:

Modern English	Middle English	Latin
debt	*dette*	*debitum*
doubt	*doute*	*dubitare*
indict	*enditen*	*indictare*

In some instances, the spelling change eventually altered pronunciation so that the modern spelling and pronunciation correspond:

Modern English	Middle English	Latin
perfect	*perfet* (Old French)	*perfectum*
falcon	*faucon*	*falcōn*
adventure	*aventure*	*aduentas*

We also find "incorrect" Latin spellings, based on false etymologies. For example, the English word *island* is a native English word, *ealand* in Old English (*ea* 'water' + *land*). Renaissance scholars assumed that the word was related to the Latin word *insula*, so they inserted the *s* back into *island*, even though it was never there!

Some odd spellings result from idiosyncratic word histories. One of the more mysterious spellings in English is the word *colonel*, pronounced /kʌrnəl/. This disjunction seems to result from a "double borrowing." In the mid-sixteenth century, English seems to have borrowed the form with "r" from the French form *coronel*, ultimately derived from the Italian form *colonello*. Then the Italian form, with the "l," was also borrowed, and the two forms seem to have coexisted for a period of time before the Italian spelling was standardized with the French pronunciation. English spellings of borrowed words often follow spelling patterns of the languages from which they were borrowed: *pneumonia, psychology, rhetoric* (all from Greek), *bizarre* (French), *borsch* (Russian), *llama* (Spanish).

Should English Spelling Be Reformed?

Efforts at reforming English spelling date back at least to the sixteenth century in Britain, when grammarians such as William Bullokar introduced new spelling systems, often employing double letters and diacritics to create a one-to-one correspondence between sound and spelling. In the United States, Noah Webster was a well-known supporter of spelling reform. Originally an advocate of more radical reforms to create logical spelling, Webster modified his position by the time he published his important 1828 *Dictionary of the American Language,* which he hoped would help establish the independence of American spelling from British spelling. Many of the spelling differences between American and British written English can be traced back to new American spellings that Webster introduced, which were then adopted by the U.S. Government Printing Office in 1864:

British	American	
-our	*-or*	(*honour* vs. *honor*)
-re	*-er*	(*centre* vs. *center*)
-ence	*-ense*	(*defence* vs. *defense*)
-ise	*-ize*	(*realise* vs. *realize*)

Webster also introduced the single *l* in inflected forms of verbs such as *travel,* so the American spelling is *traveled,* not *travelled.* He dropped the final *-k* from words such as *public,* and introduced final *-or* for *-er* when it corresponded to the Latin (e.g., *instructor*). It should be noted that Webster also introduced some spelling reforms that did not succeed, notably dropping the final *-e* to create words such as *determin, definit, medicin,* and *infinit.* The only one of these that may be succeeding now is *ax* for *axe.*

In the nineteenth century, institutions such as the American Philological Reform Association published suggested new spellings, and the American Spelling Reform Association proposed a modified alphabet with thirty-two letters. In 1906, the Simplified Spelling Board was established in the United States with $250,000 from Andrew Carnegie. While it was neither financially nor orthographically successful, its proposed reforms are responsible for the shortening of words such as *catalog* and *program,* and for the substitution of *f* for *ph* in *fantasy* (but not in other *ph* words). The Simplified Spelling Society, based in Britain, was founded in 1908 and continues to this day. And the American Literacy Council continues to advocate spelling reforms that supposedly will help English speakers learn to read and write English.

Arguments against reforming English spelling note that the language is always changing, so reformed spellings will also become out of date. In addition, whose pronunciation would become standardized in a reformed spelling system? Would *cot* and *caught* be spelled the same way or differently? Reformed spelling might also erase etymological connections that spelling preserves, such as *south* and *southern,* related words with different nuclear vowels. Spelling, it can be argued, is a museum that preserves interesting facts about the history of English (e.g., the Great Vowel Shift) and relevant etymological connections.

It is unlikely that English speakers will ever see their entire spelling system reformed—in part because it would be unfeasibly difficult and expensive to get everyone to comply or to overhaul all publications, and in part because English speakers are attached to their idiosyncratic spellings. But spelling changes are happening around us, even without explicit proposals for reform. Consider, for example, the simplified spelling *donut* for *doughnut,* and *lite* in reference to low-calorie food products, or the spelling *dawg* rather than *dog* to capture pronunciations that distinguish the meaning 'friend' from 'domestic canine'. And while the word processor on which this book was written does not like the spellings *lite* or *dawg* right now, they may be accepted reforms to English spelling in the future.

☑ Summary

- English phonology examines the distinctive categories of sounds in the English sound system, as well as how sounds combine in syllables and words.

- A phoneme is what speakers think of as a distinctive sound of a language. All the sounds in the consonant and vowel charts in this chapter are the distinctive phonemes of English. Phonemes can have subtle, predictable variants in pronunciation, called allophones, which occur in particular contexts (e.g., the beginning of a word).

- Minimal pairs involve two words that carry different meanings and vary only in one sound in the same place in the word's structure (e.g., *pat, bat*). Minimal pairs prove that these two sounds, which occur in overlapping distribution, are phonemes in the language. Allophones occur in complementary distribution (their environments do not overlap).

- Consonants generally involve stopping or impeding the airflow. Vowels involve unimpeded airflow and function as the center of syllables. The distinctive features for consonants are place of articulation, manner of articulation, and voicing. The distinctive features for vowels are height, front/back, and tense/lax.

- Natural classes of sounds share a set of features that distinguish them from all other sounds and that exclude all other sounds. Natural classes allow us to talk about sets of sounds more efficiently.

- In the application of phonological rules such as assimilation, natural classes of sounds often behave similarly or cause similar effects on other sounds.

Suggested Reading

For more details about the International Phonetic Alphabet and the symbols for phonetic transcription, the first place to turn is the *Handbook of the International Phonetic Association* (1999). April McMahon's *English Phonology* (2002) provides an excellent, more detailed overview of the sound system of English, including phonotactic constraints and stress patterns. Heinz Giegerich's *English Phonology: An Introduction* (1992) can be very valuable for more advanced students. For a more general overview of phonetics and phonology, the work of Peter Ladefoged is invaluable and often cited: his book *Vowels and Consonants* (2001) is an impressively accessible and readable discussion of many of the world's sounds and how they are produced, and it is accompanied by a CD; his textbook *A Course in Phonetics* (4th ed., 2001) provides a more comprehensive discussion of the subject. J. C. Catford's *Fundamental Problems in Phonetics* (1977) and *A Practical Introduction in Phonetics* (1988) are also excellent, as is Keith Johnson's *Acoustic and Auditory Phonetics* (2d ed., 2003). D. B. Fry's *The Physics of Speech* (1979) is a useful supplement to standard treatments of phonetics. Another standard textbook on phonetics and phonology is John Clark and Colin Yallop's *An Introduction to Phonetics and Phonology* (2d ed., 1995). Robert Stockwell and Donka Minkova, in their *English Words: History and Structure* (2001), provide a detailed account of many more phonological rules for English than discussed here. Many of the fascinating aspects of language acquisition and processing are discussed at greater length, in accessible ways, in Gerry T. M. Altmann's *The Ascent of Babel* (1997) and Steven Pinker's *The Language Instinct* (1994). Mario Pei includes an entertaining section on the history of English spelling in *The Story of the English Language* (1967), as does Bill Bryson in *The Mother Tongue: English and How It Got That Way* (1990); for a full-length book on the subject, consult D. G. Scragg's *A History of English Spelling* (1974).

Exercises

Exercise 3.1   Transcription of English Words

A few important notes before you begin the exercise:

- The goal of transcription is to represent the sounds of words using IPA symbols. Here we focus on *phonemic* transcription. In other words, the transcription represents the phonemes that occur in a word without representing the allophones of those sounds that may occur in the word. For example, the phonemic transcription (sometimes called a "broad transcription") of the word *pit* would be /pɪt/. A possible phonetic transcription (sometimes called a "narrow transcription") would be [pʰɪt˺].

- When you transcribe English words, focus on their sound, not their spelling. Read the word aloud and then transcribe what you hear. Sometimes there are silent letters in spelling that you should not transcribe. For example, *bite* should be transcribed /baɪt/. The spelling of some words does not represent all the sounds in the word. For example, *huge* contains a glide not indicated by the spelling: /hjudʒ/ (just try saying /hudʒ/!).

- You will probably discover that it is hard to decipher the vowel before the consonant /r/. This phenomenon is sometimes called "r-coloring" or "r-infection," and it means that the articulation of the vowel is affected (lowered and centralized) by the oncoming articulation of /r/. So you may find alternants such as

[or] versus [ɔr], and [ir] versus [ɪr]. The liquid /l/ can have a similar effect on preceding vowels for some speakers. The nasal /ŋ/ also affects the preceding vowel, causing it to rise slightly (so, for example, the vowel in *sing* may sound closer to /i/ than /ɪ/).

- If you compare your transcriptions with those of a classmate, you may discover that some of your vowel transcriptions vary. These differences reflect differences in your accents and your map of the vowel space.

- The transcriptions that you will be reading and producing here represent "careful pronunciation," which we know is different from naturally occurring, more rapid speech.

1. Rewrite these transcribed English sentences in normal spelling. The pronunciation of words indicated here may not completely correspond to your speech, but the words still should be recognizable. We have artificially included punctuation.

a. /wʌns əpɑn ə taɪm ðər wʌz ə kæt ɪn ə hæt hu əskeɪpt frʌm ðə wr̩ld ʌv dɑktr̩ sus ænd dəsaɪdɪd tə lɪv ɪn nu joʊrk sɪti, weɪr hi dəsaɪdɪd tə luz ðə hæt ænd bɪkʌm ə fæʃn̩ dəzaɪnr̩ ʌv filɑɪn kæʒul̩ weɪr./

_____

_____

_____

_____

b. /aɪ toʊld maɪ frɛnd ðæt maɪ noʊz wʌz rʌnɪŋ ænd ʃi æskt wɪtʃ weɪ ɪt wʌz hɛdɪd./

_____

_____

_____

c. /ju meɪ bi tu jʌŋ tə rəmɛmbr̩ tɛləvɪʒn̩ sɛts wɪθaʊt rəmoʊt kəntroʊl, rotəri foʊnz, wʌn ʌv ðə fr̩st vɪdioʊ geɪmz kɑld pɔŋ, eɪt træk teɪps, ænd laɪf bəfoʊr ðə ɪntr̩nɛt./

_____

_____

_____

d. /ɪf ju noʊ ðə ɪntr̩næʃunəl fənɛtɪk ælfɑbɛt, ju kæn ɪmprɛs ɑl jr̩ pirz baɪ jr̩ əbɪlɪti tu rid sɛntənsɪz laɪk ðiz ænd ðeɪ wɪl əndaʊtɪdli bi grin wɪθ ɛnvi./

_____

_____

_____

If you still need a challenge, think about how your transcription would change if you said these sentences quickly, so that the words ran together more.

2. Identify each of the following works of fiction.

 a. /mɪdnaɪt ɪn ðə gɑrdən əv gʊd ænd ivəl/

 b. /ə tel əv tu sɪtiz/

 c. /ðə bluəst aɪ/

 d. /ðə dʒen ɔstən bʊk klʌb/

 e. /ɪntərprɛtər əv mælədiz/

 f. /wʌðərɪŋ haɪts/

 g. /ðə brif wʌndrəs laɪf əv ɑskər waʊ/

 h. /ə kənfɛdərasi əv dʌnsəs/

 i. /ðə kʌlər pərpəl/

 j. / ðə də vɪntʃi kod/

 k. /θɪŋz fɑl əpɑrt/

 l. /laɪf əv paɪ/

3. Transcribe the words in the following lists as you would say them. Because you will be saying the words slowly in order to transcribe them, these transcriptions will probably represent your "careful pronunciation." As we noted earlier, you will probably discover that your vowels vary at least slightly from those of your classmates.

 Before you begin, you might want to read this advice (written with careful pronunciation so the words do not run together, and we have put in punctuation to help you out):

/wi rɛkəmɛnd ðæt ju dont traɪ tə du ðɪs eksr̩saɪz ɪn ə kɔfi ʃɑp, ðə laɪbrɛri, oʊr sʌm ʌðr̩ pʌblɪk pleɪs bəkʌz ju wɪl nid tə meɪk fʌni saʊndz oʊvr̩ and oʊvr̩ tə trænskraɪb ðiz wr̩dz ænd ʌðr̩ pipl̩ wɪl steɪr æt ju ænd θɪŋk ðæt ju ɑr streɪndʒ./

 a. One-syllable words

tick _____	kite _____	pat _____
key _____	man _____	teen _____
men _____	grace _____	lit _____
safe _____	zilch _____	moose _____
sole _____	push _____	house _____
soul _____	tie _____	yank _____
beige _____	vast _____	path _____
gym _____	thing _____	choice _____
shoe _____	route _____	gnat _____

chick _____   doubt _____   box _____

quiz _____   toy _____   yes _____

there _____   light _____   no _____

b. Two-syllable words

talent _____   jello _____

window _____   sweater _____

sashes _____   center _____

silky _____   relax _____

mental _____   instinct _____

answer _____   facelift _____

coffee _____   fortune _____

sofa _____   challenge _____

pencil _____   feature _____

swimming _____   fashion _____

feather _____   music _____

throttle _____   bluejeans _____

Tuesday _____   hustle _____

propose _____   sandwich _____

c. Longer, multisyllabic words

yesterday _____   ceremony _____

calibrate _____   revolution _____

maximum _____   symphony _____

genuine _____   electronic _____

December _____   sufficient _____

January _____   officer _____

February _____   pacifier _____

Wednesday _____   photograph _____

Saturday _____   Washington _____

engagement _____   hypochondria _____

antidisestablishmentarianism _____

4. Choose a short passage from a novel (about 50 words) and transcribe it using the IPA. Next, write the passage in standard spelling on the back of the page. Then exchange papers with a classmate. Read your classmate's transcription and try to write it out in standard spelling. When you finish, look at the back of the page to check your classmate's transcription. Mark where your classmate's transcription diverges from the words he or she was attempting to transcribe.

Exercise 3.2   Natural Classes

Determine which of the following are natural classes in English. For those that are natural classes, provide a description of the natural class.

a. /i, ɪ, u, ʊ/ _____

b. /i, ɪ, e, ɛ, æ/ _____

c. /i, e, u/ _____

d. /l, r/ _____

e. /m, n/ _____

f. /p, b, m, w, ʍ/ _____

g. /v, ð, z, ʒ/ _____

h. /s, ʃ, tʃ/ _____

Exercise 3.3   Phonemes and Allophones

Why *knife* but *knives*?

Present-day English differs from Old English in the distribution of phonemes and allophones. Try to figure out the differences in these two examples.

1. In Old English, [ŋ] and [n] were allophones of /n/. Look at the following transcriptions of Old English words and figure out when [ŋ] appears, and when [n]. What is the rule for their predictable distribution?

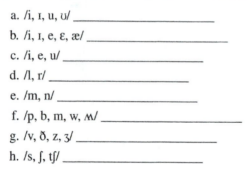

singan 'to sing'   [siŋɑn]

land 'land'   [lɑnd]

nama 'name'   [nɑmɑ]

snotor 'clever'   [snotor]

hring 'ring'	[hriŋg]
minte 'mint'	[minte]
ranc 'proud'	[raŋk]
mon 'one'	[mon]

Now you can see why, when the final /g/ was lost from words ending in *-ng*, there remained a /ŋ/ at the end.

2. In Old English, voiced fricatives were not distinctive phonemes but rather allophones of voiceless fricatives. In other words, [v] and [f] were allophones of /f/; [z] and [s] were allophones of /s/; and [ð] and [θ] were allophones of /θ/. Look at the following transcriptions of Old English words and figure out the distribution pattern of voiced and voiceless fricatives in Old English. In other words, when do the voiced fricatives appear and when do the voiceless fricatives appear? (The line over the vowel in the Old English spelling indicates a long vowel, which is transcribed phonetically with a colon after the vowel.)

heofon 'heaven'	[heəvon]
hlāf 'loaf'	[hlɑ:f]
hlāford 'lord'	[hlɑ:vord]
hlāfdige 'lady'	[hlɑ:vdije]
cēosan 'to choose'	[tʃe:əzɑn]
sēoðan 'to boil'	[se:əðɑn]
stān 'stone'	[stɑ:n]
flēogan 'to flee'	[fle:əgɑn]
læssa 'less'	[læ:ssɑ]
pæð 'path'	[pæθ]
paðas 'paths'	[paðɑs]
fæst 'firm'	[fæst]
ðone 'the'	[θone]
ðost 'dung'	[θost]
sīððan 'since'	[siθθɑn]
cnīf 'knife'	[kni:f]
cnīfas 'knifes'	[kni:vɑs]
lyft 'air'	[lyft]
āscian 'ask'	[ɑ:skiɑn]
līðnes 'mildness'	[li:ðnes]
līðsmann 'pirate'	[li:θsmann]

Now you can see the origins of *knife/knives* (as well as the pronunciation difference between *path* and *paths*). Now that /f/ and /v/ are separate phonemes, the spelling has changed to reflect the pronunciation.

3. Provide a minimal pair that demonstrates that each of the following features is phonemic in English. Remember, if the two sounds substituted for each other differ in more than one feature (e.g., place of articulation and voicing), it is impossible to know which feature the pair of words proves is phonemic.

   a. height of vowels

   b. frontness of vowels

   c. place of articulation for consonants

Exercise 3.4   Phonological Rules

1. Why might some speakers spell the word *hamster* as *hampster*? In other words, where does the *p* come from?

2. Why do some speakers delete the first /r/ in *library* ("liberry")?

3. English speakers think of the regular past-tense ending as *-ed*. In fact, there are three different phonological realizations of the regular past-tense ending: /d/, /t/, and /ɪd/. When each of these endings will occur is completely predictable. Transcribe the words below. Then, as succinctly as possible, write a set of rules that explain how we form the past tense of regular verbs in English (i.e., how we determine which of the three past-tense variants to use). Order the rules as efficiently as possible. You will discover that if you order the rules, you will be able to write them in their simplest, most general form in terms of natural classes. Two more hints:

   ■ The notion of assimilation is relevant here.

   ■ Consider /d/ as the basic past-tense ending.

     ticked

     spouted

     dozed

     added

     missed

     aimed

     pried

     counted

     watched

4. English speakers think of the regular plural noun ending as *-s*. In fact, there are three different phonological realizations of the regular plural noun ending: /z/, /s/, and /ɪz/. When each of these endings will occur is completely predictable. Transcribe the words below. Then, as succinctly as possible, write a set of rules that explains how we form the plural of regular nouns in English (i.e., how we determine which of the three plural variants to use). Order the rules as efficiently as possible. The hints provided in #3 also apply here, with /z/ as the basic plural ending.

     trees

     cats

dogs

horses

leeches

ticks

judges

cabs

cops

The variants of the past tense and plural inflectional endings in English are examples of **allomorphs**: predictable phonological variants of one morpheme. We talk more about morphemes and allomorphs in Chapter 4.

Exercise 3.5   Phonotactic Constraints

English has phonotactic constraints on three-consonant clusters in the onset of a syllable. Come up with a list of examples (e.g., *splash, straight, scream,* and *spring*), and write a rule for the composition of three-consonant clusters.

Exercise 3.6   Spelling Reform

Consider the following possible spelling reforms and argue for or against each one. Be specific in your reasoning about why you think the spelling should or should not be reformed. For example, you might specify that a word should adopt a different spelling for a specific meaning—such as adopting *lite* for low-calorie food products but maintaining *light* to refer to sources of illumination, as this spelling reform creates a useful visual distinction between the two meanings.

a. night/nite, tonight/tonite

b. cigarette/cigaret

c. catalogue/catalog, dialogue/dialog, monologue/monolog

d. judgment/judgement

e. eerie/eery

f. doughnut/donut

g. though/tho

h. through/thru, drive-thru

Chapter **4**

English Morphology

Blogs, like www.whatevs.org, have introduced or popularized new words in the English language, such as the word *whatevs*.

Bloggers have created not only a new genre of writing—the blog—but a new world of words as well. According to the new edition of the *OED*, the word *blog* is first cited in 1999. It began as the compound *weblog* and then was shortened by losing most of the first syllable. The noun *blog* quickly gave birth to the verb *to blog*, which in turn allowed the creation of *blogging* (the activity), *blogger* (the person), and *blogosphere* (the network of bloggers and blog readers all over the Web). The American Dialect Society elected *blog* as the word most likely to succeed from the year 2002.

A few years ago, one particular blogger created the blog www.whatevs.org, on which he introduced an array of new words—usually not completely made-up words, but derivations of already existing English words. For example, the shortened form *whatevs* can replace *whatever* when it is used to express the lack of a strong opinion. The shortened form *evs* is often used for *ever*: "Blogging is the best way to pass time evs." Visitors to the site report that they now find themselves using *evs*, *obvs* ('obviously'), and other new words not only in their own blogging but in their speech as well. None of these new words may stick. But then again, some of them might gain enough currency to make it into a dictionary some day. After all, *blog* already has.

Of particular interest for this chapter is that most of these "new" words are made from "old" parts. Occasionally a new word, like *quark,* is completely made up, and English speakers have borrowed many words from other languages over the centuries. But the majority of new words in English involve the combination, shortening, or other manipulation of already existing English components. We speakers of English make up new words every day, and we know how to interpret most new words when we meet them. When you surf the Web and encounter words like *bloggy* ("That's a bloggy notion"), *bloghead* ("Only a bloghead would think that"), *blogtastic* ("What he said about American foreign policy was blogtastic"), or *blogapalooza* ("Let's all meet up this weekend for a big ol' blogapalooza"), you know exactly what they mean.

We may think that we create these new words haphazardly and that they are "just slang." But in fact, the processes of creating new words follow systematic patterns. This chapter focuses specifically on how existing words are structured and classified and how new words are formed.

Morphology

The study of word structure is called **morphology**. The word *morphology* comes from the Greek word *morphē*, meaning 'form, shape', which is also related to the English verb *morph* meaning 'change'. But the study of language change is called historical linguistics, not morphology. Why not call the study of word structure "wordology" instead of "morphology"? Because many words are made up of smaller units, called morphemes, and morphology covers those units, too.

Linguists do not agree universally on a definition of *morpheme*, but the currently predominant view is that articulated by Zelig Harris (1942, 109): "Every sequence of phonemes which has meaning, and which is not composed of smaller sequences having meaning, is a morpheme." Morphemes, therefore, are the smallest meaningful units in language. Some morphemes are freestanding words, such as *small, unit, in, language.* Some morphemes are not full words but they still carry meaning, such as the superlative suffix *-est* in *smallest*, the suffixes *-ing* in *freestanding* and *-ful* in *meaningful*, and the plural suffix *-s* in *units*. In linguistic terms, all these are morphemes as well as lexical items, *small* as well as *-est*. But we call *small* and *smallest* "words"; we don't call *-est* a word. Why not? The answer lies in the roles any one of them can play in phrases, clauses, and sentences: freestanding morphemes have a different grammatical status from bound ones.

English sentences are typically constructed from multiple words, some of which contain only one morpheme and some of which combine morphemes. In some languages, words and complete utterances are often the same thing. Consider this example borrowed from Leonard Bloomfield's classic *Language* (1933, 207): the Inuit word that sounds like /aːwlisa-ut-issʔar-si-niarpu-ɔa/ apparently means 'I am looking for something suitable for a fish-line'. This one word serves the purpose of an entire English sentence. Inuit is an **agglutinative language**: a language in which words are formed from strings of relatively stable parts or morphemes. That is, in agglutinative languages, morphemes change little in the process of combination. The Inuit word is thus a string of meaningful parts, or morphemes, most of which cannot stand on their own—in other words, they cannot be Inuit words themselves.

Modern English is primarily an **analytic language**, one that depends mostly on word order for sentence structure and meaning. We usually can know a subject from an object because the subject comes before the verb and the object after the verb: As the saying goes, "The dog bit the man" is not news, but "The man bit the dog" is news—it's all about who gets to be before the verb. Other languages have more flexible word order, which is possible because endings on words indicate their grammatical function. For example, a noun will take one ending if it is the subject of the sentence, different endings if it is the direct or indirect object, and so on. Languages that employ word endings to indicate grammatical function are **synthetic languages** (e.g., Latin, Russian, German). In synthetic languages, nouns change form according to **number** (in English a matter of whether the word is singular or plural) and **case** (the grammatical function of a noun, pronoun, adjective, or determiner).

Old English was largely a synthetic language. In other words, it depended heavily on inflected forms rather than word order to convey grammatical relations among words in a sentence. Consider the made-up, highly artificial Old English sentences that follow. For each example, we have provided two variants with different word order but the same meaning, and there are other possible orders.

Se kyning seah þone hlāford.   or   Se kyning þone hlāford seah.
subject   direct object   subject   direct object
'The king saw the lord'.

Se hlāford þǣm kyninge þone hund geaf.   or   Se hlāford þone hund þǣm kyninge geaf.
subject indirect object direct object   subject direct object indirect object
'The lord gave the king the dog'.

As these sentences demonstrate, the ending on the noun changes (as does the form of the determiner 'the') depending on the function of the word in the sentence.

The story of English is partly the story of its movement from one type of language (more synthetic) to another (more analytic), and Modern English still has a few remnants from the older synthetic stage: the final *-s* to indicate plural nouns, for instance, and changing forms of pronouns to indicate whether the pronoun is singular or plural and whether it serves as a subject (e.g., *I, she, we*), an object (e.g., *me, her, us*), or a possessive (e.g., *mine, hers, ours*).

Different languages have different rules for how morphemes combine, but the categories of morphemes that we describe in the next three sections hold across languages.

Open and Closed Classes of Morphemes

Take any English sentence and you'll realize immediately that some words are susceptible to different forms and some are not. Take, for instance, "If I go to the store, then I can buy fresh milk." The conjunction *if* only appears in English in exactly that form, and so, too, the conjunction *then*, the preposition *to*, and the definite article *the*. Other words in the sentence readily form plurals (e.g., *stores*), past tense (e.g., *bought*), comparatives (e.g., *fresher*), and so on. The invariant forms belong to "closed classes" of morphemes. The forms with variants, such as nouns, verbs, adjectives, and adverbs, belong to "open classes" of morphemes.

The **closed morphological classes** in English include conjunctions, pronouns (of all kinds), auxiliary verbs (e.g., *may*, *can*), determiners (e.g., *the*, *a*), prepositions (e.g., *in*, *for*), and inflectional suffixes (see below). These classes tend not to add new members very often—that's why we call them "closed." Closed-class morphemes also tend to be invariant: they appear in the same form regardless of how they are used in a sentence (e.g., *the*, *if*). There are exceptions, however, which are mostly remnants of the earlier, synthetic stage of English. The pronoun *I*, for example, changes form according to number and case, so *I* yields *mine* in the genitive case (or possessive case), *me* in the object case, and *we*, *our*, and *us* in the plural. Similarly, the auxiliary verb *can* in some instances alters to *could*. But *can* and *could*, as auxiliaries, behave very differently from other verbs in that they do not have variant forms in the present tense (e.g., *he buys* but not *he cans* or *he coulds*).

Many word forms have remained within the same closed class throughout the history of English, from Old English (449–1066 CE), through Middle English (1100–1500 CE), then Early Modern English (1476–1776), and into Modern English. Some, like the conjunction *and*, have changed neither form nor core meaning in more than 1,500 years. Others are historically invariant as regards form, but not meaning. The preposition *with*, for instance, meant 'against, opposite, toward, in return for, along' in Old English; over time, the 'along' sense superseded the others and led to current meanings of *with*, such as 'accompanying, next to, supporting, having' (the meaning 'against' survives in phrases such as *fight with* and in compounds such as *withstand*). The preposition *to* meant everything from 'to, at, toward' to 'from' in Old English, but 'from' has fallen by the historical wayside. The meanings of these words have changed, but their forms (and their grammatical functions, or "parts of speech") have not. Prepositions and conjunctions, as classes, are open semantically, that is, in terms of meaning, but they do not tend to change, over time, with regard to grammatical situation.

Closed-class words are fundamental to the ordered structure of Modern English sentences. In a sentence, closed-class words signal important aspects of sentence-level meaning to listeners or readers. Closed-class words often show us how to understand the grammatical and semantic relationship of the words that precede and follow them. Consider, for example, *chapter <u>about</u> morphology* versus *phonology <u>and</u> morphology*: words on either side of the closed-class word in the first case stand in a different relation to each other than do those in the second. Because we depend on them for such grammatical information, closed classes tend to remain relatively stable. Hypothetically, speakers could add conjunctions beyond *and, as, but, if, for, or, nor, so, than, that, then, though, because, when, where, although, while, yet,* and a few others. But instead, speakers pack these few words with many meanings, rather than invent, borrow, or shift from another class a "new" word to cover a particular meaning.

If you glance back at Lewis Carroll's "Jabberwocky" in Chapter 1, you'll notice that most of the words you recognize are "function" words. For example, we've italicized the function words in this stanza:

'Twas brillig *and the* slithy toves
Did gyre *and* gimble *in the* wabe:
All mimsy were *the* borogoves,
And the mome raths outgrabe.

If these function words weren't retained, then Carroll's sentences wouldn't resemble English sentences enough for you to appreciate the nonsense.

The words you don't recognize in "Jabberwocky," like *brillig* and *outgrabe,* apparently belong to **open morphological classes**, those in which word forms adapt to new grammatical and semantic demands. New items can be added to or subtracted from these morphological classes—and frequently are—which is why we call them "open." These are the classes in which our vocabulary grows. The nonsense words in "Jabberwocky" wouldn't make sense if they didn't behave like members of open classes. Nouns, verbs, adjectives, and adverbs, as well as derivational affixes (which you will read more about in this chapter) all belong to open morphological classes.

In our earlier example, the words *go, store, buy, fresh,* and *milk* all belong to open classes. These words can and do change forms depending on the grammar of the sentence, and they can be used to form new words. For instance, *go* transforms into progressive *going* or past-tense *went. Store* can be compounded into *grocery store* or *hardware store. Buy* can become *bought* or *buying,* and *buying* can be a noun (e.g., *consumer buying*) as well as a verb. The word *milk* is, in its formal self, sometimes noun or verb. You can drink *milk,* or you can *milk* a cow; a cow is there for the *milking,* and once a *milk* cow is *milked,* one can produce *whole milk, 2% milk,* or *skim milk.* We can freely add new members to open-class categories, through compounding, shifting (e.g., the noun *milk* becoming a verb), and other processes described later in this chapter.

Most open-class morphemes change form depending on the grammar of the sentence (e.g., if past tense or plural is required). But there are exceptions here, too. Derivational morphemes, such as the prefix *non-,* are invariant. Some nouns have no plural form (e.g., *engineering*). And most adverbs are invariant (e.g., *really*).

While there are many more open-class words than closed-class words, the most common words in English are almost entirely closed-class. Table 4.1 shows the most common twenty words in corpora of spoken and written English, and you'll see that *the*

TABLE 4.1   **Most Frequent Words in Present-Day English**

Written English (American)[a]				Spoken English (British)[b]			
1. the	6. in	11. for	16. on	1. the	6. a	11. is	16. on
2. of	7. that	12. it	17. be	2. and	7. you	12. yes	17. well
3. and	8. is	13. with	18. at	3. I	8. that	13. was	18. he
4. to	9. was	14. as	19. by	4. to	9. in	14. this	19. have
5. a	10. he	15. his	20. I	5. of	10. it	15. but	20. for

[a]From the Brown Corpus of written American English.
[b]From the London-Lund corpus of spoken British conversation.
Source: Adapted from Greenbaum (1996, 403); and Crystal (1997, 86).

A Question to Discuss

Exceptions to the Closedness of Closed Classes?

Some closed morphological classes are more closed than others. It's been a long time since English has admitted a new preposition to that class. But other classes have been more accepting of new members. For instance, English used to distinguish between second-person singular and plural pronouns: *thou*, *thee*, and *thine*, were singular; *ye*, *you*, and *your* were plural. During the Early Modern period (beginning about 1475), the singular forms had all but dropped out of use, and the plural forms extended to cover both singular and plural uses. But speakers of English, especially American English, seem to find distinct plural forms useful and so either have retained dialectal forms of plural *you*, such as *youse* (an English dialect form) on the Mid-Atlantic seaboard and *yins/yinz* (*you ones*, from Ulster Scots) in Appalachia and Pittsburgh, or have introduced new forms, such as Southern *y'all* and general American *you guys*.

Some linguists argue that *y'all* can now be used as a singular pronoun, and some argue strenuously that it cannot. But the super-plural form *all y'all* has emerged recently, suggesting that some speakers are unsure about *y'all*'s status.

Other apparent exceptions to the typical behavior of closed-class words turn out not to be exceptions. Some word forms belong to more than one lexical category. For instance, some words that function as prepositions also function as adverbs. The preposition *by*, as in "The cat sat by the door," is not the same as the adverb *by*, as in "The days went by slowly." Adverbial *by* (an open-class morpheme) has developed into several compounds, such as *byway* and *bypass*, whereas prepositional *by*, as a member of a closed class, does not combine with other morphemes to form new words. Can you think of other possible exceptions?

tops both lists, with prepositions, articles, pronouns (all closed classes), and forms of *to be* (which can be open- or closed-class) not far behind.

Some open-class and closed-class morphemes have two or more phonological realizations or forms, called allomorphs. Much as allophones are variants of one phoneme, allomorphs are variants of one morpheme. For example, the forms *-en* and *-ed* are allomorphs of the same morpheme: the past-participle marker for verbs. Fictional British spy James Bond may have wanted his martini *shaken*, not *stirred*, but from the perspective of inflectional morphology, the *-en* on *shaken* and the *-ed* on *stirred* represent the same past-participle morpheme.

As a second example, the past-tense ending, which we usually think of as *-ed*, has four different phonological realizations or allomorphs: /t/ (*walked*), /d/ (*snored*), and /ɪd/ (*skated*), and **ablaut** (the vowel change in a verb like *sang*—for more on this, see Chapter 13). The plural marker *-s* has several allomorphs: /s/ (*cats*), /z/ (*dogs*), /ɪz/ (*horses*), /en/ (*children*), /ɑɪ/ (*alumni*), *-a* (*data*), ablaut (*mice* from *mouse*), and zero-plural (*deer*).

Use of many of these allomorphs is predictable. With the past-tense morpheme, the voiceless allomorph /t/ appears after voiceless sounds and the voiced allomorph /d/ after voiced sounds, with the exception of words ending in /t, d/, which require the ending /ɪd/ so that the past-tense marker can be distinguished from the final sound of the root word.

The plural morpheme works similarly in current Standard English: words ending with sibilants require /ɪz/ so that the final /z/ can be heard. Those exceptions aside, words ending in voiceless sounds take /s/ and those ending in voiced sounds take /z/. (You now have the answer to items 3 and 4 in Exercise 3.4.) Other plural allophones are products of borrowing or relics of early English plural systems, so behave less systematically. The /aɪ/ allomorph is sometimes borrowed from Latin or New Latin (*cacti*) or modeled on them (as in the case of *alumni*, which is an Americanism from 1696). Today, /aɪ/ is mostly facetious and active in slang (*peni* instead of *penises*, for instance), while traditionally /aɪ/ plurals are being reformed on a predictable basis (*cactuses* instead of *cacti*). Zero-plurals include historically irregular forms (e.g., *sheep*), and some new forms created through "zeroing": for instance, for many speakers, *dice* stands for both singular and plural, though the historical singular is *die*, as in what is cast. Plurals formed with /ɛn/ are relics (*children*, *brethren* and *oxen* are the only Modern English examples) and /ɛn/ is no longer productive. Plurals formed by means of ablaut are old (*mouse/mice*, *louse/lice*), and any new examples (*moose/meese*) are facetious.

Bound and Free Morphemes

Think of morphemes as making up a pie. We have discussed how the pie can be divided into "open classes" and "closed classes." But we can also divide the morpheme pie into "free morphemes" and "bound morphemes," and the dividing lines are different. The set of open-class morphemes contains both free and bound morphemes, and the same holds true for the set of closed-class morphemes.

Many morphemes in English are **free morphemes**: the word form consists of exactly one morpheme, and that morpheme functions independently as an English word (e.g., *word*). Most free morphemes can combine with at least some other morphemes to create still other words (e.g., *wordy*, *wordiness*). Closed-class morphemes are exceptions. Most morphemes in closed morphological classes—except for inflectional morphemes, as described below—are free, but they do not combine with other morphemes into new words.

Let's look at an example of free morphemes in combination. *Up* is a free morpheme: it includes more than one phonetic part, but it comprises only one morpheme, and that morpheme functions independently as an English word. When a preposition, *up* belongs to a closed morphological class (e.g., *she ran her finger up the page*). When an adverb, *up* belongs to an open morphological class (e.g., *taxes went up*), and it can combine with other morphemes into other words. *Talk* is also a free morpheme, as well as a member of an open morphological class. Hypothetically, then, *up* and *talk*, though they can perform in English sentences as single-morpheme words on their own, can also combine in other words. Indeed, they can even combine with each other, as they have in *uptalk*.

You probably hear people "uptalk" every day. A declarative sentence, such as "I really like eating out," would typically end on a low pitch. But sometimes speakers end such a statement on a higher pitch, making the statement sound like a question: "I really like eating out?" As more and more Americans started to speak in this pattern, linguists needed a name for it. Thus *uptalk* (verb and noun) was created from the two free morphemes *up* and *talk*. Because many parents and teachers object to *uptalking* (noun), they may have helped you break the habit. You may once have *uptalked* (verb) but aren't *uptalking* (verb) anymore. Or maybe you are still an *uptalker* (noun), in spite of their best efforts.

Uptalking, uptalked, and *uptalker,* though closely related to *uptalk,* both in form and in meaning, obviously incorporate morphemes other than *up* and *talk*. The suffixes *-ing*, *-ed*, and *-er* are morphemes because they are meaningful phonetic strings that contain within them no smaller meaningful strings. The suffix *-er*, for instance, means 'one who performs an action'. But these suffixes clearly aren't free morphemes because they cannot function as freestanding English words. They must always attach to a free morpheme. Morphemes that cannot stand independently as words are classified as **bound morphemes**.

Inflectional and Derivational Bound Morphemes

There are two classes of bound morphemes: inflectional and derivational.

Inflectional Morphemes

Some lexical categories, especially nouns and verbs in English, indicate certain types of meaning through the addition of **inflectional morphemes**. Consider the following paradigm (or list of related forms):

uptalk, uptalks, uptalking, uptalked

The suffixes indicated with underlining, each of them a bound morpheme, mark inflected forms of the verb *uptalk*. Meaning changes as the root adopts each suffix: *-s* indicates third-person singular present tense, *-ing* indicates the present participle or the progressive mood, *-ed* indicates the simple past tense or the past participle. But the root's meaning does not change, and neither does the lexical category—all four forms are verbs. Similarly, the noun *uptalker* can add an inflectional morpheme to indicate the plural (*uptalkers*), or the possessive (*uptalker's*), or the plural possessive (*uptalkers'*).

Inflectional morphemes in English are always suffixes, and there are no longer very many of them in English (see "Language Change at Work: The Origins of Inflectional *-s*"). Here's the full list and some examples:

Inflectional Morphemes

NOUNS → person, place, thing, idea, state of being

- plural *-s* — *uptalkers*
- possessive *-s* — *blogger's/bloggers'*

VERBS → action words

- third-person singular present tense *-s* — *she blogs*
- progressive *-ing* — *she is blogging*
- past tense *-ed* — *she blogged*
- past participle *-ed/-en* — *she has blogged/written*

ADJECTIVES → describing word

- comparative *-er* — *stinkier*
- superlative *-est* — *stinkiest*

Language Change at Work

The Origins of Inflectional -s

Although English employs a few inflected forms today, once upon a time it employed many, many more. Modern English is primarily an analytic language: it depends on word order for sentence structure and meaning. Old English was primarily a synthetic language: it depended on inflected forms rather than word order to convey grammatical relations among words in a sentence. In terms of inflectional morphology, then, Old English was considerably more complicated than Modern English.

Consider the following paradigms for the masculine nouns *guma* 'man' and *wer* 'man', which demonstrate how inflectional morphemes accounted for number (singular, plural) and case (nominative, genitive, dative, accusative) in Old English. Old English nouns were categorized in two **declensions** or types—"weak" and "strong"—descriptions that are no longer meaningful in this context. Within each declension there were masculine, feminine, and neuter nouns (much like Modern German).

In the history of English, almost all of these inflectional endings have been lost. We've underlined the ones that remain. The Modern English plurals *oxen* and *brethren* are remnants of the weak forms. Note the final *-[vowel]n* that marks the plural in *guman*. The other inflectional endings for nouns in Modern English—possessive *-'s* (and *-s'*) and plural *-s*—survive from the strong declension of masculine nouns. Note the final *-s* in the singular genitive *weres* and the final *-s* in the plural forms *weras*.

The two Old English words *guma* and *wer* have also disappeared. But we still use the word *werewolf*, an Old English compound originally meaning (obviously) 'man-wolf'. And the word *bridegroom* was originally *brydguma*, but once speakers no longer recognized *guma* as a word, the compound was changed to end in the more recognizable morpheme *groom*.

We discuss the history of English inflections in detail in Chapter 13.

	"Weak" Declension		"Strong" Declension	
	Singular	*Plural*	*Singular*	*Plural*
Nominative (subject)	*guma*	*gum<u>an</u>*	*wer*	*wera<u>s</u>*
Genitive (possessive)	*guman*	*gumena*	*were<u>s</u>*	*wera*
Dative (indirect object)	*guman*	*gumum*	*were*	*werum*
Accusative (direct object)	*guman*	*guman*	*wer*	*wera<u>s</u>*

Derivational Morphemes

Unlike *uptalked*, the word *uptalker* is not a combination of two free, open-class morphemes (*uptalk*) and an inflectional morpheme. The suffix *-er* here alters the lexical category of the word *uptalk*, from verb to noun, so the resulting term is not inflected but derived, and the suffix *-er* (in this case) is a **derivational morpheme**. An important heads-up: this derivational suffix *-er*, which creates nouns from verbs, is distinct from the inflectional suffix *-er*, which marks the comparative form of an adjective (e.g., *taller*).

Derivational morphemes often change the lexical category (or part of speech) of a word. For example, *nerd* (noun) becomes *nerdy* (adjective) with the addition of the derivational suffix *-y* and *anti-nerd* (adjective) with the addition of the derivational prefix *anti-*. When derivational morphemes do not change the lexical category of the word, they still significantly alter the meaning of the word within that lexical category. For example, *dork* (noun) becomes *dorkdom* (noun) with the addition of the derivational suffix *-dom*. Both words are nouns, but adding the *-dom* suffix to *dork* changes the meaning to 'the state or condition of being a dork'. Derivational morphemes in English can be prefixes and suffixes.

Inflectional morphemes never change the part of speech of the root word. Derivational morphemes often change the root word's part of speech, but not always. Let's look, for instance, at the derivational morpheme *-ness*, which can be combined with both adjectives and nouns to make nouns. When combined with an adjective, this derivational morpheme does change the root word's part of speech: *lovely* (adjective) becomes *loveliness* (noun). But if we combine *-ness* with *uptalker* (noun), the resulting word is still a noun: *uptalkerness*. Shown in its morphemic parts, the resulting word has been formed by combining *up* + *talk* + derivational morpheme (*-er*) + derivational morpheme (*-ness*).

There is a greater semantic difference—or difference in meaning—between these two nouns than between two inflected forms of one verb. For example, when we refer to *uptalks* and *uptalked,* we are referring to the "same" uptalking in different tenses or points in time. With *uptalker* and *uptalkerness,* however, we refer to the difference between a person who uptalks and the habitual state of being an uptalker.

A Question to Discuss

What About Complex Words That Seem to Have Only One Morpheme?

Some English words have inflected forms without the addition of any clear inflectional morpheme. For example, some verbs indicate tense not by means of inflectional suffixes, but by changes in the vowel of the stem. With *sing,* we do not have **singed,* but rather *sing, sang, sung.* Some nouns mark the plural similarly, with an internal vowel change: *tooth/teeth, mouse/mice.* And some nouns show no change at all in the plural: *deer/deer, sheep/sheep.*

Words such as these pose problems that morphologists have yet to solve. One could say that *sang* and *sung* are morphologically conditioned alternants of *sing,* altered in order to express tense. But *deer* is not as obviously an alternant of itself. Would it make sense to think of plural *deer* as deer + plural

where the plural is unrealized in any formal way? How would one express the hierarchical structure of such words in a morphological tree? It's not impossible, but we pose it to you as a challenge! Hint: Ø (the "zero morpheme") is a possible morpheme in an abstract morphology tree.

The problems multiply when we consider variation within English. For instance, while we might struggle to describe *sit* and *sat* morphologically in Standard American English, Appalachian English, in which the past tense of *sit* is often represented as *sit* (as in "My daddy sit down in his chair and told me the facts of life") could give you more problems. Should we consider *sit* in this example the past-tense form, or is present tense *sit* used to mark the past tense?

Affixes and Combining Forms

An **affix** is an element of a word joined in some fashion to a base or root word. English allows three types of affix: the prefix, the suffix, and the infix. You are probably familiar with the first two of these affixes. A **prefix** precedes the root word: for example, *a-* in *amoral*, *dis-* in *disappear*, *un-* in *uncool*. A **suffix** follows the root word: for example, *-age* in *breakage*, *-ness* in *kindness*, *-y* in *cheesy*.

All inflectional morphemes in current standard English are suffixes, such as the *'s* in *James Bond's*, *-s* in *martinis*, *-en* in *shaken*, *-ed* in *stirred*, *-er* in *drier*, *-est* in *driest*, *-s* in *drinks*, and *-ing* in *drinking*. Most derivational morphemes are suffixes. For example, *-age* derives a noun from the verb *break*, *-ness* derives a noun from the adjective *kind*, and *-y* derives an adjective from the noun *cheese*. Prefixes in current standard English are always derivational.

An **infix** is placed, given certain phonological and morphological constraints, within the root word. An example would be the infix *-fucking-* in *absofuckinglutely* or *guaranfuckingtee*. Because most infixes in English are derived from taboo words and because infixing is fairly rare in English, speakers can be surprised to discover that infixing is still highly rule-governed in English. In the **matrix** or root word (e.g., *absolutely* or *guarantee*), the infix must directly precede the stressed syllable. For example, it does not "sound right" to form **abfuckingsolutely* or **guafuckingrantee*. In other languages, infixing can be inflectional or derivational. In English, the infix "is typically an expletory intensifier, its function that of an emotive stress amplifier" (McMillan 1980, 165). In other words, the infix adds emotional emphasis to the matrix. Its meaning isn't really grammatical, and it doesn't alter the matrix's lexical category.

Is *-fucking-* a derivational morpheme then? It does not have a clear lexical meaning the way most prefixes and suffixes in English do. Neither does *-diddly-* , Ned Flanders's favorite infix, as in *weldiddlyelcome*, nor the *-ma-* in Homer Simpson's *edumacation*, nor the *-iz-* in *hizouse*. (Note that not all infixes are vulgar or profane.) As you'll discover in Chapter 8, the meaning is not lexical, but pragmatic—meaning from context— and the effect, in this case, is to add emphasis to *absolutely*, to intensify the force of this intensifier. Recently, some recorded infixes seem to carry a clearer lexical meaning. For instance, one overwhelmed participant in a high-powered snowboarding competition wrote that the event was "Absoschmuckinglutely paradise!" The writer used *schmuck* 'fool' as the base of the insert to communicate feeling foolish for trying to compete at that level. In another context, an online slang lexicographer refers to inventing new words and defining them as *lexifabricography*.

Some bound morphemes are not really affixes, but we are forced to call them something and have settled on **combining form**. For instance, *alcoholic* is formed from *alcohol* (a free, open-class morpheme) and *-ic* (a bound, derivational morpheme), but for the last few decades, *-holic* has been abstracted from *alcoholic* and combined with many other morphemes to create new words (*chocoholic*, *shopaholic*, *workaholic*). The combining form *-holic* has been abstracted so often and used so regularly that it is well on its way to being categorized as a suffix. Similarly, *-scape*, meaning 'view', was abstracted from *landscape* and combined with free morphemes to form *seascape* and *cityscape*. *Scape* is listed in some dictionaries as free in some uses, so there may be two morphemes in question, a bound *-scape* and a free *scape* derived from it.

Morphology Trees

Words are constructed hierarchically. In other words, one affix attaches itself to the root first, and then another affix attaches to that complex form—rather than both affixes attaching at the same time. For example, derivational morphemes (whether prefixes, suffixes, or combining forms) always take precedence over inflectional morphemes; in other words, derivational morphemes attach before inflectional ones. So one cannot refer to reigning monarchs who are husband and wife as their *highesness*, but only as their *highnesses*.

You can think of any complex word, one constructed of a number of morphemes, some free and some bound, in hierarchical terms. The stem takes precedence and provides the word's core lexical meaning. The derivational morphemes are next in the hierarchy, and then the inflectional morphemes. A word develops in the order of morphemic combination, and you can illustrate a word's hierarchical organization in a **morphology tree**.

The tree below charts the morphological development of *irreplaceableness,* as in this emphatic utterance: "Don't be too sure about your irreplaceableness!"

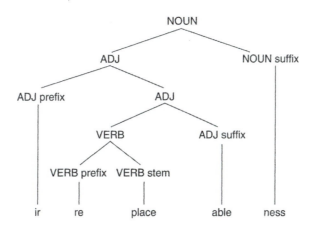

We form words that are this complex all of the time. We do so intuitively, given our experience hearing and speaking English. Yet the tree illustrates how complex our words often are, and how they conform to derivational rules. In this example, the verb *replace* is formed from the verb *place* and the verb prefix *re-* (a derivational morpheme). The first adjective stem, *replaceable*, is formed from the verb *replace* and the adjective suffix *-able* (another derivational morpheme). The second adjective stem, *irreplaceable*, is formed from the adjective *replaceable* and the adjective prefix *ir-* (also a derivational morpheme—a variant of the negative prefix *in-* that assimilates phonologically with the /r/ at the beginning of the adjective). Finally, the noun *irreplaceableness* is formed from the adjective *irreplaceable* and the noun suffix *-ness* (yet another derivational morpheme).

Usually we are not conscious that all these steps take place. Native speakers of English intuitively know that, in this case, the verb *replace* must be formed before the adjective *replaceable* because *re-* attaches only to verbs (i.e., it could not attach to the adjective *placeable*). We form *replaceable* first, rather than **irreplace*, because *-able* can attach to a verb like *replace*, but *ir-* cannot attach to a verb like *replace*: it attaches only to adjectives, so once *replaceable* is formed, we can attach *ir-* to it. Similarly, the adjective *irreplaceable* must be formed before the noun *irreplaceableness*. How do we know that? The prefix *ir-* attaches to adjectives (e.g., *irregular, irresponsible*), not to nouns (**irresponse*). If *replaceableness* were formed first, *ir-* would then have to attach to a noun.

When you are trying to unpack a complex word's structure and create a morphological tree for it, it will help if you determine the types of words to which various bound morphemes can attach (e.g., that *re-* attaches to verbs: *redo, rewrite*). This knowledge will help you figure out which morphemes attach to the stem first. For example, with the word *unpatriotic*, there are three morphemes: the noun *patriot* (a free morpheme and the stem) and the two bound derivational morphemes *un-* and *-ic*. The prefix *un-* can attach to verbs and create new verbs (e.g., *undo, unlock*) or attach to adjectives and create new adjectives (e.g., *unhappy, unsafe*); it cannot, however, attach to nouns (**uncat, *unpatriot*). The suffix *-ic* must attach to nouns and creates adjectives (e.g., *artistic, sulphuric*). If *-ic* attaches first to *patriot* to create the adjective *patriotic*, then *un-* can attach to this adjective to create a new adjective, *unpatriotic*.

Ways of Forming English Words

Speakers of English invent new words frequently. They may do so because there is no word to express an idea (i.e., they perceive a **lexical gap** and fill it), because they don't know or can't remember an already existing word to express the idea, or because, for reasons of style or whim, they prefer to make up a word. Sometimes, a newly created word is a **nonce word**—that is, a word created only once, for a specific purpose in a specific context. Over time, though, a word can be reintroduced "for the nonce" many times, and if it becomes familiar to many speakers, it may enter the common English vocabulary and even end up in dictionaries. *Bloghead* is an example of a nonce word that's likely to remain one, as would be the word *nonce-y* if we were to ask "Just how nonce-y is *bloghead*?" The word *blog,* however, started out a nonce word but then its use spread until it became generally accepted.

In English, speakers use a handful of systematic processes to create new words, and these few morphological processes can generate an infinite number of forms. The following is an account of English word formation processes.

Combining

Combining morphemes, the most productive way to make new words in English, can involve combinations of all free morphemes, free and bound morphemes, and occasionally all bound morphemes. Combining processes include compounding, prefixing, and suffixing.

Compounding   **Compounds,** or combinations of free morphemes, are frequent in Germanic languages, of which English is one. They were very frequent in Old English, and many Old English forms persist to the present day. For instance, Modern English *seaman* descends from Old English *sǣ-mann*. Old English epic poetry, of which the best-known example is *Beowulf,* employed compounds in a special type of metaphor, called a "kenning." When the Anglo-Saxon "scop," or epic poet, sang his poem at a feast, he was said to unlock his *wordhord* ('word-hoard'), the treasure of words he had at his disposal—and it was full of poetic compounds. For example, the body could be a *sawolhūs* ('soul-house') or *bānhūs* ('bone-house'), the sea a *hwælwæg* ('whale-way') or *swanrād* ('swan-road'), a warrior a *helmberend* ('helmet-bearer') and his sword a *beadolēoma* ('battle-light').

Compounding is as productive today as it was in Anglo-Saxon England (i.e., it continues to produce as many new words). Consider many recent terms that are computer-related (itself a compound adjective), for instance, *chatroom, doubleclick, newsgroup, screen saver,* and *username.* Many compounds are transparent: one of their component parts indicates the classification of the compound semantically. For example, a *newsgroup* is a kind of group and a *chatroom* is a kind of metaphorical room. But other compounds are opaque: a *hatchback* is neither a hatch nor a back but a kind of car. We also still have metaphorical compounds in everyday speech today, though we don't call them kennings: someone who dislikes what you're saying can tell you to shut your *pie hole*; if a certain type of underwear rises above the waistband, people see a *whale-tail* or *longhorn.*

How do you know if two words constitute a compound or simply a modifier preceding another word? It is often hard to tell. One way to approach the question is to examine stress patterns. In a compound, the primary stress will fall on the first part, whereas in a phrase, both words will receive almost equal stress. So we have a *'blackboard* (the traditional classroom tool) versus a *'black 'board* (a board that happens to be black); a *'jumping bean* (a type of bean) versus a *'jumping 'bean* (a bean that happens to be behaving oddly). The question of whether compounds should appear as one word, two words, or a hyphenated word is often decided word by word by lexicographers, and dictionaries do not always show consensus on the decision. The loss of 16,000 hyphens in compounds in the sixth edition of the *Shorter Oxford English Dictionary* in 2007 received some attention in the press; some of these became one word (*bumblebee*) and some two (*ice cream*).

Prefixing   Another common way to form a new word is to attach a bound morpheme at the head of an already existing word (a free morpheme or a combination of a free morpheme with other morphemes), as in *reboot, decryption, encryption, hyperlink,* and *unfriend* (possible now that *friend* has become a verb).

Suffixing   One can create a new word by attaching a bound morpheme to the foot of an already existing word, as in *diskette, hacker,* or *scrollage.* As mentioned earlier, some bound morphemes (e.g., *-holic*) combine like prefixes or suffixes even though, at least in the traditional sense, they aren't. Consider the variety of forms combined from noun + *-top,* such as *desktop, laptop,* and *palmtop.* The derivational form *-top* behaves more like a combining form than a suffix.

Infixing   Some infixing is combination pure but not so simple: in a form like *absofuck-inglutely,* all elements of the matrix and infix are maintained, as would be the case in a compounding or other affixation, but the word is divided in order to insert the bound morpheme. In other cases, though, like *lexifabricography,* the insert *fabri-* is clipped from *fabricate,* and the infixed form is a type of blend (blending is discussed below).

Language Change at Work

Where Do Contractions Fit In?

The following sentences are so typical of everyday speech that you may not see what's unexpected about them: *I'll finish reading this chapter tomorrow*, and *We've got no idea what a clitic is*. Both include words formed by combining one word (the pronouns *I* and *we*) with a reduced form of an auxiliary verb (*will* and *have* in these sentences, but others, including forms of *be*, work just as well, as in *what's*): voilà, the new words *I'll* and *we've*. "Wait a minute," you say, "those aren't single words—there are two words in each of those forms." But are there? Each of the forms can be represented as a single word phonologically: /ɑɪl/ and /wiv/. Nevertheless, your intuition is sound: while the reduced form is phonologically dependent on the preceding pronoun and so resembles an affix, it has an independent syntactic function (auxiliary verb), which distinguishes it from affixes. The reduced forms are called **clitics**. They come about because auxiliary verbs usually occur in unstressed positions, and in such positions, the auxiliaries lose initial consonants like /h/ and /w/, then their vowels; the remaining sounds attach to the preceding or following word. If the reduced form attaches to the preceding word, the reduced form is an **enclitic**; if it attaches to the following word, it's a **proclitic**. Arguably, a-prefixing, which we discuss in Chapter 12, is a proclitic reduced from *on*, but the fact that it's called *a-prefixing* proves how easy it is to confuse clitics and affixes. Often, because we represent it as a contracted form, the *-n't* in words like *haven't* and *won't* are mistaken for clitics, but linguists Arnold M. Zwicky and Geoffrey K. Pullum (1983) have demonstrated that *n't* is actually a negating suffix, and not a clitic at all.

Shortening

Existing English words can be shortened to form new words in four common ways: alphabetism, acronymy, clipping, and backformation.

TV **Alphabetism**   When a word is formed from the initials of a phrase and the word is pronounced as the resulting sequence of letters, it is called an **alphabetism** or **initialism**, as in *CPU* 'Central Processing Unit' or *URL* 'Universal Resource Locator'. When alphabetisms become common, speakers often will not know what the letters stood for in the first place. Did you know the words behind *URL* before you read them here?

Although most alphabetisms save speakers syllables, occasionally they are longer: compare *by the way* (three syllables) with *BTW* (five syllables). But speakers can always shorten again. For example, *BTW* could well consistently become "B T Dub" (see "Clipping" below).

MILF **Acronymy**   Sometimes groups of words are shortened to initials and then pronounced as though the initials were merely letters in a typical word, as in *RAM* 'Random Access Memory' and *ROM* 'Read Only Memory'. These forms are called **acronyms**. *CD-ROM* is a compound of an alphabetism with an acronym, and *e-mail* compounds an alphabetism (*e* for *electronic*) and a common noun, a reminder that words are often formed by more than one morphological process. Some acronyms are so common that speakers are no longer aware that they began as acronyms: *radar* (<u>ra</u>dio <u>d</u>etection <u>a</u>nd <u>r</u>anging), *sonar* (<u>so</u>und <u>n</u>avigation <u>a</u>nd <u>r</u>anging), and perhaps even *scuba* (<u>s</u>elf-<u>c</u>ontained <u>u</u>nderwater <u>b</u>reathing <u>a</u>pparatus) and *AIDS* (<u>A</u>cquired <u>I</u>mmune <u>D</u>eficiency <u>S</u>yndrome).

Sometimes, the difference between acronomy and alphabetism depends on English phonotactic constraints (see Chapter 3). You can pronounce *GWOT*, the acronym for 'Global War on Terror', as /gwɑt/, but *GSAVE* 'Global Struggle against Violent Extremism' is a hybrid alphabetism/acronym—/dʒisev/—because /gs/ is not an acceptable onset consonant cluster in English.

Clipping   A word is "clipped" when it loses an element, often at its primary morphemic boundary, next to the root or base. Some words are **foreclipped**, such as *net* (from *Internet*), *server* (originally *file server*), and *scanner* (from *optical scanner*). Apparently, *e-mail*, already a shortened form, isn't short enough for some who have resorted simply to *e*, a hindclipping. Other high-tech **hindclippings** are *cell* (from *cellular*) and both *comp* and *sci* in the common clipped form of *computer science*. Some clippings become lexicalized or thought of as words in and of themselves (as opposed to shortened forms of other words). For example, *mob* is a shortened form of *mobile*, a shortened form itself from the Latin *mōbile vulgus* 'moveable or excitable crowd'.

As some of these examples indicate, **innovative clippings** don't always observe the original morphemic boundaries. Other recent examples include *zine* (from *magazine*), *rents* (from *parents*), *emo music* (from *emotional music*), *mic* (from *microphone*), and *limo* (from *limousine*), as well as *blog*, *evs*, *obvs*, and *whatevs* from the chapter's opening story. To take another example, if you participate on a posting board dedicated to a popular television show, say *The X-Files*, you might have expressed on the board (a foreclipping, by the way) your desire that someday Mulder and Scully would be romantically involved, would have a relationship. In that case, you would be a Mulder/Scully *shipper*. *Shipper* is an innovative clipping from *relationshipper*. Note that the root of the word is *relationship*, not *relation* or *shipper*. As it turns out, your hopes for Mulder and Scully were at least partially realized. And *shipper* is an excellent example of a word formed to fill a lexical gap. Can you think of any other word that expresses the concept 'one who hopes that two people (actual or fictional) will develop a romantic relationship'?

Backformation   In **backformation**, a new word is formed by removing an affix (or what looks like an affix) from a word to form a word that never existed before. Usually the affix in question is a suffix or a supposed suffix. A classic example is the borrowed French word *beggar*. The word is one morpheme in French, but English speakers reinterpreted it as a suffixed form: verb + *-er*. In this way, through backformation, speakers created the new verb *beg*. Another example would be *burglar* and *burgle*. The word *couth* is a backformation from *uncouth*, and in this case the removed affix is a prefix. But let's take a more modern example.

If your computer takes a long time to find a file, perhaps it's because the file has been broken up and the parts scattered to gaps in the disk, where files have previously been deleted. The read/write head has to search all over the disk to put the file together, which causes the slowdown. This state of affairs is called *fragmentation*. You need a disk-optimizing program to *defrag*, and you need backformation (and affixation) to create the verb *defrag*. First, you have to backform (itself a backformation from

A Question to Discuss

Is It Clipping or Backformation?

Sometimes, it's difficult to determine whether a word has been formed by clipping or by backformation. *Fax* is an example of such a word. It might represent an innovative clipping from *facsimile,* one that simply ignored morphemic boundaries. But it might also be backformed: *facsimile* is borrowed from Latin *fac simile* 'make similar'. Many Latin suffixes borrowed into English (*-ity, -ism, -ible/-able*) begin with vowels. Perhaps whoever first formed *fax* assumed that **-imile* was a derivational suffix and that the root of the word was **facs*, which the word innovator may then have respelled to end with an *x*. If this scenario is true, then backformation would be the relevant morphological process behind the word *fax*.

backformation) the verb *fragment* from *fragmentation*, then apply the derivational prefix *de-*, to *fragment*, and then, in pursuit of an even shorter, slangier word, backform *defrag* from *defragment*. The process of backformation is relatively rare.

Blending

Blends are created by joining two or more words, at least one of which must be clipped: blending is a hybrid process of clipping and combining. *Internet* is a blend, derived from *inter(connected) net(work)*. *Netiquette* blends *(Inter)net* with *(et)iquette*. Some other well-known blends include *smog* (*smoke + fog*) and *motel* (*motor + hotel*). One of this book's authors is hoping her family's use of the fairly rare blend *plog* (*plug + clog*) will catch on. One's toilet can be plogged, one's nose can be plogged, and these days, one's e-mail box can all too easily become plogged. As noted earlier, infixings with meaningful inserts (like *accipurpodentally* 'accidentally on purpose') tend to be blends.

Language Change at Work

Alice in Wonderland and the Portmanteau

Blends are sometimes also called *portmanteau words,* a term we can trace back to Lewis Carroll's *Alice in Wonderland.* Humpty Dumpty, in his explanation of the poem "Jabberwocky," states, "Well, '*slithy*' means 'lithe and slimy.' 'Lithe' is the same as 'active.' You see it's like a portmanteau—there are two meanings packed up into one word." A portmanteau is a small, stiff leather piece of luggage with two equal sides that fold together and latch to create one bag. *Slithy* did not survive as a portmanteau word, but the term *portmanteau word* is still used to this day in linguistics. And some of Lewis Carroll's other portmanteau words, such as *chortle* (*snort + chuckle*), have become part of the English vocabulary.

Shifting

When a word form employed in one lexical category moves into another category, it undergoes a **functional shift**. *E-mail* began as a noun ("I love e-mail because you can communicate with family and friends more quickly than in letters") but soon shifted into a verb ("E-mail me tomorrow!"). The noun *text*, clipped from *text message*, did the same thing, quickly shifting to a verb ("Text me!"). The shortened form *e* can also be a noun or verb ("Send me some e" or "E me as soon as you can"), though we aren't sure whether noun or verb was the functional chicken or egg. Similarly vague are the origins of *doubleclick,* though one guesses that the verb ("Doubleclick on the icon") came before the noun ("That takes a doubleclick"). One Calvin and Hobbes cartoon refers to the "verbing" of words, employing the functional shift of the noun *verb* to a verb as part of the joke.

One relatively recent example of verbing that some older speakers still find jarring is the use of the noun *impact* as a verb (unless one is referring to teeth). While they might say "Computers have had an impact on the English lexicon," they would frown upon the innovative "Computers have greatly impacted the English lexicon."

Language Change at Work

Success Rates for New Words

How many new words die for every one that survives? We don't have hard numbers, but we do know that the odds of survival are, well, terrible. Allan Metcalf, in his book *Predicting New Words* (2002), writes: "The history of new words is largely a tale of failure. . . . [E]ach day in the English language at least as many thousands of new words are born [as babies in the United States]. Yet after a year's time, only a few hundred of these will remain as serious candidates for the dictionary and a place in our permanent vocabulary" (1). Occasionally a newly coined word meets almost immediate success. For example, the proposed word *skycap* won a 1940 contest calling for a suitable name for airport porters, and we continue to use the word to this day. In 1963, Murray Gell-Mann made up the word *quark* to refer to a hypothetical subatomic particle. Quarks are no longer hypothetical and Gell-Mann's name for them has persisted—undoubtedly only helped by his Nobel Prize for his work on quarks.

But the story of Gelett Burgess is more indicative of the survival rate of new words.

In 1914, he proposed one hundred new words in his *Burgess Unabridged: A New Dictionary of Words You Have Always Needed*. One such word has obviously succeeded: *blurb*. The other ninety-nine, however, will look unfamiliar. They include the likes of:

> *oofle:* a person whose name one cannot remember; to forget.
> *rawp:* a reliably unreliable person, one always late.
> *tashivation:* the art of answering without listening to questions.
> *tintiddle:* an imaginary conversation; wit coming too late.
> *wog:* food on the face; unconscious adornment of the person.
> *wumgush:* women's insincere flattery of each other.

These words, despite their flair, never caught on, but you can read more details of Burgess's story in Metcalf's book. Remember, though, that most new words are not consciously created and defined like these words invented by Burgess.

Reanalysis, Eggcorns, and Folk Etymology

Sometimes, we hear words in ways that misrepresent their etymological forms. As a result, we **reanalyze** morphemes phonologically, that is, redistribute the sounds of morphemes in ways that create new morphemes. For instance, in Old English or Middle English, speakers feared the bite of the *nædre* 'snake', made pies from *numbles* 'the internal organs of animals', and wore *naprons* to protect their clothes from flying numbles. Now, we fear the bite of *an adder* and wear *aprons* in the kitchen (but use *napkins* in the dining room and *nappies* in the nursery). In these cases, we have redistributed /n/ from the noun to the article. In any dialect of English, *a numble pie* sounds like *an umble pie*. If you speak an /h/-dropping dialect (see Chapter 3), an *umble pie* could just as likely be a *humble pie* (with the /h/ dropped), and if you aren't familiar with umbles (or numbles), then *humble pie* may make more sense as a compound and could be seen as expressing the historical relationship between low social standing and a diet of entrails or innards. How frequent is reanalysis? Not very frequent at all, but that's a whole nother story.

In September 2003, Geoffrey Pullum, a linguist at the University of Edinburgh, introduced the term **eggcorn** for phonetic reinterpretations of words (e.g., *intensive purposes* for *intents and purposes*) that create new meaningful forms made up of familiar words, words arguably more familiar to the maker of eggcorns than the ones in the original. The supposed meaning of an eggcorn is plausible in terms of the meaning of the new component parts, though often unlikely. The term *eggcorn* honors the first recorded example of the phenomenon, from 1844, when someone substituted *egg corn* for *acorn*, producing a new word for the fruit of oak trees. Other eggcorns include *duck tape* (instead of *duct tape*, a reinterpretation you should now be able to explain on phonological grounds), *hone in* (instead of *home in*), and *just desserts* (rather than *just deserts*). There are well over 600 eggcorns recorded so far. You can find out all about them (and contribute any missing eggcorns) at the Eggcorn Database (http://eggcorns.lascribe.net).

It's easy to dismiss eggcorns as mistakes, though the earlier examples of *a/an* reanalysis make it clear that mistakes count in historical language change, as they do in metathesis that holds over time. Someone has to make the mistake first, but once lots of people within a speech community shift allegiance to the new form (*aks* into *ask*, or *home in* into *hone in*), a mistake becomes a standard word form.

Once speakers hear a reanalyzed form, they may wonder about its etymology: What do acorns have to do with eggs? What do ducks have to do with duct tape? Often, speakers supply explanations for what they hear, regardless of etymology—they supply a **folk etymology,** a commonly accepted, but (strictly) historically incorrect, account of a word's origin. For instance, we call a certain insect a *praying mantis* because of how it holds its "hands" together, as though in prayer, but some speakers call it a *preying mantis*, because the females of the species devour the males, or prey on them, after sexual intercourse. The idea that *humble pie* is humble because poorer people eat it is also folk etymology. The etymology would never occur to a speaker until the word had been reanalyzed. So, in general, reanalysis occurs before folk etymology, though they cooperate to establish new words in the English lexicon.

Reduplication

Occasionally, we form new English words by repeating a morpheme, a process called **reduplication,** as in *knock-knock* or *no-no*. Some reduplicated forms are typical of infant child language and the language parents speak with them: *mama, dada, boo-boo*. Some are slangy, like *yadda yadda yadda*. Many reduplicated forms include rhyming elements that differ in their initial consonant (that is, they form a minimal pair), such as *hocus-pocus* and *hodge-podge*, not to mention *Humpty Dumpty* and *Henny Penny, Turkey Lurkey, Goosey Loosey*, and other nursery rhyme and folktale character names. Other forms alter the vowel, as in *flip-flop, hip hop, knickknack, tick-tock,* and *wishy-washy*. Historically, reduplication is a minimally productive word-formative process in English; other languages and language families, for instance, South Asian languages, reduplicate more regularly. Contact between such languages and English worldwide has introduced reduplication as a potentially productive process in these varieties of English to indicate, for example, intensification (*sweet-sweet* 'very sweet' in Singaporean English) or create adverbs (e.g., *separate-separate* 'separately' in South African English) (Nagle 2007).

Frequency of Different Word-Formation Processes

Since 1941, the quarterly journal *American Speech*, now sponsored by the American Dialect Society, has included a column called "Among the New Words" in nearly every issue. One of the column's editors, John Algeo, and his wife, Adele S. Algeo, collected the material published in the column over fifty years (Algeo and Algeo 1991) and assessed the relative importance of various word-formative processes. These statistics are listed in the first column of Table 4.2 and are compared with statistics from similar analyses of data in the *Barnhart Dictionary of New English since 1963* (1973) and the *Longman Register of New Words* (1989) (Algeo and Algeo 1991, 14).

As you can see, combining accounts for the majority of new words. And while some folks take issue with functional shifts such as *impact* as a verb, shifting is a highly productive process in English. You may wonder why in a section about forming new words, we have not discussed out-and-out creation; as the figures show, English words are rarely brought into existence from a lexical vacuum. As the word *quark* proves, however, it is far from impossible. Still, if we consider the period from 1460 to 1774,

TABLE 4.2   **Word-Formative Processes Compared by Three Sources (% by types)**

	ANW	*BDNE*	*LRNW*
Combining	68.3	63.9	54.3
Compound forms	40.3	29.8	36.3
Affixed forms	28.0	34.1	18.0
Shifting	17.4	14.2	19.4
Shortening	7.6	9.7	10.0
Blending	4.6	4.8	9.8
Borrowing	1.6	6.9	4.3
Unknown	.3	.5	2.2
Creating	.2		

ANW = "Among the New Words" column in *American Speech*
BDNE = *Barnhart Dictionary of New English since 1963*
LRNW = *Longman Register of New Words*, vol. 1

coining, reduplication, backformation, clipping, blending, and other "minor processes" (like shifting and reanalysis) contributed no more than 10 percent of new words (Nevalainen 1999). Today, they contribute more, but not much more.

Borrowing and the Multicultural Vocabulary of English

Another process by which English builds its vocabulary is **borrowing**. Sometimes, as in the case of Finnish *sauna,* we simply adopt a word without alteration. Sometimes, as in the case of *wampum,* borrowed from the Native American Massachuset *wampumpeag,* we adapt a word, not only in spelling, but also morphologically, in this case by shortening the borrowed word. In still other cases we effect a **loan translation** or **calque**, as with *groundhog,* which is a fairly literal translation of Dutch *aardvarken,* or 'earth-pig'. Although the figures in Table 4.2 show that, relative to other processes of word formation, borrowing is not currently among the most productive (i.e., it is the source of fewer new words), borrowing has historically made the English language what it is. According to one commonly quoted statistic in histories of English, of the most common 1,000 words in English, over 80 percent are native; they are Germanic words that have always been part of English. Of the most common 10,000 words in English, however, over 60 percent are borrowed. Over the centuries, English speakers have borrowed a cup of lexical sugar from nearly every global neighbor, and in some cases they have carried away a barrel.

English was influenced by other languages even before it arrived in Britain. (See Chapter 13 for more details about the historical events mentioned in this section.) Latin words like *mīl* 'mile', *weall* 'wall', and *camp* 'battle' were borrowed by German tribes from the Romans in the course of trade, well before the Angles, Saxons, and Jutes began their gradual conquest of Britain in 449 CE. Familiar words like *cheese* (from Old English *cīese,* from Latin *cāseus*) and *chalk* (from Old English *cealc,* from Latin *calx*) originate in the same pre-English period.

Latin has influenced English in waves. When Christianity was reestablished in England during the Old English period, many words came with it, such as *angel, candle, martyr,* and *priest.* Common words were borrowed from Latin texts on which, increasingly, English education was based: for instance, *circle, elephant, fever,* and *talent.* Church reform in the tenth century, which brought the English into even greater contact with Continental scholarship written in Latin, introduced legal terms like *brief,* botanical terms like *cucumber,* and medical terms like *cancer* and *paralysis.* The examples given here are but a small fraction of the many, many terms borrowed from Latin in early periods of English. Later, in the Early Modern period (1476–1776), English borrowed many more forms from Latin (or Neo-Latin, as learned Latin of the Renaissance is called), such as *compendious, extol,* and *verbosity.* Although English is now rich with Latinate loanwords as a result of these waves of borrowing, many Neo-Latin borrowings failed to survive the Renaissance—though *abambulation* may appeal to you if you like to walk away from unpleasant situations.

The Norman Conquest of England in 1066 resulted in profound lexical change. English is a Germanic language: much of its vocabulary, especially its closed lexical classes, is of German origin and has changed remarkably little over the millennia. English grammar is Germanic, too, and has remained so even as English has borrowed incessantly from other languages. But for the two centuries after the Norman Conquest, when the ruling class spoke Anglo-French, and when many functions of government, especially the law, were conducted in French, French words poured into the English word-hoard. Imagine English without *alliance, baptism, chess, dance, evidence, flower, gentle, hour, indictment, jury, kennel, labor, mayor, number, original, pheasant, quality, river, squirrel, tax, unity, vanity,* and *waste.* These represent the merest fraction of words borrowed from French in the Middle Ages.

New French words sometimes killed off native English words. For example, since 1200, we have sought *peace* in our time (from Old French *pais*), rather than *sibb*, the word we would likely use had William, Duke of Normandy, never become William the Conqueror. In other cases, the sudden competition of synonyms or near-synonyms forced semantic change, sometimes **generalization**, and sometimes **specialization** of meaning (these semantic processes are discussed at length in Chapter 7). While French and Latin have provided English with more words, prefixes, and suffixes than other languages (each contributes about 25 percent of the general English vocabulary), we must not underestimate the tendency of English to absorb whatever words it finds useful, from whatever language, for whatever reason. *Pal* comes to us from Romany, the language of the Rom (commonly, but not politely, called Gypsies). We borrowed *graffiti* from Italian; *vampire* from Serbo-Croatian; *tango* from Ibibio, a language of Nigeria; *mojo* from Fula; and *amok* from Malay.

American English has borrowed liberally from Native American languages, especially in place-names, but also terms like *bayou* (from Ojibwa, reanalyzed as a French word) and *raccoon* (from Algonquian). And it is likewise indebted to African languages imported on slave ships for terms like *bogus* (perhaps from Hausa), *banjo* (Portuguese borrowed into West African languages), and *yam* (West African borrowed into Portuguese, and introduced through English- and Portuguese-based creoles in the Caribbean).

A Question to Discuss

What's Wrong with *amorality*?

In 1926, H. W. Fowler first published his classic *Dictionary of Modern English Usage,* long considered by many prescriptivists a usage Bible, rather than a book of observations and advice, which is closer to what Fowler intended. In his article on the prefix *a-,* Fowler wrote that *a-* and *an-* "should be prefixed only to Greek stems; of such compounds there are some hundreds, whereas Latin-stemmed words having any currency even in scientific use do not exceed four. There are the botanical *acapsular & acaulous,* the biological *asexual,* & the literary *amoral.* The last, being literary, is inexcusable, & *non-moral* should be used instead. The other three should not be treated as precedents for future word-making." As with much heartfelt advice, Fowler's has fallen on deaf ears. The *American Heritage Dictionary of the English Language* (2000) illustrates its entry for the *a-* prefix with *amoral!*

Although Fowler was incensed by the mixing of Latin and Greek, he appears to have overlooked the importance of bilingual mixing in English. Even he frequently used the word *perhaps,* formed by the Latin prefix *per-* and the Old Norse root *happ* 'fortune, chance'.

It would be tedious to list even more words here, but the authors recommend that you look into Allan Metcalf's *The World in So Many Words* (1999) and *America in So Many Words* (1997), by Metcalf and David K. Barnhart, for more examples. Both of these books provide a brief essay per word. Interested in even more? To see the extent of borrowing from Native American languages in place-names, browse through William Bright's *Native American Placenames of the United States* (2004).

Special Focus: Slang and Creativity

Nowhere are English speakers more creative word formers than in their slang, a linguistic artifact for which they are famous worldwide. The *American Heritage Dictionary of the English Language* (2000) defines *slang* as "A kind of language occurring chiefly in casual and playful speech, made up typically of short-lived coinages and figures of speech that are deliberately used in place of standard terms for added raciness, humor, irreverence, or other effect." Many usage wolves howl at slang, insistent that it's "substandard," "coarse," or "lazy." Really, though, it's English through and through, and it makes morphology, well, fun.

Some of the fun is in rebellion. Slang can be rebellion against the expectation that we will use Standard English in all places and at all times. It can be rebellion against the people who embody that expectation, be they teachers or parents or other authority figures. James Sledd, in his classic essay "On Not Teaching English Usage" (1965), describes the motivations of those who use and those who suppress slang (remember this was written in 1965):

> When a teacher warns his students against slang, he reaffirms his allegiance to the social order that created him. Typically, slang is a para-code, a system of substitutes for statusful expressions which are used by people who lack conventional status and do not conduct the important affairs of established communities. Slang flourishes in the semantic areas of sex, drinking, narcotics, racing, athletics, popular music, and other crime—a "liberal" language of things done as ends in themselves by gentlemen who are not gentlemen and dislike gentility. Genteel pedagogues must naturally oppose it, precisely because slang serves the outs as a weapon against the ins. To use slang is to deny allegiance to the existing order, either jokingly or in earnest, by refusing even the words which represent convention and signal status; and those who are paid to preserve the status quo are prompted to repress slang as they are prompted to repress any other symbol of revolution. (699)

The young of every generation "lack conventional status and do not conduct the important affairs of established communities," and they enthusiastically, perhaps appropriately, wreak linguistic havoc, before they establish 401(k) plans.

About a century earlier, Walt Whitman saw verbal revolution as poetry. Whitman (1969/1885) wrote in "Slang in America":

> Slang, or indirection, [is] an attempt of common humanity to escape from bald literalism, and express itself illimitably, which in the highest walks produces poets and poems. . . . Slang, too, is the wholesome fermentation of those processes eternally active in language, by which froth and specks are thrown up, mostly to pass away, though occasionally to settle and permanently chrystallize. (58)

In one way or another, and perhaps contrary to what you've been told, slang is ennobling. Rebellious and (heaven forbid) creative, it is fundamental to the word-formation processes that are "eternally active in language."

For instance, English words have developed through functional shifts since the language's inception. But slangy functional shifts rub our noses in that process and its consequences. "That is *so* eighties," we say of teased-out hair (or legwarmers, or pink sneakers), but *so* is usually an adverb, and when it works as an adjective (e.g., *she likes her coffee to be exactly so*), it does not usually modify a noun as it does with *eighties*. And *eighties* is, in fact, best considered a noun here, just as *you* in "That is so you" is a noun. You can see the rebellion (or the poetry) creep up on you in a sequence like the following: "Do you walk often?" "Walk much?" "Mobile much?" "Pedestrian much?" Again, *much* ostensibly functions as an adverb in these sentences, yet, as an adverb, it barely collocates with *mobile* and certainly should not with *pedestrian*. Either *so* and *much* have undergone functional shifts from adverb to adjective, or a new lexical category, the "adnoun," has been invented.

Slang often communicates on the fly. It's linguistic jaywalking. When you have something to say, you can stand at the crosswalk and wait for the light to change, or you can take the shortest path between idea and utterance. When you sit in your dorm room, hungry for pizza, you can say to your roommate, "My good man, I am short of cash and wish that my parents would send me a check," or you could say, "Dude, I need fundage." The *-age* shortcut is a well-worn path of English suffixation (*baggage, blockage, breakage, clearage, parentage, vicarage*), but we have on record recently such forms as *agreeage, AIMage* (AOL *Instant Messenger-age*), *clueage, doobage, downage, droppage, lurkage* (as on a posting board), *quotage, taggage, topicage*, and *visitage*. For the purist, these are unnecessary forms. There are perfectly good conventional ways of expressing what they express, often simply by replacing the derivational suffix *-age* with an inflectional suffix (e.g., *clues* for *clueage, quotations* for *quotage, tags* or *tagging* for *taggage*). But among those positioned against the status quo, such forms are part of the "para-code" of outness. Conventional forms are for those who "conduct the important affairs of established communities." Slang establishes community among those not (yet) in charge.

Slang is essentially transgressive. It often breaks rules at the margins of meaning and form, of semantics and morphology. Consider the range of *-y* suffixation you can easily find while surfing the Web: a church can be *catholicy*, clothing styles can be *Britney Spearsy* or *Paris Hiltony*, a computer program may be incompatible with an operating system because it's too *interrupty*, some believe that the world has become *armageddony*, journalism can be *New Yorkery*, and the *Paris Review* can be accused of "*interviewy* goodness." As you know from Chapter 3, syllable nuclei are all *vowely*, and onset and coda clusters are *consonanty*. All of these words (strange as they may seem) have been used on the Web, most of them many times; they may be nonce words, but they have been created for more than one nonce. Anyone who belongs to the group that plays with word formation along the lines represented in this list of slang words will understand perfectly what you mean and will also understand that you both are members of the same social group.

Slang is often dismissed as "loose" or "bad" language, but in fact, in slang we find morphological processes at their most active. Slang works because we all share the morphological processes that create it, even if we don't all share the slang words themselves.

☑ Summary

- Morphemes are the smallest units of meaning in language. They can be classified into the following categories:

    - open-class and closed-class morphemes
    - bound and free morphemes

- Bound morphemes can be classified into the following categories:

    - derivational and inflectional morphemes
    - suffixes, prefixes, infixes, and combining forms

- When morphemes combine to form words, they do so within hierarchical structures, which we capture in morphology trees. The processes of word formation can be classified into the following categories:

    - combining (compounding, affixation)
    - shortening (alphabetism, acronymy, clipping, backformation)
    - blending
    - shifting
    - reanalysis
    - reduplication

- Historically, borrowing has been an important source of new words in English, but today native word-formation processes account for the majority of new words in English, both in slang and in more standard registers.

Suggested Reading

Much is written about morphology, but it tends toward the technical and theoretical. We recommend Laurie Bauer's *Introducing Linguistic Morphology* (1988) and J. L. Bybee's *Morphology: A Study into the Relation between Meaning and Form* (1985). If you are especially interested in morphology or think that you might actually become a linguist, then you should read P. H. Matthews's *Morphology: An Introduction to the Theory of Word-Structure* (1974). The best practical account of English derivational processes is the introduction to John Algeo and Adele S. Algeo's *Fifty Years among the New Words: A Dictionary of Neologisms, 1941–1991* (1991). For more stories about new words, turn to Allan Metcalf's *Predicting New Words* (2002). Michael Adams's *Slang: The People's Poetry* (2009) is a recent introduction to slang in all its manifestations.

Exercises

Exercise 4.1   Inflectional versus Derivational Endings

Let's practice identifying derivational and inflectional morphemes. In the following passage, indicate in the blank following each underlined suffix whether it is inflectional (I) or derivational (D). Note: some examples may involve two suffixes.

You may have notic<u>ed</u> _____ that some English speaker<u>s</u> _____ intone their declarative sentence<u>s</u> _____ as though they are questions, so that "I really like eat<u>ing</u> _____ out," a sentence which end<u>s</u> _____ on it<u>s</u> _____ lowest pitch, sound<u>s</u> _____ like "I real<u>ly</u> _____ like eating out?" and ends on one of the sentence'<u>s</u> _____ high<u>er</u> _____ pitches. As more and more American<u>s</u> _____ start<u>ed</u> _____ to speak, at least occasion<u>ally</u> _____, in this pattern, we needed a name for it. Thus *uptalk* (verb and noun) was creat<u>ed</u> _____ from the two free morphemes *up* and *talk*. Because many parents and teachers object to *uptalk<u>ing</u>* _____ (noun), they may have helped you break the habit. You may once have *uptalk<u>ed</u>* _____ but aren't *uptalk<u>ing</u>* _____ (verb) anymore. Or maybe you are still an *uptalk<u>er</u>* _____, in spite of their best efforts and care<u>ful</u> _____ monitor<u>ing</u> _____. Can you now reli<u>ably</u> _____ identify inflection<u>al</u> _____ and derivation<u>al</u> _____ morpheme<u>s</u> _____?

Exercise 4.2   Morphology Trees

1. What's wrong with each of the following morphology trees? Explain how you knew that the tree was not possible as drawn.

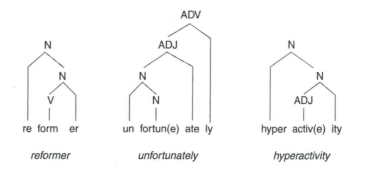

| reformer | unfortunately | hyperactivity |

2. Develop morphology trees for the following words. Be sure to label the part of speech of the stem at each level of the tree. (You can use the *OED* to determine the English roots of borrowed words.)

governmentally   unlovable
unhelpful   nationalism
depoliticize   recyclable
retroviral   geekiness
conversationally   imperfection
Bonus word: antidisestablishmentarianism

3. Create two morphology trees that demonstrate the semantic ambiguity of the word *undoable*. Can you come up with at least one other similarly morphologically ambiguous word?

Exercise 4.3   Word Formation Processes and Lexical Gaps

1. Find a copy of a newspaper of record (*New York Times, USA Today, Wall Street Journal, Christian Science Monitor*) and comb it for new words—try to find at least one new word for each of the categories discussed in the text: prefixing, suffixing, compounding, alphabetism, acronymy, clipping, backformation, blending, functional shift. Explain how each item satisfies the category to which you assign it. (Be sure to cite the source for each example.)

2. Try to discover one or more lexical gaps. By what new word could each gap be filled? By what processes are the new words you propose made?

3. One significant lexical gap seems to be the lack of a word for the first decade of the new millennium. Should we call the years 2000–2009 "the ohs"? "The zeros"? "The preteens"? How do you refer to this decade? Why do you think this gap has not been filled by one word? And what will we call this new decade, from 2010–2019?

4. This exercise is about the direction of functional firsts. When a word is used as both a noun and a verb, for example, which part of speech came first? Was *commute* first a noun or a verb? Right now, *blog* appears only as a noun in most dictionaries (if it is there at all); its use as a verb is even newer.

   Use the *OED* to determine the order in which the following words acquired their various parts of speech, at least according to the *OED*—it sometimes can miss even earlier references. (Hint: for each word, determine which part of speech has the earliest quotation.)

commute	surf
network	motor
mail	link

5. College slang is a productive source of new words and employs all the processes described in this chapter. For example, *chicktionary* ('the twenty-first-century little black book') and *chillax* are blends. The new suffix *-tastic* is the result of clipping or backformation (from *fantastic*) and can create new forms (e.g., *craptastic*) through suffixation. List three slang words used on your campus that employ the word-formation processes described in this chapter. For each word, provide a definition and explain the process by which the word was formed.

6. The suffix *-ate* is a common verb ending. A few verbs in English have developed an additional extended form with *-ate*: *comment/commentate; administer/administrate; minister/ministrate; orient/orientate*. Why do you think these particular verbs have been susceptible to the creation of an extended form? (Hint: why is it more likely that we would get *simplificate* rather than *simplifate*?) Have any of these new extended forms developed meanings that differ from the original verb?

Exercise 4.4   Borrowings

According to one statistic, of the most common 10,000 words in English, over 60 percent are borrowed. It can be hard to get out an English sentence without using a borrowed word. Try to rewrite the following paragraph using only native English words (i.e., Germanic words that have always been in English, rather than words borrowed into English). To do this, you will need a good dictionary that provides etymological information. First check to see which words are borrowed; native English words will have an Old English (OE) form as their etymology or perhaps a Germanic root. Then, for all the borrowed words, try to come up with a native English alternative (you may find that compounding will be very helpful here). You will also have to look up the alternative forms that you propose, to make sure that they are not borrowed words as well!

> When English incorporates a word from another language, why do we call it "borrowing," when English speakers rarely if ever have any intention of returning it to its proper owners? Would it be more appropriate to describe this linguistic action—this enriching of the English vocabulary through foreign expressions—as "stealing"? Some might argue that the term *stealing* implies that the word in question no longer exists in the foreign language (which, of course, it still does), but that argument applies to the term *borrowing* as well. Perhaps it is simply more polite to imagine English speakers as a community of linguistic borrowers than a bunch of word thieves.

Exercise 4.5   Where Do the Words of the Year Come From?

Every January, the American Dialect Society (ADS) votes on the Word of the Year for the previous year. The requirements are that the word be new to that year or have risen from relative obscurity to prominence during that year. For the past several years, the ADS has added several other categories of words on which the members vote, such as Most Creative Word of the Year and Word Most Likely to Succeed.

On the following pages you will find the winners and some rival candidates in many of these categories from 2002 to 2009. For each word, identify the word-formation process responsible for the creation of this word (e.g., compounding, clipping). If you are curious about the honored words in other years, visit the ADS Web site at www.americandialect.org.

Category	Winner (in bold) and Other Candidates	Word-Formation Process
Selected Words of the Year 2009		
Word of the Year	*tweet* 'short message sent via Twitter; act of sending such a message'	
Most Useful	*fail* 'noun or interjection used when something is egregiously unsuccessful, usually written as "FAIL!"'	
Most Unnecessary	*sea kittens* 'fish (according to PETA)'	

(continued)

Category	Winner (in bold) and Other Candidates	Word-Formation Process
Selected Words of the Year 2008		
Word of the Year	***bailout*** 'government rescue of a company about to fail'	
Most Creative	***recombobulation area*** 'area in which recently screened air passengers get their clothes and belongings back in order'	
Most Unnecessary	***moofing*** '"mobile out of office," or working on the go with laptop or phone'	
Selected Words of the Year 2007		
Word of the Year	***subprime*** 'risky or less than ideal loan, mortgage, or investment'	
Most Useful/Likely to Succeed	***green-*** 'prefix of combining form designating environmental concern'	
Most Creative	***googleganger*** 'person with your name who shows up when you google yourself'	
Selected Words of the Year 2006		
Word of the Year	***to pluto/be plutoed*** 'demote or devalue something, as Pluto was demoted from planet status'	
Most Useful	***climate canary*** 'organism or species whose poor health or declining numbers suggest a broader environmental change'	
Most Euphemistic	***waterboarding*** 'interrogation technique that simulates drowning'	
Selected Words of the Year 2005		
Word of the Year	***truthiness*** 'what one wishes to be the truth, regardless of the facts'	
Most Useful	***podcast*** 'audio or video file for downloading'	
Most Creative	***whale-tail*** 'appearance of thong or g-string underwear worn above the waistband'	
Most Outrageous	***crotchfruit*** 'child or children'	
Most Likely to Succeed	***sudoku*** 'number puzzle from Japan'	
Selected Words of the Year 2004		
Word of the Year	***red/blue/purple states*** 'states favoring Republicans, favoring Democrats, or undecided, respectively'	
Most Useful	***phish*** 'induce someone to reveal private information by means of a deceptive e-mail'	
Most Euphemistic	***badly sourced*** 'false'	
Most Unnecessary	***stalkette*** 'female stalker'	

Category	Winner (in bold) and Other Candidates	Word-Formation Process
Selected Words of the Year 2003		
Word of the Year	**metrosexual** 'fashion-conscious urban male'	
Most Useful	**flexitarian** 'vegetarian who occasionally eats meat'	
Most Creative	**freegan** 'person who eats only free food'	
Most Likely to Succeed	**SARS** 'Severe Acute Respiratory Syndrome'	
Selected Words of the Year 2002		
Word of the Year	**WMD** (Weapons of Mass Destruction)	
Most Useful	**google** (as a verb)	
	dataveillance 'surveillance using computer data'	
Most Creative	**Iraqnophobia** 'strong fear of Iraq'	
	dialarhoea 'inadvertent dialing of a cell phone in a pocket or handbag'	
Most Unnecessary	**Saddameter** 'meter on television showing daily likelihood of war with Iraq'	

Source: The American Dialect Society: http://www.americandialect.org.

Chapter 5

English Syntax: The Grammar of Words

I NEED HELP ON MY HOMEWORK. WHAT'S A PRONOUN?

A NOUN THAT LOST ITS AMATEUR STATUS.

MAYBE I CAN GET A POINT FOR ORIGINALITY.

Calvin and Hobbes. © 1996 Watterson. Dist. by Universal Press Syndicate. Reprinted with permission. All rights reserved.

From 1973 to 1985, 41 different *Schoolhouse Rock* educational cartoon shorts aired weekend mornings between cartoons on the ABC television network. As children sang along, they learned how a bill becomes a law, how multiplication works, and how different parts of speech function. These *Schoolhouse Rock* shorts were revived more than a decade later, and you may remember songs such as "A Noun Is a Person, Place, or Thing" or "Conjunction Junction," where conjunctions are "hooking up words and phrases and clauses." The set of these enormously successful cartoon shorts about language, known together as *Grammar Rock*, captures some fundamentals about English parts of speech: conjunctions really do hook up words, phrases, and clauses, even if kids don't know a clause from a cracker. But, for obvious reasons, these cartoons do not provide sufficiently complex descriptions of any of these parts of speech. For example, nouns are not persons, places, or things; some aren't even words for persons, places, or things. How would you classify, for example, *being, nothingness, karma, metaphor,* or *phoneme*? Are these things in any conventional sense? And while all conjunctions are "hook ups," are they all equivalent? Isn't there a big difference between the function of *and* and that of *because*?

Many college students feel shaky about their control of grammar, despite the *Grammar Rock* songs stuck in their heads. One Calvin and Hobbes cartoon captures this discomfort well. Calvin says to Hobbes, "I need help on my homework. What's a pronoun?" Hobbes replies, "A noun that lost its amateur status." With a dubious look but a scribbling pen, Calvin remarks, "Maybe I can get a point for originality."

All students know that they should know English grammar, but few feel that they have command over it—however much or little grammar they were taught in school. Many students, and you may count yourself among this group, learn the most about English grammar from studying a foreign language. Learning about direct and indirect object pronouns in French makes the distinction clear in English. Distinguishing the perfect and imperfect verb aspect in Spanish clarifies aspect in English verbs. In this chapter, we describe the grammatical categories of English words, both those that correspond to distinctions in other languages and those that are specific to English. And although we agree that Calvin should certainly get originality points for this clever description of pronouns, you will discover better reasons for calling them pronouns.

This chapter focuses on how words behave grammatically. For example, nouns all function similarly in sentences, so we can describe how the "category of nouns" behaves "syntactically." *Syntax* refers to the study of how words combine systematically to form meaningful strings such as sentences. In this chapter, we stay at the level of the word. In Chapter 6, also about syntax, the focus changes to phrases, clauses, and sentences.

In Chapters 5 and 6, we will **parse** sentences: break them down into their component parts in order to examine the form and function of each part. Parsing helps us understand how all the parts work together to create the meaning of the sentence.

Syntax and Lexical Categories

We all know grammar in the descriptive sense—it allows us to use language for communication. The technical term *syntax* can make grammar sound less familiar, but if we all know grammar, that means we all know syntax. We have to know syntax to create each and every well-formed sentence that we utter every day. The following piece of knowledge may seem obvious, but it is fundamental to English syntax: we know that words cannot appear in just any order to form a grammatical sentence.

Let's start small. If you were given the three words *book, in,* and *the* and told to place them in an order that "sounds right" or is grammatical, you would know, as a speaker of English, that there is only one possibility for a well-formed phrase: *in the book.* Now imagine being presented with the following hodge-podge of words and being told to make a grammatical sentence:

> *chapter perplexed the reread students the*

Given the requirement of grammaticality, you could not say **The reread students chapter perplexed the,* but you could go with *The perplexed students reread the chapter.*

In any context, the function of some words will help determine their placement. For example, adjectives modify nouns, and they come before the noun they modify in a noun phrase. In the collection of words above, the only adjective is *perplexed,* and the only nouns are *students* and *chapters.* Obviously, *perplexed* could only describe the students—there are no perplexed chapters! We also have two instances of *the.* The word *the* is a "determiner," a function word that introduces a noun phrase. (We'll return to determiners later in the chapter.) So we know that we have two noun phrases: *the perplexed students* and *the chapter.* If the phrase *the chapter* is the object of *reread,* then it must appear after the verb, as a requirement of English syntax (we'll talk more about direct and indirect objects later).

Then, if we wanted to combine this sentence with another one—say, *The material was challenging*—we could use a variety of conjunctions to do so: *The perplexed students reread the chapter because/if/when/and/although the material was challenging,* or *The material was challenging so/and the perplexed students reread the chapter.* Knowing, understanding, and practicing this ordering of words, even if we do it unconsciously, is knowing syntax.

Syntax describes: (1) the systematic ways in which words are combined to create well-formed phrases, clauses, and sentences; and (2) the systematic ways in which clauses and sentences combine to create more complex sentences. Before we get to how words behave in combination, we discuss the properties and behavior of different categories of words, which affect how words can and do combine with one another.

Parts of speech (the more traditional term) or **lexical categories** (the more technical linguistic term) describe classes of words that behave similarly in the grammar of a language. You may previously have thought of these classes as words that "share some kinds of meaning": for example, nouns are persons, places, or things. These semantic criteria, however, often prove unsatisfactory. For example, the word *confusion,* although definitely a noun (and perhaps a noun referring to a condition that you associate with grammar), is not a person, place, or thing (at least in any concrete sense of *thing*), nor is *tomorrow,* which is a noun but can also function as an adverbial (a word "acting like" an adverb).

Tomorrow as a noun:	<u>*Tomorrow*</u> *is my birthday.*
Tomorrow as an adverbial:	*I hope I will receive lots of presents* <u>*tomorrow*</u>*.*

We can often more precisely describe and determine lexical categories by morphological and syntactic criteria—for example, the inflectional endings that they can take or the "slots" that they can fill in a sentence (e.g., *the _____*). These criteria also allow us to test any given word of unknown or difficult categorization. For example, what part of speech is *yes?* Don't worry: we will come back to this question.

In descriptive grammar, we distinguish between a word's grammatical form and its function. **Form** refers to the grammatical or lexical class of a word—what kind of word it is (e.g., a noun or a preposition). **Function** describes the role of a word in a phrase or clause—what the word does in a grammatical environment (e.g., functions as a subject or an adverbial). An analogy may help clarify this distinction. If you were to use your economics textbook as a doorstop (we know that you would never use your linguistics textbook for this purpose), the textbook remains a textbook in form, but at that moment, it functions as a doorstop. Now back to grammar. Compare the phrases *the fast car* and *the company car.* In the first case, we have an adjective, *fast,* modifying the noun *car.* *Fast* behaves morphologically like other adjectives, for example, it takes the comparative and superlative (*faster, fastest*). *Company,* however, is a noun in form. It behaves like other nouns (e.g., *a/the company, company's*) and not like adjectives (**companier,* *companiest). But in the phrase *the company car,* the noun *company* functions as an adjectival modifier.

Be careful not to confuse lexical categories like noun and verb with descriptions of function such as subject, object, and predicate. The description *subject* or *object* refers to the function of a given word or phrase within a clause. Nouns often function as subjects and objects, but other grammatical constructions can as well. For example, in the sentence *Students say things,* the noun *things* functions as the direct object of the verb *say.* In the sentence *Students say that they never learned grammar in high school,* the direct object of *say* is the full clause *that they never learned grammar in high school.*

Students	*say*	*things.*
Subject	Verb	Direct Object (= noun)

Students	*say*	*that they never learned grammar in high school.*
Subject	Verb	Direct Object (= full clause)

We discuss functional distinctions like subject and predicate, as well as types of clauses, in Chapter 6. In this chapter, we focus primarily on describing lexical categories, which are the building blocks of phrases and clauses. These categories allow us to make generalizations about types of words and to find principles for how types of words behave.

Open-Class Lexical Categories

As we discussed in Chapter 4, open-class categories of words readily accept new members. The chart in Table 5.1 summarizes the four major lexical categories of open-class words—**nouns, adjectives, verbs,** and **adverbs**—according to two types of criteria: morphological and syntactic. Below we discuss the criteria of each lexical category in detail. You can refer back to Table 5.1 as a general reference as you read this section of the chapter.

Nouns

Certainly many nouns refer to persons, places, and things, but they also refer to ideas (*idea*), concepts (*education*), states (*confusion*), activities (*studying*), time (*yesterday*), and more. It is possible to figure out that a word is a noun, even without knowing what it means. For example, look at the word *flibs* in the following sentence:

The flibs keep me on my toes.

We don't know if *flibs* are hard questions, unpredictable children, high-heeled shoes, or something else entirely, but we do know that *flibs* is a plural noun. Several clues here signal the nounness of *flib*. It is preceded by the determiner *the,* which precedes nouns, and there is no other noun after it that *the* could be modifying. (If the sentence read "the flib questions," we could interpret *flib* as an adjective or as a noun functioning as an adjectival modifier.) *Flib* appears here with final *-s,* the typical plural inflectional ending for nouns, and *flibs* is followed by the plural form of the verb, *keep,* which allows us to interpret *flibs* as a plural form of the singular noun *flib.* Note here

TABLE 5.1   **Lexical Categories of Open-Class Words**

Lexical Category	Morphological Description	Syntactic Description
Noun	• plural form with -s (/s, z, ɪz/) • sample derivational suffixes: -ion, -ment, -ness, -er, -ity, -an, -ship, -dom	• DET ___ • DET ADJ ___ • ADJ ___
Adjective	• comparative and superlative forms with -er/-est or more/most • sample derivational suffixes: -al, -able, -like, -ful, -an	• DET ___ N • LINKING V ___ • ADV ___
Verb	• past tense form with -ed (/t, d, ɪd/) • progressive form with -ing[a] • third-person present-tense singular form with -s (/s, z, ɪz/) • sample derivational suffixes: -ize, -ify	• AUX ___ • ___! (as an imperative)
Adverb	• characteristic derivational suffix: -ly (although a few adjectives end in -ly)	• ___ADJ • ___V (or VP) • V (or VP) ___ • ___ADV

[a]See the section "Challenges to Categorization" for more details about the complicated nature of the suffix -ing.

how much we depend on closed-class forms such as inflectional endings and articles to determine phrase and clause structure.

Compare the previous example to the sentence "Bad news travels fast." In this case, the singular verb *travels* signals that the -s on *news* is not a plural inflectional ending but rather part of the root of the singular noun *news*. Just this kind of intuitive work about word classes is what makes Lewis Carroll's poem "Jabberwocky" readable, as we make assumptions about how the made-up words work. (See Exercise 1.1 in Chapter 1 for the full text of "Jabberwocky.")

Morphological Description of Nouns   Morphologically speaking, nouns in English become plural through the addition of an allomorph of the morpheme PLURAL, expressed most often by the inflectional ending -s, realized phonetically as /s/, /z/, or /ɪz/. Certain derivational endings can also signal nounness, such as the -ness on *nounness* as well as -ion, -ism, -ity, -ship, -dom, -hood, -er/-or (-er is also the comparative ending for adjectives, though it represents a different morpheme then, so beware), -an, -ist, and -age.

Syntactic Position of Nouns   Syntactically, nouns can occur after determiners (e.g., *a/an, the*), determiners plus adjectives, or just adjectives. Let's use the nouns *noun* and *weather* as examples.

Language Change at Work

Is It *fish* or *fishes*, *oxen* or *oxes*?

Irregular plurals occur in Modern English for a variety of reasons. First, in Old English, there were several plural inflectional endings that depended on the class and gender of the noun. These endings included *-(a)s* and *-en*. Over time, *-s* became the regular plural ending, but we still have three "remnant" *-en* plurals: *children*, *oxen*, and *brethren* (versus *brothers*). These last two may be on their way to obsolescence, which would leave us with only one.

Old English also had unmarked plurals for one class of nouns, including the words *sheep* and *deer*. This class has expanded rather than shrunk over time. In other words, speakers extended this pattern of zero plurals to new words by analogy. For example, *fish* used to take an inflectional ending with final *-s* to form the plural, and now it does not; it is, therefore, an old word with a new plural ending (or zero ending, to be precise). A more recent acquisition to the English vocabulary, *moose*, was borrowed from Algonquian, and it was added to this irregular class of nouns, with the plural *moose*, not **mooses*. In the case

of *fish*, the plural with a final *-s* has never completely died. For example, in the Michigan Corpus of Academic Spoken English (MICASE), although *fish* is the most common plural form, there are thirty-three examples of *fishes*. And speaking of variation in plural forms due to analogy, what is your plural form of *shrimp*?

Another set of irregular plurals comes from borrowed words that retain their foreign plural forms for a certain period of time. For example, many speakers still use Latin plural forms for *fungus/fungi*, *syllabus/syllabi*, *memorandum/memoranda*, and *datum/data*. In this last case, however, the plural *data* is now often interpreted and used by many speakers as a singular mass noun. One borrowed Latin word with four forms is causing English speakers a great deal of confusion: *alumnus* (masculine), *alumna* (feminine), *alumni* (plural generic or masculine), *alumnae* (plural feminine). *Alumni* is often used as a generic singular, sometimes with the plural *alumnis*. Some speakers dodge the issue entirely with the shortened forms *alum* and *alums*.

DET + NOUN	*a/the noun*	*the weather (*a weather)*
DET + ADJ + NOUN	*a/the troublesome noun*	*the bad weather (*a bad weather)*
ADJ + NOUN	*quirky nouns (*quirky noun)*	*good weather*

Based on the ungrammatical constructions marked with an asterisk (*), we can see how *noun* and *weather* behave differently. *Noun* is a countable noun and *weather* is uncountable. **Countable nouns** (or count nouns) are quantifiable (i.e., they can be counted). And countable nouns can take plural *-s*. **Uncountable nouns** (or mass nouns) describe ideas (*peace*) or other referents that cannot be counted (*engineering*). If you want to count *engineering*, you have to count *kinds/types of engineering*. In other words, you have to add a countable quantifier.

The linguist Ray Jackendoff has argued that, given enough context, all nouns can be countable and uncountable. You can be in love (uncountable) but have had three great loves (countable) in your life. In theory, the quantifier *fewer* modifies only countable nouns and *less* uncountable nouns. But many speakers use *less* for both types of nouns, and there are some well-known, even standard exceptions to the rule: the saying "one less thing to worry about," the common essay prompt "write an essay of 500 words or less," and the grocery store sign "10 items or less."

In the syntax of a phrase or clause, nouns can function as subjects, objects (direct and indirect objects of verbs and objects of prepositions), and complements (a term we return to in Chapter 6). One fairly reliable test for a noun is whether the word can fill any of these syntactic positions:

The _____

(The) _____ is/are

I like/want/have (the) _____

There are odd exceptions to the second test. For example, "pretty is as pretty does" has an adjective in this syntactic position, but we all recognize the construction, though acceptable, as slightly peculiar grammatically.

Adjectives

Merely establishing that adjectives "describe things" is clearly inadequate. At some level, depending on how we interpret *describe,* almost all words are describing words. In more precise linguistic terms, adjectives are words that modify the meaning of nouns.

Morphological Description of Adjectives   Morphologically, some derivational suffixes indicate adjectiveness: for example, *-al, -able, -like, -ful, -y, -an.* Most adjectives have **comparative** and **superlative** forms, which are formed either by the addition of the inflectional endings *-er/-est* or of the modifiers *more/most.* English follows the general rule that adjectives of one syllable take the inflectional endings (*tall, taller, tallest*), adjectives of three or more syllables take *more/most* (*beautiful, more beautiful, most beautiful*), and adjectives of two syllables often can do either (*gentle, gentler* or *more gentle, gentlest* or *most gentle*).

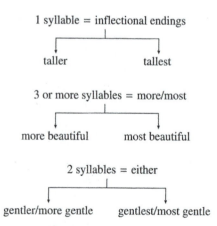

Within this general rule, there are patterns and exceptions. For example, you probably wouldn't say *pompouser* or *purpler,* and many people think that *funner* sounds terrible. The word *fun* takes *more/most* for historical reasons, as it only recently shifted from a noun to an adjective. There is a good chance that, over time, its morphological behavior will come into line with other one-syllable adjectives and it will become regular: *funner* and *funnest* may become standard.

Not all adjectives form comparatives and superlatives, for semantic reasons: adjectives must be gradable in order to have degrees of comparison. For example, the meaning of *unique*, at least in theory, resists comparison—if something is one of a kind, it cannot be compared. However, you will certainly hear "more unique" if you listen for it. Other nongradable adjectives include *pregnant, alive*, and *asleep*. And in any given context, nongradable adjectives may take a comparative or superlative form. For example, if your alarm clock goes off and you continue to sleep but your roommate wakes up, you might say, "Well, I guess I was more asleep than you were."

Some adjectives form the comparative and superlative in irregular ways, for example, *good/better/best* and *bad/worse/worst*.

Syntactic Position of Adjectives
Syntactically, adjectives can appear in **attributive** or **predicative** position. Attributive position refers to the position before the noun (and after the determiner if it is present): *fascinating adjectives*, or *the attributive adjective*. Predicative position refers to the position after the verb. (The predicate is the verb and other elements it governs in a clause. In the clause *grammar makes me happy*, *grammar* is the subject and *makes me happy* is the **predicate**.) In predicative position, the adjective can modify the subject or in some cases the object. After a linking verb such as *be* or *seem*, predicative adjectives describe the subject:

Adjectives are fascinating.

Grammar seems cooler than I remember.

After a small set of verbs, a predicative adjective can modify the object:

We called the construction grammatical.

Grammar makes me happy.

In English, some adjectives typically appear exclusively or almost exclusively in attributive or in predicative position. For example:

Predicative	Attributive
The grammarian is finally well.	**The well grammarian sang the noun's praises.*
The student was awake for class.	**The awake student wanted to learn more grammar.*
*The grammar teacher was former.	*The former grammar teacher missed studying adjectives.*
*Her interest in grammar was sheer.	*The sheer interest of grammar overwhelmed her.*

A Question to Discuss

Am I Good or Well?

Whether or not you are good or well depends on what you mean. If your health is good, then you are well. *Well* can function as an adjective meaning 'healthy', which is its meaning here. If you do something well, you are good at it. In this case, *well* is an adverb, and *good* is an adjective. So things are good and one does things well.

Confusion arises because *well*, which is usually an adverb, can also be an adjective, but only in the context of discussing one's health. So, if someone asks you how you are, what is the difference between saying "I'm good" and "I'm well"? (Hint: There is arguably a difference.) A very similar issue arises if you want to express your condolences and say that you feel bad/badly about something. Do you think it should be *bad* or *badly* here?

That said, you can imagine specific circumstances in which you could use the phrase *the awake student:* for example, *Of the two students camped out in the library, the awake student was getting more work done.*

Some adjectives have different meanings in attributive and predicative position— see Exercise 5.2. As one example, the adjective *sheer* can appear in both predicative and attributive position when it means 'transparent or thin' in reference to fabric: *his curtains are sheer,* and *the sheer curtains.* This use is historically related to the word's meaning 'absolute, pure' in *sheer interest*—a meaning that the adjective has only in attributive position.

Verbs

Modern English verbs typically have five basic morphological forms: the bare form (e.g., *nap*), the third-person singular present-tense form (*naps*), the past-tense form (*napped*), the present participle (*napping*), and the past participle (*napped*). Each form corresponds to different grammatical functions, as summarized in Table 5.2.

Before we turn to the detailed morphological description of verbs, we can state more generally that all English verbs **conjugate** (or change form) to indicate six grammatical categories: person (first, second, third), number (singular and plural), tense, aspect, voice, and mood. Whereas person and number are relatively straightforward, the other four categories may require a brief explanation.

Tense   English verbs formally have two tenses: past and present (sometimes called past and nonpast). By "formally," we are referring to tense as marked by inflectional endings. The term *present* in *present tense* is deceptive because the present-tense form can also describe the future, particularly if the future event is scheduled to occur: *The class is at 2:00 tomorrow.* The present tense can also describe the past, usually in a narrative: *So yesterday I go to class and the teacher says English formally has no future tense.*

TABLE 5.2   **Morphological Forms of Verbs**

Verb Form	Function	Examples
Bare/infinitive form (regular = zero ending)	All present tense forms except the third-person singular	I/we/you/they *nap*
	Base for infinitive form with *to* (the marked infinitive)	to *nap*
	Form after modal auxiliaries and auxiliary *do*	we must *nap* we don't *nap* / do we *nap*? / we do *nap*
	Imperative form	*nap*!
	Present subjunctive form	I recommend that she *nap*
	Complement of perception and causative verbs	we watched her *nap*
Third-person singular present tense form (regular = -*s* ending)	Third-person singular present tense forms	he/she/it/one *naps*
Past tense form (regular = -*ed* ending irregular = internal vowel change)	All past tense forms	I/we/you/she/they *napped* I/we/you/she/they *sang*
Present participle (regular = -*ing* ending)	Form for progressive constructions	we are/were/have been *napping*
Past participle (regular = -*ed* ending irregular = -*en* ending or internal vowel change)	Form for perfect constructions (with form of *have* as auxiliary)	we have/had *napped* we have/had *forgotten* we have/had *sung*
	Form for passive constructions (with form of *be* as auxiliary)	the sentence is/was *mangled* all verbs are/were *forgotten* the song is/was *sung*

Note: The third-person singular present-tense form (e.g., *naps*) and the past-tense form (*napped*) are both **finite** forms: these forms mark tense. The other three forms—the bare form (*nap*), the present participle (*napping*), and the past participle (*napped*)—are called **nonfinite** (or infinite) forms because they remain fixed: they do not mark tense.

Wait a minute. English has no future tense? Technically, or formally, no. Verbs in English do not inflect (i.e., take an inflectional ending) to indicate future time. Instead, English employs modal auxiliary verbs (usually *will*) to indicate future action.

Aspect   **Aspect** marks whether the action of the verb is completed (the perfect) or continuous (the progressive). The perfect and progressive can co-occur: *I have been loving this chapter*. Standard varieties of English mark only the present and past perfect and the progressive. Some nonstandard varieties, such as African American English, also mark habitual action and remote past perfect (see the "Auxiliary Verbs" section for details).

Voice   Voice describes the relationship of the subject to the action of the verb (e.g., agent, recipient). In English, the active voice is distinguished from the passive voice (in which the subject is acted upon by the verb) through syntactic devices including the inflection on the past participle (e.g., *I broke the record* ⟶ *The record was broken*).

Mood   The grammatical category of mood is not related to mood as we typically understand it (e.g., happy, depressed), but it does allow speakers or writers to indicate their attitude toward what they are expressing. For example, they can express a certainty, a command, or a wish. In English there are three basic moods: indicative (the mood of statements and questions, which inflects for person, number, and tense); imperative (the mood of commands, which uses the bare infinitive); and subjunctive (the mood of conditions, which employs the bare infinitive for present tense and is identical to the regular past tense in the past tense except for invariant *were* for 'to be'). The **subjunctive mood** (whose death has been predicted for decades but which, if anything, may be getting stronger) expresses something wished for (*I wish ice cream were healthier*), commanded (*let it be*), intended (*we propose that she bring ice cream*), or hypothesized (*if green beans were chocolate*). English speakers more often create conditionals, though, through the addition of modal auxiliary verbs (e.g., *might, could, would*), discussed later in this chapter. Modality allows speakers to express, grammatically, that they know something to be true, that they think something is possible or permissible, or that they think something must or should happen.

Morphological Description of Verbs   In terms of morphology, for all verbs except *be, have, do,* and *go,* the **bare infinitive** form serves as the base for the other four forms, marked by inflectional endings or internal vowel changes. In standard varieties of English, the bare infinitive functions as the present-tense form for first- and second-person singular and plural, and for third-person plural. Third-person singular requires the addition of inflectional *-s.* Many nonstandard varieties use the bare infinitive form throughout the present-tense paradigm. See Table 5.3 for examples.

Regular English verbs—the majority of verbs—form the **past tense** through the addition of the inflectional ending *-ed.* Another significant class of verbs, now seen as irregular but historically regular (see the discussion of "strong verbs" in Chapter 13),

TABLE 5.3   Present Tense of a Regular Verb

	Standard Varieties of English	*Some Nonstandard Varieties of English*	
Singular			
1st	I think	I think	I think
2nd	you think	you think	you think
3rd	he/she/it thinks	he/she/it think	he/she/it thinks
Plural			
1st	we think	we think	we think
2nd	you think	you think	you think
3rd	they think	they think	they thinks[a]

[a]Some varieties allow constructions such as *they thinks*; others extend inflectional *-s* to the third-person plural but not if the pronoun *they* occurs right next to the verb.

form the past tense through an internal vowel change: *sing/sang, swim/swam, run/ran, drive/drove.* Other minor classes of exceptions in the formation of the past tense include:

Final -(e)d + vowel change	*tell/told, sell/sold*
Final -t	*bend/bent, burn/burnt* (or *burned*)
Final -t + vowel change	*keep/kept, feel/felt, creep/crept, leap/leapt* (?*leaped*)
No change	*bet/bet, spread/spread*
Irregular	*bring/brought, think/thought, catch/caught, teach/taught, seek/sought, buy/bought*

For all these minor classes, the **past participle** is identical to the past-tense form.

The change in a verb like *go* to the very irregular past-tense form *went* is referred to as **suppletion.** *Go* and *went* are reflexes of different Old English verbs, *gan* ('to go') and *wendan* ('to follow a certain course, come about, turn'), that have merged into the same verb in Modern English. Outside the *go* conjugation, the verb *wend* (past tense *wended*) survives in phrases such as "wend one's way." Another example of suppletion is the shift in the adjective *good* to the comparative *better.*

The **present participle**, formed through the addition of the inflectional ending -*ing*, appears in progressive constructions, both past and present: *I am thinking, I was thinking.* The **progressive aspect** describes a continuing action, whether in the past or present, and is formed with the appropriate form of *be* + present participle.

The past participle appears in perfect constructions (typically used to refer to completed actions) and passive constructions. We discuss the perfect here and the passive in Chapter 6.

Present Perfect	**Past Perfect**	**Passive**
I have <u>played</u>	*I had <u>played</u>*	*the game is/was <u>played</u>*
they have <u>taken</u>	*they had <u>taken</u>*	*the money is/was <u>taken</u>*
you have <u>rung</u>	*you had <u>rung</u>*	*the bell was <u>rung</u>*

The **perfect aspect**, formed by combining the appropriate form of *have* + past participle, indicates a completed action, either before the present moment (present perfect: *we have finished studying*) or before a specific moment in the past (past perfect: *we had finished studying before the electricity went out*). The present perfect also can describe an action that began in the past and continues to the present (e.g., *I have taken dance for five years*).

For regular verbs, the past participle and the past-tense form are identical: both involve the addition of the inflectional -*ed.* The past participle of former strong verbs, irregular verbs that inflect through internal vowel changes, can be formed in six different ways:

Past participle form of irregular, "strong" verbs	(present/past/past participle)
Vowel change	*sing/sang/sung, ring/rang/rung, swim/swam/swum*
Addition of -*en* to bare infinitive form	*take/took/taken, give/gave/given, eat/ate/eaten*
Addition of -*en* to past-tense form	*break/broke/broken, bite/bit/bitten*
Addition of -*en* + vowel change	*smite/smote/smitten*
Identical to past-tense form	*feed/fed/fed, dig/dug/dug, ran/run/run/*
Identical to bare infinitive form	*become/became/become*

While this list can seem overwhelming, there are fewer than 200 of these irregular verbs in current English.

Syntactic Position of Verbs
Syntactically, verbs appear in a few distinctive spots: (1) after auxiliary verbs, (2) alone in imperative constructions, (3) alone after a **subject**, and (4) between a subject and an **object.** So a verb will typically be able to fill one of these constructions:

We must/have _____.	*We must study./We have studied.*
_____!	*Focus!*
We _____.	*We read.*
We _____ things.	*We forget things.*

These last two constructions that test "verbness" highlight another distinction among verbs: **transitivity**, or whether the verb takes a direct object. Traditionally, English verbs have been described as falling into five categories, based on the types of grammatical constructions in which they appear—or to put it differently, the kinds of complements that they entail. The **complement** of a verb is the phrase or clause that follows the verb to complete the verb phrase, by providing, for example, a direct object or both a direct object and indirect object. Here are the five basic categories of verbs:

intransitive	verbs appearing with no object (*we sleep*)
transitive	verbs appearing with a direct object (*we made cookies*)
ditransitive	verbs appearing with both a direct and indirect object (*we gave Sue the cookies*)
linking	verbs connecting a subject-predicative to a subject (*we are nice*)
object-predicative	verbs connecting an object-predicative to an object (*Sue called us nice*)

We discuss the first three categories, all related to transitivity, first. Etymology can provide a useful mnemonic here: the prefix *trans-* can mean 'across' (e.g., *transport* or *Trans Am*—the car that was supposed to take you across America). With transitive and ditransitive verbs, the subject "reaches across" the verb to have an effect on one or more objects.

Some verbs require an object. These verbs are only transitive; they are never intransitive. Consider the verbs *prohibit* and *require* in the following sentences.

The school	*prohibits*	*tank tops.*	**The school prohibits.*
(subject)	(transitive verb)	(direct object)	
Some verbs	*require*	*an object.*	**Some verbs require.*
(subject)	(transitive verb)	(direct object)	

Notice that in these sentences with objects, you can make a passive construction. In other words, you can reverse the subject and object such that the new grammatical subject is acted upon (by the former subject): *An object is required by some verbs* or *Tank tops are prohibited by the school.*

Some senses of some verbs, such as *come* and *go*, can only be intransitive; they cannot take a direct object.

We will come.

We will come for dinner.   **We will come dinner.*

We went yesterday.   **We went Toronto.*

The word *yesterday* in *We went yesterday* is functioning as an adverbial, not an object. How do you know? You cannot make a passive construction in which *yesterday* is acted upon by the verb *go*: **Yesterday was gone by us.* (Note, however, in some senses, *go* is used transitively, as in *go the distance*.)

A subset of intransitive verbs requires a prepositional phrase after the verb (e.g., *depend on, count on, campaign for*). It's also possible to argue that these verbs should constitute their own class, with a prepositional phrase as the complement—see Exercise 5.3, #7.

Many verbs in English can function both transitively and intransitively—a fact that raises the question of whether the transitive/intransitive distinction is an especially useful one for thinking about English. For example, you can study grammar (transitive), or you can just study (intransitive). You can eat your lunch (transitive), or you can eat every day (intransitive). In that last example, *every day* is not an object but an adverbial—you could not make a passive construction with it: **Every day can be eaten by you.*

Even verbs that are typically transitive or intransitive can often cross the transitivity boundary in a given context. For example:

Typically Transitive	Used Intransitively
You shouldn't hit people even if you're mad.	*Watch out! That baby hits.*
This course satisfies the requirement.	*Try this new product: it satisfies.*

Typically Intransitive	Used Transitively
We all sleep in one room.	*The house sleeps five people.*
The Cheshire cat smiled.	*The Cheshire cat smiled a big smile.*

Our description here assumes that one verb can function in grammatically different ways (e.g., transitively and/or intransitively). It's also possible to argue that the transitive and intransitive forms of the verb are two different lexical items that are homonymous (i.e., they sound the same). To translate the debate into more applied terms, the question for lexicographers would be whether the verb's transitive and intransitive uses are described under one headword or whether the transitive verb is one headword and the intransitive verb another headword. You'll notice that some verbs mean differently when they are used transitively and intransitively: compare, for example, *I broke the garbage disposal* versus *the garbage disposal broke*, or *she drinks coffee* versus *she drinks* (which colloquially implies drinking alcohol).

A smaller set of verbs can be used ditransitively—that is, with a direct and indirect object. These verbs include *give, send, promise, tell, lend, ask,* and *show*. Semantically speaking, the **direct object** is typically described as the recipient of the verb's action, and the **indirect object** is to or for whom the action is done. Two syntactic tests can help differentiate the direct and indirect object:

1. If there are two objects in a row after the verb, the indirect object comes first.

Direct object

He gave her the letter.

Indirect object

2. The indirect object can be moved to a position after the direct object with the addition of the preposition *for* or *to*.

	Indirect object	Direct object
The kind-hearted teacher gave	*her students*	*a grammar quiz.*

The kind-hearted teacher gave a grammar quiz to her students.

The last two categories of verbs require predicatives in their complements: noun or adjective phrases that modify either the subject or object of the clause. First, **linking verbs,** such as *be, appear, seem,* connect a subject to a subject-predicative: a noun or adjective phrase (and occasionally an adverbial) that modifies or describes the subject. For example:

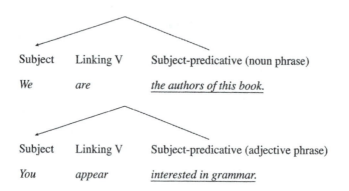

Subject	Linking V	Subject-predicative (noun phrase)
We	*are*	*the authors of this book.*

Subject	Linking V	Subject-predicative (adjective phrase)
You	*appear*	*interested in grammar.*

Second, a small set of verbs, object-predicative verbs, can link an object to an object-predicative: a noun or adjective phrase that modifies the object. For example:

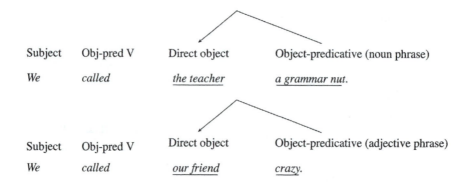

Subject	Obj-pred V	Direct object	Object-predicative (noun phrase)
We	*called*	*the teacher*	*a grammar nut.*

Subject	Obj-pred V	Direct object	Object-predicative (adjective phrase)
We	*called*	*our friend*	*crazy.*

These five types of verbs (or five ways that verbs can behave, given that many of them qualify as more than one type)—intransitive, transitive, ditransitive, linking, and object-predicative—correspond to the five basic types of clause structures we discuss in Chapter 6. You can see one way that the lexicon and syntax are interrelated, as these verbs determine syntactic aspects of the clauses in which they appear.

A Question to Discuss

Did I Lie Down or Lay Down?

You might say to your friend at the poker table, "Lay down your cards." If you lost the hand and were feeling discouraged, your friend might say to you, "Lie down for a while." The meaning of the verbs in these two commands is very similar, yet two different verbs are in play here: one transitive (*lay*) and one intransitive (*lie*). How do you know which verb to use? And do you always know? Might you be at all tempted to say "Lay down for a while"? If so, why?

The two verbs *lay* and *lie* are historically related, which is why they share such similar forms.

What gets confusing is that the past tense of the verb *lie* (*lay*) is identical to the bare/ infinitive form (and, therefore, the present tense) of the verb *lay*. So *you always lay your book*

Bare/ infinitive form	(to) lie 'to be in or assume a horizontal position'	(to) lay 'to put or set down'
Third-person singular present	lies	lays
Past tense	lay	laid
Present participle	lying	laying
Past participle	lain	laid

on the floor before you go to sleep (transitive verb *lay*, present tense), and *yesterday you lay down for a nap* (intransitive verb *lie*, past tense).

Let's now consider the sentence "Now I lay me down to sleep"? Why is that a historically correct use of *lay*?

All these categories have subcategories. For example, the verb *put* belongs to the subcategory of transitive verbs that require a direct object and a prepositional phrase in the complement: *They put the book on the shelf.* The verb *wonder* belongs to the subcategory of transitive verbs that require a full clause (rather than a noun or noun phrase): *I wonder if she will see me.*

Adverbs

Adverbs are one of the hardest lexical categories to define semantically, morphologically, or syntactically. Adverbs modify verbs (*walk quickly*), adjectives (*truly beautiful*), and other adverbs (*wonderfully quickly*). "Sentence adverbs" can modify full clauses or sentences. For example, *clearly* and *frankly* can modify the entire clause or sentence that follows them:

Frankly, adverbs seem a bit hard to pin down.

We can distinguish three general categories of adverbs:

Temporal adverbs	describe when an action or state occurs (e.g., *yesterday, soon*)
Manner adverbs	describe how an action or state occurs (e.g., *quickly, safely*)
Discourse adverbs (or **sentence adverbs**)	describe the speaker's or writer's stance on the clause or sentence (e.g., *frankly, bluntly*)

Morphological Description of Adverbs   There are no definitive morphological criteria for adverbs. Adverbs often end in the derivational suffix *-ly* (*quickly, beautifully*), but not always. Some words that end in *-ly* are adjectives (*friendly, homely*). And many adverbs do not end in *-ly* (*fast, well, often, down*). Probably based on analogy with adverbs like *fast*, speakers sometimes form other "flat adverbs," so that the adverb shares the same form as the adjective. Kanye West uses one in his song title "Drive Slow."

Adverbs form the comparative and superlative with *more* and *most*.

Syntactic Position of Adverbs   Most adverbs do not adhere to a fixed position in the sentence. They can often occur at the beginning or end of a clause, as well as directly before or after a main verb.

> *Quickly I read through the chapter.*
> *I quickly read through the chapter.*
> *I read quickly through the chapter.*
> *I read through the chapter quickly.*

There are, however, places that an adverb cannot occur. For example, an adverb cannot be placed directly between an adjective and the noun that the adjective modifies: **a long ridiculously lecture*. But an adverb can occur before an adjective as a modifier (*a ridiculously long lecture*) and before another adverb as a modifier (*she ran ridiculously quickly*). Some linguists call adverbs the "trash can" or "dustbin" category (depending on whether the linguist is a speaker of American or British English)—a catch-all for words that modify all open-class words other than nouns.

Closed-Class Lexical Categories

As we discussed in Chapter 4, closed-class categories (or what we often refer to as "function words") tend not to admit new members easily or often. Here we cover the five major closed-class categories: prepositions, conjunctions, pronouns, determiners, and auxiliary verbs.

Prepositions

Prepositions might be even harder to define than adverbs. One humorous attempt at a definition claims that a preposition is everywhere a squirrel can go with respect to a tree (e.g., *up/down/around/to/from/into/in/off the tree*). This definition captures a lot about prepositions but certainly not everything. The *American Heritage Dictionary of the English Language* (2000) provides a more precise definition:

> A word or phrase placed typically before a substantive [noun] and indicating the relation of that substantive to a verb, an adjective, or another substantive, as English *at, by, with, from,* and *in regard to*.

In other words, prepositions assist in indicating location, direction, time, duration, manner, and other relationships.

Prepositions occur before nouns or noun phrases and create a modifying connection between that noun (phrase) and a verb (*go to school, learn by rote*), an adjective (*crazy as a*

Many prepositions describe where a squirrel can go with respect to a tree, but this semantic description fails to capture all prepositions in English.

loon, bored by television), or another noun (*a book about linguistics, a definition of prepositions*). So syntactically, prepositions occur in this position (NP = noun or noun phrase):

_____ NP (e.g., *to school, about linguistics*)

As one test for "preposition-ness," many prepositions can be modified by *right*:

right _____ NP (e.g., *right around the corner*)

A Question to Discuss

What Is the *up* in *call up*?

English has a relatively large set of verbs usually called **phrasal verbs** or multipart verbs: *call up, ask out, put up with, freak out, carry on,* and so forth. All of the parts contribute to the verb's meaning, which is different from the meaning of the verb alone. The word or words after the verb look like prepositions or in some cases adverbs, but they don't act syntactically like prepositions or adverbs. Grammarians, therefore, call them **particles**. Prepositions require a noun phrase after them, but many phrasal verbs can function intransitively, for example, *he tends to freak out.* Adverbs can typically appear before the verb or elsewhere in the sentence, but particles must appear after the verb. And passive constructions demonstrate that the phrasal verb functions like a one-word verb: *someone asked out Jasmine* ⟶ *Jasmine was asked out (by someone).* The main verb and the particle are always separated when the object is a pronoun, which must appear between the verb and particle: *grammar freaks me out,* not **grammar freaks out me.* Other NPs can also appear between the main verb and particle: for example, *someone asked Jasmine out.*

Should these particles be their own lexical category?

Conjunctions

Conjunctions connect things, be they words, phrases, or clauses. There are three major types of conjunctions: coordinating, correlative, and subordinating.

English has six common **coordinating conjunctions**: *for, and, nor, but, or,* and *yet* (to create the useful acronym *FANBOY*). *So* can also be considered a coordinating conjunction (making *FANBOYS*). Coordinating conjunctions connect words or phrases of the same category (e.g., two nouns or two prepositional phrases) to create a coordinated phrase in that category. For example:

nouns and verbs	noun *and* noun = noun phrase
stay or go	verb *or* verb = verb phrase
safe yet sorry	adjective *yet* adjective = adjective phrase
over the river and to the woods	prepositional phrase (PP) *and* PP = PP

Coordinating conjunctions can also connect two clauses—what we might think of as two sentences. For example: *Coordinating conjunctions are cool, but subordinating conjunctions rock.*

Correlative conjunctions refer to paired conjunctions such as *either/or, neither/nor, not only/but also*. Correlative conjunctions function much like coordinating conjunctions except that they involve a conjunction at the beginning of each phrase or clause: e.g., *either cookies or candy*; *they not only ate the cookies, but they also drank all the milk.*

Common **subordinating conjunctions** are *because, although, when, after, before, unless, if, while, in order that, as long as,* and many others. Subordinating conjunctions connect two clauses: a main clause and a dependent or subordinate clause. A subordinate clause depends on the main clause to provide context or complete its meaning. Most subordinating conjunctions (including all the ones just listed) create subordinate clauses that function adverbially, often answering "When?" "Why?" or "Under what conditions?" For example:

> <u>After we ate all the cookies,</u> *we felt sick.*
>   subordinate clause

> *We ate all the cookies <u>because they were delicious.</u>*
>   subordinate clause

These adverbial subordinate clauses can occur before or after the main clause. You'll notice that some of these subordinating conjunctions are also prepositions. As conjunctions, they are followed by a full clause; as prepositions, they are followed by just a noun phrase (e.g., *after we learn grammar* versus *after class*). A subordinate clause cannot stand alone as a sentence:

> *After we ate all the cookies.
> *Because they were delicious.

Complementizers can also be considered subordinating conjunctions; they create subordinate clauses that function nominally (i.e., like noun phrases). The most common complementizers in English are *that*, a set of *wh-* words (*what, whether, who/whom, where, why*), and *how*, which function as complementizers when used to introduce a clause that serves nominally. Some verbs in English can require a full clause as their object, to complete their meaning in a sentence: for example, *say that . . .* or *think that . . .* (*Her roommate said that she pulled an all-nighter* or *I think that she is crazy to go without sleep*). Other verbs can take an NP or a complementizer clause as the object: for example, *I know Alicia* or *I know how it happened*. In all these constructions, the complementizer introduces the clause that is the object (or complement) of the verb—the clause that completes the verb phrase by providing the object.

Note that when *that* and *who/whom* are used as relative pronouns, they introduce a clause that modifies the preceding noun phrase and they serve as the subject or object of that clause: for example, *the book that I read* or *the teacher who has bad handwriting*. The word *that* can also function as a demonstrative pronoun and demonstrative determiner. The words *who* and *whom* can also function as interrogative pronouns.

Pronouns

Pronouns stand in for nouns or noun phrases. Given that the category "pronoun" does not readily accept new members, we classify pronouns as closed class. But syntactically, pronouns behave like nouns. So we could think of pronouns as a closed class within the open class of nouns.

If someone asked you to identify some pronouns, you might immediately think of ones such as *she, they,* or *it*—all personal pronouns. Yet there are actually five categories of pronouns.

- **Personal pronouns** have three persons (first, second, third), two numbers (singular, plural), and three cases (subject, object, possessive), as well as reflexive forms. See Table 5.4. English used to make a singular/plural distinction in the second person with the forms *thou/thee/thine* (singular) and *ye/you/yours* (plural). Many dialects have re-created a singular/plural distinction with plural forms such as *yous, you guys,* or *y'all* (with the possessive form *y'alls*).

- **Indefinite pronouns** stand in for an unknown or unspecified element in a clause. For example: *Anyone can do that*. Common indefinite pronouns include *one, anyone, someone, everyone, no one, something, neither, either, another, both, all, most, some, whoever/whomever,* and *whatever.*

TABLE 5.4 **Personal Pronouns**

	Subject	*Object*	*Possessive*	*Reflexive*
Singular 1st	I	me	mine	myself
2nd	you	you	yours	yourself
3rd	he/she/it (they?[a])	him/her/it (them?)	his/hers/its (theirs?)	himself/herself/itself (themself?)
Plural				
1st	we	us	ours	ourselves
2nd	you	you	yours	yourselves
3rd	they	them	theirs	themselves

[a]See the final section of this chapter for more discussion of singular generic *they.*

- **Interrogative pronouns** stand in for an unknown element in a clause in order to create a question. For example: *Who is coming to dinner?* Common interrogative pronouns include *who/whom/whose, what,* and *which.*

- **Demonstrative pronouns** point to things either previously mentioned in the text or in the physical environment. For example: *I took the 47 bus—that is the one that goes downtown.* Or, pointing to something: *I want that.* The demonstrative pronouns include *this, that, these,* and *those.*

- **Relative pronouns** act as the subject or object of a dependent/subordinate clause to link the clause to a preceding noun phrase. The most common relative pronouns are *who/whom/whose, that, which, whoever/whomever,* and *whichever.*

that is the object of *studying*

The grammar <u>*that we are studying*</u> is riveting. (the dependent clause modifies *grammar*)

who is the subject of *master*

Students <u>who master descriptive grammar</u> will be richly rewarded in life. (the dependent clause modifies *students*)

Language Change at Work

Himself, Hisself, Hisownself

Typically, **reflexive pronouns** are used when the object of a clause refers back to the subject. For example: *I see myself in the mirror* or *Raoul gave himself a haircut.* Technically, you do not need a reflexive pronoun in a construction such as *The work will be done by Mary, Jasmine, and me,* because the subject is *work.* However, you will also sometimes see or hear *The work will be done by Mary, Jasmine, and myself,* because although the subject of the clause is *work,* the pronoun is still referring back or reflexively in some way to the speaker of the sentence. In addition, reflexive pronouns are occasionally used for emphasis: *I did it myself,* or *He himself showed up for the opening.*

In standard varieties of English, the formation of the reflexive pronouns is not consistent. The first- and second-person reflexive pronouns are formed by POSSESSIVE FORM + SELF (*myself, yourself,* etc.). The third-person singular masculine (*himself*) and the third-person

plural (*themselves*) involve OBJECT FORM + SELF. The forms *herself* and *itself* are ambiguous as to whether they involve the possessive or object form.

Some nonstandard varieties employ possessive forms throughout the paradigm, to make the construction entirely regular: POSSESSIVE FORM + SELF. These varieties use *hisself* and *theirselves* instead of *himself* and *themselves.* Some nonstandard varieties of American English can also employ the emphatic infix *-own-* to emphasize a reflexive construction or to emphasize the subject in a nonreflexive construction: *He can't even help hisownself,* or *I hooked up the computer my own self.* It is difficult to tell, though, whether this is *hisself* (available in some varieties) infixed with emphatic *-own-,* or whether those varieties in question retain a tendency borrowed from Scots and Ulster Scots to focus the phrase with free *own: He'll be here his own self.*

A subset of indefinites, as well as some interrogatives and demonstratives, can also function as determiners.

Determiners

Determiners encompass the class of function words that introduce noun phrases, often indicating, for example:

Determinacy: e.g., indefinite articles *a/an* versus definite article *the*

Quantity: e.g., *some, many, all*

Number: e.g., *one, two, first, second*

Pragmatic functions such as specification: e.g., *this* versus *that*

Determiners precede the adjectives that modify nouns:

_____ (ADJ$^+$) N   *the car, a fast car*

The superscript + means there can be more than one of that element.

Determiners behave differently from adjectives in that they do not form comparatives or superlatives (*samer, *allest) and they cannot appear in predicative position (*car is the).

More than one determiner can introduce a single noun (e.g., <u>*a third* category</u> or <u>*all these many* years</u>), and the ordering of these determiners is fairly rigid. It has to be, for example, *all these books*, not *these all books*, or *your last date*, not *last your date*. For this reason, grammarians refer to three classes of determiners based on the order in which they appear in combination: predeterminers, central determiners, and postdeterminers. See Table 5.5 for examples.

TABLE 5.5   **Determiners**

Type of Determiner	Examples
Predeterminers	*all, both, half*
	multipliers (*twice, double, ten times*)
	fractions other than *half*
	exclamative *what*
Central determiners	articles (*a/an, the*)
	demonstratives (*this, these*)
	possessive determiners (*your, my*)
	interrogative determiners (*which, whose*)
	relative determiners (*whose, which*)
	nominal relative determiners (*whichever*)
	indefinite determiners (*some, any, no*)
Postdeterminers	cardinal numbers (*three, six*)
	ordinal numbers (*third, seventeenth*)
	general ordinals (*another, last, next*)
	primary quantifiers (*many, several, few, much*)

Source: Adapted from Sidney Greenbaum. *Oxford English Grammar*. London: Oxford University Press, pp. 213–16 (1996). © 1996 by Oxford University Press. By permission of Oxford University Press.

Several of these subsets of determiners can also function as pronouns (e.g., *all, both, some, many, one, this*). They are considered pronouns when they stand alone, and they are considered determiners when they modify a noun: *this is ridiculous* (pronoun) versus *this situation is ridiculous* (determiner). A few take a slightly different form as determiners and as pronouns: *my, your, her, our, their* (determiners) versus *mine, yours, hers, ours, theirs* (pronouns); *no* (determiner) versus *none* (pronoun).

Predeterminers and central determiners cannot co-occur with members of their own class (e.g., **your the knowledge*), whereas postdeterminers can co-occur (e.g., *the next few examples*). A possessive form of a noun (e.g., *book's* or *Michael's*) functions as a central determiner, like other possessives such as *my*.

Auxiliary Verbs

Often called "helping verbs," **auxiliary verbs** occur before main or "lexical" verbs in order to indicate time (*will give*), aspect (*have given*), modality (*might give*), or emphasis (*do give*), or to assist in the formation of negative (*don't give*), interrogative (*do you give?*), and passive constructions (*was given*). We can distinguish two main classes of auxiliary verbs: primary auxiliaries and modals (Greenbaum 1996, 153–56). There is a small group of marginal auxiliaries as well. See Table 5.6 for examples of the three categories.

Interestingly, the same **modal auxiliary** can express two very different things. For example, take the phrase *I may go* in the following two sentences:

I finally got permission: my parents said that <u>I may go</u> to the party.

<u>I may go</u> to the party, but then again I may not if I'm too busy.

TABLE 5.6   **Auxiliary Verbs**

	Auxiliary Verbs	Uses
Primary auxiliaries	*be*	Progressive aspect (*is taking*)
		Passive constructions (*was taken*)
	have	Perfect aspect (*has/had taken*)
	do	Emphatic constructions (*I did take it*)
		Negative constructions. if no other auxiliary is present[a]: (*he understands auxiliaries* ⟶ *he doesn't understand auxiliaries*)
		Interrogative constructions. if no other auxiliary is present[a]: (*he loves auxiliaries* ⟶ *does he love auxiliaries?*)
Modals	*can, could may, might shall, should will, would must*	convey possibility, necessity, permission, certainty, prediction
Marginal auxiliaries[b]	*used to (useta), ought to (oughta), dare (to), need (to), be going to (gonna), have to (hafta), supposed to (sposta), start, had better, have got to (gotta)*	

[a]These uses of auxiliary *do* are often referred to as constructions with "dummy" or **periphrastic** *do* because *do* carries no semantic content—it simply completes the grammatical construction. If another auxiliary verb is present, *not* comes after that auxiliary (e.g., *I will not go*).

[b]Marginal auxiliaries involve lexical verbs that have come to function also as auxiliaries.

Modal auxiliary verbs can be categorized as **epistemic** (or what is necessary/possible given known facts or conditions) or **deontic** (expressing obligation, permission). The following pairs help illustrate the difference (Huddleston and Pullum 2002):

Epistemic	Deontic
He must have overslept.	*He must apologize.*
She may be ill.	*She may take as many as she needs.*
You can't have read the instructions.	*You can't smoke in here.*
The storm should be over soon.	*We should call the police.*

The modals are sometimes referred to as "defective" verbs because they do not behave morphologically like other verbs:

a. they do not inflect for third-person singular: **he cans, *she mays*

b. they do not inflect for the present participle: **is shalling, *were musting*

c. they do not inflect for the past participle: **have mayed, *had could(ed)*

d. they do not form an infinitive with *to*: **to must*

Unlike lexical verbs, auxiliaries also can have negative contracted forms (*can't, isn't, won't*) and sometimes can form contractions themselves with subjects (*she will* ⟶ *she'll*).

All auxiliaries appear before the main verb of the clause. Two possible syntactic tests for all auxiliaries except *be* and *have* involve questions and negative constructions. Auxiliaries can appear in these two syntactic spots:

_____NP V$_{inf}$?	*Does he walk? Will he go?*
_____not V$_{inf}$.	*might not walk, should not go*

Although Standard English does not typically allow multiple modals in a row, it does allow multiple auxiliaries in a row. The ordering of multiple auxiliaries follows a set pattern, as described below. Each auxiliary also requires a specific form (e.g., the past participle or infinitive form) of the subsequent verb, be it another auxiliary or the main verb. The required affix hops to the next verb in the string, as shown below.

(MODAL + [INF. FORM]) + (HAVE (+ *-ed/-en*]) + (BE [+ *-ing*]) + (BE [+ *-ed/-en*]) + MAIN VERB
PERFECT   PROGRESSIVE   PASSIVE

In the equation above, the form required by the auxiliary verb (e.g., *-ed/-en* or *-ing*) distributes forward to the next verb in the sequence. For example, modals require the bare infinitive form, and the progressive *be* always requires the present participle, so you will get the following constructions:

will study (bare form)

will be (bare form) *studying* (present participle)

Four auxiliaries in a row will look like: *will have been being studied*. Here you can see how the marginal auxiliaries don't behave quite like the other auxiliaries. For example, if we insert *have to*, we can get an even longer string with a double modal: *the material will have had to have been being studied.*

Standard varieties of English do not allow double modals, but nonstandard varieties often use them systematically. For example, in Southern American English you will hear *might could* or *may can*. Southern American English also employs the modal *fixin to* to express future time (*I'm fixin to go to school*). African American English employs invariant *be* to mark habitual aspect (*I be working all the time*), *done* to mark completive aspect (*I done studied* 'I finished studying'), and stressed *BIN* to mark remote perfect aspect (*I BIN studied* 'I studied a while/long time ago').

Challenges to Categorization

In the discussion of verbs earlier, we mentioned that the transitive/intransitive categorization of verbs in English may not be especially useful, given how many verbs can be classified as both. There are many other grammatical constructions that challenge traditional grammatical categories. We discuss three here: *-ing* forms, noun modifiers, and *yes/no*.

The Suffix *-ing*

The suffix *-ing* has several functions, some of them inflectional and some derivational. The suffix *-ing* is inflectional when it signals that a verb is being used in a progressive construction, such as *The students are hoping to learn why people say hopefully is wrong*. As we discussed in Chapter 4, *-ing* can also function as a derivational suffix that creates gerunds, or nouns created from verbs. For example:

> *Studying grammar cheers me up on a gloomy day.*
>
> *We all love studying.*

The derivational *-ing* form also appears in nouns that do not refer directly to the action of the related verb but rather, for example, to a finished product or metaphorical result: *a building, an opening.*

In addition, *-ing* forms can act as modifiers:

> *Reading his grammar book over and over, he found enlightenment.*
>
> *The words streaming out of the teacher's mouth inspired the students to learn more grammar.*
>
> *The beeping phone reminded the student to call her mother to tell her all about -ing forms.*

These *-ing* forms, which function as modifiers of nouns, do not act like all other adjectives, even when they appear between the determiner and the noun in a construction like *the beeping phone*. For example, you cannot say **the very beeping phone* or **beepinger/more beeping*. So here's the open question: Should we consider this use of *-ing* derivational or inflectional? We could argue that this derivational use of *-ing* creates modifiers that function in many ways like adjectives. Or we could argue that the construction stems from an inflectional use of *-ing*, namely, the present participle: *the beeping phone* could be interpreted as a shortened and transformed (i.e., the parts have been moved) realization of *the phone that is beeping*.

Some modifying *-ing* forms have become fossilized as adjectives and behave like all other adjectives. Examples are *baffling* or *confusing*.

A Question to Discuss

What Can Phonology Reveal about Modifying *-ing* Forms?

The derivational *-ing* that creates gerunds and the inflectional *-ing* that creates present participles can be distinguished phonologically with speakers who "drop their *g*'s" or use /n/ rather than /ŋ/ on present participles. These speakers still typically use /ŋ/ in gerunds.

Where do modifying *-ing* forms fall? Do speakers who use /n/ in present participles (e.g., *the dog's barking*) also use /n/ when the *-ing* form is a modifier (e.g., *the barking dog*) or /ŋ/? What do you hear when you listen to the people around you?

Noun Modifiers

Nouns can be used as noun modifiers. Over the past two to three centuries, the use of several nouns, or strings of nouns, to modify one head noun has become increasingly common. We can now create quite long strings this way:

> *my English class textbook*
>
> *my English class textbook cover*
>
> *my English class grammar textbook cover image*
>
> *the Computer Science Department Web directory homepage search engine*
>
> *the Smithton University Computer Science Department Web directory homepage search engine*

How do we want to categorize these modifying nouns? They occur between the determiner(s) and the head noun, like adjectives. But they do not behave like adjectives morphologically (**an English class textbookest cover*), and they can appear only in attributive position (**the cover is English class textbook*). If there are adjectives describing the head noun, they typically appear before the string of modifying nouns: *my fascinating English class textbook*, not **my English class fascinating textbook*. In this way, they seem to act almost like long compound nouns. But the stress patterns indicate that they are not compound nouns. How would you categorize them?

Yes and No

What part of speech is *yes*? And what about *no*? First, we can eliminate some of the minor uses of *yes/no:*

> Noun: *There were three yeses and one no in the final vote.*
>
> Verb: *He just yeses me all day.*
>
> Interjection: *Yes! Great shot!*
>
> Noun modifier or part of noun-noun compound: *yes vote, no vote, yes-man.*

But what is *yes* doing in the following dialogue?

> *Do you have a position on what part of speech yes is?*
>
> *Yes, I do.*

Will you tell me?

<u>*Yes*</u>.

One persuasive argument is that *yes* is a sentence adverb here (an adverb modifying the whole sentence), expressing an affirmative response to a posed question, request, or invitation. In this way, it is expressing meaning tied to the pragmatics of the conversation. Given its position at the margins of the discourse, it could also arguably be a discourse marker, one of the "little words" that structure turns in conversation (see Chapter 8). Can adverbs sit alone in response to a question? Clearly. (Just to answer the question twice.) Can discourse markers? Well. Um.

These examples highlight the complexity of grammar and its ability to elude some of the categories that we create and impose on it. Some grammatical descriptions of English are still relics of early seventeenth- and eighteenth-century English grammars, which were based on Latin, and some represent earlier stages of English. In any case, the flexibility of language often bends the boundaries of the grammatical categories listed in grammar books.

Special Focus: Descriptive Syntax and Prescriptive Rules

In the context of this descriptive approach to grammatical categories and how words work grammatically, let's reexamine a few common prescriptive usage rules, including where they originated and how they correspond to usage. We've already discussed *good/well* and *lie/lay*. Here are five more contested points of usage. Much of the historical information here comes from *Merriam-Webster's Dictionary of English Usage* and the *American Heritage Book of English Usage,* both of which we encourage you to consult for similar information about other usage questions.

Hopefully

In the grammar book *Woe Is I*, Patricia O'Conner (1996, 84) writes, "By now it's probably hopeless to resist the misuse of *hopefully*." Many grammar pundits believe, or at least tell us, that we should not use *hopefully* as a sentence adverb. "In an ideal world," O'Conner goes on to say, "it wouldn't be used to replace a phrase like 'It is hoped' or 'I hope' " (84). Why does this meaning of *hopefully* get categorized as a misuse?

The adverb *hopefully* historically stems from the adjective *hopeful* and can still be used as an adverb meaning 'full of hope': *He was expecting her call, and he answered the phone hopefully.* In common usage, however, *hopefully* now most frequently functions as a sentence adverb, expressing the speaker's (or writer's) attitude rather than the grammatical subject's attitude. As a sentence adverb, *hopefully* means something like 'I/we hope that ___.' The authors of this textbook could honestly say, "Hopefully you are finding grammar more interesting than you expected." But there are also ambiguous instances in which *hopefully* could be interpreted either as 'full of hope' or as a sentence adverb: *He hopefully opened the package I sent him last week.* Many if not most speakers would first interpret this statement to mean 'I hope he opened the package'. A few might first think that *hopefully* is describing *how* he opened the package.

There is nothing wrong with sentence adverbs, and many of the older ones are well established in usage: *frankly, clearly, interestingly.* Consider Rhett Butler's line from

Gone with the Wind: "Frankly, my dear, I don't give a damn." Censors wanted to change this line, but not because of the sentence adverb. The "problem" with *hopefully* is that its use as a sentence adverb is relatively new. It was well established as a sentence adverb by the 1930s, but that use took off in the 1960s. Some people, including some grammar book writers, noticed and stigmatized the new, "trendy" usage as ungrammatical or as a misuse of *hopefully*.

Split Infinitive

A split infinitive occurs when an adverb, an adverbial, or *not* is placed between the particle *to* and the bare infinitive form of a verb, thereby splitting the two parts of the verb infinitive: *to safely return, to seriously study, to better serve*. The most famous split infinitive of them all occurs in the opening words of each *Star Trek* episode: *to boldly go where no man has gone before*.

The split infinitive has been relatively common in written English since the end of the eighteenth century, and we have evidence for it as early as the thirteenth century. Interestingly (just to use a sentence adverb), no one is sure where the condemnation of the split infinitive originates. The earliest prescription that has been located, in 1834, appears in a letter to the editor of *The New England Magazine*, and condemns the split infinitive because it is "uneducated" (Bailey 2006). In 1840, the British editor John Taylor argued against the split infinitive, as "disagreeable," because English should be truer to its Germanic roots, in which infinitives are one word (Perales-Escudero 2011).

By the end of the nineteenth century, usage guides commonly stated that "grammarians" condemned the construction, and soon the guides could look to each other for confirmation of the perceived undesirability of such a construction—even if they added a note that perhaps split infinitives weren't so terrible after all. In 1998, the newly published *Oxford American Desk Dictionary* made newspaper headlines when it stated that the ban on split infinitives can lead to "awkward, stilted sentences." Samuel Pickering, a professor of English at the University of Connecticut, is said to have responded: "I do not dine with those who split infinitives." Although many other English teachers have never heard or have chosen not to heed this official grammatical proclamation, you are "officially" free to split an infinitive if it sounds better to do so in your writing. You've probably been splitting infinitives in your speech for years anyway, as English speakers have been doing for centuries. Just be warned that you will have to forego a meal with Professor Pickering!

Sentence-Final Prepositions

In the seventeenth century, John Dryden criticized Ben Jonson's use of sentence-final prepositions in phrases such as *the bodies that those souls were frighted from*. Dryden objected to the stranded *from* at the end of the sentence. (Jonson had already died, so we cannot know how he would have defended this usage.) Commentators in the eighteenth century turned this grammatical criticism into a grammatical rule: avoid ending sentences with a preposition. But is this a rule that you must adhere to? In a sentence or a question such as the previous one, it is easy to separate the preposition from the relative pronoun (*that*) which appears at the beginning of the embedded clause. The alternate version can sound very formal: *But is this a rule to which you must adhere?*

Since the beginning of the twentieth century, many influential grammarians have accepted sentence-final prepositions, but the public perception of their wrongness persists. Some critics also object to the particles at the end of phrasal verbs (*freak out, call up*, etc.) if they appear at the end of a sentence. But these aren't really prepositions, and sometimes they truly cannot be moved anywhere else. As Winston Churchill is often quoted as saying, in response to a civil servant's criticism of a sentence Churchill had ended with a preposition: "This is the kind of pedantic nonsense up with which I will not put!" (The story survives in several versions, each with a slightly different Churchill quotation.)

Its/It's

In Boston, England, a retired copy editor and reporter named John Richards patrols the vicinity for public apostrophe misuse. Using the letterhead of the Apostrophe Protection Society, which he founded with his son, he sends letters to businesses to alert them to their incorrect usage of this punctuation mark: "apple's" in a grocery store or "shopper's car park" in a parking lot. Perhaps the most common mistake with the apostrophe is the confusion of *it's* and *its*. Why is this so confusing? The source of the mix-up is the double function of -*'s*: it marks contractions (e.g., *John's* for *John is*) and possessives (e.g., *John's*).

In the eighteenth century, the personal pronouns could be written either with or without the apostrophe: *their's* and *theirs*, *your's* and *yours*. But in current usage, the personal pronouns consistently adhere to their own rule for forming the possessive: a final -*s* with no apostrophe. None of the personal pronouns other than *it* can contract with *is* in such a way as to promote confusion between the contracted form and the possessive (e.g., *she's* versus *hers*, *he's* versus *his*).

Writers also sometimes find themselves confused about words that end with an *s*. Do they add the possessive apostrophe and then another *s*? Is it *Tess'* or *Tess's*, *Charlie Jones'* or *Charlie Jones's*? This is fundamentally a spelling convention and not a grammatical question. In these two instances, most usage guides recommend both the apostrophe and the *s*, as this additional morpheme in the spelling accurately reflects the pronunciation, which involves an additional syllable. But if all of Charlie Jones's family owned something, it would be the *Joneses' thing* (with the apostrophe but no additional *s*).

It has taken a long time in the history of English spelling for the apostrophe to settle down in its conventions. John Richards is trying to fix apostrophe rules where they are. But just over 100 miles away, the Birmingham City Council removed possessive apostrophes from its street signs in January 2009. It wouldn't be surprising if the apostrophe weren't finished moving yet.

Singular Generic They

Let's think about third-person pronouns. We have *he* for a male, *she* for a female, and *it* for a thing. But what about a person whose gender is unknown, unspecified, or irrelevant? English has no singular generic third-person pronoun for just these situations, or so some people say.

As a singular generic pronoun, the pronoun *one* can be awkward and at times too formal. It also does not work particularly well referring back to another noun: **A student should know one's grammar*. Over the past century, many new pronouns have been suggested (e.g., *heshe, E, thon*), but none has met with any success. Some middle and high schoolers in Baltimore may now use *yo* as a singular generic third-person pronoun (e.g., *Yo handin' out papers* 'She/they (the teacher) is handing out papers' and *Peep yo* 'Look at him'), but this pronoun does not (at least yet) seem to have spread beyond Baltimore (Stotko and Troyer 2007). At this point, almost all usage guides state that singular generic *he* is sexist, as it excludes females in its reference. As a replacement, we can write *he or she*, but this can be awkward and wordy. It is sometimes suggested that we alternate pronouns every paragraph or so, but this can get confusing as the gender of a referent seems to shift. Another alternative in some situations is to use the plural (e.g., *Students should know their grammar*).

What about singular *they*? Most grammar books state that *they* is grammatically incorrect in these constructions because it violates number agreement. It is often used in reference to words like *everyone* (e.g., *Everyone who went to the Trekkie conference said they loved the Klingon panel*) because *everyone* is semantically plural. However, in current spoken American English, many speakers commonly hear and use *they* in sentences such as: "I was talking to a friend of mine and they said that the movie is terrible." In this sentence, *they* is clearly singular, as it is referring back to one friend. Historical studies indicate that *they* has been used as a singular for centuries, and there is an entire Web site (www.crossmyt.com/hc/linghebr/austheir.html) cataloging Jane Austen's use of singular generic *their*.

Historically, *they* is also not the only plural pronoun to make this kind of move to a singular function. English used to make a distinction between the singular and plural in the second person with *thou* (singular) and *ye* (plural). Eventually *you* took on both singular and plural functions, and it kept its plural verb agreement in Standard English (with *are*, not *is*) even when the referent is clearly singular: e.g., *Anne, you are on your soapbox*. As the pronoun *you* proves, it is possible for a pronoun to be both singular and plural, depending on context. English had a gap in the singular third-person pronouns (generic reference), and *they* seems to have filled it more successfully than invented pronouns or the lengthier *he or she*. It may take time, however, for grammar books to endorse this spoken construction as acceptable in the written language.

☑ Summary

- Syntax describes: (1) the systematic ways in which words are combined to create well-formed phrases, clauses, and sentences; and (2) the systematic ways in which clauses and sentences are combined to create more complex sentences. Parts of speech or lexical categories describe classes of words that behave similarly in the grammar of a language.

- There are four open-class lexical categories, and there are often subcategories within each category:
  - Nouns: countable/uncountable
  - Adjectives
  - Verbs: transitive/intransitive/ditransitive/linking/object-predicative
  - Adverbs: temporal/manner/discourse

- There are five closed-class lexical categories discussed in this chapter, with some relevant subcategories:
  - Prepositions
  - Conjunctions: coordinating/correlative/subordinating (including complementizers)
  - Pronouns: personal/indefinite/interrogative/demonstrative/relative
  - Determiners: predeterminer/central determiner/postdeterminer
  - Auxiliary verbs: primary/modal/marginal
- Within all of these lexical categories, we can describe words by their morphological forms and typical syntactic position.

Suggested Reading

Comprehensive descriptive grammars are probably the best resource for more information, such as Sidney Greenbaum's *Oxford English Grammar* (1996), Rodney Huddleston and Geoffrey K. Pullum's *Cambridge Grammar of the English Language* (2002), Randolph Quirk and Sidney Greenbaum's *A Student's Grammar of the English Language* (1990), *A Comprehensive Grammar of the English Language* (1985) by Randolph Quirk et al., and *The Longman Grammar of Spoken and Written English* (1999) by Douglas Biber et al. Useful chapters on word classes can be found in *Understanding English Grammar* (1995) by Ronald Wardhaugh and in *Analyzing English Grammar* (4th ed., 2004) by Thomas P. Klammer et al.

Exercises
Exercise 5.1 Nouns

1. Are any of the following nouns exclusively countable or uncountable regardless of context?

stuff	milk	laundry	beer
snow	media	human	weather
anxiety	grammar	homework	jeans

2. Ask ten people to fill out the survey shown below. Then, check two dictionaries to see what plural forms each dictionary provides. Finally, summarize and analyze your survey results about how speakers form the plural of these borrowed and/or irregular nouns, particularly compared to the dictionary results.

   one syllabus, many _____
   one ox, many _____
   one fish, many _____
   one antenna, many _____
   one hippopotamus, many _____
   one octopus, many _____
   one nucleus, many _____
   one focus, many _____

3. A challenge: How long a string of noun modifiers, all modifying one head noun, can you create?

Exercise 5.2   Adjectives

1. Some adjectives have different meanings in attributive and predicative position. For example, these two sentences mean dramatically different things about the validity of the theory in question:

Attributive: *His theory was true hogwash.*

Predicative: *His theory was true.*

Come up with similar examples that demonstrate how the following adjectives have different meanings in attributive and predicative position: *late, big, real, perfect, apparent.*

2. Use the *OED* to determine why the adjective is placed second in *attorney general, postmaster general,* and *notary public.* What do you think the plural form is for each of these position descriptions? Now search the Corpus of Contemporary American English (COCA) to see how usage compares to your intuition about the plural forms. (The phrase *the light fantastic,* which most speakers now interpret as a noun-adjective combination, historically is an adjective-adjective combination, from the phrase *light fantastic toe.*)

3. For the following two-syllable adjectives, provide the most "natural sounding" comparative and superlative forms. Can you identify any patterns?

pleasant	baffling	focused	silly
playful	lovely	nymphlike	fussy
neutral	hopeful	manly	catlike
skinny	honest	nimble	gentle
careful	subtle	famous	
boring	faithful	grotesque	

Why can the three-syllable adjectives *unhappy* and *unhealthy* take the inflectional endings *-er* and *-est*?

Exercise 5.3   Verbs

1. Fill out the chart in Table 5.7 for the irregular verbs *be, have, do,* and *go.*

TABLE 5.7   **Irregular Verb Forms**

	be	*have*	*do*	*go*
Bare/infinitive form				
Third-person singular present tense form				
Past tense form				
Present participle				
Past participle				

2. Provide example sentences for each of the following:

   a. a form of *be* as a main verb

   b. a form of *be* as an auxiliary verb in a progressive construction

   c. a form of *be* as an auxiliary verb in a passive construction

   d. a form of *have* as a main verb

   e. a form of *have* as an auxiliary verb in a present perfect construction

   f. a form of *have* as an auxiliary verb in a past perfect construction

   g. a form of *do* as a main verb

   h. a form of *do* as an auxiliary verb in a negated construction

   i. a form of *do* as an auxiliary verb in a question

   j. a form of *do* as an auxiliary verb in an emphatic construction

3. The verb *fly* 'to move through the air on wings' is an irregular verb that forms the past tense through a vowel change (*flew*). So why, when a baseball or softball player hits a fly ball into the outfield and an outfielder catches it, do we say the player *flied out*?

4. For each of the following verbs, determine if it can be used transitively, intransitively, and/or ditransitively. Provide an example in the form of a sentence for each possible use.

to have	to sit	to keep	to forget
to lend	to receive	to buy	to make
to do	to walk		

5. The present tense can be used to express future time in some but not all circumstances. Why do two of these example sentences sound odd?

   > I take the exam tomorrow.
   > *I pass the exam tomorrow.
   >
   > We are having dinner at 7:00 tonight.
   > *We are having a good time at 7:00 tonight.

6. What is the semantic difference between the simple past and present perfect? Look at the following sentences and then describe the patterns of difference in meaning that you discover. Then compare answers with your classmates. Can you agree on differences in meaning? Do you discover that there are dialectal differences?

   > Did you ever cheat on your boyfriend?
   > Have you ever cheated on your boyfriend?
   >
   > We did our homework already.
   > We've done our homework already.
   >
   > I discovered that I love grammar.
   > I've discovered that I love grammar.
   >
   > I learned to cook Indian food.
   > I've learned to cook Indian food.

7. Let's consider the verb *depend on* as a representative of the class of verbs that require a prepositional phrase after them. These verbs are often described as a subclass of intransitive verbs because they do not take a direct object.

> I depend on my family.
> *I depend my family.

But these verbs do not behave exactly like other intransitive verbs, which could be used as evidence to argue for a sixth class of verbs: prepositional verbs. Note that these are not the same as phrasal verbs and do not behave the same way. For example, you cannot say **depend it on*. Come up with at least one convincing argument on each side (intransitive verbs versus prepositional verbs), and then argue for the one you find more convincing.

Exercise 5.4   Adverbs

1. Why should *very* and *really* be considered adverbs? Justify your answer with examples. Would you consider them typical adverbs? Why or why not?

2. Provide five examples in which *all* functions as an adverb. Ensure that your examples capture *all* modifying verbs, adjectives, and adverbs.

Exercise 5.5   Pronouns

In each of the following sentences, determine whether the grammatical construction requires a subject or object form of the pronoun. Make a note next to the sentences in which the "correct" grammatical choice feels awkward to you. Why do you think these constructions might create more confusion between pronouns than the others? Compare your results with your classmates'. Do you think you have evidence for change in progress?

a. The message was sent to _____ (*him and me, he and I, him and I, he and me*).

b. _____ went to the movies (*Me and her, I and she, She and me, She and I*).

c. No, the present is for _____ (*me, I*).

d. My parents gave _____ (*him and me, he and I, him and I, he and me*) a gift.

e. She is much faster than _____ (*me, I*).

f. If you were to ask my friends and (*me, I*), we would say pronouns are definitely confusing.

g. We lent _____ (*him, he*) a book.

h. _____ (*Who, Whom*) is this present for?

i. To _____ (*who, whom*) did you give the present?

j. I gave the present to the man _____ (*who, whom*) I love.

k. The person _____ (*who, whom*) sold me the present said it could win hearts.

l. I wish I were the person _____ (*who, whom*) received gifts from me!

Exercise 5.6   Determiners

1. What kind of determiners are *such* and *many*: predeterminers, central determiners, or postdeterminers? Justify your answer.

2. Provide evidence that the possessive form *Michael's* functions like a determiner.

3. A challenge: How many determiners can you get in a row before a noun?

Exercise 5.7   Modal Auxiliaries

Are the following modal auxiliaries epistemic or deontic?

a. I must start doing yoga.

b. Look at her touch her toes: she must be doing yoga regularly.

c. I will start doing yoga.

d. She can do yoga.

e. She can't do yoga tomorrow.

f. Yoga should be good for you.

g. The yoga class should be happening tomorrow at 5:00.

h. If he doesn't want to get injured, he should do yoga.

i. He shouldn't be doing yoga with the flu.

j. He must not have been doing yoga right to have twisted his neck like that.

k. He may go see a doctor about his neck.

l. May we please have an example sentence that does not involve yoga?

Chapter **6**

English Syntax: Phrases, Clauses, and Sentences

Is this man hunting ducks or ducking out? The syntax of garden path sentences can lead us astray.

The man who hunts ducks out occasionally. Did you read that sentence at least a couple of times before moving on to this one? Although you may not believe it, it *is* a grammatical sentence of English. It is called a "garden path sentence" because it leads you down the proverbial garden path, only for you to discover that you have misparsed the sentence—that is, misinterpreted the function of some of the words. You probably read *who hunts ducks* as a complete clause, all modifying the subject *the man*. You were, therefore, expecting another verb to come on the heels of *ducks* to indicate what the man who hunts ducks did: perhaps he headed out into the fields or decided to give up the sport. You were not expecting the words *out occasionally*—neither of which is a verb. As a speaker of English, you know that you need another verb to

163

complete the main clause, so you realize something has gone terribly wrong in your reading of this sentence.

If you are like the subjects described in the study in Steven Pinker's book *The Language Instinct* (1994), your eyes probably jumped back to the potentially ambiguous word *ducks* to see if you could find a verb for the main clause. And sure enough: *ducks* can be reparsed as a third-person singular verb in the present tense, rather than as a plural noun functioning as the object of *hunts*, such that the sentence describes a man (who hunts) who ducks out. So what happened in your original reading of the sentence? Because the verb *hunt* often functions transitively (i.e., it takes a direct object), you probably used your experience of that frequency to make a well-informed guess about how to understand the grammatically ambiguous word *ducks*, interpreting it as the object and then expecting that the verb of the main clause would come next. When that did not happen, you realized that you had made a wrong guess in parsing the structure. The point is that our brains rely on knowledge of grammatical patterns—how words combine to make grammatical phrases, clauses, and sentences—and on knowledge of the frequency of grammatical patterns, to interpret strings of words as they occur, in speech or in writing. We don't just interpret each word as it occurs; we understand words as functioning in grammatical contexts, in systematic, predictable relationships with other words. In this case, we hear or read *who hunts ducks* and parse that as a complete clause, which allows us to "close" that structure, return our focus to the main clause (*The man* . . .), and anticipate the verb for that clause.

Whenever we talk, we employ our knowledge of grammatical rules to combine some of the thousands of words that we know into new, grammatical utterances. Our audience can then interpret our brand-new combinations by employing their knowledge of the same grammatical rules. Garden path sentences can be funny because they highlight our initial grammatical parsing going astray (see if you can figure out this one: *The horse raced past the barn fell*). But we are fully capable of going back and reparsing any ambiguous sentence according to a different set of grammatical structures—that is all part of our linguistic competence.

In this chapter, we focus on these grammatical structures. How do our brains know how to generate entirely new and yet entirely grammatical sentences? How do we know how to parse the entirely new sentences created by others? The answer is syntax. Syntax encompasses the set of descriptive rules for how words can combine into phrases, phrases into clauses, and clauses into sentences. Syntax, according to Noam Chomsky, also governs the grammatical structures possible in language.

Generative Grammar

What are we trying to describe when we describe the grammar of a language? One possible answer is all the ways that words can be combined systematically into phrases, clauses, and sentences. To achieve this goal, we could collect a lot of language data (and it would take a lot) and then analyze which grammatical patterns are possible and which are not. This descriptive approach to grammar was popular in the first half of the twentieth century, particularly in the linguistic study of indigenous languages. Now, with large electronic corpora of English available, some corpus linguists are working to use corpus data to describe English grammar comprehensively as it is spoken and written (for example, in the *Longman Grammar of Spoken and Written English*).

Beginning in the 1950s, Noam Chomsky changed the linguistic playing field by changing the goals of syntactic study—and linguistics more generally. He began something of a revolution in linguistics and cognitive science. Chomsky argued that the goal is not to bring order to or find patterns in observable language behavior ("externalized language," as he called it). The goal is to describe what an individual speaker *knows*— the grammatical knowledge that allows a speaker to generate these patterns ("internalized language"). In other words, Chomsky shifted the focus of syntax from description to something more theoretical.

Chomsky has often outlined three aims for linguistic study:

1. What constitutes knowledge of language?
2. How is such knowledge acquired?
3. How is such knowledge put to use?

The second and third questions depend on the first: we need to establish what the knowledge is before we can determine how it is acquired or put to use. And, almost needless to say, the first question is an ambitious one!

In this chapter, we introduce Chomsky's approach to the first question (what constitutes knowledge of language, or linguistic competence), as well as how we would describe some of the fundamental aspects of English syntax along these lines. Chomsky's theory was originally called Generative Grammar because it aims to specify the membership of the set of all grammatical sentences in a language (an extension of the mathematical definition of *generate*)—in other words, it proposes a formal set of rules that allow all possible grammatical constructions and disallow ungrammatical ones. Remember, Chomsky's goal is to describe what speakers *know*, often subconsciously, about grammar. Today, many names apply to the web of related theories developed by Chomsky and his numerous followers: among them, Transformational Grammar, Transformational Generative Grammar, Standard Theory and Extended Standard Theory, Government and Binding Theory, and Minimalism.

Generative grammar is a scientific theory created to explain how language is possible and how it happens that any child can learn any language. As such, it is what Chomsky calls an "explanatorily adequate" theory. It is a theory that does not simply explain what is possible but rather articulates the rules that make some things possible and others not possible. For example, an explanatorily adequate theory explains why in English it is possible to say (grammatically):

What did you buy?

and why it is not possible to say (grammatically):

What did you buy bread and?

We use language every day (our linguistic performance) without thinking about what underlies our ability to speak grammatically. We don't need to explicitly describe our linguistic knowledge to use it every day. But describing the complex, often subconscious grammatical knowledge of a language—and of language generally—is central to generative grammar. For Chomsky and his followers, linguistic competence is necessarily prior to linguistic performance. They assert that linguistic competence is, therefore, more interesting than linguistic performance, and it is the obvious, logical object of linguistic study. These Chomskyan models of syntactic knowledge will be our primary focus here.

Universal Grammar

Universal Grammar is fundamental to Chomsky's conception of linguistic competence. Language distinguishes human beings from all other animals. And all human beings, unless they suffer circumstances of extreme deprivation, acquire language in similar ways. All human languages share certain fundamental structural properties. How do we explain this phenomenon? To answer this question, Chomsky proposed the concept of **Universal Grammar**: "the system of principles, conditions, and rules that are elements or properties of all human languages" (1975, 29). This system guides the acquisition of any language and, essentially, defines what language is.

Universal Grammar is *not* the grammar of any one language—it is not nearly that specific. For example, one fundamental principle holds that in all human languages, sentence structure depends on groupings of words rather than linear strings. Linear strings are like numbered lists of equal elements: word #1, word #2, word #3, and so on. Computers rely on linear strings (0 1 1 0 0 1 1 1 0 1 and so on), but the human language faculty does not. The human language faculty groups strings of words into phrases. For example, if we want to make a yes-no question from a statement, sometimes we reverse the first and second words:

Syntax will change my life. ⟶ *Will syntax change my life?*

But no human grammar would count on that kind of linear order to create a rule such as "Always reverse the first and second word for yes-no questions." Often reversing the first and second words creates nonsense:

The syntax book was dog-eared from heavy use. ⟶
* Syntax the book was dog-eared from heavy use?

We know that we need to move the whole phrase *the syntax book* together, reversing that phrase with the verb, because it functions as one unit in the sentence:

Was the syntax book dog-eared from heavy use?

The rules of language—of all languages—depend on these smaller units or groupings, not on strict linear order. (We talk more about these groupings, or constituents, in the next section.)

So Universal Grammar could be thought of more like a toolkit in the brain that allows human babies to acquire the grammar of whatever language they encounter. As we discuss in Chapter 10, babies do not just imitate adults when they learn language: they seem to use

A Scholar to Know

Noam Chomsky (1928–)

Noam Chomsky was born in Philadelphia in 1928 and earned his undergraduate and graduate degrees in linguistics from the University of Pennsylvania. He joined the faculty of the Massachusetts Institute of Technology in 1955; he retired from teaching there in 1988 but remains a very active scholar. Chomsky is among the ten most cited authors of all time, up there with Freud and Aristotle.

Generative grammar began with Chomsky's dissertation, *Transformational Analysis* (1955), which formed the basis for his first book, *Syntactic Structures* (1957), and a book of broader scope, *The Logical Structure of Linguistic Theory*, published in 1975 but first circulated in 1955. He refined his theory in several other books, notably *Aspects of the Theory of Syntax* (1965), *Cartesian Linguistics* (1966), *Language and the Mind* (1968), *Rules and Representations* (1980), *Lectures on Government and Binding* (1981), and *The Minimalist Program* (1995). He has written extensively, not only on language, mind, and philosophy but also on social and political issues, especially as a critic of America's foreign policy, from the Vietnam War to the present day.

Among modern thinkers, Chomsky most resembles Bertrand Russell (1872–1970), the British logician, philosopher, and social theorist. Both began their careers by pointing out new directions in technical subfields of established disciplines (mathematics for Russell, linguistics for Chomsky), but later both wrote more generally about their professional subjects and also about social and political activity in the world around them. They became public intellectuals, not only professors but also protestors profoundly committed to both Truth and Justice. As they voiced dissenting views often uncomfortably at odds with conventional wisdom, they became controversial figures. Russell wrote more books than he lived years (he lived ninety-eight of them), and Chomsky is likely to clear that bar as well.

language data to figure out the grammatical rules of a language—rules that allow them to create new, never-heard-before utterances.

Constituents and Hierarchies

The syntax of all languages depends on groupings of words, called constituents. **Constituents** are syntactic units (words that work together) that fit into larger units that in turn fit into or constitute sentences. Sentences are not like trains. Trains depend on linear order. A train is built by hooking one car onto the next until the train is complete, and each car is hooked as closely to the car before it as the car after it. In a sentence, some words are more closely related to each other than to the words on either side of them; together, these make a unit or constituent, which then may be closely related to a neighboring constituent to form an even larger constituent. Take the sentence:

The perplexed students reread the chapter in the book.

Clearly, *the, perplexed,* and *students* are all closely related and work together as a unit—in this case, a noun phrase. *The* and *chapter,* as well as *the* and *book,* work together the same way. The word *in* is working together with *the book* (already a constituent), rather than with the preceding noun phrase *the chapter*, to make a prepositional phrase, which then connects with *the chapter* to make an even bigger noun phrase: *the chapter in the book*. Finally, *reread* connects with *the chapter in the book* to create a verb phrase with a verb and a direct object. We could represent this constituent structure by underlining the constituents, first the smallest ones and then the bigger ones in which they fit:

The perplexed students reread the chapter in <u>the book</u>.

———————

—————————

———————————

As you can see, some constituents are embedded within other constituents, in a hierarchical structure.

Constituent Hierarchies

There are constituents at every level of structure. Arguably, every word is a constituent in and of itself. Words are then combined into **phrases,** and phrases are combined to form **clauses.** A **sentence** can be one or more clauses. The relations among words, phrases, clauses, and sentences are hierarchical:

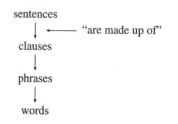

In Chapter 5, we covered the major types of lexical categories, both open and closed class. In English, there are five types of phrases: noun phrase (NP), verb phrase (VP), adjective phrase (ADJP), adverb phrase (ADVP), and prepositional phrase (PP). Every full clause is composed of an NP that functions as the subject and a VP that functions as the predicate. Other types of phrases and even clauses can be embedded in those.

Clauses and Sentences

Every sentence contains at least one clause, and many, like this sentence itself, contain more. Some clauses are independent, and some are dependent or subordinate. An **independent clause** may be a sentence itself, as in *The perplexed students reread the chapter.* Two or more independent clauses can be combined into a **compound sentence,** joined either by a coordinating conjunction or, in the written language, by punctuation like the semicolon or colon.

Coordinating conjunction:	*The students were perplexed and they reread the chapter.*
	The chapter perplexed the students, so they reread it.
Punctuation:	*The students were perplexed; they reread the chapter.*

A **dependent** or **subordinate clause** is not itself a sentence—it cannot stand alone. Dependent clauses are embedded or inserted into an independent clause and often modify a constituent in it or the entire independent clause. For example:

The students, who were perplexed by the material, decided to reread the chapter.

Because they remained perplexed, the students decided to reread the chapter.

These examples show how an independent clause can be combined with a dependent or subordinate clause to form a **complex sentence**. Note how the dependent clauses (*who were perplexed by the material* or *because they remained perplexed*) could not stand alone as sentences. Instead, they modify and are embedded in the **main clause**: *the students decided to reread the chapter.*

In English, subordinate clauses fall into three main types.

1. **Adverbial clauses,** often introduced by a subordinating conjunction (e.g., *when, because, after, if, although*), which modify the verb of the main clause:

   After they reread the chapter, the students felt much less perplexed.

2. **Relative clauses,** typically introduced by relative pronouns (*that, which, who, whom, whose*), and typically functioning as adjectivals (constituents that modify nouns or NPs):

   The instructor, who loved syntax, tried to make that love contagious.

3. **Complementizer clauses,** often introduced by *that* or a set of *wh-* words (e.g., *whether, what, when*), which fill the slot of an NP, often to complete a VP (a "complement" is something that completes the structural requirements of a phrase or clause—a complementizer clause can complete a VP):

   The students thought that the instructor was a little off her rocker.

These three types of subordinate clauses can be reduced into participial, gerund, and infinitive phrases, which we discuss later in the chapter. The point here is that these reduced clauses are simply variants of the three main types of subordinate clauses. Here are versions of the three example sentences above with reduced clauses:

Having reread the chapter, the students felt much less perplexed.

The instructor, loving syntax, tried to make that love contagious.

The students thought the instructor to be a little off her rocker.

So let's summarize the two types of hierarchies we have discussed. First, in the constituent hierarchy, words are combined to make phrases, which are combined to make clauses and sentences. Second, clauses alone can compose simple sentences, or they can be combined to create compound or complex sentences.

Constituency Tests

How do you know what is a constituent and what isn't? Below are four generally accepted constituency tests. But before we give these to you, we must issue a warning: these tests are not determinative. Some constituents will satisfy all four; many will satisfy two or maybe only one. Occasionally, a constituent may not satisfy any of these tests. The tests are a helpful guide, however, and work best when complemented by intuition and critical analysis.

Substitution Test Many constituents can be replaced by a single word that does the same syntactic work as the longer constituent and retains a similar meaning. For example, a pronoun can be substituted for a noun phrase. The word *so* can be substituted for many adverb phrases. The auxiliary *do* can be substituted for many verb phrases. If we return to our example sentence, we can insert substitutes for several of the constituents:

		Replaced constituent
They reread the chapter in the book.	$\longrightarrow$	*the perplexed students*
The perplexed students reread it.	$\longrightarrow$	*the chapter in the book*
The perplexed students did.	$\longrightarrow$	*reread the chapter in the book*

There is no substitute for *reread the* or *the perplexed* or *chapter in* because these are not constituents. Yet, there is also no good substitute for *in the book*, but it is still a constituent—illustrating how this test is helpful, but not entirely determinative.

Stand-alone Test Constituents can often stand alone as the response to a question. In fact, the question word also acts as a kind of substitute for the constituent itself. For example:

	Constituent (standing alone)
Who reread the chapter in the book?	*The perplexed students.*
What did the perplexed students reread?	*The chapter in the book.*
What did the perplexed students do?	*Reread the chapter in the book.*

Notice, though, that the constituent *in the book* does not work particularly well with this test. The question "Where did the perplexed students read the chapter?" implies a location for the activity rather than for the chapter. If there were a different prepositional phrase at the end, say *in the library*, that phrase could stand alone as a constituent in response. The prepositional phrase *in the book* can stand alone as a response to the question "Which chapter?" or "Where was the chapter?"—which is arguably a fair question if there is an understood "that is" between *the chapter* and *in the book*.

Movement Test Constituents can sometimes be moved as units. Sometimes this rearrangement of the words sounds awkward but not entirely ungrammatical (especially with properly placed emphasis). For example:

> *The chapter in the book, the students reread.*

Two similar constructions can test for movement:

> *"it is/was _____ that/who . . ."*
> *"_____ is/are who/what . . ."*

For example:

> *It is <u>the perplexed students</u> who reread the chapter in the book.*
> *<u>The chapter in the book</u> is what the perplexed students reread.*

Coordination Test Coordinated structures can also be a useful constituent test. The coordinating conjunctions *and* and *or* must connect equal units. So you can try balancing a unit you think is a constituent with a word whose lexical category you know. For example: *complained and reread the chapter* or *my friends and the perplexed students* or *in their heads or in the book.*

Now that we've established what counts as a constituent and the hierarchical relationship of various constituents, we can return to one of the central questions of generative grammar: How are constituents systematically combined into well-formed, grammatical strings?

Phrase Structure Rules

We know, at such a fundamental level that it seems beyond obvious, that in English *the fabulous teacher* is an acceptable noun phrase. Just as clearly, we know that **fabulous teacher the, *fabulous the teacher, *teacher fabulous the,* and **the teacher fabulous* are not acceptable noun phrases. We also know that if we want to say something more about the fabulous teacher in the form of a sentence, the verb must come after the subject, followed by the direct object if there is one: *the fabulous teacher explained grammar to me,* not **explained the fabulous teacher grammar to me,* or some other variation. Here's the interesting question: How can we systematically account for this knowledge about how to combine words into well-formed phrases, clauses, and sentences, in a way that captures the knowledge of native speakers and that accounts for child language acquisition?

In generative grammar, **phrase structure rules** describe allowable constituents within the syntax of a language. Phrase structure rules are different in every language, but all languages have them. Phrase structure rules, building on the fundamentals of lexical categories, dictate the parts and ordering of different kinds of phrases. These phrases can then be combined and embedded within each other to create clauses and sentences. Phrase structure rules are written this way:

Type of phrase $\longrightarrow$ allowable elements in phrase

The arrow indicates 'consists of'. So NP $\longrightarrow$ DET N would be read "a noun phrase consists of a determiner and a noun." If an element is in parentheses, it is optional. A superscript + means there can be more than one of that element. So NP $\longrightarrow$ (DET) (ADJ$^+$) N (PP$^+$) would be read "a noun phrase consists of a noun possibly preceded by a determiner and/or one or more adjectives and possibly followed by one or more prepositional phrases." Here are some sample NPs:

NP $\longrightarrow$ N	*smoke*
NP $\longrightarrow$ DET N	*the smoke*
NP $\longrightarrow$ DET ADJ N	*the thick smoke*
NP $\longrightarrow$ DET ADJ ADJ N PP	*the thick, smelly smoke in the kitchen*

Phrase structure rules are models of grammatical knowledge, and different theoretical approaches differ in the details and complexity of the rules they present. Below we summarize one relatively basic set of phrase structure rules for the major types of constituent phrases to give you an idea of how these rules work—this list is not exhaustive. (The S stands for sentence or clause.)

S $\longrightarrow$ NP VP

NP $\longrightarrow$ (DET) (ADJ$^+$) N (PP$^+$)

$$\text{ADJP} \longrightarrow (\text{ADV}) \text{ ADJ}$$

$$\text{VP} \longrightarrow (\text{ADVP}^+) \text{ V } (\text{NP/S}) (\text{PP}^+) (\text{ADVP}^+)$$

$$\text{ADVP} \longrightarrow (\text{ADV}) \text{ ADV}$$

$$\text{PP} \longrightarrow \text{P NP}$$

The phrase structure rule for a sentence or clause ($\text{S} \longrightarrow \text{NP VP}$) represents, in a different form, the requirement of a clause we discussed earlier: that it has a subject (the NP) followed by a predicate (the VP).

The rule for the noun phrase above captures the behavior of uncountable nouns and plural countable nouns. Singular countable nouns require a determiner, so you could write a more specific phrase structure rule:

$$\text{NP} \longrightarrow \text{DET } (\text{ADJ}^+) \text{ N}_{\text{sg. count}} (\text{PP}^+)$$

Proper nouns also behave differently in that they typically do not take determiners. They rarely take modifying adjectives or prepositional phrases, but you can imagine possible examples (e.g., *Cher in that dress was quite a sight to see*). A noun phrase can also consist of a pronoun (e.g., *me*):

$$\text{NP} \longrightarrow \text{N}_{\text{pro}}$$

Adjective and adverb phrases are relatively straightforward in this representation. Both can involve adverb modifiers. These adverb modifiers may be intensifiers (*very thoughtful*, *really quickly*), qualifiers (*sort of thoughtful*, *kind of quickly*), or other adverbs (*intensely thoughtful*, *incredibly quickly*). The complicated nature of noun modifiers (e.g., *textbook cover*), which we discussed in Chapter 5, eludes the phrase structure rules for NPs and ADJPs as described earlier.

The majority of prepositional phrases consist of a preposition followed by a noun phrase (e.g., *in my coffee*). But PPs can also combine a preposition with an adverb (*until recently*) or another PP (*from on high*, *from in the car*).

The verb phrase is also more complicated than is captured by the basic rule above: $\text{VP} \longrightarrow (\text{ADVP}^+) \text{ V } (\text{NP}) (\text{PP}^+) (\text{ADVP}^+)$. The rule as it is written captures the behavior of intransitive and transitive verbs. A verb used transitively appears in $\text{V} \longrightarrow \text{V NP}$, and a verb used intransitively in $\text{V} \longrightarrow \text{V}$. Ditransitive verbs take two NPs: $\text{VP} \longrightarrow (\text{ADVP}^+) \text{ V } \text{NP NP } (\text{PP}^+) (\text{ADVP}^+)$. Linking verbs take an NP, an ADJP, or an ADVP. Object-predicative verbs take two NPs or an NP and an ADJP. The general rule captures some of the mobility of the ADVP, which can appear both at the beginning and end of the VP. That the ADVP can also appear before PPs, within the VP (e.g., *He sat down hurriedly in the chair*), raises a question to which we will return: Should the phrase structure rules present every possible location of the ADVP or should there be an additional rule that states that the ADVP can move to a given set of locations?

Syntax is also closely tied to the lexicon. Any given word specifies the type of phrase(s) in which it can appear. For example, the verb *sleep* (in the sense of 'to rest in a state of suspended consciousness') specifies VPs only of the type $\text{VP} \longrightarrow (\text{ADVP}^+) \text{ V } (\text{PP}^+) (\text{ADVP}^+)$. We can sleep on the floor restlessly. The verb *predict* specifies VPs of the type $\text{VP} \longrightarrow (\text{ADVP}^+) \text{ V NP } (\text{PP}^+) (\text{ADVP}^+)$. We typically don't just predict; we predict something.

As we discuss in later sections, subordinate clauses can be embedded in phrases or function like a phrase within a clause. For example, a complementizer clause functions nominally, like an NP.

Form and Function

As we discussed in Chapter 5, it is important always to distinguish form and function with words, and the same holds true with phrases and clauses. For example, an NP typically functions like a noun, which means that within a clause, it can function as the subject, direct or indirect object, subject or object predicative, or object of a preposition. But sometimes an NP modifies another noun, acting more like an adjective in terms of its function. All constituents, no matter their form, that function to modify nouns are called **adjectivals**, some of which will appear after the noun, such as modifying prepositional phrases. In addition, constituents other than NPs can function like nouns (e.g., complementizer clauses). For this reason, we sometimes refer to the category of **nominals**, or all constituents functioning in a sentence like a noun. And all constituents that function like adverbs in modifying verbs and full clauses or sentences are called **adverbials**. We work through the different types of nominals, adjectivals, and adverbials in the next few sections; for a summary chart, see Table 6.1.

Clause Types

We can describe five basic clause patterns for declarative sentences in English, as shown in Table 6.2 in terms of phrase structure and the function of the parts. Note that in Table 6.2, the S represents a subject, not a sentence or clause. These basic clause patterns can appear in both independent clauses and all types of subordinate clauses.

One or more adverbials (A) can be added to any of these clauses. *Adverbial*, as we discussed, is a cover term for several types of constituents that can function like adverbs, modifying the verb or the entire clause—for example, adverb phrases, prepositional phrases, and adverbial clauses.

TABLE 6.1   **Phrase and Clause Functions**

	Types of Phrases and Clauses	*Example Sentence*
Nominals	NP	I heard *this weird noise*.
	PP	The noise came from *in the car*.
	complementizer clause	I know *that the noise came from there*.
	infinitive phrase	I want *to know what the noise is*.
	gerund phrase	*Hearing the noise* freaked me out.
Adjectivals	ADJP	I have an *incredibly crazy* cat.
	NP	I found my cat in the *school* basement.
	PP	My cat likes twist-ties *from plastic bags*.
	relative clause	She eats cereal *that falls on the floor*.
	infinitive phrase	She disobeys my command *to stop biting my feet*.
	participial phrase	She is a cat *possessed by imaginary friends*.
Adverbials	ADVP	She swims in arctic waters *ridiculously often*.
	PP	She protects her face *with petroleum jelly*.
	NP	She plans to swim *tomorrow*.
	adverbial clause	Doctors were stunned *when they heard about her*.
	infinitive phrase	They ran tests *to figure out how she does it*.
	participial phrase	She went *swimming in an icy lake*.

Source: Adapted from material by Mark Canada (http://www.uncp.edu/home/canada/work/markport/language/aspects/spg2003/05syntax.htm).

TABLE 6.2   **Basic Clause Types**

Phrase Structure Description	Functional Description	Type of Verb	Example Sentence
NP VP	S V	intransitive	We studied.
NP [V NP]$_{VP}$	S V O$_d$	transitive	We studied grammar.
NP [V NP NP]$_{VP}$	S V O$_i$ O$_d$	ditransitive	We gave her our homework.
NP [V NP/ADJP]$_{VP}$	S V PRED	linking	We are good students.
NP [V NP NP/ADJP]$_{VP}$	S V O PRED	object-predicative	She called us brilliant.

S = subject, O$_d$ = direct object, O$_i$ = indirect object, PRED = predicative.

Adverb phrase	*We studied <u>incredibly hard</u>.* (S V A)
Prepositional phrase	*We brought our books <u>to the library</u>.* (S V O A)
Adverbial clause	*We aced the test <u>because we knew our stuff</u>.* (S V O A)

In all these cases, the adverbial is optional. But some verbs require an adverbial to complete the clause—for example, the verb *put* requires the clause structure S V O A. As this example shows, there are additional clause types beyond these basic five. Verbs that require prepositional phrases (e.g., *rely on*) provide another example: here the required clause structure is S V A. In these cases, grammarians often refer to the adverbial as an adverbial complement, as it is required to complete the verb phrase.

With phrase structure rules, we can now visually represent in sentence trees the structure of all of these clause types, as described in the next section.

Basic Phrase Structure Trees

Phrase structure trees are visual representations of the hierarchical structure of constituents within phrases and clauses: they represent how some constituents are embedded inside other ones as we proceed from the level of the word to the phrase to the clause and sentence. You could show the same information with brackets (the traditional method in phrase structure grammar before Chomsky), as we demonstrate below, but that can be confusing. In a phrase structure tree (first drawn this way by Chomsky), the lines are called **branches** and there is a constituent label (e.g., NP, S) at the end of every branch (which is often an intersection of branches) called a **node**.

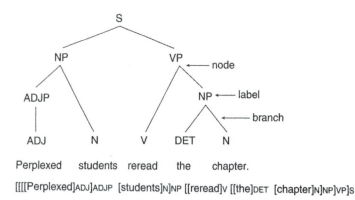

[[[[Perplexed]ADJ]ADJP [students]N]NP [[reread]V [[the]DET [chapter]N]NP]VP]S

You can check, using the phrase structure rules, that each constituent is allow-able—for example, an NP can consist of ADJP + N. We know that an NP can also include a prepositional phrase, as the following tree structure represents, in which we specify that the students, given their perplexed state, are rereading the chapter *in the book*.

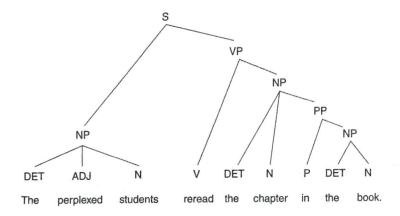

The structure of the noun phrases in this sentence merits more discussion. We have represented them here as "flat" trees in which the determiner, adjective or other modifier like a prepositional phrase, and the head noun all appear on the same level, as "sister" nodes. Some grammarians employ hierarchical structures within these kinds of noun phrases, creating trees like these:

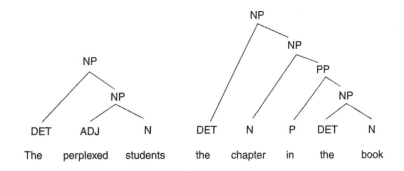

In these tree structures, *perplexed students* and *chapter in the book* are constituents, which are then combined with the determiner to create a larger constituent. These exam-ples do not behave very clearly like constituents, according to our constituency tests (e.g., you cannot move them without the determiner), but in some contexts, substitution tests seem to indicate this kind of hierarchical structure for similar NPs. For example:

> We understand <u>this complicated tree structure</u> but not <u>that one</u>.

In this sentence, *one* substitutes for *complicated tree structure*, which seems to indicate that *complicated tree structure* acts as a constituent that is then combined with the determiner *this*.

In some cases, tree structures can disambiguate potentially ambiguous noun phrases. In other words, in an ambiguous phrase, the tree can indicate what modifies what within a constituent. Consider the noun phrase *old horse farm*. Two different tree structures visually disambiguate a farm for old horses (the tree on the left) and a horse farm with a long history (the tree on the right):

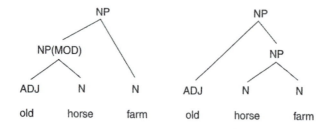

What about a noun phrase like *big, complicated trees*? In this case, if both *big* and *complicated* modify *trees* (in other words, if the adjectives are equally weighted), it would indicate the following tree structure:

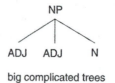

If the phrase describes complicated trees that are big (rather than small), it could arguably support this tree structure:

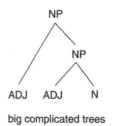

Some forms of generative grammar, such as Minimalism, rely solely on binary tree structures in which all nodes have only two branches. These models thus would disallow the kind of flat tree above with the two equally weighted adjectives and the noun all connected at the same level. Binary models create hierarchical trees in which the rightmost adjective and noun always form a constituent (e.g., *complicated trees*), which is then modified by the preceding adjective (in this case, *big*), such as the tree directly above.

The "golden rule of tree structures" (a term coined by linguist Andrew Carnie) states that modifiers must always attach within the phrase that they modify. Consider the following two sentences:

The perplexed students reread the chapter in the book.

The perplexed students reread the chapter over the weekend.

In the first sentence, the prepositional phrase *in the book* attaches within the noun phrase, because it modifies *the chapter*. In the second sentence, however, the prepositional phrase *over the weekend* acts like an adverb (or adverbial), modifying the verb (*reread*) within the verb phrase, so we get a very different tree structure:

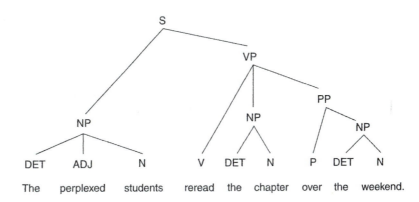

The stand-alone constituency tests could also justify a tree structure in which the verb and direct object (in this case, *the chapter*) form a VP constituent, which then attaches to the prepositional phrase. What did the perplexed students do over the weekend? *Reread the chapter.* The key is that you must be able to justify, using principles of constituency structure, the representation of the sentence's structure captured in any given tree.

Phrase structure trees allow us to show visually the different meanings of a potentially ambiguous sentence. Take a sentence such as *The unpredictable actress tripped the cop with the prop.* If the cop is holding the prop, and the actress sticks out her foot to trip him, we get this tree structure:

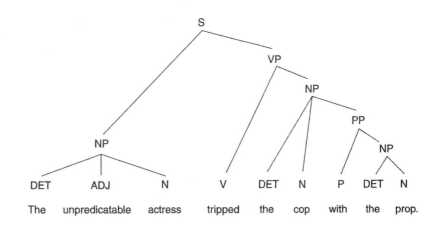

If the actress uses the prop to trip the cop, we get this tree structure:

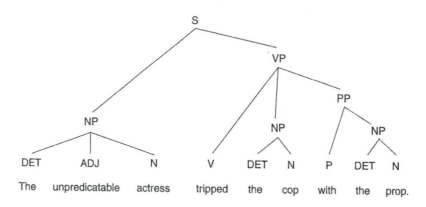

Another potentially ambiguous structure, which phrase structure trees allow us to disambiguate visually, involves coordinating conjunctions. In a phrase such as *old men and women*, how old are the women? Consider the following two possible phrase structure trees:

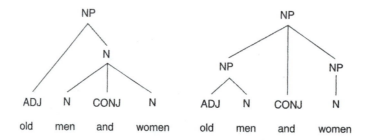

Coordinating conjunctions connect two words or phrases of the same category to create a larger constituent in that category. In the left-hand structure, the adjective *old* modifies the coordinated noun phrase *men and women*, so it could refer to, for example, your grandparents, if they are both "of a certain age." The right-hand structure indicates that *old* modifies only *men*, which forms a noun phrase that is conjoined with *women*—so this could refer to your elderly grandparents or it could refer to elderly men and their younger trophy wives, as the age of the women is unspecified.

A **compound sentence** (e.g., *I read the chapter, and I went to bed*) with two independent clauses reflects the same balanced structure as a coordinated phrase:

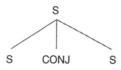

In these coordinated structures, there can be more than two sister nodes in addition to the coordinating conjunction. For example, imagine the phrase structure tree for the NP *perplexity, bewilderment, and mass confusion* (not that you are experiencing any of these right now), or for the sentence *I came, I ate, and I left.*

Complex sentences, with an independent and one or more dependent clauses, require more complicated representation, which we turn to now.

Complex Phrase Structure Trees

Clauses can be embedded within clauses to create a complex sentence: a sentence with one or more subordinated clauses in addition to the main clause. Although sometimes complex sentences may look long and complicated, they are composed of familiar parts. They involve the combination or rearrangement of the now familiar clause types that we have been discussing.

Embedded clauses, or dependent/subordinate clauses, within complex sentences take many forms. In this section, we cover three major ones: adverbial clauses with subordinating conjunctions, relative clauses (which function as adjectivals), and complementizer clauses (which function as nominals). In the next section, we discuss three forms of reduced subordinate clauses: infinitive phrases (which can function as nominals, adjectivals, and adverbials), gerund phrases (which function as nominals), and participial phrases (which can function as adjectivals and adverbials). There are many other kinds of complex sentences, but this material should give you a toolkit with which to analyze the component parts of any complex sentence.

Adverbial Clauses

Sentences with an adverbial clause, introduced by a subordinating conjunction (e.g., *when, because, while, if*), are a common type of complex sentence. Adverbial clauses are generally optional and provide circumstantial information about the proposition of the main clause (e.g., how, why, where, when something happened). A phrase structure tree demonstrates how the entire subordinate clause functions as an adverbial within the predicate VP.

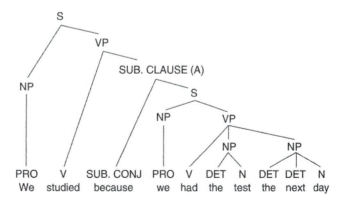

Some grammarians argue that adverbial clauses like this one are sentence modifiers, modifying the entire main clause rather than being embedded in the verb phrase.

Relative Clauses

Relative clauses, typically introduced by the relative pronouns *who/whom/whose, which,* and *that,* modify preceding nouns. In this way, the basic phrase structure tree resembles one in which a prepositional phrase modifies a preceding noun phrase.

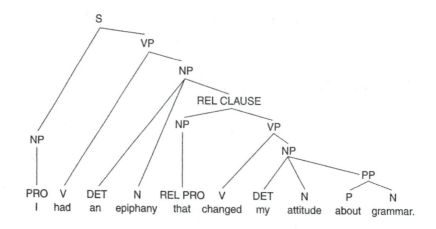

In this case, the relative pronoun functions as the subject of the relative clause, so the phrase structure tree of the relative clause is straightforward. Trees become more complicated when the relative pronoun is the object in the relative clause. For example:

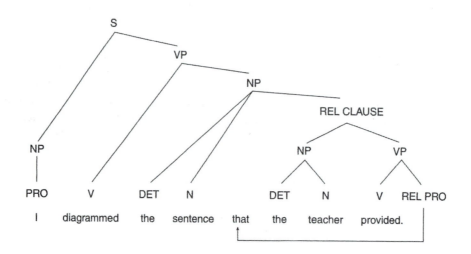

We draw the phrase structure tree with all the constituents in positions that correspond to the basic clause types and phrase structure rules. So in this case, the relative pronoun node and label occur in the VP of the relative clause. We then draw an arrow to show the movement of the relative pronoun to the beginning of the relative clause—where all relative pronouns must occur in English in the realization of a complex sentence with a relative clause. This kind of movement is called a transformation—a term and process we will discuss in detail later in the chapter.

Why not just put the relative pronoun in this example at the beginning of the relative clause in the phrase structure tree? There are two reasons. First, the branches of a phrase structure tree are not allowed to cross: it violates the principles for how constituents embed in other constituents in an orderly hierarchy. In this case, the NP branch in the VP cannot cross the subject NP branch.

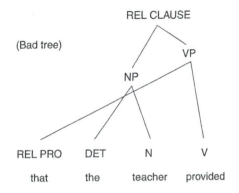

(Bad tree)

REL CLAUSE

NP

VP

REL PRO   DET   N   V

that   the   teacher   provided

Second, all constituents in a phrase structure tree must correspond to phrase structure rules. There is no phrase structure rule in English that states s ⟶ NP NP VP. This phrase structure rule would allow *that the teacher provided,* but it would also allow many ungrammatical clauses such as **students the light at the end of the tunnel saw.*

More advanced generative grammar refers to "traces," which stand in for an element that has been moved elsewhere or been deleted—like a shadow or ghost of an element that used to appear at that node in the phrase structure tree. So, for example, in the sentence *I diagrammed the sentence that the teacher provided,* there would be a trace after *provided,* where the relative pronoun *that* would occur as the object of the verb except that it has moved to the head of the relative clause.

The two sentences shown in the trees above both involve **restrictive relative clauses,** or clauses that specify the referent of the noun or noun phrase that they modify. In other words, *that the teacher provided* specifies which particular sentence we are referring to here (*the one that the teacher provided*) out of the set of all possible sentences in the world. A **nonrestrictive clause** provides additional information about the noun or noun phrase it modifies but does not work to specify or restrict the referent. An example will help here:

Restrictive: *Hannah needs to buy the grammar book that she saw at the university bookstore.*

Nonrestrictive: *Hannah needs to buy the required grammar book, which she saw at the university bookstore.*

In the first sentence, the relative clause specifies what grammar book Hannah needs to buy—it restricts the referent of the phrase *the grammar book* to the one that Hannah saw at the bookstore. In the second sentence, the relative clause provides additional information about the required grammar book (i.e., that Hannah saw it at the university bookstore), but the referent is already specified and is not further restricted by the relative clause. One common rule of thumb is that you can usually add a comma before a nonrestrictive relative clause (which is where you would pause if you read the sentence aloud) but not before a restrictive one.

Sometimes relative clauses modify full clauses, rather than noun phrases. For example:

Niko ate twelve hotdogs yesterday, which must be some kind of record.

The relative clause is always nonrestrictive in these cases, adding an optional comment about the main clause.

Language Change at Work

Which Is It, *Which* or *That?*

Many style guides have extended and sometimes complicated descriptions of the "proper" use of *which* and *that* for nonrestrictive and restrictive clauses respectively. Historically, *that* and *which* were used interchangeably in the seventeenth century, and then *that* seems to have dropped out of at least literary use. When *that* resurfaced as a relative pronoun in the eighteenth and nineteenth centuries, it was fairly well restricted to restrictive clauses. This fact allowed H. W. Fowler, in his influential style guide of 1926, to propose that if *that* was already used only for restrictive clauses, then *which* should be used only for nonrestrictive clauses, as "there would be much gain both in lucidity & in ease." However, *which* has not been restricted by style guide recommendations, and it continues to be used freely to introduce both restrictive and nonrestrictive clauses. In fact, in a study by Virginia McDavid in 1977, 75 percent of the instances of relative pronoun *which* introduced restrictive clauses (cited in Gilman 1994, 894).

The ability to distinguish between the "proper" use of *which* and *that* continues to be reason enough, though, for some prescriptive grammarians to judge the ability of other English users. In his *A Dictionary of Modern American Usage* (1998), Bryan Garner writes these strong words (probably more seriously than not):

> You'll encounter two schools of thought on this point. First are those who don't care about any distinction between these words, who think that *which* is more formal than *that*, and who point to many historical examples of copious *whiches*. They say that modern usage is a muddle. Second are those who insist that both words have useful functions that ought to be separated, and who observe the distinction rigorously in their own writing. They view departures from this distinction as "mistakes."
>
> Before reading any further, you ought to know something more about these two groups: those in the first probably don't write very well; those in the second just might. (647)

The knowledge to make informed decisions about prescriptive rules and the ability to write good prose are not, however, mutually exclusive. It is almost always unjustified to prejudge writers based on their adherence to one prescriptive grammatical rule.

Complementizer Clauses

Complementizer clauses are dependent clauses that fill an NP position. For this reason, they are sometimes called nominal clauses. They are typically introduced by *that* or *wh*-words (*what, whether, who/whom, where, why*) or *how*. If they serve as the object of the verb, complementizer clauses complete the predicate; if they serve as the object of a preposition, they complete the prepositional phrase. Complementizer clauses can also serve as the subject, completing the subject-predicate structure of the clause or sentence. For example:

The teacher said <u>that complementizer clauses are not that difficult</u>.

<u>That grammar is fascinating</u> surprises us a little.

We know <u>what a complementizer is</u>.

We talk about <u>whether the grammar fairy has all the answers</u>.

A sample phrase structure tree looks like this:

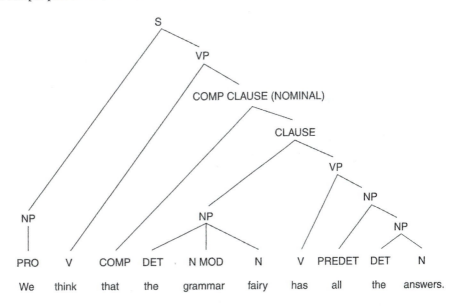

Sometimes the complementizer *that* is absent: *We hope the grammar fairy has all the answers*. We talk more about deleting words and constituents in the section on transformations. Object or predicative *wh-* words in complementizer clauses undergo movement to the beginning of the clause similar to object relative pronouns in relative clauses (e.g., *We know what a complementizer is*).

Reduced Subordinate Clauses

In the two preceding sections, on relative clauses and complementizer clauses, we have seen that these clauses can be reduced through the deletion of *that* (or *which*). Some subordinate clauses can be reduced even further, to phrases: infinitive phrases, gerund phrases, and participial phrases.

Infinitive Phrases

In generative grammar, infinitive phrases are considered reduced forms of full subordinate clauses or of full clauses substituted for a pronoun. For example:

We know ~~that we should~~ do all our syntax homework.

↓

We know to do all our syntax homework.

Our job is this: ~~we must~~ safeguard the answer key.

↓

Our job is to safeguard the answer key.

Infinitive phrases can function as NPs, adverbials, and occasionally as adjectivals (reduced from relative clauses).

NP:	*We want to know the intricacies of grammar.*
	To know grammar is to love grammar.
Adverbial:	*Jose learned grammar to impress all his friends.*
	To be honest, I diagram sentences for fun.
Adjectival:	*Amelia followed the instructions to start drawing tree structures.*

These infinitive phrases are labeled *phrases* rather than clauses because there is no finite verb in the VP (i.e., there is no predicate). In the first two examples, we know that these grammatical constructions require an NP in these positions, and the infinitive phrase functions as the NP. In these examples, there is also no subject NP, but it is possible to have an infinitive phrase with a subject NP: *We want Jamie to give us all the answers.* Adverbial infinitive phrases, except for those that modify the entire sentence, can be preceded by *in order to*.

Here's an example of a phrase structure tree with an infinitive phrase:

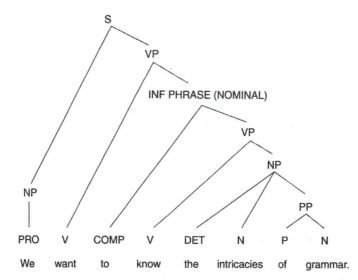

The reduction of an embedded clause to a phrase represents another kind of transformation, which we discuss in detail below.

Gerund and Participial Phrases

Gerund and participial phrases can also be framed as reduced forms of full clauses. For example:

We like it. We study gerund phrases.

↓

We like studying gerund phrases.

We used the book that contains goofy example sentences.

↓

We used the book containing goofy example sentences.

We were stunned by the phrase structure tree ~~that was~~ drawn on the board.

↓

We were stunned by the phrase structure tree drawn on the board.

Gerund phrases can function as NPs, and participial phrases (both present and past) function as adjectivals when they are reduced relative clauses.

Gerund Phrase

We absolutely love <u>learning grammar</u>. (S V O)

Gerunds make <u>learning grammar</u> fun. (S V O PRED)

<u>Writing example sentences</u> is harder than you think. (S V PRED)

Present Participle Phrase

We need sentences <u>exemplifying present participle phrases</u>. (S V O)

I want answers <u>falling out of the sky</u>. (S V O)

Past Participle Phrase

The answers <u>provided in the book</u> did not fall from the sky. (S V A)

The trees <u>drawn below</u> should help. (S V)

For a brief summary, see Table 6.1.

Tense and Auxiliaries

You may have noticed that all the example sentences in the phrase structure trees so far have employed the simple present or simple past tense—there have been no auxiliary verbs. The phrase structure rules for VP do not even include an auxiliary. Why not? Most generative grammar approaches position AUX/TENSE as an additional node directly dominated by S:

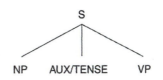

If there is an auxiliary verb (or more than one), the auxiliary carries the tense marking and determines the form of the main verb. For example:

I	*have*	*run*	*ten miles.*
	AUX: present tense	MAIN VERB: past participle	
My legs	*did not*	*want*	*to run anymore.*
	AUX: past tense	MAIN VERB: infinitive form	

If there is no auxiliary verb present, the tense hops to the main verb so that it appears in the present or past tense.

Why put tense and auxiliaries on this separate node between the NP and VP? Of the many theoretical justifications, one of the critical ones is that "tense" is always indicated in the main clause, and it appears either in the form of the auxiliary or in the form of the main verb, but never in the form of both. For example, Standard English does not allow *I did not jogged yesterday*, in which both the auxiliary and the main verb are marked for past tense. The auxiliary verb also moves independent of the VP in transformations like yes-no questions. And if there is no auxiliary verb for these transformations, auxiliary *do* is added to fill this position. For example: *Randy jogged* ⟶ *Did Randy jog?* That said, some theoretical approaches include AUX as the left-most node of the VP.

A Question to Discuss

What Is the *It* in "It Is Raining"?

In Standard English, we can rearrange basic clause types by employing two "empty" or expletive subjects—positions filled by *it* and *there*. (Here *expletive* refers to 'a word used to fill a syntactic vacancy' rather than 'an obscene exclamatory word'.) These constructions with expletive subjects shift the emphasis to the complement, which is particularly useful when the complement contains new or important information. For example, if you are trying to draw attention to beverages in the refrigerator that you would like your friend to consume, you would probably use *There are three beers in the fridge* rather than *Three beers are in the fridge.*

"Heavy" (i.e., long) phrases and clauses also tend to get shifted into final position. For this reason, subject complementizer clauses that are predicated by an adjective often get moved into final position in a construction with expletive *it*. For example:

> That new information tends to occur in the predicate is commonly accepted.

> It is commonly accepted that new information tends to occur in the predicate.

And some idiomatic expressions, such as *It is raining*, require the expletive *it*.

Both *it* and *there* function like subjects grammatically. They both undergo reversal with the verb to form questions:

> It is . . . ⟶ Is it . . . ?
> There is . . . ⟶ Is there . . . ?

Expletive *it* also controls the required singular verb agreement. With *there*, however, verb agreement is typically controlled by the number of the predicate noun, so we find:

> There is only one verb in this sentence.
> There are seven words in this sentence.

But the construction *there is/there's* is such a common empty subject that sometimes it occurs with plural predicate nouns as well. For example:

> There's many reasons to study grammar, including fun, fascination, and fulfillment.

In African American English, expletive *it* systematically appears in constructions that take expletive *there* in standard varieties to create sentences such as *It is a lot of information in this chapter.* In Appalachian English, expletive *they* can appear in *there* constructions. It is just as systematic and rule-governed to use *it* or *they* in such a construction as it is to use *there*.

Transformations

There is a fundamental problem with the set of phrase structure rules as we have described them thus far: they cannot account for all the various kinds of grammatical sentences we can create—which is, after all, the goal of generative grammar. Hence the need for **transformations**, or processes that change "underlying" sentences (which adhere to phrase structure rules) to "surface" realizations (which are systematically related to the underlying structures but whose structures do not adhere to phrase structure rules). For example, our phrase structure rules dictate that an object NP appears after the verb, but in this question, the object NP appears first:

What are you saying?

Not only that, but the auxiliary verb in this question is also clearly "in the wrong place." According to phrase structure rules, *are* should come after the subject (*you*) and before the main verb (*saying*). At the same time, this question is equally clearly systematically related to its declarative counterpart:

You are saying what.

A transformation can show the relationship between the declarative version and the interrogative version.

Do we as speakers actually transform clauses when we construct and interpret sentences? In other words, do we begin with a declarative sentence and then transform it into a question? The evidence suggests not. We process language in real time, rather than waiting to hear or read the full sentence before processing it. In other words, we produce and interpret the "transformed" clauses as spontaneously as any other clauses. But transformations usefully reveal the systematic relationships among different kinds of clauses.

Wh- Questions

To make a *wh-* question, the *wh-* word is fronted to the beginning of the sentence, and the subject NP and first auxiliary verb are reversed. If there is no auxiliary verb, *do* is added in AUX position and then reversed with the subject NP. You may notice that the tense hops from the main verb to *do* in these cases: *you said what* ⟶ *what did you say?* All these steps are critical components of the *wh-* question transformation. The fronting of *wh-* words in questions should remind you of the fronting of relative pronouns in relative clauses, which we mentioned earlier in the chapter.

Transformations can be and have been described in extensive theoretical detail, and the exact details have been the source of much discussion and debate in the history of generative grammar. Chomsky began by describing the underlying structure as the "deep structure," which was transformed into the "surface structure." These terms were later changed to *d-structure* and *s-structure*, to avoid the connotations about language processing in the brain itself. Questions such as exactly how constituents move, what is left at the node once the constituent moves, constraints on transformations, and much more are beyond an introductory treatment of transformations. Below we outline how four other fundamental sentence structures can be derived from phrase structure rules in combination with transformations: negation, yes-no questions, passive constructions, and relative pronoun deletion. These descriptions capture the systematicity of transformations without going into the technicalities of various theoretical approaches to transformations or the syntactic tree representations of transformations.

Negation

Negation can be viewed as a transformation or as a feature of phrase structure trees, similar to tense. Here we outline how it is sometimes treated as a transformation. Negative constructions in standard varieties of English involve the insertion of *not,* typically after the first auxiliary verb. So if there are auxiliaries present in the related affirmative clause or sentence, *not* is inserted after the first auxiliary verb:

>   *I had heard about Chomsky before.* $\longrightarrow$ *I had not heard about Chomsky before.*

If the main verb is a form of *be,* however, and there are no auxiliaries present, *not* is inserted after the *be* verb form:

>   *Transformations are confusing.* $\longrightarrow$ *Transformations are not confusing.*

With any other main verb, if there are no auxiliaries present, the appropriate form of *do* is inserted as an auxiliary and then *not* is inserted after auxiliary *do.* Again, the tense hops from the main verb to *do:*

>   *We revised the chapter.* $\longrightarrow$ *We did not revise the chapter.*

It would be possible to reorder these steps more efficiently: if there is no auxiliary present for all main verbs except *be,* insert the appropriate form of the auxiliary *do;* insert *not* after the first auxiliary or form of *be* if there is no auxiliary present.

Many nonstandard varieties of English insert a second (or third) negative element as part of the negative transformation, including adverbs (e.g., *never*), determiners (e.g., *no*), and negative indefinite pronouns (e.g., *nobody, none*). For example:

>   *We don't have none.*
>
>   *Don't nobody go there no more.*

You'll notice that in the second example, the negative indefinite pronoun (*nobody*) and the negated auxiliary verb (*don't*) are also reversed. Multiple negation is as systematic and grammatically rule-governed as single negation.

Yes-No Questions

The process of creating yes-no questions by rearrangement of constituents (rather than by rising intonation) parallels the *wh-* question transformation, without the movement of the *wh-* form. If there is no auxiliary verb before any main verb except *be,* the auxiliary *do* (in the appropriate tense) is inserted. The subject NP and the first auxiliary are then reversed. The one exception again involves the copula (or linking verb) *be,* which can reverse positions with the subject NP like an auxiliary.

>   *The students should have questions.* $\longrightarrow$ *Should the students have questions?*
>
>   *You have a question.* $\longrightarrow$ *Do you have a question?*
>
>   *That question was brilliant.* $\longrightarrow$ *Was that question brilliant?*

The verb *be* behaves anomalously in several transformations. As we discuss in Chapter 7, *be* is a complicated verb semantically (what exactly does it mean?), and many languages (e.g., Russian, Chinese) often do not employ a copula between a subject and a complement in a clause such as *that question is brilliant*.

Given this description, you can now probably figure out the transformation involved in **tag questions** such as *Your mom works in Dallas now, doesn't she?* and *The car won't be fixed tomorrow, will it?*

Passive Constructions

In passive constructions, the direct object becomes the grammatical subject and the agent subject NP is moved to the end of the sentence—or deleted entirely. "Moved or deleted by whom?" you might ask in reference to the previous sentence. This is a good example of a passive construction in which the agent NP has been deleted. Here are three more examples of passive sentences:

The instructor assigned homework. ⟶ *Homework was assigned by the instructor.*

I have completed the homework. ⟶ *The homework has been completed by me.*

The homework takes up my nights. ⟶ *My nights are taken up by the homework.*

The passive construction involves the fronting of the direct object NP to the grammatical subject position, and the movement of the subject NP to a position after the verb with the insertion of the preposition *by* before this NP to create a PP. The form of the main verb changes to the past participle, and a form of the auxiliary verb *be* (in the appropriate tense, person, and number) is inserted. If other auxiliaries are already present, passive auxiliary *be* will be the last one before the main verb (see Chapter 5 about the order of multiple auxiliary verbs), and its form will be controlled by the preceding auxiliary verb. If passive *be* is the only auxiliary verb, tense marking hops from the main verb to auxiliary *be*.

The deletion of the *by* prepositional phrase, which captures agency, is optional. For example, we could say *My car was hit* or *My car was hit by another car.* Most of the components of the transformations that we have discussed so far have been syntactically required to create grammatical utterances of that type. But many transformations (or particular components of transformations) are optional: they create alternate grammatical constructions.

A Question to Discuss

How Did This Passive Sentence *Get* Constructed?

In English it is possible to create passive sentences through the insertion of auxiliary *get* instead of *be*:

A mad bicyclist hit my car. ⟶

    My car was hit by a mad bicyclist.
    My car got hit by a mad bicyclist.

It has been argued (to use an effective passive construction) that there is a subtle semantic difference between passives with *be* and with *get*. Create a list of examples, and find some additional examples in the Corpus of Contemporary American English (COCA). Can you make an argument for a semantic difference?

Relative Pronoun Deletion

Standard English allows the deletion of relative pronouns in restrictive clauses when they function grammatically as objects in the subordinate clause (remember, these relative pronouns get fronted to the beginning of the clause). So Standard English allows either of the following sentences:

> I understood the last section *that I read*.
>
> I understood the last section *I read*.

Or either of these sentences:

> I raved about the instructor *whom I had for my syntax class*.
>
> I raved about the instructor *I had for syntax class*.

In Standard English, the relative pronoun cannot be deleted from a restrictive clause when it serves as the subject of the relative clause. For example:

> I felt sorry for the fly *that landed in my latte*.
>
> *I felt sorry for the fly ~~that~~ *landed in my latte*.

But some nonstandard varieties allow the deletion of relative pronouns in restrictive clauses when they function grammatically as subjects of the subordinate clauses. In these varieties, either of these two sentences is grammatical:

> The person *who speaks out of turn* will get in trouble.
>
> The person *speaks out of turn* will get in trouble.

In Standard English, the relative pronoun can also be deleted if it functions as the object of a preposition, but only if the preposition is left stranded at the end of the subordinate clause; if the preposition is fronted (sometimes called "pied piping" because the preposition follows the relative pronoun to the beginning of the subordinate clause), the relative pronoun must remain:

> I threw out the coffee ~~that~~ *the fly drowned in*.
>
> *I threw out the coffee in ~~which~~ *the fly drowned*.

You'll notice that when we front the preposition in the subordinate clause, *that* becomes *which*, no matter whether the clause is restrictive or nonrestrictive. It's just one of those things about English grammar.

When the relative clause is nonrestrictive, the relative pronoun cannot be deleted, as in the following sentences:

> I poured myself a cup of mocha, *which is my favorite drink*.
>
> *I poured myself a cup of mocha, ~~which~~ *is my favorite drink*.

These transformations only begin to account for the rich array of sentences that you know how to create grammatically without a conscious thought. We also have not discussed some of the important restrictions on transformations. For example, a *wh-* form cannot undergo fronting out of a conjoined construction:

> You are buying pencils and what. → *What are you buying pencils and?*

This transformed sentence obviously does not work.

These examples should give you a general understanding of how transformations interact with phrase structure rules and how transformations explain the systematic relationship between types of grammatical constructions, such as declarative statements and yes-no questions. These examples should also give you the tools to figure out the transformations involved in other constructions.

Does Generative Grammar Succeed?

Most of the grammatical descriptions in this chapter, from phrase structure rules to transformations, have relied on the theory of generative grammar. Generative grammar aims not simply to describe what occurs in a language or even only what is possible in a language; generative grammar aims to articulate the rules that make some grammatical structures possible and others not possible in a language.

Generative grammar is a powerful theory of language as a human mental faculty, and especially of language acquisition. It is also a powerful analytical method for understanding syntactic structures. That said, it has its critics, and it does not adequately account for many aspects of language.

If we conceive of language as a set of conventions learned from experience, generative grammar cannot provide adequate explanations. And the role of convention in language use, the social basis for language, discourse, and variation, is interesting and important. It's a matter of getting the right questions aligned with the right methods for the right reasons.

One alternate approach to grammar, espoused by linguist Paul J. Hopper among others, is Usage-Based Linguistics. It takes seriously the premise that language is, first and foremost, a spoken phenomenon and focuses primarily on what speakers actually do with language, rather than what they can theoretically do. Hopper (2007, 239) summarizes his challenge to generative grammar as follows: "Is it a question of what people are able to do under optimal conditions of isolation and setting and education and literacy, or is it rather what people habitually say under ordinary everyday conditions? If, as I think, the investigation of language includes the crucial question of why grammar is the way that it is, it would seem that a study of how people habitually talk with one another must be given priority over what they *could* say in idealized circumstances." As a result, Usage-Based Linguistics targets dialogical discourse—that is, conversation—as a primary unit for analysis and examines, for example, the importance of fixed phrases (e.g., *what I mean/said/[another expressive verb] is*) in the grammar we use every day. Along these lines, American linguist Barbara Johnstone, in her book *Discourse Analysis* (2002), describes *grammar* as the "easily available set of conventions for constructing phrases, clauses, and sentences." In other words, grammar consists of patterns that are set from conventional, regular use in actual discourse. Usage-based approaches also try to account for the many fragments and grammatical exceptions (e.g., *there's* + a plural noun: *There's four doughnuts left*) that characterize language as we actually use it.

This approach to grammar echoes work by the Prague School linguists and British linguist Michael Halliday, whose approach to grammar is labeled functional linguistics or "functional grammar"—a school of thought overshadowed by the rise of generative grammar but still very much alive as a theoretical approach. Functionalism emphasizes the effect of choices on the structure of language. Each time a speaker utters a sentence, he or she creates reusable ways of speaking and reinforces particular structures as grammatical. As Johnstone (2002, 41) explains, "each time a particular choice is made, the possibility of making that choice is highlighted. In other words, each use of an element of grammar in one text makes it more salient, more available for another use, or a slightly different use, in another text." As a theory, functionalism may be descriptively adequate (it successfully accounts for what occurs), but it is not explanatorily adequate (it does not necessarily account for what is possible and not possible), which Chomsky established clearly as a requisite for a successful grammatical theory.

Recent work in cognitive linguistics has produced fascinating empirical results about how our brains process language. Some of these findings seem to support tenets of generative grammar. For example, if a click is superimposed on a sentence as we hear it spoken, we think we hear the click at breaks between constituents rather than in the middle of constituents (even if this is where the click occurs). Other findings about the cognitive processing of language present challenges to generative grammar. For example, we process language in real time; that is, we process words wherever they appear in the s-structure (the utterance as it is spoken, signed, or written) rather than waiting for the entire sentence to determine where they might fit most appropriately in the d-structure (or underlying structure). Cognitive scientists like Steven Pinker, working in the generative tradition, bring together such findings and generative grammar, and we foresee lively conversations in this realm as technology allows ever more sophisticated access to the syntactic happenings in our brains.

There are also cogent rival theories within cognitive approaches to language. For instance, Alison Gopnik and her colleagues have argued, partly on the basis of experiment, that infants have innate theoretical ability (see Gopnik 2003): they emerge from the womb with a theoretical framework and then develop and test theories about everything they encounter, including language. Thus Universal Grammar may be part of a larger theoretical competence that is innate, and infant theories about language, once tested, may generate viable syntactic structures. These structures would not be isolated from the world, neither from referential semantics, nor from social conventions of meaning, nor from cultural construction of meaning. The Theory Theory, as it's called, is much more tolerant of functional interaction, potentially mixing many more ingredients into the recipe for language than does generative grammar.

The cognitive workings of language may be fundamentally more complicated than any linguistic theory. We may have difficulty even comprehending the speed, complexity, and level of cognitive activity of which our brains are capable (we discuss this more in Chapter 10). Linguistic theories of grammar may also fall short of the workings of our brains because theory has a tendency to reduce explanatory assumptions and propositions to the minimum. Indeed, according to the principle called Occam's Razor, the best theory is that with the fewest assumptions (as is the best mathematical proof the one with the fewest steps). Our brains, however, may not necessarily follow Occam's Razor. To take one example, the interaction of syntax, lexicon, and discourse is clearly more complex than any theory we have to date. Does a fully explanatory theory take as its center words, syntactic structures, or discourse? Words to some extent determine the grammar of the phrases in which they appear, but syntactic structures also disallow words from combining in particular ways, and all naturally occurring uses of language are created to fulfill a communicative purpose in interaction. What would it mean for grammatical theory to balance all these factors?

The volume *Chomsky and His Critics* (2003), edited by Louise M. Anthony and Norbert Hornstein, contains multiple articles that challenge Chomsky or offer alternative solutions to Chomsky's original questions. In the next generation or so, a new theory may well challenge generative grammar and perhaps even supercede it, but it will do so only *because of* generative grammar and all the insights it has provided about the systematicity of grammatical structure and acquisition.

Special Focus: Syntax and Prescriptive Grammar

This chapter has focused on the "well-formedness" of sentences, or on what kinds of sentences speakers accept as grammatical—in the descriptive sense of "grammatical." Many basic prescriptive rules of English grammar also deal with this issue of what constitutes a well-formed sentence, often from a more stylistic perspective. In other words, which grammatical structures are preferred, typically in the written language? Unlike descriptive grammatical rules, stylistic restrictions sometimes allow some well-formed sentences and criticize or disallow other equally well-formed ones.

Sentence Fragments and Run-on Sentences

By definition, **sentence fragments** are not well formed: they are missing a subject (*Called him up*) or a predicate (*The woman in the sports car*) or both (*Out of the blue*); or they are a subordinate rather than an independent clause (*If he'd only known*). We often speak in sentence fragments because context allows us to supply the missing sentence parts in our own and in others' utterances. But grammar books and style guides typically condemn fragments as unacceptable in written usage, except for instances when context justifies them or when listeners or readers are likely easily to understand the fragment's rhetorical purpose. For example, in this excerpt from Yann Martel's best-selling book *Life of Pi* (2001), a sentence fragment emphasizes the importance of the sloth's slowness.

> How does it [the sloth] survive, you might ask.
>   Precisely by being so slow. Sleepiness and slothfulness keep it out of harm's way, away from the notice of jaguars, ocelots, harpy eagles and anacondas. (4)

Run-on sentences typically run into one of two problems: either they do not use the appropriate or enough conjunctions/punctuation to join clauses, or they use too many conjunctions, joining too many clauses. In the first category, run-on sentences are sometimes badly formed sentences because they combine two or more sentences into one sentence without any hierarchical markers:

> *The students were perplexed, they reread the chapter they still didn't understand it.*

As we have discussed, sentences can be composed of multiple clauses, either conjoined or in a hierarchical relation to one another. So this run-on sentence could be broken into two sentences, one of which could be compound as in the following:

> *The students were perplexed. They reread the chapter, but they still didn't understand it.*

The second category of run-on sentences is condemned on stylistic rather than grammatical grounds. If you write a sentence with multiple clauses connected by coordinating conjunctions (e.g., *I began studying syntax <u>and</u> I loved it <u>and</u> so I went to the* *bookstore <u>and</u> I bought every book on Chomsky that I could find <u>but</u> I soon discovered that my passion lay in phonology instead*), your writing instructor or editor will probably pull out the red pen. There is nothing grammatically wrong or badly formed about this sentence; in fact, in Old English prose, you can find long coordinated sentences like this all the time in formal writing. Contemporary stylistic conventions, however, prefer subordination over coordination for eloquent prose, and if you are going to use coordination, the imposed stylistic limit is typically two coordinated clauses.

Colons, Semicolons, and Comma Splices

Both the semicolon and the colon can serve to connect two independent clauses. A semicolon (;) can join two closely related independent clauses, as in this example: *Punctuation is relatively arbitrary; grammarians have made it up over the centuries.* When a colon (:) connects two closely related independent clauses, it typically indicates that the second clause explains, exemplifies, or describes a consequence of the first. For example: *The idea that two negatives always make a positive in language makes no sense: language is not like math and negatives do not necessarily cancel each other out.* A comma, while a very useful and versatile punctuation mark, cannot work like a colon or a semicolon: it cannot connect two independent clauses all by itself.

A **comma splice** occurs when two independent clauses are joined by a comma without a coordinating conjunction (so splice in the sense of 'join' with a comma). In other words, in a sentence with a comma splice, the comma is trying to function like a semicolon or colon. Modern punctuation conventions do not allow commas to join two independent clauses with no help from a coordinating conjunction. So a comma splice is a species of run-on sentence, as in *The students were perplexed, they reread the chapter.*

There are several easy ways to undo a comma splice. Is the second clause an explanation or consequence of the first clause? If so, insert a colon in place of the comma in order to express that hierarchical relation: *The students were perplexed: the chapter was full of complex information.* Or you could express the semantic relationship by choosing an appropriate conjunction: *The students were perplexed, so they reread the chapter.* Perhaps the two clauses are meant to coordinate "as equals" rather than as marking cause and effect: *The students were perplexed, and they reread the chapter* or *The students were perplexed; they reread the chapter.* In any case, you cannot simply splice two independent clauses together with a comma.

It is perfectly reasonable to wonder why a colon and a semicolon are allowed to connect two independent clauses, whereas a comma is not. Punctuation is fully conventional: over the years, it has been created by grammarians to mark specific syntactic relationships and structures, as well as to indicate prosodic contours. For example, a "?" indicates rising intonation. In medieval manuscripts, punctuation is minimal, and you frequently encounter conjoined clauses with different subjects written without the comma we expect today. So you might see the equivalent of "The chapter perplexed them and they reread it" rather than "The chapter perplexed them, and they reread it." These manuscripts also contain sentences we would consider run-ons, and into which we would insert a semicolon.

Many punctuation marks were historically used differently from the way they are today. For example, before the standardization of most English punctuation in the eighteenth century, the slash (/) was sometimes used where today we would use a comma.

Because hierarchical relations aren't always transparent, grammarians developed punctuation to clarify them. But the assignment of one punctuation mark to one clarification rather than another (e.g., the slash versus the comma) is arbitrary, in the way that assigning one letter form (e.g., f) and not another to represent a phoneme or group of phonemes is arbitrary. But the fact that punctuation is purely conventional does not mean that you can violate it at will. Successful convention rests on consensus and adherence. And punctuation usefully clarifies syntactic structures in many instances. In addition, you—or your education—may be judged on how well you follow conventional punctuation rules.

Dangling Participles

Dangling or **misplaced participles** can create ambiguous or unintended meanings: (a) by having a participial phrase that does not modify anything in the main clause (hence it is "dangling"); or (b) by placing the participial phrase next to a constituent (e.g., a noun phrase) that it does not modify (hence it is "misplaced"). Let's start with an example of a dangling participle:

Considering the weather conditions, the commute could have been much worse.

The participial phrase (*considering the weather conditions*) functions as an adjectival and should, prescriptive grammar tells us, modify the noun phrase next to it (in this case, *the commute*). But the commute is not actually considering the weather conditions. Most of us would read this sentence to mean that the weather conditions are a condition on which the commute depends, but what syntactically governs what?

The example here is modeled on one given in the entry "danglers," in Bryan A. Garner's *Dictionary of Modern American Usage* (1998): "Considering the current atmosphere in the legislature, the bill probably won't pass." Of such danglers, Garner writes, "Some danglers, though, are acceptable because of longstanding usage." In other words, dangling participles beginning with *considering* are so common that they no longer even seem to be dangling or to be a grammatical "error." In this case, the phrase beginning with *considering* functions much like *hopefully* (discussed in Chapter 5), as a sentence modifier. Most style guides grant as acceptable a certain set of participial phrases (e.g., *considering, assuming, barring, taking [into account], returning to [a point]*), those that have clearly understood referents, typically all the participants in the discourse (i.e., the author and the audience).

Other dangling modifiers are often seen as less acceptable because the syntax implies semantic relations that are incongruous if not impossible. Let's take the sentence *Having read over the chapter, syntax is still a little fuzzy.* Syntax does not read, although the placement of this participial phrase suggests that it does. (Or does it? Did you interpret the sentence as syntax reading or did you supply an understood referent for "having read," such as students?)

Some misplaced modifiers create memorable images:

Clinging to the side of the aquarium, Mary saw a starfish.

Barreling down the tracks, the conductor saw the runaway train.

From our experience with the world, we know that probably the starfish, not Mary, was clinging to the side of the aquarium, and that the train is barreling down the tracks, not the conductor. This knowledge means that we may not even notice the dangling modifier. One

Dangling or misplaced modifiers can create amusing images, such as a woman clinging to the side of an aquarium.

could argue that this knowledge is what allows us to put the participial phrase in the front of the sentence in the first place. Prescriptive rules about dangling modifiers sometimes reflect concerted attempts to minimize in writing the ambiguity that characterizes much of spoken language. But that some dangling modifiers become accepted in style guides over time, whereas others do not, also reflects arbitrary preferences about which kinds of ambiguity are acceptable and which are not, rather than the systematic nature of syntax.

☑ Summary

- This chapter has described grammatical rules for how words combine systematically into phrases, clauses, and sentences. Grammar is hierarchical, based on a constituent structure: words combine into constituents called phrases, and phrases combine into larger phrases and into clauses; clauses can be sentences in and of themselves or they can combine into compound or complex sentences.

- The chapter presents many important distinctions related to phrases and clauses:
  - There are five types of phrases in English: NP, VP, ADJP, ADVP, PP.
  - A clause is composed of a NP and a VP.
  - There are two main types of clauses: independent clauses, dependent clauses.
  - Independent clauses can be joined to form compound sentences; subordinate/dependent clauses can be joined to an independent clause to form complex sentences.
  - Subordinate/dependent clauses can sometimes be reduced to infinitive phrases, gerund phrases, and participial phrases.
  - Different phrases and clauses can function in a sentence as nominals, adjectivals, and adverbials.

- Phrase structure rules describe the types and order of constituents that are possible for a given kind of phrase or clause. Phrase structure trees visually represent the hierarchical structure of a phrase, clause, or sentence, showing which words combine into phrases and then how those phrases combine into clauses and sentences. Transformations show the relationships between "underlying" grammatical structures, which adhere to phrase structure rules, and "surface" grammatical realizations, which are systematically related to the underlying structures but no longer adhere to phrase structure rules.

Suggested Reading

Chomsky's Universal Grammar: An Introduction (2nd ed., 1996), by V. J. Cook and Mark Newson, provides an excellent introductory but detailed overview of Chomskyan theory, as does Andrew Carnie's *Syntax: A Generative Introduction* (2002). Max Morenberg's *Doing Grammar* (2d ed., 1997) is a very accessible treatment of syntactic trees; it covers extremely complex sentences without the technical language of generative theory. For a comprehensive and fascinating overview and analysis of the interaction of cognitive and linguistic theory, including Universal Grammar, see Ray Jackendoff's *Foundations of Language* (2002). For more on competing theories to generative approaches, see *Chomsky and His Critics* (2003), edited by Louise M. Anthony and Norbert Hornstein. For detailed descriptive accounts of English grammar, you can turn to Rodney Huddleston and Geoffrey Pullum's *Cambridge Grammar of the English Language* (2002), Douglas Biber et al.'s *Longman Grammar of Spoken and Written English* (1999), and Sidney Greenbaum's *Oxford English Grammar* (1996).

Exercises
Exercise 6.1   Identifying Constituents

1. Decide which of the following are constituents. Then choose five and explain your answer using constituency tests.

    a. One day I took my car in for <u>an oil change</u>.

    b. The <u>serviceman asked</u> if I wanted to replace the air filter, too.

    c. When he <u>opened the airbox</u>, he doubled over with laughter.

    d. I walked <u>toward the front hood</u>.

    e. The airbox <u>was full of</u> acorns!

    f. There must have been <u>hundreds of acorns</u>.

    g. He also replaced <u>the windshield washer fluid</u>.

    h. He charged me an <u>outrageously large</u> sum for all of these services.

    i. The left turn signal seemed to be blinking <u>too fast</u>.

    j. So I took <u>my car to the car dealership</u>.

    k. <u>The serviceman at the car dealership</u> tested the bulb.

    l. The bulb <u>was fine</u>.

    m. We looked at each other, and <u>he shrugged</u>.

    n. I got in <u>my car</u> and drove away.

2. Identify each underlined constituent as a NP, VP, ADJP, ADVP, PP, S.

    a. The guy then pulled out the bulb <u>with its wires</u>.

    b. The critter that had left acorns in my airbox <u>had chewed through the wires</u>!

    c. This <u>very nice</u> guy replaced the wires for free.

d. As <u>I drove home</u>, I tried to wash the windshield.

e. No fluid squirted <u>onto the windshield</u>.

f. But I <u>had refilled the container only three hours earlier</u>.

g. <u>The annoying critter</u> had chewed through that tube, too.

h. But my revenge was that I had cleared out <u>the critter's pantry</u>.

i. And he never munched on <u>the wires and tubes in my car</u> again.

j. Here's the odd part: I always parked <u>in different parking spaces</u>.

k. How did he recognize my car <u>so consistently</u>?

l. Or perhaps lots of cars in the parking lot had <u>acorn-full airboxes and malfunctioning turn signals</u>.

Exercise 6.2   Basic Phrase Structure Trees

1. Draw phrase structure trees for the following basic sentences. You may find it easiest to draw the trees from the bottom to the top, first labeling all the words and then connecting them into constituents, which may then be embedded in other constituents. Remember that every sentence consists of a NP and a VP (so these will be the two constituents at the second-to-the-top level).

   a. We went to a party.

   b. The party was fun.

   c. My friend swallowed a goldfish.

   d. This friend swallowed the goldfish at the fun party.

   e. The goldfish wiggled in his throat.

   f. He looked frightened.

   g. The very scared goldfish leapt from his mouth into its bowl.

   h. Everyone laughed.

   i. The resourceful goldfish swam happily in its bowl.

   j. The sympathetic partygoers put the bowl on the mantel over the fireplace.

2. Provide two tree structures for each of the following phrases or clauses that disambiguate the two possible readings. The last one is a well-known ambiguous example in linguistics circles.

   a. My husband hit the car with the antenna ball.

   b. My Chinese literature instructor makes the readings fascinating.

   c. I spoke to the emcee with the microphone.

   d. The British left waffles on the Falkland Islands.

Exercise 6.3   Coordination

Draw phrase structure trees for the following sentences that involve coordination of NPs, PPs, ADJPs, and ss. Remember, a coordinated sentence can involve two clauses (usually still labeled s) connected by a conjunction.

a. The teacher assigned homework and papers.

b. The paper assignments were challenging but fun.

c. I write papers on my laptop or on a campus computer.

d. I lost my disk and my hard-drive crashed.

e. Lost disks and cranky computers ruined my day entirely.

Exercise 6.4   Relative Clauses

1. Identify which of the following relative clauses are restrictive and which are non-restrictive.

a. Yesterday afternoon I watched the television, which was tuned to *Friends*.

b. At the appliance store, Will watched the television that was tuned to *Friends*.

c. I enjoyed meeting Alex, who is also trained as a linguist.

d. Linguists, who sometimes speak multiple languages, are almost always asked how many languages they speak.

e. Some people are very impressed by linguists who speak many languages.

f. I would love to show you my collection of dictionaries, which is at my office.

g. The collection of dictionaries which I have at my office is bigger than this one at home.

h. Provide phrase structure trees that disambiguate the following sentences.

2. Draw phrase structure trees for the following sentences with restrictive relative clauses.

a. You drew syntactic trees that disambiguated the sentences in the exercise.

b. The homework that the instructor assigned was very challenging.

c. My friend who is a linguistics major helped me with the trees.

d. The trees that I drew looked sick and droopy.

Exercise 6.5   Complementizer Clauses

Draw phrase structure trees for the following sentences with complementizer clauses.

a. My instructor said that my sick trees needed more work.

b. I told him that my trees are an artistic statement.

c. I think that I understand what he wants.

Exercise 6.6   Infinitive and Participial Phrases

1. Identify which infinitive phrases function as nominals and which as adverbials.

a. I really want to work out five times a week.

b. I need more resolve to make this happen.

c. I planned to go to the gym last night.

d. I stayed home to hang out with my roommates and eat pizza.

e. I feel certain that my roommates ordered the pizza to tempt me.

f. It's not my fault that I like to eat pizza more than I like to go to the gym.

2. Identify which -*ing* forms occur in gerund phrases and which in participial phrases.

a. I remember taking my first linguistics class in college.

b. The instructor liked polling us about new college slang.

c. She would create handouts defining slang expressions, with short usage quizzes.

d. Seeing the slang we used in the dorm on a class handout was a bit disconcerting.

e. I still remember the instructor saying that a word means what people use it to mean.

f. Students enrolling in linguistics courses should expect surprises.

Exercise 6.7   Transformations

In her book *African American English: A Linguistic Introduction* (2002), linguist Lisa Green describes the grammatical rules of African American English (AAE) using phrase structure rules and transformations, as is so often done with Standard English. Many English speakers are not used to seeing AAE constructions described using the same grammatical terminology used for Standard English; in this way, Green aims to demonstrate the grammatical systematicity of African American English. AAE constructions are as grammatical in the descriptive sense as Standard English constructions, and they can be described using generative grammar. Let's look at an example.

In African American English, negative constructions with a negative indefinite noun phrase (e.g., *nobody, no game*) can undergo a transformation that does not occur in Standard English in these constructions: the auxiliary verb and the negative indefinite noun phrase can reverse positions. The result is sentences such as the following (from Green 2002, 78):

> *Don't no game last all night long.*
>
> *Can't nobody tell you it wasn't meant for you.*
>
> *Ain't nothing you can do.*
>
> *Don't nothing come to a sleeper but a dream.*

Let's look at two other systematic differences between AAE and Standard English. In the chapter, we described some transformations that occur in Standard English. Here we are asking you to describe some transformations in African American English.

1. Look at the following constructions in AAE and in Standard English (from Green 2002, 85–86). Describe the transformation for creating *wh-* questions in AAE, which is systematically different from the transformation in Standard English.

AAE	StE
Who you be talking to like that?	Who are you usually talking to like that?
What they was doing?	What were they doing?
What we gon get out the deal since we left everything?	What are we going to get out of the deal since we have left everything?

Why they ain't growing?	Why aren't they growing?
Why you looking like that?	Why are you looking like that?
Why those people don't want to take that car?	Why don't those people want to take that car?
Where your part be at?	Usually where is your part?

2. Examine the following examples of "indirect questions"—questions that occur within a sentence when you are describing a question you or someone else has. (The examples are from Green [2002, 87].) In Standard English, the embedded clause begins with *if* and the word order of the subordinate clause remains unchanged. For African American English, it works better to describe the structure of embedded indirect-question clauses as the result of a transformation. Describe the transformation in the following AAE examples.

AAE	StE
It's gonna ask you do you wanna make a transfer.	It's going to ask you if you want to make a transfer.
I wanted to see was it the one we bought.	I wanted to see if it was the one we bought.
They don't ask you did you sit on the choir.	They don't ask you if you were a member of the choir.
Go over there and see did they bring my car in.	Go over there and see if they brought my car in.
I meant to ask her did she want it.	I meant to ask her if she wanted it.
I wanted to know could they do it for me.	I wanted to know if they could do it for me.
You gotta wonder is the fear based on shame.	You've got to wonder if the fear is based on shame.
I wonder am I helping anybody yet.	I wonder if I am helping anybody yet.

Chapter 7

Semantics

The language of "Jabberwocky" was so vivid that readers invented meanings for *chortle* and other nonsense words—and over the years, some of them have even created images of the fictitious Jabberwock.

D o you chortle? How does your chortle compare to your friends' chortles? Although they all probably sound different, they are enough the same all to count as chortles. But what does it mean for chortles to be "the same"? They aren't really "the same" because a chortle, once chortled, cannot be reused (unless it is recorded). And when does a chortle become a giggle or a laugh? How does this word mean anyway?

When the word *chortle* was first introduced to English speakers in Lewis Carroll's "Jabberwocky," from *Through the Looking-Glass*, it didn't mean anything. Carroll made it up; it was a nonsense word. And yet readers of his poem were able to come up with a meaning for it—and that meaning ('to chuckle gleefully') can now be found in any standard dictionary. Readers made sense from nonsense. How?

The line in question reads: "He chortled in his joy." The syntax and morphology of the sentence make it clear that *chortle* needs to be a verb—and a happy verb, as "in his joy" indicates. So readers could guess that *chortle* might be a blend of *chuckle* and *snort*, as opposed to, say, a blend of *chocolate* and *turtle*.

The whole poem works this way. (You can find the full text in Exercise 1.1 in this book.) Here is the first stanza:

> 'Twas brillig and the slithy toves
> Did gyre and gimble in the wabe:
> All mimsy were the borogoves
> And the mome raths outgrabe.

You see from the start that plenty of words in the poem make little or no sense, at least not in English—they look and sound like words you know (is *brillig* like *bright* or *brilliant*? is *slithy* like *slithery*?), but finally, you can't attribute any meaning to them. You just as quickly realize that the lines aren't complete nonsense: many of the words in "Jabberwocky" are perfectly good English words.

You'll note that the words you recognize tend to be from closed morphological classes, words we use to organize sentences and larger segments of speech: *'Twas, and* (CONJ), *the* (DET), *did* (AUX), *in* (PREP). As a result, we can identify lexical categories for otherwise meaningless words. For example:

> 'Twas ADJ and the ADJ N
> Did V and V in the N

In other words, meaning isn't confined to lexical meaning: it develops from the relations of words, morphosyntax, and syntax in specific contexts, dependent also on relationships among speakers. The poem begins as advice and warning from father to son, then progresses to congratulation: you recognize these forms of discourse because of phrases like *my son* (later in the poem) and the verb *chortle*, even though you don't know much about the content of the advice or the congratulation.

Most of the time, we speak and understand speech perfectly well without consciously considering all these levels of meaning. But from a linguistic point of view, the nature of meaning cannot be taken for granted.

This chapter explains some fundamental semantic relationships among words, as well as some important theories of how meaning works, not only at the lexical level but beyond it, at the intersection of words, syntax, and discourse. Currently, no semantic theory proves that semantics is as systematic as phonology, morphology, or syntax;

words and sentences in context do not behave as predictably as phonemes, morphemes, or syntactic structures. During the twentieth century, philosophers and linguists made considerable progress toward an adequate semantic theory. Nevertheless, meaning may ultimately prove too slippery for any theory to hold.

Semantics

Semantics is the study of meaning in language. We can break it down further into two subfields: lexical semantics, which is the study of how words mean; and compositional semantics, which is the study of how words and syntax work together to make sentences mean. Words and syntax aren't just abstractions, though; we utter them in speech contexts, and rules of discourse further amplify and modify meaning when we use language to communicate. We focus primarily on lexical semantics here, but how words mean, how words mean in sentences, and how sentences mean are all essentially intertwined.

So what exactly does "the study of meaning" mean? One commonsense answer is that studying meaning is studying how words refer to things. Consider an old-fashioned definition of *semantics*, from Mario Pei and Frank Gaynor's *Dictionary of Linguistics* (1954), which makes the concept of reference central to semantics:

> **semantics** . . . A science dealing with the relation between *referents* and *referends*— linguistic symbols (words, expressions, phrases) and the objects or concepts to which they refer—and with the history and changes in the meaning of words.

At first glance, this account seems right: a dog is a thing to which the word *dog* refers; and *dog* is a word that refers to an object with certain qualities typical of dogs but not typical of things that aren't dogs, like cats.

Dictionaries do a lot of this kind of semantic work. Many dictionary definitions, especially of nouns, attempt to describe the relationship between a word and the thing to which it supposedly refers. The *American Heritage Dictionary of the English Language* (2000) defines *dog* in its most common sense as follows:

> **dog** . . . *n.* 1a. A domesticated carnivorous mammal (*Canus familiaris*) related to the foxes and wolves and raised in a wide variety of breeds.

The referential relationship between dog and *dog* seems transparent, but that transparency is, in fact, an illusion.

How is reference not transparent with a word like *dog*? Let's start with the definition. When you see a dog, do you think, "Ah, a domesticated carnivorous mammal"? When you see the word *dog*, do you register the variety of breeds? Somehow, reference seems to be an operation both completely tied to and yet detached from our experience. We meet dogs, we learn to call dogs "dogs," and we know to call a new dog "a dog" because, apparently, there is a meaningful mental and linguistic category of "dogs" to which we know that this new dog belongs. Now here's the hard part to explain: we each meet different dogs when we learn the word *dog*, and we each have our own image of a typical dog; yet we all share an understanding of the category "dog" that allows us all to share the same meaning for the word *dog*. So, as the Pei/Gaynor definition suggests, sometimes words refer to things in the world, and sometimes they refer to "concepts" or "categories" in the mind. And how we create and/or understand those concepts and categories is complex.

The concept of reference that seems plausible for nouns seems less able to account fully for the meaning of words in other lexical categories. To what does *above* refer? How about *meanwhile*? The best answer to these questions is probably, "Don't think in terms of words referring to things." The problem is that we are taught to think this way, and common sense superficially confirms what we're taught.

Reference plays a role in some lexical meaning, but the relationship between words and things isn't nearly as straightforward as we assume in our daily lives. And talking about the meaning of words, isolated from each other and any other context, may be a problematic enterprise. In order to rely less on reference in semantics, we start by outlining ways of thinking about meaning that go beyond any theory of reference. Then we'll go through a brief history of theories of reference to see how they have developed and how semantic theory has progressed from there.

The Limits of Reference

Here are three general observations that point to the limits of a theory of pure reference. First, the meaning of words has a complex relationship with each of our experiences in the world and how we categorize that world cognitively. In other words, lexical meaning is embedded in human thought and understanding. Second, words don't mean in isolation from sentences and discourse (the subject of the next chapter). Lexical meaning is somehow related to syntax and discourse, and any adequate theory of lexical meaning must account for those relationships. Third, words mean in physical and cultural context. When we isolate words from the contexts in which they occur, we lose part of their meaning. Already you can see that when we talk about the meaning of "a word," we are artificially abstracting the word from the contexts—cognitive, linguistic, and experiential—in which the word means.

The Role of Cognition

When someone asks, "Would you like to adopt a stray dog?", what runs through your mind? Whatever it is, it's probably not a dictionary definition. You have considerable experience of dogs, and chances are that you associate the term with dogs you have known personally, or those you've encountered in books (Lassie, Old Yeller, Odie), or in movies (Benji, K-9, Lady, or the Tramp), or on television (Scooby Doo, Snoopy). The mental "picture" you associate with the word depends on that experience, as well as experience of things similar to dogs that are not dogs (cats, for instance) and things that are dogs but not domestic ones (foxes and wolves).

Understanding what a word means, then, depends on cognitively sorting through alternative meanings and selecting the most appropriate meaning for the context in which the word is used or understood. When you use *dog*, or when you understand what someone else means by the word, to which dog in all the world does the term refer? Or does it refer to the class of dogs that includes those you've known personally or encountered through the media? The answer will vary, but here's the critical problem for a theory of semantics: you can point to a dog, but you'll have trouble pointing to the class of dogs, whatever that is.

Meaning may well depend at least as much on the way our minds understand and categorize the world around us as on the relations between objects/concepts and the symbols we assign to represent them. We have cognitive skills with which we make sense of the world. They help us categorize what we encounter as "like" and "not like" other things we have encountered. These cognitive skills are reflected in our language and how words mean. Words develop in response to our experience of the world, but our experience is always subject to cognitive processes and mental content.

The Role of Linguistic Context

Semantics is a matter of knowing not only how words mean, but how sentences mean as well. The meaning of sentences cannot be determined by just adding up the meaning of the words. Otherwise, the two sentences *Jessie doesn't like beer* and *Beer doesn't like Jessie* would mean the same thing. But we know that one sentence describes Jessie's preferences, and the other implies some nasty bodily reactions for poor Jessie after drinking beer.

Syntax matters in determining what sentences mean. But we can turn that statement around to argue that syntax is part of how words mean. In other words, the syntactic roles that a word can play and the syntactic structures that a word requires are part of the word's meaning. For example, the verb *read* that occurs intransitively, without an object ("Most three-year-olds don't know how to read"), carries a different meaning

---

A Question to Discuss

How Do Function Words Mean?

Some words simultaneously help sentences mean and gain their own meanings from their functions within sentences. These words mean without even a hint of reference, unless the words refer to the concepts of their functions. For example, the *American Heritage Dictionary of the English Language* defines the infinitive marker *to* (for instance, in "She wanted to learn all about English linguistics") simply as "Used before a verb to indicate an infinitive." The *New Oxford American Dictionary* (*NOAD*), on the other hand, while defining the term in essentially the same way, itemizes various implications of infinitives, for example, "expressing purpose or intention: *I set out to buy food | we tried to help | I am going to tell you a story.*"

Although infinitives do certainly mean in various, definable ways, to what extent does *to* carry any of the infinitive's meaning? Is the meaning a feature of the noninfinitive verb (*set out* or *tried*) or the infinitive marker in

combination with a verb? But then, which verb? As the *NOAD* examples indicate, though *to* marks *tell* as an infinitive, the *going* and *to* cooperate semantically at least as much as *to* and *tell*. You set out to do what? *I set out to buy food.* It would be difficult to describe any self-sufficient semantic role played by *to* in such cases.

For different reasons, words like *and* and *or* describe functions rather than refer, unless they refer to the concepts of the functions they perform. In formal logic (which formal semanticists often employ to disambiguate sentence meaning), the functions are indefinable and accepted as "self-evident" (even when, to many of us, they are not!). When expressed by the symbols "&" and "v," they avoid associations with natural language and mean 'conjunction' and 'disjunction', merely the connective functions they perform within sentences. But do we want to say that these conjunctions have no lexical meaning?

from *read* before an object ("If you want to know about semantics, you should read this chapter"). To take another example, the word *dog* after the determiner *the* typically carries a specific reference to one animal, whereas after the indefinite article *a,* it describes a representative of a class.

The Role of Physical and Cultural Context

Polysemy is the linguistic term for one word carrying multiple historically related meanings. If you walk down the street with an animal-loving friend, he might point to a dog and say, "Hey, that's a cool looking dog!" He might bend down, scratch the dog behind the ears, and say something like, "How are you doin', dog? What's your name, dog?" If he knows the owner well, he might say to him, "Yo, wassup dawg?" but he's unlikely to address the dog this way, except as a self-conscious joke. A few minutes later, hungry, your friend may stop at a vendor's cart: "Dog me!" he'll exclaim, but he means 'Serve me a hot dog', rather than 'follow me around like a dog'. After a while, he may suggest that you both sit down and rest. "My dogs are barkin'!" he explains. In purely formal terms, such sentences are ambiguous. But successful users of a language know how to assign various meanings to the same symbol or signifier, depending on context. We observe physical context; we watch for discourse cues like tone and gesture; we guess at speakers' intentions, and much more.

Sometimes understanding an utterance depends on a very complex system of shared cultural context. When you finally get back to your friend's apartment, you suggest a video, but he can't hang out: he has to go to work. "It's a dog's life," he says jokingly. In such a sentence, to what does the word *dog* refer? To what does the sentence refer? There's no literal dog in question. The statement itself is metaphorical, although

---

Language Change at Work

The Formation of Idioms

An idiom is an expression whose meaning cannot be derived directly from the string of words that make up the expression. For example, if something is *a piece of cake*, it is easy to do (not frosted or iced). If an idea is completely *off the wall*, you may not be able *to make heads or tails* of it. Whether you *hit the books* or *hit the sack,* you aren't actually physically hitting anything. Your hands are similarly not physically involved in *lending someone a hand* (luckily! What if the person did not return it?) or *having your hands full*.

Many idioms, such as *lending someone a hand* or *having one's hands full*—but not all idioms—derive their meaning from metaphor.

For example, *being saved by the bell* has been metaphorically extended from boxing to any situation in which one is saved at the last minute. *Down to the wire* also comes from sports (horse racing), and *chip off the old block* from carpentry. The origin of some idioms lies in literature, rather than metaphor. For example, we can trace *what the dickens* back to Shakespeare. And some idioms are metaphorical and are first recorded in literature, such as *to be tongue-tied,* also from Shakespeare. Other idioms come neither from literature or metaphor but rely on shared cultural knowledge for their meaning, such as *what's up?*

most speakers now probably don't immediately process it as a metaphor. The origins of the metaphor rely on a cultural understanding of the miserable life that a dog leads—or at least led in the sixteenth century when the expression is first recorded. Now it is an idiom: a fixed expression whose meaning is understood through shared cultural context.

A theory of linguistic reference takes us some distance toward an intelligent semantics, but not far enough. It is the semantic theory, however, with the longest history. We now trace the development of theories of reference to see where they take us.

A Brief History of Theories of Reference

Much of what linguists study now was historically the domain of philosophers. Even today, especially in syntax and semantics, the interests of current linguists and philosophers often overlap.

Deixis

Let's start with a very straightforward kind of reference. In speech, we sometimes make reference clear with what linguists call **deixis**, from the Ancient Greek adjective *deiktikos* 'pointing'. All personal pronouns "point" to specific people and are markers of **personal deixis**: "*I* want the dog that *you* found in the alley." Demonstrative pronouns mark **spatial deixis**: "I want *that* dog" (i.e., the one over there, or near you) or "I want *this* dog" (i.e., the one near me). Certain adverbs of time indicate **temporal deixis**: "I want the dog *now*" or "I will pick up the dog *tomorrow*." (See Figure 7.1.)

Deictic reference, however, is very limited in speech and isn't the type of reference we assume endows most of our vocabulary with meaning. We can't point to everything we mean. Nonetheless, until the twentieth century, philosophers and linguists tried to explain how words carried meaning through a kind of extended deixis, following in the tradition of Plato.

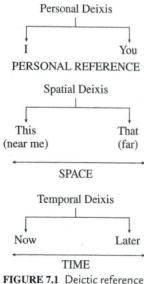

FIGURE 7.1 Deictic reference involves pointing to people (e.g., *you*), to things at a specific point in space (e.g., *that*), or to a specific point in time (e.g., *now*).

Plato and Forms

Attempts at semantic explanation based on extended deixis began very early in the history of Western ideas. Plato, for instance, thought that our everyday conception of things referred to Forms or Ideas. If you have a mental representation of a dog, it refers to an ideal dog in the world of Ideas, what you might call "dogness"—that is, there's a difference between anyone's idea of a dog and the Idea of Dog. Our mental representations are closer to the Ideas than real things are to the Forms: the mental dog mediates between the perfect Idea of Dog and the imperfect dog, napping in the sun. The word *dog* does not refer to a dog but to our mental representations of dogs.

We now generally reject the notion that our words represent mental images that in turn represent pure exemplars of concepts beyond experience. But we are just as likely, when we're not doing philosophy, to think that words, especially nouns, refer to things (or classes of things) with definable properties. This is obvious in a case like *dog*, but take a time-worn example of a sentence that doesn't actually refer to anything: "The present king of France is bald." There is no present king of France—that is, the sentence doesn't refer to any real state of affairs. Is the sentence meaningless, then, even though, word by word, we think we know what it means?

Repairing Plato

Viennese philosopher Alexius Meinong (1853–1920) had an approach to meaning resembling Plato's. In order for a sentence like "The present king of France is bald" to mean anything, Meinong argued, there had to be referents for each word in the sentence. True, there is no object in everyday experience to which *the, present, of, is,* or *bald* refers; but there are concepts of these "things" to which such words refer, like "of-ness" and "existence" and "baldness," for instance.

The problems with such a theory of meaning are probably obvious to you. How do we know to refer to these concepts or ideas with the words we use? And how do we know that the concepts exist in the first place? The tendency in theories of meaning like Meinong's was to assume reference and then argue that the concepts must exist so that words could refer to them. The logic of such a position isn't defensible. If we are really interested in determining what exists and in the relations among existing things, then we want logical or empirical proof that, for example, "presentness" is real enough for *present* to refer to it.

Bertrand Russell (1872–1970), one of the most significant of twentieth-century philosophers, developed a "theory of descriptions" to answer Meinong and like-minded philosophers. Russell attempted to explain the relationship between word and sentence meaning without presupposing, as Meinong had done, imaginary referents for words that do not have obvious referents given our experience in the world.

Once a word is used in a phrase, Russell argued, it no longer functions as a name, unless the statement is trivial (e.g., "Michael is Michael"). If the statement is otherwise meaningful, as in "Anne and Michael are the authors of this book," then phrases like "Anne and Michael" and "the authors of this book" are not names but "descriptions." They don't refer to things, but within the sentence they help to describe a state of affairs. If the sentence in question corresponds accurately to affairs in the world ("Anne and Michael are the authors of this book"), then the statement is meaningful and true. If the sentence in question does not correspond accurately to the world ("The present king of France is bald"—there is no present king of France, so he certainly isn't bald), then the sentence is false but still meaningful; it is meaningful in some context other than correspondence to actual events or circumstances (say, to false belief or fiction).

This theory of meaning, although less naive than Plato's, is nonetheless referential: "correspondence" is a more sophisticated version of "reference." It's just that, according to Russell, reference is accomplished at the sentence level. And the fundamental issue is the "truth condition" of the sentence—that is, what would have to be the case in order for the sentence to be true or false (or, in logics that allow more truth values, "neither true nor false," "both true and false," etc.).

From Reference to Discourse

P. F. Strawson (1919–), another British philosopher, lodged two significant objections against Russell's theory. First, Strawson argued, Russell had not accounted for the fact that the same sentence can be put to different uses. (Consider the sentence "That's my dog!" in which *dog* could mean 'domestic canine' and the aim of the utterance is to identify that particular canine as yours, or *dog* could mean 'guy friend'—sometimes spelled *dawg*—and the utterance could express enthusiastic approval.) Second, Strawson denied that every proposition was necessarily either true or false. Strawson used the test sentence "The present King of France is wise." He pointed out that, had someone uttered the sentence during the reign of Louis XIV, the person would have put it to one use, referring to an actual king with properties that might be described in a sentence. If anyone used the sentence today, however, it would have a different meaning because it has a different use. As Strawson explained it,

> if one man uttered it in the reign of Louis XIV and another man uttered it in the reign of Louis XV, it would be natural to say (to assume) that they were respectively talking about different people; and it might be held that the first man, in using the sentence, made a true assertion, while the second man, in using the same sentence, made a false assertion. If on the other hand two different men simultaneously uttered the sentence (*e.g.* if one wrote it and the other spoke it) during the reign of Louis XIV, it would be natural to say (assume) that they were both talking about the same person, and, in that case, in using the sentence, they *must* either both have made a true assertion or both have made a false assertion. And this illustrates what I mean by *a use* of a sentence. The two men who uttered the sentence, one in the reign of Louis XV and one in the reign of Louis XIV, each made a different use of the same sentence; whereas the two men who uttered the sentence simultaneously in the reign of Louis XIV, made the same use of the same sentence. Obviously in the case of this sentence, and equally obvious in the case of many others, we cannot talk of *the sentence* being true or false, but only of its being used to make a true or false assertion. (Strawson 1965, 320)

Indeed, because there is no king of France today, and because the sentence in question presupposes the existence of such a king, and because the presupposition is clearly false, were the sentence used today, Strawson argued, it would be neither true nor false—truth and falsity aren't relevant categories of explanation for such a sentence. In other words, Russell's theory of descriptions isn't necessary, because he had misunderstood the semantic problem.

Meinong and Russell were formal semanticists: they viewed meaning in language as a self-contained system. Strawson, though nominally a formal semanticist, nonetheless points toward a functional approach to meaning: that language carries meaning when used in a given context. His use of the term *use* in the quotation says it all.

From Reference to Translation

The American philosopher Willard van Orman Quine (1908–2000) argued that all semantics is a matter of translation—in other words, we understand a word in terms of other words. Suppose, he argued, that someone who spoke a language different from yours uttered *gavagai* while pointing to a rabbit. How would you know whether the word meant 'rabbit' or 'part of a rabbit' or 'behavior of a rabbit'? You wouldn't. The only way to know is to discuss or explain the reference, using words, to clarify the exact meaning of *gavagai. All reference, in other words, is circular:

> A question of the form "What is an F?" can be answered only by recourse to a further term: "An F is a G." The answer makes only relative sense: sense relative to the uncritical acceptance of "G." (Quine 1969, 53)

Quine proposed an essentially formalist position. Within language, terms are only understood according to circular definitions: meaning consists in the translation we provide for terms. It is a self-contained linguistic sphere, dependent on shared lexical meanings.

The circularity on which Quine focused is manifest throughout the vocabulary of English and every other language. Consider complex words, like adverbs or prepositions, rather than nouns. The adverbial sense of *inside* doesn't refer to a thing but to a spatial relation. What does it mean? Dictionaries often define it as 'within', which you will admit doesn't exactly pin the meaning down. One dictionary the authors consulted defines *within* as "In or into the inner part; inside"—you can't get more circular than that! Good dictionaries rely on a **defining vocabulary**: essentially all definitions are written in words also entered in the dictionary, so that users puzzled by words in definitions can look them up. Terms like *within* and *inside* may be especially susceptible to very obvious circularity. But a defining vocabulary, while it doesn't necessarily lead to tight circles like that of *within* and *inside*, is really just one big circle: in the end, all words are defined by other words. If we understand word meanings in spite of this circularity, something besides lexical reference must determine semantic relations, both among words and between words and "things."

Words gain most of their meaning from participating in sentences. Sentences, though they can be described in a symbolic fashion, mean most when they are uttered—that is, when their abstract syntactic structures are embodied in speech, in the social use of language where meaning actually counts. When we define words, we do so by examining how they operate in speech. We don't start with the lexical meaning and move "forward" to sentences and discourse; rather, we move "backward" from discourse and sentences to understand the meanings of words. In any event, attempts to defend the commonsense notion that words mean simply because they refer have only proved that semantics must be larger and more complicated than a theory of reference.

Lexical Fields

Lexical meaning is arguably at least as relational as it is referential. One way to think about how words mean in relation to other words exploits clusters of related items in the lexicon, relying more on shared than contrasting features. Our sense of a word's meaning derives in part from where it fits into the web of words and meanings. As mentioned earlier, part of what we mean by *dog* is determined by its semantic relationship to *cat*, because dogs aren't cats. Of course, dogs aren't motorcycles either, but the relationship between *dog* and *motorcycle* is quite different from that between *dog* and *cat*.

Dog and *cat* belong to the same **lexical field**, or set of words that somehow belong together. In fact, *dog* and *cat* belong potentially to several lexical fields, together and individually. *Summer, doormat, cookie, book, fire, dime,* and *DVD* do not constitute a lexical field, because the terms are not conceptually related in any obvious way. The relationship among items in a lexical field is conceptual and not referential. Consider the following (very incomplete) descriptions of three lexical fields:

Field 1: *dog, cat, hamster, parakeet, goldfish*

Field 2: *gryphon, phoenix, satyr, siren, centaur*

Field 3: *journal, newspaper, annual, magazine, review*

All of the items in Field 1 are words that represent household pets (see Figure 7.2). We could say that they are all terms that refer to household pets, but that misses the point. The field is governed, not by the reference of words to things, but by the quality of pet-ness shared among items in the list. *Aardvark* does not belong in Field 1, not because as a term it refers any less than the items listed, but because it's unlikely that anyone keeps an aardvark as a pet. The items in Field 2, all mythological creatures, refer to nothing, if we expect reference to join a word with a "thing." At best they refer to concepts, but the key here is that they share the semantic feature "mythological creatures."

The relations among terms in Field 3 are semantically more complicated than those among terms in the other groups. For instance, because you can form mental pictures that correspond with *dog* and *cat, gryphon* and *phoenix*, you can say that one word does not mean the other because the pictures are different. But items in Field 3 are words that represent types of periodical: the differences among them are definable, but mostly the items aren't physically or even visually distinct. A maga-zine doesn't look like a newspaper, unless it's a tabloid (we could add *tabloid* to Field 3). What is the discernible difference among journals, annuals, and reviews? A journal publishes articles of professional concern for a certain group. For example, doctors and others interested in medicine and health subscribe to the *New England Journal of Medicine*. A review publishes literary and critical essays, as well as works of literature, as in the *American Poetry Review* or the *Gettysburg Review*. But then

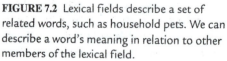

FIGURE 7.2 Lexical fields describe a set of related words, such as household pets. We can describe a word's meaning in relation to other members of the lexical field.

how do we explain the scholarly journal of Middle English literature called the *Chaucer Review*? Are *journal* and *review* synonyms? An annual is merely a journal (or maybe a review) published once a year. The distinction here is not one of type or purpose, but of frequency.

Words inevitably belong to lexical fields, and part of knowing their meaning is understanding their relationship to other words in their lexical fields. To talk precisely about lexical meaning, then, we need to distinguish among several possible meaningful relationships that words can have with one another besides simply belonging to the same lexical field.

Hyponym to Homonym (and Other Nyms)

In the sections that follow, we examine several types of semantic relationships: hyponymy, meronymy, synonymy, antonymy, and homonymy.

Hyponymy

Hyponymy denotes a set of hierarchical semantic relationships. A **hypernym** or **superordinate** is a more general term than its **hyponyms.** Looked at from the other direction, hyponyms are subordinate to their hypernym. Take *dog* as a superordinate: subordinate to it are words for all kinds of dogs, like *Pekingese, mutt, terrier,* and *Labrador*—these are the hyponyms. Hyponymy simultaneously expresses a hierarchical and several parallel semantic relationships, as illustrated in the following diagram:

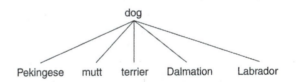

Note here that the relationship described is not conceptual but semantic, a matter of words in relation to other words. *Pekingese* and *Labrador* are both words for kinds of dogs and, in relation to *dog,* belong at the same level of meaning; they are specific examples of a more general term. Obviously, though, *dog* is also a hyponym:

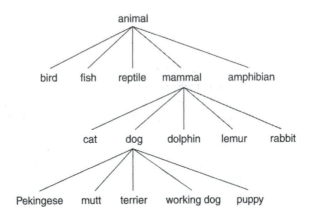

Superordinate to kinds of dogs, *dog* is a hyponym under the superordinate *mammal*, itself a hyponym of *animal*. Some words are more general in their meanings than others, but the generality or specificity is relative, depending on where a word falls in the complete hierarchical tree of animal terms.

Sometimes hyponymy fails us. For example, *aunt* and *uncle*, although clearly hyponyms in relation to each other, lack an immediate superordinate term. They are clearly subordinate to superordinates: *aunt* and *uncle* are types of *relative/relation,* and they are also examples of *person/human*. There is, however, no term parallel to *parent,* the immediate superordinate for *mother* and *father,* that serves as a superordinate for *aunt* and *uncle*. The missing stage in the hierarchical tree is a lexical gap: there's a thing or concept, but there's no lexical item to cover it. Thirtysomethings who don't like the terms *partner* or *significant other* sometimes complain that there is no good immediate hypernym for *boyfriend* and *girlfriend*.

Meronymy

Another hierarchical semantic relationship is the **meronym**, which figures in the relation of whole to part: *tail, whiskers, paw, ears,* and *snout* all represent parts of a dog (well, most dogs—some Welsh Corgi, for example, lack tails), and so stand in a subordinate semantic relationship to the word *dog*. The meronymic relationship is not hyponymic: hyponyms represent kinds of a superordinate; *paw* and *whiskers* are not kinds of dogs, so their relationship to *dog* is categorically distinct from hyponymy.

Now we're getting somewhere: *weasel* is superordinate to *stoat* and *ermine* (as well as other types of weasels). Thus, *stoat* and *ermine* are hyponyms under that superordinate. Or are they? They don't stand in the same relation to each other as the hyponyms arranged under *dog*—they don't represent different "types" of weasel, but two states of the same type. Perhaps *ermine* and *stoat* both originated to fill perceived lexical gaps: folks thought they needed one word for the animal they encountered in summer, another for the one they saw in winter. But if they hadn't experienced two apparently different animals, they wouldn't have identified two gaps and created two words. Perhaps *stoat* and *ermine* are both hyponyms of *stoat* (it is, after all, brown three seasons out of the year), which is itself a hyponym of *weasel*. Can a word be a hyponym of itself? Well, *lion* in reference to a male lion, as opposed to *lioness*, is a hyponym of *lion*. Perhaps *ermine* and *stoat* are meronyms, since the words identify the color of the animal's fur— but it's the *fur* that's the part, not the color of the fur. Come to think of it, we haven't come very far at all!

Synonymy

Synonymy is one of the semantic relationships with which you are already familiar. **Synonyms** are words that supposedly mean the same thing, but that very explanation exposes the problem with synonymy. True, synonyms refer to the same thing, but much of their relative meaning isn't referential. Words denote according to their point of reference; a word's **denotative meaning** is referential (and what we sometimes more loosely refer to as "literal"). Words connote according to associations that arise from their use; **connotative meaning**, then, is determined by speaker experience and intention, auditor reaction, context, and shared cultural understanding. So, for instance, *dog/dawg, dude, companion/associate,* and *friend* are all synonyms that denote the same thing but that carry with them quite different connotations. **What's up, my associate?* is an unlikely greeting, to say the least.

Synonyms, then, do not easily replace each other. Because of the distance between denotation and connotation, because meaning is so much more than mere reference, there are very few true synonyms in English—if there are any at all. If you imagine a *jacket* and a *coat* (arguably two close synonyms), do you conjure up the same mental image? Is one heavier or more fashionable or more weatherproof? Even *stoat* and *ermine,* which we used to illustrate the relationship between phonemes and allophones in Chapter 3, don't denote exactly the same thing, since both terms apply to the same animal, but not in the same season. There are arguably a few pairs (or sets) of true synonyms, like *cemetery* and *graveyard,* but most true synonyms are words that differ by geographic region, such as *pop* versus *soda, firebug* versus *firefly,* or *dragonfly* versus *mosquito hawk* (or *skeeter hawk*) versus *snake feeder* versus *snake doctor* versus *darning needle* (or *darner*). In most of these cases, however, speakers typically use only one of the forms in their dialect.

Antonymy

Antonymy is another familiar semantic relationship; **antonyms** are words that mean the opposite of each other. Unlike synonymy and hyponymy, antonymy is a binary relationship—only two words at a time. Some antonyms are **gradable:** that is, while conceptually opposites, they represent values at two ends of a spectrum, with many values in between them. For instance, dogs can be *fat* or *thin,* and many dogs fall somewhere in between: *pudgy, chunky, plump, healthy, slender, lean.* Other gradable antonyms include *hot* and *cold, good* and *bad, slow* and *fast.*

Nongradable (or **complementary**) **antonyms** are those that admit no more or less, just absolutes at opposite conceptual poles: *single* and *married, awake* and *asleep,* and *dead* and *alive* are nongradable. Legend has it that one can also be *undead,* like a vampire or demon, but this "middle" term doesn't affect the nongradable status of *dead* and *alive.* Instead, it suggests other antonymic pairs, like *dead* and *undead,* though the semantic relationship seems not to be transitive; in other words, *undead* is obviously not an antonym of *alive,* anymore than the "middle" term *drowsy* is the antonym of either *awake* or *asleep.*

Converseness is also a semantic relation of opposites, a feature of some (but by no means all, or even most) antonymy. Converse pairs are semantically reciprocal. *Male* and *female* are not a converse pair, because a male is not necessarily joined to a female, and vice versa; but *parent* and *child* are converse, because *parent* means a person with a child, and *child* means a person with a parent. In other words, the opposite of each word is implied in the meaning of each word. Although *good* and *evil* are antonyms, it's not clear that they are a converse pair; some have argued that good cannot exist without evil, but that conclusion is not necessary—conceivably, good and evil each could exist without the other. Although not every evil requires a correspondent good, every teacher requires a correspondent student. Here again we see how lexical meaning is at least as relational as it is referential: at least part of the meaning of either *teacher* or *student* has to do, not with the correspondence of word and thing, but with the meaning of the other term.

A Question to Discuss

Does the Thesaurus Have a Bad Name?

When you are writing a paper and need a different word that means something like a word you've already used, where do you turn? To a thesaurus, of course. But have you ever noticed that certain risks attend use of a thesaurus? The synonyms you find under this or that heading are all related semantically, some more, some less. They tend to share a referent, so they also share a denotation. But since each synonym carries a slightly to grossly different connotation from the others, context and tone and audience and other subtle influences on meaning are difficult to gauge and can interfere with the correct application of one word or another. There are few true synonyms, so synonyms listed in a thesaurus aren't automatically replacements for one another. If you think that you need a synonym for *happy*, you can't just insert *glad, jolly, jubilant*, or *merry* into your sentence—none of these words means exactly the same as the others.

The original *Thesaurus of English Words and Phrases* (1852) was compiled by Peter Mark Roget (1779–1869), a British physician. As Simon Winchester (of *The Professor and the Madman* fame) has recently pointed out,

Roget's *Thesaurus* was not intended as a dictionary of synonyms, but as a vast, interconnected system of classification of terms in English. It was an intellectual enterprise: the question was, "In what ways are words related to one another?"

The thesaurus on your desk doesn't resemble Roget's, though the name *Roget* may be in the title, just as the name *Webster* may figure in the title of a dictionary not published by the G. & C. Merriam Company—if not protected as trademarks, such terms can be used by anyone. In fact, nearly all books sold under the name "thesaurus" today are really "synonym finders." J. I. Rodale's *The Synonym Finder*, first published in 1947 and still in print, is the most honestly titled of such books.

Many teachers claim they can tell when students use (or misuse) words suggested by a word processing program's thesaurus. Some teachers tell their students not to use the thesaurus and not to plug in words with which they are not comfortable. Do you think this is good advice? How can students benefit from using the thesaurus? What guidance would you give them?

Homonymy

As we mentioned earlier, a word is polysemous when it carries more than one meaning—typically meanings that are relatively transparently related because some developed out of others over time. (In fact, the development of new senses of a word is always historical, but when words develop quickly in our own experience, we find it difficult to think of it that way.) It's useful to have polysemy in mind when we consider homonymy.

Homonyms are words of radically different meaning that share a word form: either the same spelling, or the same pronunciation, or both. For instance, *sink* can mean a basin connected to plumbing (among some other things), and it can also mean to fall to a lower level (among many other verb senses). *Sink* the noun and *sink* the verb are homonyms because they share a spelling and a pronunciation but have different meanings. You can also be *in sync*, where *sync* is a clipping of *synchrony* (**synch* might be a homonym of *cinch*, so the spelling *sync* is preferred). *Sink* and *sync* are spelled differently but are homonyms because they share a pronunciation and have different meanings. They are also etymologically distinct, which is not true of *sink* and *sink*, where the noun derives from the verb.

Sometimes homonyms are both **homophones** (words that have the same pronunciations) and **homographs** (words that share the same form), as in the case of *sink* (noun) and *sink* (verb). In other cases, like *dove* 'bird' and *dove* 'past tense of *dive*', homonyms are homographs but not homophones. In other cases, homonyms such as *to, too,* and *two*, are homophones but not homographs. Confused yet? Unfortunately, it may only get more confusing if you look at enough linguistics books, because some equate homonyms with homographs and some require that homonyms be both homographs and homophones. In any case, most dictionaries enter homonyms separately, so that they are not taken as semantic developments of the same word.

Organization of the Mental Lexicon

The mental lexicon is often compared to a dictionary, but that metaphor creates a false impression of how words are organized in the brain. The standard English dictionary organizes words alphabetically, in columns and from left to right, so words are stored near other words that are spelled similarly. This kind of organization is not irrelevant to the organization of words in the brain, but it is only the beginning. One type of thesaurus organizes words into lexical fields, so words that mean similar things appear near each other. Rhyming dictionaries put words that rhyme together. The brain does all of these things. Studies of brain activity (as well as of aphasia) indicate that we process open-class and closed-class words in different parts of the brain. By the time you finish reading about the organization of the mental lexicon and all the activity that takes place in your brain when you access a word, you may be amazed that your head doesn't explode, let alone that you can walk, talk on your cell, watch out for oncoming pedestrians, and butter your bagel all at the same time.

Many studies of the organization of lexical knowledge rely on a technique called **priming**, which tests the activation of the lexicon in our brains. This test provides

The word *pot* primes all its meanings, including a cooking pot, a planting pot, and marijuana.

evidence about how speakers access the meaning of a given word. Subjects watch a computer screen as words and nonwords flash onto it. Their task (for English speakers) is to determine whether the word is a "real" English word or a nonword and then hit the appropriate button under their hand. This typically takes a few hundred milliseconds, which is significantly slower than the brain's recognition speed, but you have to allow time for motor reflexes like lifting the finger. Priming tests generally show that reaction time for real words is faster if the word is "related" to a recently presented word. Related how? There are many possibilities.

Let's imagine that a subject sees the word *pot* and a few milliseconds later identifies it as a real word. The speaker's reaction time will then be faster for words in the following categories:

- Synonyms: e.g., *pan, container, vessel, marijuana.*
- Collocates: e.g., *cook, hot, pan, smoke, plants* (**collocates** are words that often occur in proximity to each other—*cooking pots, hot pots, pots and pans, smoke pot, pot plants*; these are all not only recorded but typical combinations of words).
- Rhymes: e.g., *cot, tot, lot.*
- Phonologically similar words: e.g., *pod* (a common example is *sympathy* priming *symphony*).

The word *pot* is polysemous, and, as you can see from this list, there is priming for all of its meanings, including its use as a noun (e.g., *pots and pans, smoke pot*) and as a verb (*to pot plants*). Studies also indicate that if the syllable *pot* appears in another word like *pothole*, all this priming still occurs.

What happens when we see or hear a word? We often use the verb *access* to refer to retrieving meaning, but many scholars note that the verb *activate* may be more appropriate. When we see or hear a word, we activate the web of relationships around it—its homonyms, synonyms, collocates, and rhymes. Further studies indicate that hearing a word activates all possibilities, and we then eliminate the irrelevant ones as we get more information. For example, with the word *possibility*, after the first syllable, our minds would activate words like *possible, possum, posse*—as well as their primes. These words would then be deactivated as we hear more of the word and eliminate these other possibilities (e.g., the second syllable of *possibility* would eliminate *possum* and *posse*). Researchers test these relationships by flashing up primes of, say, *possum* before the subject has heard all of the word *possibility*. With a polysemous word like *pot*, all its meanings (in all syntactic categories) are activated, even if context makes clear what meaning is meant. For example, if you hear or read "I put spaghetti in the pot," primes like *marijuana* will still be activated. But two or three syllables later, these irrelevant primes are deactivated.

Why might our minds prime so exhaustively every time we hear a word? Although it may seem like a lot of extra work, it could actually be a mechanism for speeding language processing. Because priming activates words that are likely to appear in the immediate context of the word you have just read or heard, you will be able to process the entire utterance more quickly as you are "prepared" for what is likely to follow.

Prototype Semantics

Prototype semantics assumes a connection between cognitive and linguistic categories. It emphasizes the centrality of "best examples" or **prototypes** that allow language users to structure linguistic categories and create meaningful semantic relationships. Categories structured around prototypes have "fuzzy edges" as opposed to clear-cut semantic boundaries.

Lexical Prototype Semantics

Lexical prototype semantics proposes that prototypes (sometimes called "image schemas") are fundamental to lexical meaning. According to this theory, prototypes develop as our innate linguistic competence comes into contact with experience of the world around us. Meaning, then, is not with us from the outset of our linguistic activity. Instead, it is a lifelong, ongoing interface of the mind with the world through experience.

Prototype theory asserts that lexical categories are organized around prototypes. For example, each of us has developed a notion of the prototypical dog, and although some of the details may differ (such as color), given our varied experience of the world, our prototypical understandings of "dog" probably share many features, including particularly doglike shapes and sizes, fur, lolling tongue, wagging tail, and so on. Prototype theory proposes a graded relationship (*graded* in the sense we used above for antonyms) among things that belong to a prototype's category: some items in the category are more prototypical than others. Thus, a spaniel may be closer to prototypical "dog" than a hairless dog, but the hairless dog shares enough features of the prototype to be in the "dog" category.

In prototype theory, not all members of a category have to share features with each other, as long as they share features with the prototype. In this way, ice skating can be a sport and football can be a sport, even though the two may share little to nothing with each other. "Sport" is a fuzzy category. If you and your friend decide to have a contest to see who can spit cherry pits the farthest, is that a sport? Or is sport a metaphor to describe this activity? It is difficult to see how man's best friend and aching feet could share any semantic features, but, as George Lakoff (1987) has pointed out, prototype theory better explains metaphor—metaphorical extension is one of the ways that categories can have fuzzy boundaries.

Analogical Mapping

Prototypes are very useful in explaining meaning difficult to explain by other theoretical means. For instance, prepositions aren't adequately accounted for by reference or lexical semantic relationships. Consider a small portion of the range of prepositional meanings (there are twenty-nine in all) encompassed by *on* in the *American Heritage Dictionary of the English Language*:

> **1a.** Used to indicate position above and supported by or in contact with: *The vase is on the table* . . . **b.** Used to indicate contact with or extent over (a surface) regardless of position: *a picture on the wall* . . . **c.** Used to indicate location at or along: *the pasture on the south side of the river* . . . **d.** Used to indicate proximity: *a town on the border.*

e. Used to indicate attachment to or suspension from: *beads on a string*. **f.** Used to indicate figurative or abstract positions: *on the young side*.

Is 'above' a component of *on*'s meaning? It certainly would be one for *on* in sense **1a**. But 'above' plays no role in *on* in sense **1b**. We need something further to explain the polysemy of *on*.

That something is **analogical mapping**: arguably, we draw relations among meanings within cognitively based patterns of spatial, temporal, or logical relations. Such a cognitive process would help to explain the meaning of many items in closed morphological classes, like prepositions. A vase sits above a table, given a horizontal plane as a frame of reference. A picture on the wall is not above the wall, but that's because the frame of reference is vertical. Yet the positions are similar, given the frames of reference. That is, a vase is to a table as a picture is to a wall—and this is the closest possible relationship among all available prepositional relationships. The picture isn't *in* the wall, because *in* requires a container—*in* participates in a "containment prototype," whereas *on* does not. Admitting certain distinctions, *on* is the word for the picture as well as the vase.

Analogy guarantees the semantic flexibility that allows us to encounter an infinite number of spatial situations in experience and then position among prototypes, so that we know *on* from *in, above* from *below, to* from *into*. Such mapping cannot explain all prepositional meanings, however. How can you be *in trouble* or *on the lam*? In order to use prepositions flexibly within the constraints of syntactic structures, we depend on metaphor, which may also have its basis in prototypes.

Conceptual Metaphor

We often think of metaphor as just a poetic device, but in fact, metaphor is so embedded in our language that we do not notice most of it. We mentioned that metaphor sometimes connects meanings within a semantic category organized around a prototype. Metaphor also plays a key role in language describing abstract concepts. One way to talk about abstract concepts is to relate them to known, more concrete objects and experiences—to create a conceptual metaphor for what the abstract concept "is like." For example, speakers often talk about the abstract concept of "more" in terms of "up" (MORE IS UP)—in other words, in terms of our experience with verticality and with the vertical rising of piles with "more" physical things added to them. When we add gas to the tank or pour more water into a glass, we "fill it up." A highway accident involving more cars than you could easily count is a "pileup," even though the cars aren't literally piled on top of one another. In this way, conceptual metaphors structure talk about abstract concepts.

Let's take a few examples from George Lakoff and Mark Johnson's book *Metaphors We Live By* (1980, 4). Their first example is the conceptual metaphor ARGUMENT IS WAR. In everyday language, we say:

Your claims are *indefensible*.

He *attacked every weak point* in my argument.

His criticisms were *right on target*.

I've never *won* an argument with him.

He *shot down* all of my arguments.

The conceptual metaphor TIME IS MONEY surfaces in our language: we *spend time* or *save* it; we *invest time, budget time,* and sometimes *run out of time;* we can *borrow time,* especially if someone else can *spare* it. And while you may not consciously think of ideas as plants, the conceptual metaphor IDEAS ARE PLANTS allows us to *plant ideas,* watch them *grow,* and hope that they come to *fruition.*

The Intersection of Semantics, Syntax, and Discourse

We pointed out earlier that syntax and discourse play a part in how words mean. The syntactic roles that a word can fulfill and the syntactic structures that a word requires are part of the word's meaning. The theoretical approaches to this relationship between words and syntax are varied and complex, and we sketch a few of them here before turning briefly to discourse.

Projection Rules

Jerrold Katz developed a semantic theory compatible with (and dependent on) Chomsky's theory of sentence meaning. A system of **projection rules** guides words into appropriate syntactic roles. In other words, these rules specify how a word can be used in a phrase and clause.

For Chomskyans, the mental lexicon is a database from which we draw to compose sentences, material separate from our grammatical ability, an ability natural to all humans. Grammar is universal, but the lexicon is particular to the speech community. The lexicon is "tagged" and thus accessible to the grammatical code. The tagging, according to this theory, is componential, and it indicates where certain features fit and how what's tagged will be expressed. Words of various functions fit into syntactic structures in limited ways. For instance, adverbs are not objects of prepositions, though they can figure in prepositional phrases as modifiers of adjectives. In other words, there is a relationship between lexical categories as an aspect of lexical meaning and the functional roles that words play in syntactic structures.

How Sentences Mean

Most theories of sentence meaning rely on **compositionality**, the idea that *both* the meaning of the parts *and* how they are put together determine the meaning of the sentence. Compositional semantics and truth conditional semantics are often combined to provide a framework for understanding the meaning of a sentence—a framework that returns to theories of reference in some aspects. Let's continue with our example sentence *The perplexed students reread the chapter* to outline this approach to sentence meaning, in a highly simplified form.

First, we must determine the sets to which the components, especially the subject NP and predicate VP, of the sentence refer. *The perplexed students* refers to a particular set of students (just as *the chapter* refers to a particular chapter), and *reread the chapter* refers to the set of individuals who reread the chapter. (There are, of course, other ways to understand the meaning of the predicate, but relating it to sets proves critical to this framework.) Next, we must determine the **truth conditions** of the sentence: in other words, what must be true for the sentence to be true. In the case of this sentence, we have at least two important truth conditions: the perplexed students must belong to the set of individuals who reread the chapter; and within the NP itself, the students in question must belong to the set of perplexed individuals. Finally, we determine the truth value: whether or not the truth conditions are met.

Of course, many sentences do not express propositions that are so easily associated with truth conditions and truth values. We can return to the sentence *The present king of France is bald*. To talk about sentences that refer to fictional entities, we can add to this semantic theory the idea of **presuppositions**: what is presupposed by the sentence in order to make a proposition. This sentence presupposes a king of France and perhaps even a fictional context in which there is a king of France which allows us to discuss, within that context, the proposition that the king of France is bald. And *The present king of France is bald* is by no means the only sentence of its type. Many other sentences seem barely related, if related at all, to propositions with truth values.

Sentences and Context

A more functional approach to sentence meaning emphasizes the ways in which sentences mean when uttered, in context, rather than the way that they mean formally, in the abstract. Consider the utterance "Show me the money!" If you bet on a basketball game with an unreliable friend, you might say "Show me the money" and mean it literally: 'Show me the money (before I will enter this bet with you)'. In an illicit sale (of drugs, information, etc.), the seller would mean "Show me the money" literally, too: '(Open that black briefcase and) show me the money (before I hand over the goods)'. But when the football player Rod Tidwell (Cuba Gooding Jr.) yells this phrase at his agent Jerry Maguire (Tom Cruise) in the movie *Jerry Maguire,* he is not asking to see dollar bills or to have a briefcase opened at that very moment. He is urging Maguire to get him a lucrative contract. The use of the word *money* here is more abstract: the promise of money. And what exactly does *show* mean here? Is it a metaphor? Can we isolate its meaning outside the utterance? Since the movie, the phrase *show me the money* has taken on yet another life: you might use it as a joke about someone being greedy or as a humorous plea to get paid or as an expression of exasperation for work that you do without compensation. The utterance is more than merely the sum of its lexical parts, more than syntax can convey: context helps to determine a sentence's meaning, whether literal or metaphorical or idiomatic, and it guides audiences to interpret utterances appropriately.

In real speech, meaning is the product of all relevant cognitively based lexical and syntactic knowledge. But clearly, lexical and syntactic knowledge are not enough to explain all meaning; that knowledge is a precondition to our more complex and subtle understanding of meaning created in social context. Ultimately, all the linguistic levels you've studied so far cooperate, to a greater or lesser extent, in the production of meaning, and we need to understand "meaning" as encompassing how words mean in and of themselves, in sentences, and in real discourse contexts. We'll continue with the discussion of how utterances mean in Chapter 8.

Processes of Semantic Change

As speakers use words in their day-to-day lives, the words can subtly change meaning through use. For example, a word like *see*, which as we discussed earlier can now mean 'understand', becomes polysemous over time through the process of semantic change, or the acquisition and/or loss of new meanings. Words can change meanings in a variety of ways and often unpredictably, but we can create general categories for directions of semantic change.

Generalization and Specialization

Two fundamental processes of semantic change are **generalization** and **specialization**, which mean just what they seem to mean: in the former process, a word's meaning becomes more general, encompasses more meaning; in the latter, meaning narrows, or becomes specialized. In the history of any particular word, these processes can alternate or occur simultaneously.

C. S. Lewis, whom you probably know as the author of *The Chronicles of Narnia*, wrote in *Studies in Words* (1960):

> If a man had time to study the history of one word only, *wit* would perhaps be the best word he could choose. Its fortunes provide almost perfect examples of the main principles at work in semantic development. Its early life was happy and free from complications. It then acquired a sense which brought into full play the difference between the word's and the speaker's meanings. It also suffered the worst fate any word has to fear; it became the fashionable term of approval among critics. (86)

Ever since Lewis wrote about *wit*, it has been a staple example of generalization and specialization, the example given in nearly every textbook. It seems unnecessary to break with that tradition here.

Old English *gewit* was already polysemous: it meant 'mind, or an aspect of mind', 'understanding, intelligence, reason', and 'right mind, sanity'. Over the next several centuries, the semantic character of *wit* changed frequently (as semantic change goes) and dramatically, as the *Wit* Timeline demonstrates (see Figure 7.3). Senses of *wit* (by no means all of them) listed on the left are adapted from the *Oxford English Dictionary*, in which you can find an exhaustive account of the word's history.

From roughly 1200 well into the eighteenth century, *wit* generalizes, adding a number of senses derived from those available in Old English. Some of these developments are surprising—for instance, the sense from 1200 meaning 'the five senses (i.e., sight, touch, hearing, smell, and taste)' because Old English *wit* is clearly a mental capacity, not a physical one. Even though the sense 'senses', which refers to inward (like common sense) as well as outward senses, is dated slightly later in the *OED*, we must assume that it developed first and that once *wit* had extended to all senses, folks used it rather loosely to refer to the physical ones alone. The sense 'genius, talent, mental quickness' draws apt use of them from the earlier faculties 'understanding, intelligence, reason'. The sense most common today, 'quality of speech or writing which consists in the apt association of thought and expression', itemizes just one of the 'talents' of a 'genius'.

After the period of greatest generalization, after *wit* had embraced the greatest number of senses historically, many of those senses were used less and less until, finally, they disappeared from use altogether. In other words, *wit*, having lost most of the meanings it once encompassed, began to specialize. We still have remnants of some older senses in current English, preserved in fixed idioms. If you are reminded to *keep your wits about you*, no one cares if you are especially clever, but only that you are sufficiently aware (due to your five outward senses) and prepared mentally and spiritually

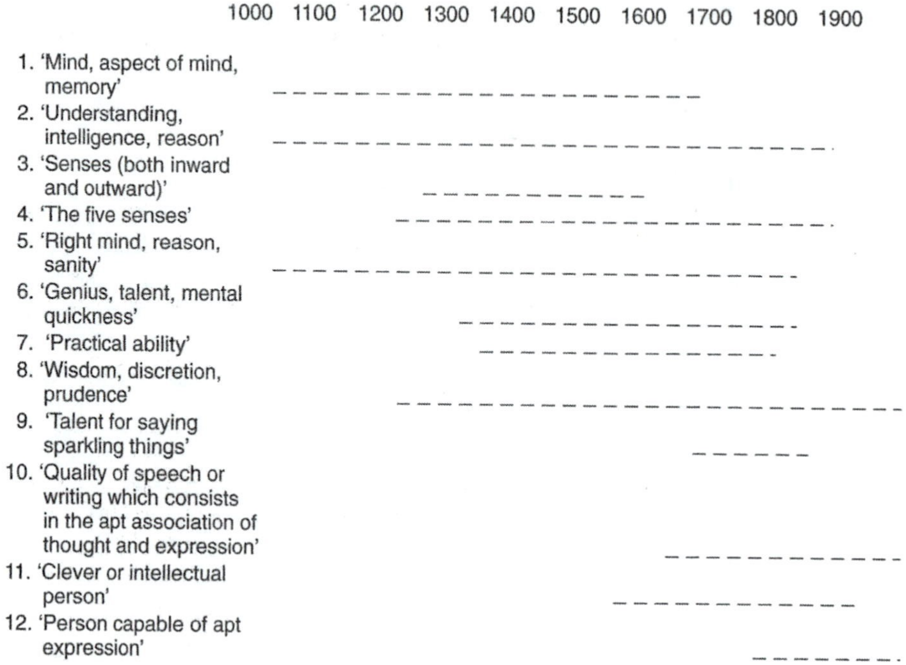

```
                    1000  1100  1200  1300  1400  1500  1600  1700  1800  1900
```

1. 'Mind, aspect of mind, memory'
2. 'Understanding, intelligence, reason'
3. 'Senses (both inward and outward)'
4. 'The five senses'
5. 'Right mind, reason, sanity'
6. 'Genius, talent, mental quickness'
7. 'Practical ability'
8. 'Wisdom, discretion, prudence'
9. 'Talent for saying sparkling things'
10. 'Quality of speech or writing which consists in the apt association of thought and expression'
11. 'Clever or intellectual person'
12. 'Person capable of apt expression'

FIGURE 7.3 *Wit* Timeline.

(because of your five inward senses) for the dangers you will encounter in the world around you. If someone claims that you are *out of your wits,* they mean you are 'crazy', though not that you are 'certifiably insane', as they might have in any year from 1000 to 1724. If you are *at your wits' end,* then you have discovered the limit of your 'understanding, intelligence, or reason'. You probably reached that point *unwittingly* 'without awareness', that is, without having kept your wits about you as you had been advised.

It is perfectly reasonable to ask what motivates such semantic expansion and contraction. Many linguistic processes, like metathesis (discussed in Chapters 1 and 3), don't seem to happen for any reason at all—they just happen. Not so, though, with generalization and specialization of the kind illustrated in *wit.* Here the motivation is often synonymic pressure, a reminder that semantic relations and semantic processes are constantly at play with one another, not operating in isolation. Consider the glosses in the left-hand column of the *Wit* Timeline (Figure 7.3). Many of the words used to define *wit* are of Latin or Anglo-French origin, absorbed into English after the Norman Conquest and during the Renaissance:

> *memory* < L *memoria* via AF *memorie*
>
> *intelligence* < L *intelligens*
>
> *sense* < L *sensus* via AF *sens*
>
> *reason* < AF *raison*
>
> *genius* or *ingenuity* (as well as 'practical ability') < L *ingenium* via AF *ingenios*
>
> *discretion* < L *discrētus* via AF *discret*
>
> *prudence* < L *prudens* via AF (?).

Of the core terms used to define *wit*, only *mind* < OE *gemynd*, *understand* < OE *understonden*, and *wisdom* < OE *wīsdōm* were uttered alongside *gewit* in Old English sentences. The Anglo-French and Latin synonyms for *wit* were all introduced into English during the period of *wit*'s great generalization (1200–1700) and competed for use by English speakers.

Gradually, some of these Romance terms won the competition, becoming, ultimately, Modern English words for Old and Middle English things. In the Early Modern English period, the prevalent senses of *wit* narrowed to those developed from Middle English *wit*, essentially 'quality of speech or writing which consists in the apt association of thought and expression' and 'person of apt expression'. Why accept a confusing polysemy when distribution of senses among the available synonyms would allow a more precise connection between word and meaning? The result of the competition among *wit*'s several senses, however, isn't quite that tidy. Although each word took over one primary sense from *wit*, apparently resolving confusion among related senses, their meanings overlap some, too—*intelligence* and *ingenuity* are nearly synonyms, as are *prudence* and *discretion*, *clever* and *witty*. In any event, words mean what they do partly as a consequence of their histories: formal and functional semantics ultimately intersect with the histories of particular languages, like English.

Metaphorical Extension

Another semantic process that promotes polysemy is **metaphorical extension**, when a word reaches beyond its primary meaning and applies to something perceived imaginatively as similar to what the word usually represents. The moon in the sky is not a big pizza pie, but if it looks that way to someone, then a metaphor is born. Metaphor thrives on similarity between fundamentally dissimilar things. So a detective *dogs* 'pursues' a *dogged* 'persevering' criminal; so we soften to the appeal of *puppy eyes,* even if they are in a child's rather than a puppy's face. An expression such as *you can't have your cake and eat it too* reminds us that metaphor, while often a matter of lexical semantics, also applies at the level of utterance.

Many meanings that originated in metaphorical extension are now so entrenched that we forget they are even metaphors. When you see a *crane* in a construction site, do

you think of the bird from which it got its name? What about a *leaf* in a book? A *lame* idea? Much of the computer jargon with which we are all now familiar results from metaphorical extension: *web, surf, windows, mouse.*

Euphemism and Dysphemism

Sometimes, a metaphor is a **euphemism**, a word or phrase meant to sound better than the literal alternative. For instance, when people die, we say that they *pass away*, or *cross the river*, or that we have *lost* them—but it would be sloppy, perhaps even criminally negligent, literally to lose a loved one. It's difficult to know exactly how to categorize *kick the bucket* or *croaked*—sometimes humor helps us to deal with loss. According to the *American Heritage Dictionary of Idioms* (Ammer 1997), *kick the bucket* may have originated in suicide (someone stands on a bucket to hang him- or herself and then kicks the bucket away) or in the slaughter of pigs—a slaughtered pig was hung by its feet from a beam called a *bucket*, so could be said to kick it. When *croak* emerged in the nineteenth century, it may have been a synonym for "death rattle." Later, it shifted functionally from noun to verb and even later shifted semantically into a somewhat crass, somewhat humorous term for dying.

Such idioms are certainly metaphorical and probably euphemistic, but their complex histories put them in a different class from transparent euphemisms like *cross the river*, because they originated as literalisms rather than metaphors. It is tempting to say that a given word is a euphemism, but more often we should say that a word is being used euphemistically. Euphemism is more a matter of context and utterance than a property of a word. You can, after all, literally kick a bucket or cross to the other side. Your fish can't literally kick buckets, though you could say they had if you found them floating at the top of the aquarium.

Euphemism is by no means always metaphorical, however. We buy *life insurance*, when what we really mean is **death insurance*, but we'd rather not think of it that way, so we enlist an antonym as a euphemism. And you are probably well versed in the various euphemisms for the once (and for many, still) taboo *fucking*, like *frigging, freaking,* and *effing*. If you aren't inclined to use *fucking* or any of the alternatives just listed, you may refer to the *F-word,* itself a euphemism.

Dysphemisms are just what you'd expect—words or phrases meant to sound worse in some context than when used literally. When angry Americans resist the influx of undocumented workers from south of the border, they say things like, "We don't want Mexicans taking our jobs." There is nothing naturally dysphemistic about *Mexican*, but it can be used with disgust and becomes offensive. You can easily list racial epithets and dysphemistic ethnic labels, though we hope that you don't use them: *mick* 'Irish or Irish American person', *yid* 'Jewish or Jewish American person', *PR* 'Puerto Rican or Puerto Rican American person', *chink* 'Chinese or Chinese American person', *gook* 'Vietnamese or Vietnamese American person', *jap* 'Japanese or Japanese American person', and *JAP* 'Jewish American Princess' are all terms designed to harm. Consider how often such racial and ethnic labels collocate with *dirty* or *filthy*. Of course, some may object that the authors are just being *politically correct* in characterizing these terms as dysphemistic and harmful. With this dismissal, these objectors would exemplify dysphemism in their use of *politically* *correct.* They could use *liberal* to the same effect. However, the denotation of these terms, *politically correct* and *liberal,* is not offensive.

Pejoration and Amelioration

Some dysphemisms are offensive the first times they are used (the word *kike* never had a neutral meaning), but some undergo a process called **pejoration**: they start as neutral terms and end up pejorative or dysphemistic. The word *nigger* is a powerful example of pejoration. It originated as a loan word (perhaps from Portuguese) meaning 'black in color', from Latin *niger.* When it was borrowed into English in the late sixteenth century, it was essentially neutral. But, fairly quickly, it took on extremely negative connotations—those associated with slavery and the supposed inferiority of African Americans—and the highly pejorative, offensive connotations have been associated with *nigger* ever since. Its pejoration accelerated during the twentieth century. Many speakers now will not utter the word because it is seen as so offensive, and we discussed the public debate about how the word should be defined in dictionaries in Chapter 2.

However, some African American speakers have claimed the word as their own, though in a reanalyzed form. A phonological reanalysis of *nigger,* in effect *nigga,* is a term of address, endearment, and solidarity for some speakers within the African American community. They have brought *nigger* out of pejoration into **amelioration**, the development of positive or socially accepted senses from negative or socially unacceptable senses or from simply neutral senses. The process of claiming or reclaiming a historically derogatory term by a community that has been oppressed or stigmatized by the term is usually called **reappropriation** (and sometimes reclamation). However, this use of *nigga* in an ameliorated form is not available to all speakers: it's not currently available to non-African Americans, except perhaps as represented in various media, like hip hop lyrics, film, and stand-up comedy routines. The use of *nigga,* given its history, is also debated within the African American community. Maya Angelou, for example, has called the *N-word* (a euphemism), in any form, "poison."

Another word that has undergone amelioration is *fuck.* At one point, *fuck* was clearly taboo, so much so that, though the word may have been in English since Anglo-Saxon times, we can't prove it—there's no evidence of *fuck* until about 1500, and even then it appears in a Latinized form, *fuccant,* effectively a euphemism. Although used fairly often for the next few centuries, *fuck* was almost always given a euphemistic form (e.g., *f****) until the late nineteenth century. The euphemism was necessary because the word's meaning was sexual, and Anglo-American culture has maintained a taboo about referring to sexual activity, with more or less determination, into the current century. Nonetheless, as you can tell by browsing through Jesse Sheidlower's *The F Word* (2009), *fuck* developed dramatically during the twentieth century, and one effect of its increased and increasingly diverse use (forms of *fuck* can be used as a verb, noun, adjective, adverb, and conjunction, if not more) has been "devulgarization," a species of amelioration. When rain begins to pour and an umbrellaless pedestrian far from home exclaims "Fuck!", there's no suggestion of sexual activity. Once socially dangerous to utter, the F-word, for good or ill, is common in casual speech for many speakers and has sloughed off at least some of its profanity.

More words seem to undergo pejoration than amelioration. The acquisition of negative meanings is powerful and can kill off (to use a metaphor) more neutral or positive meanings. But sometimes semantic change is idiosyncratic and hard to predict—just compare the results of being 'full of awe': *awful* and *awesome*.

Linguistic Relativity

Throughout this chapter, we've talked about the relationship of meaning and cognition, and we've addressed one difficult philosophical question after the next. Why stop now? So let's approach the relationship of language and thought. Can we think outside language? Does language determine thought? Or, if we don't want to go that far, can we say that language influences thought?

The precise intersections of language and thought are still mysterious, but it's almost impossible to assume, once you take a functionalist approach to language, at least, that there is no connection. At the most basic level, to say that linguistic categories are cognitive categories is to say that linguistic categories are one way that we categorize and understand—that is, think about—our experience in the world. But do different languages cause people to think differently?

In the heyday of German Romanticism, Wilhelm von Humboldt (1767–1835) argued that language determined the capacity of a language group's worldview (*Weltansicht*): you couldn't intellectually consider things about which you couldn't talk. This limitation was associated with views about relative cultural superiority. The great civilizations engaged in philosophical speculation; they had developed languages in which to philosophize. Lesser civilizations weren't much good at philosophy, and their languages didn't wield the tools necessary for philosophical discourse. An advanced civilization would need morphological processes like compounding, so that it could talk about *Zeitgeist* 'time-spirit, spirit of an age' and similarly complex ideas. Supposedly, language families like Semitic were less capable of expressing advanced ideas, and the Semitic mind less philosophical than, say, the Aryan mind. Aryan culture was, evidently, superior to Semitic culture. This naive theory of the relationships among language, intelligence, and culture (and many other aspects of Romantic ideology) fertilized the ground in which German Nationalism took root. It is an especially vicious association of language, thought, and culture and thus a useful contrast to the Sapir-Whorf Hypothesis.

The Sapir-Whorf Hypothesis is named for two of its early and best-known advocates, Edward Sapir (1884–1939) and his student, Benjamin Lee Whorf (1897–1941). Sometimes it is referred to as the Whorfian hypothesis, because Whorf developed the hypothesis more fully and articulated it at times more adamantly. Sapir was an anthropologist when anthropology was an infant science, and his investigations of Native American culture were among the most important of early anthropological studies because they helped to establish the field's methodology. In "The Status of Linguistics as a Science" (1929), Sapir proposed the earliest version of the hypothesis:

> Human beings do not live in the objective world alone, nor alone in the world of social activity as ordinarily understood, but are very much at the mercy of the particular language which has become the medium of expression for their society. It is quite an illusion to imagine that one adjusts to reality essentially without the use of language and that language is merely an incidental means of solving problems of communication or

reflection. The fact of the matter is that the "real world" is to a large extent unconsciously built up on the language habits of the group. No two languages are ever sufficiently similar to be considered as representing the same social reality. The worlds in which different societies live are distinct worlds, not merely the same world with different labels attached. (209)

No mention of cultural superiority here, but Sapir's claim about the relations of thought and language were provocative, nonetheless.

Whorf studied with Sapir at Yale. In his work on Hopi, among other Native American languages, Whorf contrasted the ways in which Hopi expresses, for example, days and seasons as adverbs, not as nouns, as in most Indo-European languages. Hopi does not employ "imaginary plurals," so that an English expression such as "five days" would be expressed along the lines of "until the fifth day." Hopi does not atomize as much of the world into nouns as does, say, English; it puts more functional weight on verbs. Whorf came to the conclusion: "We dissect nature along the lines laid down by our native languages."

Whorf was a relatively prolific writer, and depending on what parts of his work you quote, you can frame him as an advocate of linguistic determinism or linguistic relativity—although the majority of his work puts him in the latter camp. Jerry Gill (1997) usefully outlines the continuum of theoretical possibilities for the relationship of language and thought:

- **Objectivism**: There is a reality out there that we can access, bypassing language, and language describes that world.
- **Linguistic relativity**: Differences in language create differences in thought.
- **Linguistic determinism**: Thought is determined by the categories available in language.

Linguistic determinism is relatively easy to shoot down as a theory; linguistic relativity is much harder. We know that the world can always surprise us with things that we've never thought of. Studies also indicate that speakers can think "outside" their language. For example, the Mundurukú, an Amazonian indigene group, can exploit basic geometric concepts in solving problems even though their language has few specific words for these geometrical concepts (Dehaene et al. 2006). It also seems clear that the linguistic categories and metaphors that structure our language influence the ways in which we categorize and understand the world. The extent to which they shape our reality, however, will probably remain unknowable.

A study published by Lera Boroditsky in 2009 generated some media buzz about linguistic relativity. Her study suggests that grammatical gender influences how speakers think about objects. For example, the word for 'key' in German is masculine, and German speakers were more likely to describe keys as "hard," "heavy," "jagged," "metal," "serrated," and "useful"; Spanish speakers, whose word for 'key' is feminine, more often described keys as "golden," "intricate," "little," "lovely," "shiny," and "tiny."

A study by Susan Hespos and Elizabeth Spelke, reported in the July 2004 issue of *Nature*, provides evidence that babies have a rich conceptual life before they acquire language and that language shapes what we notice once we acquire it. Their study exploited a linguistic difference between English and Korean: English distinguishes between objects being *in* versus *on* other objects, whereas Korean distinguishes between a *tight* and *loose fit* between two objects. All the babies in the study (in both Korean- and English-speaking homes) noticed and were interested in the contrast between objects being put on versus in other objects as well as in the contrast between tight and loose fits between objects. They became bored if shown the same relationship over and over. English-speaking adults, however, when shown a series of relationships that contrasted tight versus loose fit, did not pick up this contrast but noticed things like the colors of the objects instead. In other words, it appears that because the structure of English emphasizes the relationship of objects as containers and supports but not the relationship of fit, English speakers tend to notice the former relationship in their experience of the world and not the latter. This is not to say that English-speakers *cannot* notice the difference between loose and tight fit, but it does not appear to be a fundamental way in which English speakers categorize or experience the world.

It is important to remember two things. First, all languages are capable of expressing anything that their speakers need to express. Second, we should never make assumptions about how speakers view the world based on the structure of their language. Just imagine what people could say about English speakers based on the fact that English technically has no future tense: "Those people can only think about the future in terms of what they want or wish to happen." Even though English does not express the future with tense like many of the world's languages, English speakers nevertheless express futurity and conceive of future time. This is an important lesson to bear in mind whenever we're tempted to make judgments about how other speakers think based on our understanding of their language's structure.

To sum up, Sapir and Whorf, in the Humboldtian tradition, argued that study of a culture entails study of its language—the two cannot be separated artificially—and the converse would also seem true, that understanding a language entails study of the culture that uses it. Without denying the existence of a material world outside human minds, Sapir and Whorf also proposed that "reality" is a construction, a mediation of experience, language, and thought.

So if experience influences language, and language influences mind, and experience and mind and language influence culture, couldn't calculated semantic change influence culture?

Special Focus: Politically Correct Language

The term *politically correct*, or *PC*, was originally used by the American political left to describe believing, saying, or doing things according to the liberal agenda automatically or mindlessly. The term was brought to new life in the 1980s by the American political right to describe what they took as thoughtless, knee-jerk liberalism. *Politically correct* is generally a dysphemism, although the *American Heritage Dictionary of the English Language* defines it neutrally: "Of, relating to, or supporting broad social, political, and educational change, especially to redress historical injustices in matters such as race, class, gender, and sexual orientation."

Politically correct language reform rests on premises that echo aspects of Whorfian thought: language encodes certain cultural beliefs and biases and by changing language, you can change attitudes. Put in a different way, if you want to effect broad social change, one approach is to change the language, which may have the power gradually to alter the way a society thinks about its social relations and to promote different cultural practices.

The American political right often asserts that liberals are the ones who engage in politically correct speech. Liberals, for example, write manuals of gender-neutral language: *chair* or *chairperson* rather than *chairman; firefighter* instead of *fireman; he or she* or *s/he* in place of the traditional *he* as the generic singular third-person pronoun. Some view such usage as amusing and trivial; others see it as dangerously subversive. Those who promote these changes see such reform as desirable, if not necessary to a good society that respects equal rights and allows equal opportunities. The absurd "PC reforms," such as *personhole cover* or *vertically challenged,* are almost all made up by opponents of PC language reform in order to ridicule the project.

Opponents of PC language reform often argue that people are "reading too much into" words. Deborah Cameron points out that what many people dislike or feel uneasy about is "the politicizing of words against their will" (1995, 119). This politicizing of words means that whether you use the "traditional" word or the "PC" word, either way you are declaring a political position. Another common argument asserts that PC language reform distracts people from the very real social issues we face—or perhaps even covers up problems with euphemisms—but language reformers aren't arguing that we should change the language but ignore social injustice or inequity. A third objection to PC reforms adopts the line that language is "just language": it really doesn't matter. This objection actually sets up its own rebuttal: if language really doesn't matter, then let's just agree to do it the PC way since the PC advocates feel so strongly about it. Of course language does matter, and debates about PC language are about much more than language.

Many arguments for politically correct speech are not "knee-jerk liberalism" but are carefully considered and theoretically grounded. Geneva Smitherman, in an article titled "'What Is Africa to Me?': Language, Ideology, and *African American*" (1991), argues the case for preferring *African American* over *African, Black, Colored,* and *Negro* as the racial terminology applied to Americans of African descent. She accounts for the history of each term and then reports the results of a five-city survey of attitudes among African Americans toward the term *African American*. At the outset of the article, Smitherman makes her theoretical presuppositions clear:

> reality is not merely SOCIALLY, but SOCIOLINGUISTICALLY, constructed. Real-world experience and phenomena do not exist in some raw, undifferentiated form. Rather, reality is always filtered, apprehended, encoded, codified, and conveyed via some linguistic shape. This linguistic form exists in a dialectical relationship with social cognition and social behavior. While Humboldtian linguists (and most Whorfians, for that matter) overstate the case for language as THE determiner of thought, consciousness, and behavior, nonetheless language DOES play a dominant role in the formation of ideology, consciousness, and class relations. . . . Thus my contention is that consciousness and ideology are largely the products of what I call the SOCIOLINGUISTIC CONSTRUCTION OF REALITY. (117)

Preference of one term over another by African Americans speaks to their sense of identity. Use of *African American* by non-African Americans registers respect for that preference and the identity it constructs. The term's use by all Americans acknowledges the historical asymmetry of *Colored* or *Black* versus *Irish American* or *Polish American* and redresses it by reconstructing social reality through semantic change. Smitherman's conclusion is a plain statement of political correctness as defined by the *American Heritage Dictionary*. She writes:

> As an African American womanist linguist, it is clear to me that this is not a debate about semantics at the expense of addressing the plight of the community, as some intellectuals fear. Rather, this new racial designation can lead to the construction of an identity to facilitate the creation of policy, tactics, strategies, and programs to address that plight—that is, the use of language to create a new theory of reality. (129)

Even if they aren't politically correct, some arguments for curbing such change equally rely on a Whorfian view of language. In order to conserve the traditional order of things, the argument goes, we need to resist change in the language; if people adopt new language, they will erode traditional values. Each issue of the *Vocabula Review*, an online journal about English usage, opens with the aphorism: "A society is generally as lax as its language." If you don't want a lax society, according to the aphorism, then don't allow too much language variety or language change.

The conservative concern about language change is sincere. The liberal concern about promoting a fairer society through fairer language is equally heartfelt. The dysphemistic use of *politically correct* is unfortunate because it glibly tosses the political opposition's views aside and impedes serious argument in an important cultural debate. In fact, what we choose to say and how we choose to say it can make a big difference in the lives of those around us. If nothing else, PC language can demonstrate respect for those asking to be referred to in a particular way. And changing the terms of public discussion can eventually change attitudes. As Deborah Cameron (1995, 143) points out, "Changing what counts as acceptable public behaviour is one of the ways you go about changing prevailing attitudes—ask anyone who still smokes cigarettes." Linguistic habits, like smoking, die hard, but changing the norms for "acceptable public behavior" does have an effect.

☑ Summary

- Semantics is the study of meaning in language. In this chapter, you have learned about several different ways of analyzing lexical meaning.

- While words seem to refer to things and concepts, the nature of lexical meaning is more complicated than mere reference allows.

- Lexical meaning depends partly on relations among words, for instance as described by lexical fields, hyponymy, antonymy, synonymy, meronymy, and homonymy.

- Lexical meaning is partly determined by syntactic structures.

- Lexical meaning is also very likely influenced by cognitive structures and processes by which the mind interprets human experience.

- Lexical meaning depends partly on semantic processes that occur over time, such as specialization, generalization, amelioration, pejoration, and metaphorical extension.

■ Lexical meaning is sometimes socially and culturally significant; at least, our understanding of what and how words mean influences our political and cultural conversations.

Suggested Reading

There are many formidable expositions of semantic theory, including, but by no means limited to, the following: John Lyons's two-volume *Semantics* (1977), Keith Allan's two-volume *Linguistic Meaning* (1986), and Leonard Talmy's two-volume *Toward a Cognitive Semantics* (2000). From philosophical logic to cognitive theory, and roughly parallel to syntactic theory, semantics has become an intensively active and increasingly systematic field during the last few decades—all of this activity is difficult to summarize in a single textbook chapter.

Some books on semantics are more accessible and manageable than those mentioned above, especially John Saeed's recent general introduction, *Semantics* (2003). Lexical semantics is well represented by D. A. Cruse's *Lexical Semantics* (1986). Several more recent studies of compositional and cognitive semantics are especially interesting, among them R. M. W. Dixon's *A New Approach to English Grammar on Semantic Principles* (1991), Ray Jackendoff's *Semantic Structures* (1990), and Anna Wierzbicka's *Semantics, Culture, and Cognition: Universal Concepts in Culture-Specific Configurations* (1992).

Charles J. Fillmore's *Lectures on Deixis* (1997) is currently the standard work on deixis. Both George Lakoff and Mark Johnson's *Metaphors We Live By* (1980) and Eva Kittay's *Metaphor: Its Cognitive Force and Linguistic Structure* (1987) are classic discussions of their subject. Thematic roles and the intersection of word and sentence meaning are discussed in many of the works mentioned, as well as in Edwin Williams's *Thematic Structure in Syntax* (1994). Those interested in the Sapir-Whorf Hypothesis can turn to Edward Sapir's *Language: An Introduction to the Study of Speech* (1949), as well as *Language, Thought, and Reality: Selected Writings of Benjamin Lee Whorf*, edited by John B. Carroll (1956), and *Rethinking Linguistic Relativity*, edited by John J. Gumperz and Stephen C. Levinson (1996).

Exercises
Exercise 7.1   How Do Words Refer?

Consider this paragraph opening from Chapter 1:

> Language inundates us, and every one of us is not only inundated but an inundator. Few of us wake up to silence; most of us groan out of our sleep to the jarring noise of morning radio blaring from our alarm clock. Whether in our kitchen at home or in the cafeteria at school, many of us eat a rushed breakfast (if we eat breakfast at all!) between sleepy conversations about the day ahead and a rushed glance through the morning paper. Sometimes the television drones in the background. Once at school, the flood of language continues: lectures, classroom discussions, campus meetings—during all of which we may not only listen but also have much to say. Who doesn't also steal snatches of the day to send text messages or surf the Internet?

Categorize each word in the paragraph as one of the following:

- Refers to an object I could point to if it were in the room.
- Refers to a concept.
- Doesn't obviously refer to anything.

Given the distribution of your findings among these categories, what would you conclude about the relationship of word meaning and reference?

Exercise 7.2   Construct Your Own Hyponymic Tree

Construct your own hyponymic trees that include:

motorcycle

washing machine, dishwasher

washing machine, dishwasher, blender, hair dryer

bicycle, car, SUV, sedan

Exercise 7.3   Semantic Relationships

1. Provide four additional examples of each of these semantic relationships, and explain if necessary:

   a. synonyms

   b. gradable antonyms

   c. complementary antonyms

   d. converse antonyms

   e. homonyms that are homophones and homographs

   f. homonyms that are homophones but not homographs

   g. homonyms that are homographs but not homophones

2. In order to make the best argument you can that there are "true synonyms," come up with three pairs (or sets) of words not mentioned in the chapter that you think mean exactly the same thing, in both denotation and connotation(s).

3. In the following passage, identify all of the lexical semantic relationships (the ones we describe in this chapter as "nyms") among open-class words:

   Hugh took his ax into the woods in search of firewood, cutting his way through brambles, hedges, and undergrowth in his path until he came across the perfect tree. Finding his ax a little dull, he took a whetstone and made the edge sharp, after which he proceeded to hew at the tree. Once it was on the ground, he lopped off the limbs and branches and set about trimming twigs from the branches, after which he cut the trunk into lengths. Then it occurred to him: how was he going to carry all of this firewood back to the cabin?

4. Identify all of the metaphors in the following passage. Remember, many of these are part of conceptual metaphors and may at first strike you as literal (e.g., *see* meaning 'understand').

Mary is one of our top executives, and she's famous for her hardball tactics. She was on the team that built the company from scratch, and it is like a child to her. She is willing to make the hard decisions, be that cutting the budget or ending a long-standing relationship with a client or firing a hard-working but unsuccessful employee. I vividly remember my job interview with her: she was calm and unbelievably eloquent, while I was tripping over my words and generally making myself look stupid. She asked me to solve a complex marketing problem, to showcase all the skills that I acquired in business school, and I panicked! I did manage, however, to resist the urge to leap up from my chair and run out of the interview. Silence filled the room as I desperately searched my brain for any relevant information. I suddenly hit on an idea and launched into a brilliant explanation of one marketing strategy. Or at least it seemed brilliant at the time. Mary was kind enough not to shoot me down then and there; it was not until several weeks into the job that she told me that she almost burst with laughter in the middle of my far-fetched, yet "confidently presented" and "creatively conceived" answer.

5. For each of the following conceptual metaphors, list at least six everyday expressions that depend on the underlying metaphor:

   a. IDEAS ARE FOOD.

   b. IDEAS ARE COMMODITIES.

   c. IDEAS ARE PRODUCTS.

   d. LIFE IS A JOURNEY.

   e. IMPORTANT/SIGNIFICANT IS BIG.

   f. TREATING A DISEASE IS FIGHTING A BATTLE.

Exercise 7.4   Mapping Processes of Semantic Change

1. Consult the *OED* and other sources, and construct a figure illustrating the semantic development of the word *peace* parallel to the treatment of *wit* presented here. Then write a brief summary of the semantic changes and how you would explain the relationships between various historical meanings.

2. For each of these four words, examine the historical meanings in the *OED* and rely on your own observations of how the words are used now to describe the semantic processes involved in the development of these words in the nineteenth, twentieth, and twenty-first centuries: *gay, bitch, geek, nerd.*

Chapter 8

Spoken Discourse

The rules of cooperative conversation can turn the bank machine and your forgetfulness into a ten-dollar loan for a movie ticket without your ever directly asking for money.

Y‌ou and a friend are standing in line to buy movie tickets. You reach for your wallet and suddenly exclaim, "Dang! I forgot to go to the bank machine." Your friend opens her wallet and says, "I can lend you ten dollars." This interaction seems perfectly normal and logical until we look carefully at the sequence of utterances. How does your statement about the errand that you forgot to do lead your friend to offer you money?

Now here's a different version: You return home after running errands all morning. You put the groceries down in the kitchen and suddenly exclaim, "Dang! I forgot to go to the bank machine." Your roommate, who does not budge from the couch, replies, "Huh. What a hassle." Why is this response, to exactly the same sequence of words in your utterance, acceptable from your roommate in this context? If your friend in the movie line had the same response, that would be downright rude! Clearly your utterance means differently in the two contexts.

Sentences, when uttered, can mean much more than the denotational meaning of the words they contain, and they can do more than describe or refer to the world around us. The utterance "There is a coffee shop on the corner" can function as a referential statement about the shop's location, as a request for the driver of a car to slow down to find parking, or as a suggestion to go get coffee. Language users exploit and interpret the implications of sentences in context, and utterances can perform actions in and of themselves.

Scholars who focus on meaning in context have a set of frameworks and methods for examining these kinds of questions about both speech and writing, which are captured under the term *discourse analysis*. This chapter focuses primarily on the systematic examination of oral discourse, and Chapter 9 focuses on written discourse. Any line between the analysis of spoken and written discourse is blurry, and some of the material in both chapters applies to both spoken and written text.

In Chapters 3–7, we examined different levels of our linguistic knowledge or competence, from sounds to words to sentences to meaning. This chapter focuses on different components of our **communicative competence**: the knowledge that we bring to using language as a communicative tool in conversation with other speakers. The chapter addresses several different aspects of spoken discourse: how we accomplish actions with words; how we successfully convey information and negotiate relationships in conversation; how conversations are organized; and how we perform identities through speech.

Defining Discourse Analysis

One of the most basic definitions of **discourse** is connected text (spoken, written, or signed) above the level of the sentence. A piece of discourse can be a letter, a speech, a conversation, an essay, a story, an interview, a novel, even a toast. The description "connected text" means that it is continuous and that the sentences function coherently together, in succession, as a unit. The basic unit of spoken discourse is the **utterance**: the realization of a unit of speech on a specific occasion in a specific context. For example, a clause (e.g., "you rock") becomes an utterance when someone utters it on a particular occasion (e.g., when you say "You rock" to your friend after she wins her soccer game). Utterances more extended or more complex than "You rock!" can be broken down into phrases and clauses, even into words, for closer analysis: lexical semantics and meaning introduced at the level of syntax both participate in the meaning of discourse, but they do not determine it.

Discourse analysis (DA) is the systematic study of connected text, or units of language above the level of the sentence, and the utterances of which they are composed. Some scholars define DA more broadly as the study of "language use" or as an even broader range of social practices, but here we focus on discourse as connected text. Pragmatics studies utterances in particular contexts.

Critical discourse analysis (CDA) connects systematic analysis of features within a discourse to the larger sociopolitical context in which the discourse occurs. It rests on the idea that ways of talking create, maintain, and reinforce ways of thinking. CDA often focuses on "institutional discourse"—the media, the language of courtrooms, and political language, for instance. The analysis typically relates features of discourse to questions of power and ideology (i.e., prevailing belief systems) and examines how language is manipulated in order to produce, reproduce, maintain, and/or resist particular power structures and relationships. For example, in a critical discourse analysis of the Senate hearings regarding Clarence Thomas's appointment to the Supreme Court, Norma Mendoza-Denton (1995) examines the length of pauses and the ratio of yes-no questions, concise answers, and topic shifts in the questioning of Clarence Thomas and Anita Hill, a former staffer who accused Thomas of sexual harassment. Mendoza-Denton argues that, for example, false presuppositions in questions addressed to Hill and abrupt topic shifts diminished the rhetorical and persuasive power of Hill's testimony, whereas Thomas made powerful use of both concise answers and African American speech styles. CDA examines language use and the manipulation (and often misuse) of power, calling for social engagement and change. CDA is thus often viewed as "politically invested" scholarship.

Should we consider discourse analysis a field of inquiry (like phonology or morphology) or a methodology for inquiry? It is clearly interdisciplinary in its origins, applications, and methods: its approaches and applications span anthropology, sociology, philosophy, speech communications, rhetoric, and linguistics, as well as the study of many specific languages. The following sections treat discourse analysis primarily as a methodology or heuristic (i.e., a method for interpreting). They focus on the kinds of questions about spoken (and written) language prompted by various discourse analysis approaches.

Speech Act Theory: Accomplishing Things with Words

How do words "do things"? **Speech act theory** works from the premise that language performs actions: when we speak, we are "doing things," not just talking about them. In some cases, speaking actually changes the status of the world around us. For example, if a minister declares two people husband and wife, they are legally partnered in a way they were not before that utterance. If the umpire yells "Strike three!" after a pitch, then the batter is out. (The batter can then use words to protest the call and try to change the umpire's mind, but in most cases, the umpire's words represent the final ruling.) If you bet the person sitting next to you five dollars that you will get more of the exercises in this chapter right than he or she will, then you have five dollars on the line in a way you did not before you opened your mouth. In less obvious ways, all of our utterances perform actions, from asking questions to making assertions to making requests. Speech act theory examines how language is related to action—how utterances accomplish things, especially things that surpass the referential meaning of the words in the utterance.

Speech act theory originated in philosophy, in the works of J. L. Austin and John Searle. The title *How to Do Things with Words* (1962) captures Austin's argument that all utterances perform speech acts, which are parallel to other forms of action. Searle, a student of Austin at Oxford, extended and revised many of Austin's arguments in *Speech Acts* (1969), as well as in numerous complementary articles. We treat Austin's and Searle's work together, but we also point to some fundamental differences between them.

Components of Speech Acts

Austin distinguished three different acts involved in any given speech act; these three differentiate referential meaning, intended meaning, and understood meaning:

- **Locutionary act**: the production of the sounds and words that make up an utterance and its referential meaning.

Scholars to Know

J. L. Austin (1911–1960)

The British philosopher J. L. Austin died at a relatively young age, and although he published some of his philosophical work during his lifetime, some of his very influential papers were gathered and published by his students after his death. Austin put forward most of his theories in lectures and seminars in the 1940s and 1950s, first at Oxford and later in the United States, where he became something of a celebrity. His best-known book, *How to Do Things with Words* (1962), is actually a transcription of his William James lectures at Harvard. (This story should remind you of how Ferdinand de Saussure's lectures were published.)

John Searle (1932–)

John Searle, born in Colorado, received a Ph.D. in philosophy from Oxford, where he studied with Austin. His influential book *Speech Acts* (1969) made use of ideas first proposed by Austin but also established Searle as an independent scholar in the field. After his important work on speech act theory, Searle turned his scholarly attention primarily to the philosophy of mind. He is now a professor of philosophy at the University of California at Berkeley—a university that actively courted Austin to join the faculty before his untimely death.

- **Illocutionary act**: the intended meaning of the utterance or the conventional force that an utterance is understood to have.
- **Perlocutionary act**: the effect achieved by an utterance on the hearer.

The speech act is not complete until someone receives and interprets the utterance. Sometimes illocutionary and perlocutionary acts are closely aligned; at other times, though, the two are misaligned, and communication breaks down—the hearer takes from the speech act an illocutionary meaning different from what the speaker intended, or the hearer overlooks illocutionary meaning conventionally associated with certain types of utterance.

To explain these concepts, let's return to our opening example from the movie line: "Dang! I forgot to go to the bank machine." Uttering these nine words in this particular order is the locutionary act and indicates just what it appears to say: that you forgot to go to the bank machine. The illocutionary act is the intended meaning of those nine words in this context, something along the lines of 'please lend me some cash so I can buy a ticket because I do not have any/enough cash because I forgot to go to the bank machine where I could get cash'. The perlocutionary act is in the effect: your friend thinks that, because you forgot to go to the bank machine, you do not have enough money to buy the ticket, so she offers to lend you ten dollars.

Sometimes the illocutionary and perlocutionary acts are combined and referred to as *illocutionary force*. But, as mentioned earlier, because the intended illocutionary force may not be identical with the perceived illocutionary force, the perlocutionary act may or may not correspond to the intended illocutionary act. For example, you may say to your friend, "There's a coffee shop on the corner" only to alert her to its location because it is near her house. She, on the other hand, may interpret the illocutionary act of your utterance as a request to stop and may reply, "I have twenty minutes to grab a cup of coffee with you."

TABLE 8.1   **Types of Illocutionary Acts**

Type of Illocutionary Act	Description	Example Verbs	Associated Grammatical Form
Representatives (or assertives)	Illocutionary acts that represent a state of affairs	stating, claiming, hypothe-sizing, describing, telling, insisting, suggesting, asserting, or swearing that something is the case	Declarative/indicative
Directives	Illocutionary acts designed to get the addressee to do something	ordering, commanding, asking, daring, challenging	Imperative Interrogative (for questions)
Commissives	Illocutionary acts designed to get the speaker (i.e., the one performing the act) to do something	promising, threatening, intending, vowing to do or to refrain from doing something	
Expressives	Illocutionary acts that express the mental state of the speaker	congratulating, thanking, deploring, condoling, welcoming, apologizing	
Declarations	Illocutionary acts that bring about the state of affairs to which they refer	blessing, firing, baptizing, bidding, passing sentence, excommunicating	

Source: Adapted from material by Sanford Schane, Homepage for Logistics 105: Law and Languages, http://ling.ucsd.edu/courses/ling105/illoc.htm.

Searle outlined five categories of illocutionary acts: **representatives** (or **assertives**), **directives**, **commissives**, **expressives**, and **declarations**. See Table 8.1 for brief descriptions and some of the verbs associated with each act. Some scholars have altered these categories slightly—for example, expanding them to six to include questions and/or verdictives. The sixth category, **verdictives**, describes illocutionary acts that pass judgment (e.g., judge, assess, rank). You can see the possible overlap of verdictives with both declarations and representatives.

In the speech acts described earlier, the illocutionary acts are probably directives. If you say "There's a coffee shop on the corner" and really do hope your friend will stop for a cup of coffee, you are proposing a coffee break, and proposing to do something is directive (as opposed to proposing that something is the case, which is assertive). If you say "Dang! I forgot to go the bank machine" because you want your friend to lend you money for the movie, you aren't merely describing a fact about your day, the illocutionary force of which would be representative or assertive—you are asking for a little financial support, and asking is a type of directive.

Why is "asking" considered directive? Most questions are intended to elicit information from the hearer. So, their illocutionary force is directive: "Tell me . . ." For example, the question "What time is it?" could be reframed as "Tell me what time it is" in order to make its illocutionary force more obvious. Rhetorical questions, such as "Why is 'asking' considered a directive?" (at the beginning of this paragraph) is not a directive. It isn't intended to elicit information from you—it is a stylistic device for opening and focusing the paragraph. If you answer a rhetorical question (Ellen: "Why do I always forget my password?" Tyler: "Because you are scatterbrained."), you have misunderstood the question's illocutionary force.

Direct and Indirect Speech Acts

When the form of the locutionary act corresponds directly with the illocutionary act, the utterance is called a **direct speech act**. In the second opening scenario, the exclamation to a roommate that you forgot to go to the bank machine while you were running errands is a direct speech act. The locutionary act is a declarative statement or exclamation. The illocutionary force is that of a representative or assertion. You are not asking your roommate to do anything in particular about the situation; you simply suddenly remember what you have forgotten to do and announce that fact. In other words, the intended meaning of the utterance corresponds directly to the propositional meaning.

Indirect speech acts involve intended meanings different from the locutionary act or the literal meaning of the words. The movie-line utterance is clearly one example: an assertion about a bank machine acts as a request to borrow money. We use indirect speech acts all the time (listen and you will hear them all around you). They are especially useful when we try to be polite—for example, when we make requests. We also use them when we are being impolite—for example, when we are sarcastic. We discuss the concept of politeness in more detail below, but it is clear that in many Western cultures, indirectness is considered an integral part of respecting others' needs and feelings. However, indirection is used for many social purposes, not all of them so polite.

Imagine a scene in which a woman named Monique sits at the breakfast table with a cup of coffee. She wants milk for her coffee, but she doesn't want to get up. Instead, she hopes her husband will get it for her. She asks, "Could you get me some milk?" On the surface, this seems like a fairly direct request—we frequently make requests in just this way. But in fact it is a question about possibility or willingness (depending on how one interprets *could*): Is Monique's husband Gary able or willing to get her some milk?

Gary could mull the question over, then answer as though it were a direct speech act: "Yes," he might say, "I would be willing to get milk for you, if you ask." Monique might be taken aback by this response, as she thought she had asked! If her husband were simply to say "Yes" and then remain seated at the table with her, Monique probably also wouldn't be pleased—she probably thought that her question indirectly did request the milk. With an exasperated sigh, she might end up getting the milk for herself. Consider the following examples of other possible indirect speech acts Monique could make in this context:

- "Do we have any milk?"
- "I was wondering if you would mind getting me some milk."
- "Are you getting up?"

The direct speech act for Monique, in this case, would be: "Get me some milk (please)" or, using a performative verb, "I ask/request that you get me some milk." These utterances may sound rude or overly authoritative to you because you are accustomed to the politeness conventions that encourage indirect requests.

Performative Speech Acts

J. L. Austin coined the term *performative* (which he described as "an ugly word"). **Performative speech acts** are utterances that accomplish the acts they describe just by being uttered. If you say to a friend, "I bet you dinner that you will now start noticing indirect speech acts all around you," you are making a statement about placing a bet, and you are also actually placing one. Some performative speech acts directly change the status of the world surrounding the discourse, either by judging something to be the case or by making something the case. For example, if you uttered the bet in the sentence, there would now be a dinner riding on your friend's observational skills. Other performative speech acts that clearly change the status of the world of the participants are "I christen this boat the Please Don't Sink" and "I dub you Sir Harry Potter." Another set of performative speech acts "announce" their illocutionary force (they are asking, requesting, etc.) and thereby perform that action: "I request that you stop jumping on the bed" or "I tell you I have seen this before."

The most obviously performative speech acts:

1. employ first-person subjects (*I*, *we*), and

2. employ present-tense verbs that describe the speech act.

Generally, speakers use the first person in order to perform the act themselves (or to act as the representative of a group). Otherwise, they are simply describing the actions of others. Compare, for example, the performative speech act "I promise to stop smoking" (which creates a promise) and the referential assertion "She promises to stop smoking" (which describes someone else's promise). Performative verbs are often in the present tense because otherwise the speech act describes a past or future action ("I promised to stop smoking" or "I will promise to stop smoking") rather than constituting the action in the moment of utterance. One common test of a performative speech act is to try inserting "hereby" after the subject (e.g., "I hereby promise . . . "). If you can logically use "hereby," it is probably a performative speech act. However, many utterances are performative even though they don't follow the formula described here—we provide an example in Chapter 9.

Performative speech acts are unlike other utterances: they are not referential. Instead, performative speech acts accomplish what they say they are accomplishing, just because they are uttered. As you learned in Chapter 7, the meaning of many sentences is "propositional": propositions propose something, so can be evaluated in terms of truth conditions—the conditions that must hold for a statement to be true. Utterances that can be evaluated as true or false are called **constative speech acts**. For performative speech acts, however, it is not logical to ask whether or not they are "true"—the question is whether or not they successfully accomplish their purpose. Austin's great contribution to our knowledge about language was to notice that propositions weren't the only utterances in use, and that the alternative, performative speech acts, test our assumptions about what meaning is and how language works.

Searle, building on work by Austin, outlined conditions, called **felicity conditions**, that determine whether or not a performative speech act, or any illocutionary act, is successful. In other words, what conditions are required for an utterance to achieve its intended illocutionary force? A felicitous utterance successfully performs its illocutionary force. Searle outlined specific felicity conditions for each speech act, which are fundamentally about authority (does the speaker have the authority to perform this speech act?), context (is this an appropriate context for the speech act?), and recognizability. Consider the following conditions you would have to meet in order to successfully promise your roommate that you will make dinner for him tonight:

- You must say to your roommate something along the lines of "I promise I will make you dinner tonight," a performative speech act that predicates a future action of which you are capable and that is recognizably a promise.
- You must believe your roommate would like you to make dinner, and your roommate must actually want this.
- It must be obvious that you would not normally cook dinner for him.
- You must truly intend to make dinner and be willing to be obligated to making dinner.

These conditions reveal how close a promise is to a threat: for a threat, the second condition above would change to "You must believe your roommate would prefer that you not make dinner, and your roommate must actually not want you to cook dinner." If you are a terrible cook and your roommate was violently ill the last time you cooked him dinner, the promise to cook him dinner could actually be a threat. Similar kinds of conditions can be mapped for vows, bets, pledges, and other performative speech acts.

These felicity conditions highlight the importance of a speaker's intentions in speech act theory. But if a hearer does not recognize a speaker's intentions, is it a successful speech act? A good case study is the debate over Bill Clinton's "apology" after the Monica Lewinsky scandal (Lakoff 2000). It took Clinton several attempts to satisfy the public that he had successfully apologized for his actions. In his first speech, he used the words "wrong" and "inappropriate" to describe his behavior, but he did not utter the words "apologize" or "sorry." Two weeks later, he said, "I have acknowledged that I made a mistake, said that I regretted it, asked to be forgiven." The past tense in these statements prevents them from being performative speech acts that function as an apology; rather, they describe past conditions that would hold for an apology to be successful. In his third attempt, a few days later, President Clinton said he was "very sorry" about the affair, but he said it in Europe, not to the American people. About a week later, he said, "I don't think there is a fancy way to say that I have sinned" and "I have asked all for their forgiveness." Finally, the public seems to have felt that he had apologized, although if you look carefully at these utterances, you will see that they report on past speech acts and do not themselves function performatively as apologies. But if the addressees accept the indirect speech act as an apology, no matter what the speaker intended, has it been successful?

Evaluating Speech Act Theory

Austin introduced speech act theory to provide a systematic account of meaning at the level of utterance. Such an account of utterance in a language would be predictive: given certain conditions, speakers could predict certain semantic results from certain types of utterance. Austin had a very narrow notion of what counted as speech acts and how they worked: he had to keep it narrow, so that it would remain systematic; if he loosened the notion of illocutionary force to include all utterances, the model would not always behave in predictable ways.

Austin's early version of speech act theory wasn't fully successful. In 1971, P. F. Strawson (introduced in Chapter 7) objected that the relations Austin proposed among locution, illocution, and perlocution, and especially the range of illocutionary acts, have little to do with the way people speak most of the time in conversation (declarations are relatively rare, for instance), so speech acts as Austin described them could play only a limited role in the communicative aspect of language. Searle's improvements to Austin's theory were meant to overcome the objections of Strawson and others. Linguists and philosophers still argue about how successful speech act theory on Austin and Searle's terms really is.

For instance, a lot of our conversation consists of nonsentences, such as *Hello, Mikey*, and *Whatever*. You might be tempted to think of these as sentence fragments, but they're only sentence fragments if they are part of elliptical sentences, those to which hearers correctly supply the missing parts in their minds on the basis of syntactic, semantic, and contextual clues. These nonsentence utterances stand alone. Speech act theory accounts only for utterances that *are* sentences—it's the only way for illocutionary acts to correspond to typical verbs like those listed in Table 8.1. Does this mean that nonsentence utterances aren't speech acts, that is, can't be understood in terms of locution, illocution, and perlocution? The linguist Robert J. Stainton (2004) has argued the case that, in fact, they are speech acts.

Let's consider the two nonsentence utterances above in more detail. If the person in question is generally called *Mikey*, the first example is probably a simple greeting, one in which what *Mikey* hears is what the greeter intended, which is also the straightforward locutionary sense of the utterance. But what if the speaker is a killer, a serial killer right out of the movies, with Michael (not Mikey) as his next victim? The utterance is threatening and diminishing at the same time: it enacts the speaker's power over the victim. Of course, that meaning doesn't come up much in everyday conversation, but as we mentioned in Chapter 1, nicknames can be put-downs, definitely speech as an act—a speech act. So if the speaker addresses a bona fide Michael as *Mikey*, the utterance's illocutionary act might be a "dismissive." Or, *Mikey* could be used as a term of endearment—it depends on the context. But Michael (or Mikey) has to interpret the illocutionary force of the utterance and its relationship to the locutionary act, *Hello, Mikey*.

Whatever can be said without attitude: the speaker is asked to make a choice or to affirm a plan of action; uncommitted to any option, the speaker responds, "Whatever." Effectively, this means 'I don't care, so go ahead and choose (or plan) whatever you like'. This version of *Whatever* might, in fact, be an elliptical sentence, not really a nonsentence utterance. But you are familiar with the mildly dismissive, shoulder-shrugging, uncooperative *Whatever* (Monique: "I can't believe you used up all of the milk!" Monique's husband, Gary: "Whatever."), as well as the exclamatory, unbelieving, or extremely uncooperative *Whatever,* the one with extra stress on the second syllable (Monique: "You're going out to get more milk!" Gary: "Whatever! Get it yourself!")

Arguably, *Whatever* is loaded with illocutionary force, but classic speech act theory doesn't account for it. Nonsentence speech acts, like the classic ones, are associated with conventional meanings, but they are also more heavily dependent on context. As a result, the semantics of utterances may not be as systematic as Austin, Searle, and others have hoped. Linguists have used speech act theory flexibly in recent years in order to account for the extraordinary range of illocutionary and perlocutionary meaning that underlies utterances of all kinds.

In discourse analysis, the meaning of primary interest is at the level of the whole utterance in context. And, although that discourse meaning is never merely the sum of phonological, morphological, lexical semantic, and syntactic parts, all of those levels can contribute to the meaning of an utterance. For instance, the illocutionary force of *Whatever* is expressed in intonation and the intensity of stress, a phonological property of the utterance (not of the word used in the utterance). The illocutionary force depends partly on the morphology of *Mikey*, where Mike is clipped from Michael and Mikey is derived with the suffix *-ie/-ey*, which can be diminutive in some cases ("How much is that doggie in the window?"), familiar or intimate in others (Monique: "Do we have any milk?" Gary: "Would you like some milk, sweetie?"), and threatening in others ("Hello, Mikey."). All linguistic levels participate in making meaning, but some kinds of meaning belong to discourse itself.

The Cooperative Principle: Successfully Exchanging Information

In order to exchange information successfully, speakers must cooperate both in creating meaningful utterances in specific contexts and in working to interpret other speakers' utterances as meaningful. The British philosopher H. P. Grice describes the **Cooperative Principle** as follows:

> Make your conversational contribution such as is required, at the stage at which it occurs, by the accepted purpose or direction of the talk exchange in which you are engaged. (1989, 26)

In order for conversation to happen successfully, all participants or interlocutors must cooperate. Hearers must assume that speakers are making contributions that serve a purpose within the context of the discourse, and hearers must seek out that purpose. Just as essentially, speakers must actually speak with a purpose.

Conversational Maxims

Grice proposed four categories of maxims critical to the cooperative principle (from the perspective of the speaker):

Maxims of Quantity

1. Make your contribution as informative as required.

2. Do not make your contribution more informative than is required.

Maxims of Quality

1. Do not say what you believe to be false.

2. Do not say that for which you lack adequate evidence.

Maxim of Relation

1. Be relevant.

Maxims of Manner

1. Avoid obscurity of expression.

2. Avoid ambiguity.

3. Be brief.

4. Be orderly.

Imagine that a friend asks you what you did last Saturday night. You reply, "I washed my hair and watched some TV." If these were your primary two activities on Saturday night, then your response seems to follow the maxims. But your friend then says, "Didn't I see you at the salsa dance party?" You reply, "Yeah. After I watched some TV, I went to the movies and then to the party." Given these new facts, your first response seems to violate a maxim of quantity: it does not provide as much information as was requested. If you did not, in fact, wash your hair, your response also violates a maxim of quality: it provides information that you know to be false.

Of course, speakers violate these maxims all the time. And, given social conventions and the requirements or pressing needs of particular conversations, many of these violations actually facilitate conversational interaction. One major cause for such violations is politeness, which we discuss in more detail below. We also employ "white lies," for example, to avoid hurting people's feelings or to avoid unnecessarily complicating an answer. Though warned to avoid it in writing, we exploit ambiguity in conversation all the time. Usually, when someone asks you how you are, you say "Fine" and leave it at that. If you say much more, you might violate a maxim of quantity by providing what we call colloquially TMI ('Too Much Information').

Conversational Implicature

The cooperative principle extends to all participants in a conversation—speakers and hearers. Such reciprocal cooperation helps explain how many utterances in conversation are connected and how indirect speech acts work. Grice used the term **conversational implicature** to describe the way an utterance can carry implied meaning in a particular conversation, which may be very different from its propositional content (or what is entailed in an utterance). Conversational implicature works if the implied meanings somehow belong in the conversation, that is, if:

a. a speaker, knowing that his or her utterance implies X, makes the utterance with the assumption that given its implicatures it conforms with the cooperative principle and with the belief that the hearer will interpret the utterance and implicature in such a way that it conforms with the cooperative principle; and

b. the hearer interprets the utterance's implicatures in such a way that it conforms with the cooperative principle.

For example, imagine that a stranger stops you on the street and asks, "Do you know where I can buy a university sweatshirt?" You reply, "The university bookstore is right down the street." The implication of your utterance is that the university bookstore sells university sweatshirts. You also have responded to the implied request for information (the utterance is literally a yes-no question) as well as to the question's implication that the stranger is looking for a university sweatshirt in the near future and from a store in close proximity (otherwise you might respond that they sell such sweatshirts in, say, a neighboring town).

Let's take another example. You ask a good friend to go bowling with you on Saturday. He replies, "I'm busy. Sorry." And you say, "No problem—maybe we can go next week." Why did you interpret his statement about his state of busy-ness as relevant to bowling on Saturday? Because you are a cooperative speaker looking for and interpreting conversational implicatures and because you assume your friend is as well, you address the implied meaning of the utterance: you assume that this statement is relevant to your invitation (your friend is busy on Saturday, not just busy in general), provides as much information as is necessary (your friend is busy on Saturday in such a way that prevents him from going bowling with you), and is truthful. If your friend had responded, "My parents are coming to town—sorry," the conversational implication would have been that his parents will be in town on Saturday and your friend, therefore, will need to entertain them rather than go bowling with you.

Being a cooperative participant in conversation also means responding to the culturally understood illocutionary force of utterances rather than only to the locutionary force. When a speaker chooses to ignore the illocutionary force of an utterance, we often take it as a joke (or as exceptionally rude):

Speaker A (calling on the telephone): "Is Rachel home?"

Speaker B: "Yes" (and then remains on the phone).

Cultural differences sometimes create miscommunication around indirect speech acts, for what seems obvious to some speakers may be hidden to others if they do not

A Question to Discuss

Entailment and Implicature

Conversational implicature is one specific kind of implicature, specific to how an utterance can have implied meaning beyond the propositional meaning of its words within the context of a conversation. Implicature, as an umbrella term, refers to any kind of implied meaning beyond the propositional meaning of a sentence (or longer stretch of discourse) in terms of truth conditions. Entailment refers to the truth-conditional meaning of the proposition; in other words, what conditions must hold for a sentence (or longer stretch of discourse) to be true.

Let's take an example. Your instructor hands back a set of quizzes and says, "Not everyone did very well on this quiz." The implication here is that a lot of the class did not do very well. But the statement entails only that at least one person did not do very well on the quiz. So if only you did poorly on the quiz and everyone else got an A, the statement would still be true.

The difference between entailment and implicature is often exploited in advertising. An ad for an air purifier which states that the filter "removes small airborne particles" with "less noise" implies that it removes all of them with very little noise, but really it only entails that it removes some of them with an unclear amount of noise (less than what?). In the fine print, the ad states that the air purifier is "99.97% effective at removing particles as small as 0.3 microns that pass through the filter." The implication is that it is 99.97 percent effective at removing particles as small as 0.3 microns. In fact, however, the statement entails that the particles must pass through the filter and it's unclear how effective the purifier is at sucking in these particles so that they must pass through the filter. You can see why people tell you to read the fine print carefully.

Browse through a few magazines and newspapers and find at least two ads that you think are interesting in terms of the difference between what they entail and what they imply. How do the ads exploit implicature for their purposes? Come to class prepared to discuss your analysis of the ads' aims and effectiveness.

share an understanding of an utterance's illocutionary force and conversational implicatures. Shared cultural understandings among speakers are critical to implicature and successful conversation.

Relevance

Fundamental to the successful use and interpretation of implicature, **relevance** helps discourse (whether spoken or written) to cohere. In any conversation, for instance, we assume that anything any party to the conversation says is relevant to that conversation. Discourse presumably rises to optimal relevance. If we couldn't assume that, we wouldn't bother to engage in conversation at all.

Consider the following conversation:

Jenny: What are we having for dinner?

Michael: Paul just pulled in.

Jenny: I was hoping that you'd make macaroni and cheese.

Michael: Did you replace the lightbulb in the hall?

Clearly, Jenny is trying to construct a conversation about dinner, but Michael's responses are not optimally relevant to that conversation—indeed, they're wholly irrelevant. Generally, we don't accept conversation of this kind, unless, as dialogue in a play or novel, it serves some literary function. You can probably imagine Jenny trying to interpret Michael's utterances as relevant to her conversation about dinner. For example:

Jenny: What are we having for dinner?

Michael: Paul just pulled in.

Jenny: Oh, is he joining us for dinner?

Michael: Did you replace the lightbulb in the hall?

Jenny: Will Paul not be able to find his way in if it's too dark?

Now reconsider Monique's request for milk, in a slightly different context:

Monique: I'm in the mood for some milk.

Gary: I think there's some in the fridge.

Monique: Are you getting up?

On the face of it, her husband's getting up has nothing to do with Monique's desire for milk, but because we assume optimal relevance in discourse, her husband will understand the implicit request that he bring her some milk (whether or not he had intended to leave his recliner before this conversation).

What if there were no milk in the house? Then the conversation between Monique and her husband might go something like this:

Gary: I'll go to the store and get some milk.

Monique: But it's raining so hard!

On the face of it, the rain has nothing to do with getting milk. The *but* (a "discourse marker"—more on this later in the chapter) indicates relevance, however. In Chapter 7, we discussed whether function words, like conjunctions (i.e., like *but*), refer to anything. The study of discourse clarifies the issue somewhat: function words need not refer; one of their key functions is to mark discourse in terms of categories like relevance.

Relevance is partly a cognitive matter. What we hear in a conversation must fit into conceptual frames and contexts in order for us to comprehend it. We prefer to comprehend with the least possible effort; we resist spending great effort to understand conversation. Relevance is thus a measure of effort in communication: the more relevant an element of conversation is, the less cognitive effort it requires of the participants. As you know from experience, most conversations are composed partly of sentence fragments and indirect comments. Such conversations assume a high degree of relevance. Because the participants find it easy to understand one another, they can take syntactic shortcuts.

Conversation doesn't always conform to the cooperative principle. Indeed, a sizeable number of interactions involve disputes in which speakers' aims may not be cooperative. For instance, strategic rudeness can be seen as a reflection of pragmatic competence (Beebe 1995). The question "What's your point?" can effectively shape the contribution of an interlocutor. Cussing someone out can vent negative feelings. Rather than assuming that these utterances fail to adhere to the maxims that encourage clarity, politeness, directness, relevance, and truthfulness, we could view them as successfully fulfilling other important social and conversational functions.

Remember that in conversation all participants are working to achieve desired ends, from presenting themselves in specific ways to creating or maintaining relationships, from trying to elicit information to trying to persuade others to think or act in certain ways. Linguist Robin Lakoff (1990) describes all language as political. In other words, every time we talk (whether an intimate conversation with someone close to us or a speech before an audience), we are being strategic and trying to accomplish a purpose—even when we think that we are just being spontaneous and innocent. That purpose does not have to be a negative one, and "political" should be understood here without the negative connotations that the term has acquired in other contexts. Our purposes can be to persuade, to acquire information, to maintain a friendship, to have people like us. The point is that we are always using language toward particular ends—ends that go far beyond the literal meaning of the words we utter.

Politeness and Face: Negotiating Relationships in Speaking

Grice's conversational maxims emphasize being clear and direct in our speech—saying no more and no less than required, being relevant, and unambiguous. The maxims aren't meant to prescribe conversational etiquette, but explain the rational basis of human speech interaction. As Grice puts it, "I would like to be able to think of the standard type of conversational practice not merely as something that all or most of us do *in fact* but as something that it is *reasonable* for us to follow, that we *should* not abandon" (1989, 29).

Of course, much of the time, we as speakers are much more circuitous, ambiguous, and long-winded than the maxims propose we would be. Grice was well aware that speakers find it useful to deviate from the maxims, to various degrees, which he called "flouting," "clashing," "opting out," and "violating" maxims (1989, 30). The terms for all of these conversational strategies are negative, the strategies not preferred and inadvisable if your goal is a successful conversation. As Robin Lakoff observes, however, "There are in ordinary conversation higher obligations than clarity" (1990, 30). One of the most important of these obligations is politeness. We as speakers often go to significant conversational lengths to be polite because we understand the needs and wants of those with whom we speak, as well as the power dynamics of the situation.

A Scholar to Know

Robin Tolmach Lakoff (1942–)

American linguist Robin Tolmach Lakoff, a professor of linguistics at the University of California, Berkeley, earned her Ph.D. in linguistics at Harvard University in 1967, with a dissertation later published as *Abstract Syntax and Latin Complementation* (1968). She quickly turned to discourse analysis, however, an emerging field of which she was a leader. Her *The Logic of Politeness* (1973) challenged the status of Grice's maxims and proposed a politeness principle to supplement Grice's cooperative principle (see below for the three maxims of politeness). Lakoff's most famous (and infamous) work is *Language and Woman's Place* (1975), a book that is often framed as initiating the modern field of language and gender (see the "Special Focus" section of this chapter). Though Lakoff's argument has been criticized (her approach is intuitive rather than empirical, her experience drawn from a narrow social context), it has been extremely important to the development of discourse analysis and sociolinguistics. In 2004, *Language and Woman's Place* was republished in an edition by Mary Bucholtz that includes essays by linguists like Janet Holmes and Penelope Eckert, who explain the important role Lakoff's early work on language and gender played in their own significant contributions to the field. Lakoff's most recent books, including *The Language War* (2000), examine the politics of language and the relationship of language and power more generally.

Positive and Negative Politeness and Face

In discourse studies, **politeness** encompasses all the ways in which speakers adapt (or don't adapt) to the needs and wants of the other speakers involved in a conversational exchange (often referred to as *interlocutors*). Penelope Brown (1980) describes politeness as a special way of treating people, saying and doing things in such a way as to take into account the other person's feelings. Lakoff outlines three general rules of politeness:

1. Formality/distance: don't impose; be sufficiently aloof.
2. Hesitancy/deference: give addressees options about how to respond.
3. Equality/camaraderie: act like equals; make others feel good.

Penelope Brown and Stephen Levinson, in their work on communicative strategies and politeness, frame these kinds of politeness principles in terms of **face**. (We commonly use the word *face* this way in the colloquial expression "to save face.") All participants in conversations have two kinds of desires or "face-wants":

1. **Positive face**, or the desire to be approved of and/or liked.
2. **Negative face**, or the desire to be unimpeded in one's actions.

Politeness revolves around respecting the face-wants of others. **Positive politeness** is enhancing the positive face of others: giving them compliments; using terms of address or other markers that indicate friendliness, equality, or camaraderie; thanking

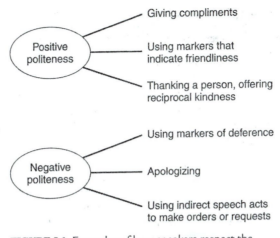

FIGURE 8.1 Examples of how speakers respect the face-wants of other speakers through both positive and negative politeness. Positive politeness helps others feel approved of or liked; negative politeness helps others feel unimpeded in their desired actions.

them and offering reciprocal kindness; and so on (see Figure 8.1). These speech acts and features can make one's interlocutors feel liked, appreciated, and on equal (if not higher) footing. **Negative politeness** is respecting the negative face of others: using markers of deference; apologizing; using indirect speech acts to make requests or orders; and so on. These speech acts and features can make one's interlocutors feel that their needs are being respected and that they are not being unduly imposed upon. For example, an indirect request, which may allow the other person to turn it down without directly refusing, reflects the speaker's desire not to impose the request as a directive.

Face-Threatening Acts

Any utterance can potentially be a **face-threatening act** (**FTA**), and speakers must determine whether, given the context and their relationship with the addressee, there is a need to mitigate the act. If speakers have to perform a highly face-threatening act, they typically employ a high level of politeness in order to mitigate the force of the act or utterance. Highly threatening FTAs include telling people things they do not want to hear, as well as making certain kinds of requests/orders.

Imagine that you need to borrow your friend's car. Clearly, this kind of request will impose on the negative face of your friend. If you were not particularly interested in being polite about the request (and if you thought you could get away with such impoliteness and still use the car), you might simply use a declarative sentence or a bald imperative: "I need to borrow your car" or "Lend me your car." You could soften or make the imperative more polite by adding "please." If you were trying to be even more polite, you could employ an apology ("I am so sorry to impose . . ."), an indirect request ("I was wondering if I could . . ." or "Would you mind if I . . ."), another marker of deference or a recognition of the imposition ("I know that this is probably going to be a hassle for you . . ."), or a combination of these strategies.

A Question to Discuss

How Do Compliments Work?

Although compliments are typically intended to make others feel good, to praise them, and to create solidarity or positive relations between the speaker and addressee, compliments can be interpreted as patronizing or as "brown-nosing" if there is a power differential between the speakers. Scholars have noted that a compliment can even be face-threatening if it implies that the complimenter envies the addressee in some way (especially in a culture where compliments imply debt).

In a study of speakers of New Zealand English, Janet Holmes (1995) examined whether men or women use more compliments. She found that the women in her study gave and received significantly more compliments than the men did. Men gave more compliments to women than they did to other men. Holmes argues that women use compliments as a positive politeness strategy and to create solidarity, whereas men may be more likely to take compliments as evaluative and possibly even face-threatening (in that compliments may imply jealousy).

Holmes's study indicates how formulaic compliments tend to be. More than half of the compliments in her study involve the words *good, nice, great, beautiful,* and *pretty* (with even gender distribution). Women tend to use the formula "What a _____!" more (e.g., "What a great car!"), while men more often use "Adj Noun" (e.g., "Nice shirt."), which could be read as a reduced form of a more emphatic compliment. Women give and receive more compliments on their appearance; men compliment other men on their possessions. This finding calls attention to the social belief systems that may prevent men from complimenting other men on their appearance.

On the whole, the speakers in Holmes's study paid the most compliments to their equals. Higher-status females were twice as likely to receive compliments from their subordinates as higher-status males. How would you explain this finding?

You also might try a series of positive face moves: "Chris, we're real buddies, aren't we, and I'm really impressed with what a generous and carefree person you are. Will you let me use your car?" Power dynamics and politeness are clearly interrelated, and speakers choose politeness strategies—and then the linguistic forms that correlate with those strategies—based on their understanding of what is required and what will be effective. In general, we tend to be more polite to people who are socially or institutionally superior to us and to people we don't know well.

Cultural differences affect what kinds of acts are considered face-threatening and what linguistic forms and strategies are seen as polite. For example, many Americans consider asking how much money a person makes a face-threatening act. In parts of China, this question is not necessarily seen as more face-threatening than asking someone what his or her job is. In another example, the novelist Isabel Allende (2003, 172) writes about her move from Chile to Caracas, Venezuela: "Accustomed to euphemisms, we were offended by the frankness of speech." In some cultures, one accepts compliments; in others, one rejects them.

Differences in communicative background and expectations across different speakers and across different cultures are the focus of interactional sociolinguistics and other anthropological approaches. Politeness, like conversational implicature, rests on shared cultural knowledge. Allende puts it well when she writes:

> Each country has its customs, its manias, its complexes. I know the idiosyncrasies of mine like the palm of my hand; nothing surprises me, I can anticipate others' reactions. I understand what gestures mean, silences, formulas of courtesy, ambiguous responses. Only there do I feel comfortable socially—despite the fact that I rarely behave as I'm expected to—because there I know how to behave and my good manners rarely fail me. (132)

Discourse Markers: Signaling Discourse Organization and Authority

In naturally occurring conversation, many words do not seem to carry any propositional content. Consider, for example, how this section might have started if it were being delivered orally as a lecture: "So, the next topic is how we signal to listeners what is coming in our utterances and how we involve our listeners in what we're saying. So we're going to look at discourse markers. Now, discourse markers function differently from other lexical categories." What is the function of *so* in the first sentence? In the second sentence? What about *now* in the third sentence? In this utterance, these words are functioning as discourse markers: they are organizing the presentation of the discourse, providing clues to listeners about what to expect next and how it is related to what came before. Most discourse markers occur at the "periphery" of the discourse:

Language Change at Work

Discourse Markers from *Beowulf* to *Dude*

The Anglo-Saxon epic poem *Beowulf* begins with a discourse marker: *hwæt*. Many modern translations turn this first word into "lo" or "hark." The Nobel Prize–winning poet Seamus Heaney, in his best-selling translation of the poem, translates the word as "so." He explains that in Hiberno-English, as in other varieties of English, "so" works as an expression "which obliterates all previous discourse and narrative, and at the same time functions as an exclamation calling for immediate attention" (2000, xxvii). Linguists would call it a focuser, but most of us think of it as the first step in telling a story.

In the twenty-first century, some young people in the United States use the word *dude* in telling stories—in all kinds of ways. A study by

Scott Kiesling (2004) describes how *dude* has moved from being a term of address (originally by men to men but now by men and women to men and women, and now usually signaling affiliation or connection) to encompassing all of these additional functions: an exclamation (both positive and negative); a marker structuring discourse (e.g., to signal an important event in a story), much like *so*; a marker mitigating confrontational stance, much like *well*, as in "Dude, I guess I don't agree with you"; and a marker of agreement, like *totally*. The use of *dude* usually signals a speaker's stance toward the addressee(s), typically, Kiesling argues, one of "cool solidarity." These last three functions of *dude* all arguably mean that *dude* now functions as a discourse marker.

often at the beginning or end of turns in a conversation, or—in this example—at the beginning of sentences in a sequence of moves by one speaker.

Function of Discourse Markers

Discourse markers are typically defined as the seemingly meaningless elements that tend to occur in spoken language, that are nonobligatory, and that carry out pragmatic functions rather than convey semantic or truth-conditional meaning. They signal to a listener how to understand an utterance in relation to the utterances that precede and follow it, as well as how to understand the utterance in the context of the relationship being negotiated between the speaker and the listener. Examples include *now, so, and, well, I mean, however, then, you know,* and many more. That said, there is actually not much agreement among linguists about: (1) exactly how to define "discourse markers" (as well as whether to call them discourse markers, discourse particles, pragmatic markers, etc.); and (2) which words count as discourse markers. The arguments and counterarguments are fascinating and complex. Here, we provide a general framework in which you can think about words that structure discourse.

Discourse markers often signal the sequential relationship of utterances. In other words, they link a given utterance to those that precede it. Importantly, they are optional and do not affect the propositional meaning of an utterance—their presence does not change the truth-condition of a statement. If we take an extreme example, consider the utterance: "Well, like, I mean, you know, yeah." The string of discourse markers at the beginning of that utterance does not change the propositional content of the message, which is the affirmative "yeah." The discourse markers do indicate the utterance's relationship to previous messages, as well as (potentially) the speaker's stance and understanding of his or her relationship with the hearer(s).

Types of Discourse Markers

Discourse markers include many parts of speech:

- adverbs (*so, however, then*)
- interjections (*oh, geez*)
- verbs (*say, look*)
- conjunctions (*and, but*)
- lexicalized clauses (*you know, I mean*)

They can serve many functions. For example:

> *Now*: The discourse marker *now* typically functions as a focuser. In the example at the beginning of this section, in which the lecturer states, "Now, discourse markers ...," *now* signals to the audience that an important piece of information is coming on this new topic.

> *And*: *And* often shows continuity within the discourse, either by one speaker in a monologue or between two speakers, if one is continuing a thought by the other. For example:

> > Karen: I remember when he came up to you all like cool and acting like he-being like I know I'm hot.

Language Change at Work

Like, I was like, what is going on with the word *like*?

The word *like* in current American English has taken on multiple meanings and functions in addition to its "dictionary definitions" as a verb, noun, conjunction, and preposition. One of its common new uses is often called "quotative *like*": *like* used to introduce direct speech or thought, and sometimes even a gesture, as in:

> She was *like*, can't you buy the beer? (introducing speech)
>
> And I was *like*, how old does she think I am? (introducing thought)
>
> He was *like*. [shrugs] (introducing gesture)

Like also functions as a hedge, to qualify a claim:

> Cigarettes now cost *like* seven dollars in New York.

As a discourse marker, *like* is often used as a "focuser," a marker of new information or focus, for example, "Well, it's not *like* wonderful, but it's okay."

It is commonly believed that younger people use *like* more than older people, and women use *like* more than men. A study of thirty speakers in Southeastern Michigan in 1995 found that the younger speakers (ages fourteen to twenty-nine) used quotative and focuser *like* more often than the older speakers. The study did not find, however, any significant difference between use by men and women in any of the age groups (Dailey-O'Cain 2000). A second part of the study surveyed forty speakers' attitudes about the use of *like*. The majority of informants agreed that younger people and women use *like* more often, although when asked whether they used *like*, young men and women responded affirmatively in approximately equal numbers. The majority of informants also expressed generally negative feelings about the use of *like*, often because it makes people sound uneducated or lazy. A few informants noted that *like* was okay when "imitating an airhead" or "telling a story," and several of the informants associated the word with "Valley girls." When asked to rate tape-recorded speakers, the informants rated speakers who used *like* frequently as more attractive, more cheerful, more friendly, and more successful, but less educated. The use of *like* seems to be associated with "solidarity," but not with "status." It is associated with informality and bad grammar, but it clearly carries positive meanings for many speakers in terms of friendly and polite interaction.

Though most Americans associate quotative *like* with youth, and with good reason, it has been around for a long time, and not just in America. Linguist Alexandra D'Arcy (2007) found evidence of its use in nineteenth-century England!

Kim: And then tripped on that barstool and I think he like broke his nose or something.

So: *So* serves many functions: to show effects or logical consequences; to introduce summaries or rephrasings; and, within an extended narrative, to indicate "parts of the story," much like signaling the beginning of a new paragraph. In the example at the beginning of this section, from the opening of a possible lecture, the first *so* opens the narrative progression of the lecture. The second *so* indicates a logical progression.

Well: Four distinct uses of *well* include: (1) introducing a new topic or directly reported speech; (2) prefacing a partial answer to a question; (3) prefacing a response that expresses disagreement and/or is face-threatening; and (4) filling a pause (Jucker 1997). (Many scholars categorize the "filler" use of *well, um, like* separately from their uses as discourse markers.) If we return to your friend's declining your invitation to go bowling with "Well, actually, I'm already busy," the *well* is working to mitigate the FTA involved in turning down your invitation.

You know (y'know): *You know* can conclude an argument, introduce a new referent, introduce a story, and serve to establish solidarity with the audience. If you were to turn to your classmate and say, "I am, you know, pretty into these discourse markers," the *you know* could function to establish shared ground with your classmate to help make your newly acquired fascination understandable. It could also help introduce this new fascination into the discourse.

I mean: *I mean* can signal an upcoming adjustment. It can also help minimize the authority of the speaker, which speakers often choose to do to make their audience feel more equal. For example: "I think that's the answer. I mean, it's kind of hard to say, but I think so."

At the end of his or her turn in a conversation, a speaker may use various discourse markers to "turn over the floor": *so, you know*, and so on. The next section provides more details about the conversational floor.

Conversation Analysis: Taking Turns and the Conversational Floor

Conversation analysis (CA) examines the structure of conversation, one specific type of discourse. The basic unit of conversation, given that there is typically more than one speaker, is the **turn**. Just as words are created from morphemes and sentences from words, conversations are created from sequences of turns. Conversations involve the negotiation of turns as speakers take and give up the **conversational floor**. Discourse markers provide one kind of organizational resource in conversation, and there are many more. Conversation analysis provides a framework for analyzing the structure of conversations.

Structure of Conversation

The basic structure of most conversations consists of the opening moves, the body of the conversation with turns taken by all speakers, and the closing moves (see Figure 8.2). Conversational openings and closings tend to be highly ritualized. In English, we have typical ways of beginning a conversation, such as "Hi," "Hey," "Yo," "How are you?" "What's up?" "'sup?" And we have typical ways of responding to these opening gambits, for example "Hi" as a response to "Hi," "Yo" as a response to "Yo," "Fine" as a response to "How are you?" and "Nothing" or "Not much" or perhaps "'sup?" as responses to "What's up?" Sometimes you will even hear speakers mix up these fairly meaningless opening moves, as they have misanticipated the opening question: for example, "Nothing" as a response to "How are you?" We notice, and can sometimes be disconcerted or even annoyed, when interlocutors do not follow convention here and

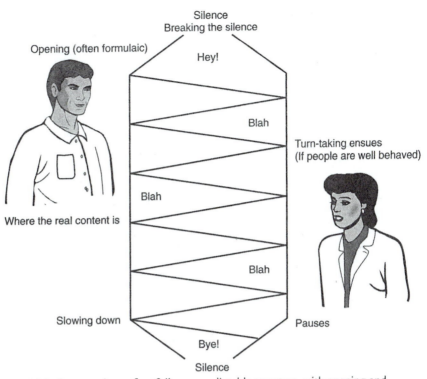

FIGURE 8.2 Conversations often follow a predictable structure, with opening and closing moves framing an exchange of information in which speakers negotiate turns on the conversational floor.

provide truly informative answers to opening questions such as "How are you?" rather than simply answering "Fine."

Speakers of other languages follow different opening conventions. In Chinese, one form of greeting translates as "Are you well?" with the reciprocal response "Are you well?" In Chile, the answer to "How are you?" is different from that in the United States: "In Chile it is bad manners to acknowledge that you're overly satisfied because that can irritate the less fortunate, which is why for us the correct answer to the question 'How are you?' is 'So-so.' . . . That is the sense of 'So-so' that can sometimes confuse visiting foreigners: it gives us time to feel out the ground and avoid a faux pas" (Allende 2003, 133).

Closing a conversation is a delicate business—as one linguist describes it, "negotiating our way to silence." We are generally trying to make sure that all interlocutors have a chance to say what they need or want to say and that everyone is ready to close the conversation. Conversation analysts have discovered that pauses often get longer near the end of conversations, speakers employ discourse markers such as *well* followed by a pause, and speakers often provide almost ritualized reasons to close such as "I should get going" or "It's been nice talking to you" or "So we'll talk again next week." These moves lead to the highly ritualized leave-taking turns such as "Bye" and "See you later." Obviously, conversations are much easier to end when speakers can physically leave as well (or hang up a phone). Ending a conversation with someone sitting next to you on a plane, when you must remain seated next to that person after the conversation, is trickier.

Turn-Taking

Throughout a conversation, speakers negotiate turn-taking. There are many ways for a speaker to indicate that someone else can take the floor:

- **Silence**: When a speaker finishes speaking, he or she can simply stop, creating a pause that allows someone else to take the floor. Different cultures are more and less comfortable with pauses of varying durations. Many American cultures are notably intolerant of—or at least uncomfortable with—silence, and speakers often jump in to fill gaps in conversations.

- **Questions**: A speaker can direct a question to another interlocutor, sometimes even using that person's name. Requests and invitations work similarly. These are often called **adjacency pairs**, or the combination of utterances that conventionally require a direct response and the response. Questions call for answers; invitations call for acceptance and decline. Again, cultural differences will affect adjacency pairs. For example, how one responds to a compliment (deny it? compliment the speaker? thank the speaker?) or a thank-you ("thank you"? "you're welcome"? "no problem"? say nothing at all?) will vary depending on cultural expectations and politeness conventions. Other kinds of sequencing involve, for example, preannouncements: "Guess what" or "You're not going to believe this" signal an upcoming announcement. In some ways, these preannouncements also ask for permission to take a longer turn and may be used by speakers with less power (institutional, social, cultural) in a given situation.

- **Gestures**: Many speakers use their hands, heads, and/or posture to indicate that another speaker can or should take the floor. Some speakers, if they tend to gesticulate when they speak, quiet their hands as they come to the end of a turn; some gesture toward an interlocutor. Some speakers lean forward to indicate attention to an interlocutor they are inviting to take the floor.

- **Eye contact**: Studies suggest that when we speak to other interlocutors, our eyes flit; when we are ready to turn the floor over to another speaker, we make direct and more prolonged eye contact.

- **Intonation**: Typically, falling intonation signals that a speaker is prepared to give up the floor, and rising intonation (other than that associated with questions) often signals that a speaker wishes to keep the floor.

You can undoubtedly come up with other turn-taking devices.

Different situations are often characterized by particular kinds of exchanges. For example, in classrooms, teachers frequently initiate interaction with questions. Students respond, and then teachers make another move, often repeating or rephrasing what the student has said and providing evaluative feedback (e.g., "Good," "Yes," "Almost").

Turn-Taking Violations

Speakers violate orderly turn-taking on a regular basis. If you listen carefully to naturally occurring conversation, many times you will hear "simultaneous talk": in other words, at least two speakers are talking at the same time. Conversation analysts distinguish between two major kinds of simultaneous talk, which are described below. Both are attempts by speakers to take the floor, but only interruptions are a **turn-taking violation**.

- **Overlap**: Overlap occurs when a speaker enters the conversation at what he or she thinks is a natural turn-taking moment but overlaps with the current speaker in the process. In the example, the brackets ([ ]) indicate simultaneous talk:

  Speaker A: It's so rude to interrupt [you know?]

  Speaker B: [Yeah I know] I hate it when
          people interrupt

  Speaker B has probably anticipated that the utterance is going to end after "interrupt," so she begins to speak just as Speaker A finishes the word "interrupt," thereby overlapping with the tag question at the end of Speaker A's utterance. We would typically not consider that an interruption, as it occurs at a natural turn-taking moment.

- **Interruption**: Interruptions typically occur in the middle of another speaker's turn where there is no indication that the speaker is prepared to give up the floor. When another speaker interrupts, the first speaker can either break off and thereby give up the floor or continue to speak and see if the interrupter will cease his or her attempt to take the floor. Interruptions can indicate power differentials in conversation and they can be disruptive. But interruptions can also demonstrate high involvement by participants in a conversation. Some speakers and cultures typically use highly involved speech styles that are characterized by high levels of interruption, which other speakers may interpret as disruptive rather than supportive.

Simultaneous speech can also occur at a turn-taking boundary if two or more speakers all try to take the floor at the same time. This kind of turn-taking violation often results in attempts to repair the conversational structure, as speakers explicitly cede the floor to others or request the floor. Another kind of turn-taking violation is not responding to an explicit conversational move by an interlocutor that invites the other speaker to take the floor.

Maintenance and Repair

Successfully maintaining a conversation can be hard work. All participants have to work to keep up their ends in a successful conversation. If one speaker asks a question, the other should answer. If one offers an invitation, the other should respond. In addition, speakers must continue to introduce and develop topics—both those that they introduce and those that others introduce—for a conversation to proceed. This conversational work may not always be evenly distributed. For example, some speakers may find themselves responsible in a conversation for asking all the questions or introducing most of the topics. (See the last section of this chapter for more details about how gender plays into the distribution of conversational work.)

Some forms of conversational maintenance in English are quite conventional. For instance, in conversation, speakers often provide vocal feedback, called **back-channeling** or **minimal responses**, to indicate that they are listening: "yeah," "uh huh," "ummm," "I know," and the like (as well as gestures such as head nodding). These responses are not meant as attempts to take the floor; they are typically interpreted as moves by hearers to indicate support of or agreement with the speaker. Many linguists have noted that these minimal responses don't necessarily indicate agreement—even if it involves head nodding and "yeah"—but rather acknowledgment of listening, and they are sometimes misinterpreted. Research on language and gender suggests that women back-channel more than men (more on language and gender research below). Almost all of us back-channel on the phone to indicate that we are still present. If you experiment with not back-channeling on the phone, you gradually may feel uncomfortable because you feel the urge to intrude your presence, and the person on the other end will probably pause at some point and ask if you are still there.

Speakers also **repair** conversation, their own utterances and those of others. Sometimes the repair work happens almost immediately, within one utterance, for example, when a person misspeaks and begins again. Sometimes a speaker clarifies an earlier utterance, especially if it becomes clear that others have not understood. Or the speaker may qualify or contradict an earlier utterance, especially if others indicate that the speaker is wrong or has unintentionally committed a face-threatening act.

Repairs can be self-initiated or other-initiated, as well as self-completed or other-completed. An example of an other-initiated repair is a question in response to an utterance, which asks for clarification or indicates that something was wrong with the utterance. Classrooms often involve a good amount of other-initiated repair by the instructor in response to the students, if they make mistakes. Ongoing educational research focuses on how to make classrooms, particularly ESL classrooms, more conducive to self-initiated, self-completed repair, or to other-initiated, other-completed repair in which the "other" is a student rather than the teacher.

Style Shifting: Negotiating Social Meaning

Style encompasses not only how we look—for example, what we wear, how we do our hair—but also how we talk. Style in language often refers to informal versus formal speech, but it can also refer to more specific kinds of speech along and beyond this spectrum, for example, formal academic speech versus formal social occasion speech, or informal sports speech versus informal gossip-session speech. Style is one way we convey meaning that surpasses the denotational meaning of the words we utter. As sociolinguist John Gumperz describes it, spoken interaction is "an ongoing process of negotiation, both to infer what others intend to convey and to monitor how one's own contributions are received" (2001, 218). In order to do this successfully, we need to share background knowledge about how to interpret others' utterances, including what various styles "mean."

Indexical Meaning

How does style "mean"? It means very differently from how words and clauses mean. Style has **indexical meaning**. In other words, its meaning is derived from its direct association with context. In reference to language, to "index" is to point outside the discourse for meaning. So words like *here* and *there* are indexical in that their meaning depends on the context of the utterance: *here*, for example, points to the location of the speaker and it can be used more locally or more globally. If you say, "I am studying here," *here* might refer to the library in which you are studying, the school that you attend, or the country in which you go to school, depending on the context of the utterance. Words like *here* and *there*, or *you* and *I*, potentially change their referent with every utterance.

In context, various styles can index social meanings. Styles indicate the purposes for which a speaker is using language and how the speaker is positioning himself or herself within understood social identities. All speakers **style-shift**, moving from more formal to less formal, for example, or from more local to more supralocal styles, depending on the context and purpose of their interactions, as well as the other interlocutors.

Let's consider an example. Many younger speakers use *like* frequently as a discourse marker. The word indexes youth. It also indexes informality and a deemphasizing of education. In serious settings, however, teenagers sometimes dramatically reduce their use of *like*. The context and the seriousness of the topic can cause these younger speakers to style-shift. A professor, who tends not to use *like* very often in interactions with other faculty, may use quotative *like* in lectures with students in order to establish a level of solidarity and friendliness with students (but perhaps not focuser *like* because of its strong indexicality of youth). These strategic uses of stylistic features are sometimes conscious but often unconscious.

Style and Creativity

Style can involve mixtures of linguistic features, many of which may index different social identities and/or contexts, in order to index in new and creative ways. Penelope Eckert's study of two high school girls in California in 1985 provides a useful analogy (see also Figure 8.3):

> These two best friends were part of the main preppy group. . . . However, they felt some admiration for the new wavers, who were a prominent counter-cultural group in their high school, because of their autonomy—their unwillingness to be dominated by "the school thing." The new wavers wore dark eye makeup and black clothing, most notably black

Indexes   Indexes

New Wave Identity   Preppy Identity

FIGURE 8.3 Clothing and makeup can index specific social identities, such as new wave or preppy.

pegged jeans, while the preppies stayed away from dark colors and wore straight legged designer blue jeans and light or bright colored name brand shirts and jackets. These two girls found a way to align themselves slightly with the new wavers without moving too far from the preppy mainstream, by pegging [that is, tapering the legs of] their blue jeans. This stylistic move was completely conscious and completely rational. The girls saw it as a social strategy, and were able to tell me about it unselfconsciously, and to tell me what each element represented. Certain aspects of linguistic style also work this way—those aspects of style that are most easily controlled and most easily associated with parts of the social landscape. Thus people adopt lexical items, expressions, intonation patterns, and pronunciations, at least of particular words, in a quite conscious construction of style whether momentary or as part of a trajectory. One might, for example, combine uses of "cool," "dude," or "whatever" with otherwise fairly standard English to achieve a "with it" image— to show that one is in tune with, but not limited to, vernacular culture. (Eckert 2000, 214)

This argument for stylistic creativity on the part of speakers breaks with some traditional arguments about style. Traditional arguments frame style primarily as a response to context. In other words, presented with a specific context and its requirements, speakers respond with appropriate speech styles. One school of thought explains stylistic difference as dependent on the amount of attention paid to speech, on the parts both of speaker and audience: formal speech shows a high level of attention and casual speech a low level of attention. Another school of thought explains stylistic difference as dependent on relationships among groups and between groups and individual speakers: speakers speak differently to different audiences, given their understanding of how language varies by social group. Recent work on style, like Eckert's, frames style as a linguistic resource on which speakers can draw in order to construct social meaning and present themselves in certain ways.

Natalie Schilling-Estes (1998) presents a case study of Rex, a native of the fairly isolated island of Ocracoke off the coast of North Carolina, who uses more pronounced Ocracoke dialect features when talking to outsiders. He uses vowels, for example, that make *high tide* sound more like *hoi toide*. By employing these features, Rex presents himself as the "quintessential islander," an identity clearly important to him in such situations (see also Figure 8.4). Studies like this one have stressed the importance of audience, not just topic, to style-shifting.

Another study examines two interviews by Stanford researchers with an eighteen-year-old African American woman, Foxy, from East Palo Alto (Rickford and McNair-Knox 1994). The first interview was conducted by Faye, a forty-one-year-old African American woman, and Faye's daughter; Foxy already knew Faye and felt comfortable with her. In this first interview, Foxy employed many more features of African American English (e.g., absence of third-person singular -s, zero is/are, invariant be) than she did in a subsequent interview with a twenty-five-year-old European American whom she had not met before. But in two earlier interviews with Faye, one when Foxy was thirteen and one when she was fifteen, Foxy had also shown a stylistic shift away from AAE features. The researchers hypothesize that at least in the second of these early interviews, when she was fifteen, Foxy may have been making an "initiative style shift," asserting her intellectual authority and her association with Stanford (where she had attended a summer program) in this situation with a Stanford interviewer. In the interview with Faye when Foxy was eighteen, Foxy, who was then president of the Black Student Union and seemed very comfortable with her background and identity, returned to her more distinctively African American language and style, though she had shifted away from it when thirteen and fifteen years old.

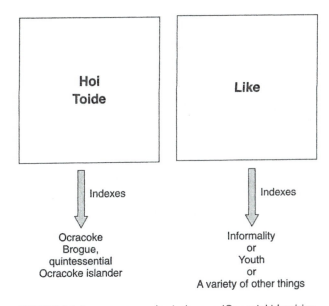

FIGURE 8.4 Language can also index specific social identities.

All speakers can style-shift. Many speakers can also code-switch. **Code-switching** is defined as switching between or mixing dialects and/or languages within one sentence, within one utterance, or within one conversation. Sometimes the line between style-shifting and code-switching is blurry. For example, if a speaker of a nonstandard dialect that employs double negation uses a double negative to create emphasis in an otherwise more Standard English context, does that constitute a style-shift toward a more informal or colloquial style or a code-switch to a different dialect? In either case, it represents the speaker's use of his or her available linguistic resources to create meaning within that context, dependent on shared knowledge of the indexicality of double negation. We discuss code-switching in more detail in Chapter 11.

Special Focus: Do Men and Women Speak Differently?

We live in a culture fascinated by differences between the sexes. In 1993, the book *Men Are from Mars, Women Are from Venus,* which is all about understanding the hidden differences of the opposite sex, became a best seller. In linguistics, the central question has been whether men and women speak differently.

There is no easy answer to this question. Many studies have explored differences between men's and women's patterns of speech, and although differences have been found, it's not always clear how we should interpret these results—in part because the questions researchers ask affect the answers that they get. If, for example, you study a population of high school students and ask whether the boys and girls speak differently, the answer will probably be yes. But, as Penelope Eckert demonstrates in her study of a high school population outside Detroit, if you examine the same population and ask whether the "jocks" speak differently from the "burn-outs," the answer is also yes—and this group identity seems to be at least as powerful as the students' identities as males and females in terms of how they talk.

Studies of gender difference in language have focused on two areas:

1. The use of standard and nonstandard features (e.g., *-ing* vs. *-in'*) by males and females.
2. Conversational patterns by males and females.

We discuss the first area in Chapter 11, as it is closely related to questions of dialect difference. Here we focus on the question of whether men and women speak differently in conversation.

Performing Gender

We are born with biological sex; we learn to perform gender. We perform gender every day not just in how we dress or do our hair but also in subtle ways like how we check our fingernails, carry our books, and look to see if something is stuck on the bottom of our shoe. We also perform gender through how we talk. We learn to do this by watching those around us and determining what performances are gendered as masculine and feminine. Gender is "socially constructed" in that it refers to the characteristics that a society sees as distinguishing men and women; these vary over time and from culture to culture, as they are not biologically determined.

So language and gender research aims to uncover how gender, and expectations about gendered speech, affect how men and women talk. It is important to remember that men and women don't "naturally" speak differently; if they speak differently, it is because they learned how to make that gendered distinction.

Early Language and Gender Research

Modern interest in the conversational behavior of men and women is usually traced back to Robin Lakoff's book *Language and Woman's Place* (1975). She described what she saw as "women's features" in language, which included the following (summarized in O'Barr and Atkins 1980):

- Hedges (e.g., "It's sort of hot in here.")
- (Super)polite forms (e.g., "Would you please open the door, if you don't mind?")
- Tag questions (e.g., "John is here, isn't he?")
- Speaking in italics (e.g., emphatic *so* and *very*)
- Empty adjectives (e.g., *divine, charming*)
- Hypercorrect grammar and pronunciation
- Lack of sense of humor
- Direct quotations (rather than paraphrasing what others have said)
- Special lexicon (e.g., more specific color terms like *mauve*)
- Question intonation in declarative contexts.

Subsequent research attempted to quantify these differences, with mixed results. For example, there has never been convincing evidence that women use more tag questions. And as discussed in Chapter 4, question intonation in declarative contexts (or "uptalking") has become characteristic of young people of both sexes. On the other hand, some studies showed women using more polite forms and more standard grammar and pronunciation than men.

A study of men and women serving as witnesses in court trials showed that both women and men who had less education and were less comfortable in a courtroom setting used many of these "women's features," such as hedges and emphatic forms (O'Barr and Atkins 1980). So perhaps the features are better thought of as "powerless features," with the recognition that gender and power often correlate. Cross-cultural studies, however, question even this description. For example, in Japan, indirectness, tag questions, and back-channeling characterize valued, powerful forms of communication (Wetzel 1988). "Powerless" or "women's" features are not universal.

Different Models for Gender Difference

Much of this early work in the field adheres to a "deficit model" of gender differences, which frames women's language as lacking or deficient compared to men's. One response to this model was scholarship focused more on a "difference model." Deborah Tannen's early work is a very good example of this approach. She argues that boys and girls—later men and women—are raised and live in different worlds. To oversimplify, we might say that boys are brought up to be competitive, while girls are brought up to be cooperative; men and women live, work, and play in cultures of gender that reflect that difference. As a result, there is miscommunication, just as there is in all cross-cultural communication. Here is one example from Tannen's book *That's Not What I Meant* (1986):

> If talks (of any kind) do get going, men's and women's ideas about how to conduct them may be very different. For example, Diana is feeling comfortable and close to Tom. She settles into a chair after dinner and begins to tell him about a problem at work. She expects him to ask questions to show he's interested; reassure her that he understands and that what she feels is normal; and return the intimacy by telling her a problem of his. Instead, Tom sidetracks her story, cracks jokes about it, questions her interpretation of the problem, and gives her advice about how to solve it and avoid such problems in the future.
>
> All of these responses, natural to men, are unexpected to women, who interpret them in terms of their own habits—negatively. When Tom comments on side issues or cracks jokes, Diana thinks he doesn't care about what she's saying and isn't really listening. If he challenges her reading of what went on, she feels he is criticizing her and telling her she's crazy, when what she wants is to be reassured that she's not. If he tells her how to solve the problem, it makes her feel as if she's the patient to his doctor—a metamessage of condescension, echoing male one-upmanship compared to the female etiquette of equality. Because he doesn't volunteer information about his problems, she feels he's implying he doesn't have any. (136–37)

One of the critiques of this kind of explanatory model has been that it does not address the power dynamic of gender relations. In the example, is Tom's challenge just a different yet equal communicative style, or do power dynamics allow him to be more aggressive than equality would permit? It is also fair to ask just how separate boys' and girls' worlds are growing up; is this really cross-cultural communication?

As a response, some scholars have explored a "dominance model" as a way to explain gender differences: differences in power result in speakers' exploiting different communicative strategies. In a study of three heterosexual couples talking in their homes, Pamela

Fishman (1983) argues that women do most of the "shitwork" in conversation. In other words, they are more actively engaged in making sure that conversational interaction is successful. For example:

- Women asked two and a half times as many questions.
- Women used more back-channeling to express interest; men used more minimal turns.
- Women introduced more than half the topics but most of their topics failed; men's topics were picked up and discussed in almost all cases.

Subsequent studies have supported many of these findings and added evidence that women tend to be interrupted more often than men. Women tend to work harder in conversation than men but aren't appreciated equally—an imbalance that mirrors much of women's experience in American culture.

Recent work in the field has focused on intra-sex talk: women talking with other women and men talking with other men. These studies often describe women as maintaining a "collaborative floor," in which they jointly produce discourse, support each other's turns with back-channeling, and gradually transition from one topic to the next (Coates 1996). Men, on the other hand, communicate more "competitively," with more interruptions and abrupt topic shifts. The many exceptions to these patterns indicate that the studies may oversimplify gender differences and not adequately address context and other factors in identity such as socioeconomic class, race and ethnicity, and age. Deborah Cameron (1997), for example, shows how an all-male conversation that one of her students interpreted as a case of competitive one-upmanship could persuasively be reinterpreted as a more cooperative gossip session among heterosexual men.

Language, Sexuality, and Desire

Most of the early work in language and gender focused on heterosexual speakers, but did not foreground sexuality as a factor. Pioneering work in queer sociolinguistics (the preferred scholarly term for referring to the systematic examination of language use in the queer community) has importantly complicated what we mean by the question: Do men and women speak differently? (*Queer* in this context serves as an umbrella term for the lesbian, gay, bisexual, and transgender communities.) This research has emphasized the idea of performance, looking at how speakers exploit the conventionalized meanings that come with specific ways of speaking in order to express sexuality and desire. Don Kulick (2000, 247) reminds us: "There is no such thing as gay or lesbian language. . . . [T]o say that some self-identified gay men and lesbians may sometimes use language in certain ways in certain contexts is not the same thing as saying that there is a gay or lesbian language."

Studies indicate that members of the queer community, for example, play with combinations of stereotypically heterosexual male and female speech, as well as stereotypical gay male speech, in order to construct their own gendered and sexual identities (Barrett 1997; Queen 1997). A mixture of linguistic features may "index" or indicate a queer identity. For example, in a study of how African American drag queens in Texas construct and maintain their identities, Rusty Barrett investigates the use of features such as "women's lexical items" (as listed by Lakoff), lexical items specific to gay men, hypercorrect pronunciation, a high-low pitch contour (often with an extended vowel, as in "FAABulous"), a generally wider pitch range of intonational contours, and features of African American English. Code-switching and style-shifting are clearly critical for most of these speakers, to determine the sexual orientation of an interlocutor and to navigate the fluid speech communities in which these speakers participate. Recent research has argued that to understand language and sexuality, we must understand the relationship of language and desire (e.g., how speakers use language to express desire), as desire is fundamental to sexuality (Cameron and Kulick 2003).

Language and Identity

Many of these studies highlight the complexity of identity as well as what we communicate beyond identity categories. Language is a critical component of our identities and how we perform them: we present ourselves in particular ways through language and others judge us by the language we use. As speakers, we all are members of multiple speech communities or "communities of practice" (Eckert and McConnell-Ginet 1992). As a result, we are always negotiating among these various identities—for example, as a male or female, as gay or straight, as a student, as a person from a specific part of the country, as a person of a specific ethnicity, as a person of a specific socioeconomic class, perhaps as a person in the workforce, perhaps as a person identifying with other specific local groups. Gender is clearly an important part of our identity and how we talk, but so are all these other parts of our identities.

At the same time, to return to the beginning of this section, many speakers believe strongly in gender difference. Speakers recognize certain language features as stereotypically "male" or "female" or "gay" or "straight," whether or not empirical findings confirm these stereotypes. As a result, speakers sometimes incorporate or perform toward these stereotypes, thereby enacting these features—and making them available to reinforce the stereotypes. It is a complex process and a dynamic one, in that all of us are using the spoken language to indicate important parts of our identities every time we speak.

☑ *Summary*

In this chapter, you have learned about several different ways to analyze spoken discourse.

- Utterances can be analyzed as speech acts, which involve locutionary, illocutionary, and perlocutionary acts. Speech acts can be direct or indirect, and speakers make strategic choices within any given context about how to formulate specific speech acts in order to be successful.

- Speakers cooperate in the creation of meaningful discourse: all participants must assume that the others are contributing relevant and purposeful information and interpret their utterances accordingly.

- Politeness is a crucial force in many interactions and speakers often shape their speech to respect the face-wants of interlocutors, depending on the power dynamics and cultural norms involved.

- Discourse markers help organize spoken discourse and often indicate the relationship being negotiated by speakers, both to what they are saying and to their interlocutors.

- Conversations themselves are highly structured, in terms of how speakers negotiate turns on the conversational floor.
- All speakers control multiple speech styles and style-shift in meaningful ways.

Suggested Reading

Two popular general treatments of discourse analysis are Barbara Johnstone's *Discourse Analysis* (2002) and Deborah Schiffrin's *Approaches to Discourse* (1994). *The Handbook of Discourse Analysis* (2001), edited by Deborah Schiffrin, Deborah Tannen, and Heidi E. Hamilton, and the two volumes of *Discourse Studies* (1999), edited by Teun van Dijk, both contain valuable collections of essays by many of the leading scholars in the field about topics in the analysis of both spoken and written discourse, including discourse markers, politeness, critical discourse analysis, and interactional sociolinguistics. Penelope Eckert's book *Linguistic Variation as Social Practice* (2000) provides an extended study of style-shifting. The reader *Language and Gender* (1998), edited by Jennifer Coates, contains many of the foundational articles in the field, although some are truncated. For a comprehensive look at recent language and gender research, see *The Handbook of Language and Gender* (2003), edited by Janet Holmes and Miriam Meyerhoff.

Exercises
Exercise 8.1   Speech Acts

1. For each of the utterances below:

   - Identify the grammatical form of the utterance: declarative, interrogative, imperative.
   - Describe the locutionary act and illocutionary act involved.
   - Identify the utterance as a direct or indirect speech act.

   If you think there is more than one possible answer in the case of different contexts, explain. Then use three of these utterances as examples of how meaning is context-dependent.

   a. "Do you know when the final exam is?"

   b. "Could I have a beer and a chicken sandwich?"

   c. "Is Carol home?" (on the phone)

   d. "I was wondering what the homework was for tomorrow."

   e. "Please don't leave."

   f. "Where is El Paso?"

   g. "I need help putting on these cufflinks."

   h. "Do you have ten dollars that I could borrow?"

      i. "Do you think I'm fat?"

      j. "I was hoping you could call me tonight."

      k. "I need two pounds of salami." (standing in front of the deli counter at the supermarket)

      l. "Thanks a lot."

2. What circumstances would need to apply for these utterances to be direct speech acts?

      a. Justin and his family are all sitting at dinner. Justin sees the ketchup at the far end of the table and asks his dad, "Can you pass me the ketchup?"

      b. Jessica and Paul are sitting on a park bench chatting. Jessica suddenly pinches Paul hard on the arm and says, "You asked for it."

3. Describe three different possible illocutionary acts that could be accomplished by each of the following utterances.

      a. "I will call the doctor."

      b. "Can I use your cell phone to make a call to Mexico?"

      c. "I hear that is a great movie."

      d. "Has the muffler fallen off your car?"

4. What are some ways to make a promise using an indirect speech act? Explain.

5. Asking another person out on a date can involve elaborate conversational strategies, particularly among younger speakers.

      a. Imagine a scenario in which two undergraduates, who know each other slightly, see each other at the gym after they have both finished working out. Construct a reasonably natural-sounding dialogue between the two, in which one maneuvers the conversation to ask the other to a movie on Friday night.

      b. Look back at your dialogue and underline all the indirect speech acts. Why do you think these more indirect formulas are so typical in such a conversation?

      c. Rewrite the conversation using only direct speech acts. Evaluate the result.

6. Outline a set of conditions that must hold true between a speaker and a hearer for each of the following speech acts to be successful: an expression of thanks; an expression of congratulations.

Exercise 8.2   The Cooperative Principle

1. Create examples of conversations that violate each of the four conversational maxims described on page 245 (some of your conversations may violate more than one principle). Share your conversations with a classmate and see if he or she agrees about which maxim(s) they violate.

2. Imagine this scene: At the grocery store, you see someone you have met there once before. You are going in opposite directions with your carts. As he passes, he asks, "How are you?" In fact, you have had a terrible week: you bombed an English quiz, your favorite football team lost its playoff game, your roommate isn't speaking to you, and you have had three bad hair days in a row.

    a. You reply, "Fine, thanks." Do you think this reply violates the maxims of the cooperative principle? Explain.

    b. You reply, "Actually, since you asked, just terrible. I can't even describe to you how awful my life is right now." Do you think this response violates the maxims of the cooperative principle? Explain.

    Hint: in thinking through your answers, consider the illocutionary force of your acquaintance's question.

3. Look back at the "natural-sounding" conversation that you created in Exercise 8.1, in which one undergraduate asks another out on a date. Describe the conversational implicatures at work in each stage of the conversation.

4. Come up with your best counterexample to the argument that all language use is political. In other words, do your best to provide an example of an utterance or conversation that is "neutral" or not strategically motivated. In class, exchange examples with a classmate and try to refute the example he or she provides. In other words, try to provide an argument for how the utterance or conversation could be read as strategic.

Exercise 8.3   Politeness

1. First, provide five "more polite" ways to make the following request: "Give me a double cappuccino, no whip." Then answer the questions below.

    a. How many of the five are indirect speech acts?

    b. Are there circumstances in which you can imagine any of these five being "too polite" or "oddly polite"?

2. Terms of address are a vital part of politeness. Do you address someone by his or her first name, with Mr./Mrs./Ms., or with his or her professional title (e.g., Doctor, Professor)? List the categories of people who fall into each of these forms of address for you, right now. Have some people moved from one category to another as you have gotten older? Why do you think that some have moved, or not moved, and how is it related to politeness?

3. In her memoir *My Invented Country,* Isabel Allende (2003, 173–74) describes one form of politeness in Venezuela that, at first, she did not know how to interpret:

    I didn't know their customs; for example, they rarely say no because they think it's rude: they would rather say "Come back tomorrow." I would go to look for a job and they would interview me with a great show of friendliness, offer me coffee, and say good-bye with a firm handshake and that "Come back tomorrow." So I would come back the next day, and the same routine would be repeated until finally I gave up.

Think about the politeness conventions that you know. Create a list of four polite expressions whose precise meaning you think outsiders to your culture might not understand, and explain why you think these might cause miscommunication. (Hint: it may help to think about social situations or interviews or classrooms.)

4. Run a small test with ten people to see how they respond to compliments. For each person, record his or her age, gender, and culture or ethnicity—after you have gotten his or her response. For the first five speakers, at some point in a conversation, say to them, "I really like your (a piece of clothing)." For the second five, say, "What a great (possession of theirs)." Record their responses. Then compare your results with those of your classmates and compile more comprehensive results. Can you find any patterns, by gender (of complimenter and/or complimentee), by culture or ethnicity, by age, or by type of compliment?

5. When might a compliment not be a compliment? It is possible to imagine ways in which a higher-status woman might use compliments directed toward men as a power play. For example, a female senior consultant at a consulting firm is convening the first team meeting for a project, and the team is composed of three male junior consultants. Before the meeting, she says to one of the men, "Good choice of tie." How might this utterance function in this context? Explain.

6. When a woman receives "positive" comments about her appearance from strangers as she walks down the street, do these "stranger compliments" really count as compliments? Why or why not? Justify your answer in relation to a specific definition of a compliment.

Exercise 8.4   Discourse Markers

1. Select one transcript from the Michigan Corpus of Academic Spoken English (http://www.hti.umich.edu/m/micase/). It can be either primarily monologic (e.g., a lecture) or primarily dialogic (e.g., office hours or a seminar). Find all hits of the discourse marker *well*. Try to categorize each instance within the four proposed functional categories of *well*. Make a list of any instances that you had trouble categorizing. How would you describe the use of *well* in these instances?

2. Select any discourse marker of particular interest to you. Select one transcript from MICASE, locate all the instances of this discourse marker, and try to categorize the functions of the discourse marker systematically.

Exercise 8.5   Conversation Analysis

1. Examine the following conversation (adapted from West and Zimmerman 1998/1977, 172). See Exercise 8.7 for the transcription conventions. Color-code and then provide specific labels for each of the following:

   - Types of adjacency pairs (in blue)
   - Types of turn-taking devices (in red)
   - Types of conversational overlap (in green)
   - Topic introduction (in yellow)

Provide a brief analysis of what is happening in this conversation, based on your findings.

```
 1 Female: How's your paper coming?
 2 Male:   All right I guess (#) I haven't done much in the
 3          past two weeks
 4          (1.8)
 5 Female: Yeah::: know how that [can]
 6 Male:                        [Hey] ya' got an extra cigarette?
 7          (#)
 8 Female: Oh uh sure ((hands him the pack))
 9          like my [pa ]
10 Male:           [How] 'bout a match?
11          (1.2)
12 Female: Ere ya go uh like my [pa ]
13 Male:                        [Thanks]
14          (1.8)
15 Female: Sure (#) I was gonna tell you [my ]
16 Male:                                 [Hey] I'd really like
17          ta' talk but I gotta run (#) see ya
18          (3.2)
19 Female: Yeah
```

Exercise 8.6   Style

In a short essay, describe the range of spoken style-shifting that you do every day. When and with whom do you style-shift? How would you describe these different styles? What specific words or other linguistic features strongly characterize these different styles? Feel free to use these styles themselves in the writing.

Exercise 8.7   Transcribing Conversation

Tape and transcribe a conversation among two to five people. You will need to get permission from the participants to tape their conversation for a classroom project. Use the conventions listed below to transcribe an interesting excerpt of the conversation (approximately two single-spaced pages of text). These conventions allow you to indicate overlap, pauses, extralinguistic features such as laughter, unintelligible segments, and intonation. No transcription will ever be "fully accurate"—you always choose to represent some features and ignore others. For these transcriptions, use standard spellings unless you think a pronunciation feature is especially relevant. Once you have finished the transcription, use the information in this chapter (e.g., about politeness, turn-taking, discourse markers) to write a focused analysis of one significant feature of the excerpt—or perhaps a cluster of related features—that you think are most interesting. Remember to consider context and the relationship of the interlocutors.

Transcription conventions (adapted from Coates 1998, xviii–xix):

A: I had [them] B: [Did] you	Brackets around portions of utterances indicate overlap
A: 'swhat I said= B: =But you didn't	Equal signs indicate "latching": no interval between the end of one turn and the beginning of the next
THIRteen	Capital letters indicate louder speech
°thirteen	A degree sign indicates quieter speech
thirteen	Italics indicate emphasis
?,!.	Punctuation is used to mark intonation
(2)	Numbers in parenthesis denote the length in seconds of a pause
(#)	The number sign in parenthesis indicates a pause of one second or less
we:::ll	Colons indicate that the sound before the colons is lengthened
but-	A hyphen marks an abrupt cut-off point in the utterance
((singing))	Double parentheses mark transcriber's comments
(only)	Single parentheses indicate that the transcriber is uncertain of the exact words uttered (but he/she is taking a stab at it anyway)
(xxxxx)	Parentheses around x's indicate untranscribable material
.hh	An inbreath
hhh	An outbreath

Chapter 9

Stylistics

Alice and Humpty Dumpty engage in a stylistic analysis of "Jabberwocky."

Poems can be hard to talk about. So, to discuss a poem in an English classroom, a teacher will frequently start with the question: "What do you think this poem is about?" And it turns out that tens of thousands of helpful Web sites about how to read poetry, aimed at students from Kindergarten to college, give the same advice (though not only that advice, of course).

"What is the poem about?" can be a productive question. It prompts consideration of the poem's subject: love, politics, history, mortality, truth, or beauty. But there's a difference between understanding a poem's subject and a poem's meaning. As you know from previous chapters, meaning is accomplished at several linguistic "levels" and you can't separate "what the poem is about" from the language in which the "what" is expressed. To consider *what* a poem—or any other work of literature, or any other written text—means, you must also consider *how* it means: how it is structured and how it draws on the phonological, lexical, syntactic, and pragmatic resources of English (or any other language in which it is written).

When Alice asks Humpty Dumpty to explain "Jabberwocky" to her, he defines the unfamiliar words. He asks, "Who's been repeating all that hard stuff to you?" (Carroll 1998, 189). When Alice first encountered the poem, she remarked, "It seems very pretty . . . but it's *rather* hard to understand. . . . Somehow it seems to fill my head with ideas—only I don't know exactly what they are! However, *somebody* killed *something:* that's clear at any rate" (Carroll 1998, 134). Alice and Humpty Dumpty are linguistic readers of poetry. Humpty Dumpty starts with morphology and lexical semantics: "Well, *slithy* means 'lithe' and 'slimy'. 'Lithe' is the same as 'active'. You see, it's like a portmanteau—there are two meanings packed up into one word" (Carroll 1998, 187). Alice finds a different way into the poem's meaning: she starts with syntax, recognizing familiar English subject/object positions in the structure of the poem's sentences.

This chapter focuses on stylistics, on the application of linguistic knowledge to help us discover what texts mean by explaining how they mean. Linguistic knowledge can also lead us beyond obvious meaning to feel the emotional affects of literature and also to appreciate its aesthetic value, though literature isn't always as "pretty" as Alice thought "Jabberwocky" to be.

The sections of this chapter move from the more general to the more specific questions that you can ask of a text. The chapter begins with a discussion of how to analyze the "world" of the text, then moves through examining the structure of the text as a whole, and then continues down to its parts, from sentences to words to sounds.

Stylistics

Stylistics is traditionally defined as the study of language and craft in literature, but it now includes other written texts such as advertisements, letters, song lyrics, and the like. Here, we focus primarily on written texts, but much of this material is relevant to spoken discourse as well. In truth, the line between discourse analysis, usually applied to spoken English, and stylistics, usually applied to self-conscious literary language, is blurry—aspects of one often transfer to the other.

Stylistics, like discourse analysis more generally, is as much a methodology as a field. It is a process of carefully examining the language in a given text to understand how the various components function and to explain the structure and effects of the text, not to mention its affect—the way that style provokes emotional response in readers.

Systematicity and Choice

Stylistics is *systematic* application of linguistic knowledge, both the formal and the social aspects of language, to the analysis of texts. It applies our knowledge of how language works generally to a specific text. Thus, we can examine the choices that any writer has made: why the text is written the way that it is and not in some other way, and what the effects of an author's stylistic choices are.

Systematicity is a key component of stylistics. When we read a piece of literature, we all have individual, subjective responses to the text, and we all notice and respond to different aspects of the work. By establishing a clear methodology for examining textual features, stylistics aims to create shared, "objective" material from which to draw conclusions about the text's effects. In other words, if we all systematically examine and describe specific features of the text, then we can all draw conclusions from a common place. Our conclusions may be different, but we have a scientific, shared, and verifiable basis for the discussion.

Thus, stylistic analysis involves two steps:

1. A systematic description of linguistic features of a specific text.
2. A critical analysis of the effects of these features, working together, in this specific text.

The first, empirically rigorous step creates the shared, verifiable results about how language works in a text. The second, subjective step examines the implications of the empirical results from a reader's perspective. Both steps are essential. Without the first step, there is no systematic basis for analysis of the language in a text. The first step allows us to agree on what questions to ask, even if we disagree ultimately about the answers. Without the second step, there is only a straightforward description of a text's language, a labeling of features without insight into the implications of linguistic description for a text's meaning. The fusion of these two functions is exactly what makes literature innovative and studying it so exciting.

The notion of style rests on the notion of choice. Every author, like every speaker, is always making choices about which word to use, which construction to employ, which structure to follow. These choices create patterns that can be examined. While some of the variation will be individual to an author, some of it will be characteristic of a type of text.

The World of Texts: Genres and Registers

Of course, not all texts are the same. A poem is not a novel, a textbook is not a play, and a letter is not a will. Texts can generally be categorized into groups that share formal features (e.g., lexical items, grammatical features, textual structures) and textual functions (e.g., informational, artistic). When literary scholars refer to genres, they mean literary subtypes. A student of poetry, for instance, would distinguish among sonnets, epics, romances, rondeaux, villanelles, and other types of poetry—each type constitutes a genre. Linguists, on the other hand, describe **genres** as types of texts that tend to occur in or are associated with specific contexts or social occasions and serve identifiable purposes within those contexts (e.g., the editorial, the résumé, the student expository essay).

Registers are varieties of a language defined by use, as opposed to dialects, which are varieties defined by user. A register like "Business English" is typical of text types or genres like the commercial letter and the résumé; a register like "Journalese" is typical of text types like the editorial and the feature story. But *register* can be identified not only by genre but also by social level or mode as well: most of us speak in an informal register among family and friends but in a formal register (at least some of the time) at school or work. Though some language scholars use the terms *genre* and *register* interchangeably, we recommend employing them carefully, aware of the audience and context. Careful use of these terms is, itself, a stylistic issue.

In linguistics, the terms *genre* and *register* capture two different directions of scholarly inquiry. Genre studies often move from the text toward its historical and conventional contexts, examining, first, how the text shapes audience response and, second, the social work it performs. Register studies often move from the text to its specific components, examining what features characterize a given text. Genres tend to be defined not only by the structure of the text but, more importantly, by the situation that requires the text. Registers are kinds of texts characterized by their purpose or use.

The first step in understanding a text stylistically is to identify its genre or register. A text may very well be described in terms of genre *and* in terms of register—any text might be considered from either or both perspectives:

- What type of text is it? That is, to what register or genre does it belong?
- How does genre/register identify a text's audience?
- How does genre/register identify a text's purpose?
- How does genre/register influence a reader's expectations of a text?

With answers to these questions, you can then analyze the text's relationship to its social context.

For example, in a study of patient intake forms, Anis Bawarshi (2003) argues that the patient medical history form (PMHF) shapes the subsequent interaction between the patient and the doctor. The form asks for only certain kinds of information—age, sex, height, weight, past physical conditions and treatments, and current symptoms—thereby establishing what information is considered relevant, both by the doctor and by the patient, to the interaction. The PMHF does not ask about, for example, how things are going at home or at work. In this way, Bawarshi argues, the form and the subsequent interaction reinforce a larger ideology of Western medicine that privileges physical symptoms and minimizes discussion of emotional and mental states, that assumes that we can treat the body separately from the mind—and this ideology, in an almost circular way, underlies the form. As you can see, one critical component of arguments about genres is the power of the genre to maintain the social conditions that allow its existence.

Variation among Text Types

One kind of register study examines the systematic variation among different text types. For example, if novels, essays, letters, and the PMHF are all text types of different registers, then systematic linguistic differences among them ought to account for at least part of what distinguishes one register from another. Douglas Biber has done extensive corpus-based studies of differences among registers and what features tend to co-occur. For example, informational texts such as academic prose and official documents tend to have a higher percentage of nouns and of relative clauses, which identify or elaborate on the referent. Conversation shows a higher percentage of causative adverbial subordinate clauses, which explain why, when, or how things happened. Here are two examples (Biber et al. 1998, 140):

Geology Textbook. In 1904 Jukes-Browne had completed his survey of the cretaceous rocks (1900–4), which includes description of sections west of the area dealt with in the sheet memoir.

Conversation. Do ring Cathy if you feel like it, because I'm sure she won't mind.

Texts focused more on interpersonal communication, rather than on informational communication, demonstrate a high co-occurrence of other features: contractions, second-person pronouns, discourse markers, semimodals (*have to, need to*), and *wh*-complement clauses (e.g., *what you need to do is . . .*). Informational texts more often employ agentless passives (e.g., *dealt with* in the earlier example), attributive adjectives, and prepositions, often modifying nouns. (See the last section of this chapter for more details on scientific registers.)

Which Comes First?

Here's a mind-bending question: do we manipulate genres and registers, or do they shape our linguistic products, even in terms of "creativity" with language? This is a complicated and still debated question in genre studies. The answer is probably "yes" —to both questions.

Let's start with a not very creative text type: the résumé (see Figure 9.1). As writers, we understand that future employers, the audience for résumés, look for particular kinds of information: education, work experience, relevant skills, and references. All of this information is supposed to appear as lists. Think how differently our résumés might read if they were framed as narratives, explaining how we have acquired our skills and experience (the challenges, successes, and insights we have gained), rather than as lists of isolated items. It would frame us as stories more than as sets of skills. The form of the résumé helps reinforce the idea, both for employers and applicants, that applicants' present skills are of more importance than their learning process, their ability to overcome obstacles, and so on. If you were to be "creative" with your résumé and make it a narrative, your creativity would lie in mixing conventions: importing features of narrative texts into this genre/register. But we could not take responsibility for any potential employer's response to your creative impulse!

For a second example, let's consider the five- to seven-page argumentative paper for an English literature course. Students are usually asked to construct original, creative arguments—but, of course, only within the expected conventions of the student argumentative paper. For instance, it should be thesis-driven, with sequential paragraphs controlled by transitional sentences, written in the style expected of college papers—rather than, say, journal entries, e-mail messages, or newspaper columns. These conventions reinforce for us the idea that an argument about literature can be captured successfully in a sentence or two and then supported with a linear progression of evidence. The conventions respond to and mold our conception of what constitutes an effectively presented argument.

Not all cultures share these conventions for effective argumentation. Another valued form of argument involves the subtle revelation of the thesis through examples and an exposition of the reasoning, so that readers "discover" the argument without any explicit statement of the thesis.

Text types respond to rhetorical situations, but they also help us to make sense of the situations in which we use them. Sometimes they even shape those situations—for instance, in terms of the interaction between author and audience, or the relation of one text to past and future texts that all together constitute a literary tradition. As readers, we bring expectations to texts that affect how we read them. As authors, we make assumptions about our audience and their expectations. And in texts, we can locate assumptions about what readers are expected to know and believe.

Kyle I. Hope

Campus Address:
424 East University St.
Collegeville, MI 49334
(616) 222-4744
kihope@univ.edu

Permanent address:
11245 Rosewood Ave.
Hometown, IN 46258
(219) 398-1120
kylehope@gmail.com

OBJECTIVE: Editing position at a publishing house in the New York/New Jersey area.

SUMMARY:
- Two years as Chief Editor of *Collage* literary magazine.
- Four years as staff sportswriter for *Lake Michigan State Daily* newspaper.
- Internship for two summers at *Cosmopolitan Magazine*.
- Proficient with MS Office, Windows 2000/XP, Photoshop and Internet design.

EDUCATION: **Bachelor of Arts in English, June 2010**
Lake Michigan State, Collegeville, Michigan
Graduated *cum laude* with a GPA of 3.4 on a 4.0 scale

Courses taken included:
American Literature (Contemporary Poetry, 19th-Century Literature,
20th-Century African American Literature, Asian American Women's Literature),
British Literature (Medieval Literature, Shakespeare's plays, Victorian Novel),
English Linguistics (Introduction, History of English, English Grammar),
Journalism I & II

EXPERIENCE: **Internship, June–August 2008, 2009**
***Cosmopolitan Magazine*, New York City, New York**
- Provided initial copy-editing of columns and selected feature articles.
- Assisted with page layout and photo selection.

Chief Editor, 2008–2010
***Collage* literary magazine, Lake Michigan State University**
- Read all submissions and chaired selection committee.
- Oversaw the magazine's budget, staffing, and production.

ACTIVITIES:
- Varsity tennis team, 2007–2010.
- Writing Center tutor, 2007–2010.
- Staff sportswriter, *Lake Michigan State Daily*, 2007–2010.

FIGURE 9.1 The form of the résumé emphasizes our present skills and degrees over our process of acquiring those skills and degrees. The form reinforces shared ideas about relevant job skills and experiences.

Textual Unity: Cohesion

Texts are not haphazard collections of words, but words collected for a purpose, to convey an idea or message. As such, they must cohere enough to communicate purposefully, but coherence is a somewhat elusive textual attribute. What makes a text an identifiable entity? In other words, how do we recognize that a sequence of sentences constitutes a unified text rather than a collection of unrelated sentences? One answer is cohesion.

Cohesion describes the set of linguistic features or forms that create ties across sentences and thereby join them together into one text. Most speakers intuitively know how to identify texts as texts when they encounter them; the theory of cohesion aims to make this knowledge explicit. Cohesion focuses on linguistic forms. The term *coherence* is sometimes used to refer to the logical connections between the assertions and presuppositions of sentences—the logical structure of a text. Here we focus on cohesion.

It is important to remember that with cohesion, we are focused on ties across sentences, rather than within them. We assume that the grammatical structure of the sentence creates unity for all its components. Cohesion refers to the ties that link structurally unrelated sentences. M. A. K. Halliday and Ruqaiya Hasan in the most influential work on cohesion, *Cohesion in English* (1976), identify five major types of cohesive ties: reference, ellipsis, substitution, conjunction, and lexical cohesion. In his later work, Halliday (1985) collapsed the five into four categories, combining ellipsis and substitution.

Elements of Cohesion

The first step in studying cohesion in a text is to identify the different types of ties, which is a process of finding and labeling. You can then examine patterns and discuss possible interpretations, as the example at the end of this section demonstrates.

Reference   Reference items are those that depend on antecedents for their interpretation. For example, *she* or *here* or *that* must refer to something to have meaning in a given sentence. When the referring form (e.g., a pronoun) and the antecedent to which it refers (e.g., the name of a specific person) occur in different sentences, that relationship creates a cohesive tie between the two sentences. For example, take the sentences "Pronouns can refer back to nouns representing people or things. The nouns that they refer back to are called antecedents." The pronoun *they* in the second sentence refers back to the noun *pronouns* (its antecedent) in the first sentence, thereby connecting the two sentences.

There are two general forms of reference: **exophoric** (*exo*- 'outside') and **endophoric** (*endo*- 'inside'). Cohesion depends on endophoric reference because it alone is textual.

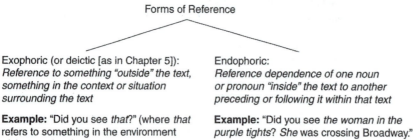

Forms of Reference

Exophoric (or deictic [as in Chapter 5]): *Reference to something "outside" the text, something in the context or situation surrounding the text*

Example: "Did you see *that*?" (where *that* refers to something in the environment of the speakers)

Endophoric: *Reference dependence of one noun or pronoun "inside" the text to another preceding or following it within that text*

Example: "Did you see *the woman in the purple tights*? *She* was crossing Broadway."

Types of Endophoric Reference

Anaphoric reference
Reference backward

Example: "Let me tell you about fish. *They* lead boring lives."

Cataphoric reference
Reference forward

Example: "*It* is the best. My new computer can do it all."

TABLE 9.1   **Devices That Refer**

Referring Devices	Forms	Examples
Personal reference	*I, me, mine, my, we, us, ours, our, you, yours, your, she/he/it, her/him, hers/his/its, they, them, theirs, their, one, one's*	"My new running shoes don't fit quite right. *They* seem to be giving *me* blisters."
Demonstrative reference	*this, these, that, those, here, there, then, the*	"A lieutenant in the army proposed to fifty women. *These* women found out and then wanted him put in jail."
		"In the United States, we are always rushed for time. *Here*, we opt for snacks over meals."
Comparative reference	*same, identical(ly), equal(ly), similar(ly), additional(ly), likewise, so, such, other, different(ly), else, otherwise, better, more, less* (and all comparative and superlative adjectives)	"They served us fish and peas again. It was the *same* meal we get every time we visit."
		"She got a 95 on the exam. But I am proud to say that I did *better*."

There are three main categories of devices that refer: personal pronouns (e.g., *I, we*), demonstratives (e.g., *this, that*), and comparatives (e.g., *such, another*). Table 9.1 lists their forms and provides examples. By referring to elements in the preceding and/or following text, these forms of reference create ties across sentences, showing relationships (e.g., comparing things) or pointing to them as the focus of reference.

Ellipsis and Substitution   **Ellipsis** involves leaving out something mentioned earlier. For example, in the two sentences "Would you like to go? I would," the rest of the verb phrase has been elided or left off (it could read "I would like to go"). It is possible to elide the entire verb phrase: "Who saw the tooth fairy? Bob." Ellipsis creates cohesion because it is clearly dependent on the earlier utterance to fill in the missing information (e.g., in the second example, *saw the tooth fairy*).

Substitution is a variation of ellipsis. Rather than completely leaving out the information, a "holding item" like *so* or *one* or *do* is inserted in its place. Here's an example: "Who took out the garbage? She did." In this example, *did* takes the place of *took out the garbage*.

Conjunction   Conjunction across sentences is very similar to conjunction within sentences: through the use of a conjunctive adverbial, a prepositional phrase, or a conjunction, a logical-semantic relationship is expressed between the two sentences. In other words, the conjunctive expression (e.g., *yet, therefore*) shows the way in which the second sentence is related to the first (e.g., it stands in opposition, it is a result). In the sentence you just read, the phrase *in other words* functions as a conjunction—it says this sentence will help explain the sentence that came before.

There are three main categories of conjunction:

- **Elaboration**: material is either re-presented or clarified (e.g., *in other words, that is, for example, to be more precise, by the way, or rather, in short, in fact*).
- **Extension**: material is added or qualified (*and, also, but, yet, on the other hand, alternatively, instead*).
- **Enhancement**: material is related in terms of time, space, manner, or cause (*then, next, finally, soon, meanwhile, likewise, so, as a result, because, in this way*).

These categories overlap some, and sometimes such conjunctive relationships are expressed implicitly rather than with a conjunction. For instance (to use a conjunction of elaboration), punctuation can imply conjunction without expressing it: colons often do so, as do semicolons and dashes.

Lexical Cohesion   Lexical cohesion ties parts of a text to one another principally through the following means:

- Repetition of words across sentences.
- Use of synonyms to create semantic connections.
- Use of collocations.

Repeating a word from sentence to sentence is a very straightforward way to tie the sentences together. Synonyms and collocations similarly draw on semantic and syntactic relations among words to show relationships among sentences.

Cohesion at Work

Let's look at some of the ties in an excerpt from the book *Naked* by David Sedaris (see Figure 9.2). *It* (reference) opens the second essay in *the* (reference) *book* (lexical cohesion), which is an intentionally outrageous and funny memoir of *his* (reference) childhood through early adulthood.

You'll notice that there are not many conjunctions in this excerpt. The progression of the dialogue does a lot of that connective work.

Different registers or genres of texts often employ different ratios of cohesive ties. For example, sermons are often characterized by high levels of repetition (lexical cohesion), and narratives are often characterized by high levels of conjunction and reference. Consider the different patterns of cohesion in an excerpt from Martin Luther King Jr.'s "I Have a Dream" speech (see Figure 9.3).

"Five score years ago" and "one hundred years later" amount to the same number of years, but the rhetorical difference is significant: the shift in style suggests the difference between a historical promise and the current situation. Even stylistic contrast within a text can contribute to that text's cohesion. The conjunction *but* sets up this contrast, and the repetition in the three "one hundred years later" sentences builds powerfully to the concluding sentence, introduced by the resultative *so*. As you can see, when you begin labeling and analyzing cohesion, at once a rhetorical and a linguistic structure, you can uncover the mechanics of effective stylistic craft.

From David Sedaris's *Naked*:

When the teacher asked if she might visit with my mother, I touched my nose eight times to the surface of my desk.

"May I take *that* as a 'yes'?" she asked.

According to her calculations, I had left my chair twenty-eight times that day. "You're up and down like a flea. I turn my back for two minutes and there you are with your tongue pressed against that light switch. Maybe they do *that* where you come from, but here in my classroom we don't leave our seats and lick things whenever we please. *That* is Miss Chestnut's light switch, and she likes to keep it dry. Would you like me to come over to *your* house and put my tongue on your light switches? Well, would you?"

I tried to picture **her** in action, but my shoe was calling. *Take me off,* it whispered. *Tap* **my** *heel against* **your** *forehead three times. Do* **it** *now, quick, no one will notice.*

"Well?" Miss Chestnut raised her faint, penciled eyebrows. "I'm asking you a question. Would you or would you not want me licking the light switches in your house?"

I slipped off my shoe, pretending to examine the imprint on the heel.

"You're going to hit yourself over the head with that shoe, aren't you?"

It wasn't "hitting," it was tapping; but still, how had **she** known what I was about to do?

"Heel marks all over **your** forehead," **she** said, answering my silent question.

"**You** should take a look in the mirror sometime. Shoes are dirty things. We wear **them** on our feet to protect **ourselves** against the soil. It's not healthy to hit **ourselves** over the head with shoes, is it?"

I guessed that **it** was not.

"Guess? *This* is not a game to be guessed at. I don't 'guess' that it's dangerous to run into traffic with a paper sack over my head. There's no guesswork involved. *These* things are facts, not riddles." **She** sat at her desk, continuing her lecture as she penned a brief letter. "I'd like to have a word with your mother. You do have one, don't you? I'm assuming you weren't raised by animals. Is **she** blind, your mother? Can she see the way you behave, or do you reserve your antics exclusively for Miss Chestnut?" **She** handed **me** the folded slip of paper. "You may go now, and on your way out the door I'm asking you please not to bathe my light switch with your germ-ridden tongue. **It**'s had a long day; we both have." (7–8)

Key:

Personal reference   Ellipsis

Demonstrative reference   Substitution

Lexical cohesion

FIGURE 9.2 An excerpt from David Sedaris's novel *Naked*, marked up for cohesive devices. Once you have identified the words involved in cohesion, it can be helpful to draw lines that show the cohesive ties between lexically related words and between pronouns and their antecedents—as we have done for some of the cohesive ties above.

Five score years ago, a great American, in whose symbolic shadow we stand signed the Emancipation Proclamation. These momentous decrees came as a great beacon light of hope to millions of Negro slaves who had been seared in the flames of withering injustice. **It** came as a joyous daybreak to end the long night of captivity.

But **one hundred** years **later,** we must face the tragic fact that **the Negro** is still not free. **One hundred** years **later,** the life of **the Negro** is still sadly crippled by the manacles of segregation and the chains of discrimination. **One hundred years later, the Negro** lives on a lonely island of poverty in the midst of a vast ocean of material prosperity. **One hundred years later, the Negro** is still languishing in the corners of American society and find himself an exile in his own land. So we have come here today to dramatize an appalling condition.

Repetition   Other types of lexical cohesion

Conjunction

FIGURE 9.3 An excerpt from Martin Luther King Jr.'s "I Have a Dream" speech, marked up to show some of the cohesive ties.

Telling Stories: The Structure of Narratives

Stories or narratives take a specific form in many Western cultures, including those of North America. Stories from other parts of the world have different structures, but, for our purposes, we'll focus on those taken to represent the West. A **narrative** is "a text in which something humanly interesting has happened, or a significant change in the situation has occurred" (Toolan 1996, 137).

A narrative is a way for speakers to relate past experiences or imagined ones. It is critical to the structure of a successful narrative that something take place or that the situation change, and it is a social requirement that that something be of some interest. A narrative is different from:

- **Description**: a telling of how things are, were, or will be.
- **Exposition**: an explanation of how things are, were, or will be.
- **Persuasion**: an argument for how things were, are, or should be.

The Components of a Narrative

In their foundational work on narrative, William Labov and Joshua Waletzky (1967) examined the oral narratives of young African American men in New York City. They argue that fully formed narratives of personal experience have six basic parts, and subsequent scholars have applied this structure to a wider range of narratives.

Abstract	A short introductory summary of what happened or an overview statement that captures the interest of the narrative.
Orientation	Background information to orient the audience about when and where the narrative occurs and who the major actors are.

Complicating action	The moment(s) in the ordering of events where "something happens" or the situation changes.
Evaluation	Comments potentially throughout the narrative that address why the story is interesting, the narrator's attitude toward or reaction to the events, anticipated reactions of the audience, etc.
Resolution	Closing material about what finally happens in the narrative or how events play out.
Coda	A final summary or comment, which may provide a moral or lesson or may connect the narrative to the current context.

Let's examine a short narrative provided by Ronald Macaulay (1994, 119), from an interview in which a man was asked if he had ever been in a situation where he thought he might be killed. This "near-death" question is a standard question in sociolinguistic interviews. The hope is that if a speaker gets involved in telling a story, especially an emotional one, the speaker will use more natural language patterns. This speaker tells a story about nearly drowning and then says the following:

1 another time I was in a car smash with a—
2 a friend of mine had just got a new Baby Austin with a sunshine roof
3 which fortunately was open
4 and there were five of us in this
5 and he was going out by Butlins
6 and suddenly he turned round and says
7 "See I told you we could do fifty-five"
8 and he skidded
9 and we went over on our side
10 and we slid for seventy-five feet—
11 the police measured it—
12 on our side
13 and then the car caught fire
14 and we climbed out the sunshine roof
15 I got a bit of a fright that time too.

The first line acts as the abstract, providing the topic of the story. Lines 2–5 are arguably all orientation, explaining who (and what: the new Baby Austin) is involved and where they were. The complicating action begins with the skid in line 8 (or arguably with the driver's turning around in line 6, which caused the skid). The resolution occurs in line 14, with the five people climbing out of the car, and line 15 acts as a coda. Evaluation occurs in line 11, with the comment about the police measuring the distance of the skid, and in line 15, when the author describes his reaction. The word *fortunately* in line 3 is also a source of evaluation.

Some critics have argued that the presence of an abstract and orientation in this model is the result of an interview situation, in which a speaker more consciously starts a story. In naturally occurring conversation, narratives often begin more abruptly with the sequence of actions or events. One study of women's narratives presents evidence for abrupt narrative openings even in interviews, perhaps to prevent interruption from another participant (Sawin 1999). Some scholars have examined collaborative story-telling by several speakers, creating one narrative, such as "kernel stories" in women rap groups (Kalcik 1975).

Although some of the listed features of narrative may be optional, complicating action is a critical component of a successful narrative. "Shaggy dog" stories are the most extreme example of extended narratives with no complicating action, but shorter versions occur regularly in conversation and often leave listeners waiting for that expected narrative moment: "And then what happened?" In other words, this general narrative structure shapes our expectations of any text that seems to present itself as a narrative, and our reading of the text will at least in part depend on our expectations.

Even fairly young children seem to grasp narrative and its components, probably partly from listening to adults tell stories and partly from reading storybooks. Michael Toolan (1996, 146) provides the following example of a narrative written by a six-year-old (in six-year-old spelling):

The Big Nose

1 ouns a pon a time
2 ther was a big Nose.
3 Now lets get on to the
4 ril story. ther was
5 a skelatn thet lost
6 his Nose, 'wer is ~~me~~ my
7 Nose' a van piae
8 fand the big Nose
9 and ~~tok~~ took it to
10 it's carsll he was
11 abaot to have it
12 for dinir. 'Narsty ~~him~~ me
13 he gobld to him self
14 he lost the Nose. 'wer
15 did it go the skelatn
16 fand ita gen and thae livd
17 haply evr arfd

The fairy tale conventions "once upon a time" and "lived happily ever after" frame the narrative. Perhaps most interesting is the move in lines 3–4: "Now lets get on to the ril story." The child recognizes the need for an opening abstract and also acknowledges that the "real" story in terms of what happened does not begin until after that opening. Losing the nose, which the vampire does in line 14, is a complicating action; finding it again, which the skeleton does in lines 15 and 16, is a resolution that leads into a "happily ever after" coda.

Literature and Speech Acts

Toward the beginning of *How to Do Things with Words* (1975), which we introduced in Chapter 8, J. L. Austin excluded literature from his argument about performative speech acts. The language of poetry, fiction, and drama, he claimed, "is parasitic on its normal use," so "our performative utterances, felicitous or not, are to be understood as issued in ordinary circumstances" (22). What Austin implies, but doesn't say directly, is that literature doesn't help draw distinctions about propositions, utterances, and performatives, because literature is *all* speech act.

Of course, there are speech acts *in* literature: in drama and fiction characters have conversations, formalized as dialogue, and their fictional utterances can be understood as speech acts within the fictional world and evaluated as such. In fiction, dialogue is framed by narrative commentary, spoken by a narrator to readers. This narrative intervention is thus a set of speech acts initiated by the narrator (as locutionary act) and interpreted by the reader (as perlocutionary act), with lots of illocutionary activity in between. In the end, one could argue, a whole literary work is a very complex speech act between author and readers.

Speech Acts and Narrative Perspective

A story is told; it requires a narrator. Narrators are not (as many readers naively believe) passive, merely conduits leading from an author's mind onto the page. Even in an oral literary tradition, the poet adopts a persona to recite his or her work. The cautious reader or listener asks certain questions about perspective when encountering a story: From whose perspective is the text presented? What relationship does perspective construct between the text and readers? How are speech and thought presented?

When we read a text, usually the narrator is speaking to us, presented either as a first-person "I" within the text (as in the Sedaris passage) or as an omniscient ('all-knowing') presence who is not an actor in the text itself.

The following famous opening lines of celebrated novels suggest that narrative perspective can be usefully interpreted as speech act, such that reader and text are in a relationship similar to that of speakers making and interpreting utterances in everyday speech:

> "It is a truth universally acknowledged, that a single man in possession of a good fortune, must be in want of a wife." (Jane Austen, *Pride and Prejudice*)

> "Whether I shall turn out to be the hero of my own life, or whether that station will be held by anybody else, these pages must show." (Charles Dickens, *David Copperfield*)

> "Lyra and her daemon moved through the darkening hall, taking care to keep to one side, out of sight of the kitchen." (Philip Pullman, *The Golden Compass*)

Austen's opening sentence isn't just about the supposed condition of single men, but also about the conventional wisdom that rich young men look for wives. The narrator of *Pride and Prejudice* proposes the truth with great assurance and with her tongue in her cheek: it is an indirect speech act (a verdictive one), and readers must settle the implications in a perlocutionary act, as well as judge the truth of the narrator's proposition, which is a constative act.

Unlike the narrator of *Pride and Prejudice*, David Copperfield tells his own story. He claims that he might not be his own story's hero, but there seems to be a performative aspect to this opening. Copperfield claims that identifying the hero of his life will take the whole narrative, but doesn't the sentence itself, as a speech act, establish him in the hero's role? How convenient. From the beginning, we as readers know to be suspicious of this first-person narrative perspective, as narrators telling their own story can look better than they would from an omniscient perspective.

Successful interpretation of *Pride and Prejudice* and *David Copperfield* requires illocutionary awareness and perlocutionary stamina: readers have to resist those narrators and establish a readerly, interpretive perspective that takes into account the narrative (locutionary) perspective. In many cases, narrative is composed of indirect speech acts—but not always. Pullman opens *The Golden Compass* with a "mere" assertive, a description of something we can only see through the narrator's perspective. Arguably, then, it is a direct speech act, in which the locution, illocution, and perlocution are perfectly aligned.

These are just three examples of the speech act character of literary style. There are as many examples as there are works of literature, and the problems the acts pose for narratives and readers are to some degree idiosyncratic. We can use speech acts to interpret nonliterary texts as well, as literary critic J. Hillis Miller cleverly shows us with the opening passage of Austin's *How to Do Things with Words* (1975). Miller notes:

> Austin wants to find out the truth about performative utterances and to tell the truth. The lecture series is firmly put under the aegis of truth or falsehood by the admirably ironic first sentence of the first lecture: "What I shall have to say here is neither difficult nor contentious: the only merit I should like to claim for it is that of being true, at least in parts" . . . This seems clearly enough to say that the whole book is intended to be constative. (2001, 21)

But, as Miller goes on to suggest, it isn't. Because the lectures are both difficult and contentious, and because Austin believes they are (no matter what he says), the lectures start off with two lies. So we as readers must then determine how to interpret the function of that speech act.

Speech Acts in Literature

Speech acts can be integral to a work of fiction, certainly in dialogue, but also in some expected ways. For instance, a complex speech act is at the center of Muriel Spark's dark, witty short novel, *Memento Mori*, first published in 1959. In the story, a group of friends and relatives well advanced in age are harassed by someone who calls them on the telephone and announces, "Remember that you must die." The act is strongly (though not absolutely) performative: if we take it to mean 'I remind you that you must die', then we accept its performativity, even though, in the locutionary act, there is no first person pronoun, no verb that describes the speaker's act. Also, the statement is imperative, so structured as a directive. Once uttered, it causes anyone who hears it to remember that he or she must die, so the statement has a declarative illocutionary force. Many characters in *Memento Mori*, however, refuse (or pretend to refuse) to be so prompted. Those who do are "good" interpreters of speech acts; the others have a perlocutionary problem of not knowing a performative or declarative act when they encounter it. So, the story plays with relations among directive, performative, and declarative speech acts bound up in a *memento mori*, or reminder of mortality. As such, it is also "about" speech acts and what makes them felicitous.

We are most familiar with speech acts in dialogue. In Anthony Powell's *The Soldier's Art* (1966), the narrator, Nick Jenkins, discovers that one of his sisters-in-law has been unfaithful; he learns it from his jilted brother-in-law, Chips Lovell, who explains of his rival, "He did rather well—was it the Lofoten raid? That sort of thing. He's a hero on top of everything else. I suppose if I were to do something where I could get killed, instead of composing lists of signal equipment and such like, I might make a more interesting husband" (1995, 108–9). Jenkins replies, "I don't think so for a moment" (109). Is Jenkins's comment a direct or an indirect speech act?

One might take it as indirect. As a locutionary act it seems to validate Lovell's qualities as a man and husband: he's already so virtuous that becoming a hero wouldn't make him any more interesting. Its illocutionary force, however, might be much less complimentary: even if he *were* a hero, he'd be as dull as ever. Lovell can hear the tone of Jenkins's voice and look him in the eye as he comes to his perlocutionary conclusions. We don't have that advantage, and Jenkins, the narrator, realizes that we might hear his comment as a face threatening act, so he proceeds in the narrative with something parallel to conversational repair: "In giving this answer, I spoke a decided opinion. To assume such a thing was a typical instance of Lovell's taste, mentioned earlier, for the obvious" (109). So, the answer "I don't think so for a moment" was a decided opinion—to what effect? As readers, we are now responsible for unraveling the illocutionary force behind Jenkins the character's comment and the illocutionary force behind his narrative explanation of the comment!

In sum, fictional style is always partly a matter of speech acts, and reading fiction requires a grasp of how speech acts work. You can try it out on your favorite work of fiction or on the next novel or short story assigned in your literature class.

Investigating Dialogue

Dialogue isn't natural conversation, but a stylized representation of conversation. Sometimes, given the aims of the literary work in question, dialogue closely resembles conversation—it's realistic and imitates the real thing. In other cases, though, dialogue is deliberately artificial. We measure speech and speakers against our intuition about how conversation *ought* to go.

Conversational Structure and Politeness

When H. P. Grice proposed his Cooperative Principle and the accompanying conversational maxims (see Chapter 8), he was explaining how ideal conversation would function, how, as he put it, we *should* conduct ourselves in conversation. The Cooperative Principle is meant to allow participants in a conversation each to achieve their conversational goals without conflict. Conflict is at the heart of any fiction and it is often enacted in dialogue. It follows, then, that literary dialogue is built partly on violations of conversational maxims and on face-threatening acts. Applying linguistic models for conversation can help you interpret the nuances of literary dialogue, as the following example demonstrates.

In Charles Dickens's incomplete last novel, *The Mystery of Edwin Drood* (1870), the central character, John Jasper, is secretly in love with his nephew Edwin Drood's finacée. Drood knows Jasper loves Rosa (Jasper is also her music teacher) and goads him with it—which is why Jasper is a prime suspect in Drood's death. On the surface, though, Jasper and Drood are best friends. Consider the following excerpts from a conversation between them:

Mr. Jasper listens, starts from his chair, and catches a young fellow in his arms, exclaiming:

"My dear Edwin!"
"My dear Jack! So glad to see you!"

What could be a more convivial start to conversation? Jasper and Drood take turns as they greet each other; their parallel "My dears" compose an adjacency pair. But there is a difference between their greetings, one that might count as a face-threatening act: Drood is "Edwin," but Jasper is "Jack," a nickname. Drood emphasizes this sign of familiarity (or is it condescension?): "My dear Jack, I'm as dry as a bone"; "Now I am right, and now I'll take my corner, Jack. Any dinner, Jack?"; "What a jolly old Jack it is! . . . Look here, Jack; tell me; whose birthday is it" (1996, 9). Drood is so intent on the performative act of nicknaming—making Jasper "Jack" by calling him *Jack*—that Jasper barely gets a word into the conversation.

The less than reciprocal familiarity imposed by Drood's nicknaming violates one of Lakoff's politeness maxims; Drood's tendency to rattle on violates some of Grice's maxims and the basic etiquette of turn-taking. In all of this, Dickens is building the conflict between the two characters.

Drood has a nickname for Rosa, too: *Pussy*. As they are about to drink, Drood interjects:

"Halloa, Jack! Don't drink."
"Why not?"
"Asks why not, on Pussy's birthday, and no Happy returns proposed! Pussy, Jack, and many of 'em! Happy returns I mean."

This is all a means of provoking Jasper, who must hear the undeserving Drood treat Rosa, the woman he also loves, impolitely, behind her back; Jasper must bear all of this while preserving politeness conventions.

Still, in the end, their conversation breaks down; neither can maintain and repair the conversation patiently past a certain point. After dinner, with their wine, they eat some nuts, for which they each have a nutcracker.

"How's Pussy getting on, Jack."
"With her music? Fairly."
"What a dreadfully conscientious fellow you are, Jack! But I know, Lord bless you! Inattentive, isn't she?"

(It is worth interrupting here to note that Drood may be hinting at her lack of romantic interest in Jasper. There is an illocutionary force to be resolved in Jasper's perlocutionary response.)

"She can learn anything, if she will."
"*If* she will! Egad, that's it. But if she won't?"
Crack!—on Mr. Jasper's part.
"How's she looking, Jack?"
Mr. Jasper's concentrated face again includes the portrait as he returns: "Very like your sketch indeed."
"I am a little proud of it," says the young fellow, glancing up at the sketch with complacency, and then shutting one eye, and taking a corrected prospect of it over a level bridge of nut-crackers in the air: "Not badly hit off from memory. But I ought to have caught that expression pretty well, for I have seen it often enough."
Crack!—on Edwin Drood's part.
Crack!— on Mr. Jasper's part.

"In point of fact," the former resumes, after some silent dipping among his fragments of walnut with an air of pique, "I see it whenever I go to see Pussy. If I don't find it on her face, I leave it there.—You know I do, Miss Scornful Pert. Booh!" With a twirl of the nutcrackers at the portrait.

Crack! Crack! Crack. Slowly, on Mr. Jasper's part.

Crack. Sharply on the part of Edwin Drood.

Silence on both sides.

"Have you lost your tongue, Jack?"

The conflict between them becomes so intense that it becomes a duel of nutcracking and silence, in which each crack is face-threatening, as it represents a "no response": a refusal to do the conversational work of continuing someone else's topic. Obviously, they understand each other's cracks and silences well enough, and one of them ends up dead anyway, though whether by John Jasper's hand we'll never know.

As with other cases of pragmatics and discourse in literature investigated here, this is only one example, and there are as many examples as there are conversations in books. Brown and Levinson's *Politeness* (1987) could serve as a handbook for fiction writers in search of strategies for developing conflict by means of dialogue. This example demonstrates how you can apply what you know about pragmatics and discourse to enrich your understanding of the texts you read and write about, perhaps someday teach about, too.

Reporting Speech: Direct and Indirect

The type of speech employed in a text—**direct speech** (quoted verbatim, with quotation marks) or **indirect speech** (reported secondhand, with no quotation marks)—is a significant aspect of style. The distinction between direct and indirect speech seems simple enough. For example, the omniscient narrator in the passage above from *The Mystery of Edwin Drood* records direct speech, the dialogue between Jasper and Drood. But the line between the two is sometimes blurry. Consider the following sentence:

She said, well, she sure wasn't going to let some bozo stand in her way.

There are features of both direct and indirect discourse here. The third-person pronouns (*she, her*) indicate that it is indirect, reported speech. But "well" and the phrasing of the utterance (e.g., "sure wasn't going to" and "some bozo") suggest that her words are being captured as she said them.

The relationship between speech and thought is sometimes even trickier to define. Some of the humor in the passage from Sedaris's *Naked* plays on blurriness between the two. Look again at these lines:

"You should take a look in the mirror sometime. Shoes are dirty things. We wear them on our feet to protect ourselves against the soil. It's not healthy to hit ourselves over the head with shoes, is it?"

I guessed that it was not.

"Guess? This is not a game to be guessed at."

The verb *guess* can function as both a thinking and a saying verb. Because there are no quotation marks near it, we as readers may first assume that we are seeing into the narrator's head, as he reacts to the teacher's question. The teacher's follow-up question suddenly makes it clear that the narrator has uttered the guess—but in our reading, it also seems that the teacher has read his mind. Either way, Sedaris's sleight of hand with perspective reminds us to read carefully: he has more up his sleeve than we may imagine initially. That fact influences our relationship with the text and with the narrative perspective in which it's composed.

Investigating Word Choice

Choosing the right words for calculated effects is at the heart of writing. Accuracy of description or exposition and force of persuasion depend absolutely on the words in which ideas, attitudes, perspectives, and feelings are conveyed.

Diction

The passage from Sedaris's *Naked* demonstrates the power of diction in an especially useful way because, more than an exercise in word choice, it is an indirect commentary on the significance of choosing the right word. Sedaris refuses to accept that he *hit* his head with his shoe, even though his teacher prefers that word: "It wasn't 'hitting,' it was tapping," he insists. Who is narrating his childhood behavior? The teacher? Word choice is intimately involved in the development of perspective.

Like all great essayists, Sedaris has a remarkable memory, yet we have to assume that he is reconstructing events in the passage quoted, not reporting them verbatim. "I guessed that it was not"—the choice of *guess* is essential to the narrative's coherence and perspective: one can *suppose, reckon,* or *insist,* as well as *guess.* But consider the consequences of any choice of synonym besides *guess.*

- "Suppose? This is not a game to be supposed at."
- "Reckon? This is not a game to be reckoned at."
- "Insist? This is not a game to be insisted at."

The problem is deeply semantic: *guess* is polysemous in a way that the alternatives (*suppose, reckon, insist*) are not. The problem is also syntactic: we *guess at* things, but *insist on* others, and *suppose* or *reckon* without prepositional help.

And the choice of *guess* is not only semantically significant, but morphologically significant as well. The teacher derives *guesswork* from *guess:* she couldn't very well move from *suppose* to **supposework,* or *reckon* to **reckonwork,* or *insist* to **insistwork.* Compounds of VERB + NOUN are strange in English, and we are reluctant to accept them, but *guesswork* is historically accepted. The passage couldn't cohere in the same way, the teacher couldn't work up the same lather, unless *guess* had prompted her reaction. We all approve of semantic and morphological clarity, but it is exactly the "open" nature of *guess* that allows Sedaris (or any other author in a similar circumstance) his creative opportunity.

Metaphor

Daily language, as described in Chapter 7, is filled with metaphors that we no longer notice—like the ones that "fill" this sentence itself. Literature, and poetry especially, often employs novel, more dramatic metaphors that draw our attention and ask us to make new, unfamiliar connections among things and notice new aspects of familiar things.

In Old English, when the *Beowulf* poet describes the sea as a "swan-road" or a "whale-way," or our bodies as "soul-houses," he provides us a new way to see these entities. When Martin Luther King Jr. describes the "manacles of segregation" and "the chains of discrimination," the metaphors force us to see the connections and similarities between ongoing segregation and slavery. King presupposes the shared cultural knowledge required to make these connections. His use of metaphors like "lonely island," "corners," and "exile" give a spatial, geographic reality to the effects of the poverty and discrimination that African Americans experience. The evocative metaphor in the title of Maya Angelou's book *I Know Why the Caged Bird Sings* creates a powerful context in which we then read and understand her autobiography.

Modality

Verbs often reveal speaker attitudes and opinions, beyond the choice of the verb itself (e.g., *venture* versus *say* versus *assert*). Modality gives us a way to qualify a claim or commitment linguistically. Consider these examples:

> *I know what I'm doing.*
>
> *I might know what I'm doing.*   (expresses speaker's sense of doubt)
>
> *I should know what I'm doing.*   (expresses speaker's sense of obligation)
>
> *I must know what I'm doing.*   (expresses speaker's sense of need—before, perhaps, an exam)

Halliday (1985, 1994) outlines four types of qualification that modals can express:

1. Probability (e.g., *may, might,* and now *can, could*).
2. Obligation (e.g., *should, must, ought,* and the semimodals *have to, got to*).
3. Willingness or inclination (e.g., *can, could*).
4. Usuality (e.g., *may, will*—as in, "I often will go to the store when I have nothing better to do," or "When I have nothing better to do, I may even go to the store").

Although we have put particular modals as examples for each category, in fact, many modals can express all four categories. For example, "You should tell her" expresses obligation, whereas "It should rain" expresses probability. All these can also be expressed by adverbs such as *possibly, maybe, surely, necessarily, perhaps, definitely,* and *often*. These modal verbs and adverbs help speakers position themselves in relation to the information or assertions that they present, as well as to other speakers or their audience.

In a study of scientific articles, Greg Myers (1989) applies politeness theory (see Chapter 8) to examine modals and other expressions of qualification. He notes that many new claims in scientific articles are made with modals and hedges (e.g., "this would suggest . . ."), a kind of negative politeness strategy. Other strategies mitigate possible face-threatening acts toward other scholars, as when an author criticizes previous work: "Robin Lakoff's analysis of this . . . *seems to us* counterintuitive" (Brown and Levinson 290n, qtd. in Myers 1989, 16). Scholars may also mitigate a criticism by using "we," in order to suggest their solidarity with others in the field who now join to prove a previously shared set of beliefs or assumptions wrong: for example, "Previous studies had led us to believe . . ." Scholars also can use modals to frame statements as obligations: "We should note . . ." or "It must be added . . ."

Written texts still participate in conversations, and authors use the linguistic resources available to negotiate face while, for example, supporting an argument. Anyone who says that scientific writing is entirely "objective" or "dispassionate" hasn't looked at scientific writing as discourse or style.

Language Variation at Work

Literary Forensics

The 1996 publication of *Primary Colors*, an insider's exposé of the 1992 Clinton presidential campaign, generated much speculation about the identity of "Anonymous," the novel's author. Some members of the media asked Vassar English professor Donald Foster to try and identify the author using the "textual analysis" methodologies he had devised. Foster used a computer to compare the stylistic choices in *Primary Colors* to the style of over fifty writers identified as possible "suspects." When he tried Joe Klein, a political reporter and columnist for *Newsweek*, the comparison set "the lights flashing and the bells ringing." He describes the combination of stylistic similarities:

> Like Anonymous, Klein favors adverbs made from -y adjectives: *crazily, eerily, goofily, handily, huffily, juicily, scarily, spottily, uncannily,* etc. Both Klein and Anonymous added letters to their interjections: *ahh, aww, naww.* Both were into "modes": *listening mode, opaque mode, mega-explain mode, filial mode, mega-vulture mode* (Anon.); *uplift mode, crisis mode, campaign mode* (Klein). . . . Both Klein and Anonymous loved to coin words beginning in *hyper-, mega-, non-, post-, quasi-,* and *semi-.* (Klein, like

Anonymous, coined more words using these prefixes than all the other authors combined.) So too for words ending in *-ish.* . . . I found that Klein and Anonymous borrowed or invented similar compound adjectives. There's *melanin-deprived* (Anon.) and *gadfly-deprived* (Klein); *well-oiled* (Anon.) and *well-greased* (Klein); *not-very-convincing* (Anon.) and *not-so-funny* or *not-so-modest* (Klein). (Foster 2000, 66)

Joe Klein initially strongly denied that he was the author, at one point shouting, "For god's sake, definitely, I didn't write it!" About six months later, he was "outed" with evidence from handwriting on the original manuscript and he admitted to being Anonymous.

But as is true of all detective work, clues, in this case stylistic ones, can lead us astray. In 1989, Donald Foster published the book *Elegy by W. S.*, in which he presents stylistic evidence suggesting that Shakespeare is the likely author of "A Funeral Elegy," written by "W. S." and printed in 1612. In 2002 he recanted his attribution after a French scholar published persuasive evidence that John Foster (1586–1640) wrote the elegy.

Linguistics into Poetics

If you have taken many literature courses, you have probably been asked to do a "close reading" of a poem or story. Close reading of a literary text is, at base, linguistic reading. Obviously, our understanding of literature surpasses any systematic study of the words and sentences it contains, but systematic study provides a crucial foundation. As the master linguist Roman Jakobson argued in his foundational essay "Linguistics and Poetics" (1987a/1958, 94): "A linguist deaf to the poetic function of language and a literary scholar indifferent to linguistic problems and unconversant with linguistic methods are equally flagrant anachronisms." The poetic functions of language are not confined to poetry. For instance, as poet Walt Whitman observed, slang is poetic language in everyday speech (see Chapter 4). This chapter is devoted to style in all types of text, and after considering résumés, essays, and stories, we turn our attention to poetry, at last.

Reading like Alice, Humpty Dumpty, and Michael Toolan

Well, mostly reading like stylistics expert Michael Toolan, who takes a more systematic approach to reading literature than Alice or Humpty Dumpty, when they discuss the meaning of "Jabberwocky"—though, as we suggested, they were on the right, that is, the stylistic, track. In order to follow Toolan, though, we need to have a poem in mind. We have chosen e.e. cummings's "anyone lived in a pretty how town" because it provides more opportunities for linguistic intervention than most poems, and certainly an unusual variety of them. So, here we go.

anyone lived in a pretty how town

anyone lived in a pretty how town
(with up so floating many bells down)
spring summer autumn winter
he sang his didn't he danced his did.

Women and men(both little and small)
cared for anyone not at all
they sowed their isn't they reaped their same
sun moon stars rain

children guessed(but only a few
and down they forgot as up they grew
autumn winter spring summer)
that noone loved him more by more

when by now and tree by leaf
she laughed his joy she cried his grief
bird by snow and stir by still
anyone's any was all to her

someones married their everyones
laughed their cryings and did their dance
(sleep wake hope and then) they
said their nevers they slept their dream

stars rain sun moon
(and only the snow can begin to explain
how children are apt to forget to remember
with up so floating many bells down)

one day anyone died i guess
(and noone stooped to kiss his face)
busy folk buried them side by side
little by little and was by was

all by all and deep by deep
and more by more they dream their sleep
noone and anyone earth by april
wish by spirit and if by yes.

Women and men(both dong and ding)
summer autumn winter spring
reaped their sowing and went their came
sun moon stars rain

A good place to start your analysis, Toolan (1996) recommends, is with one of the most fundamental questions in stylistics: "What do you notice about this text?" Toolan then outlines five categories of things you might look for in a text:

- repetition;
- patterns;
- recurrent structures;
- ungrammatical or "language-stretching" structures;
- large internal contrasts of content or presentation.

What are some things you might notice in this poem?

Repetition/patterns/recurrent structures

- The seasons (*spring, summer, fall, winter*) rotate in the course of the poem. Other items, like *stars rain sun moon*, also rotate. The parallel suggests that *star, rain, sun,* and *moon* are hyponyms that share a superordinate term like *season* (see Figure 9.4), but that term remains a mystery.

- The poem uses rhythmic pairings, like *when by now* and *tree by leaf*, in which the preposition or another function word serves as a rhythmic axis. Rhythmic relationships in English poetry and prose are partly syllabic, so they are also partly phonological.

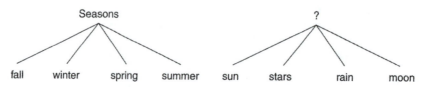

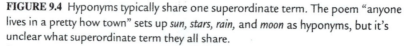

FIGURE 9.4 Hyponyms typically share one superordinate term. The poem "anyone lives in a pretty how town" sets up *sun, stars, rain,* and *moon* as hyponyms, but it's unclear what superordinate term they all share.

- Some rhythmic pairings are also repetitions, as in *all by all and deep by deep*. Such pairings, though they seem innocent, subsist on the edges of morphology, syntax, and semantics. After all, there's a difference, maybe several differences, between an idiomatic pairing, like *drop by drop* (which indicates progressive action), and an unidiomatic one, like *all by all*. Literary use of language challenges our linguistic expectations just as often as it follows them.

Just as Toolan suggests, repetition folds into pattern, and pattern folds into structure. At first, each instance looks like "simple" repetition. In fact, though, repetition in "anyone lived in a pretty how town" is creative, surprising, even meaningful because it plays on linguistic principles outlined in Chapters 3 through 7.

Stretching of Language

- The indefinite pronouns in the poem work in surprising ways: for example, *anyone* and *noone* refer to specific characters, while *someone* and *everyone* take plural *-s*, an essentially ungrammatical application of inflectional morphemes, since singular indefinite pronouns usually aren't pluralized.

- Familiar parts of speech are in unusual syntactic positions: for example, *his didn't* puts an auxiliary verb (*didn't*) where we would expect a noun; *pretty how town* puts an interrogative pronoun (*how*) where we would expect an adjective.

- Familiar collocations take unfamiliar collocational structures: for example, *laugh* and *joy* as well as *cry* and *grief* are familiar collocates, but *laugh* and *cry* are typically intransitive verbs and would not take *joy* and *grief* as direct objects.

- When items like *nevers, dream*, and *came* become direct objects, they take on a metaphorical quality unlikely in everyday speech.

- Converse terms are placed in a paradoxical sequence (*went their came*), a construction for which, surely, there are no projection rules in English, but which nonetheless makes sense.

Cummings guides this poem's effect by playing with linguistic expectations outlined earlier in this book, from those of inflectional morphology (Chapter 4), to those of phrase structure (Chapter 6), to conventions of collocation (Chapter 7). He pulls language tricks out of his hat constantly and without remorse. Imaginative literature often treads the fine line between challenging convention and adhering to it (remember Walt Whitman's praise of slang, quoted in Chapter 4).

A text's meaning is ultimately "whole." When you read a poem, you try to understand what the whole poem means, not just this phrase or that word. Generally, though, we assemble the whole text from our experience of its parts. With poetry, in addition to phrases and words and the like, we need to pay attention to rhythm and rhyme.

Although prose has its distinctive cadences, poetry operates by formal conventions—such as meter, rhythm, and rhyme—quite unlike those of prose. Each convention adds meaning (whether denotative, connotative, or "emotional") mostly unavailable in other genres. For example, the mostly iambic meter of cummings's "anyone lived in a pretty how town" thrums along, reinforcing the idea of inevitable change, the point at the poem's thematic center. Analyzing the interaction of meter, rhythm, rhyme, and other phonological connections along with the poem's semantics adds layers of meaning and makes the poem whole.

Poeticity and Its Axes

Poetry asks us to focus on sounds as sounds, and words as words—not just as ways to refer to the world. In poetry the form, the type and structure of the poem, is foregrounded and meaningful. According to Roman Jakobson, one of the most important figures in twentieth-century poetics, "focus on the message itself for its own sake, is the *poetic* function of language" (1987a, 69). He also writes:

> *Poeticity* is present when the word is felt as a word and not a mere representation of the object being named or an outburst of emotion, when words and their composition, their meaning, their external and inner form, acquire a weight and value of their own instead of referring indifferently to reality. (378)

Poetry adds weight to words beyond reference, namely, the weight of their own forms.

How does poetry achieve this effect? Jakobson explains the poetic function using two axes.

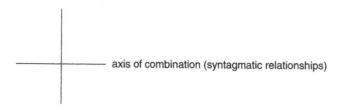

axis of selection (associative or paradigmatic relationships)

Units are combined into longer units (e.g., words into clauses) along the axis of combination, based on the relationships allowed, for example, by phonology, morphology, and syntax among words and phrases. Each unit in a given position along the axis of combination is related to many other equivalent units that could also have been selected or could be substituted to fill that position. These other possible units exist on the axis of selection. For example, if a particular syntactic construction specifies a slot for an attributive personal adjective, that slot could be filled by a range of adjectives, from which one is selected (e.g., *beautiful, gorgeous, striking, pretty*).

Jakobson then describes the projection principle, which is critical to poetry: "The poetic function projects the principle of equivalence from the axis of selection into the axis of combination." What does that mean? It is, in typical Jakobsonian fashion, a highly complex statement, and we hope you will spend some time thinking through what *you* think it means. One possible way to interpret it is that in poetry units that appear next to each other (on the axis of combination) become equivalent in ways that they normally would not. Poetry creates parallels among words of different classes by their juxtaposition.

We focus next on two ways that your linguistic toolbox can enhance the ways in which you do a close reading of poetry. First, you can examine meter and rhythm in relation to prosody and phrasing. Second, you can systematically examine phonological connections.

A Scholar to Know

Roman Jakobson (1896–1982)

Roman Jakobson once said, "I am a linguist and hold nothing that has to do with language to be alien to me" (qtd. in Bradford 1994, 7). The breadth of his interests spanned literature, poetry, phonology, semantics, folklore, language acquisition, and beyond. Born in Moscow, Jakobson was a professor in Moscow and then in Prague, where he was sent on the first Soviet mission to Czechoslovakia. He was one of the primary founders of the Prague linguistic circle, which influenced much of European structuralism. Jakobson's work on aphasia and its relationship to the poetic function occurred primarily when he was in Scandinavia, after having been driven from Czechoslovakia by the Nazis in 1939 and before moving to the United States in 1941. He subsequently served on the faculty at Columbia (1943–1949), Harvard (1950–1967), and MIT (1957–1967).

In 1958, in Bloomington, Indiana, Jakobson gave his famous "Linguistics and Poetics" paper, sometimes cited as the distillation of some of his fundamental contributions to the linguistic study of literature. For Jakobson, poetry and language, like meaning and form, are intertwined: form carries meaning, and poetry, rather than being only a specialized genre, is fundamental to all language. Above all, Jakobson envisioned the broadest possible linguistics, the sort of unifying theory of language against which even Chomsky's Standard Theory (see Chapter 6) pales in comparison.

Meter, Rhythm, and Scansion

Meter is an ideal, invariant rhythmic pattern that actual poetic rhythms approximate. In other words, meter is roughly analogous to phonemic or morphemic representation: the rules can be understood in the abstract, but just as every phoneme or morpheme must be realized in speech, meter must be realized in rhythm. **Rhythm** is the arrangement of stress in speech. Meter is an abstract scheme; rhythm is an aspect, not only of poetry, but of prose, conversation, and even nonlinguistic media like music. **Prosody** is the structure of sound in speech, but in poetics it is the systematic arrangement of intonation and stress.

Scansion represents meter symbolically. It counts units and/or marks stress, but it does so in the abstract—scansion does not account for rhythm or prosody. Three common kinds of metrical systems are:

- **Pure accentual meter**: based only on stressed syllables. Much oral poetry follows a pure accentual meter. In Old English poetry, there are four stressed syllables per line (two per half-line). Old English poetry is alliterative, and the alliteration has a systematic relationship to stress.

- **Pure syllabic meter**: based only on the number of syllables per line. Haiku, with its 5-7-5 syllable per line pattern, is a good example of pure syllabic meter.

- **Accentual-syllabic meter**: distributes stress and syllables into different kinds of feet. A **foot** is a metrical unit composed of a certain number of syllables arranged in a certain pattern of stress. Most English poetry is accentual-syllabic.

We cannot cover all the intricacies of metrical scansion (and many of you have probably studied meter in literature classes), but here are some of the most common types of feet in accentual-syllabic meter (x indicates an unstressed syllable, and / indicates a stressed syllable):

Iambic foot (iamb)	x /
Trochaic foot (trochee)	/ x
Anapestic foot (anapest)	x x /
Dactylic foot (dactyl)	/ x x
Pyrrhic foot (pyrrhic)	x x
Spondaic foot (spondee)	/ /

Types of lines are named by how many feet there are, so pentameter has five feet, tetrameter has four feet, and so on. To look at poetic lines from a different angle, though, iambic pentameter has ten syllables, whereas anapestic pentameter has fifteen syllables. Different forms (e.g., the Shakespearean sonnet, rhyme royal) are characterized by the number of lines, types of lines, and rhyme schemes.

The iambic pentameter of much English verse is not necessarily a "natural" meter for the language. It became an institution during the Renaissance, when scholars began analyzing English poetry within classical frameworks based on Latin meter. As a stress-timed language, English is arguably still effectively described with pure accentual meter, but this is open to dispute.

Prosody and Verse Structure

Now here's where your knowledge of linguistics can be especially illuminating. In any poem, we can read two rhythmic systems at work. The language itself, actualized in English prosody, challenges the meter, an idealized pattern of stress. Prosody follows not only word stress, but also phrasing: the contours of a phrase or clause. Sometimes prosody and meter line up, and sometimes there is tension and interplay between the two, as demonstrated by the following examples adapted from material by Richard Cureton (the x's indicate unstressed syllables, the /'s stressed syllables):

```
Phrasal stress or prosody      x  /  x  /  x  /  x  /  x  /
Meter (pentameter)             x  /  x  /  x  /  x  /  x  /

                               At once with joy and fear his heart rebounds
                                 PP          PP          NP        VP


Phrasal stress or prosody      /  x  x  /  x  x  x  /  x  /
Meter (pentameter)             x  /  x  /  x  /  x  /  x  /

                               Downward to darkness on extended wings
                               _____PP__  _____NP_____
                                        ADVP              PP
```

In the first example, *At once with joy and fear his heart rebounds,* the contours of the phrases coincide with the boundaries of the metrical feet. In the second example, *Downward to darkness on extended wings,* the phrasing may break in the middle foot (creating a pause in the meter at the end of a description of downward movement), or it may somewhat unnaturally emphasize the *ex-* syllable in *extended.* The meter stresses *on,* but the phrasing rushes the second half of the line, which is all one prepositional phrase (*on extended wings*), toward the next stress in the phrasing (and toward a description of flying). The competing stress pattern on *downward* potentially gives the word even more weight as the second syllable receives more than typical stress.

Some of the vocabulary of metrical analysis describes the tension between phrasing and meter. The term **caesura** indicates a pause in a line created by natural phrasing rather than by the meter. **Enjambment** occurs when the poetic line and syntax are asynchronous, that is, when a phrase, clause, or sentence isn't complete at the end of a line of poetry but instead spills over into the next line. It happens in these lines from Robert Frost's "On a Tree Fallen across the Road":

> The tree the tempest with a crash of wood
> Throws down in front of us is not to bar
> Our passage to our journey's end for good.

Enjambment can serve various purposes. In the first instance here, for example, it certainly supports the violent emphasis on *Throws* at the beginning of the second line.

Not all stresses in a clause or sentence are equal. Work in poetics by scholars like Derek Attridge (1982) has drawn on music theory to explain the different kinds of rhythms and pulses in poetic meter, as well as the importance and complexities of phrasing.

Sound, Meaning, and Poetic Technique

In addition to meter, much English verse is characterized by **rhyme** or other phonological connections. And rhyme, like meter, helps to organize verse. All rhymes in poetry create possible semantic relationships. Rhyme links words in a way that creates an association that can then be interpreted as meaningful.

There are other kinds of rhymes in addition to full word rhymes. **Eye rhymes,** for instance, are those where words look as though they would rhyme exactly, but actually don't—*move* and *glove* are eye rhymes. "Come live with me and be my love / And we will all the pleasures prove," insists Christopher Marlowe's passionate shepherd. Today, *love* and *prove* are eye rhymes, but they were true rhymes in the sixteenth century, when Marlowe wrote these lines. Particular rhymes and patterns of stress, it's important to remember when reading poetry, aren't constant over time—they change along with English phonology. But whether exact or approximate, rhyme connects and contrasts poetic ideas. Marlowe's poem is all about the shepherd proving his love, and though one must read the whole poem to judge the shepherd's success, the tension between loving and proving it is present from the beginning, suggested in the rhyme.

In much poetry, **alliteration** draws words into semantic relationships. When the speakers of Gwendolyn Brooks's poem "We Real Cool" say they "Sing sin," they yoke *sing,* a word with positive connotations, like 'celebration', with one of very negative denotation, *sin.* The contrast is informative, evocative, and troubling at the same time. *Sing/sin* is an example of **consonance**, alliteration based on consonant sounds. Much more rarely, poets alliterate vowel sounds, for which the precise term is **assonance**.

Alliteration has many uses and many effects. Whereas most modern English poetry through much of the twentieth century was metrical and rhymed, Old English and early Middle English poetry was generally alliterative. In such poetry, alliteration governs the line. First, it provides a sense of movement across the line, as the reader anticipates the next repetition of the alliterated sound. In modern English poetry, meter provides that sense of movement. Second, alliteration can provide a sense of closure, since each successive line of an alliterative poem typically relies on a different sound. In much modern English poetry, rhyme provides a parallel sense of linear closure. These effects are peculiar to poetry, but alliteration is not. Alliteration figures (usually very lightly) in English prose, both fiction and nonfiction.

In some poems, alliteration and other manipulations of sound amount to a type of symbolism, what we might call "sound symbolism." You are probably already aware of one, very restricted case of sound symbolism, **onomatopoeia**, in which a word (*slurp, squish, buzz,* for instance) sounds like what it means, perhaps the only instance that confounds the structuralist principle that language always and only arbitrarily couples sound and meaning. Such words could also be called **mimetic**, or 'imitative'. But poetry can be mimetic without indulging in onomatopoeia. In the first stanza of his poem "Upper Lambourne," John Betjeman draws the imagination's eye upward along the trunk of an ash tree covered with ivy, and then further upward, toward the sun. The first line begins with the phrase "Up the ash tree"; the second line begins with the phrase "Up the sun." The reader's visual imagination, though, may be stimulated by what the reader hears. In the initial position of these lines, *up* is literally an uplifting sound; as a syllable, it is stressed and, depending on how you vocalize it, air rises from the diaphragm, lifts the chest, and raises the tone of the vowel even as you say it aloud. The repetition of *up* in the second line suggests further ascent, from the treetop into the sky. (Repetition of an initial word or phrase in a poetic line is called **anaphora**. There are many poetical and rhetorical figures like anaphora, significant techniques of literary style, but well beyond the scope

A Question to Discuss

Hip Hop Rhymes

When people think about poetic rhyme, sometimes they just think about end rhymes of perhaps one or two syllables. But, of course, poetic rhyme can be much more complicated. Hip hop lyrics often demonstrate enormously complex rhyme tactics. As a study by H. Samy Alim (2003) demonstrates, they capitalize not only on the one-syllable rhymes (like *hip/trip*), and two-syllable rhymes with the stress on the first syllable (like *filling/chilling*), but also on triple, quadruple, quintuple, and even sextuple rhymes (like *declare which object/the Blair Witch Project*).

Hip hop poets are creating exciting poetry in their songs, with complex multisyllabic rhymes, extended strings of alliteration, and many other kinds of wordplay. Check it out in a song of your choosing. How does the song exploit these poetic devices? Hip hop style plays with phonology to accomplish much of its "language stretching" as well as much of its critique, implict or explicit, of Standard English and the ideology that accompanies it.

of this chapter. The Suggested Reading section at the end of this chapter includes books devoted to explaining such elements of rhetoric and poetics.)

A poem shouldn't be reduced to alliteration or meter, metaphor, or rhyme. It isn't even the sum of all the poetic features that cooperate in its meaning, a meaning much larger than denotation or reference to the world of things outside the poem. Poeticity is holistic, and each poem must be read as a whole, with every relevant linguistic feature interpreted in the context of all the others.

Special Focus: What Makes "Good Writing"?

We strive to write well in academia—or at least we should—whether we are students or faculty. But what exactly makes academic writing "good"?

There is no one answer to what makes "good writing" in academia. Effective cohesion is a start, but far from an end. We could think about trying to answer the question at two related levels: expectations for content and rhetorical strategies and expectations for language. In academia, those expectations depend in part on the conventions of the discipline and of the register or genre in which we are writing. As we suggested earlier, choice of genre probably determines what we say and how we say it just as much as what we say and how we say it characterize the various genres.

To start, all genres have consistent themes and conventions, and this is in no way a criticism. The themes and conventions are part of how genres help us make sense of the world and allow us to write in ways that make sense to particular audiences in particular situations. To take one example with which many of you may be familiar, literary criticism has its own characteristic features. One study of "lit crit" articles published between 1978 and 1982 describes several topoi (or themes) that appear consistently (Fahnestock and Secor 1991):

- Ubiquity: critics either find many examples of the same thing in a text or find one thing in many forms in a text.
- Paradox: critics often bring together apparently irreconcilable opposites in order to examine the "startling dualism" they create.
- "*Contemptus mundi*": critics work from an assumption of shared despair (with the audience) over the condition of modern society, which is seen as in decline.
- Paradigm: much criticism is an elucidation of a structure in a literary text.
- Complexity: critics explain where to locate the complexity of a text (e.g., in the historical moment, in the author's psyche or background, in the text itself).

Fundamental to all such critical inquiry is the assumption that literature is complex. To understand literature requires "patient unraveling, translating, decoding, interpreting and analyzing" (Fahnestock and Secor 1991, 89). Critical articles don't usually praise literary pieces for simplicity or transparency, though there are exceptions—sometimes texts are deliberately simple, in order to challenge the assumption that complication is necessarily a good thing. Critics who pay attention will notice this and locate the "simple" text in the context of that argument.

At the level of language, how would those critics locate their points about a simple text in the context of arguments about the value of complexity? How do they effectively opinions and engage the opinions of others? Scholars in systemic functional linguistics (see Chapter 6) talk about features of "stance" and "engagement" to help specify how we as writers use specific language resources to position ourselves in the scholarly conversation (see Hyland 2005). Student writers, it turns out, don't always seem to see themselves as full participants in that conversation and do not exploit stance and engagement features the way that expert writers do. What do we mean?

Stance markers, through which we express our opinions and judgments, include hedges (e.g., *may*, *arguably*), boosters (*certainly*), first person references (*I think*), and the like. Students, who are often told to make strong, convincing arguments, sometimes don't hedge as much as experts do through subtle devices such as modals; and when writers are expressing certainty, a word like *clearly* may sound more expert than the phrase *I believe*.

Engagement refers to the ways we acknowledge and relate to others, be those our readers or other scholars. Engagement markers include reader pronouns (*we*, *you*), directives (*Note that . . .*), questions, appeals to shared knowledge, and the like. Less expert writers in a field may feel less comfortable using a directive to readers like *Consider*, but these kinds of directives are characteristic of successful writing in many academic fields. Students also more often rely on a generalized *we* (e.g., society as a whole) rather than using *we* to refer to, for example, scholars in a specific discipline. This is certainly understandable, as students may not feel they have the right to position themselves as a scholar in the field; there is no question that student writers are often put in a difficult bind when trying to write authoritatively without always having the authority they feel they need to do so.

When we write, we are not just asserting claims—we are negotiating them with other scholars and our readers. Aware of this need for negotiation, successful texts tend to be "dialogic." They acknowledge contrary points of view and "deal with" them by making concessions, offering counters, endorsing others' arguments, and so on. Studies show that more successful student writers tend to make more liberal use of these strategies (Wu 2007). Studies also show that expert writers often use the rhetorical strategy of "problematization" to set up their arguments, and students who use this strategy in their papers tend to score better (Barton 1993). Expert writers use contrastive language such as *nonetheless*, *however*, and *yet* in order to mark counterclaims; you can see how these kinds of words help writers recognize the claims of others and then qualify or reject them as part of the scholarly conversation. Making those kinds of connections in writing is clearly part of "good" academic writing across fields.

Other linguistic features may vary by discipline. Scholars in the humanities and social sciences tend to take more explicitly personal and involved positions (Hyland 2005). More objectivity is supposedly reflected in the scientists' use of the passive voice: *It was observed . . .* or *It was proved . . .* for example. The choice of passive over active voice doesn't eliminate the subjective element in scientific experiment. At its best, it places an emphasis on outcome over agency; at its worst, it denies subjectivity nonetheless present. Scientific writing is also characterized by a high frequency of nominalizations (e.g., *the transferal of energy, the fermentation of the yeast, the stimulation of the rats by loud noises*), which also hide agency and frame actions as entities rather than processes—and can create very dense prose.

Across disciplines, though, writers must master the devices that help organize the text—creating cohesion and engaging readers. Certain conjunctive devices are more characteristic of academic prose (e.g., *therefore, in other words, as a result, in contrast, however, indeed*), and one of the transitions for student writers is adopting these conventions over more spoken equivalents (e.g., *so, but, and*).

Part of succeeding in whatever discipline you select is acquiring literacy in that discipline. You must learn the technical vocabulary of the field, in addition to the facts and arguments. You must also learn the conventions for writing: What form do arguments take? What kinds of evidence are credible? How are the relevant genres of texts structured? How do authors construct their authority in the text and engage the arguments of others? Armed with answers to these questions, you can begin to construct your own authority and style to write effective texts within the conventions of the genre.

☑ Summary

In this chapter, you have learned about several linguistic ways of analyzing literary and nonliterary texts.

- Genres and registers are characterized partly by the linguistic practices typical of them. As a result, because genres and registers are conventional, they promote certain linguistic behaviors. But we often manipulate genres and registers creatively, by means of linguistic behavior unusual within them. What constitutes "good writing" depends on the genre and register in which one works, as stylistic conventions vary from genre to genre.

- Cohesion is a fundamental characteristic of texts. Texts achieve cohesion through any or all of the following linguistic strategies: reference, ellipsis and substitution, conjunction, and lexical cohesion.

- Narrative is structured in predictable ways and can be understood in terms of its parts and progress among them. Audiences expect stories to work in conventional ways.

- Any narrative is told from a narrator's perspective, which can be analyzed as a type of discourse, as discussed in Chapter 8. Narrative perspective often provokes audience response, whether intellectual or emotional, by means of a reader's relationship to the narrator, pace and voice within the narrative, and the relation between direct and indirect speech in the narrative.

- Literary dialogue can be interpreted in terms of speech acts, conversational maxims, and politeness principles and maxims.

- Poetry (also, to a lesser extent, prose) depends on creative choice of diction, metaphor, and phonological aspects of language like rhyme and prosody to promote intellectual and emotional responses in its audience.

Suggested Reading

One very accessible introduction to stylistics, structured around methodological approaches and text applications, is Michael Toolan's *Language in Literature: An Introduction* ᴜtylistics (1996). Sara Mills provides an introduction to stylistics from a feminist perspective in *Feminist Stylistics* (1995). For more on cohesion, readers may want to turn to *Cohesion in English* (1976) by M. A. K. Halliday and Ruqaiya Hasan. A shorter, revised description of cohesion is also included in Chapter 9 of Halliday's *An Introduction to Functional Grammar* (1985). In *Discourse Analysis* (2002), Barbara Johnstone provides useful discussions of cohesion, register and genre, and narrative structure. The foundational work for this kind of narrative analysis is William Labov and Joshua Waletzky's "Narrative Analysis: Oral Versions of Personal Experience," in *Essays on the Verbal and Visual Arts: Proceedings of the 1966 Annual Spring Meeting of the American Ethnological Association* (1967). The first volume in *Discourse Studies* (1997) edited by Teun A. Van Dijk, titled *Discourse as Structure and Process*, contains informative chapters on narrative as well as register and genre. J. Hillis Miller's *Speech Acts in Literature* (2001) and Mary Louise Pratt's *Toward a Speech Act Theory of Literary Discourse* (1977) are excellent treatments of the subject, though the former requires some experience with postmodern literary theory. For further information about poetics and rhetoric, see Richard A. Lanham's *A Handlist of Rhetorical Terms* (2d ed., 1991), *The New Princeton Encyclopedia of Poetics*, edited by Alex Preminger, T. V. F. Brogan, and others (3d ed., 1993), and Paul Fussell's *Poetic Meter and Poetic Form* (rev. ed., 1979). H. Samy Alim writes about hip hop's poetic form in "On Some Serious Next Millennium Rap Ishhh: Pharoahe Monch, Hip Hop Poetics, and the Internal Rhymes of Internal Affairs," in the *Journal of English Linguistics* 31 (March 2003): 60–84.

Exercises
Exercise 9.1   Cohesion

1. Choose excerpts of about 300 words from two texts that represent distinctly different genres or registers. Using different colored pens or pencils for each type of cohesive tie, identify all the forms of cohesion in each text. Then compare the patterns of cohesion. What conclusions can you draw from your comparison?

2. Using the same mark-up conventions that you used in question 1, identify the cohesive ties in the following conversational excerpt (from Tannen 1986, 119).

Mike: What kind of salad dressing should I make?
Ken: Oil and vinegar, what else?
Mike: What do you mean, "what else?"
Ken: Well, I always make oil and vinegar, but if you want, we could try something else.
Mike: Does that mean you don't like it when I make other dressings?
Ken: No, I like it. Go ahead. Make something else.
Mike: Not if you want oil and vinegar.
Ken: I don't. Make a yogurt dressing.
(Mike makes a yogurt dressing, tastes it, and makes a face.)
Ken: Isn't it good?

Mike: I don't know how to make a yogurt dressing.
Ken: Well, if you don't like it, throw it out.
Mike: You're making a big deal about nothing.
Ken: *You* are!

Exercise 9.2   Narratives

1. Choose a young children's book (i.e., a book that is mostly pictures with a very simple narrative). Retype the narrative so that you can see it all at once. Then identify the narrative parts, using the model proposed by Labov and Waletzky. Is anything missing, and if so, what? What might children be learning about storytelling from this kind of narrative?

2. Print out a copy of the six-year-old's story (page 286), which you are now going to mark up with different colors and/or different symbols. Identify all the different types of cohesive ties in the story (use the mark-up of the passage from David Sedaris's book *Naked* as an example). How does cohesion in the child's story compare to that in the Sedaris passage? How does it compare to cohesion in Martin Luther King Jr.'s "I Have a Dream" speech? Are cohesive strategies among the three texts similar, or do they help to distinguish one text from another?

3. Tape an interview in which you ask someone to tell you a story about a near-death experience or one of the most frightening moments of his or her life. Transcribe the narrative—including your part, if you participate. Then analyze the structure of the narrative using the model proposed by Labov and Waletzky. You could address questions like the following: Is anything missing? Is there any joint storytelling? Do any parts of the narrative merit their own description in a model for narratives?

Exercise 9.3   Representing Speech

Listen to the people around you use quotative *like* and jot down examples. Given your evidence (and your intuitions as a speaker of English—but never trust these too much!), can quotative *like* be used for both direct and indirect speech? For both speech and thought? For other things? What restrictions do you find? If you want to test your conclusions, create a survey in which you ask native speakers to identify a set of sentences with quotative *like* as acceptable or unacceptable (in the descriptive sense). Use some of the sentences from your evidence and make some up to test your hypotheses.

Exercise 9.4   Analyzing Dialogue

Select a passage of dialogue from a work of fiction, drama, film, or television. Analyze it in terms of conversational principles and maxims (cooperation, Grice's maxims, adjacency, implicature, etc.), discourse features (discourse markers, etc.), and politeness. What are your conclusions about the success of the conversation, its role in the story, and in the development of characters.

Poetics

1. Scan the meter of "The Tyger" by William Blake (1757–1827), both the classical meter and the prosody of the phrasing.

The Tyger

Tyger! Tyger! burning bright,
In the forests of the night,
What immortal hand or eye
Could frame thy fearful symmetry?

In what distant deeps or skies
Burnt the fire in thine eyes?
On what wings dare he aspire?
What the hand dare seize the fire?

And what shoulder, and what art?
Could twist the sinews of thy heart?
And when thy heart began to beat,
What dread hand, and what dread feet?

What the hammer? What the chain?
In what furnace was thy brain?
What the anvil? What dread grasp
Dare its deadly terrors clasp?

When the stars threw down their spears,
And watered heaven with their tears,
Did he smile his work to see?
Did he who made the Lamb, make thee?

Tyger! Tyger! burning bright,
In the forests of the night,
What immortal hand or eye
Dare frame thy fearful symmetry?

2. Now analyze the rhymes. Do they create any notable semantic connections? What is the effect of the near-rhyme between *eye* and *symmetry*?

Exercise 9.6   Stylistic Analysis

1. Interview various experts in an academic field (perhaps in your major) about the kinds of writing they do. How would they define good writing?

    Then select one genre of writing from that discipline. Collect examples and analyze the conventions. From this analysis, what can you conclude about the nature of the interaction it sets up among the author, text, and audience?

2. In consultation with your instructor, choose a text (other than transcribed conversation) on which to perform a stylistic analysis. Try to employ all of the linguistics you've studied so far (phonology, morphology, semantics, syntax, pragmatics, and speech act theory) in making sense of the text in question.

Chapter **10**

Language Acquisition

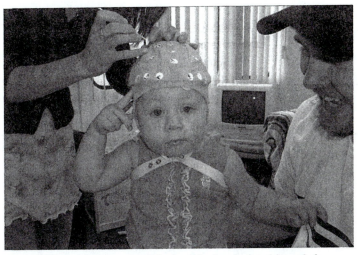

These fashionable caps record the brain's electrical activity to help researchers learn more about what is happening in babies' brains when they are learning language.

If you have tried learning a second or third language in high school or college, then you probably know just how hard, and sometimes frustrating, that process can be. It takes years to learn a language, and even then, you rarely achieve nativelike fluency. Given this experience, it can seem all the more amazing that you learned to speak your native language(s) fluently by the age of about four—four years that you mostly can't remember because of infantile amnesia. How does this happen? And why is it so hard to learn languages later in life?

Children's acquisition of language is one of the most normal and most amazing feats of the human mind. No one explicitly teaches children how to talk. Parents don't typically say "Now honey, to make a yes-no question, just take that auxiliary verb and move it before the subject, and if there is no auxiliary verb, then add *do*." Yet children babble, learn their first words, suddenly start speaking in sentences, and add new words to their vocabularies during every waking hour. Children do make mistakes, but they are often predictable mistakes and not ones they would have heard from adults. For example, children might call the woman who comes to babysit "Mommy" or a gerbil "kitty" or broccoli "trees." Or they might talk about how they "taked" their shoes off their two "foots."

How do children know, for example, to add -s to make plural nouns? No adult said to them "Just put that -s on the end of that noun" (and, of course, we know that it's not nearly that easy, given that -s can be [s] or [z] or [ɪz]). The infants themselves deduced the rule from the language input with which they were (unsystematically) presented in their day-to-day interactions with adults and older children. The substitution of *trees* for *broccoli* might be evidence in the case for prototype semantics (see Chapter 7), and **taked* and **foots* for the power of analogy in word formation (see Chapter 4). Modern linguistic theory often turns to research on language acquisition for confirmation, even inspiration.

Language learning follows its own systematic timeline, with little or no regard for prescriptive grammar intervention by adults. Let's take an example. Here is an exchange between a parent and a two-and-a-half-year-old child:

Child: Macy don't have one.
Parent: Macy *doesn't* have one.
Child: Macy don't have one.
Parent: Doesn't.
Child: Doesn't.
Parent: Macy doesn't have one.
Child: Macy don't have one.

In this example, the parent attempts to correct the child's grammar toward a standard form: *doesn't* for *don't*. The child can repeat the word *doesn't*, but when she returns to the full sentence and the grammatical rule as she presently understands it, she reverts to *don't*. Some varieties of English systematically use *don't* in this construction; standard English uses *doesn't*. What is happening in the child's mind?

In this chapter, we begin with a general look at studies of language acquisition. Then we consider the stages that babies and young children go through in the acquisition of first languages. These stages raise important questions about the brain and whether it has an innate capacity for language (and whether that capacity has a "biological clock"). To address these questions, we look at examples from pidgins and creole languages, sign languages, and special circumstances in which children are deprived of normal language input. We conclude with a discussion of second-language acquisition, both at a young age and at an older age, and educational questions related to learning languages and bilingual education.

Theories about Children's Language Acquisition

Linguists and psychologists have learned most of what they know about children's language acquisition in the last fifty years. Researchers have been keeping diaries of children's behavior for over one hundred years, but modern technology has revolutionized the field. Video recorders allow researchers to capture children's learning, from their babbling to their responses to language (e.g., eye movements)—to be studied over and over again in slow motion. Technologies such as neuroimaging and electroencephalography (EEG) can localize brain activity in response to stimuli. Digital computers allow researchers to synthesize speech to study the intricacies of what children hear, and when. It's not quite right to say the brain is "like a computer," but the computer has shown us much about the brain.

Imitation versus Instinct

At first glance, children's language acquisition may seem simple. Many people, including perhaps you up to this point, assume that children simply imitate the language that they hear (or see, in the case of deaf children) all around them. But imitation cannot account for many of the facts of children's language acquisition. For example:

- Children get imperfect input from adults (e.g., speech errors, imprecise enunciation) but do not necessarily repeat these errors.
- Children make mistakes they have not heard from adults (e.g., "I eated it," "I no go").
- Children around the world follow similar stages in the acquisition of language.
- Most importantly, children learn to produce an infinite number of creative utterances—so "learning language" means acquiring the "rules" to produce these utterances, yet these are rules that most adult speakers do not consciously know, let alone explicitly teach their children.

Thus, it seems, there must be something innate in the human brain that allows children to take the language input they receive and construct grammar. Out of the generative tradition came the term *language acquisition device,* which provides the general principles of Universal Grammar for parsing and structuring language. Noam Chomsky coined the term Universal Grammar. Steven Pinker, a well-known linguist at Harvard University, calls it a "language instinct." Some researchers are searching for a language gene. And others argue that linguistic competence depends on innate cognitive abilities broader than those focused on language alone. Imitation is clearly important to language acquisition: it is, for example, how children know which sounds to practice through babbling, how children learn words, and how children gain much of their communicative competence (e.g., politeness conventions). But learning a language involves much more than imitation. Modern linguists have been debating the following questions for more than four decades: how much of language is part of our cognitive abilities when we're born, and how much do we learn from hearing spoken language?

Early hypotheses about language learning echo theories that you read about in Chapter 7 on semantics. One theory, which can be traced back to John Locke's idea of children as "blank tablets," suggests that ideas and words are copies of sensory impressions. A second theory proposes that we learn words by associating sounds with visual stimuli. Both extend naive theories of reference. But blind children learn language without visual stimuli, and all children learn words for things for which there is no visual stimuli (e.g., 'love').

Behaviorism, a school of thought that had its heyday in the first half of the twentieth century, assumes that humans are complex machines, that stimuli lead people to speak, and that "conditioning" can explain language learning: rewards for correct language use (e.g., getting what we want, having others understand our utterances) reinforce grammatical rules and lead to consistent grammar usage. Behavioral theories are not based on inferences about what happens in people's minds; they rely strictly on data that can be observed directly (in this case, language behavior in given contexts).

Noam Chomsky and Universal Grammar

In 1959, these theories were turned on their heads by Noam Chomsky's systematic and devastating critique of *Verbal Behavior*, a book by B. F. Skinner, one of the leading proponents of behaviorism. Chomsky's theories about the mind, language acquisition, and Universal Grammar were the key trigger for modern studies of language acquisition. He focused on the fact that children learn a set of rules to combine linguistic elements in order to produce an infinite number of utterances. Previous theories, and behaviorism in particular, simply could not explain that fact. He argued that linguistics should focus on the mind and the linguistic competence of the ideal speaker-listener. (See also Chapters 1 and 6.) He asked, how do children discover the grammatical rules that allow them to create and parse an infinite number of linguistic combinations? And what are these rules? To answer these questions, linguists must often rely on introspection—that is, looking into their own minds and examining their own intuitions about grammaticality—rather than simply observing language behavior. As a result of this Chomskyan revolution, modern theories have focused primarily on language learning as an active process in which children reinvent language rather than merely acquire it.

Reinventing language? Yes—every minute of every day, children around the world reinvent language as they acquire it. Most children are "bathed" in language from the moment they are born, and from this vast amount of input, they figure out a set of rules to understand the language they hear and to create utterances with which they can communicate with other speakers. No one gives them the rules of language; they must deduce the rules underlying the language they hear (or see, in the case of sign languages). How else are you going to make sure that you get apple juice instead of orange juice or tell your father that your stomach hurts? So children use language input to reinvent the language around them—or they reinvent a very close approximation of this language.

Like human fingerprints, the language learning process is unique to each individual. Every child's version of his or her native language will be slightly different from his or her parents' versions. This is an important part of how language varies from speaker to speaker and how it changes from generation to generation. For example, a child may simply understand a word's meaning differently from his or her parents (remember the example from Chapter 2 of *peruse*, whose meaning has been reversed within a generation or two). Or a child could extend a grammatical rule in innovative ways: for example, extending the regular plural rule to *ox* to make it a regular noun (*ox/oxes*, rather than *ox/oxen*). A child might interpret a new construction as part of the grammar: for example, *you guys* as one grammatical form of the second-person plural pronoun. Or a child might learn to produce a set of vowels slightly higher or more front than his or her parents'. One generation's *larynx* may become the next generation's *larnyx* (see Chapter 3, page 82). Although language change often looks dramatic in retrospect, it typically happens gradually over several generations of speakers.

Debates about Language "Hard Wiring"

The proposition that humans have an innate capacity or "hard wiring" for language remains contested. The debate centers on whether the hard wiring is specifically for language or represents a more general cognitive ability that supports our ability to learn languages. Chomsky and Pinker are two of the strongest advocates of the theory that babies are born with some linguistic knowledge that allows them to process language and create grammar. According to Chomsky and those who follow him, this knowledge, called Universal Grammar, is general (or universal) enough to cover any language that the infant encounters. For example, babies would know that there are the categories noun and verb, that a subject can come either before or after the verb, and that there are grammatical roles that correspond to subject or agent. Infants would also know to expect phrases and clauses in their language.

Another school of thought, voiced by scholars such as Lila Gleitman, views language acquisition as tied to an innate cognitive ability to map or create associations—in this case, between language and the world. These scholars argue that language takes the form that it does in part because that is how our brains map more generally. Prototype semantics, for example, is closely aligned with this approach to language learning.

As with any theory about the brain and cognitive abilities, these two competing theories are both hard to prove and hard to refute. And the acquisition of different aspects of language may require different cognitive abilities, some more targeted than others. In this chapter, we're certainly not going to solve the question of whether humans have innate cognitive capacities designed specifically for language acquisition, but we do present evidence that is relevant to any eventual answer. Pidgins and creole languages, for example, provide compelling evidence for innate linguistic knowledge in children.

Language and the Brain

Whether hard-wired, as Chomsky and Pinker argue, or not, language is clearly associated with certain functions and areas of the adult brain. We have learned the extent to which certain areas of the brain are involved in both linguistic processing and production, partly by examining the impaired speech of those who have suffered damage to specific parts of the brain—for instance, the speech of aphasics. **Aphasia** is the partial or total loss of the power of speech, specifically the ability to articulate thoughts or comprehend spoken or written language, typically as the result of a brain injury or disease.

The brain is divided into two halves: the **right hemisphere** and the **left hemisphere**. Between the two hemispheres is the median longitudinal fissure (the groove that divides the brain in two), and underneath that is a thick bundle of nerve fibers called the **corpus callosum**. The two hemispheres take on different aspects of the cognitive load by a process called **lateralization**. Scientists have known since the nineteenth century that the left hemisphere of the brain controls the right side of the body and the right hemisphere of the brain controls the left side of the body. The corpus callosum allows communication between the two hemispheres.

Modularity of the mind, sometimes known as **localization**, refers to the general scientific belief that specific parts of the mind (or modules) are responsible for specific kinds of processing. For example, vision is processed near the back of the brain. Music and human faces (yes, we seem to have a specific part of the brain dedicated to processing human faces) are interpreted primarily in parts of the right hemisphere, as are spatial relationships and the understanding of jokes and irony. For most speakers, language processing primarily occurs in parts of the left hemisphere, as does mathematical calculation. There are exceptions, particularly related to handedness: about 15 percent of left-handed people process language primarily in the right hemisphere, and about 15 percent of left-handed people process language in both hemispheres. Right-handed people vastly outnumber left-handed people, and, all told, over 95 percent of the population handles most language processing in the left hemisphere.

How early in life does the human brain become lateralized? In one experiment, infants less than four days old seemed more sensitive to linguistic contrasts in the sound signal (i.e., differences between phonemes) when presented to the right ear and more discerning of musical notes when presented to the left ear (Mehler and Dupoux 1994). But we also know that up to about the age of three, children can recover to almost full if not fully normal functioning after many kinds of brain injuries, as other modules in the brain take on new specialized functions to compensate for damaged areas. So, while infants' brains develop lateralization, they remain highly plastic for at least some period of time.

The cerebrum, the largest part of the brain, is covered by a layer of gray matter known as the cerebral cortex, which is 2–6 millimeters thick. Fissures among the many

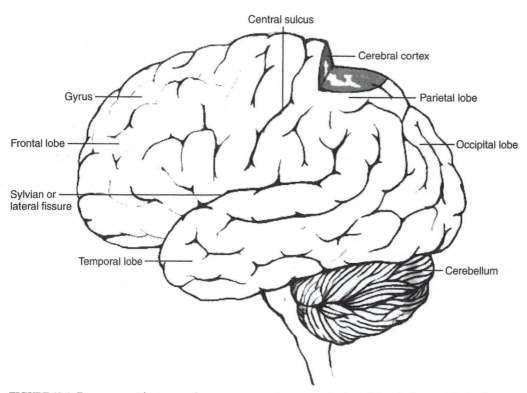

FIGURE 10.1 For most speakers, most language processing occurs in the left hemisphere of the brain. The left and right hemispheres are connected by the corpus callosum.

folds in the cerebrum define major functional areas called lobes. The left hemisphere of the human brain (depicted in Figure 10.1) includes:

- The **frontal lobe**, responsible for, among other things, some language and some motor functions.
- The **parietal lobe**, responsible for, among other things, bodily sensations such as touch, pain, and temperature.
- The **occipital lobe**, responsible for, among other things, vision.
- The **temporal lobe**, responsible for, among other things, hearing and aspects of memory storage.

The frontal lobe is a distinct attribute of *Homo sapiens*. It developed some 100,000 years ago. Though separated from the rest of each hemisphere by the **Sylvian fissure**, the frontal lobe of the left hemisphere is not solely responsible for human linguistic ability—some language functions are just beyond the fissure, in the other lobes. Studies of different kinds of aphasia have allowed brain scientists to locate certain language functions in specific areas of the left hemisphere, as we discuss later in this chapter. To fully understand language processing, we may also need to study further the role of other parts of the brain, such as the basal ganglia, nuclei of gray matter interconnected with the cerebral cortex, that help control sequential movements such as walking.

A Question to Discuss

Why Do We Talk with Our Hands?

When you try to do something with your hands that requires fine motor skills, like untangle a knot or move a block in a game of Jenga, do you do funny things with your mouth? Bite your lip or put your tongue in your cheek or purse your lips? Our hands and mouth seem to be connected such that these kinds of activities trigger mouth movements. Speech is also often accompanied by, and may trigger, hand movements.

Why do we use our hands when we talk? Sometimes gestures provide supplementary information to listeners. For example, if we say "She has long hair" while using our index fingers to make a corkscrew gesture, we are adding the information that her long hair is curly. But not all our gestures have as clear semantic content (for example, thrusting your hands forward, palms up, while making a point), and we still make gestures when we're talking on the phone and our audience cannot see them.

Some research suggests that gesturing while talking helps reduce the cognitive load of speech production. In one study, children and adults were asked to solve a math problem, after which they were given a list of words or letters and told to try to remember them. They then were asked to explain their solution to the math problem. Both adults and children could remember more words or letters later if they gestured during their explanations (Goldin-Meadow et al. 2001). In other words, the use of gestures eased the load of producing the speech required to explain the math problem, which freed up more cognitive resources to remember the letters or words.

How do you use your hands when you talk? What happens if you force yourself not to use your hands?

The fact that all children acquire language in predictable stages, uniformly across language communities, provides further evidence that there is something biological, a process of brain development, deeply implicated in language acquisition. In the next three sections, we consider some of the steps children go through in acquiring (or reinventing) language. As you read, remember that this developmental timeline is approximate and variable. Different children reach each of these stages on their own timelines, and the milestones of language acquisition can vary by many months from child to child. Some children speak their first word at six months, and some wait for over two years. New parents should not panic that their child has somehow fallen behind the curve, nor should they become excessively swaggering that their child is light-years ahead. Some children take their time starting to speak (while keeping up with their peers in terms of comprehension), especially if they are very physically active and are devoting much of their attention and energy to developing motor skills.

Children Learning Sounds

When a baby is born (assuming the baby is not deaf), she (or he) hears all kinds of noises, for example, the doctor discussing the birth with her mother, her father weeping tears of joy and exhaustion, her grandmother cooing over her tiny feet and hands, the wheels of the dinner cart coming down the hall, the whir of the air conditioning, the buzz of the neon lights, and the beeps of the monitor in the next room. How does the baby know to pay particular attention to the language noises?

Perhaps babies have a language instinct, but as you now know, not everyone agrees that such an instinct exists. In any case, children do seem to have an instinct to pay special attention to features and behaviors of other humans. For example, part of the right hemisphere of the brain specializes in the recognition of human faces. And babies seem to know to tune in to the sounds that other humans make when communicating with each other in context. Language learning, from what cognitive scientists can tell, is all about real humans using language around infants, spoken either to them or to others. (There are cultures in which children are not spoken to and yet they learn language along a similar timeline.) Children do not seem to learn language from the radio or language tapes, where the language is disembodied and decontextualized. Young children can learn some language from television, but hearing language from real humans, in person, seems to be critical to language acquisition.

Somewhere between four days and two months old, babies can distinguish between their native language and other languages by intonation patterns (but they cannot distinguish among unfamiliar languages—they are all just "other" undifferentiated noise). How is this possible? Babies actually begin hearing before they are born. By about seven months in gestation, babies in the womb can hear, although their hearing is distorted by the amniotic fluid. They mostly hear low frequencies; thus they can hear the intonation and stress patterns of the language, particularly the language spoken by their mothers.

In other words, for at least a couple of months before they are born, children learn the prosody (the patterns of stress and intonation) of the language spoken around them, and specifically about the prosody of their mothers. The usefulness of prosody in children's language acquisition has been another bone of contention among researchers. Some argue that prosody provides critical clues to infants about word, phrase, and clause breaks. Others acknowledge that although this may be true, prosody appreciation does not account for how children figure out grammatical rules.

By three and a half months after their birth, and maybe much earlier, babies are more attentive to their mothers' voices than a stranger's. By four months, babies prefer listening to words over other sounds, and they prefer voices speaking parentese—sometimes called motherese—over other voices. (We talk more about parentese below.)

Language Acquisition Tests

How do we know these facts about what babies think? Babies this young certainly can't *tell* researchers what they notice or what they like. And researchers do not try to read babies' minds either. For very young babies, the most commonly used method for determining babies' reactions is "the suck test." (See also Chapter 3.) Babies are given a special pacifier attached to a monitor that senses whether the baby has compressed the pacifier nipple and records how fast the baby is sucking. Some of the tests are designed so that if babies suck slower, they will hear one sound or recording (e.g., the researcher's voice), and if they suck faster, they will hear a different one (e.g., their mother's voice). By this method, researchers draw conclusions about whether, for example, babies prefer their mothers' voices—will they do the sucking work required to hear them? Other tests are structured so that each time the babies suck, they hear a sound. When babies first hear the sound, they show interest in it and suck faster to hear it more often. After they hear the same sound for a while, they become habituated to it (or bored by it, depending on how you want to think about it) and their sucking slows down. But if the sound suddenly changes, their interest will be rekindled and they will suck faster again.

As babies get a bit older (say, six months), the sucking tests can be less effective, and researchers have devised other ways to test infants' preferences. For example, an infant sitting on a parent's lap is presented with a toy that is being moved about by a research assistant on the right, while on the left sits a stereo speaker with a dark box or an unmoving Mr. Potato Head on top. The infant usually looks at the moving toy,

Mr. Potato Head: You'd look over at him too, wouldn't you?

as the same sound (e.g., /lo/) is repeated out of the speaker. After all, which is more interesting? But if the sound coming out of the speaker changes (e.g., from /lo/ to /ro/) and the child looks over, he or she will discover that the box has lit up and there is a moving toy inside or that Mr. Potato Head is glowing. Then it all goes dark as the sound is repeated. Children quickly learn that if they hear a new sound, they can look over and see something interesting; otherwise, nothing interesting is happening on the speaker. This way, researchers can tell if children hear the distinctions among different sounds.

Acquisition of Phonemic Differences

Why should we care if and when infants hear different sounds? One of the intriguing questions in research on language acquisition has been when and how infants figure out the distinctive sounds or phonemes of their native languages. As we discussed in Chapter 3, when we hear people talk, we actually hear a continuous stream of sound, which we break up into words and syllables and phonemes. Babies know to pay attention to language coming from other humans differently from, say, the sound of a washing machine. By four months, they prefer listening to language over listening to the washing machine or other noise—or silence.

When babies are born, they are able to hear the phonemic distinctions of all the known languages of the world. They are prepared to learn whatever language the adults around them are speaking. Using the suck test, researchers have determined that all hearing infants detect changes from one phoneme to another in any language. If the researchers play one phoneme repeatedly, the child's sucking slows; then, when a new phoneme is introduced, the baby's sucking speeds up until he or she becomes habituated to the new sound. A baby born in a Japanese-speaking home can hear the difference between /l/ and /r/, and a baby born in an English-speaking home can hear the difference between aspirated and unaspirated /p/—unlike most monolingual adult speakers of these respective languages.

During these first few months, infants start to figure out which sounds are distinctive in their native languages (i.e., the languages being spoken by the adults around them). By around ten months, infants have learned to pay attention only to the phonemic distinctions relevant to their native languages, and they no longer respond to sound changes that are not distinctive in their language. Japanese-learning babies, for example, no longer respond to a shift from /l/ to /r/ because they have learned to process both these sounds as variants of one phoneme. In these ten months, the babies have learned to sort sounds into the stable categories of phonemes relevant to their languages.

Although young babies are attuned to the phonemic distinctions relevant to all the world's languages, they are not attuned to acoustic distinctions that are equally "real" but not phonemic in any language. This phenomenon is probably related to the shape of the human ear and the nature of the connections in the nervous system, which distort the acoustic signals that humans perceive. Sound systems in the world's languages probably capitalize on the distinctions that are most prominent to the human ear and do not depend on distinctions that are difficult for the human ear to pick up. The question that researchers are still trying to answer is how babies know to adjust for the differences that come with every speaker and every change in a speaker's rate of speech. Men, women, and children, because of the size and shape of their oral cavities among other things, all produce very different sound waves, yet babies learn to categorize, for example, all these different variants of [i] as /i/. In this respect, young children far surpass even the most sophisticated speech-recognition computers.

The bottom line: babies have figured out all of this relevant information about the sound system of their native language(s) before or just as they say their first words.

Children Learning Words

Children start to coo (uttering consonant-like sounds in the back of the mouth and a range of vowels) when they are about three months old. By this age, they also seem to understand a bit about turn-taking in conversation: we coo, they coo, we giggle, they coo, we coo, they reach out a hand. In other words, they are already developing their communicative competence in addition to their linguistic competence. Parents often unconsciously model turn-taking behavior for the baby as they interpret a gesture or a gurgle as a full-fledged turn and respond accordingly.

Babbling and First Words

Around seven or eight months of age, children start babbling, producing strings of consonants and vowels. Some researchers argue that for babies learning any language, those consonants are often [b, d, m, g] and the vowel is often [a] or [ɑ], but not all studies agree that there is a clear order of sound acquisition. Children babble for at least two reasons. First, they are doing the equivalent of calisthenics with their vocal cords, giving them a workout as they prepare to speak. Second, they are probably experimenting in the production of the sounds they hear. As we discussed in the previous section, around this age, children are figuring out the prototypical sounds or phonemes of their native languages. When they babble, they may well be trying to match specific movements of their lips, tongues, and other articulators with the sounds they hear, in order to figure out how to produce those sounds themselves.

Children get some visual help in figuring out how to produce sounds from watching the adults around them. This visual input is, however, obviously not necessary, as blind children babble and learn words in ways almost identical to sighted children. Tests indicate that by five months old, children associate specific mouth movements with specific sounds. When presented with two images of a face producing two sounds and a recording of one sound, the children, after looking between the two images, focus on the one producing the sound they hear. In other words, they are already doing some lip reading.

When they are about a year old, children start consistently to make the sounds distinctive to their native languages and say their first words (although some children may be closer to twenty months when they say their first words). The period from about twelve to eighteen months is typically referred to as the "one-word stage," during which infants produce simple, one-word utterances. Children's first words, especially if they

Language Acquisition at Work

Imitating Faces

For babies to use lip reading to inform their own production of sounds, they must understand that the faces they see on adults are like their own faces. This is actually quite sophisticated knowledge. If you have never looked in a mirror or extensively studied your face with your hands, how would you know that you have a face and a mouth like those of the other humans that you see? Andrew Meltzoff, a developmental psychologist at the University of Washington, has done extensive studies on how early babies can imitate. His research, in the 1970s through 1990s, involved convincing mothers that they wanted an unknown researcher to be one of the first faces their baby saw. It also involved many rushed trips to the hospital to study newborn babies.

Meltzoff's findings indicate that within hours of birth, infants can imitate: if an adult sticks out his or her tongue, the infant does, too; if the adult opens his or her mouth, so does the infant. Although this kind of imitation may not seem like a big deal, it really is. It means that infants know there is something unique about a human face (and a human face much bigger than their own): they know that it reflects what they themselves have. It also means that babies can observe the movements of another person's face and "turn it around," to know that if they make similar movements—say, of the tongue— then a similar thing will happen. Studies indicate that a part of the right hemisphere of the brain specializes in the recognition of human faces, and the ability to imitate human faces seems to be available within hours of, if not at, birth.

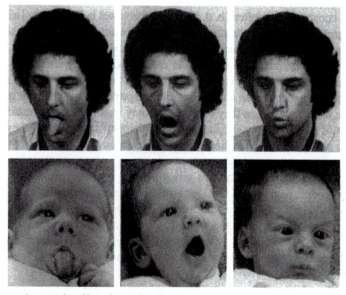

Andrew Meltzoff performed a series of experiments to see how early babies can imitate adult faces, as this baby is doing.

Source: A. N. Meltzoff and M. K. Moore, "Imitation of Facial and Manual Gestures by Human Neonates," *Science* 198 (1977): 75–78.

are learning a language like English, are often mostly nouns—one scholar says 50 percent. And these first nouns typically (in all languages) refer to people (*Mama*, *Dada*, *Papa*), animals, food, toys and other objects in the house, body parts, and clothing. Children acquire a few words for motion or activity (e.g., *up*) as well as some modifiers (e.g., *more*).

At this stage, children also sometimes produce short phrases, which they treat as one word (e.g., *what's-that*) rather than parsing for meaningful components. Another good example of this kind of lexicalization of phrases is the child who first understood "Daddyscar" as the way to refer to all cars, so there was "Mommy's Daddyscar" and "Gramma's Daddyscar." At this stage, children also typically use words in nonadult ways. For example, *there* may be used to indicate success while *uh-oh* is used to indicate failure. The word *gone* may describe any object that disappeared from view, whether it was eaten, taken away, hidden, or left of its own accord (Gopnik et al. 1999).

At the one-word stage, young children also generalize or extend the vocabulary they have to encompass items for which they have no other name. At the beginning of this chapter, we considered the examples of children calling other women "Mommy" and a whole range of animals "kitty." The child who calls broccoli "trees" has put that word through semantic extension to refer to all plants of a specific shape. There are stories of babies who call all round things "moon" and all long stringlike things "hair." These patterns of learning provide interesting evidence to anyone promoting prototype semantics (see Chapter 7).

Some scholars studying the relationship of language and gesture argue that the first signs of language may be gestures, and gestures can facilitate or provide scaffolding for language learning. In the one-word stage, the combination of a word and a supplementary gesture allows children to communicate information they cannot yet express verbally: for example, a child says "Mommy" and points to a cup to capture both the agent (Mommy) and the object (cup), with an understood action (probably bring or give) and recipient (me). The ability to express this kind of sentence-level information with a word and gesture seems to be predictive of the child's developing the ability to produce two-word utterances; in other words, the word-gesture combination generally occurs several months before the child combines two words to express similar information (Özçalişkan and Goldin-Meadow 2005).

At about eighteen months, most children undergo the "naming explosion," as they discover that all the objects around them have names. The process involved is sometimes called "fast mapping," as children (like adults) only need to hear one instance of a word to create a memory of its association with a specific referent. Studies have shown that this process of learning words goes far beyond hearing a word and seeing a thing. For example, in one study a researcher plays with a child in a room full of toys, and the researcher clearly looks at each toy. The researcher then leaves and someone else comes and adds a new toy to the collection. Then the researcher returns and says, "Look! A dax!" And the child, when asked to show the researcher the dax, assumes that the new toy is the dax (Gopnik et al. 1999, 116–17). The child has figured out that we often talk about new things rather than familiar things and, therefore, associates the new word with the new thing in the room. At this stage, children have also figured out how to use the speaker's intentions to help understand meaning, so they will look to see where the speaker is looking when he or she says a word.

Around eighteen months, most children have also entered the two-word stage, in which they combine words in predictable patterns. For example:

Subject—Verb	"Kitty run"
Verb—Object	"Find Mommy"
Noun—Modifier	"Hotdog allgone"

By this stage, children demonstrate an understanding of basic grammatical relationships. In English, these relationships are expressed by word order, and children put subjects before verbs and objects after verbs. Even at this age, "Mommy find" and "find Mommy" mean different things. They also seem to understand that some word orders are allowable and some are disallowed. For example, children do not typically say "juice more" or "cat the" (after they have acquired the determiner *the*).

At eighteen months, English-speaking children rarely use inflectional endings (e.g., third-person singular *-s* on verbs) or function words (e.g., *a*, *the*). There are, of course, exceptions. At fourteen months, the nephew of one of the authors attached *the* to the beginning of almost all nouns: for example, "the car" for every car he saw on the street. Children learning languages in which inflectional endings play a more vital role in grammar than they do in English start using these endings earlier.

Deaf children (and hearing children exposed to sign language consistently as a form of communication) go through similar stages of language acquisition. Assuming they are exposed to sign language in their early years, deaf children first babble with their hands. Studies indicate that babies learning sign languages start making comparatively slow (compared to children learning spoken language) rhythmic hand gestures that imitate the rhythms of sign languages. These gestures mostly occur in front of their bodies, in the typical "signing space" of sign languages. Babies acquiring sign languages then produce one-sign and later two-sign utterances. Their sentences get longer and more complex at a rate comparable to that of hearing children.

Deaf children also struggle with some of the same grammatical constructions as hearing children. In American Sign Language, first- and second-person pronouns, which are called deictic ('pointing') forms in all languages, involve physical pointing. The sign for 'I' is the index finger pointing in toward the speaker; the sign for 'you' is the index finger pointing straight out toward the hearer. So it seems as if these signs' meanings might be transparent to deaf infants. Yet both hearing and deaf children tend not to use these pronouns during their second year, and when they do, they sometimes confuse the two. After all, the pronouns 'I' and 'you' are confusing: the referent is always shifting depending on who is speaking to whom. By the age of two and a half, both groups have sorted out these personal pronouns (Cattell 2000).

At all these early stages of the language acquisition process, children's production (what they say) lags behind their comprehension (what they understand). This gap is one clue to the distinction between linguistic competence and linguistic performance. At twelve months old, when children are producing maybe ten words, they probably comprehend between 50 and 200 words. When children are only combining two words in their own speech, they can understand sentences of much greater complexity. Some psychologists argue that part of the "terrible twos" is the frustration of knowing there are so many things that others can communicate and not yet having the grammatical knowledge to do so. Steven Pinker (1988) points out that by the two-word stage, children have many of the components of more complex utterances, but they have not yet mastered the grammar needed to

Language Acquisition at Work

Deaf Children Learning ASL

American Sign Language (ASL) is a language like any other, with its own lexicon and grammar. It is different from other sign languages around the world, such as British Sign Language and German Sign Language, and it is not related to American English. While users of ASL will sometimes spell out English words that do not have a sign, ASL is not "English told in signs." It has its own lexicon and grammar.

The roots of ASL go as far back as the late 1700s, and one of the most significant factors in its development was the establishment of a school for the deaf in 1817 by American Thomas Hopkins Gallaudet and Frenchman Laurent Clerc. This joint educational merger introduced French Sign Language to the Americas as the language of instruction, and it led to a mixing of French Sign Language and the sign language already used in the Americas to create what is known as American Sign Language. In the almost two centuries since then, ASL has diverged from French Sign Language, although the two still share some vocabulary items and grammatical structures.

Every sign in ASL is distinguished by three elements:

1. The configuration and orientation of the hand (e.g., palm up or down).

2. The position of the hand in the signing space (which is generally between the waist and head and just past the shoulders on each side).

3. The movement of the hand.

Like any other language, American Sign Language has grammatical rules for word order (in statements, questions, etc.) and for expressing negation, tense, modality, and so on. For example, to express negation, the sign for 'not' can be placed either before the verb or at the end of the sentence; all negative sentences are accompanied by a headshake and a squeezing together of the eyebrows. The signs for some verbs such as 'know' and 'want' have related variants, which include

Family

Mother

FIGURE 10.2 The American Sign Language (ASL) sign for "family" involves both hands, with three fingers extended and the index finger and thumb touching, beginning palm out and then moving in a circle until they face palm in. For the sign "mother," all fingers on the right hand are extended with the palm facing left, and the hand moves so the thumb touches or nears the chin twice.

(continued)

Deaf Children Learning ASL (continued)

an outward twisting motion that captures the negative meaning (e.g., 'not know' or 'not want'). Tense is typically expressed through "tense indicator" signs that can be translated as, for example, 'recently', 'in the distant past', 'in the near future', 'in the far future', and 'tomorrow'.

ASL is different from "signed English," a system devised by the hearing to help deaf children learn English. It has long been feared that deaf children would fall behind by learning ASL (but see the final section of

this chapter on bilingualism). Signed English draws many of its signs from ASL but adds signs for function words (e.g., *the*), affixes, tense, and other elements. So in signed English there is a sign to match every English word, including all function words and forms of *to be* (which ASL does not use). Some signs from finger spelling have been borrowed into ASL, but ASL remains a language independent of English. Some deaf speakers can code-switch between ASL and signed English.

put them all together in combination. Table 10.1, from a study by Roger Brown, shows utterances by three children that capture all the necessary parts of a complex sentence like *Mom gave John lunch in the kitchen*, but mostly only in two- and three-word bundles.

Acquisition of Words and Word Meaning

The average twelve-month-old knows between 50 and 200 words. According to one estimate, the average eighteen-year-old graduate from high school uses 60,000 words on a regular basis. That's a lot of words to learn over seventeen years! Although we often refer

TABLE 10.1   **Constituent Combinations That Occur and Constituents That Are Omitted from the Main Verb Paradigm**

Ordered Constituents Present	Constituents Omitted	Example
Agent-action-dative-object-locative	None	*Mother gave Jon lunch in the kitchen.* (nonoccurring)
Agent-action	Object	*Mommy fix.* (Eve I)
Agent-object	Action	*Mommy pumpkin.* (Eve I; *is cutting a*)
Agent-locative	Action	*Baby table.* (Eve I; *is eating at a*)
Action-dative	Agent, object	*Give doggie.* (Adam I; *you give it to*)
Action-object	Agent	*Hit ball.* (Adam I; *I*)
	Agent, locative	*Put light.* (Adam I; *I, there*)
Action-locative	Agent-object	*Put floor.* (Adam I; *I, it*)
Agent-action-object	None	*I ride horsie.* (Sarah I)
Agent-action-locative	None	*Tractor go floor.* (Adam I)
Action-dative-object	Agent	*Give doggie paper.* (Adam I)
Action-object-locative	Agent	*Put truck window.* (Adam I)
Agent-action-object-locative	None	*Adam put it box.* (Adam I)

Source: Reprinted and adapted by permission of the publisher from Roger Brown, *A First Language: The Early Stages*, 205. © 1973 by the President and Fellows of Harvard College.

to a word explosion or spurt starting around eighteen months, some scholars propose that young children's vocabulary growth may show a more gradual linear increase rather than an explosion (see Bloom 2000). It may feel like an explosion because if the child only has 100 words and learns 100 more, the child has doubled his or her vocabulary. But estimates of children's vocabulary development through elementary school show that they are learning the largest number of new words (over 12 per day) from eight- to ten years old, but fewer than two words a day at two-years-old (see Table 10.2). For eight-year-olds, that is almost one word per waking hour, according to an often quoted calculation by Susan Carey (1978). Word learning remains highly active throughout adolescence—after all, there are still approximately 20,000 words to learn to get to the 60,000 high school graduate average.

This description of lexical acquisition has left a fundamental question unanswered: How do children learn to associate particular sequences of sounds with specific things and ideas? It's a very complicated process. Let's imagine that you are playing with a small baby when your pet cat enters the room. You point and say, "Look! Cat." The child looks at the cat, but how does the child know what the word *cat* actually refers to? It could, of course, refer to the whole cat, but it could refer only to this specific cat (like the name *Morris*). It could refer to the cat's ear or tail or fur. It could refer to all furry things or all four-legged things or all breathing things or all moving things. It could also refer to the act of walking on four legs, given that this is what the cat is doing. (This conundrum should remind you of Quine's example of *gavagai* in Chapter 7.)

English-speaking children, at least, learn more nouns than verbs, adjectives, or adverbs at the early stages of language acquisition. At least two basic assumptions seem to inform children's lexical acquisition at early stages (Altmann 1997):

1. The word refers to the whole thing (e.g., the whole cat as opposed to its tail or fur).
2. If the child already knows a word for that thing, the new word is assumed to refer to a part of the thing—as opposed to, for example, being a synonym for the thing. Children growing up bilingual, however, learn that each language will have a different term for a given object.

Children also seem to show a bias toward assuming that a word refers to a class or kind of thing, rather than, for example, just that one instance of the class (e.g., *cat,* as opposed to Paws, the neighbor's cat). Researchers have been trying to figure out if children also tend to classify objects primarily at the "basic level," and if they do, why they do so. As we discussed in Chapter 7, there are hierarchies of classification, so that some

TABLE 10.2   **Approximate Rate of Word Acquisition for Children**

Child's Age	Approximate Rate of Word Acquisition
12 months–16 months	0.3 word per day
16 months–23 months	0.8 word per day
23 months–30 months	1.6 words per day
30 months–6 years	3.6 words per day
6 years–8 years	6.6 words per day
8 years–10 years	12.1 words per day

Source: Bloom (2000), 44.

words are hyponyms of others. To take an example with animals, linguists refer to categories at the species level, such as *cat,* as "basic": more specific than the more encompassing or more abstract (in terms of shared properties) *animal,* but more general than a specific kind of cat like *Siamese* or the name of one cat like *Mittens.* At the basic level, members of the category share relatively obvious features that are distinctive from other categories at that level—you can think of this as sharing features of the prototype of the category (see Chapter 7). In the example of *Daddyscar,* the child has assumed the basic-level category meaning of 'car' for the phrase, as opposed to the more specific reference to one particular car.

Children Learning Grammar

In their late twos through their mid threes, children become more and more fluent in their grammatical utterances, moving through the three-word stage to ever more complex grammatical constructions. This process often happens with such exponential growth that linguists have yet to discern all its stages. It is clear that sentence length continues to increase, as does the number of types of sentences a child controls (e.g., questions with *wh-* words, conjoined sentences). By the time most children are in their threes, they are using inflectional endings and function words more often than not (Pinker 1988).

Patterns of Children's Errors

None of these facts about acquisition means that children don't produce many ungrammatical utterances—because, in fact, they do. Why? And what are the patterns?

Some early sentences are ungrammatical because they do not yet contain all the necessary inflectional endings or function words. So a child may say, "Yesterday I play" without the inflectional *-ed,* or "You find shoe" without *the.* In the example at the beginning of the chapter, the child has not yet mastered all the regularities and irregularities of the third-person singular present-tense inflections in Standard English and is using *don't* rather than *doesn't* ("Macy don't have one"). Of course, if the child is learning a variety of English that has leveled all present-tense inflections, "Macy don't" is perfectly grammatical and regular in that variety.

Some sentences are ungrammatical because children seem to follow their own timeline, with predictable patterns, in terms of acquiring more complex constructions. For example, most researchers agree that children follow a predictable pattern of development in expressing negative sentences (Cattell 2000). There are three general stages:

1. The negative element occurs outside the main part of the utterance: "No you go" or "No shoe off."

2. The negative element becomes internal to the clause but typically without *do* support (some sentences will show *can't* and *don't*): "Car no go" or "Pizza not here," but also "Car can't go."

3. All the relevant auxiliaries are acquired and the negative element is consistently put after the auxiliary, as is done by adult speakers: "The car doesn't go" or "The pizza isn't here."

English has a relatively complex set of auxiliary verbs, and children have to master many aspects of auxiliary use in order to fully master negation in English. There is some dispute about whether the negative particle is always outside the utterance in stage 1. For example, "No you go" could represent "(I) no (want) you go."

Some sentences are ungrammatical because children overgeneralize or overextend rules once they acquire them. In this respect, children can appear to go backward in their learning curve. Linguists have described this learning curve, with its three major stages, as "u-shaped." When children are first learning verbs, for example, they are imitating what they hear. So they say "brought" when they hear it, along with "ate" and "went." Then, in the second stage, they figure out the general rule that the past tense for verbs in English is formed by adding the morpheme -ed (or more technically, one of its three allomorphs). Researchers test to see if children have acquired the rules for creating noun plurals and verb past tense by giving them made-up words and eliciting these forms: so "He ricks, and yesterday he _____" or "Here's a wug, and here are many _____" (you can now see why it is called the "wug-test").

Once they have acquired these rules, children from their late ones through late twos sometimes overapply them. They apply the past-tense rule to some irregular verbs as well as all regular ones, so they may say "bringed," "eated," and "goed." Sometimes this regularized form will override the exception they learned earlier, and sometimes the child will produce both. These errors are not as common as people think they are. In one study, they occurred with a mean of 4.2 percent and a median of 2.5 percent (Pinker 1988). Finally, in the third stage (and usually within a relatively short period of time), children have reached the other side of the "u" and produce irregular past-tense forms consistently.

How do children learn the exceptions? Is it that, when they say an overregularized, incorrect form like "goed" or "eated," a parental figure says, "No, no, it's *went*" or "It's *ate*"? Perhaps, but evidence indicates that this kind of correction does not actually occur that often or that consistently. Parents seem to let grammatical errors go, while correcting factual errors. Roger Brown commented on the odd outcome of this situation:

> this leads to an interesting paradox: if children are corrected for producing untruths, and are not corrected for producing bad grammar, how is it that the result of this regime is an adult who is adept at telling untruths but whose sentences are perfectly grammatical? (qtd. in Altmann 1997, 43)

Steven Pinker argues that children (and adults) follow a "blocking principle"—which he argues is innate. If the child knows an exception to a rule (e.g., that the past tense of *eat* is *ate*), this knowledge will block the application of the rule (e.g., that verbs form the past tense with a form of -ed) to this exceptional word. Early in their language learning, children may have only a weak memory trace to the irregular form that they have heard (e.g., *ate*), so the rule can override the trace (which would result in *eated*), until they have heard the irregular form more often.

Acquisition of Complex Grammatical Constructions

By the age of four, children have mastered most of the central structures of English syntax. For example, many of them have mastered passive constructions as well as yes-no questions and *wh-* questions. They continue to master some of the more complex constructions over the next five years or so (e.g., reflexive pronouns). By six years, most children stop assuming that the first event in a grammatical construction happened chronologically first—thus, they can consistently, correctly parse sentences that employ *before* and *after,* such as "Many linguists try out their own personal language acquisition experiments after they have children."

As even these brief descriptions of children's language acquisition indicate, the amount of learning that takes place in a child's mind during these early years is stunning. It may or may not surprise you to learn that by the age of two, a child's brain has reached adult levels of energy consumption. What may also surprise you is that by the age of three, the child's brain is twice as active as an average adult's brain, and it stays at this level until the child is nine or ten. Brain activity then gradually decreases until about eighteen, when it levels off at average adult levels (and when many students head to college). During these adolescent years, the brain is building neural connections and killing off little-used ones, thereby creating the neural pathways that characterize each person's brain.

Can we really be getting smarter as our brains get slower? Here's how three researchers of cognitive development explain it:

> If you combine the psychological and neurological evidence, it is hard to avoid concluding that babies are just plain smarter than we are, at least if being smart means being able to learn something new. The advantage we adults have comes precisely from the fact that we once were babies. We can use the finely tuned, specialized, well-oiled mental machinery we constructed when we were very young to do all sorts of things that babies can't. (Gopnik et al. 1999, 196)

This explanation is certainly food for thought, especially as you put hours into studying this book so that you can acquire conscious knowledge of linguistic information that your infant self learned with no conscious effort.

The Role of Parents in Language Acquisition

What exactly is the role of parents' speech to children in their language acquisition process? Clearly children need language input to learn. Children do not need specialized speech in order to learn language. In cultures in which parents do not typically speak directly to children or do not alter their speech to children, children learn the language with full fluency. But the fact is that around the world, in most cultures, adults speak to small children differently from the way they speak to each other.

Even the most articulate, highfalutin of speakers seem to abandon their skills in the vicinity of infants. The quality of our voices changes (the pitch rises and intonation becomes more dramatic). We lose our pronouns ("Look at Alexandra! What is Alexandra doing? Aunt Annie is here to visit!"). We use short sentences and repeat ourselves. And babies love it when we talk this way. In tests, they will choose to listen to "parentese," regardless of the content, over other kinds of speech.

What is it about putting a baby in our arms or sitting us on the floor with a toddler and a pile of toys that makes us talk like this? Right now, researchers do not have a definitive answer to the *why* question, but they have identified many characteristic features of "parentese."

Features of Parentese

The term **parentese** refers to the special version of a language that adults (parents and nonparents alike), and even older siblings (sometimes as young as four), use when talking to small children. It is sometimes referred to as "motherese" or as "child-directed speech" (CDS). We are using "parentese" because fathers do it, too, and they now often take on many of the duties involved in raising children. Parentese is much more than—and some would say very different from—the garbled utterances that adults some-times use with children, with mispronunciations and nonsense words (e.g., "Do-ee duckie-wuckies swim? What about a wabbit?"). Some of the typical features of parentese include:

- *More limited vocabulary.* The focus is often on body parts, food, names for people, animals, clothing, and similar local objects.

- *Repetition.* Adults may repeat up to 23 percent of their utterances when talk-ing with small children, according to one study (cited in Cattell 2000).

- *Slower rate of speech.* Slower speech facilitates more precise articulation.

- *Exaggerated intonation.* These more dramatic intonation patterns may help children hear "breaks" between phrases and clauses. The more "sing-songy" intonation patterns can also be comforting for children.

- *Lengthened vowels.* Some researchers argue that our vowels are more "pre-cise" or cleaned up in parentese, which could help children figure out proto-typical vowel forms.

- *Higher pitch.* Adults have lower pitch than children, and some researchers point out that by raising their pitch, adults are almost meeting children "halfway." It also can make speech highly expressive of emotional content and can capture children's attention.

- *Fewer verbs.* Parentese can be "noun-heavy," except for verbs like *do* and *go*.

- *Focus on the "here and now."* Talking about what is happening in the child's immediate vicinity at that moment makes more referents available and obvi-ous for figuring out meaning.

- *Names rather than pronouns.* Adults often substitute proper names or repeated nouns for pronouns. Pronouns are relatively difficult for children to understand because they do not have a consistent referent or meaning (e.g., "I" can mean Mommy or Daddy or anyone else, just as "he" can refer to all kinds of males).

- *Phonetic simplification of some words.* Sometimes words will be made pho-netically "easier"—for example, by shortening them ("Gramma") or by sub-stituting another word ("boo-boo").

You may already have realized that many of these features also characterize the way some adults talk to animals—as well as to other adults who happen to be their girlfriends or boyfriends, spouses or partners—which suggests that intimacy is central to the success of parentese as an element in child language acquisition.

Role of Parentese

One controversial question about parentese is how necessary or useful it is for child lan-guage acquisition. As we discussed earlier, it seems that children can learn language just from listening to adults talk with other adults as well as from listening to adults talk to them as though they were adults. Parentese provides simplified structures from which children can learn (e.g., shorter sentences, fewer verbs, few pronouns) and clarification of structures (vowel elongation, word and sentence repetition, exaggerated intonation). Children obviously need to hear all the complex kinds of sentences involved in a language in order to figure out how to create them, but parentese may provide helpful input at the early stages, when children are figuring out the "language code."

Language Acquisition in Special Circumstances

Not all children have access to full-fledged languages when they are young. For example, deaf children born to hearing parents who don't know or don't use sign language may have only a simplified set of home signs with which to communicate until they get access to other language instruction. Other children, in specific kinds of language contact situations, are born into communities where a pidgin language is spoken.

Pidgins and Creoles

Pidgins are highly simplified communicative systems that arise when adult speakers who share no common language need to communicate with each other. Pidgins have been created historically in trading communities (e.g., on the west coast of Africa) and on plantations when workers were brought from a range of language communities (e.g., in Jamaica and Hawaii), among other circumstances. Pidgins tend to employ many nouns, and their content tends to be highly functional in terms of ways to refer to place, time, direction, or relevant actions. Pidgins typically employ few if any grammatical forms such as tense markers or pronouns. Speakers of pidgins may not use the same word order—or the same set of words—to express a given meaning. Pidgins are never the native language of any of their speakers.

If speakers in a stable pidgin-speaking community have children and the children are exposed to the pidgin as their home language, the language that the children create as their native language is called a **creole**. Creoles are full-fledged languages. They retain much of the vocabulary of the pidgin, but they have productive grammatical systems that include, for example, rules for word order, the use of pronouns, and the use of tense. So Hawaiian Pidgin is actually a creole, and it is now often referred to in the literature as Hawaiian Creole English.

As the outcome of contact between two or more languages, the lexicon of creoles will typically be based on one language—usually called the "lexifier language" because that is where much of the vocabulary originates. Some of the grammatical rules may resemble grammatical rules in one of the contact languages, but other grammatical rules are typically unique to the creole (and sometimes shared with other creole languages around the world). There are English-based, French-based, Portuguese-based, and many other types of creoles around the world.

We talk more about pidgins and creoles in Chapter 11, but the relevant question here is: where does the grammar of creole languages come from? Although much of the vocabulary originates in the contact languages, there will often be other forms, particularly grammatical forms, that cannot be found in any of the contact languages. In addition, the rules for word order, the inflectional system, the pronouns, and other parts of the language may differ from any of the source contact languages. What seems to happen is that the children, who are communicating with each other and thereby reinforcing the system that they create, impose or invent grammar for the language input that they hear, in this case the simplified input of a pidgin.

Many creoles around the world share features with one another—features that they do not necessarily share with their contact languages. These common features may be one useful window onto the "hard wiring" for language in the human brain, but that remains a disputed question among researchers of these language varieties.

Let's look at one example of a creole language that many linguists think has been "born" in the past thirty years.

Nicaraguan Sign Language

A potentially dramatic example of "the birth of a language" has been recorded in Nicaragua over the past three decades. Until the Sandinista revolution in 1979, deaf children in Nicaragua were highly stigmatized and usually kept at home; they received no schooling and were not allowed to marry. To be deaf was to be isolated from language and from the learning that can happen through language. Deaf children often had a few home signs, but they had no full-fledged sign language. In the 1980s, the first schools for the deaf were opened in Managua, and adolescents from around the country were brought to the school. Within a very short period of time, the teenagers were communicating with each other using a combination of the home signs that different students had brought with them, along with other signs that they created. It was, from all reports, a signed pidgin. The teachers, with very little training in the teaching of the deaf, were using primarily signed Spanish with the students (despite the fact that the students had had no prior exposure to Spanish), which seems to have had little effect on the communicative system that they developed.

In the 1980s, deaf children and adolescents in Nicaragua were brought together in schools, and they created a new sign language. These children sign with the new creole sign language, Idioma de Signos Nicaraguenese (ISN) or Nicaraguan Sign Language (NSL).

Within a few years, younger children were enrolled in the school. In 1986, Judy Kegl, a professor at the University of Southern Maine, went to Nicaragua to consult with the school about their program, and she describes her amazement at what she saw happening at the school. After arriving at the school and seeing the sign system used by the older students, the young students were signing with each other fluently, using a system clearly related to but different from the older students' language. These children appeared to have created grammar. The language is called Idioma de Signos Nicaraguense (ISN) or Nicaraguan Sign Language (NSL). With other creole languages, there is always the question of whether children have learned grammar from other languages spoken in the home or community and have then applied that knowledge to the pidgin input. In the situation in Nicaragua, however, these young children did not have access to any other languages from which to learn about grammatical structures, and yet NSL shares grammatical features with other creoles and other sign languages.

While some scholars assert that the development of ISN supports the existence of an innate, "universal grammar" in humans, other scholars disagree. Another team of researchers from the University of Haifa are examining the Al Sayyid Bedouin Sign Language, which also seems to have developed spontaneously, in this case in an isolated village in the Negev Desert (Sandler et al. 2005). It is not related to Israeli or Jordanian sign languages, and it does not seem to have been influenced by spoken languages in the region. Of particular interest, this new sign language uses subject-object-verb word order, which is the most common word order in the world's languages. These new languages will undoubtedly continue to be the focus of serious study for years to come.

Critical Age Hypothesis

Is there an age at which it becomes more difficult if not almost impossible for us to learn another language with nativelike fluency? Many of us have anecdotal evidence that this seems to be the case. Families move to another country and, within very short periods of time, the five- and six-year-old children have made friends at school, talk fluently with neighbors and shopkeepers, and translate for their parents, who have struggled to pick up a few words and phrases to get by. When we're children, we seem to learn language just by being exposed to it. As adults, while we certainly seem to do better when we're immersed in a language, we still seem to require more explicit instruction, and even then we do not become as fluent or sound as native as do children. Of course, other factors may inhibit adult language learning: distractions, fear of embarrassing ourselves by making mistakes, or more limited exposure. But many linguists believe there is more going on than just external factors.

Critical Periods

Critical periods for learning are attested in other species. One of the most often cited examples is the white-crowned male sparrow, which must hear and learn the sparrows' song within the first twenty to fifty days of its life or the sparrow will not be able to sing it like the other sparrows.

Perhaps unsurprisingly, given the number of changes going on in the human body, puberty seems to be an important time in terms of language learning. The critical age for learning languages with fluency, many linguists argue, seems to be before puberty. Here is a summary of findings from three leading researchers in the field (Gopnik et al. 1999):

- From ages three to seven, children learning a second language perform on tests like native speakers.

- From age eight to puberty, children's performance on these kinds of second-language tests gradually declines.

- After puberty, there is no correlation between age and linguistic skill; overall, older speakers' performance with a second (or third, etc.) language is worse than children's performance.

Testing the critical age hypothesis for first-language acquisition is difficult because it would require systematically depriving children of language input until a specific age. So most studies focus on exceptional, and usually very sad, circumstances in which children have been deprived of language for other reasons. The language-learning situation of Nicaraguan Sign Language provides one kind of evidence for the critical age hypothesis. The young children at the school became fluent speakers of a sign language, with additional grammar, in ways that the older children did not. The best-known case study of critical age and language learning involves Genie, sometimes referred to as a modern-day "wild child" because of her lack of human contact and language input until a relatively late age.

A Case Study: Genie

Genie was found in California in 1970 at the age of thirteen and a half, when her mother, who was almost blind, left her abusive husband and went to a government office, with Genie, about receiving assistance. It turned out to be a horrific case of child abuse. Until that time, Genie had spent most of her life tied to a potty chair in a closed room by herself. At night she slept confined in a sleeping bag in a crib. Her father and brother sometimes barked at her, but she received no other language input. She was beaten if she made noise. When she was found, her physical development was that of about a six-year-old, and she had trouble walking because of her confinement. She also had no language.

A set of psychologists and linguists began studying Genie's development in a world with physical freedom, human contact, and language. She lived with one researcher as a foster parent, and her progress was carefully recorded and studied (with a series of grants from 1970 to 1975), as much as the researchers felt was ethical while trying to provide her with a caring home. The major linguistic question was whether, at this age, Genie could learn language as other children do. The overall findings indicate that she could not. After four years, she had produced only about 2,500 spontaneous utterances of two or more words. She acquired a vocabulary that, while limited compared to another speaker her age, allowed her basic communication. But she never mastered many of the fundamental grammatical structures of English, including negation, question formation, relative clauses, passives, and tense and aspect distinctions.

Genie's case seems to indicate that she may have come to language too late, that she did not have sufficient exposure to language during the critical years to become a fluent speaker. But her case is complicated because we do not know whether her difficulties were caused by brain damage (her father claimed, before he committed suicide preceding the trial, that she was mentally retarded) or emotional damage—or both. The unfortunate end to the story is that after her mother gave up custody, Genie went through a series of foster homes in which she sometimes suffered abuse and other trauma. She is now in an adult-care home.

Genie's case is often contrasted with that of Isabelle, an illegitimate child who was hidden in a closed, dark room with her deaf-mute mother until she was found at the age of six. Isabelle underwent intensive training and language exposure. She learned physically to articulate words and went on to acquire language rapidly. She spoke like her peers, in terms of grammar and vocabulary, within about two years. Researchers working on another case suggest the age for relatively normal language acquisition could be raised to about nine years old (Vargha-Khadem et al. 1997). Alex, a boy with Sturge-Weber syndrome who failed to develop speech, had his left cerebral hemisphere removed and was taken off anticonvulsants at the age of nine. He quickly acquired language, and by the age of fifteen, he achieved language comprehension and production (including fluent phonology and syntax) that placed him at the level of normally developing children eight to ten years old. Complicating factors in this case include Alex's low IQ, the extent to which the right hemisphere had been reorganized for language processing at an earlier age, and the linguistic capacity of an isolated right hemisphere.

Acquisition of Languages Later in Life

Linguists are not sure how to explain what happens in the human brain that makes learning a language later in life so difficult. Findings in neuroscience suggest that experience changes our brains, as certain pathways or synapses are formed to facilitate processing and others die off (or never form). Children's brains seem to be more plastic than adults' brains—more able to adapt to new experiences and lay down new circuitry. As you can see, the analogy to computers really has been useful.

Another possible analogy for language learning is mapping. When we learn languages early in life, we create a map for the grammar (including phonology, morphology, and syntax) and lexicon. If we learn multiple languages while we are young, we create a map for each one. At some point, these maps become more fixed and we become less able to create new maps, so if we learn a new language, we are to some extent mapping through the grammar of the language(s) that we already know. Yet "mapping" is undoubtedly still an imperfect analogy. It remains very difficult to know exactly how our brains learn—and struggle to learn—languages.

Studies using brain imaging suggest that something different is happening in the brain when speakers learn a language (in this case, typically a second language) before versus after puberty. As you will read in the next section, it appears that different modules in our left hemisphere take on the primary responsibility for processing open-class words (nouns, verbs, adjectives, adverbs, derivational morphemes) and for processing closed-class words (function words, inflectional morphemes). One study documented on the video *Pieces of Mind* (1997) examines two bilingual speakers, both students in the United States at the time. Arthur Goh, born in Singapore, first learned English in school at the age of three or four. Nick Hong, born in Vietnam, began learning English around the age of ten. The pictures of brain activity for Arthur when he is processing language input resemble those for monolingual native speakers of English, with a division of processing in terms of brain activity. Open-class words are processed in one area of the brain and closed-class words in another. Nick, who learned English later in life, shows brain activity all over the left hemisphere for both classes of words. In other words, his brain has not cognitively made the grammatical distinctions for English that he has made for his native language.

Learning a language later in life usually also means having a nonnative accent. As we discussed earlier in this chapter, infants learn to pay attention to the phonemic distinctions in their own language(s) and ignore those that are not relevant. At some point, it becomes very difficult for adult speakers to hear phonemic distinctions present in other languages but not in their own, which makes producing these distinctions difficult as well. In addition, speakers of syllable-time languages (in which all syllables receive equal weight in terms of timing) such as French or Hindi will often impose this prosodic structure on stress-timed languages (in which primary stress occurs at regular intervals) such as English, and vice versa. Phonology from one's native language interferes with pronunciation of a new one.

When Things Go Wrong

A number of conditions can impair language acquisition. Among the more well known are aphasia and dyslexia. Research on these conditions has led to insights about language acquisition and processing. For example, study of aphasia—the study of language loss rather than acquisition—has allowed scientists to locate some linguistic brain functions relatively precisely within the brain's geography. Aphasia can result from strokes or "highly targeted" injuries to the brain (e.g., an arrow piercing one part of the brain). The two types of aphasia that have received the most attention in language research are Broca's aphasia and Wernicke's aphasia.

Broca's Aphasia

Broca's aphasia affects language production more than language comprehension. Broca's aphasia and the part of the left hemisphere called Broca's area are named for the French physician Pierre-Paul Broca (1824–1880), who discovered its influence on language (see Figure 10.3). If someone sustains damage to Broca's area, in the frontal lobe, he or she loses some degree of syntactic ability. People with Broca's aphasia typically understand and use open-class words, but they find it difficult, sometimes impossible, to construct comprehensible sentences. They lose the capacity to apply inflectional morphemes, so that number and tense and verbal aspect may disappear from their speech. They drop function words, like prepositions and articles, from their sentences. In other words, Broca's aphasics seem to lose access to many if not most closed-class morphemes or words. Here's an often cited example of the speech of a Broca's aphasic, who seems to be trying to say that he, or his father, had a dentist's appointment (Carroll 1999):

> Yes . . . ah . . . Monday . . . er Dad and Peter H . . . [the patient's name], and Dad . . . er hospital . . . and ah . . . Wednesday . . . Wednesday nine o'clock . . . and oh . . . Thursday . . . ten o'clock, ah doctors . . . two . . . an' doctors . . . and er . . . teeth . . . yah.

Sometimes Broca's aphasics also invert terms, as in *Dirt dig shovel.* However, not all aphasics exhibit all symptoms of their syndromes.

Broca's aphasics maintain a reasonable level of language comprehension, particularly with sentences with subject-verb-object order. With SVO order, the listener can assume who/what acts upon who/what based on the order of the words. So a sentence such as *Susan ate spaghetti last night* is fairly easy to understand in terms of general meaning, even without access to tense. However, a sentences such as *Susan was hit by a bicycle last night* relies much more heavily on syntax for meaning (if one relied on word order, it might seem that Susan hit a bicycle), and Broca's aphasics struggle more with comprehension of such sentences.

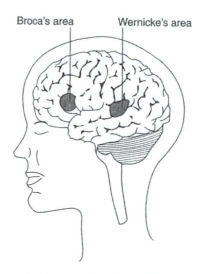

Broca's area   Wernicke's area

FIGURE 10.3 Wernicke's area and
Broca's area refer to specific parts of
the left hemisphere of the brain that
are responsible for different aspects
of language processing.
From the Dr. Joseph E. Smith Medical Library.

Broca's area is immediately next to a center of motor control essential to speech
production, one responsible for the jaws, lips, and tongue. For a long time, brain scientists
assumed that damage to Broca's area resulted in the usually slow, labored speech of
Broca's aphasics because it affected motor control, but Broca's area is probably not involved
in the physical aspects of speech production: Broca's aphasics exhibit the same difficulties with written language and (where relevant) with signing as they do with speech.

Broca's area is probably not uniquely responsible for syntactic abilities, although it
is a center of such activity in the brain. Stroke victims, for instance, who may suffer
damage there, often fully recover their powers of speech after therapy. But those who
suffer damage both to Broca's area and to other parts of the surrounding **cortex**, the tissue composed of "gray matter" that folds in on itself over and over (so that a very large
brain can fit into the shapely human head), endure catastrophic language loss. It is by no
means clear how the cortex is involved in language acquisition, development, or use.

Wernicke's Aphasia

Wernicke's area, named for Carl Wernicke (1848–1904), the physician who discovered
the relation of the area to language, lies just across the Sylvian fissure from Broca's area
(Figure 10.3). Damage to Wernicke's area also produces an aphasia, but of a kind significantly different from Broca's aphasia. Speakers who suffer from **Wernicke's aphasia** usually speak fluidly, but their sentences contain misapplied words or nonsense words that
substitute for the intended ones. In other words, the fluency of their speech production is
not impaired, but their ability to create substantively meaningful utterances is. Wernicke's
aphasics also seem to lose much of their ability to comprehend the language of others.

Language Variation at Work

Verbal Slips

Sometimes we seem to get ahead of ourselves, anticipating a sound to come, so we might say "wish a brush" rather than "with a brush." Sometimes we do the opposite and hold onto a sound from an earlier word: "big bilch" for "big belch." And sometimes we reverse sounds or words: "crockers and braccoli" for "crackers and broccoli," "wall on the picture" for "picture on the wall." The first two kinds of verbal slips are called **anticipation** and **preservation**, respectively. The third kind of verbal slip, which involves metathesis, is sometimes known as a **Spoonerism**, when the reversal results in meaningful English words that create a humorous meaning. Reverend William Archibald Spooner (1844–1930), a professor at Oxford University, was well known among the undergraduates for his outrageous verbal slips of this type: "You have hissed all my mystery lectures"; "a well-boiled icicle" (a well-oiled bicycle); and "Give three cheers for our queer old dean" when toasting Queen Victoria. We learn several things from these three kinds of verbal slips: we already have words in mind before we utter them; phonemes (and clusters of phonemes) exist as independent units that can be moved; slips involve equivalent units, so we do not exchange, for example, a phoneme and a word or a preposition and a noun.

Another kind of verbal slip, a **malapropism**, indicates that words with similar phonological structure are connected somehow in language processing. In Richard Sheridan's eighteenth-century play *The Rivals* (1775), Mrs. Malaprop (whose name is derived from French *mal a propos* 'inappropriate'), in her attempt to use highfalutin words, has a tendency to use the wrong—but similar-sounding—word: *pineapple* for *pinnacle*, *hydrostatics* for *hysterics*. Although we may not slip this way as often as Mrs. Malaprop, we all use an infectious—oops, infelicitous—word now and again.

Sometimes Wernicke's aphasics replace a word with one related from the same lexical field, like *cat* for *dog,* in a sentence like *I wish the cat would stop barking.* Or they invert sounds within a word, as one does in metathesis: *birds* can become *brids,* and so on. Or a child will throw a *rantrum* rather than a *tantrum,* partly because the two words rhyme, partly because ranting is part of a tantrum; at times, a semantic relationship between the alternates is brought out in a bit of creative morphology. Some Wernicke's aphasics use few content words at all, repeating syntactic variations of phrases with little meaning (e.g., "for the cat with the cat for the cat with him from there"). So Wernicke's aphasia seems to affect one's lexical abilities: the "look-up" function necessary to choose aptly from the mental dictionary malfunctions.

Studies of brain activity, as well as of aphasia, indicate that we process open-class and closed-class words in different parts of the brain. In a famous article titled "Two Aspects of Language and Two Types of Aphasic Disturbances," Roman Jakobson discusses these two kinds of aphasia in relation to the two axes of language that he proposed: metaphoric/paradigmatic and metonymic/syntagmatic (see Chapter 9). Wernicke's aphasia affects the metaphoric/paradigmatic axis or the ability to select among similar words, while the ability to create contiguous strings of words remains relatively intact. Broca's aphasia affects the metonymic/syntagmatic axis or the ability to create contiguous strings of words, yet the ability to select appropriate lexical items for reference remains relatively intact. Jakobson argues that these two kinds of aphasia demonstrate the separateness of the two functions in language: selection and combination.

Dyslexia

The definition of dyslexia goes far beyond the letter reversals or mirror images most commonly associated with the disorder. **Dyslexia** can refer to deficits that impair a person's ability to understand written language (i.e., reading and writing), or it can be defined more broadly. The International Dyslexia Association provides the following definition:

> Dyslexia is a specific learning disability that is neurological in origin. It is characterized by difficulties with accurate and/or fluent word recognition and by poor spelling and decoding abilities. These difficulties typically result from a deficit in the phonological component of language that is often unexpected in relation to other cognitive abilities and the provision of effective classroom instruction.

The exact cause of dyslexia is unknown. It seems to have genetic links, so people with a dyslexic relative have higher odds of also being dyslexic. It is not linked to intelligence. And it is relatively common, affecting 4–10 percent of the population. Ads to raise awareness of dyslexia highlight the many famous and very successful people with dyslexia—Whoopi Goldberg, Tom Cruise, Albert Einstein, and many more.

To understand the categories of dyslexia, you need some information about how humans learn to read. Unlike speaking, reading and writing must be taught to children. First, children must realize that the written symbols correspond in some consistent way to spoken language, be that sounds or syllables. Gerry Altmann (1997, 168–70) outlines two basic steps that most children then go through in learning to read:

1. Children develop a "sight" vocabulary. That is, they associate the shape of a word as it appears on the page with a spoken word, but they do not necessarily parse the written word letter by letter and sound by sound. (It is unclear if children taught from the beginning with phonics go through this stage in the same way.)

2. As they read more, children develop their understanding of the letter-to-sound correspondence (i.e., they "spell out" the sounds of a written word), using this as an additional route to word recognition.

Proficient adult readers rely primarily on their sight vocabulary as the direct route to word meanings, especially for more commonly encountered words, which involves recognizing the shape of the word. For less familiar and unknown words, adults must rely on an understanding of the letter-to-sound correspondence. And as we all know from trying to pronounce words we have never seen before, we do not always get it right. Many of us probably would not guess that *epitome,* for example, has four syllables, or that *victuals* is pronounced the same way as the revised spelling in the cat food "Tender Vittles."

There are two basic types of dyslexia: (1) developmental dyslexia, which children have from birth; and (2) acquired dyslexia, which can be caused by damage to the left hemisphere. Acquired dyslexia can take at least three different forms (Altmann 1997):

- **Deep dyslexia**: when reading aloud, speakers substitute either a synonym or a phonologically similar word (e.g., *sympathy* for *symphony*) for the word on the page.

- **Phonological dyslexia**: speakers struggle with reading aloud unfamiliar and nonsense words, as they seem to have impaired access to the letter-to-sound correspondence.

- **Surface dyslexia**: speakers have significant trouble reading aloud words with irregular spellings, as they rely heavily on the letter-to-sound correspondence and seem to have impaired access to a sight vocabulary (the direct association between the shape of a word and its meaning and sound).

Developmental dyslexia is diagnosed primarily through comparison with other children of a similar age: typically, when a child is eighteen to twenty-four months behind in reading skills and shows no other signs of development deficits. For many children, dyslexia involves a phonological deficit. Dyslexic children may have trouble playing games that involve breaking a word into its component sounds or rhyming words. Dyslexic children would struggle to answer the question "What is *bat* without 'b'?" At a later age, dyslexic children may have trouble naming the letters of the alphabet from a written source. In terms of reading, dyslexic children often struggle with the letter-to-sound correspondence in a language like English. But even these general assertions about dyslexia are controversial, as some dyslexic children do not seem to develop a sight vocabulary (Altmann 1997). For some dyslexics, every time they see a written word, it is as if they have never seen that word before, even if it is a common word. New studies are examining whether intensive, systematic instruction in phonics and phonemic awareness can help change the brain activation patterns in dyslexic children and thereby help them read more like unimpaired children.

In an interview for the Academy of Achievement in 1994, Whoopi Goldberg described her childhood experience with dyslexia:

> When I was a kid they didn't call it dyslexia. They called it . . . you know, you were slow, or you were retarded, or whatever. And so, I learned from a guy who was running a program who I met one day and he had written out on a board a sentence.
> And I said to him, "You know, I can't read that."
> And he said, "Why not?" And I said, "Because it doesn't make any sense to me." So he said, "Well, write down what you see under each. Whatever you see, write exactly what you see underneath." And so, he brought me to letters by coordinating what I saw to something called an A, or a B, or a C, or a D, and that was pretty cool. . . .
> What you can never change is the effect that the words "dumb" and "stupid" have on young people. So we must always be vigilant when those two words get stuck in our throat. "Hey, dummy! God, you're so stupid." You know. Just remember that what those leave you with are forever, you know.

Every child's experience with dyslexia is different, as are the teaching methods that work for each child. But we should always be aware of the potentially destructive consequences of not understanding dyslexia as a neurological condition that affects the way children process written language and of categorizing these children as "slow" or "dumb." Sally Shaywitz, a neuroscientist and professor of pediatrics at Yale who specializes in dyslexia, explains: "Dyslexic readers can be as smart as anything, but they can't read fast. Schools, universities, employers need to accommodate their need for extra time; it's as physiological as a diabetic's need for insulin" (Ackerman 2004, 54).

Special Focus: Children and Bilingualism

Given all this information about child language acquisition, you may wonder: Should children be raised bilingually? At what age should they learn other languages? It used to be believed that a child's attempt to learn more than one language hindered his or her cognitive development, but these theories have been discredited. Some scholars even argue now that multilingual children often do better in some subjects, like math, because they already understand the nature of symbolic systems, including the arbitrary relationship in a sign between the signifier and signified.

Children Learning Two Languages

Children raised in bilingual homes or communities often pass through the early stages of language acquisition later than other children. After all, they have two sets of language input to sort through in figuring out how to construct grammatical utterances in both languages. Some studies indicate that children achieve these milestones more quickly if they can link a language to a person. For example, Mom speaks English and Dad speaks Swahili, or Mom speaks Korean and Teacher Joe speaks English. But even if the languages are mixed, the children sort them out and catch up quickly in terms of fluency (in this case, in two languages) with their monolingual peers.

In many cultures and countries around the world, multilingualism is a part of daily life and constitutes "normal" language acquisition for all children—not necessarily either a cognitive feat or hindrance. In countries like India, South Africa, Malaysia, Switzerland, and many more, speakers learn multiple languages because they participate in multilingual communities in which different languages are used by various speakers for different purposes. In many countries where English is not the primary language, children start learning English as an additional language fairly early and intensively in their schooling. For example, in Sweden, English instruction is part of the mandatory curriculum for children starting at the age of seven. Required foreign-language classes for K–12 students in the United States start comparatively late, typically when students are somewhere between twelve and fifteen years of age.

Bilingual Education Programs

In the United States, bilingual education has become a controversial political issue. At stake in the debate for many Americans is national unity: How can the United States stand united if people don't all speak the same language? Multilingualism has a long history in the United States. At present, Spanish is the second most commonly spoken language in the country, behind English, but for a long time it was German. At this moment in the United States, despite the concerns voiced in debates over bilingual education and the increasing linguistic diversity of the population, the status of English as a shared language does not appear to be threatened by other languages. Although many immigrants bring other languages with them and may speak them at home or at work, census data indicate over 95 percent of American citizens report speaking at least good or very good English.

The burden for educating all U.S. children in English and the question of whether to promote childhood bilingualism fall to the schools. Bilingual education programs can take many forms. We provide only a brief overview of three possibilities here.

- Immersion programs (sometimes referred to as "sink-or-swim" programs) and early-exit programs: These programs are designed to mainstream Limited English Proficiency (LEP) children as quickly as possible. The rationale is that children learn best if immersed in the foreign language (in this case, English). For example, Proposition 227 in California, which was passed in

1998, mandates that children can receive native-language instruction in all their school subjects for a maximum of one school year, unless there are special circumstances. After that, they study all subjects with their native English-speaking peers.

- Developmental or late-exit programs: These programs are designed to move children into an all-English curriculum gradually. The rationale is that children can transfer literacy in a home language to English and that if they understand a subject matter in part through their home language, they will be better able to study it in English as well. In these programs, after first receiving instruction primarily in their home language, children begin to move to English-based instruction in subjects like math and science and finally in subjects like history and language arts.

- Dual-language programs: In one form of these programs, all children in a given school—native speakers of English and of other languages—receive instruction in two languages. The goal is to make *all* the children bilingual. Some programs split the day between languages or teach different subjects in different languages. Some programs move from instruction primarily in one language in early grades (e.g., Spanish) to a more split language curriculum in middle years and to a more English-dominant curriculum later. And there are many other variations.

The aim of all bilingual programs is to educate children in fluent academic English. Another goal of many bilingual programs is the maintenance of home languages. So the question becomes, how can children's home languages be reinforced as valuable parts of their culture, their identity, and their linguistic repertoire if they are taught only in English and allowed to speak only English at school?

Needless to say, bilingual education is an enormously complicated issue. There are school districts across the United States in which the children bring up to 100 different home languages to school. Studies assessing the effectiveness of both early-exit and late-exit bilingual programs are contested. And the political debate about bilingual education has intensified, with ballot initiatives in several states over whether to fund bilingual education programs.

Do you speak more than one language fluently? Do you wish you did? Many of you will undoubtedly become involved in these complicated questions as parents, voters, and educators, if not policy makers. Knowledge about how language acquisition works will help make for an ever better informed debate about these important topics.

☑ Summary

This chapter has described children's early stages of language acquisition and what language acquisition and loss can reveal about how language is processed in the human brain.

- For most speakers, the majority of language processing occurs in the left hemisphere of the brain. Specific areas in the left hemisphere are responsible for particular kinds of language (e.g., closed- versus open-class morphemes).

- Imitation alone cannot explain children's acquisition of language. Humans seem to have an innate cognitive capacity for language.

- Young children actively construct grammar from the language input they receive—and in the case of some creole languages, children receive more limited input and still create complex grammar.

- Young children undergo predictable stages in the acquisition of language: the identification and articulation of the phonemes of their native language(s); the one-word stage, the two-word stage, and then an exponential growth in vocabulary; the gradual acquisition of more complex grammatical forms, including both the regular patterns and the exceptions.

- After a certain critical age, around puberty, language acquisition seems to become more difficult for most speakers; to what extent the causes are cognitive and to what extent social remains an open question.

Suggested Reading

Several highly accessible and interesting books about language acquisition are currently available, including *Ascent of Babel* (1997) by Gerry T. M. Altmann, *What Infants Know: The New Cognitive Science of Early Development* (1994) by J. Mehler and E. Dupoux, *Children's Language: Consensus and Controversy* (2000) by Ray Cattell, and *The Scientist in the Crib* (1999) by Alison Gopnik, Andrew Meltzoff, and Patricia Kuhl. Steven Pinker's *Language Instinct* (1994) summarizes many of his and others' studies about language acquisition. For an authoritative treatment of word acquisition, see Paul Bloom's *How Children Learn the Meaning of Words* (2000). *First Language Acquisition: The Essential Readings* (2004), edited by Barbara C. Lust and Claire Foley, and *The Child Language Reader* (2004), edited by Kate Trott et al., contain articles not only on many of the topics covered here, but also on children's acquisition of, for example, communicative competence, narrative structure, and metaphor. Eve V. Clark's "Morphology in Language Acquisition," in *The Handbook of Morphology* (1998), edited by Andrew Spencer and Arnold M. Zwicky, is an excellent summary of issues in the field. A useful one-hour television program about Genie, prepared for WGBH in Boston, is "Secret of the Wild Child" (1994) by Jane Garmon. Michael Erard's *Um . . . Slips, Stumbles, and Verbal Blunders, and What They Mean* (2007) is full of entertaining information about verbal slips. James Crawford's book *Bilingual Education: History, Politics, Theory, and Practice* (4th ed., 1999) provides a useful introduction to the topic of bilingual education.

Exercises
Exercise 10.1   Learning Sounds

This exercise provides a brief review of phonology. At ten months old, a baby in a family that speaks American English will hear and respond to which of the following distinctions?

a. [m] and [n]

b. [n] and [ŋ]

c. [p] and [b]

d. [p] and [pʰ]

e. [l] and [r]

f. [w] and [ʍ]

g. [ɑ] and [ɔ]

h. [i] and [ɪ]

i. [ɛ] and [ɪ]

Exercise 10.2   Learning Words

When children are acquiring words, there will be large lexical gaps, or things for which they have no words. Given what you know about how children learn words, explain why you think they might fill gaps in the following ways (examples from Clark 1988):

a. New verbs:

"You have to scale it."

"I'm crackering my soup."

"We already decorationed the tree."

"We're going to cast it." (in reference to a broken arm)

b. New subcategories of things:

"plate-egg" and "cup-egg"

"house-smoke" (from chimney) and "car-smoke" (from tailpipe)

"fire-dog" (for dog found at the site of a fire)

c. New agent nouns:

"garden-man" (gardener)

"rat-man" (man who works with rats in a psychology lab)

"smile-person" (someone who smiles at people)

Exercise 10.3   Learning Grammar

1. What kind of overregularization has happened in this sentence produced by a young child (Pinker 1988)?

I love cut-upped egg.

2. A computational study of the Brown corpus of written texts (cited in Pinker 1988) provided a list of the top ten most common verbs:

be	go
have	take
do	come
say	see
make	get

   a. You will notice that all of these verbs are irregular in the formation of the past tense and/or past participle, if not more. So all ten of the most common verbs in English are irregular. How would you explain this correlation?

   b. For each verb, predict an overregularization error that a child might make.

3. Imagine that you are interested in determining how early children can comprehend (not produce) passive constructions. When children are first learning language, they interpret nouns that come before the verb as subjects, and nouns that come after the verb as objects. So they parse a noun-verb-noun sentence as S-V-O, no matter what grammatical forms might be present to indicate otherwise (for example, *kissed* versus *was kissed* or the presence of *by* before the second noun).

   Given what you have learned so far about how studies of child language acquisition are often designed, design your own study to test children's comprehension of the passive. Be specific about what children will hear, see, touch, do—whatever is relevant to the study you design.

Exercise 10.4   Parentese

Identify features of parentese in the following excerpt (from Ninio and Bruner 1988):

   Mother: Look!
   Child: (Touches picture)
   Mother: What are those?
   Child: (Vocalizes and smiles)
   Mother: Yes, they are rabbits.
   Child: (Vocalizes, smiles, and looks up at mother)
   Mother: (Laughs) Yes, rabbit.
   Child: (Vocalizes, smiles)
   Mother: Yes (Laughs)

Exercise 10.5   Types of Aphasia

Examine the following two excerpts of speech by two French aphasic patients, translated into English below (from A. R. Lecours et al. 1983, quoted in Crystal 1997, 273). Identify whether the speech patterns seem consistent with Broca's or Wernicke's aphasia and provide a detailed explanation why. (The symbol / represents an abnormal drop in pitch; italics represent strong stress.)

Yes I have another *woman* who has remained since the /bœtʀe/ of the child of *my son.* He is/she was ten years old when my /fɛs/ died. And then, she is there now. She will soon be /syz/ years old. She is still going to school since she presents herself the / I had sent her to school since I myself was indeed working in the /syz/ /—uh—at the /faʀmid/ of / of /syz/ isn't it, of two /ɛtmiʀ/. And then, I / This /mwazɛ/—there uh, *Ginette* is her name—she / she / abil/ ...

Uh, hemiplegia, uh, fulgurant, uh Pasteur Hospital, Nice, Nice. Uh, Doctor Dupont, uh, uh, examinations / finally, examinations, uh, finally, a coma, uh, a little bit. Uh, a month / a month, uh, pavilion F-3 /dy/ uh, Doctor Durand. My kidneys. Uh, physiotherapist. Walk uh, uh, very well, a little, a little. Uh, November first, medica / The / Giscard / Doctor Giscard uh, therapy. Uh, uh, yes, uh physio / no, eight o'clock, physio, uh a quarter of an hour ...

Chapter 11

Language Variation

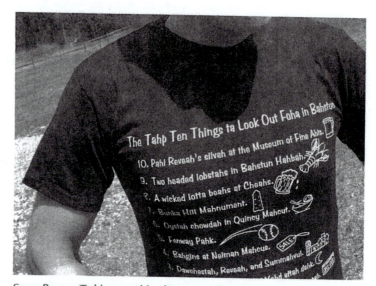

The Tahp Ten Things ta Look Out Foha in Bahstun

10. Pahl Reveah's sllvah at the Museum of Fine Ahts.

9. Two headed lobstahs in Bahstun Hahbah.

8. A wicked lotta beahs at Cheahs.

7. Bunka Hill Mahnument.

6. Oyetah chowdah in Quincy Mahcut.

5. Fenway Pahk.

4. Bahgins at Neiman Mahcus.

3. Dawchestah, Reveah, and Summahvul.

Some Boston T-shirts combine humor and local pride in the /r/-less pronunciations typical of many dialects in the area.

Some Bostonians famously "pahk the cah," and if you want to be more specific about the location of the vehicle, they "pahk the cah in Hahvahd Yahd." This expression captures something important about Boston pronunciation in an amusing way, but it isn't exactly right: while many Bostonians drop their /r/s after vowels, they do so only when the /r/ is followed by a consonant or a pause. So the /r/ is lost in *park*, *Harvard*, and *yard*—and *car* when it appears at the end of a sentence. But when *car* is followed by a word beginning with a vowel, like *in*, the /r/ is pronounced. This is why Bostonians and other similar /r/-droppers sometimes insert /r/s at the end of words that end with vowels, for example, "idear" and "lore ('law') and order."

Variation in the pronunciation of /r/ is not limited to Boston: it occurs throughout the United States. Many speakers of Southern American English, African American English, and New York English also do not pronounce postvocalic /r/ (/r/ after a vowel). But not all New Yorkers call themselves "New Yawkers": you'll find lots of variation with /r/ within the city, among New York City natives. If you ask directions in coastal Maine ("down East"), you might learn that you can't get "theyuh" from "heeuh"—the /r/ is, in a sense, still present, but its effect is to introduce an additional vowel syllable in words that Iowans, Philadelphians, and Californians end in liquid /r/. As though all of that variation and its history weren't complicated enough, /r/ sometimes appears where we don't expect: in small dialect areas across the United States, speakers "warsh" their cars and send their senators to "Warshington."

We know that geography affects language variation: people in different parts of the United States often speak differently. When folks emigrated from the British Isles to America, they packed light but brought their accents with them. Immigrants from Scotland and Northern England imported an /r/-full manner of speaking. Those from Southern England tended to blur (or bluh) postvocalic /r/. As a result, throughout much of the United States, especially the North, the Midlands, and the West, postvocalic /r/ is voiced distinctly. In the South, parts of New England, and New York City, however, postvocalic /r/ is often not distinct.

Attitudes about /r/-dropping vary. When Franklin Delano Roosevelt said that "we have nothing to feah but feah itself," his accent was heard as aristocratic. Today, many New Yorkers take accent reduction courses to get their /r/s back.

It turns out that factors of speakers' identities such as gender, class, age, and race or ethnicity affect how they speak. Within any geographic region, we still find lots of language variation among speakers. This variation serves important social functions and is integral to language change.

In this chapter, we describe the major factors relevant to language variation, as well as major approaches to recording variation and studying it. We then discuss language or dialect mixing, both when two different speech communities come into contact and when one speaker mixes two or more language varieties in his or her speech. In Chapter 12, we look specifically at American dialects and their history.

Dialect

A **dialect** is a variety of a language spoken by a group of people that is systematically different from other varieties of the language in terms of structural (e.g., phonological, morphological, syntactic) or lexical features. Most speakers of American English are familiar with regional variation in American English—the differences, for instance, between language in the North and in the South. Language can also vary for social reasons, as in the case of African American English—variation partially rooted in geography, but now largely independent of region. The term **accent** refers to differences in pronunciation, or, to put it more technically, to systematic phonological variation. Many dialects involve accent differences, but they also involve differences at the levels of morphology, syntax, and lexicon.

Below are some examples of accent and dialect differences in American English. These examples are just a small sampling: they merely indicate the types of features that can distinguish one accent or dialect from others. Chapter 12 provides a much fuller sample of American dialect characteristics.

Sample Phonological Differences

- /r/-less pronunciations in parts of the Northeast (e.g., *car* as /kɑ/)
- Monophthongization of some diphthongs in Southern American English (e.g., /aɪ/ as [a] in a word like *right*)
- Loss of initial /h/ in *huge* /juǰ/ and *humid* /jumɪd/ in many urban areas on the East Coast
- Realization of /ð/ as [d] in African American English and other dialects

Sample Morphological Differences

- Second-person plural forms *youse* (Boston), *y'all* (Southern American English), or *yinz* (Pittsburgh)
- *a*-prefixing in Appalachian English (e.g., "We were a-huntin'.")
- Zero-ending for third-person singular present tense in African American English, some varieties of English in the Caribbean, and some dialects in East Anglia in Britain (*he walk* vs. *he walks*)
- Extension of inflectional *-s* to all present-tense forms in some British dialects, as well as in some areas of Appalachia and the Outer Banks (e.g., *I walks, you walks, he/she walks, we walks, the ducks walks*)
- Generalization of *-s* in possessive pronouns to *mines*, by analogy with *yours, ours, his, hers, theirs*, in some urban areas on the East Coast

Sample Syntactic Differences

- Multiple negation in many varieties of American English
- Use of habitual *be* in African American English (e.g., "He be working at school these days.")
- *need* + past-participle constructions in areas from Colorado to Pennsylvania (e.g., "The car needs washed.")

Sample Lexical Differences

- *Fireflies* vs. *firebugs* vs. *lightning bugs*
- *Afeard* vs. *afraid* (past participle reflexes of nearly synonymous verbs, the first from Old English *afæren* 'frighten, terrify', the second from Anglo-French *afrayer* 'disturb, startle, frighten')
- *Gumbands* vs. *rubberbands*
- *Fixin' to* vs. *about to/intend to/prepare to*

Sample Discourse-level Differences

- Sentence-final *eh* (or *hey*) in the Upper Peninsula of Michigan to invite or suggest agreement (e.g., "See you tonight, eh.")

■ "Please?" to request that someone repeat an utterance, in parts of Ohio and other regions influenced by German (from German "Bitte?")

Not all speakers of any of the dialects represented here necessarily use all of the variants listed, nor any one of the variants all of the time. These features are typical of one or another dialect, on terms described in more detail below.

Dialects versus Languages

The linguistic distinction between a dialect and a language can be a blurry one. Sometimes the distinction is based on social and political factors instead of linguistic ones. The primary criterion for distinguishing a dialect from a language is mutual comprehensibility. Generally, speakers of different dialects of one language can understand each other, although perhaps with some difficulty. Speakers of different languages generally cannot understand each other, except with instruction in the other language. For example, dialects of British English show a great deal of variability, both geographically and socially, but most speakers can understand the speech of other dialect speakers (and often identify their origins and/or social class through their speech patterns). But without studying French, most speakers of any dialect of British English cannot understand the speech of the French, who live only a few miles away, on the other side of the English Channel (or *La Manche* 'the sleeve', as the French would put it).

Exceptions to the mutual intelligibility criterion highlight the political and social factors sometimes involved in labeling a language variety a "dialect" or a "language." In China, speakers in Shanghai (in the north) generally cannot understand the variety of Chinese spoken by residents of Changsha (in the south). Students learn the Beijing dialect (or standard Mandarin) in school as the standard language so that they will be able to communicate with speakers of other Chinese dialects. However, despite this mutual unintelligibility among many varieties of the language(s) spoken in China, they are referred to as dialects of the language "Chinese" because they are all spoken within the country of China; they also all share a written form. On the other hand, many speakers of Danish can understand Norwegian and vice versa, but these two language varieties are referred to as two languages—rather than two dialects of one language—because they are spoken in two different countries.

Capturing the sometimes political nature of the distinction in 1945, Max Weinreich, a scholar of Yiddish, described a language as a dialect with an army and a navy (translated from Yiddish; cited in Lippi-Green 1997, 43). Rosina Lippi-Green (1997, 43) turns that description on its head, noting that a dialect is "perhaps nothing more than a language that gets no respect."

Standard and Nonstandard Dialects

Standard English, like the standard variety of any language, is one dialect among the many dialects of the language, which has been elevated for social and political reasons. The standard variety tends to be the language of instruction in schools (or the target language, even if instruction occurs in another variety), the language of the wider community's media and governance, and often the language of upper-middle- and upper-class speakers. Many linguists argue that standard varieties are idealizations: no speaker speaks "perfect Standard English," for example, and there is more variation within Standard English than the term suggests. The written standard is easier to identify, although

A Question to Discuss

Is American English a Dialect or a Language?

American English can be traced back to the first English-speaking settlers who sailed over from Britain, as you will read more about in Chapter 12. The geographic separation from Britain and new kinds of language and dialect mixing that happened in the colonies meant that English in the Americas began to change in different ways from the English in Britain. After the United States declared independence, Noah Webster published *An American Dictionary of the English Language* (1828) to help establish American English as independent of British English. In 1923, the state of Illinois declared "American" its official language. (The state passed a statute in 1969 repealing this declaration and establishing "English" as the official language.)

Standard American and British English differ in accent as well as in some grammatical and lexical features. However, for most speakers, the two varieties are mutually intelligible. Would you describe them as two dialects of "English" or as two languages spoken in two different countries? How would you defend your answer?

it, too, accommodates some variation. (Refer back to Chapter 2 for more discussion of the definition of Standard English.)

Nonstandard varieties are linguistically equal to standard varieties at the structural and communicative level. In other words, nonstandard varieties are just as systematic grammatically and just as expressive and responsive to their speakers' communicative needs as standard varieties. Some formal registers use primarily standard varieties (e.g., medical and legal texts), because they must maintain an unusual consistency over time and place. Nonstandard varieties may not have developed the working vocabulary for these registers, but no purely linguistic or grammatical facts preclude them from doing so.

At the same time, nonstandard varieties are often not socially equal to standard varieties. Nonstandard varieties are often stigmatized as "bad," "ungrammatical," "sloppy," "uneducated," or otherwise inferior to standard varieties. One result of the power of Standard English ideology—the idea that Standard English is more correct and preferable in most if not all contexts—is that the equally functional linguistic systems of nonstandard varieties of English become stigmatized.

Given the stigmas attached to nonstandard varieties, why don't they disappear? Why don't all speakers want to and attempt to speak only Standard English? There are many reasons. Perhaps most importantly, few speakers try to speak Standard English all of the time, if any of the time. Standard English is not always the preferable or appropriate variety for a social situation. In some contexts, for instance, it may be considered affected, or "stuck up" to satisfy perfectly the phonological, morphological, syntactic, and lexical demands of the standard. Within specific communities, other varieties of English carry more value—not to mention personal meaning—than Standard English. Speakers can use nonstandard varieties to express local pride, to identify their membership in a particular social group, to express solidarity, to draw on cultural values associated with a dialect, or a host of other reasons. For some speakers, Standard English serves several of these functions simultaneously.

Overt prestige refers to the more widely recognized value given to standards that supposedly transcend conditions like place or social status. Language varieties with overt prestige are those that speakers use or aim for in order to gain status in the "wider community," and Standard English is an example of a variety with considerable overt prestige. **Covert prestige** refers to the value that nonstandard varieties carry within specific communities. The covert prestige of nonstandard varieties has the power to define membership within communities and mark group identification, as do standard varieties in some contexts. When, for example, young white teenagers who are not native speakers of African American English adopt features of African American English, these teenagers are responding to the covert prestige of this dialect within both youth and popular cultures.

Dialectology

Geography is one of the most obvious factors in language variation, though any language varies socially as well as geographically. Traditionally, dialectology has focused on mapping geographic variation within a language. Speakers separated by geographic boundaries—bodies of water, mountain ranges—may have limited contact with each other; thus, their varieties of the language can drift apart linguistically. As linguist Roger Shuy puts it, the Connecticut River still divides people who "park your car" from those who "pahk yah cah." Dialect boundaries like this one can also reflect patterns of migration: speakers brought dialect features with them when they arrived in America, some of which persist even today. Social variation, by contrast, is *not* primarily geographical, though regional and social variation often both intersect and interact.

Early dialectologists (like the Brothers Grimm in Germany) recorded "folk dialects" in order to trace the histories of their respective languages. Dialectology in the United States can be traced back at least into the nineteenth century. By the twentieth century, this interest in what were viewed as historically conservative dialects (dialects that retain many older features) often focused on NORMs—nonmobile older rural males—whose age and geographic isolation meant that their dialect might be more "genuine" in its difference from more urban and standard varieties. Current dialectology questions the notion of "genuine" dialects, however, since city-dwellers speak dialects, too. And though Standard American English may not be the norm among NORMs, it is nonetheless as legitimate and useful a dialect as any other, given the right social circumstances, for instance, at work or school.

Under the influence of nineteenth-century German linguistic geography, twentieth-century scholars in North America began to map the full range of dialects in U.S. and Canadian English. The American Dialect Society was founded in 1889 with the explicit goal of investigating American dialects—which it still does. Large-scale dialect projects such as the Linguistic Atlas of the United States and Canada, undertaken in 1928 by Hans Kurath, set out to gather systematic data from "old-fashioned" and "modern" speakers in order to map dialects geographically. This project is still not complete, but parts of the data are described in smaller atlases such as the *Linguistic Atlas of New*

England (LANE) and the *Linguistic Atlas of the Gulf States* (LAGS). The *Linguistic Atlas of the Middle and South Atlantic States* (LAMSAS) works from material first gathered by Kurath's team, as well as more recent material, to map the use of a range of lexical items (e.g., *quarter of/till/to, pail/bucket*) in these states.

Data for these kinds of dialect projects are typically gathered either by questionnaires sent and returned by mail or by fieldworkers transcribing or audio-recording informants' responses in person. The *Dictionary of American Regional English* (DARE), which you read about in Chapter 2, has published four of its five volumes of comprehensive data about dialectal words and their meanings around the United States. The maps generated by some of the atlas projects can be found online, a significant advance for students of American regional dialects, professional or amateur.

Much dialectology has focused on lexical items, but phonological and grammatical differences have been mapped as well. The TELSUR (TELephone SURvey) project, under the direction of William Labov, used random telephone surveys to collect

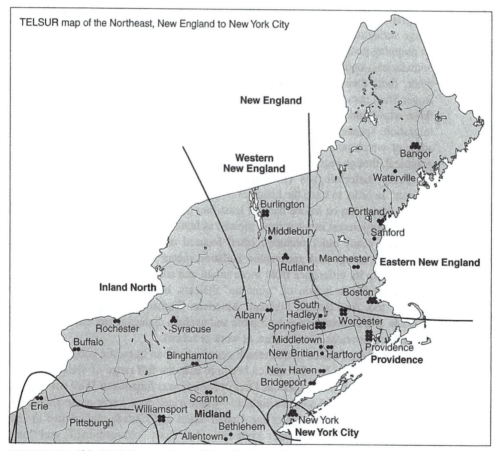

FIGURE 11.1 This TELSUR map shows dialect divisions within New England, the New York City area, and into the Inland North.

FIGURE 11.2 All DARE maps are drawn on this contorted map of the United States in order to reflect relative population among the states.

Source: Reprinted with permission of the publisher from *Dictionary of American Regional English, Volume I: A–C,* edited by Frederic G. Cassidy, Cambridge, Mass.: The Belknap Press of Harvard University Press, Copyright © 1985 by the President and Fellows of Harvard College, p. xxiv.

DARE's Map of the United States

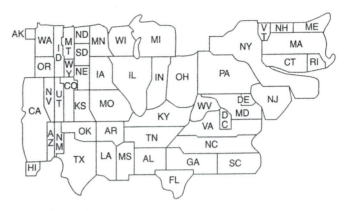

information about regional pronunciations across North America. TELSUR provides maps of variants of specific linguistic variables such as the vowels involved in the *cot/caught* merger, and William Labov and his colleagues drew from the TELSUR data to create the authoritative *Atlas of North American English* (Labov, Ash, and Boberg 2005).

Figure 11.1 shows a TELSUR map of dialect divisions in the northeastern United States. Contrast that with the DARE map of the United States shown in Figure 11.2. All DARE maps use this somewhat contorted representation of the states: it captures the relative population rather than the land area of the states. The DARE map in Figure 11.3 shows where in the United States people say *dropped egg* rather than *poached egg.*

When dialectologists map dialects, they often draw **isoglosses,** lines that separate areas that use one lexical item, grammatical construction, or pronunciation from another that uses a different lexical, syntactic, or phonetic form for the same purpose. Lines in the geography where many isoglosses coincide are typically called "dialect boundaries"

FIGURE 11.3 This DARE map shows where speakers say *dropped egg* instead of *poached egg.*

Source: Reprinted with permission of the publisher from *Dictionary of American Regional English, Volume II: D–H,* edited by Frederic G. Cassidy, Cambridge, Mass.: The Belknap Press of Harvard University Press, Copyright © 1985 by the President and Fellows of Harvard College, p. 207.

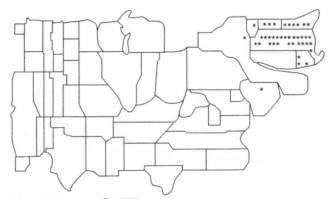

*dropped egg + varr (Qu. H35)

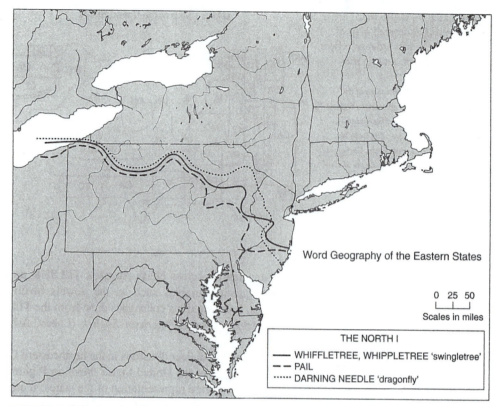

FIGURE 11.4 The bundle of isoglosses for *whiffletree/whippletree*, *pail*, and *darning needle* suggests a dialect boundary.

Source: Kurath (1949).

(see Figure 11.4). Dialect boundaries often occur along physical geographic boundaries (bodies of water, mountain ranges), along political boundaries, or along migration boundaries. Of course, isoglosses do not create definite lines where one linguistic feature stops and another begins. In linguistic atlas maps, isoglosses separate regions where there is a majority tendency to use one feature or another, but there will still be variation within the region. Different dialects, regional or social, rarely disagree absolutely; they tend to disagree at a certain statistical frequency. Thus, some dialectologists prefer to map survey responses rather than to generalize them, in order to represent intraregional variety.

Variationist Sociolinguistics

Many factors other than geography play into language variation. The field of **sociolinguistics** encompasses all subfields of linguistics that examine language use in social contexts and in speech communities, including conversation analysis and other types of discourse analysis. **Variationist sociolinguistics** specifically examines distributional patterns of linguistic variables within speech communities (e.g., use of /r/ vs. absence of /r/) in order to analyze the effect of age, gender, class, ethnicity, and other factors on how people speak. At a more abstract level, variationist sociolinguistics examines the relationship of language behavior

Language Variation at Work

Pop versus *Soda*

One of the best-known lexical differences among varieties of English in the United States is how speakers refer to carbonated beverages (see Figure 11.5). In the Midwest and Northwest, *pop* rules. In the Northeast and on the West Coast, speakers tend to order *soda*, though some speakers still prefer *tonic.* Mid-Atlantic speakers sometimes prefer *soft drinks,* and in the South, the question "What kind of *coke* do you want?" makes sense.

Exploiting the new technology of the Internet, the Web site "The Great Pop vs. Soda Controversy" (http://www.popvssoda .com/) solicited information about this usage from visitors to the site and in October 2002 mapped over 130,000 responses onto a dialect map. The Web page acknowledges the less-than-ideal rigor of its methodology, as it relies on informants to be honest about their hometowns and usage.

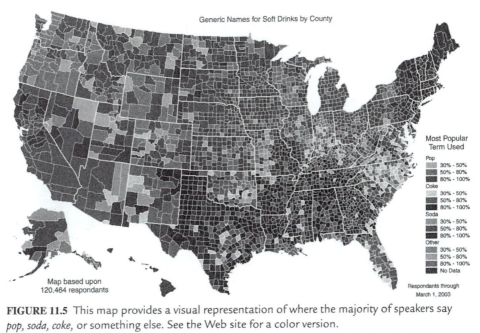

Generic Names for Soft Drinks by County

Most Popular Term Used

Pop
30% - 50%
50% - 80%
80% - 100%
Coke
30% - 50%
50% - 80%
80% - 100%
Soda
30% - 50%
50% - 80%
80% - 100%
Other
30% - 50%
50% - 80%
80% - 100%
No Data

Map based upon 120.464 respondants

Respondants through March 1, 2003

FIGURE 11.5 This map provides a visual representation of where the majority of speakers say *pop, soda, coke,* or something else. See the Web site for a color version.

Source: Courtesy of Greg Plumb, Department of Cartography and Geography, East Central University, Ada, Oklahoma.

to speaker identity. It is described as an empirical field because it works from observations of language use to analysis of those observational data. Variationist sociolinguistics works from the premise that language variation is structured or systematic, rather than random. In other words, if we take into account a speaker's age, gender, class, race, ethnicity, geographic location, and other factors such as group identities, usually we can explain why some speakers speak differently from others.

Sociolinguistic studies also often try to explain how language change begins and spreads. Historical linguistics had traditionally postulated that language change was unobservable. It argued that language develops just as a plant grows—you can see the growth, but the growth is continuous, and it would be difficult to say that one stage of growth begins here and another ends there. Thus, historical linguists argued that language change could be mapped only in retrospect, given knowledge of the language in question both before and after any change. Sociolinguists, on the other hand, postulate that in structured variation, we can often analyze language change in progress. For example, if in your town some speakers say *cot* and *caught* the same way and others still pronounce the two words differently, we may be witnessing the spread of the *cot/caught* merger in your town. We can see a change spreading through a community as some speakers use innovative patterns and some use older patterns.

William Labov's Research

William Labov is often credited with founding modern variationist sociolinguistics in the early 1960s—with his master's thesis! The study examined language use on Martha's Vineyard, specifically the different use of the centralized diphthongs of /ɑɪ/ and /ɑʊ/ (in words such as *right* and *out*), distinctive Vineyard pronunciations, by different groups of speakers on the island. The most cited result of the study was that residents who felt a strong affiliation with the island—who had strong local identities and expressed resistance about tourist encroachments on the island—had the most centralized vowels, whereas younger speakers and others with more ties to the mainland produced vowels closer to the standard. The variation reflected, below the level of consciousness, different assertions of identity with respect to the local community. The variation among speakers was far from random.

A Scholar to Know

William Labov (1927–)

After majoring in English and philosophy at Harvard, William Labov (pronounced /labov/) worked in "the real world" for more than ten years, first at a series of writing-oriented jobs and then for the longest period of time as an industrial inkmaker at a small company. These jobs, as he describes in an autobiographical essay, reinforced for him that working-class people "have a lot to say," and that linguistics would be better served if it were based on what people actually say and were subjected to rigorous experimental techniques. He attended graduate school at Columbia to study linguistics, where he wrote up his famous studies of language variation in Martha's Vineyard and New York City. In the past four decades, he

has published well over one hundred articles and is currently finishing a three-volume work on processes of language change. He has publicly refuted the claim that he "founded" sociolinguistics, given earlier work like that of Swiss linguist Louis Gauchet. He explains that the field was not a "virgin field" but "more like an abandoned back yard, overgrown with various kind of tangled, secondary scholarship" (1972, 260; qtd. in McMahon 1994, 232). Nonetheless, Labov has gone a long way to cleaning up the mess, and his work has shaped research in many areas of sociolinguistics for the past five decades.

Labov's doctoral research focused on class differences and style shifting in New York City, specifically on the use or nonuse of /r/. One of Labov's working hypotheses was that, although socioeconomic indexes would imply that all salesclerks, generally members of the lower middle class, should share the same pronunciation of a feature like /r/ (in this case a tendency to drop /r/), clerks working in department stores catering to clienteles of higher status than their own might speak differently in contact with those clienteles. Labov selected three department stores—Saks (high class), Macy's (middle class), and S. Klein (lower class)—and asked clerks in each store a question that would elicit the answer "fourth floor" (which has two potential realizations of /r/). In each case, he would pretend not to hear the response clearly and ask, "Excuse me?" in order to confirm the pronunciation. He would then jot down what he had heard (he was working without a tape recorder). This elicitation technique was another important contribution to the developing field, as a way to produce "naturally occurring" speech outside the interview setting.

As it turned out, the salesclerks *did* speak differently. The Saks employees produced /r/ more often than the Macy's employees, who produced /r/ more often than the S. Klein employees. Labov concluded that the clerks' perceptions of high-status linguistic forms and their efforts to accommodate to clientele of a particular class affected their speech. Labov's theories describe the lower middle class (which includes white-collar jobs like salesclerk) as the group of people who show the most variation through accommodation to higher-status speech patterns. Thus, members of the working class are critical contributors to the spread of language change.

A Methodological Issue

Sociolinguists like Labov often want to focus on "natural" or colloquial speech. But here's the problem: when people are being interviewed or taped or asked to read words, they tend to use more formal language. Linguists call this problem "the **observer's paradox**": they need to observe people to see/hear how they speak in natural conditions, but people do not tend to speak naturally when being observed. Ideally, sociolinguists want to observe how people speak when they are not being observed. As a result, they have developed methodologies to minimize the effect of the observer and to compare more formal speech with less formal speech.

The researchers often ask participants to complete three tasks:

1. Read off words on a list (the most formal speech).
2. Read a passage (formal speech, but not as careful as the word list).
3. Converse with the fieldworker (the most casual or "vernacular" speech).

With these three tasks, linguists can record style-shifting or code-switching, often learning about speakers' perceptions of "formal" language given what pronunciations they target in the formal settings.

In the conversations, interviewers try to ask questions that will encourage the subject to produce long strings of speech and that will elicit excited or emotional responses, because we all tend to speak more naturally if we become emotionally involved in what we are saying. For this reason, the "danger of death" question—in which the interviewer asks the subject about a time when he or she felt at risk of dying—is often used in sociolinguistic interviews. (But many researchers note that, in some communities, this question seems to be less effective.)

Analyzing Variation

Some linguistic variables demonstrate stable variation; they show the same patterns of stratification from generation to generation. For example, the absence of third-person singular present-tense -s in the Detroit African American community (e.g., *She drive too fast*) drops sharply from the upper working class to the lower middle class. In other words, lower-middle-class speakers more often use the form with -s (Wolfram 1969). It appears to be a social marker. Some variation reflects language change in progress. With a change in progress, some speakers are more advanced than others in adopting the innovative linguistic variable, and the patterns of variation shift with each generation as the change spreads.

Some changes involve speakers adopting linguistic variables that are recognized in the community as social markers. For example, many speakers in New York are aware that /r/-lessness is a nonstandard and socially stigmatized feature. When speakers adopt innovative variables (e.g., inserting /r/) in these kinds of situations of language variation, linguists call it **change from above**. It is change above the level of consciousness, involving deliberate choices of variables on the parts of speakers hoping to represent themselves socially in particular ways. Change from above often involves socially mobile speakers adopting more socially prestigious variants, but not always.

Change from below often involves phonological shifts happening below the level of consciousness. For example, the Northern Cities Vowel Shift is currently affecting many of the vowels of speakers in Midwestern urban areas (see Figure 11.6). This "rotation of vowels" means that many Detroiters and Chicagoans say, for example, [bɛg] or [beɪg] for *bag* and [hæt] for *hot*. This vowel change is spreading variably according to region, class, gender, and ethnicity, but the innovative pronunciations involved are not consciously marked as socially significant—the shift seems still to be happening below the level of consciousness for most speakers.

In any given study, sociolinguists must determine which kinds of variation the patterns reflect. Researchers sometimes supplement quantitative studies of linguistic variables with attitude surveys, to gather more data about the social significance of a linguistic variable. Interviews can reveal whether speakers consciously associate certain pronunciations or grammatical constructions with rural or urban speakers, with educated or uneducated speakers, and so on. Speaker attitudes can help sociolinguists make sense of the patterns they find, and these attitudes can affect the ongoing distribution of the linguistic variables themselves. In interviews, speakers will often be very forthcoming about the kinds of language they see as "lazy," "bad," "snooty," "hick," or otherwise socially marked.

Sociolinguistics versus Generative Grammar

Labov's sociolinguistics contrasts sharply with Chomsky's formal linguistics (discussed in Chapter 6). Each is revolutionary but from quite different motives and to entirely different effects. Chomsky argued that linguists should focus on linguistic competence, not on linguistic performance, and he advocated introspective methods for analysis. Given his assertion that the focus of linguistic inquiry should be "an ideal speaker-listener, in a completely homogeneous speech-community" (1965, 3), linguists could rely on native-speaker intuitions about the structure and use of language. Variation by real speakers in real speech communities was not the focus of linguistic theory. Variationist sociolinguistics challenges this assumption, foregrounding real speakers and speech communities and shifting the focus of linguistic inquiry to the structure of language variation. Many sociolinguists question the

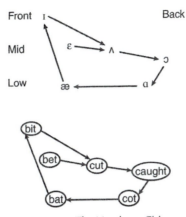

FIGURE 11.6 The Northern Cities Vowel Shift involves a rotation of low vowels in cities such as Detroit, Chicago, and Buffalo.
Source: Gordon (2006, 109).

competence/performance distinction of generative linguistics, asserting that speakers' use of variation is part of their linguistic competence, not just part of their performance.

The disagreement between sociolinguistics and generative linguistics is thus profound, as practitioners of either are well aware. Labov once wrote, "I have resisted the term *sociolinguistics* for many years, since it implies that there can be a successful linguistic theory or practice which is not social" (1972, xiii). Of course, Chomsky and other generative linguists could not disagree more.

Speech Communities and Communities of Practice

Sociolinguistics has often focused on **speech communities**, or groups of speakers who share linguistic norms and ideologies. In the studies described earlier, Labov studied the speech communities of Martha's Vineyard and New York City. Obviously, speech communities can vary dramatically in size and often contain smaller speech communities. Speech communities tend to involve speakers who share a common region, race, or ethnicity.

Linguists like Penelope Eckert have shifted the focus from speech communities to **communities of practice**. They argue that our speech can be influenced by the people we do things with. A community of practice is an "aggregate of people who come together around some enterprise" (2000, 35). Unlike a speech community, a community of practice is not defined by region, race, or ethnicity: "United by a common enterprise, people come to develop and share ways of doing things, ways of talking, beliefs, values—in short, practices—as a function of their joint engagement in activity" (2000, 35). Your college or university may constitute a community of practice, as may the band, the student government, the local public-interest research group, the college Republicans, or an Internet chat room.

Within the community of practice, speakers simultaneously fashion their own identities and contribute to the group's identity. Language is a key part of "doing identity."

So how you talk is part of the community's identity; and how you talk reflects your understanding of the community's identity. Speakers come together as communities of practice intentionally, not as an accident of birth or location. Inevitably, any speaker participates in many communities of practice.

Major Factors in Language Variation within Speech Communities

Your age, gender, socioeconomic class, race, ethnicity, and social networks can all have an effect on how you speak.

Age

Do you speak differently from your parents and from your grandparents? Many young speakers can identify differences between their speech and that of their elders. And many elders lament the changes they hear in young people's speech. Sociolinguists must grapple with the question of whether younger speakers use particular linguistic variables because they are young or because they have adopted a new linguistic form, indicating a linguistic change in progress.

Labov pioneered the use of age differences within a community as a way to study language change in progress. In a form of research called "apparent-time studies," linguists assume that the speech of a seventy-year-old speaker represents the speech of a twenty-year-old speaker fifty years ago. So if we compare a seventy-year-old, a forty-five-year-old, and a twenty-year-old speaker within one community, differences among them may reflect the adoption of a new linguistic variable within the community. For example, in communities affected by the *cot/caught* merger, older speakers may preserve the distinction between [ɑ] and [ɔ], middle-aged speakers may show variation as a group (for reasons discussed below), and almost all young speakers may have merged the vowels. Apparent-time studies allow researchers to track change without having to carry out studies that last two or three generations.

On the other hand, young speakers may use different linguistic forms from the rest of the community simply because they are young. "Age-grading" refers to shifts in individual speakers' linguistic behavior over the course of their lifetimes. For example, a study by Makiko Takekuro (2000) of young Japanese women revealed that, as the women progressed from their early to late twenties, they came to use more honorifics and feminine forms of sentence-final particles. In other words, the innovative use of fewer feminine forms and honorifics appears to be an age-graded phenomenon rather than a change in progress.

Gender

If men are from Mars and women from Venus, do they speak Martian and Venusian English? Research on gender as a factor in language variation has discovered differences between male and female speech patterns, and the differences consistently raise an interesting paradox. Women tend to use more standard forms than men—in other words, they are more conservative speakers. Yet women also tend to use more innovative forms—in other words, they are leaders of linguistic change.

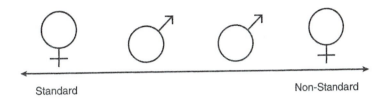

Standard   Non-Standard

It seems that with stable variation in which one variant is established as standard and the other as nonstandard (e.g., standard *-ing* vs. nonstandard *-in'*), women tend to use the more standard form. With newer changes, such as the vowel changes in the northern cities, women are often in the lead.

Many studies have established women's use of more standard forms. Further up the socioeconomic ladder, all speakers tend to show a higher percentage of standard forms, but women more so than men. For example, Peter Trudgill (1983), in a study of men and women speakers in Norwich, England, found that the use of [n] (or *-in'*) for the *-ing* ending characterized the speech both of the working class and of males. Women tended to use the more standard [ŋ] for *-ing*. He explains, "WC [working class] speech, like other aspects of WC culture, appears, at least in some western societies, to have connotations of masculinity . . . probably because it is associated with the roughness and toughness supposedly characteristic of WC life which are, stereotypically and to a certain extent, often considered to be desirable masculine attributes" (23). In other words, there is a "hidden" prestige associated with working-class speech that can help explain why it continues and why men of other socioeconomic classes may use features of working-class speech.

Women, however, may need to use more standard language for upward mobility. A study of eight African American speakers in rural South Carolina examines the differences between speakers on the mainland and on a river island accessible only by boat (Nichols 1982). The women from the island community seemed to be moving faster toward "standard forms" than the men from the island as well as the women on the mainland. The proposed explanation is the existence of very real differences in occupations and opportunities across sexes and locations. All island women worked outside the home at some point in time, and the most attractive available jobs were white-collar and required standard English. The top occupations for black men on the island were blue-collar ones that required few language-related tasks. Thus, there was incentive for families to invest in the education of daughters and for women to train for these higher-paying jobs. On the mainland, women with low education were often limited to domestic work and were not, therefore, necessarily using language for upward mobility. So the study indicates that women tend to lag behind in the adoption of innovative forms when they are limited to occupations within the home. In societies where women have more mobility through the acquisition of office work, they show more innovative and standard forms.

In a study of Belten High (a pseudonym for a high school outside Detroit), Penelope Eckert (2000) examined other factors that may affect differences between the speech of male and female high school students. She found that the most relevant social groups in the school were the "jocks" (college-bound students who participated in many of the school teams and extracurricular activities) and "burn-outs" (students who planned to take blue-collar jobs and were not invested in school activities). Within each of these groups, the girls were at the extremes. The jock girls spoke with the most standard forms, and the burn-out girls spoke with the most nonstandard forms. Her hypothesis is that boys can rely on their activities (e.g., sports) to establish their identities, whereas girls must rely more on language as a symbolic means for establishing their identities within particular groups. So the Eckert study looked at how language patterns are related to establishing group membership given the complicated interaction of various components of identity (e.g., class, gender, race, social group).

Class

In the movie *My Fair Lady*, adapted from George Bernard Shaw's play *Pygmalion*, Professor Henry Higgins claims that his expertise in phonetics allows him to place a speaker within six miles—and sometimes even within just a few streets in London—of his or her birthplace. It turns out that this pinpointing of speakers to neighborhoods is as much about class as about location. He condemns the flower-selling Eliza Doolittle's pronunciations as crude and disgusting, and he makes it an issue of class.

She says words like *'ow* and *garn,* both of them supposedly subliterate exclamations. Higgins claims that such speech determines more about her social status than does either her shabby clothing or poor hygiene. In fact, it is difficult to tell whether language marks social difference or results from it, but the relationship is certainly more complicated than Henry Higgins thinks. It would be more accurate to say that speech is "implicated" in class distinctions; it marks them but it also reinforces them.

Class distinctions have always been stronger in Britain than in the United States, but it may be a relevant factor in language variation in both. At least, Americans hear some class distinctions in speech and remark on them. Sociolinguists, though, are committed to studying the intersections of class, age, gender, ethnicity, and region—measuring any one of them in isolation can lead to the sort of self-assured stereotyping of which Higgins is guilty. Among other things, the following chapter discusses stereotype, humor, and prejudice in the context of American dialects, as well as the impulse on the part of more educated speakers to "raise" less educated speakers to a standard variety English by means of education. For sociolinguists, however, the "verbal class distinction" is not about criticizing the pronunciation, grammar, or lexical choices of any group (or its members) but about explaining variation within a larger community of speakers.

Labov's studies of language variation and change rely heavily on the concept of class as a critical factor in the actuation of language change. Class is obviously a very difficult entity to define, and studies that rely heavily on class have sometimes been criticized on this count. The categorization of people by class tends to focus on speakers' occupations, as opposed to their upbringing (if, for example, their occupation is in a higher or lower socioeconomic status group than their parents'). Despite the many issues that linguists have raised about class as a category of analysis, it has proved consistently relevant to sociolinguistic patterns of variation in many studies. Labov provides the following breakdown of class categories (qtd. in Eckert 2000, 26):

Upper class	First-rate professional, manager, official, or proprietor of a large business.
Upper middle class	Careermen in professions, managerial, official, or large business positions.

Lower middle class	Semiprofessionals, petty businessmen, white collar, foremen, and craftsmen.
Working class	Operatives: blue-collar workers at the mercy of the labor market.
Lower class	Laborers: last to be hired and first to be fired. Frequent job shifts.

Historically, women were categorized by the occupation of their husbands—a method that has rightly come under scrutiny after significant criticism.

Penelope Eckert explains the relationship of class to linguistic variation in terms of **linguistic markets**: "the value of a speaker's verbal offerings—the likelihood that these offerings will be heard and heeded—depends on the linguistic variety in which they are encoded" (Eckert 2000, 13). Language is part of a broader symbolic market of identification, which includes clothes, hairstyles, material possessions, and other indicators. Some clothes are approved in certain subcultures but not in others; similarly, some language appeals to members of one subculture but not to those of another. The standard language variety is associated with institutions of power and, therefore, those higher in the social hierarchy. Nonstandard varieties often symbolize membership in the local community and its economic and social marketplace.

Working- and middle-class communities have been the focus of most studies for their participation in language variation between standard and nonstandard forms and the spread of language change. The lower middle class seems to reside between the more standard language market of the upper middle class and the more nonstandard language market of the working class. The pull or tension between the two linguistic markets often results in lower-middle-class speakers producing "hyper-standard" forms in some contexts and "hyper-nonstandard" forms in others, as they choose to participate in either of the adjoining class categories. On the hyper-standard end of the spectrum, a speaker, from linguistic and social insecurity, might say to someone of supposedly higher social status, "Please come to dinner on Saturday with my wife and I," rather than "Please come to dinner on Saturday with my wife and me." On the hyper-nonstandard end of things, the same speaker might emphasize features that are clearly *not* standard, like *-in'* rather than *-ing*, in order to distance himself from that social and linguistic insecurity on his own ground. As we discussed in the previous section, women show similar patterns of variation. Eckert notes that women, adolescents, and lower-middle-class speakers occupy spaces on the margins of society.

In Figure 11.7, we can see the interaction of class and gender in Labov's study of negative concord in Philadelphia. High percentages reflect a high use of what is commonly referred to as "multiple negation" (here called "negative concord"). As in Eckert's study, the women in Labov's study show the highest rates of nonstandard use and the highest rates of standard use. Still other studies suggest that, in all class groups, the teens use more nonstandard forms (for instance /ɪn/ instead of /ɪŋ/) than the adults, and the men use more nonstandard forms than the women. A rise in use of nonstandard forms for middle-class male teens in these studies is similar to the rise in the use of multiple negation by upper-middle-class males in Labov's study. Nonstandard forms may index masculinity in a way that is relevant to all males, especially those who already have social status and can "afford" to use nonstandard forms.

Status, whether real or perceived (and it's not clear that there's much difference between the two), both drives and reflects variation of many kinds, whether at the level

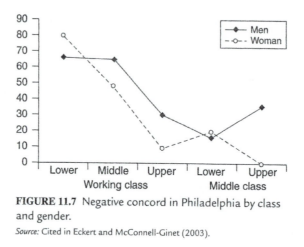

FIGURE 11.7 Negative concord in Philadelphia by class and gender.

Source: Cited in Eckert and McConnell-Ginet (2003).

of lexis, dialect, or discourse. In the end, Americans may not hear all class distinctions, but in fact they hear and express them in speech every day.

Race and Ethnicity

Race and ethnicity, as salient social categories, influence language variation. The most studied dialect of American English, regional or ethnic, is African American English. Not all African Americans speak AAE, and not all speakers of AAE are African American, but the majority of the dialect's speakers are African American and its roots are in the South, as the dialect developed by slaves, who brought African languages to the United States and then learned English. Chicano English is another important ethnic dialect. (We discuss African American English and Chicano English in more detail in Chapter 12.) In time, New World varieties of Spanish brought to the United States recently may also influence American English and promote still other dialects. Many ethnic dialects also demonstrate regional variation, which has historically been understudied, as the focus has been on the ethnic dialect as a systematic whole.

Some features of ethnic dialects can be traced back to historical causes. Many linguists believe that African American English reflects a mixture of Southern varieties and African languages, as well as some creole varieties. The English spoken by the "Pennsylvania Dutch" reflects the influence of earlier English-German bilingualism. For some ethnic varieties such as Chicano English in some parts of the United States, ongoing bilingualism affects the structure and lexicon of the English dialect. In other cases, ethnic groups like the Lumbee Indians in North Carolina, who have lost their native language, adopt a distinctive mixture of variants from other English dialects to maintain a distinctive linguistic identity (Wolfram and Schilling-Estes 1998, 182).

Social Networks

Age, gender, class, race, and ethnicity, along with geography, provide "macro-level" categories for analyzing language variation. When language is studied at that level of generality, research can overlook variation at the "microlevel," where individuals interact with other speakers. It can also fail to account for how language changes—or how it's maintained—among communities of speakers. **Social network theory** offers an alternative perspective for thinking about language variation in speech communities and the spread of language change. Developed in linguistics primarily by Lesley Milroy (her foundational book on the topic, *Language and Social Networks,* was published in 1980), social network theory draws heavily on earlier work in anthropology. Social network theory focuses on the networks of relationships that govern one speaker's regular interactions with others.

Social networks are defined by their density and multiplexity. **Density** refers to how many of the people one person knows and interacts with also know and interact with one another. In a high-density network, many if not most of the people one person interacts with also have independent relationships with each other. **Multiplexity** refers to the number of capacities in which people know each other. In highly multiplex networks, people interact at many levels, such as at work and socially and within the neighborhood. For example, if all your closest friends become friends with each other, you together form a high-density social network. If you all work together, socialize together, live in the same neighborhood, and all attend PTA meetings together at your children's school, you also form a highly multiplex social network.

Highly dense and multiplex social networks seem to help maintain vernacular dialects. Working-class communities, given the local nature of much of the employment, often foster dense and multiplex networks and often demonstrate consistently high use of vernacular forms. Men in particular may have closer-knit social networks in the working class than do women, a fact that helps to explain why women do not participate as much in the maintenance of vernacular dialects. On the other side of the coin, looser-knit networks may facilitate language change, as more socially mobile speakers participate in multiple networks and potentially serve as innovators.

Effects of Language Contact

Contact among languages and dialects sometimes smoothes variation, sometimes creates new variation, sometimes gives birth to new languages, and sometimes kills languages.

Dialect Contact

Dialects of any given language typically exist in close proximity, geographically or socially. Dialect contact can introduce new linguistic variants into a community that may get picked up by other speakers, thereby changing the patterns of variation in the community. For example, a study of the town of Corby, England, shows how native British English speakers have picked up certain Scottish pronunciations (e.g., merging the vowels in the *good* and *food* classes), historically introduced into the community by Scottish workers (Wassink and Dyer 2004). As part of the process, these pronunciations have taken on new social meanings. For younger speakers, these pronunciations signal not a Scottish identity (as they would for their parents) but a local Corby identity, in contrast to that of any neighboring town.

Sometimes dialect contact can erase a distinction, as the adoption of a feature from one dialect to another levels what used to be a difference between them. To take just one example of how this can happen, one proposed principle of change from dialect to dialect is that "mergers spread at the expense of distinctions." Dialects with phonological mergers, for example, can influence similar mergers in neighboring dialects. We can see this principle at work in American English as the *cot/caught* merger spreads across the country (see the map in Chapter 3).

A Question to Discuss

Should We Preserve Endangered Dialects?

Some smaller dialects of English, like the Ocracoke brogue, are endangered. With the greater mobility of younger generations of speakers, the value placed on general or standard varieties in education, and much nonlocal employment, some dialects have fewer and fewer speakers with each successive generation. Modern sociolinguists try to record endangered dialects before they disappear, for the historical record of dialect diversity. Some sociolinguists argue that they also have a responsibility to local communities to help preserve their dialects through, for example, dialect education programs in the schools or preservation societies. They argue that local dialects are critical to local community identities and that dialect diversity, like language diversity more generally, is a general good: a cultural resource to be protected, analogous to ecological diversity.

On the other side are those who argue that the spread of regional or national standard varieties of English, sometimes at the expense of other dialects, is a natural part of language change. They believe that sociolinguists should not interfere with what seems a natural process. What do you think? Should resources be focused on dialect preservation? Why or why not?

Language Contact

Language-contact situations often result in bi- or multilingualism. Many communities are stably multilingual across many generations of speakers. Other language-contact situations result in language change in one or more languages. Where the languages have unequal status, the dominant language is typically called the L2 language, and the subordinate language the L1 language. Thomason and Kaufman (1988) outline two fundamental language-change outcomes in such a situation (in addition to pidgins and creoles, discussed below):

1. Borrowing from L2 into L1, with the maintenance of L1.
2. Interference from L1 under a shift to L2.

As an example of the first outcome, lexical borrowing involves the incorporation of foreign words into a language, usually adapting them to the phonological and morphological patterns of that language. After the Norman Conquest in 1066, French became the language of government and the court (i.e,. the dominant language), but the majority of the population still spoke English. English borrowed an enormous number of French words during this period (including the words *govern* and *court*), and they are now pronounced in "English" ways. In the second outcome, phonological and grammatical interference results in the imposition of certain features of speakers' native language onto the learned dominant language as part of the shift to that language. For example, the syllable-timed prosody of Indian English reflects interference from native languages spoken in India, and Singaporean English incorporates the discourse marker *lah* from southern varieties of Chinese (an example of outcome 2).

As English has spread around the world, through colonialism, trade, business, and technology, English has participated in both categories of change. One of the concerns with shift is the loss of native languages as speakers shift to a second language. Speakers of minority languages like Irish Gaelic struggle to maintain their languages in the face of the social and economic power of English.

Pidgins and Creoles

As we discussed in Chapter 10, in some situations, when speakers of two different, mutually unintelligible languages come into contact over a prolonged period of time, for a specific purpose (e.g., trade), a simplified but stable language of communication will develop, called a pidgin. Pidgins are not any speaker's native language, and while they are a simplified and often more transparent communication system, they are rule-governed (they are not "broken" forms of a language). Pidgins typically have a restricted lexicon (due to their restricted contexts of use) and very few words or morphemes that indicate grammatical structure (e.g., prepositions, articles, inflectional affixes). Pidgins tend also to exhibit a relatively simple phonological system: they usually have five or fewer vowels and a reduced set of consonants. For example, Tok Pisin, an English-based pidgin spoken in Papua New Guinea (where there is a high concentration of mutually unintelligible indigenous languages) collapses /s, ʃ, tʃ/ into /s/.

Tok Pisin, which has been a stable pidgin for almost a century, is undergoing creolization. Creoles are "born" in communities when they become the native language of children of pidgin-speaking parents. With the pidgin input, children develop a full-fledged language, called a creole, that fulfills all of their communicative needs in ways that a pidgin can't. As a result of its communicative sufficiency, the creole may be their only native language. Creoles are grammatically rule-governed, and both the syntax and lexicon develop rapidly during creolization. Creoles typically employ embedded subordinate clauses and morphological marking. For example, as Tok Pisin creolizes, it has developed the morphological marker *ol* before a noun to indicate plurality; in the pidgin, one can determine plurality only by context or the presence of a numeral or qualifier before the noun (Mühlhaüsler 1986). The new systems of morphology and syntax arise in part from features of the native languages already spoken in the community (and may reflect the proportion of speakers of one versus another) and in part from the innate cognitive capacities of children related to language (see Chapters 6 and 10). Thomason and Kaufman (1988) argue that creoles are "nongenetic" languages; in other words, they assert that creoles cannot be mapped into historical language trees (see Chapter 1) as "daughter nodes" from existing languages. Creoles are discontinuous in their transmission and therefore disrupt straightforward family relationships among languages.

Estimates vary from 120 to 200 known pidgin and creole languages spoken around the world. (We do not know how many of today's "languages" came into being as creoles.) Some languages called pidgins are actually creoles (e.g., Hawaiian Pidgin, sometimes also called Hawaiian Creole or Hawaiian Creole English). Given different contact situations, creoles are related to different **lexifier languages**—the languages from which the bulk of the vocabulary comes. Haitian Creole is historically related to French, and Jamaican Creole is historically related to English; both are also related to several West African languages. Creoles often exist on a continuum, from the **basilect** (the variety with the most creole features) to the **acrolect** (the variety closest to the lexifier language—e.g., "Jamaican English" in Jamaica), with a range of **mesolects** in between. Many speakers can shift along the continuum, from varieties close to the lexifier language to varieties unintelligible to speakers of the lexifier language, and all of these varieties carry different social meanings.

To take Jamaican creole as one example—a creole related to English—we find the following distinctive features (from Wassink 2005):

- lexical items from West African languages: for example, *nyam* 'eat' from Ewe;
- English words that carry different meanings: for example, *dem* as a plural marker, as in *wuman-dem* 'the women';
- English words that carry the same meaning but are pronounced quite differently: for example, *di* 'the', *wata* 'water';
- different grammatical constructions: for example, *a* to signal the progressive: "Mi a nyam di bammy" = 'I am eating the cassava patty';
- different intonational patterns: for example, rising intonation in interrogatives versus falling intonation in declaratives constitutes the sole distinction between the syntactic structures, as the subject appears before the verb or auxiliary verb in both cases "Mi a nyam di bammy" can be either a question ('Am I eating the cassava patty?') or a statement ('I am eating the cassava patty'), depending on intonation alone.

This brief list captures elements of the distinctive lexicon, prosody, and systematic grammar of Jamaican creole. When hip hop artist Sean Paul sings "Get Busy," not all American listeners realize that they can hear some of these features of Jamaican creole in the lyrics, such as the progressive in "Me lyrics a provide electricity" (as well as the nonstandard possessive *me*).

Speaker Attitudes and Language Variation

We all judge other people based on the way they speak. As soon as someone begins speaking, we make judgments about the person's origins, education, sexual orientation, and social affiliations—not to mention his or her personality. We often make these judgments based on subtle linguistic variables such as pronunciation and grammatical features—the *way* someone speaks rather than what the person says. Even if we're not aware of it, we can put a lot of weight on whether speakers differentiate *pin* and *pen*, whether they say *greasy* or *greazy*, or whether they use one negative or two.

Dennis Preston has carried out extensive studies in **perceptual dialectology** (or "folk dialectology"), which examines where speakers perceive dialects to be, as well as their attitudes toward those dialects. In one of his best-known studies, Preston asks speakers in different states to rate the standardness of other regions in the United States. As the maps in Figures 11.8 and 11.9 indicate, speakers often agree about areas that speak nonstandard varieties: "the South" (although the boundaries of the South vary and tend to exclude Florida), New York, and the Boston area. Areas of the Midwest and Pacific Northwest often get fairly high ratings for standardness. Residents of Michigan believe that their own English is the most standard, but other states don't share that perception. Students at Auburn, Alabama, do not identify Southern English as standard (Preston diagnoses it as a case of "linguistic insecurity") but look instead to Washington, D.C., as the standard.

Many of these studies ask respondents to describe other varieties with adjectives. While Southerners may not consider their English standard, they do consider it pleasant and friendly, and their ratings of other dialects on both those counts get consistently

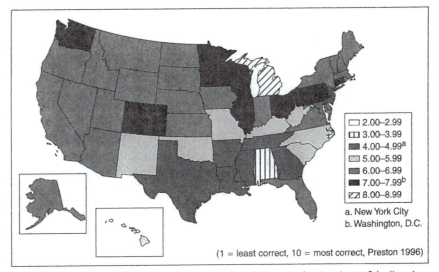

FIGURE 11.8 This map illustrates the means of Michigan speakers' ratings of the linguistic correctness of the English spoken in all 50 states (1 = least correct, 10 = most correct).

Source: Courtesy of Dennis Preston.

lower the farther north the dialect (see Figure 11.10). Midwesterners rate their own speech as pleasant. The dialect area that suffers the lowest pleasantness ratings from both Southern and Midwestern respondents is New York.

Beliefs about the correctness of Standard English and its superiority over nonstandard varieties are so pervasive that they can seem like common sense or obvious truths. As a

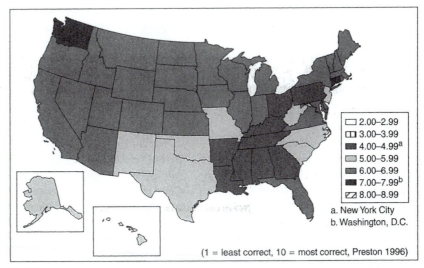

FIGURE 11.9 This map illustrates the means of Indiana speakers' ratings of the linguistic correctness of the English spoken in all 50 states (1 = least correct, 10 = most correct).

Source: Courtesy of Dennis Preston.

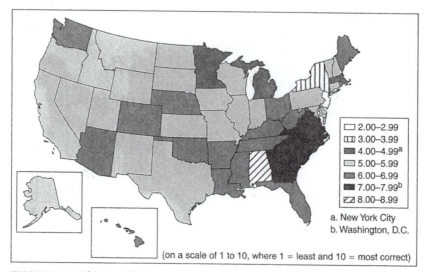

FIGURE 11.10 This map illustrates the means of Alabama speakers' ratings of the pleasantness of the English spoken in all fifty states (1 = least pleasant, 10 = most pleasant).

Source: Courtesy of Dennis Preston.

result, linguists trying to explain that all dialects are equally systematic in their structures, that they are equally communicative and expressive, and that they all deserve respect, are sometimes dismissed as overly liberal, trying to legitimize the illegitimate. For example, in 1999, Margalit Fox wrote in the *New York Times Sunday Magazine* about the linguistic equality of all dialects. She quoted several prominent sociolinguists and made claims about language that most sociolinguists see as uncontroversial. Two weeks later, the letters to the editor were all negative, attacking "ultra-liberal" linguists who were willing to let language standards fall to the point that all dialects might be considered legitimate.

A Question to Discuss

What Does "Linguistic Equality" Mean?

When linguists describe all varieties of a language, both standard and nonstandard, as "linguistically equal," they are typically referring to the fact that all varieties are equally rule-governed and logical, as well as responsive to speakers' needs. All varieties of a language are often not socially equal, however. Some nonstandard varieties may be widely considered "bad." And some standard varieties may have been extended lexically and stylistically to serve formal and academic purposes.

Sociolinguists argue that "the social" is part of "the linguistic," so social judgments cannot be excluded from "the linguistic." Given this premise, should we use a more specific term than "linguistically equal"? What are some other terms we could use instead to communicate the point that sociolinguists are trying to make? What would be gained by using each of those terms? What would be lost?

That same year, the *New York Times* ran a story about Kirk Hazen, a sociolinguist at West Virginia University, who gives talks at local K–12 schools about the legitimacy of Appalachian English as the language of students' communities. The article described the letters that some state residents had sent to the president of the university demanding Hazen's resignation for teaching such improper material. Beliefs about "proper" and "improper" English are powerful, and the social inequality of dialects can overwhelm statements about their linguistic equality. Given these kinds of public reactions, sociolinguists discuss how they might most effectively approach the education of the public about the linguistic equality of standard and nonstandard varieties.

Special Focus: Code-switching

A bilingual college student on the phone with her parents speaks mostly Spanish, but every few sentences she inserts a few English words (e.g., *train station, four o'clock*) and sometimes a full English clause (e.g., *Oh, I don't care*). It's not that she can't say these things in Spanish. And when asked about these language switches later, she doesn't realize that she used English in the conversation with her parents. What is happening here?

In Chapter 8, we discussed how all speakers style-shift. Many bidialectal or bilingual speakers also code-switch. Code-switching (sometimes also referred to as **code-mixing**) refers to speakers' alternating between two codes (usually between distinct dialects or languages) within one stretch of discourse or conversation, within one turn, or within one sentence. Thus variation can occur not only across populations, within speech communities or communities of practice, and within the speech of a single person over time, but also within a single communicative act. Code-switching is yet another result of language contact. This kind of language mixing sometimes develops names specific to the languages involved, such as Spanglish. (Note the difference between Spanglish and Chicano English.)

Many bilingual speakers who code-switch are not consciously aware that they are doing so at any given moment. And some code-switching speakers will deny code-switching at all if they feel that using one specific language or that mixing languages is stigmatized. A student of one of the authors of this book once studied the code-switching in his home, where both Korean and English were spoken. In one tape recording, his mother stated directly that she herself did not code-switch—in a sentence in which she used both Korean and English.

Although code-switching has sometimes been viewed as a result of insufficient bilingualism, studies suggest that intrasentential code-switching (switching languages within a sentence) requires high proficiency in both languages. Code-switching does not just happen when a speaker cannot think of a word in one language, or because one language does not have an appropriate word. As you can see in the following two examples, speakers often code-switch for very basic words and phrases, which clearly exist in both languages.

Why make Carol *sentarse atras pa'que* everybody has to move *pa'que se salga?*

'Why make Carol sit at the back so that everybody has to move so that she can get out?' (English/Spanish; Poplack 1980, 589)

You didn't have to worry que *somebody* te iba a tirar con cerveza o una botella *or something like that.*

'You didn't have to worry that somebody was going to throw beer or a bottle at you or something like that'. (Spanish/English; Poplack 1981, 170)

Code-switching is often the unmarked or expected form of communication in some communities and contexts, rather than an exceptional occurrence.

In the two examples, we see code-switching at the level of the word, phrase, and clause. Code-switching also sometimes occurs at the level of the utterance or turn in a conversation. Consider the following excerpt from a conversation between two bilingual Mandarin Chinese-English youths (Wei 2002). Speaker A seems to be trying to persuade B to tell Tim that A does not want to lend him his bike.

A: Tim rang [and (.) wanted to borrow me bike.
B: [oh yeah?
(1.0)
A: <u>again</u> you know?
B: (1.0)
A: You're seeing him tonight, aren't you.
B: Yup.
A: (1.0) ohhh dunno (.) I think I'm going to ask Susan to tell him.
B: (0.6) *Rang Susan shuo shenma.*
        let   say   what
        'What do you want Susan to say?'
A: He broke the bloody gear you know? (.) [I mean . . .
B: [mm
A: *Ni gen ta shuo wo yao chuqu* [*yitang.*
   you PREP. him say I want go-out once
   'You tell him that I'm going out'.
B: [*Susan buhui guan de.*
                                won't bother PA.
                                'Susan won't bother (about that).'
A: (1.5)
B: What do you want me to say.

As Wei points out, we see the speakers making many strategic moves to negotiate the making and turning down of this request: for example, B's pauses early in the episode (not acknowledging the implicit request—a dispreferred response); A's use of discourse markers like *you know;* both speakers switching between Chinese and English. When Speaker A changes tactics and says he is going to ask Susan to tell Tim, B not only pauses but then switches to Chinese, again not providing a preferred response (which would probably be something like "You don't have to ask Susan—I'll do it"). A then has to make his request explicitly, asking B to tell Tim, and you'll notice that B follows A's switch to Chinese in making this direct request. In the end, B finally acknowledges the request, in English.

Over the past three decades, studies of code-switching have tried to isolate the grammatical constraints affecting code-switching: where in a sentence or utterance can code-switching occur? Most proposed constraints do not hold across all possible language-mixing situations, however.

Pieter Muysken, after surveying many of the published studies, suggests that three processes—insertion, alternation, and congruent lexicalization—are at work in code-mixing (his preferred term).

With insertion speakers insert words or phrases from one language into the structure of another, for example (from Muysken 2000, 5):

Yo anduve *in a state of shock* por dos dias.

'I walked in a state of shock for two days'. (Spanish/English; Pfaff 1979, 296)

Insertion can look like borrowing, but inserted forms, unlike borrowed forms, are not adapted to the phonological or grammatical patterns of the dominant language. And they are more spontaneous—they do not become a stable part of the dominant language's lexicon. Insertion is more common in bilingual communities where speakers are more proficient in one of the two languages. As a result of its status, the dominant language incorporates relatively small units from the language speakers use less or less comfortably.

In **alternation** speakers switch between grammatical structures from two languages, for example (from Muysken 2000, 5):

Les femmes et le vin, *ne ponimayu.*

'Women and wine, I don't understand'. (French/Russian; Timm 1975, 312)

Andale pues *and do come again.*

'That's all right then, and do come again'. (Spanish/English; Gumperz and
    Hernández-Chavez 1971, 118)

Alternation is more frequent in stable bilingual communities, those with strong traditions of maintaining both languages. In such communities, speakers are secure in both languages, and switching in the form of alternation is a relatively common speech practice.

When the two languages spoken in a bilingual community share the same basic grammatical structure, speakers can switch between the two lexicons within a sentence or utterance: this is called **congruent lexicalization**. Switching between dialects (as well as, perhaps, style-shifting) tends to fall into this category, as the fundamental grammatical structure is typically shared. Here is an example from English and Dutch, and you can see the structural similarities (from Muysken 2000, 11):

Wan ik komt *home from school.*

'When I come home from school'. (Dutch/English; Clyne 1987, 759)

In all of these examples, the shift must be grammatical in both languages, in terms of word order. So, for example, an English adjective would not be inserted after a noun in code-switching with a language like French, which tends to use post–noun modifiers: *le vin red* ('the red wine').

Some scholars argue that code-switching, like style-shifting, is a response to a situation or speech-activity type: shifts in topic or audience can lead to switches in language. But this may not be the whole story. Bilingual speakers sometimes code-switch and sometimes do not in the same register or with the same topic. Other scholars frame code-switching as a strategic use of available language resources to achieve specific interactional goals—strategic choices happening primarily below the level of consciousness. The key point: code-switching demonstrates multiple fluencies, not any disfluencies. Bilingualism is sometimes framed only as fluency in two discrete, different languages. But for many speakers, bilingualism also involves the productive mixing of the two languages in interactions with other bilingual speakers.

☑ Summary

Dialectology and sociolinguistics are two methods of studying language variation. Dialectology is the older tradition of scholarship and involves, among other subjects, linguistic geography of the type behind the Linguistic Atlas Projects. Sociolinguistics studies variation in terms of speech communities and, more recently, communities of practice and linguistic markets. In this chapter, you have encountered several fundamental principles of language variation and research about it, including the following:

- All speakers of a language speak a dialect of that language. Dialectal variation is a natural, indeed, an essential, aspect of language.

- In any particular place and at any particular time, one or more dialects of language may have more prestige among speakers than others, but judgments about prestige are social and political, rather than linguistic. At the level of linguistic systematicity, all varieties of a language are equal.

- Language variation correlates social factors, such as age, gender, class, race and ethnicity, and social network, as well as with geographical factors and settlement history.

- Most language change occurs below the level of consciousness ("change from below"). Speakers can also influence language change deliberately, or above the level of consciousness ("change from above").

- Contact among languages influences their development and, in certain cases, produces pidgins and creoles.

Suggested Reading

Helpful introductory textbooks on sociolinguistics include J. K. Chambers's *Socioloinguistic Theory: Linguistic Variation and Its Social Significance* (1995) and Lesley Milroy and Matthew Gordon's *Sociolinguistics: Method and Interpretation* (2003). Anyone planning to pursue a sociolinguistic project would do well to read Barbara Johnstone's *Qualitative Methods in Sociolinguistics* (2000), which outlines qualitative research techniques with a combination of practical advice and more theoretical context. Penelope Eckert's *Linguistic Variation as Social Practice* (2000) describes the Belten High study in terms of communities of practice and linguistic markets. *American English* (2005), by Walt Wolfram and Natalie Schilling-Estes, provides detailed treatments of sociolinguistic variables relevant to variation in American English, as well as detailed descriptions of the history and features of many dialect varieties. Dennis Preston has reflected on his work in perceptual dialectology in the journal *American Speech* (2000, 2003). *Language Contact, Creolization, and Genetic Linguistics* (1988), by Sarah Grey Thomason and Terrence Kaufman, is a central work in the field of language contact and change. Two still important books on pidgins and creoles are Suzanne Romaine's *Pidgin and Creole Languages* (1988) and Peter Mühlhaüsler's *Pidgin and Creole Linguistics* (1986); Salikoko Mufwene provides a different perspective on the development of creoles in *The Ecology of Language Evolution* (2001). Pieter Muysken's *Bilingual Speech: A Typology of Code-Mixing* (2000) includes a very useful overview of research on code-switching and detailed descriptions. Carol Myers-Scotton's *Duelling Languages: Grammatical Structure in Codeswitching* (1993) remains a key text, and she has more recently published *Contact Linguistics: Bilingual Encounters and Grammatical Outcomes* (2002). If you are interested in William Labov's groundbreaking work, start with *Sociolinguistic Patterns* (1972). If you are ambitious, you can tackle his major recent books: *Principles of Linguistic Change,* vol. 1, *Internal Factors* (1994), and vol. 2, *Social Factors* (2001); vol. 3, *Cognitive Factors,* is yet to come.

Exercises

Exercise 11.1   Communities of Practice

Describe some of the communities of practice in which you participate. What are your intuitions about whether you speak differently in different communities? Provide specific examples.

Exercise 11.2   American Dialects

1. On the Web site of the Linguistic Atlas of the Middle and South Atlantic States (LAMSAS) (http://www.lap.uga.edu), generate maps for the different versions of "quarter of." Where would you draw isoglosses?

2. Some forms in American dialects reflect the workings of analogy: changes in irregular forms to make them consistent with the rest of the regular forms in the paradigm. For example, dialects that use the forms *hisself* and *theirself* show the effects of analogy on the reflexive pronoun paradigm: all other reflexive pronouns are created by POSSESSIVE + SELF (*myself, yourself, ourselves*), so *himself* and *themselves* have been changed to become regular.

   Think about how the past tense and past perfect are related for regular verbs. How is analogy relevant in dialects that use past-perfect forms like the following: *had went, had came, had rang, had swam*?

Exercise 11.3   Dialect Attitudes

1. Ask five speakers at your school who are from the state where your school is located to locate dialect areas on a blank map of the United States. Then ask each speaker to label and describe the dialect areas they have identified. Summarize your results with specific examples.

2. Ask five speakers at your school who are from the state where your school is located to locate dialect areas on a blank map of your state. Then ask each speaker to label and describe the dialect areas they have identified. Summarize your results with specific examples. (It can be interesting to do this with the same five speakers you asked for (1), so that you can compare how they draw more global and more local dialect areas.)

3. Describe two moments in your own life when you have judged other people by the way they speak. It may have been when you first met someone or when you spoke to someone on the phone. (These may be positive, negative, or neutral judgments.) What associations were you making between specific linguistic variables and personal characteristics?

4. Imagine that in a conversation with a friend, you describe what you have been reading about in this book: that all dialects, both standard and nonstandard, are linguistically equal. Your friend says, "Oh come on, that is just not true. Those nonstandard dialects are just ignorant—people who don't know how to use English right." How would you explain to your friend the linguistic equality of dialects? What examples or analogies do you think might be useful in making the case?

5. In your experience, what phonological, lexical, syntactic, or discourse features mark class differences? Ask six speakers at your school to name at least six language features they consider important in marking class. Examine the similarities and differences in their responses in relation to the material in this chapter. What do your results suggest about the relationship between class and speech? (If any respondents had a strong reaction to being asked this question about class, feel free to incorporate those findings into your response.)

Chapter 12

American Dialects

The most obviously nonstandard speaker on *The Simpsons*, Cletus looks as stereotyped as his speech sounds.

D ialect has long been a source of humor. Chaucer, writing in fourteenth-century London, in the south of England, made fun of northern dialects of Middle English in *The Reeve's Tale*. During this same period, the Wakefield Master (a northerner) joked about southern dialect in *The Second Shepherd's Play*. In the twenty-first century, American speakers may poke fun at the nasality of Midwesterners ("They sound like they always have a cold!"), the "tawk" of New Yorkers, or the drawl of Southerners. Sometimes this kind of criticism draws connections between language and cultural stereotypes: for instance, that New Yorkers clip their speech because they are rude, or that Southerners drawl because they are lazy.

Let's consider Cletus the Slack-Jawed Yokel from *The Simpsons*. Cletus is unshaven, dirty, lazy, and (unduly) procreative. He is a stereotype of a kind of American (on *Simpsons* Web sites, he is often referred to as a "redneck"), and his language contributes to the stereotype. To most television viewers, Cletus sounds like a "hillbilly." In fact, his Appalachian speech is exaggerated. For example, Cletus drawls more broadly and nasally than most speakers of Appalachian English. But many listeners may not think that the speech is inauthentic, so inaccuracy paradoxically reinforces the negative stereotype. Cletus also uses double modals, as in "I might could do that," which does accurately represent some Appalachian speech. Because many Americans may never have heard anyone use double modals in everyday speech, however, they may consider it ignorant speech—not merely nonstandard, but substandard.

African American English has also often been the object of unfair stereotypes and jokes. During the controversy over Ebonics in 1997 (which we discuss later in the chapter), some commentators framed the whole idea of Ebonics as laughable and constructed complex jokes about it. As John Baugh recounts in *Beyond Ebonics* (2000, 94):

> It didn't take long before other comedians began to generate a series of satirical Ebonic spin-offs for other groups: Jews were said to speak "Hebonics," and Italians were said to speak "Italionics," while residents of Utah were said to speak "Utahonics," and gay men were alleged to speak "Shebonics."

Such jokes at the expense of speakers of Appalachian and African American English may be funny to some people, but they are also socially antagonistic. They assert the ultimate validity of mainstream speech, or (more accurately) what most Americans take to be mainstream speech. What's at stake in humor about dialect, whether regional or social, is who gets to call the linguistic shots— whose position of cultural authority allows them to trivialize the speech of other Americans.

This chapter focuses specifically on American dialects. We look first at the politics of dialects in the United States and some of the social consequences of dialect competition. Next we discuss regional variation in the United States, looking specifically at Appalachian English and California English as case studies. We then turn to social variation in the United States and look specifically at Chicano English and African American English as case studies. Appalachian English and African American English are the two most studied dialects of American English in linguistic research, while California English and Chicano English are two dialects receiving increasing attention.

The Politics of American Dialects

Everyone speaks a dialect. As Walt Wolfram has written, "to speak a language is to speak some dialect of that language" (1991, 2). All speakers of American English speak a dialect of American English in any situation, even if not the same dialect in every situation. Standard American English is one dialect among many in the United States. And in fact, few of us speak pure Standard American English while about our daily business, though some of us switch easily from a familiar dialect to the standard, in order to accomplish certain social, political, or commercial ends.

Speakers in some parts of the United States, such as the Midwest and Pacific Northwest, sometimes describe their English as "plain English" or "normal English"—American English with no accent or distinctive dialect features. But "nondialectal" American English is a myth. That some speakers' dialect is closer to a standard form of American English does not mean that it has no accent or distinctive features. If these speakers go to the South or to Britain, they are the ones whose accents and grammar sound out of place, as, literally, they are. Every dialect, even the dialect called Standard English, has features that distinguish it from other dialects.

Speakers Who Control Multiple Dialects

Many speakers of American English control more than one dialect. For many native speakers of nonstandard varieties of English, one of their other dialects is Standard American English—the result of years of schooling and the dominance of the standard in the professional world, in the media, and elsewhere. The code-switching in which these speakers engage involves shifting not only from variety to variety within a particular instance of discourse, but also often between a home or "private" dialect and a professional or "public" one. For example, African American or Appalachian bankers, brokers, college professors, psychiatrists, and bureaucrats may speak one variety of American English among the African American or Appalachian communities and another when operating within the dominant speech community.

The terms of code-switching are not reciprocal, for two reasons. First, speakers in the dominant group typically assume that they do not have to switch to a nonstandard dialect to achieve specific communicative goals, and in practice they almost never do. Everyone for whom the dominant dialect is secondary is expected to switch toward the "standard" when required to do so. Consider all of the implications (social, political, economic, and linguistic) embedded in this too often asked question: "Why can't the person behind the counter at [name the establishment] speak so that I can understand her?" In fact, it would take very little for a mainstream speaker to understand most nonstandard varieties of American English—one need merely listen carefully and interpret the speech in context. It is not parallel to learning two languages, as residents of Quebec must, or three languages, as must many Swiss.

Second, when members of the culturally dominant group attempt to switch toward a nonstandard, and often supposedly inferior, variety of American English, the attempt can be seen as offensive by the culturally subordinate group. "Wiggas," the suburban, white kids who admire and attempt to participate in some aspects of African American culture (usually via hip hop), are often mocked for their use of AAE, and some AAE speakers express anger about such appropriation of their language. Many speakers of

Standard American English who borrow from AAE also do so selectively—not truly code-switching but adopting some lexical items, a few phonological features (but often not consistently), and sometimes some grammatical features (again, not always consistently or grammatically). For example, speakers may use "da" for "the" in some expressions (e.g., "da man" or "da basement"), but not use /d/ for /ð/ in all contexts. Some of these speakers use *be* in reference to vigorous action (e.g., "We be bringing down the house"), without knowledge of how *be* is used in AAE to indicate habitual activity, not vigorous activity. Times are changing, though, and AAE may be spreading to use by non–African American speakers, especially in urban settings.

Judgments and Humor about Dialects

Preference for one variety of any language over others is social and political. As we discussed in Chapter 11, from a linguistic perspective, all varieties are equal—that is, from a structural perspective, no variety is superior to any other. Most linguists view this statement about the structural equality of dialects as a linguistic fact, but it is often framed by non-linguists as a very liberal political position. It challenges many speakers' long-standing beliefs about the standard variety as inherently more logical, more eloquent, or in some other way better than other varieties. The standard variety is certainly more rule-governed in terms of prescriptive rules, but all dialects are equally rule-governed in terms of descriptive rules (e.g., in Chapter 5 we discussed how some nonstandard varieties apply the reflexive pronoun rule POSSESSIVE + SELF across the board to create *hisself* and *theirselves*). Because the standard variety is used in a wider variety of contexts, it has developed specialized vocabularies and registers. But linguists argue that any language variety could and would develop similarly if its speakers needed to use the variety in similar contexts.

None of these statements is meant to argue that there is no value to a standard variety or that the standard variety should be abandoned. Variation within a language is unavoidable, and one variety may be selected and developed into a "standard" and thereby serve as a "common ground" among other varieties—which can be very useful. But standard dialects tend also to be seen as superior compared to other varieties, and, for political and social reasons, dialects of a language often stand in unequal relations to one another. The linguistically unwarranted jump is to insist that some varieties of American English—because they are closer to the standard or because they carry social prestige—are structurally superior to others, and that, by extension, some speakers are, too.

Standard American English, a social dialect that lives side by side with other social and regional dialects in the United States, is subject to criticism and stereotype by speakers of other dialects as well. After all, speaking close to the standard is one thing, but speaking "perfectly" is quite another. When someone too well schooled in Standard American English practices it in speech and writing every day (someone, say, like an English professor), those forced to listen to him or her may think "Stuck Up American English" (SUAE), rather than Standard American English. If someone says, "Were I in your position, that's not to whom I would turn," listeners may find it pretentious, yet that sentence is certainly "standard." Most current speakers avoid the subjunctive (*were* rather than *was* in hypothetical statements), regularly end sentences with prepositions, fail to distinguish between *who* and *whom* and *that* and *which,* and on and on. The colloquial speaker rightly thinks, "Just because someone speaks Standard American English doesn't mean he's better than *me*," while the speaker of SUAE insists that it's "better than *I*."

Were your speech so standard as to carry every one of these markers, you would probably invite a smile, if not a joke at your expense. American speech is often colloquial, and 100 percent certified Standard American English is a rare phenomenon. The pristine standard is a social dialect, just as is AAE. It invites stereotype and humor. Indeed, it's a stereotype on which speakers of colloquial American English, AAE, Appalachian English, and just about everybody else can agree. The difference, of course, is that those secure in the Ivory Tower, or in national media, government, or the learned professions, don't suffer in those settings from the stigma that attaches to SUAE. But others speaking other dialects, both regional and social, can suffer from more negative stigmas.

Dialect Diversity and National Unity

One of our national mottos is *E pluribus unum*—"From many, one." It's a cryptic assertion. It could mean that many cultures melt together in the American "pot," from which we forge a national metal both unusually strong and flexible. But it isn't obvious that either American experience or American character consists of just one substance. When it comes to language, Standard American English is no longer flexible enough to enfold all the nonstandard alternatives in other dialects, and many speakers resist any such mixture. Occasionally nonstandard features become standardized, but more often they remain "nonstandard" in comparison to Standard American English. A proposal that we should all speak a single variety of American English composed of all American English dialects in proportion to population (x percent AAE, y percent Appalachian English, z percent Pennsylvania German-influenced English, etc.) is unthinkable.

Language Change at Work

The Inconsistency of Language Attitudes

Single words and pronunciation patterns can carry a lot of social baggage. In Chapter 1, we discussed the social judgments that can be attached to the use of *aks*. Interestingly, nonstandard forms from the same dialect can carry different stigmas. Here, a speaker from Portage, Michigan, describes the difference between a root and a creek:

> I grew up saying root to rhyme with *foot*, and *roof, room,* and *broom* with essentially the same vowel. At the same time, I was taught not to say creek as *crick*. Both pronunciations come from the same language heritage, that of Scots and Scots-Irish. *Crick,* however, marked social inferiority: supposedly, only the uneducated would use it rather than

standard *creek*. How one pronounced that word announced to all where one stood in the social pecking order within our region. Saying *root* to rhyme with *foot,* however, didn't raise any eyebrows. It wasn't until I started teaching in another state and my students mocked my pronunciation of *root* that I realized this pronunciation might sound strange, and even funny, to others.

The same pronunciation in different places can also carry different social meaning. For example, /r/-lessness marks working-class speech in New York City but upper-class speech in areas of Britain where they speak RP (Received Pronunciation).

An alternative reading of *E pluribus unum* is that we are one nation even though we retain a certain diversity. Diversity may be more desirable, a greater asset, than uniformity. Perhaps unity from diversity is more like working from a bag of wooden blocks than from molten culture: we build our culture and our political republic from a miscellaneous array of blocks, but the blocks retain their colors and shapes. The successful culture isn't constructed *in spite* of diversity but *because* of it. If we acknowledge the United States' inevitable pluralism, the motto can be seen as true and inspiring because it's a paradox. When it comes to language as part of this equation, we hit another paradox. Americans have generally become more and more welcoming of cultural diversity or multiculturalism when it involves, for example, dress, customs, food, and holidays. Language falls outside this multicultural embrace, and linguistic homogeneity is still generally perceived as preferable. However, almost any definition of culture you can find has language at its core. How does or should linguistic diversity play into the multiculturalism of the United States? It is a question that confronts all Americans, and we return to it in Chapter 14.

Regional Variation

We can generalize about regional variation using isoglosses on a map that neatly divide regions from each other, but in the real world of speakers, variation actually occurs on a much smaller scale than can be marked off by isoglosses. When people hear the phrase "American dialects," they may first think of the South or New York City or Boston— some of the more famous regional dialects. But dialects and dialect variations are all around you, wherever you are. Informally, we often say, "Oh, they use *that word* there" or "They say their a's differently there," without realizing we're talking about exactly the kinds of subtle differences that add up to make dialects distinctive.

Keep your ear to the ground as you walk in any direction from your home, and you'll hear minor speech differences along the way. If you are from the North, the differences won't suddenly sound like Southern speech, though, and vice versa. Variation is gradual, and for someone living on the Mason-Dixon line, the difference between North and South, in linguistic terms, is negligible at best.

Today, travel, media, and education allow dialect features to migrate more easily from community to community and can blur sharp boundaries. Nevertheless, regional dialects are alive and well in the United States. The dialect regions established by a history of migration from one to another part of the country do not seem to be eroding through the influence of television. Just as you can hear differences in the pronunciation of /r/ from a Manhattan diner to a Brooklyn subway station, you can expect to hear subtle variation wherever you turn: variation still operates on a very small scale in twenty-first-century America. Dialect differences remain fundamental parts of speakers' identities and definition of communities, and they adhere as much to local norms for speech as to more widespread "standard" norms.

The small-scale dialect differences all around you suggest one fundamental principle about regional variation:

Regional variation is generally continuous.

Isoglosses usually do not correspond to sharp breaks between how neighboring communities speak. As you travel, you are more likely to hear accents shift gradually, and to hear new words and grammatical features introduced into use and dropped from use gradually, than you are to cross an imaginary line and encounter sudden, wholesale change. There are, of course, exceptions, as when a community is isolated enough regionally (e.g., on an island) to develop dialect features more radically different from neighboring communities. For the most part, however, dialects differ as much quantitatively (how often a specific feature appears) as qualitatively (the existence of a specific feature).

A Sample Walk

Let's turn to a less well-known dialect area, specifically to Berks County, Pennsylvania (see Figure 12.1), and take a short walk among the distinctive dialect variants there. As you'll read about later in the chapter, Pennsylvania actually plays a central role in the history of American dialects, particularly of the Midland varieties. (For the purposes of dialectology, the term "Midlands" represents a large area running from the eastern seaboard to the middle of the country, including Pennsylvania, Ohio, Indiana, Illinois, Iowa, and states or parts of states often thought of as southern, like Kentucky and Arkansas.) A long walk through Berks County uncovers variation everywhere and provides a more detailed sense of subtle regional variation. The experience isn't exotic: you won't climb Mount Everest or hear the cockatoo or encounter people speaking Basque. But if you start your journey in a city like Reading, you will encounter dialectal variation by the time you reach the outskirts of the town.

Wallace Stevens (1879–1955), one of America's great poets, was born and raised in Reading, Pennsylvania. His journals recount extensive walks across Berks County, in which Reading is situated, during his high school and college years. A day's strenuous walk will take you out of Berks into Lancaster or Lebanon Counties. All three counties

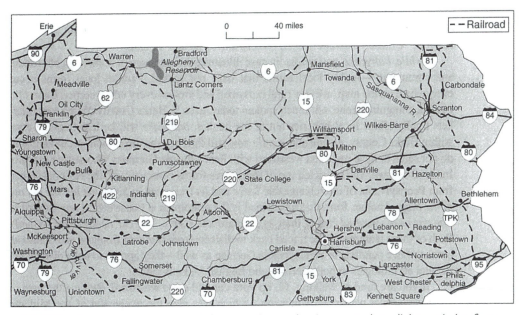

FIGURE 12.1 If you walk or drive around the state of Pennsylvania, you can hear dialect variation from town to town, county to county.

include large German-descended populations, and the American English there is strongly German influenced. Some communities in these counties also continue to speak a dialect of German sometimes called "Pennsylvania Dutch."

Many lexical items unfamiliar to most Americans are shared across these three counties. For example, if there isn't any more salt for your eggs and *scrapple* ('seasoned, molded mixture of ground meat and cornmeal'), then *The salt is all* ('The salt is all gone'). Or perhaps a friend stops by for a trip to the mall. If she retrieves your morning newspaper from the front step on the way into your house, you ask her to *let*—rather than *leave*—it on the table. Or you might think you need some new clothes, but your parents may not support the day's shopping, though they'll make sure you have what you need *till* ('by the time that') school starts in the fall.

The temporal adverb *awhile* also works differently in these counties—explicable once you know the history of the dialect. Pennsylvania German includes the term *alleweil* 'immediately', and it is likely that German speakers associated it with the similar-sounding adverbial *in a while* 'after some lapse in time'. As a result, a Berks County shopkeeper can ask, "Can I ring you up awhile?" with the innovative adverb *awhile* 'now, at this moment', a centuries-certified item of regional vocabulary. The variant form *awhile now* is recorded from Lebanon County, and as you walk west in Berks County, the more likely you are to hear *awhile now* spoken in close proximity to *awhile*, sometimes even in the same conversation!

Food terms are often very local, at least until their referents are mass-produced and marketed nationwide. *Gumbo* and *jambalaya*, for example, were rarely heard outside New Orleans and French Louisiana until recently, but now you can find them on restaurant menus in Reading, Pennsylvania. In Reading, if you stop at a local bakery, you might try a small, plain-flavored sugar cookie cut into a vaguely human shape—a *babycake*. You can buy babycakes in Reading, but you won't find them in Lancaster or in Lebanon County, just next door. If the person behind the bakery counter gives you a complimentary babycake to share more of this local delicacy, she might put it in a bag for you, "Unless you want it later," where *unless* means 'in case'.

Awhile, babycake, and *unless* 'in case' illustrate the language of home, neighborhood, and community—highly local forms that have not spread. Parallel local forms occur everywhere on the map, at every rural crossroad and around every urban corner. *Unless* 'in case' is a linguistic relic, not much spoken today, even in Berks County. When supermarkets finally elbow local bakeries out of the market, *babycake* will be less frequent even within Berks County. *Awhile* and *awhile now* still thrive in the three counties, though they do not seem to have migrated westward with Pennsylvania Germans who settled in Ohio, Indiana, or Iowa. The restricted use of these three forms contrasts with the regional spread from Pennsylvania of interchangeable *leave* and *let* (reflected in *Someone left the cat out of the bag*). Another form that has spread is the grammatical construction represented in *The car needs washed* (rather than its standard alternative, *The car needs to be washed*). Both of these features can be traced back to dialects from northern England and Scotland, but they have parallels in Pennsylvania German as well—they appear to have distinct but parallel etymologies in both German and English (Adams 2000).

If you are tired of walking, fill up your car and drive westward. Retrace the path of America's great westward expansion—which was also the expansion of the Midland dialects—along the Forbes Road, between Philadelphia and Pittsburgh. Opportunities on what was still the American frontier attracted English- and German-speaking

Language Change at Work

Why Does *unless* Mean 'in case' in Pennsylvania?

Dialectal features are often formed from the pressure of languages in contact. *Unless* 'in case' is a typical example of this phenomenon. It is the consequence of German speakers attempting to understand an English word that looks simple, but is actually quite complicated (Adams and Perrin 1995).

Unless has embedded in it a sense of exception: "I will take this away unless [except in the case that] you still want it." Why *unless* should have such a complex meaning isn't obvious, but it is the product of semantic and morphosyntactic history. *Unless* derives from the Middle English comparative phrase *on lesse than* 'on a less condition than'. In late Middle English, *on* compounded with *lesse* into *onlesse,* and (because of the weak initial stress) *onlesse* became *unless.* In the sixteenth century, *than* disappeared from the phrase and the conjunction *unless* was born.

In German, there are several ways to say *unless,* and most are formed as negatives. They correspond to English *unless,* apparently (but not really) because *un-* usually indicates a negative or opposite. That said, the German form that may be the source of confusion is *außer wenn* 'unless'. The word *außer* alone means 'apart [from]', and *wenn* alone means 'in case'. If German speakers took *unless* as an equivalent for *wenn,* that would explain the use of *unless* 'in case', *unless* without a negative or sense of exception, in contrast to standard American English *unless* 'except in the case that'.

Americans, who migrated west along that road; so did Scots and Scots-Irish newly disembarked at the ports of Baltimore and Philadelphia. Now, however, you'll have to take the Pennsylvania Turnpike, I-76.

Stopping along the turnpike, you can experience variation similar to that within Berks County and those counties immediately surrounding it, but at wider intervals. German-influenced speakers who stopped to farm in the middle of Pennsylvania, rather than proceeding to Pittsburgh and beyond, carried forms typical of their emerging American English dialect westward. Scots-Irish settling alongside them introduced *redd up* 'clean', as in "Take that pail and redd up the barn." Many current residents of mid-Pennsylvania (from Harrisburg to the west) are convinced that *redd up* is Pennsylvania German-influenced English, but it isn't. The Scots-Irish and German-descended settlers mingled so completely that they blurred the lines of linguistic influence, about as close as we get to fulfilling the "melting pot" metaphor.

If you travel as far as Pittsburgh, you'll hear *yinz* ('you ones') instead of Boston/Philadelphia/New Jersey *youse,* Southern *y'all,* or the widespread American *you guys* for the plural second-person pronoun. This particular set of divergent forms reminds us how quickly language varies: *youse* and *yinz* are separated by only five or so turnpike hours, but I-76 runs just north of the West Virginia border, so the trip to *y'all* from either east or west is more or less the same five hours. Speakers of standard varieties of American English are sprinkled among the speakers of local dialects, so that variation between *yinz, youse,* or *y'all* and *you guys* is typical. If you are hungry when you finally reach Pittsburgh, you can buy some *jumbo,* but if you stop half an hour east or west of Pittsburgh, you'll have to settle for bologna—same thing, different word.

All of these discrete examples, though encountered along the same road, make dialect sound random—but it isn't completely random. Synchronic variation, such as that you would encounter on the Pennsylvania Turnpike, is often the result of historical patterns of speaker migration and language contact.

Defining Regions

Dialect maps capture the boundaries where many dialect differences approximately line up. But remember that the boundaries are much blurrier than they seem on a map, and smaller dialect differences distinguish locally salient communities from each other in ways that only the residents understand. For example, the South is a culturally salient region, and most Americans can associate a particular kind of speech with the South. Within a geographic region as big as the South, there exist many smaller dialect regions, sometimes defined by state boundaries, sometimes by geographical boundaries, and sometimes by historical boundaries. Within any one of these geographical areas, more subtle dialect differences may mark one town from another. For instance, certainly not all Bostonians say *Pahk the cah,* and while the majority of Bostonians don't find the stereotypical dialect odd, they can tell you in which neighborhoods it's natural. Even if you're a Tarheel (someone from North Carolina), you may not feel entirely at home among speakers of Ocracoke Island (off the North Carolina coast), where *high tide* is *hoi toide.*

Sometimes dialect boundaries reflect cultural identity and attitudes as much as linguistic features. For example, the Linguistic Atlas project treats Oklahoma as its own region, though some East Texans must speak a dialect nearly indistinguishable from that of Oklahomans. But the border between Texas and Oklahoma is culturally salient. Texas singer/songwriter Nanci Griffith captures social attitudes about the border in the introduction to her song "Trouble in the Fields," on the live album *One Fair Summer Evening* (Rounder Records, 1990); she explains that her Aunt Tootie had a lot of sympathy for family farmers in the 1980s because of her own experience of the Dust Bowl years, during which "the winds blew so strong that she was afraid that she'd wake up of a morning and find herself in Oklahoma, and she, by God, didn't want to live in Oklahoma!"

There are often exceptions to generalized regional boundaries that are drawn from linguistic isoglosses. A *Dictionary of American Regional English* (DARE) map, or a map from any of the Linguistic Atlas projects, will mark a few outliers, such as instances of Southern American English somehow spoken in the North. Even more frequently, they will illustrate areas in which classically divergent features mesh: the line between Northern *pail* and Southern *bucket* is not absolute, and along the fringe of the two regions, *bucket* and *pail* are interchangeable.

The Emergence of Regional Dialects

Given that "to speak a language is to speak some dialect of that language," all change within a language is fundamentally at the level of the dialect. Historically, regional dialects emerge because related cultural or social groups, who speak a common language, diverge geographically. Each group's language keeps changing over time, as language always does, and given geographical isolation or distance from the others, each group's language changes in different ways. Given enough time and isolation, dialects can become distinct languages—indeed, historically, they have often done so.

Dialects change by means of linguistic processes described throughout this book, and here we bring this material together to describe five general processes that result in many of the particular features of regional dialects.

- **Retention**—Speakers bring features of their original dialects/languages with them at emigration/migration.

- **Naturally occurring internal language change**—Some regional features result from the ongoing variation and change that occur within any speech community, at the phonological, morphological, and syntactic level. A form first occurs in a locality or region and is maintained there; it may then spread to other regions or remain a more localized form.

- **Language contact**—Speakers of a variety encounter speakers of another language (or another dialect of their language), and contact with this other language affects the dialect.

  - **Borrowing**—Speakers borrow lexical items wholesale from contact languages or adapt borrowed words phonologically and morphologically to fit their language. Speakers may borrow terms for things previously unknown to them or borrow terms that are synonymous with words they already have in their language.

  - **Structural influence**—The phonology, morphology, or syntax of a variety is affected by the phonology, morphology, or syntax of a contact language.

- **Coining**—Speakers create new words or phrases, sometimes as a way to name something previously unknown to them and often as part of the creativity that is human language.

- **Social factors**—Language marks identity and community, and communities may adopt or retain (usually below the level of consciousness) specific features in relation to their social significance.

These five processes are explained in more detail below.

Retention

Much variation in American English reflects the linguistic heritage of speakers living in a given area. After a while, dialectal features of one group may spread, to belong to all speakers living in that area, regardless of heritage. For instance, double modals (*might could, might should*) belonged to specific dialects of English in the British Isles (Scots, Scots-Irish) before they arrived in Appalachia and on the south Atlantic coast when these British dialect-speakers emigrated to America. Double modals are strongly associated with this heritage, even though they are heard in Texas and North Carolina as often as they are throughout Appalachia. Similarly, *redd up* entered American English with the Scots-Irish, but today it is less strongly associated with that heritage. Any rural, mid-Pennsylvania speaker might use *redd up,* whether he or she is of German, English, Scots-Irish, or any other descent.

Naturally Occurring Internal Language Change

Sometimes formal linguistic processes prompt development in directions different from mainstream speech. For instance, some Southerners call a woodpecker a *peckerwood* and a grasshopper a *hoppergrass.* If you aren't familiar with these terms, you might think a speaker is being deliberately humorous in using them. However, these forms are probably morphemic inversions, parallel to phonological metathesis, as in *brid* into *bird* and *larynx* into *larnyx,* as discussed in Chapter 3.

Phonological variation among dialects can be the result of heritage, development, or some combination of the two. Features such as the presence or absence of /r/ on the eastern coast of the United States can be traced back to the English dialects of early settlers. How patterns of /r/ use spread or receded thereafter is unique to the history of American dialects. Through contact, dialects of a language constantly diverge from and converge toward one another. As we discussed in Chapter 11, phonological mergers tend to spread at the expense of phonological distinctions. Sociolinguists have observed this phenomenon in the spread of the *cot/caught* merger. This spread has been generally geographically contiguous, although California may be further along in the merger than some of the states to its east, closer to the origins of the merger. The Northern Cities Vowel Shift (described in Chapter 11) has spread from one urban area in the Midwest to another—a convergence of urban dialects and a divergence from nonurban dialects (social factors may be relevant here—see below). The vowel rotation may now be spreading into geographically contiguous nonurban areas (Gordon 2001).

Language Change at Work

Regional Food Terms

Some originally local food terms are now used nationwide (e.g., *gumbo, jambalaya*), as certain originally ethnic foods are now eaten across the United States. Let's look at *cruller,* from Dutch *krulle* 'curly cake'. This word retained a narrow and localized meaning early in its history, but later it was marketed nationwide in a nonethnic form. There was no such thing as a *French cruller* until doughnut chains associated *French* with 'fancy' and added it to the Dutch term.

Some food terms, such as *babycake,* retain their primarily local or regional character. Here are a few more examples:

Term	Language	Region
beignet 'fritter'	American French	Louisiana (esp. New Orleans)
lutefisk 'lye-cured fish'	Norwegian	Great Lakes States
pasty 'meat/vegetable turnover'	English (from French)	Northern Michigan
pho 'noodle soup'	Vietnamese	Northern Pacific Coast

Term	Language	Region
linguica 'sausage'	Portuguese	New England
bialy 'breakfast roll'	Yiddish	New York City (primarily)

You can undoubtedly come up with more. See if you (and your classmates) can list local food terms and map them as specifically as you can to areas of the United States. You can view this as a partial guide to immigration and migration routes of these language speakers.

Language Contact

In the United States, dialect development has often been spurred by language contact, from English speakers' contact with Native American languages, Spanish, African languages, and Asian languages, to name a few. Here are just a few historical numbers to drive home the importance of other languages to American English (from Algeo 2001). By 1850, of the half-million residents in New York City, 45 percent were foreign born (some in English-speaking countries and many not). Between 1880 and 1900, the population of the United States increased by 50 percent, in large part because of 9 million immigrants, many of them from non-English-speaking areas of Europe.

The New World was a land of fresh encounters for immigrants to its eastern shore, and for those who explored the continent westward. Unknown things need names, so early settlers in New England borrowed and adapted Native American (in these cases, Algonquian) words like *raccoon* and *opossum.* English-speaking pioneers in the West borrowed words such as *canyon* from Spanish speakers already settled there. In California, Texas, and much of the Southwest of the United States, ongoing contact with Spanish brought many Spanish words into these dialects. Some of the words remain more restricted to these regions (e.g., *arroyo* 'stream, brook'), and some have gained wide currency in American English (e.g., *macho, siesta, tortilla, taco*). In eastern Pennsylvania, native English speakers and German speakers learning English interacted and produced unexpected forms, such as *all* (for *all gone*), adverbial *awhile* 'now, immediately', *unless* 'in case', and *until* 'by the time that', all encountered on our earlier walking tour. Hawaiian English has incorporated words from Hawaiian Creole, such as *pau* 'finished' and *haole* 'foreigner' or 'Caucasian, blond'.

As time passes, such borrowed items may become less the property of the group that originally performed the borrowing or adaptation and more the property of speakers in the region, regardless of heritage—and then sometimes beyond that region. Folk names for animal or plant species often vary by region, however. Some of these names are borrowed. For instance, *Quahog* (from Naragansett, another Amerindian language) is an unfamiliar term outside New England, because the species of thick-shelled clam to which it refers is available only there. Sometimes one thing is called by different names in different places, not simply as a result of a settler's "first encounter" with the thing, but of many encounters by many people who didn't know (or didn't remember) the standard English term for that thing, frequently because there wasn't one. Did you know a *woodchuck* (borrowed from Algonquian) and a *groundhog* (a loan translation from Dutch *aardvark*) are the same critter?

Coining

Speakers often use the linguistic resources native to their own language to coin new terms, through compounding, affixing, and other methods (as discussed in Chapter 4). These processes can contribute to dialect variation. For example, pioneers in the West invented the commonsensical *tumbleweed* to represent exactly what it says. But not all things named are found; some are created. Whoever made the first babycake may not have named it *babycake,* but sooner or later, someone saw the resemblance between it and a baby (the term is very like *gingerbread man*), or someone thought it a good food for a baby. The culinary term *babycake* is recorded only in Berks County, Pennsylvania, but it's possible that *babycakes,* the term of endearment used nationwide, represents a

Language Variation at Work

A Dragonfly by Any Other Name

In the South, what standard American English refers to as a *dragonfly* is usually called a *mosquito hawk* (or *skeeter hawk*) or a *snake doctor* (from a folk belief that dragonflies look out for snakes). In the Midland region and the North, *snake feeder* is a variant, and so is *darner* or *darning needle*. All of these forms reflect immediate experience. A dragonfly is an imposing fly with big wings—like a dragon, hence the name. *Mosquito hawk* draws on the metaphor of the hawk, given the size of the insect, and *mosquito hawks* really do eat mosquitoes. The insect's slender body and its darting movement reminded others who encountered it of a large needle, like that for darning. The *Dictionary of American Regional English* includes more than eighty regional variants for *dragonfly*—we encourage you to see how many sound familiar.

semantic shift from the regional term. In the South, *hopping John* is a dish made of ground meat, peas, and hot red pepper. Just as someone can be *hopping mad,* food can be so hot that it's angry in the mouth and *hopping,* too. Perhaps the dish turns one who eats it into a *hopping John,* or perhaps *John* here is just as mysterious as *johnny* in *johnnycake.*

Occasionally, speakers invent words they don't need, just for the fun of it, or to establish a regional status for a common thing. Pittsburgh's *jumbo* is nothing more than *bologna,* the term by which every American except Pittsburghers calls the cold meat. Who knows how *jumbo* came into the lexicon? It certainly wasn't because residents of Pittsburgh and the surrounding area hadn't heard the word *bologna* or suddenly encountered bologna for the first time. Humor and a sense of style most likely motivate substitution of such regional or local terms for widely recognized standard ones. Of all processes leading to dialectal forms, this is the least productive.

Social Factors

Differentiation is not usually a matter of conscious choice. Just as speakers like to associate with others in groups (a preference that leads to convergence), speakers like their own groups to remain distinct from other groups (a preference that leads to divergence). Speech patterns contribute both to personal and group identity, often below the level of consciousness.

Certainly, dialects develop and maintain themselves partly from isolation. American English and British English diverged partly because American speakers of English lived on one side of the Atlantic Ocean and their British counterparts on the other. After a while, without much contact, varieties of a language develop independently of one another. The same was true of, say, New England speech and speech in Chicago a century ago. But even when isolation is no longer a factor (and it still is for some varieties of American English, for instance, the Ocracoke brogue and Appalachian speech), cultural identity remains an influence. If your folks say *root* to rhyme with *foot,* or speak Pennsylvania German-influenced English, or "drawl," you are likely to have learned that pronunciation as an infant, and you may well identify with that speech community and honor that tradition, at least when you speak at home. If you've moved away from home to a place that diverges from your native dialect, don't features of your home dialect surface when you're on the telephone with your parents or friends from home? Most of us adapt our speech toward the standard dialect or toward the local dialect where we find ourselves, because it's useful to do so, not because we speak it naturally or all of the time. These adaptations, as dialects come into contact, can influence the development of dialects as well.

The History of Regional Dialects in the United States

Despite the fact that variation continuously rolls along the road and every beaten path, American dialects can be mapped into regions, at least in general terms. The outlines of America's major dialect regions were drawn by settlement, by successive waves of immigration to North America and then migration within (though mainly across) the United States and its territories. Dialect surveys of the United States typically describe four major dialect regions: Northern, Southern, Midland, and Western. There are many smaller dialect areas within each of these regions, as we'll discuss below.

The Beginnings of American English

The original settlement of British colonies that later became the United States began almost simultaneously on the northeastern and southeastern shores. Dialect differences of these original settlers, as well as their subsequent language encounters, are reflected in ongoing differences between the North and South. Jamestown was established in what is now Virginia in 1607. The Pilgrims landed at Plymouth, in what is now Massachusetts, in 1620. From those dates forward there was continual European settlement of coastal America. And no sooner had settlers arrived than some, like Huckleberry Finn, "lit out for the territories," establishing speech communities not only at their ultimate destinations but also along the way.

Speakers of languages other than English were in North America long before English speakers arrived. To begin with, millions of speakers of hundreds of Native American languages were spread all over the continent. Most of these languages underwent language death in the centuries that followed, to the point where there are only an estimated 200 or so Native American languages remaining in the United States. The influence of these Native American languages on American English was primarily lexical. Twenty-six states have Indian names, including *Massachusetts, Mississippi, Iowa,* and *Ohio.* Flora and fauna native to the United States also often have Indian names, such as *squash, hickory, raccoon, opossum, caribou,* and *skunk.* Some American expressions are calques (loan translations) from Native American languages, such as *fire water, to bury the hatchet, to speak with forked tongue,* and *warpath* (Romaine 2001, 166).

Other European traders and colonizers reached North America before the English. By the time that the English had settled the eastern coast, the Spanish were already in Texas, New Mexico, and parts of the South. The French had established themselves in the South, as well as throughout much of Canada. The Dutch had settled New York, and Swedes could be found in Delaware. These language influences, along with waves of immigrants to follow, shaped regional American dialects. Some loanwords in American English date back to this colonial period, such as *smorgasbord* (Swedish) and *boss* and *waffle* (Dutch). French spellings of Native American words, such as *Illinois* and *Sioux,* also come from these early encounters.

The Northern Dialect Region

After the original settlement of Plymouth in 1620, over 20,000 Puritans, primarily from eastern and southeastern England, arrived in New England in the 1630s. The /r/-lessness that we still find in eastern New England reflects the dialect of these first settlers. Speakers of /r/-full British dialects came in subsequent waves of immigration and surrounded these /r/-less areas. In fact, New York City used to be /r/-full until it converged with New England dialects on this feature. Another piece of this linguistic heritage—the high-pitched nasality associated with the "Yankee twang"—originated in the "Norfolk whine" from England (Algeo 2001, 9).

By a century and a half later, restless citizens from the northeast had begun to move westward across northern Pennsylvania into the Great Lakes region and Iowa. They expanded the dialect area with them. The Northern dialect region now stretches from Maine to Iowa to Minnesota and the Dakotas, and it includes northern Ohio, Indiana, Illinois, Michigan, and Wisconsin.

Some general phonological features are shared across the area: for example, [s] in *greasy*, [ð] in *with*, and the contrast of /o/ and /ɔ/ in *hoarse/horse, fourteen/forty* (Pederson 2001). The pronunciation of /r/ varies across the region. For example, in coastal areas (as well as in New York City and the Hudson Valley), words like *beard* and *bear* are often pronounced with a central vowel where other dialects would have a postvocalic /r/: [bɪəd] ("beahd") and [bɛə] ("beah"). The Northern Cities Vowel Shift affects urban centers such as Detroit, Chicago, Cleveland, and Milwaukee, but you may hear these pronunciations outside the cities as well. In the Midwestern states, a subregion often called the Inland North, postvocalic /r/ is preserved in all contexts—as it is in upstate New York (Pederson 2001).

"Positive *anymore*" is distinctive for speakers outside this dialect region, who can use *anymore* only in negative constructions (e.g., *They don't live there anymore*) and questions (*Do they live there anymore?*). Speakers in some areas of the North can use *anymore* relatively synonymously with 'nowadays', as in *Gas is just too expensive anymore* or *I stay up so late doing homework anymore.*

The Southern Dialect Region

In broad terms, the Southern dialect extends from the southeastern coast through Texas, the result of westward expansion within the South. The earliest settlers along the southeastern coast, including Jamestown, were elite gentry and their servants (almost three out of every four southern colonists in this period were indentured servants), typically coming from southeastern England. Unlike the Puritans in Massachusetts, who arrived mostly in family groups and often emigrated for religious and political reasons, the Virginia colonists were overwhelmingly male and farmers who arrived to establish a royal colony affiliated with the Church of England. The r-lessness of parts of the South can be traced back to these early English dialects.

Beginning in 1619, through 1807, over 400,000 Africans were brought to the United States, primarily to the South, and sold as slaves. By 1850, two out of every five people in the South were African slaves. Many of the African words in American English and the linguistic features shared between Southern dialects and African American English can be traced back to the history of slavery in the United States. (You'll read more details about the history of African American English later in the chapter.)

Many speakers recognize the phonological and lexical differences between the North and the South. For example, in the South, food is *greazy,* but in the North, it's *greasy,* and speakers in the Midland region go either way. In terms of lexicon, it's a *faucet* in the North, but a *spicket* or *spigot* in the South; you put things in a *pail* or in a *bag* in the North and in a *bucket* or in a *sack* in the South. In the North, you're *sick to the stomach,* and in the South, you're *sick at the stomach.* And if there are more than one of you, then it's *y'all* in the South.

Some general phonological features, in addition to the [z] in *greasy,* include clear /l/ between front vowels (e.g., in *silly*), the monophthongization of /aɪ/ to [ɑ] in words like *night,* and the merger of /ɛ/ and /ɪ/ before /n/ in words such as *pin* and *pen* (discussed in Chapter 3). As a result, in the North you could order a box of *tin pins* as an aid to sewing, but in the South you might just as easily mean *ten pens* for writing. Southern dialects (though not Southern Appalachian speech) also often delete /l/ before /p, b, f/, in words such as *help, golf,* or *bulb.* And the Southern vowel /ɛ/ now often adds a glide to become [ɛɪ], as in *bed* [bɛɪd]—which is part of the larger Southern Vowel Shift.

Morphologically, dialects throughout the South witness the deletion of "be" forms and auxiliaries in the third person (e.g., *he gonna do it, he done it*). Other elements of Southern dialects are *ain't,* intensifier *right* (e.g., *right hot*), and perfective *done* as in *done gone* (Pederson 2001). You'll see many of these features again in the discussion of African American English.

The Midland Dialect Region

In the last quarter of the seventeenth century, Quakers began arriving in the Delaware Valley, particularly in Pennsylvania. These early settlers included English from England's North Midlands, Welsh, and Scots-Irish—people of Scottish descent who settled in Ulster in the north of Ireland, also sometimes known as Ulster Scots. All were mostly of the lower middle class. William Penn, the Quaker proprietor of the commonwealth that would later take his name, welcomed German religious dissenters into the area as well. The Amish, Mennonites, and many other Protestant sects persecuted in Catholic areas of Germany found freedom of worship under Penn's protection. Thus, from an early date, eastern Pennsylvania speech developed from contact between English and German speakers and acquired a character quite different from dialects to the north and south.

English and German-descended speakers of English, as well as German speakers, migrated west through Pennsylvania and into Ohio, Indiana, Illinois, and farther across the American midlands, contributing to what are now the Midland dialects. The mid-eighteenth century saw a wave of Scots-Irish immigration via Philadelphia and Baltimore. These newly arrived speakers, with their strongly marked Old World dialect, took advantage of the great Forbes Road between Philadelphia and Pittsburgh. They migrated west and then south and west into the Appalachian Valley, as far west as the Ozark mountains, to what we now call Arkansas and Missouri—states that straddle the political fence between North and South erected by the Missouri Compromise, the Civil War, and Reconstruction.

Phonologically, the Midland dialects have postvocalic /r/. They also sometimes feature intrusive /r/ (e.g., *warsh*), which is different from the "linking r" between vowels that sometimes appears in coastal Northern dialects (e.g., *sor on and so forth*). The word *with* is pronounced with [θ]. The words *Mary*, *merry*, and *marry* are typically not all distinguished (as they are for some speakers on the east coast): all may take [ɛ] or *Mary* and *merry* may take [ɛ] while *marry* takes [æ]. Lexically, the northern Midland dialects tend to pattern with Northern dialects, and the southern Midland dialects tend to pattern with Southern dialects. The Midland area is perhaps best known "timewise," as there it's often *quarter till* the hour, rather than *quarter to* or *quarter of.*

The Western Dialect Region

The West has been less studied than other dialect regions of the United States. It has been settled by English speakers for only a hundred and fifty years or so, so the dialects that developed there are in their infancy, at least relative to those first established in Virginia and the Massachusetts Bay Colony. The development of dialects in the West is typically described as a mixture or convergence of the dialects from the east, including the North, South, and Midland regions, as pioneers moved west. Northerners migrated to the Pacific Northwest, Montana, Idaho, Utah, and California. Southerners spread from Texas and Oklahoma into adjoining states. And folks from the Midland region settled states like Colorado.

Some historical phonological features resonate of Southern American English. For instance, in the West, the /ɑɪ/ in *ride* and *fire* still sounds vaguely like Southern /ɑ/ in the mouths of some speakers. And Western speech was, once upon a time, relatively /r/-less, as when *horse* sounded like *hoss* and *partner* sounded like *pahdnah.* Such pronunciations are now relics of an earlier time. As mentioned in Chapter 11, Northern California vowels also seem to be undergoing a rotation such that, for example, the word *bed* can sound more like *bad* (in mainstream English), *hat* more like *hot, stand* like "stee-and" and so on.

Spanish has been resident in the West much longer than English (in fact, since the sixteenth century), and patterns of settlement and immigration have made it a significant influence. Some Spanish food terms, originally part of Western American English, are now familiar nationwide, such as *tortilla, burrito, enchilada, taco,* and *chili.* From *mesa* to *canyon* to the *Rio Grande,* Spanish topographical terms and place names useful in the West have persisted there. By now, most Americans know these words well enough, even if they've never ridden into the Grand Canyon on the back of a *burro.* We return to the political and social questions about the status of the Spanish language in the United States in Chapter 14.

In spite of its brief history, the West has contributed a surprising amount to American colloquial speech. When you *high-tail* it out of some difficult situation, you may not realize that you are responding like a startled mustang, whose tail springs up before it runs away from danger. Schools no longer have *lunch rooms* but *cafeterias,* an even more common Westernism gone east.

Historically, Spanish has been the largest "contributing language" to western dialects. In the twenty-first century, it's likely that Asian languages will contribute significantly to the vocabulary of northern California and the Pacific Northwest. At this point, however, the extent to which Chinese, Korean, and Japanese have influenced American English is unclear. If you are interested in borrowing as a lexical process, you should keep your eye on America's western coast.

Dialects within Dialect Regions

All these large dialect regions include smaller ones, also easily distinguishable from those surrounding them (see Figure 12.2). For instance, Northern dialect includes several subdialects, such as Northeastern, Southeastern, and Southwestern New England dialects, while Inland North dialect comprises western Vermont, Upstate New York, and targets of western migration from these points of origin, such as the Great Lakes region. New York City is its own dialect area. Immigrants poured into New York City from all over the world over the past 200 years, and many of them stayed. It is not surprising, then, that the English spoken in New York City is distinctive. To take just one example from the hundreds of "loaner" languages, Yiddish has contributed the words *mishuggah* 'crazy', *kibitzer* 'one who offers unsolicited advice', and *schlepp* 'carry, drag'. These words have currency in New York City but not in most other parts of the country (Romaine 2001, 178).

Some regional dialects do not fit neatly into the major dialect divisions. For instance, Appalachia is not exclusively Southern. Indeed, the mountain range from which the area takes its name stretches into Maine, though the federally designated region reaches only as far as New York (see Figure 12.3). Athens, Ohio, is in the foothills of the Appalachians, and speakers there share dialect with folks as far west as the Ozarks and as far south as the Georgia and Alabama highlands—yet southern Ohio isn't in the South. Pittsburgh and southwestern Pennsylvania are the original points of settlement in the Appalachian Valley, the home of Appalachian English, but they aren't in the South either. We return to Appalachian English below.

Dialect subregions in many other areas of the United States possess distinctive features derived from specific immigrant contributions to American speech. Finns influenced speech in Minnesota, and the Portuguese who settled in Massachusetts and Connecticut contributed to the speech surrounding them. Swedes and Norwegians in Wisconsin, Germans in Iowa, Polish in Chicago and Detroit, and Ukrainians in Cleveland

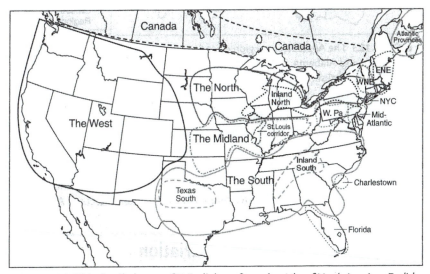

FIGURE 12.2 This detailed map of U.S. dialects from the *Atlas of North American English* (Labov, Ash, and Boberg 2005) captures major regional dialect boundaries as well as many subregional boundaries.

FIGURE 12.3 The Appalachian region extends as far north as New York and as far south as Mississippi and Alabama, and it's characterized by a distinctive regional dialect referred to as Appalachian English.

all began with their native languages and adopted American English as they assimilated into American culture. And all donated something from the old country, usually food and speech, to American culture in the transaction.

Speech in such locations generally conforms to the regional patterns described earlier, but there is a difference between local and regional speech. Today, speakers of Spanish, Chinese, Vietnamese, Korean, Russian, Arabic, Swahili, and many other languages continue to influence the development of particular dialects of American English.

Two Case Studies of Regional Variation

It would be impossible to itemize here all the features, phonological, morphological, lexical, and syntactic, that distinguish one dialect region (let alone subregion) from another. Many excellent books supply that information, some of which are in the "Suggested

Reading" section at the end of this chapter. Nonetheless, it is important to see how dialects are described, so two case studies—one on Appalachian English and one on California English—seem appropriate at this point.

Appalachian English

Geographically and historically significant, Appalachian English provides a useful case study of an American regional dialect. It has historically been more isolated than many other regional dialects, so it demonstrates relatively more distinctive features. One point to remember is that the following descriptions pull together many linguistic features of the dialect; not all speakers of Appalachian English have all these features in their speech, and they may use some features variably (i.e., in some contexts but not in others).

Phonological Features Appalachian speech includes many phonological features that, although not necessarily unique to the variety, figure more prominently in it than in other American dialects. Let's consider a few of the more characteristic ones. Appalachian English exhibits deletion of several sounds, like voiced /ð/ in *they* and *them*, producing *'ey* and *'em* instead, especially within phrases like *bought 'em, caught 'em, sold 'em*. Similarly, *was* can become *'uz* through deleted /w/. A different sort of deletion occurs with unstressed initial syllables, yielding *'member, 'posed*, and *'fessed* where others would use *remember, supposed*, and *confessed*. The last item, *'fess*, as in "First he said he called his mom, but then he 'fessed up and said he didn't," is commonly associated with stereotyped Appalachian speech, one of the features to which the dialect is reduced in the popular imagination. Deletion of initial segments in words such as *remember* and *suppose* is found to varying extents in most dialects of English.

Most Appalachian speakers on most occasions tend (at rates above 80 percent) to produce the final nasal in *coming, running*, and *singing* as /n/ rather than /ŋ/, yielding the forms *comin', runnin'*, and *singin'*. This feature holds true for speech from around Pittsburgh to the Ozarks. This feature is not unique to Appalachian English, however: the use of [n] rather than [ŋ] appears with varying frequency in almost all varieties of English.

One ubiquitous measure of variation in the United States is rhoticity, or the relative /r/-fullness or /r/-lessness of a dialect. Even though Appalachian speakers often live in the South, and most Southern dialects are at least somewhat /r/-less (especially when /r/ is in a word-final position), Appalachian English isn't generally /r/-less, perhaps a legacy from the Scots and Scots-Irish dialects from which it is descended, both of which are /r/-full compared to other British dialects. Pronunciation of some words seems to contradict this claim, as when *further* becomes *fuhthuh*, as it has in some Appalachian speech. But most words in which such /r/ deletion *could* occur remain /r/-full.

This /r/-fullness produces some other characteristic features of Appalachian speech. It influences preceding vowel sounds, for example. Older (especially Southern) Appalachian speakers may say the words *tire* and *fire* more like *tar* and *far* as pronounced in mainstream American English. In others words, the diphthong /ɑɪ/ undergoes monophthonization or becomes closer to a pure vowel, in this case /ɑ/. In fact, there are phonemic differences between Appalachian *tire* and *tar*. While outsiders are likely to hear them as merged, like Southern *pin/pen*, natives won't, and if you try to talk Appalachian while visiting, your inability to hear the difference will give you away. As Walt Wolfram and Donna Christian explain (1976, 65): "For one, the vowel of *tire* and *fire* is produced more front in the mouth than the vowel of *tar* and *far*, which is typically like the *a* of *father.* In addition, the vowel in *tire* and *fire* is usually of slightly longer duration than the corresponding vowel on *tar* and *far.*" When /r/ follows /ɛ/, as in *bear,* or /ɪ/ as in *hill,* the vowels verge on breaking into two syllables, as in *bayer* and *heal* (Mallinson et al. 2006).

As in other dialects, /r/ can be intrusive in Appalachian English, but with different patterns. A New Englander may ask, "What's the big idear?" but the Appalachian speaker is more likely to substitute /r/ for /o/ (or /oʊ/), as in "I went down to the holler" (for *hollow*) and "My sister follered me all over the house" (for *follow*). Appalachian speakers form some words with an intrusive /t/, as in "I eat an apple oncet a day," or "The store is acrosst the street from the post office."

Many of the features discussed above are much less prominent features of Appalachian speech than they once were, and it's unlikely that any Appalachian speaker would utter a sentence that simultaneously includes so many markers of the historical dialect. Much of Appalachia is less isolated than it used to be, and, as speakers of the dialect come into continual contact with neighboring dialects, Appalachian speech converges in some ways with their dialects, just as the neighbors have adopted once exclusively Appalachian features (like double modals) into their speech.

Morphological and Syntactic Features   It's often hard to separate the phonological from the morphological, or the morphological from the syntactic. Appalachian speech includes several features that straddle linguistic categories. For instance, historically there was a tendency to replace the inflectional plural /s/ or /z/ of most dialects with an additional syllable /ɪz/ with words ending in /st/ or similar consonant clusters: for example, *ghosts* becomes *ghostes.* This phonological rule is no longer productive for many speakers of Appalachian English. Appalachian speakers may also employ irregular verbs in nonstandard ways, especially regarding tense and inflectional markers of tense, as in "He give it to me yesterday," rather than standard "He gave it to me yesterday." Some verbs show different past-tense forms, created through analogy with regular or irregular verbs: for example, *throwed* in "He throwed that stone into the lake" (where *throw* is conjugated like a regular verb) or *drug* in "He drug that chair over the floor" (where *drag* is conjugated like an irregular verb, analogous to *ran/run*). It is important to note that Appalachian speakers who use one of these forms may not use all of them.

Perhaps the most famous Appalachian feature on the lines that divide phonology, morphology, and syntax is *a*-prefixing. Appalachian speakers still go *a-walkin'* or *a-fishin',* though increasingly they *walk* or *fish.* A-prefixing is strictly rule governed. In other words, Appalachian speakers know the constraints on *a*-prefixing: that *a-* only attaches to participles (*They are a-fishin'* or *They go a-fishin',* but not **The a-fishin' is fine*) and to verbs with stress on the first syllable (*a-fishin'* and *a-followin',* but not **a-repeatin'*). Although this feature may seem quaint to speakers of other American dialects (and is often stereotyped), it reflects a straightforward development of Middle English phonology and syntax with a morphological effect. It is a historical English pattern retained by northerners in England and by the Scots; it was brought to Appalachia by the speakers of these dialects who settled there. In Middle English, progressive verbs were formed with prepositional *on,* as in "After he rose that morning, he went on hunting." The nasal in *on* gradually eroded to *a* and then the *a* became the verbal prefix, *a-.* (This development is parallel to that which led from Middle English *on lesse than* to Modern English *unless,* though different prefixes result in each case.) *A*-prefixed forms have disappeared from most other English dialects worldwide.

Appalachian English and adjacent Southern dialects have a history of shared linguistic features, introduced one to the other in both directions. For example, *a*-prefixing extends into the South, wherever Scots-Irish speakers settled. Scots-Irish speakers and their descendents undoubtedly introduced double modals (*might could, might should,* etc.) into the South, for they were common in earlier Scots, and still occur in Scotland and Northern Ireland. But double modals, though a stereotyped feature of Appalachian speech, are much less frequent today in Appalachia than they are in the South generally, especially in Texas. Southern speech converged with Appalachian speech with regard to double modals, and then Appalachian speech diverged from Southern American English with regard to the feature it introduced. Perfective *done,* as in "He done mailed that check yesterday," yet another syntactic feature characteristic of Appalachian speech, was likely adopted from Southern speech, and it's by no means uniquely Appalachian. Still employed by many Southerners, it also figures prominently in African American English, which adopted it from general Southern speech.

Comparable to Southern *peckerwood* and other similarly inverted forms, forms like *everwhat* and *everhow,* instead of *whatever* and *however,* are peculiarities of Appalachian syntax. (We should note here that **Everwhat!* has not become Appalachia's dismissive exclamation.) Visitors often encounter *ever* out of its expected place in other constructions in Appalachian English: for example, "That was the scariest thing ever I seen," rather than "That was the scariest thing I ever saw." In fact, Appalachian adverbs generally can surprise nonnative speakers, because Appalachian speakers find things *worser* or *more worse*—when *worser* comes to *worstest,* visitors may cringe at the dialect's "incorrectness." Such reactions, though, are *right* foolish (or, in the sense 'completely', *plumb* foolish), because the relevant "correctness" is conformity with the rules of Appalachian speech, not with those of other American varieties.

Even prepositions, which seem the most stable lexical category in Modern English, are susceptible to variation, as we saw with Berks County *unless* earlier. If you ever visit Appalachia, you may wake up *of* a morning and realize that this is true, though Nanci Griffith, a Texan, proved earlier in this chapter that *of* used in this way is a Southern characteristic, not merely an Appalachian one.

Lexical Features Like most regional American dialects, Appalachian English varies from the others not only in its sound and structure but also in its lexicon. Not all Appalachian speakers use all historically Appalachian words, and some of the words listed here can be heard in other areas of the United States. If you *reckoned* that you'd get hungry at work, you'd take a *piece* 'snack' in a *poke* 'sack, bag'. Juvenile delinquents throw stones at *boomers* 'red squirrels' and *grinnies* 'ground squirrels'. The *-ie* in *grinnie* is preserved from Appalachia's Scots-Irish heritage (as is a verb like *redd up*): *-ie* is the favorite diminutive suffix in Scots (*laddie* and *lassie* are familiar examples). *Gap* 'mountain pass' and *dulcimer* 'stringed musical instrument' are originally Appalachian, though now generally known. In fact, *gap* has become the standard term for the item named. A ghost is sometimes called a *haint* (from *haunt*), and in parts of Appalachia you must be *afeared* instead of *afraid* of one.

Once upon a time, you might *brogue* 'walk' around the lake (a *brogue* can be a 'shoe' in Scots and Ulster Scots, as well as an accent or dialect). And you might have carried supplies for the hike in a *budget* 'bag' (from Middle English *budget* 'purse', whence also the Modern English *budget* 'financial plan') rather than a *poke*. If you were

---

Language Change at Work

Jack, Will, and Jenny in the Swamp

Marshes across Great Britain exhale methane gas and sometimes that gas ignites. At night, when viewed from a distance, these explosions are disconcerting unless you know the physical facts. It's easy to imagine, as generations have done, that the light generated by the explosions, which seems to move from one part of the marsh to another, is carried by someone who lives in the marsh, someone on the cusp of the supernatural. For many, this imaginary figment was Will o' the Wisp; others called him Jack o'Lantern. In Scotland, he was a she: Jenny of the Burnt Tail, or Jenny Buntail. *Will* and *Jack* are like every other *Tom, Dick,* or *Harry*—common names for the marsh spirit next door. *Jenny,* among Scots names, serves the same purpose: it humanizes the frightening by means of the familiar.

We have marshes in America, but we call them swamps (*swamp,* in fact, is an Americanism). English settlers brought Will and Jack to America along with the rest of their cultural baggage. When Ulster Scots settled Appalachia, they saw lights in the swamps just like those in the marshes of the Old Country, and they called the light-bearer Jenny Buntail, just as their ancestors had done. *Jenny Buntail* is now a term of folklore, not a living word, part of the history of Appalachian speech. And junior high school science obviates the need for any supernatural explanation of swamp gas. The next time you visit a swamp at night, though, when you see a light wandering among the reeds, you'll remember the folklore and, just for a flicker, Jenny Buntail will live again and need her name.

---

out all night, you could cook stew for dinner in a *blackie* 'cast iron pot'. These words are generally in decline, though—relics of Appalachia's original speech, some of them superseded by other dialect words (*poke* for *budget*), and some replaced by words available in all American dialects (like *hike* and *pot*).

The above description of Appalachian English is selective: there are many interesting features of the dialect for which there isn't space here. But even a small sample demonstrates the systematic and multilayered nature of dialect variation. A dialect is not merely a collection of words or an accent. It is the language of a community. As Tony Earley (1998, 80) writes of *poke* 'bag' and *quare* 'queer, strange' and other features of Appalachian English with which he grew up: "They were part of the language around me, and I breathed them like air." Dialects, like languages, can and do die, because the communities that speak them disappear, if only to be absorbed into a larger, vital, related speech community. Some dialects hang on by a feature or two, otherwise converging fully with another dialect. Others, Appalachian speech among them, maintain themselves as distinct varieties.

California English

In the minds of most Americans, Appalachian and California speech are about as different as two varieties of a language can be. In terms of their features, they are indeed distinct, yet both are the subject of outrageous stereotypes, Cletus in the case of Appalachian English and Cher Horowitz, the heroine of Amy Heckerling's film *Clueless* (1995), in the case of

California English. In fact, though it is a relatively new dialect—California was not widely settled by English speakers until late in the nineteenth century—California English has developed many notable characteristics, some of them unique to the dialect and some associated with California (rightly or wrongly) but now used across America.

Phonological Features California vowels tend to be articulated forward in the mouth from their historical positions, so, like most Americans, Californians merge the vowels in *cot* and *caught*. Vowel fronting is much more profound in California speech than in other American dialects, however. (See Figure 12.4 for a summary of the Northern California Vowel Shift.) Younger speakers generally shift the vowel of *dude* so that it comes close to "did," and *move* can sound like "mi-oov"; the vowel of *boat* is fronted as part of a diphthong to something like "beut," and *but* resembles *bet*.

Front vowels are also on the move in parts of California. For example, as you can see in Figure 12.4, /ɪ/ shifts in different directions depending on the environment: before /ŋ/, it raises and fronts so that *think* sounds more like "theenk"; before other consonants, it lowers such that *him* sounds more like "hem." The vowel /æ/ is also raised or lowered and backed depending on the environment: before a nasal, it raises and diphthongizes so that *can* sounds more like "cay-un"; before other consonants, it becomes lower and more back, so *hat* sounds like "hot."

California consonants are typically described as similar to those of many other varieties of American English. But especially in southern California, /s/ can become [ʃ] when preceding /t/: rather than shopping at Nordstrom's on Lake Street in Pasadena, younger speakers shop at Nordshtrom's. Sometimes /z/ follows suit and becomes [ʒ], as in "I can't afford those shoes, they're 200 dollarzh!"

Lexical Features Some California words are associated with the *SoCal* 'southern California' stereotype, especially surfer speech like *dude* (in every sense described in Chapter 8), *gnarly* 'unpleasant, difficult', *hot dogging* 'showing off', and *tubular*

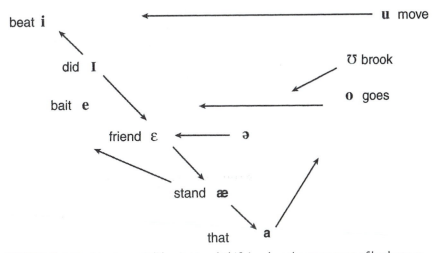

FIGURE 12.4 The Northern California Vowel Shift involves the movement of both tense and lax vowels, creating a distinctive northern California pronunciation.
Source: Eckert (2004).

'outstanding, excellent'. *Gnarly* and *tubular* respectively first described especially challenging and especially pleasant waves for *boarders* to *ride,* but now they have generalized to describe anything especially difficult or *awesome.* This is the vocabulary of "linguistic icons" like Jeff Spicoli in the film *Fast Times at Ridgemont High* (1982), who brought the speech of southern California to life for all sorts of Americans. Some items of California English, like *awesome, boarder,* and *ride* (which, influenced by surfboarding, belong to the lexicons of skateboarders and snowboarders, as well) as well as *dude* have spread throughout the country. Cher Horowitz is a similar icon, having brought to the rest of America items originally associated with California, like *as if!* and *bitchin'.*

Of course, these California meanings developed for words already used elsewhere to mean other things: *dude* originally meant 'sharp-dressed man' but has become remarkably polysemous. California, like many other parts of the country, has borrowed much of its characteristic vocabulary and developed it over time. Southern California, under a strong Spanish influence (Spanish has been spoken in the region that became California for more than 250 years), calls its strong, hot winds *Santa Anas*; many who live from Los Angeles to the south eat *frijoles* rather than beans.

When people outside California think of California, SoCal usually comes to mind, but, from a linguistic perspective, the north is just as interesting. Italian, rather than Spanish, influenced San Francisco and gave us the tomato-based fish stew called *cioppino.* In the nineteenth century, something like a hundred Native American languages were spoken in what became California. Nahuatl *tullin* 'bulrushes' was borrowed into northern California English as *tule* to mean 'swamp, marsh' and contributed to compounds like *tule grass, tule land,* and *tule swamp.* Similarly, *Chesterfield* 'sofa', used generally in Canada, is typical of northern California but not in other areas of the United States. Recently, *hella,* as in "That was a hella good concert!" has become a primary marker of northern California speech; it's not used in the southern half of the state, but speakers from the south identify it as especially characteristic of their northern counterparts (Bucholtz et al. 2007).

Syntax and Discourse Features   Syntax in California is much like that throughout the country, but some peculiar discourse features are worth noting. For instance, many English speakers worldwide associate *like* used as a discourse marker ("Like, it was the best concert I've ever been to"), focuser ("It was, like, the best concert I've ever been to"), and quotative ("I'm like, 'That was the best concert I've ever been to' and she's like, 'Totally'") with Southern California dialect. In fact, all of these uses have been available in English (not just American English) at least from the nineteenth century and are not unique to California (D'Arcy 2007). Nevertheless, 1980s popular use of *like* in California certainly influenced the frequency of its use in these senses throughout American English since. Quotative *all,* by contrast, as in "She was all, 'It was the best concert ever' ") is undoubtedly Californian in origin but seems to have all but disappeared from use, even in California (Rickford et al. 2007).

Social Variation

Not all dialects are geographically based. Shared physical space clearly often creates cohesive speech communities that share a dialect, but social and cultural factors, such as race and ethnicity, can also create distinct speech communities. Social variation can jump across geographical boundaries to create geographically discontinuous speech communities. Earlier in the chapter, we stated a fundamental principle about language variation:

> Regional variation is generally continuous.

Here is a second principle:

> Social variation is often not geographically continuous.

Some social variation is dialectal and some is not. Social variation includes slang, jargon, and dialects, and it is critical to distinguish among these three categories. Dialects, both regional and social, are often (dismissively) referred to as "slang," which reflects widespread misunderstandings about the nature of dialects. All dialects have slang—the informal language often used by young people—but the dialects themselves are not slang.

Slang and Jargon versus Dialects

Slang and jargon are types of social variation, but they aren't dialects. The variation they represent is almost exclusively lexical. They are usually restricted to particular professions or age groups, and they tend to be restricted by context and formality. For example, servers in restaurants nationwide, when they suddenly have more work than can be accomplished easily, say that they are *in the weeds,* an intensive formed metaphorically on *swamped* (in effect, "I'm not just busy and I'm not just swamped—I'm in the weeds!"). Servers in California say *in the weeds,* as do those in Iowa, Alabama, and New Jersey. Like all jargon, the term belongs to a profession or avocation, not to a "community" in the conventional sense, and most members of the profession use its jargon, regardless of location. There's football jargon, NASCAR jargon, computer hacker jargon, literary theory jargon, and countless others. Such jargon can be very specific and useful within the community; it can also serve as a marker of insider or outsider status.

Slang is somewhat different from jargon because it isn't connected to a specific occupation or activity. Any item of slang has to start somewhere, and some slang has a regional or local character. But slang typically travels in one of two directions: either it takes an intense but brief journey until it reaches the end of its road and disappears, or it is recognized and adopted by all speakers of a language, or at least those speakers of a certain generation, whether Whitman's poets or Sledd's social underdogs (see Chapter 4), and it ceases to be slang.

In 1982, Moon Unit Zappa released a song called "Valley Girl," which partly reflected and partly invented "Valley Speak," the slang of young women living in the San Fernando Valley, in Los Angeles. Some forms typical of Valley Speak have all but vanished. Who says "Eeeew! Gag me with a spoon!" in the twenty-first century? Other forms have migrated from the Valley into mainstream American slang, mainly via film and television. The phrases "What's your damage?" "What's the sitch?" and "Pathetic much?" for instance, came to national attention in the movie *Heathers* (1989) and then became staples of "slayer slang" when they resurfaced in *Buffy the Vampire Slayer* (film 1992, television series 1997–2003). Still other Valley Speak items, like *space cadet,* are now in common use. As mentioned earlier, the movie *Clueless* added popularity to (young female) slang such as *totally buggin'* ('freaked out') and "As if!"

So slang begins locally but acts globally. Its speech community is bound to a time, but not to a place. "What's the sitch?" works as well for a teen in the Great Appalachian

Valley as for another in the San Fernando Valley. Double modals and *a*-prefixing, on the other hand, do not, because they reflect regional, even historical identity, rather than a more or less consciously adopted style of speech.

Social Dialects

What is the difference between slang or jargon and a social dialect? African American English (AAE), the most prominent of American nonstandard social dialects, helps us to answer the question. First, like other social variation, social dialects may include local and regional variation but generally are spoken by members of the relevant social group without regard to location. Naturally, AAE converges to some degree with Southern American English in the South and with Midland speech in the Midland region. Across regions, it also demonstrates systematic differences from any other variety of American English.

Second, AAE is not slang. It includes African American English slang, of course, but many speakers have assumed that AAE is *only* slang. Indeed, the fact that AAE includes a slang of its own is one indication that it's a dialect. AAE operates by distinct phonological, morphological, and syntactic rules, and it possesses extensive lexical differences from other varieties of American English. We can examine it systematically from every linguistic angle described so far in this book, from phonology to discourse theory. It has all the features of a dialect, but it is a dialect without clear-cut geographical isoglosses.

What are other social dialects? Standard English itself is a social dialect. One of its defining features is that it does not have regionally distinctive forms. Chicano English is also a social dialect. Both Chicano English and African American English are discussed more fully in the case studies that follow.

Two Case Studies of Social Variation

Chicano English

Spanish has been spoken in what is now the southwestern United States (Texas, Arizona, New Mexico, southern California) much longer than English because of early Spanish exploration and settlement and subsequent control of much of the region by Mexico before the territory was annexed to the United States. The Spanish-language influence in the region is largely Mexican, and the variety of English spoken by many descendents of Mexican settlers and immigrants is now usually called Chicano English. *Chicano* is a more specific term than either *Latino* or *Hispanic*, which both refer to speakers from anywhere in the Spanish-speaking western hemisphere and their descendents in the United States.

The relationship of Chicano English to other varieties of American English poses some complex questions. For instance, some features of Chicano English are strongly influenced by African American English; in other respects, features of California Chicano English resemble features of California English generally. It is nearly impossible to know which dialect influenced the other; probably their relationship is one of ongoing, mutual influence. There is also no reason to assume that Chicano English in Texas is exactly like that in southern California, and, in fact, differences have been observed.

Some impressive research has been done on Chicano English—notably Carmen Fought's *Chicano English in Context* (2003), which focuses on Los Angeles, and many articles by Robert Bayley and colleagues, which focus on Chicano English in Texas.

However, compared to other social and regional dialects, Chicano English is very understudied. The following facts may surprise you: the U.S. Census Bureau estimates that the overall Hispanic population in America in 2006 was 44.3 million, or 15 percent of the total U.S. population. Americans of Mexican heritage constitute 64 percent of the larger Hispanic group. In 2005, the United States ranked third among Hispanic countries worldwide: only Mexico (106.2 million) and Colombia (42.7 million) ranked higher. By 2050, the Census Bureau projects that Hispanics overall will make up 25 percent of the total U.S. population. It makes sense, then, to study Chicano English, among other dialects spoken by Americans of Hispanic origin, much more intensively than we have.

Phonological Features   It's natural to assume that Chicano English owes much of its phonology to Spanish, but the facts are surprising. For instance, in Chicano English, the vowel in *school* shortens (it also fronts and relaxes) to sound like "skul," but in Spanish the vowel would tend to lengthen further than in English. Similarly, *keys* can sound more like "kiss" in some Chicano English. Nevertheless, sometimes Chicano English vowels are very like Spanish ones: *talkin'* sounds more like "talkeen," to some degree like the vowel discussed earlier as a feature of southern California dialect, on which Chicano English presumably exerts some influence. As in Spanish, the low front vowel of *lamp* centralizes in Chicano English.

Spanish has no /ʃ/ phoneme. Many Chicano English speakers sometimes replace /ʃ/ with [tʃ], so that *shop* sounds like "chop." Some Chicano English also has a tendency to unvoice /z/ into [s], so that, for instance, *raise* can sound like "race"; similarly, the affricate /dʒ/ can unvoice to [tʃ], so that *language* becomes "langwich." None of these alternations and replacements seems to work predictably, however. Fought (2003, 80–86) notes the difference between nonnative speakers (who tend to produce the features described here) and Chicano English speakers (who tend not to produce them) in Los Angeles, and it's possible that earlier studies reporting these features as typical of Chicano English had overlooked this important difference between speaker populations.

In many American dialects, including those surrounding Chicano English in southern California, speakers produce glides alongside vowels, not only onglides that occur in some speakers' *Tuesday* (discussed in Chapter 3), but the offglides characteristic of most American speech. As Fought (2003) explains, Chicano English often deletes the offglides typical in words with high vowels, like *least* and *ago*. Because, like African American English, Chicano English tends to reduce some word-final consonant clusters, *least* may be pronounced as /lis/. Indeed, Chicano English speakers often delete single word-final consonants, for instance, so that *beat* is spoken as /bi/.

Intonation is an important distinctive feature of Chicano English. Speakers tend to "uptalk," to speak with rising intonations, for instance, at the ends of declarative sentences. As a result, non-Chicano English speakers often assume that Chicano English speakers are Spanish speakers speaking English with a Spanish accent. In fact, though, many Chicano English speakers are not Spanish speakers; their accent is as American as the German-influenced accent of some Pennsylvanians, the French-influenced accents of some New Englanders, and the Swedish- or Norwegian-influenced accents of some Minnesotans.

Lexical Features   Among lexical features that distinguish Chicano English from other dialects in California and the American Southwest, words borrowed from Spanish figure prominently—*abuela* 'grandmother', for instance, or *cholo* 'gang member'.

Chicano English has also developed new meanings for familiar English items: *barely* 'just recently', as in "I barely found out about them being together"; *tell* 'ask', as in "How many times you gonna tell me that?"; *talk to* 'date', as in "I barely found out that she was talking to him"; and *from somewhere*, a euphemism for 'gang member'. Fought (2003, 100–101) notes that many Chicano English speakers use prepositions in unidiomatic ways that reflect Spanish influence. For instance (these are Fought's examples), "Must have been on the fifth grade or so," where other dialects of American English expect *in*, and "He was *in* a beer run," instead of *on*, can be explained by Spanish *en*, which stands for either *in* or *on*, depending on context. Within the Chicano community, once these prepositions were introduced, they became idiomatic within the dialect, and they mark Chicano English in contrast to other dialects of American English.

African American English

More research has been done on African American English than on any other American dialect. The dialect's history goes back to the earliest days of the United States. With such a long history and so much detailed linguistic description available, AAE makes a good case study of a social dialect in the United States. It is important to remember that while the majority of AAE speakers are African American, not all African Americans speak AAE and not all speakers of AAE are African American. Also, not all speakers of AAE share the features described below, and some speakers use them variably. AAE also encompasses geographical variation, as we discussed with Chicano English, although such variation remains understudied. You will hear other labels for this dialect, including Black English, Black English Vernacular, African American Vernacular English, and Ebonics.

Historical Origins   Linguists continue to debate the origins of AAE, specifically its relationship to other nonstandard varieties of English, to English-based creoles in the Caribbean and elsewhere, and to various West African languages. AAE can be traced back to the variety of English spoken by slaves in the South, who came to the American colonies/states speaking many West African languages (e.g., Mende, Mandinka, Gola) and were required to learn English on the plantations. In twentieth-century scholarship on the origins of AAE, there have been two competing hypotheses, often called (1) the "Anglicist" or "Dialectologist" hypothesis, and (2) the "Creolist" hypothesis.

The Anglicist hypothesis proposes that AAE can be traced back to the dialects of Britain, parallel to many other nonstandard varieties of American English. On the plantations, African slaves learned the local American dialects and abandoned their native languages, with little to no influence on the English that they acquired. The Creolist hypothesis proposes that AAE has developed from a creole spoken on the Southern plantations, when speakers of different West African languages were thrown together in an English-speaking environment. English-based creoles with African languages are attested in similar situations in the Caribbean, and with Gullah, spoken on the Sea Islands off the coast of South Carolina and Georgia. Scholars who adopt this position argue that AAE then underwent decreolization and converged with other varieties of American English.

Recent evidence from ex-slave recordings and enclaves of ex-slaves in isolated areas of North America seems to contradict decreolization arguments. If anything, AAE in the twentieth and twenty-first centuries seems to have diverged from other varieties of American English compared with AAE in the nineteenth century. Recent research in North Carolina suggests that while AAE shows many grammatical similarities to varieties of Southern American English, some phonological and grammatical features have differentiated black and white varieties of English in the region for centuries: for example, the absence of *is* in a construction such as *She nice* (possible in AAE but not typical of other varieties). It may be possible to trace some of these features back to the influence of West African languages. Whether or not AAE was ever a creole language, like the languages spoken in Jamaica, Trinidad, and Barbados, and whether it was influenced by contact with these creole languages in the South, remains an open question. It is certainly possible to argue for the influence of African languages, as "substrate languages" (see Chapter 11), on the history and development of AAE without arguing for creole origins.

Some of the historical conjecture involved in the discussion of the origins of AAE must be tentative. Some words in AAE (many of which have then been borrowed into other varieties of English) may have West African ancestries, but we lack records of West African languages from the centuries when African slaves were brought to North America. And some proposed correspondences between American words spoken primarily by African Americans and words from West African lexicons are problematic. Sometimes we can be sure of West African origins, as in the cases of the words *okra* and *gumbo*, both developments of West African words for okra. Sometimes we cannot be sure, as in the cases of *jazz* and *O.K.*, both of which have complicated etymologies that may or may not include African language influence—there's no evidence that they do, and there are cogent explanations of each word's etymology that do not rely on African languages.

These specifics aside, we know that African Americans were brought to North America with linguistic heritages that in all likelihood affected the structure and development of AAE. The dialect then spread from the South to areas around the United States as freed African Americans migrated north and west. AAE now demonstrates regional variation, although this variation within the dialect has yet to be studied in much detail.

Phonological Features   Here we describe just three distinctive phonological features of AAE—only the beginning of a complete description of AAE phonology. AAE shares some phonological features with Southern dialects, but it exhibits other distinctive features as well.

The hip hop artist 50 Cent's hit song "It's Ur Birthday" captures one characteristic phonological feature of AAE: the realization of /θ/ and /ð/. 50 Cent sings one line as *like it's your birfday,* very distinctly employing AAE phonology in the final word. In AAE, the voiceless /θ/ is often realized as [t] (word initially or word finally) or [f] (word medially or word finally), as in *wit* 'with', *baf* 'bath', or *birfday.* Voiced /ð/ can be realized as [d] (word initially or word finally) or [v] (word medially or word finally), as in *dem* 'them' or *bav* 'bathe'.

Final consonant clusters in AAE are sometimes reduced to one consonant (the first consonant in the cluster) when the two consonants share the same voicing value—that is, they are either both voiced or both unvoiced. So *list* can be reduced to *lis* and *hand* to *han,* but words such as *jump* or *paint* do not undergo consonant-cluster reduction. As you can see, it is a rule-governed phonological process. This consonant-cluster reduction can affect past-tense forms—for example, *pas* ([pæs]) rather than *passed* [pæst]—although some studies show that past-tense forms are less likely to undergo cluster reduction because of the semantic load carried by the inflectional ending.

Final voiced stops in stressed syllables can also undergo devoicing in AAE, so a word such as *bid* is realized as [bɪt], or *pig* as [pɪk]. These phonological differences can sometimes give AAE-speaking children pause on a spelling quiz: when presented with the sounds [pɪk], there are two possible spellings of this word for these children: *pig* and *pick*.

We encourage you to check out the "Suggested Reading" section for works that provide more details about AAE phonology, morphology, and syntax.

Morphological and Syntactic Features   The verb system of AAE has received a lot of scholarly attention, as it makes distinctions of tense and aspect that Standard English does not. For example, AAE "habitual *be*" communicates habitual aspect: for example, "I be cooking [all day every day]" or "He be sleeping in the afternoons." Invariant *be* can also mark future resultant states (events completed in the future): for example, "I be done cooking [when I am]." Stressed BIN marks the remote past (as opposed to the recent past): for example, "I BIN cooking" (where the stress is essential to marking the aspect). All three of these constructions involve aspect unmarked grammatically in other dialects of American English (see Chapter 5). Some scholars argue that the aspectual system of the verb *be* that operates in AAE, but not in other dialects of American English, is the result of generalized African language influence. Many West African languages mark aspect with a particularity unknown to standard American English.

AAE is also characterized by the absence of third-person singular -*s* in the present tense (*he/she raise*) and the possible deletion of forms of *to be* in the third person, as well as in the second person. Some Southern dialects delete *are* in the second person as well, as in *You bad*. Both Southern dialects and AAE tend to avoid deleting *am* (**I tired*). And while some Southern dialects also delete *is* before *gonna* in the third person (e.g., *He gonna get to that*), AAE is unusual in deleting *is* when it stands alone in the third person (e.g., *She nice*).

AAE, like many regional varieties of American English, employs multiple negation, combining negative markers on the auxiliary verb and other forms: so *not, can't, don't, won't, ain't* with *no, nothing, nobody, never, neither* (e.g., *I ain't never seen nobody shout that loud*). In AAE, it is also possible to invert two negative elements (a negative indefinite noun phrase and a negative auxiliary verb) at the beginning of a sentence or clause (e.g., *Ain't nothing you can do* or *Don't no house get built that fast*). The form *ain'(t)* serves as a negative auxiliary for Standard English *am not, isn't, aren't, hasn't, haven't,* and *didn't* (e.g., *he ain't here* or *I ain't been there* or *she ain't do it*). Many other nonstandard dialects of English use *ain't* as a negative auxiliary with most of these meanings, except for *didn't*, which is more specific to AAE. In existential constructions, where standard varieties employ *there*, AAE employs *it* (e.g., *It's a lot of people in the hall*). In both existential constructions, *it* and *there* are "empty subjects," and it makes just as much sense to use one as the other.

Lexical Features   There are many words and phrases typical of AAE and not typical of Standard English. Let's consider a few examples from Lisa Green's book *African American English* (2003). If you *get over on* someone, you take advantage of them, and if that person were to find out, she might say, with indignation, "Don't *come* telling me that you haven't cheated." The word *some* can be used as an intensifier, similar to *very*, rather than as a qualifier (e.g., *LeBron James is some tall*), and the word *steady* describes an action carried out in an intense, consistent, and continuous manner (e.g., *Her mouth is steady runnin'*). *Come* and *steady* in AAE could also be categorized as syntactic features of the dialect, given that *come* functions as a modal and *steady* expresses verbal aspect.

AAE, then, is a dialect with a history. It has developed continually over the course of American history, and it possesses its own regular phonological, morphological, and syntactic features, as well as some distinctive lexical items, some of which have influenced American English generally, standard or slang (*okra, gumbo, jukebox, dis, all that, the Man*), and some of which are still restricted to the African American community (*Amen corner, forty acres and a mule, Are you right?*). Why, then, doesn't AAE receive the same sort of respect as other historical American dialects? The answer returns us to the politics of dialects and the fact that judgments about language are usually more about social and political factors than purely linguistic ones.

The Future of AAE   This robustly distinctive version of AAE hasn't always existed: some of its features can be traced back to the seventeenth century, but many emerged from African American culture in the twentieth century, as AAE diverged from Southern Vernacular English when rural African Americans moved to urban centers all over the country. As we noted earlier, dialects can "die"—sometimes they disappear altogether, and sometimes they converge with other forms of speech, new dialects or old ones, and lose their distinctiveness. AAE, however, appears to be gaining features that distinguish it from other varieties.

Recent research suggests that AAE is now used as a home or native dialect by non-African American speakers, particularly Latino speakers in urban contexts, and may be emerging as an urban dialect without clear association with a specific racial or ethnic group (Wolford and Evans 2007). For some time, non-African American speakers have adopted lexical, syntactic, and prosodic elements of African American English, constructing racial identities by linguistic means. Mary Bucholtz (1999) calls this intermediate variety of American English CRAAVE—Cross-Racial African American Vernacular English. As Elaine W. Chun (2001) observed, not only white Americans but Korean Americans cross by borrowing items from the African American English lexicon. Both Bucholtz and Chun identify hip hop as a source of information about African American speech for non-African American speakers. As hip hop spreads into youth culture worldwide, some features of AAE, particularly lexical ones, are also entering global English. For instance, *whut* and *yo* (as discourse markers), *ill* 'excellent, awesome', *flow* 'rap well', *phat* 'excellent', and even *y'all* (as well as plenty of American profanity) are regular features of current Korean hip hop (Lee 2007). By the middle of the twenty-first century, AAE may develop far beyond the AAE recorded and analyzed in late twentieth-century scholarship.

Special Focus: The Ebonics Controversy

The most dramatic conflict over the status of a social dialect in recent years erupted when the Oakland, California, Unified School District passed its resolution on Ebonics on December 18, 1996. The amended version was issued shortly thereafter, to clarify the resolution's aims after much confusion and controversy in the mainstream media. The Ebonics resolution was designed to provide teachers in the Oakland school district with linguistic training so that they understood the structural differences between AAE and mainstream English. Armed with this knowledge and with related teacher training, these teachers could better help AAE-speaking students master Standard English. The goal was to help all students master Standard English. The resolution did not propose "teaching AAE" in the schools or teaching other subjects in AAE. If you only had access to mainstream media, however, you would never have known that. The media portrayed the resolution as something quite different from what it was, and it did not treat AAE as a systematic dialect of American English.

In order to understand the controversy, it is useful to consider the resolution in its entirety, and you can find it easily on the Web or in Perry and Delpit (1998, 143–47). In summary, the resolution argued that

- African American students in the Oakland school district were not learning Standard American English well.
- AAE is not merely a dialect of English; it is a social dialect that retains numerous features from African languages.
- Because it partly descends "genetically" (in a linguistic, not a biological sense) from African languages, AAE diverges so strongly from other American English dialects that it is more like another language than a "mere" dialect, and African American students might learn Standard English more readily if they were taught as though they were in a bilingual program.
- Thus Oakland would develop a "bilingual" program for African American students staffed by teachers with a thorough linguistic understanding of both AAE and Standard American English, so that African American students could negotiate what might be considered a daunting language difference.

Many Americans, upon hearing of the resolution with the media's spin on it, were outraged at the notion that AAE would actually be taught in schools. Cartoons depicted math being taught in AAE, as well as tourists with guidebooks trying to "talk Ebonics"—the debate and the jokes at the expense of AAE quickly moved beyond educational questions. This widespread misunderstanding of what the Oakland school board proposed erased from public view all the language in the resolution that emphasized that the goal was to facilitate the mastery of Standard English. Much of the resistance came from those who viewed AAE as "bad" or "debased" or "corrupt" versions of Standard American English, which made it unacceptable even as an instrument for teaching the standard variety.

Resistance to the Oakland decision united the political left and right. In editorials in local newspapers all over the country, as well as national newspapers including the more conservative *Wall Street Journal* and the more liberal *New York Times,* Ebonics (or AAE) was described as "broken English," "street slang," "corrupt English," and other such derogatory labels. The resolution was condemned as misguided if not ridiculous—and potentially racist for not teaching AAE-speaking students Standard English. On his Web site John Rickford, an expert on AAE at Stanford, describes his and other linguists' experience as they attempted to respond to the controversy ("The Ebonics Controversy"). They tried to clarify the school board's goal of teaching Standard English by using AAE as a bridge. They tried to legitimize AAE as a full-fledged dialect of American English. They wrote many editorials that were never published; they taped television interviews that were never aired.

In the end, after a hearing on Ebonics in the U.S. Senate on January 23, 1997, the Oakland School District was allowed to keep its Standard English Proficiency funding for such educational purposes, and a line item in the 1997 appropriations budget provided $1 million for research on the relation between the home language of African American students and their success in learning Standard English. In 1998, California voters passed Proposition 227, which banned most forms of bilingual education in the state.

The controversy over Ebonics raises several interesting questions. First, why do even well-educated people know so relatively little about language variation? Many linguists argue that dialect education represents a serious gap in the language arts curriculum. The only "linguistics" most Americans study, if they have any explicit instruction in language at all, is prescriptive grammar, the grammar of the standard variety as presented in grades 8–12, then perhaps reinforced in a college composition class. As you might guess, the authors of this book wish that more college students, and especially more future teachers (and not only English teachers), took at least one serious, informed course on language. Any language is a bundle of dialects, and learning about the systematic nature of all dialects can make it more difficult to dismiss nonstandard varieties as inherently inferior, even if one promotes the teaching of standard varieties.

Second, if you accept that AAE is a systematic dialect of American English, what would be wrong with teaching AAE (or any nonstandard dialect) to any given student population? Theoretically, of course, there is nothing at all wrong with teaching about AAE. Colleges and universities offer courses in AAE, in Appalachian English, in language variation and dialects, as well as courses in the history of the English language, American English, and so on. AAE is interesting from a linguistic point of view, but it is also a part of American history and American culture. It can (and should) be a subject (long or short) in many courses, not just those concerned with language variation or American English. Practically, though, the public school day may not be long enough to accommodate serious study of AAE, any more than a public school curriculum can offer a course on, say, Berks County dialect or Appalachian speech. Nevertheless, local dialect may well come up in classes, and there is no reason not to treat any dialect with linguistic respect in a classroom.

Third, even if one didn't agree that AAE should be taught as an independent subject, a subject on a par with Standard American English, why couldn't it be used in classrooms both as a language of instruction and as a linguistic point of comparison? In other words, if students are being asked to move from Language A to Language B, why not teach about the linguistic differences between A and B? In still other words, why is it necessary, in teaching B, to pretend that A doesn't exist, or, at least, that it has no value? Some people worry that legitimizing the value of a variety like AAE would "send the wrong message" to kids that they do not have to learn Standard English. But students can as effectively become bidialectal as bilingual, and most students understand the political, social, and economic reasons to master Standard English.

Would it seem offensive to most Americans if English grammar were clarified by comparison with French or German? If not, then why not refer explicitly to AAE as a legitimate variety of American English that can help speakers grasp the standard variety? Some preliminary studies indicate that such a comparative approach effectively helps AAE-speaking students learn to code-switch in and out of Standard English more successfully. With such an approach, standard grammatical features would be framed as one possible construction, as grammatically "logical" as nonstandard alternatives. It would lead to important questions such as: Are double negatives wrong because they are "illogical"? Then why does French form negatives with two markers rather than one? *Je ne sais pas* ('I don't know')! And if French is no less logical than Standard American English, then why do we so easily deplore double negatives in AAE, or in other varieties of American English?

Most linguists describe AAE as a dialect rather than as a separate language, as the Oakland resolution did—which stemmed in part from the desire to qualify for federal Special English Proficiency funds. But as the resolution passed by the Linguistic Society of America in 1997 in response to the Oakland decision made clear, linguists do support using AAE as a "bridging dialect" in classrooms—employing the language of home and community as one way to explore the wider world. In Berks County, Pennsylvania, students are told to "Erase the board awhile," so why can't African American teachers use the whole aspectual gamut of *be* to help students feel comfortable in school? Teachers can still require that students master speaking and writing Standard English, but it does not have to occur at the expense of or exclusion of all other varieties of English.

Standard English's monopoly on academic discourse is not unchallengeable. You could effectively write a dissertation in AAE instead of Standard American English, if your readers knew the nonstandard variety and accepted it as appropriate for the genre. Geneva Smitherman, a pioneering scholar of AAE and an advocate of students' right to their own language, frequently, if only temporarily, code-shifts in her books and scholarly articles, to reinforce the truth that AAE is the peer, for intellectual purposes, of any variety of American English, even the standard variety. In an article about the Ebonics controversy (1998, 99), she writes:

> today's negative pronouncements on Ebonics reveal a serious lack of knowledge about the scientific approach to language as well as galling ignorance about what Ebonics is (more than "slang") and who speaks it (at some point in their lives, 90 percent of African Americans). Most critically, these pronouncements reveal an appalling rejection of the language of everyday Black people. See, when you lambaste the home language that kids bring to school, you ain just dissin dem, you talkin bout they mommas! Check out the concept of "*Mother* Tongue."

Language is about identity, family, and community. As Smitherman forcefully points out, you cannot reject a language without dissing the speakers. And there is no reason schools cannot recognize both standard and nonstandard varieties of English as legitimate and expressive—not to mention meaningful to their speakers—while simultaneously asking students to master Standard English.

A Scholar to Know

Geneva Smitherman (1940–)

Since her first book in 1975, Geneva Smitherman has been a leading voice in the study of African American language and its relation to African American culture and the lived experience of African Americans. Her book *Talkin and Testifyin: The Language of Black America* (1986/1977) covers African American language at every structural level, from phonology to discourse and style. Much of her writing also tackles educational and political questions wrapped up in language variation. Smitherman's best-known book may be *Black Talk: Words and Phrases from the Hood to the Amen Corner* (2000a/1994). Smitherman has long made the case that African American English is not slang; it's got slang, but it's a social dialect spoken by a group of Americans central to American history and culture, yet with a culture of its own. She has always

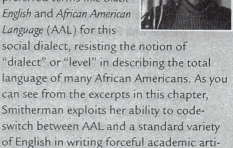

preferred terms like *Black English* and *African American Language* (AAL) for this social dialect, resisting the notion of "dialect" or "level" in describing the total language of many African Americans. As you can see from the excerpts in this chapter, Smitherman exploits her ability to code-switch between AAL and a standard variety of English in writing forceful academic articles about language, education, and language politics.

Currently University Distinguished Professor at Michigan State University, Smitherman has been an activist in Michigan education throughout her career. She has also taken on the role of a public intellectual, informing the general public, court judges, and others about discrimination in education.

American dialects, both regional and social, can be studied scientifically and historically, but they also pose immediate social challenges. American dialects lie at the intersection of linguistics and American life in our daily encounters with language and language policy.

This book has provided you a linguistically informed perspective on language variation. In the process, it has made an argument for the structural equality of dialects. Linguists continue to strive to make this information publicly available in more effective ways, so that it can productively inform public debates about language and education, such as the debate over the Oakland resolution on Ebonics. No student benefits from having his or her home language variety dissed at school.

☑ Summary

In this chapter, you have learned about several characteristics of American dialects.

- To speak a language is to speak a dialect of that language.

- American English includes regional dialects (like Appalachian English, California English, and American English in Berks County, Pennsylvania) and social dialects (like African American English, Chicago English, and Standard American English).

- Regional dialects of American English reflect patterns of settlement and contact with languages other than English, including Native American, European, African, and Asian languages.

- Regional variation is generally continuous.

- Social variation is often not geographically continuous.

- Variation among dialects boils down to variation among phonological, morphological, syntactic, and lexical features.

Suggested Reading

Given a serious interest in American dialects, you should first turn to the *Dictionary of American Regional English,* edited by Frederic G. Cassidy, Joan Houston Hall, and others; the Linguistic Atlas project materials, both published and unpublished; and the *Atlas of North American English* by William Labov, Sharon Ash, and Charles Boberg (2005). The best books about American regional dialects generally are Walt Wolfram and Natalie Schilling-Estes, *American English: Dialects and Variation* (2005); Edward Finegan and John Rickford, eds., *Language in the USA;* Craig M. Carver, *American English Dialects* (1987); Allan Metcalf, *How We Talk: American Regional English Today* (2000); and Walt Wolfram and Ben Ward, eds., *American Voices: How Dialects Differ from Coast to Coast* (2006). Among the excellent books about regional dialects are Norman Eliason's *Tarheel Talk* (1956), E. Bagby Atwood's *The Regional Vocabulary of Texas* (1962), and Wolfram and Schilling-Estes's *Hoi Toide on the Outer Banks* (1997). There are dictionaries of particular varieties that extend DARE's reach, like the *Dictionary of Smoky Mountain English,* edited by Michael Montgomery and Joseph S. Hall (2004). And there are many popular accounts of local dialects available on the

Web—many of these are less than accurate, however, and some are downright hateful, so use them with care.

The standard account of contemporary Chicano English is Carmen Fought's *Chicano English in Context* (2003); Allan A. Metcalf's *Chicano English* (1979) summarizes fieldwork on this variety from the 1930s through the 1970s and is still useful, though, like all living dialects, Chicano English has developed since then. Essential resources for the study of African American English include *African American English*, edited by Salikoko S. Mufwene, John R. Rickford, Guy Bailey, and John Baugh (1998); John R. Rickford's *African American Vernacular English* (1999); Lisa Green's *African American English* (2002); John Baugh's *Out of the Mouths of Slaves* (1999); several works by Geneva Smitherman, including *Black Talk: Words and Phrases from the Hood to the Amen Corner* (2nd ed., 2000), *Talkin and Testifyin: The Language of Black America* (1977), and *Talkin That Talk: Language Culture and Education in African America* (2000). You will be delighted, as well as informed, by John Rickford and Russell Rickford's *Spoken Soul: The Story of Black English* (2000).

The Ebonics controversy figures centrally in John Baugh's *Beyond Ebonics: Linguistic Pride and Racial Prejudice* (2000) and Theresa Perry and Lisa Delpit's *The Real Ebonics Debate: Power, Language, and the Education of African-American Children* (1998). John Rickford describes his and other linguists' experiences with the media during the controversy in the essay "The Ebonics Controversy in My Backyard," available at http://www.Stanford.edu/~rickford/papers/EbonicsInMyBackyard.html.

Exercises

Exercise 12.1 Dialect Attitudes

Survey family, friends, and acquaintances about what makes a dialect acceptable, quaint, or "bad" American English. First, come up with a set of questions that you think will elicit the relevant information. Second, survey enough speakers that you can make some generalizations about your results. Then address these questions:

a. Do you discover any regularities among the responses?

b. Are there any strong differences in opinion?

c. How do you account for either result? (Language attitudes are often influenced by the same factors that contribute to variation: gender, race, ethnicity, age, education, place of origin, etc.)

Exercise 12.2 Perceptual Dialectology

Practice a little perceptual dialectology, along the lines of Dennis Preston's work (see Chapter 11).

a. If you attend a college or university close to your hometown, what distinguishes your native speech from those who live only a county away? If you can, find a local map and take it to other natives of your hometown. Do they draw dialect boundaries along the same lines?

b. If you attend a college or university some distance from your home (more than an hour's drive away), what differences do you observe between your home dialect and that of the town where you attend college? Remember, these differences could be phonological, morphological, syntactic, or morphosyntactic, as well as lexical. Be sure to discuss dialect, that is, systematic variation, not slang or jargon.

Exercise 12.3   Regional Forms

1. You already know that some people call a nonalcoholic carbonated beverage by one word, and others by another. Similarly, folks in different dialect regions call a sandwich on an elongated roll by different names. Take a look at the *Dictionary of American Regional English* (DARE). What are the variant terms for the sandwich? How well do their distributions conform to the regions described here?

2. The *American Heritage Dictionary* asserts that *fixin' to* is a reliable marker of Southern speech. But look at the entry for *fixing* in DARE. How do you explain evidence for the item (or forms closely related to it, like New England *fixing for*) from areas beyond the South?

3. a. The form *y'all* is the characteristic second-person plural pronoun of African American English. Given what you've read in this chapter, how do you think this fact might play into the spread of *y'all?*

   b. In June 2004, Marc Anthony (the singer) said on the *Today Show,* "Y'all know I don't talk about my personal life." Anthony is a native of New York and is of Puerto Rican descent. So what explains his use of *y'all?*

   c. Linguist Jan Tillery describes the use of *y'all* as a second-person singular pronoun in Texas as a "counter-reaction to the mass appropriation" of *y'all* in the plural around the country. How can you relate this new development to the principles involved in dialect change?

   d. Linguists Guy Bailey and Jan Tillery have been researching the spread of *y'all* beyond the South. First, they've discovered that states like Kansas and New Mexico show higher proportions of "y'all use" over the past fifty years. How would you explain this phenomenon, given what you've read in this chapter?

4. Use the *Oxford English Dictionary* to determine the origins of each of the following words. For each word, speculate what its origins reflect about the effect of settlement patterns of speakers of different languages on the English vocabulary.

   a. coyote

   b. lodge

   c. Iroquois

   d. chocolate

   e. canoe

   f. tomato

Exercise 12.4   Describing Your Own Dialect

In Chapters 3–6, we describe the phonology, morphology, and syntax of primarily Standard American English. Review these chapters, and describe at least one way in which the dialect that you speak differs (or can differ in some contexts) from the description of the "standard" in each of these categories: phonology, inflectional morphology, pronouns, auxiliary verbs, adverbs, prepositions.

Exercise 12.5   African American English and Appalachian English

1. Given what you have read about the grammar of AAE, what has caused the misunderstanding in these two dialogues, between a teacher who speaks Standard English and a student who speaks AAE (from Smitherman 2000b, 25)?

   Scene 1: Elementary school, Los Angeles.

   Teacher: Bobby, what does your mother do every day? (Teacher apparently wanted to call Bobby's parents.)

   Bobby: She be at home!

   Teacher: You mean, she *is* at home.

   Bobby: No, she ain't, 'cause she took my grandmother to the hospital this morning.

   Teacher: You know what I meant. You are not supposed to say "she *be* at home." You are to say "she *is* at home."

   Bobby: Why you trying to make me lie? She ain't at home.

   Scene 2: First-grade classroom, Detroit.

   Teacher: Where is Mary?

   Student: She not here.

   Teacher: (exasperatedly) She is *never* here!

   Student: Yeah, she be here.

   Teacher: Where? You just said she wasn't here.

2. Using the *Dictionary of American Regional English*, the *Oxford English Dictionary*, and, if you can, *The Dictionary of Smoky Mountain English*, explain the meaning of the Appalachian English terms in this passage by Tony Earley (1998, 80).

   Nor is "quare" the only word still hiding out in my grandmother's house which dictionaries assure us lost currency years ago. If I brought a quare person to Sunday dinner at Granny's and he ate something that disagreed with him, we might say that he looked a little peaked. Of course, we might decide that he was peaked not because he had eaten something that disagreed with him but because he had eaten a bait of something he liked. We would say, Why, he was just too trifling to leave the table. He ate almost the whole mess by himself. And now we have this quare, peaked, trifling person on our hands. How do we get him to leave? Do we job him in the stomach? Do we hit him with a stob? No, we are kinder than that. We tell him, "Brother, you liked to have stayed too long." We put his dessert in a poke and send him on his way.

Chapter **13**

History of English:
Old to Early Modern English

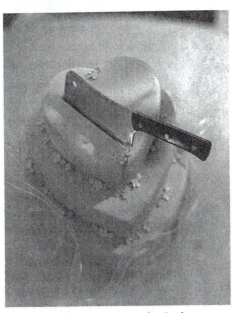

Lovers can cleave to one another in the sense of 'cling', or an unfaithful lover can cleave ('split') a loved one's heart—breaking the heart with a metaphorical cleaver.

In Modern English, you can cleave to someone or something (i.e., 'be joined to another') and also can cleave something in two (i.e., 'break or sunder something into parts'). The Web site of the Cleave Counter Agency (http://www.cleave.com) states playfully: "We put things together. We take things apart." How is it that Modern English uses the same verb to mean contradictory things: to bring things together and to separate things permanently?

In fact, *cleave* is two different verbs, and they were not always identical. They derive from two distinct Old English verbs, one "strong" and one "weak." These two verbs were significantly different in Old English, but over time, the pronunciations and inflections of the two forms converged. The Old English verb from which *cleave* 'break into parts' developed was *clēofan,* a "strong" verb that marked tense by changes in the internal vowel, rather than by adding an inflectional suffix. The past tense of this *cleave* was *clove*. The past participle was *cloven*, from which the adjective *cloven* (as in the *cloven hooves* of ungulates and the Devil) derives. The adjective *cleft* (as in a *cleft chin*) also can be traced back to the Old English "strong" verb paradigm.

If you *cleave* to someone or something, you do so with the descendent of the Old English "weak" verb *clīfan*. As a "weak" verb, *clīfan* formed the past tense by adding an inflectional suffix, which is where we get *cleave*, *cleaved*, and *had cleaved* (rather than *cleave*, *clove*, and *had cloven*). These two contradictory meanings can lead to potentially confusing sentences: for example, an unfaithful lover takes a metaphorical *cleaver* (imagine a butcher's knife) to the heart of the one to whom he or she should *cleave* in the sense of clinging, not butchering.

Many of the regularities and idiosyncrasies of Modern English can be traced back through the centuries, sometimes as far back as Old English—one reason the history of English is essential to the study of English linguistics. Sometimes history is framed primarily as knowledge of the past. The story of English, however, is living history. Current English is only one stage in an ongoing process of language change.

This chapter and the next one summarize the story of English—both of the language and of its speakers—relating historical facts to current features and then looking forward to the future.

A note before we begin: Historians typically divide the history of a language into periods, such as Old, Middle, Early Modern, and Modern. The lines between these periods are somewhat artificial, no more accurate than an isogloss (see Chapters 11 and 12). As with regional variation, chronological development is continuous. So a history of English can say that Middle English, for instance, "begins" in 1066 after the Norman Conquest, but features of Middle English are already in play before that date, and features of Old English persist well into the Middle English period in different dialects. Some historians choose an important historical event as the dividing line between periods. Speakers, however, wake up the day after these events speaking the same version of the language that they spoke the day before.

Old English (449–1066): History of Its Speakers

Old English, which Modern English speakers barely recognize as related to their language, originally developed from a group of Germanic dialects. In spite of later influence, English is fundamentally a Germanic language, a member of the same language family as Dutch, Modern High German, Pennsylvania German, and Yiddish, among others.

When Did English Begin?

In his *Ecclesiastical History of the English People* (731), the medieval scholar known as the Venerable Bede reports that in 449 CE Britain was invaded and settled by representatives of three Germanic tribes: the Angles, the Saxons, and the Jutes. Historians are not

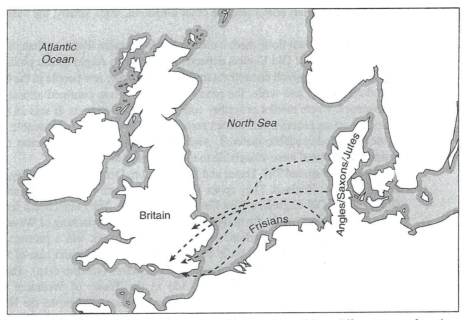

FIGURE 13.1 The Angles, Saxons, Jutes, and Frisians migrated from different parts of northern Europe to the southeastern part of Britain beginning in the middle of the fifth century.

entirely sure who the invaders were, but they believe that the Angles and Jutes hailed from what is now Denmark, and the Saxons from northwest Germany, between Denmark and the Netherlands (see Figure 13.1). Jutes settled in Kent, in the southeast corner of the island, during the fifth century. Later in the same century, Saxons established themselves in the south and west. Angles took control of the eastern coast by the middle of the sixth century. By the end of that century, many (though not all) of the Celts, who had lived in Britain for nearly a millennium, were driven into what became Wales, and the speakers of Germanic dialects occupied nearly all of what we now call England.

When the Germanic tribes arrived in Britain in 449, they spoke the same Germanic dialects that they spoke when they were on the European continent. Historians use 449 as the "beginning" of English because from that time onward, the Germanic dialect speakers in Britain were geographically isolated from the Germanic dialect speakers on the continent. The dialects spoken in Britain, through natural processes of language change and through language contact, began to drift away from their "sister" dialects on the continent to become a distinct language, which we call "English."

Which Germanic Dialect Is "Old English"?

"Old English" was actually a collection of several Germanic dialects that developed from the dialects that the waves of Germanic settlers spoke. By the seventh century, England was divided into seven kingdoms, known as the Heptarchy. Angles ruled in Northumbria, Mercia, and East Anglia; Saxons in Essex, Sussex, and Wessex (names meaning 'East Saxony', 'South Saxony', and 'West Saxony'); and the Jutes stayed in Kent. The fortunes of these kingdoms rose and fell. Initially, the Jutes were ascendant, but, in the seventh through the early ninth centuries, Northumbria and

Mercia (in that order) dominated the other kingdoms, until, finally, the Saxons became preeminent.

When a kingdom flourished, it usually produced more literature than its neighbors, so our knowledge of Old English depends somewhat on Anglo-Saxon political history. It also depends on which documents survived. Since very few people in the Old English period could read and write, the production of texts was confined almost entirely to monasteries, where monks or scribes composed or copied texts. It was an enormously time-consuming process, and written texts were relatively few and valuable. Texts were written on biodegradable material. And the monasteries in which most texts of the period were housed were vulnerable to the ravages of military attack.

Beginning around 787, Danes and Vikings, from Denmark and Norway, harried the eastern coast of England. They spoke Old Norse, a North Germanic language and distant cousin of Old English, a West Germanic language. They launched a serious attack against the English late in the ninth century, when Alfred was king of Wessex, the then ascendant Old English kingdom. Aware that he could not win a protracted conflict, Alfred allowed the Danes to settle the area north of London and east of the Watling Road—the Roman road between London and Chester (see the map). This area was designated the Danelaw (see Figure 13.2) in the Treaty of Wedmore (878). The Danelaw isolated Northumbria from the other kingdoms and broke the Heptarchy. It ensured a strong Old Norse influence on Old English, as Old Norse speakers settled throughout the Danelaw, living side by side (and intermarrying) with Old English speakers, in what may have been bilingual communities. The Viking raids and the battles

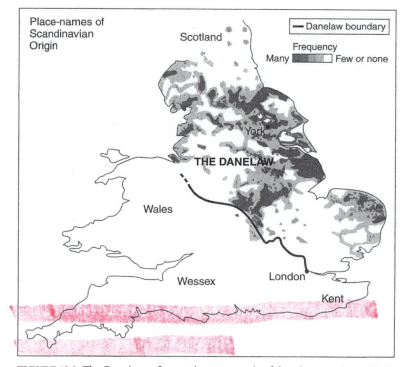

FIGURE 13.2 The Danelaw refers to the area north of the Thames River ceded to the Danes after the Treaty of Wedmore in 878 CE.

with Alfred also resulted in the burning of many monasteries, which dramatically affected the existing record of Old English texts. In 1016, the Danish king Cnut became king of England, and England became a province of Denmark. The Saxons regained control in 1042, with the accession of Edward the Confessor, only to lose it again in the Norman Conquest of 1066.

Before the Viking raids, Northumbria was a major European intellectual center, with important monasteries in Wearmouth, Jarrow, and Lindisfarne. Bede was resident at Jarrow, and, for a while, so was Alcuin, a formidable scholar who developed Europe's finest library, in York, before the emperor Charlemagne invited him to lead the school at his imperial court in France. When Mercia was in the fore, it produced the *Vespasian*

Language Change at Work

How English Was Written Down

From the seventh century on, the Latin-speaking Christian missionaries not only brought new words into English but also introduced the Latin alphabet, which was adopted for writing down English. Before the adoption of the Latin alphabet, English was written with the runic alphabet, which was used, in whole or in part, in Scandinavia, Iceland, and Britain from the third to the seventeenth centuries. The runic alphabet included twenty-four characters.

Even after the adoption of the Latin letters, English scribes kept a few runes in order to transcribe sounds unique to English. For example, Latin does not have the sounds /θ/ or /ð/, so scribes continued to use the symbols "thorn" (þ) and "eth" (ð)—often interchangeably—for what we now spell *th*. Scribes also maintained the symbol "ash" (æ) and "wynn" (which looks much like thorn, but without the rising staff at the top).

The evolution of thorn's written form is thought to explain the "ye" in store and brand names that aim to sound archaic, such as "Ye Olde Tea Shoppe" (the extra letters at the end of words seem to be inserted for a similar effect). Over time, the script form of thorn "opened up" on the top such that the curved line on the right did not necessarily touch the vertical stroke—which allowed it to be reinterpreted as a "y." So the "ye" here originates as "the."

Carved on the Ruthwell Cross is one of the earliest surviving runic inscriptions of Old English.

Psalter, a Latin version of the Psalms with interlinear glosses in Mercian dialect. When the Saxons led the Heptarchy, from the reign of Alfred (871–899), West Saxon became the most influential literary dialect of Old English. Most of the Old English documents that survive are from the late ninth and tenth centuries and are written in the West Saxon dialect. Alfred, a scholar as well as a great warrior and diplomat, translated Boethius's *The Consolation of Philosophy* and Pope Gregory's *Pastoral Care* into English, and he also sponsored many other translations from Latin into English.

Alfred's reign, late in the ninth century, is the golden age of Old English prose, and the texts translated then are crucially important to our knowledge of Old English syntax, since we know the Latin texts from which the Old English ones were translated. That the "Old English" we know is mostly late West Saxon is partly a matter of accident: more texts from the period of West Saxon dominance have survived the ravages of time. *Beowulf*, at least as we have it today, is a product of the tenth century. So is the poetic account of the *Battle of Brunanburh*, which celebrated the English king Athelstan's victory over an army of Danes and Scots (937). In the poem *The Battle of Maldon*, Byrtnoth, earl of Essex, succumbs to Olag Tryggvason, a Viking invader. The actual battle occurred on August 11, 991, so the poem may date from the eleventh century. Remember, though, that almost all of these epic poems were probably sung for decades if not centuries before they were written down in the form we know today.

By the tenth century, something like a literary standard had emerged, best exemplified and possibly created by Ælfric (ca. 955–1010), abbot of the monastery at Eynsham. Ælfric was a prolific writer. He produced many theological works, including a collection of homilies, another of saints' lives, and Old English versions of several books of the Bible (though none of these survived). Most important, though, Ælfric's language was notably consistent, not only in syntax and morphology, but also in orthography, or the method of writing. By the eleventh century, Ælfric's language was the literary language of England.

Where Do the Names *English* and *England* Originate?

Until the Germanic tribes invaded the British Isles, what we now call England was known as "Britain," because it was a large area occupied by Brythonic Celts. The Celts spoke what we now call Welsh, Gaelic, and Cornish. After the Romans occupied Great Britain in 55 BCE, Latin was spoken in Britain as well. But in 449 CE, Brythonic languages dominated the island. When the Germanic tribes began to invade the island and drove the native inhabitants to the island's geographic peripheries, the balance shifted, and Germanic dialects dominated all other languages.

In 601, Pope Gregory named Æthelbert *rex Anglorum* 'king of the English', and Bede titled his work *Historia Ecclesiastica Gentis Anglorum* 'An Ecclesiastical History of the English People' a century or so later. Historians suspect, though they have no definitive evidence, that by the seventh century, *Englisc* had been derived from the name of the tribe predominant at that time, the *Engle*, or Angles. At some point, the Germanic settlers began to call themselves the *Angelcynn: Angel* 'Angle' + *-cynn* (= Modern English *kin* 'people'). By 1000, the island had taken the name *Englalond* ('land of the Angles'), replacing *Angelcynn*. Ironically, in more recent history, as people realized that the British Isles were composed of more than Angles, *Great Britain* once again became the name of the political entity once known as *England*.

Old English Lexicon

The Renaissance is well known as the period of massive borrowing of foreign words into the English vocabulary, but even in Old English, language contact resulted in extensive foreign borrowing. Although Celtic languages had little influence on Old English, two other languages, Latin and Old Norse, were significant influences.

Latin Borrowing

Approximately 25 percent of English vocabulary derives from Latin, and a significant proportion of that borrowing dates from the Old English period. That is, Latin influence significantly predates the Norman Conquest, let alone the Renaissance. Latin influenced Old English in four different stages.

The first is known as the "Zero period," because the Germanic tribes weren't in Britain when it occurred. The Germanic people alternately fought and traded with the Romans for centuries, and their conflict and commerce drew some Latin words into German. Here are some Old English words borrowed from Latin before the Germanic tribes invaded England, with their Modern English descendents:

Old English, from Latin		Modern English
camp	'battle'	*camp* 'place of temporary shelter'
cēap	'bargain'	*cheap*
cīese	'cheese'	*cheese*
cytel	'kettle'	*kettle*
flasce	'bottle'	*flask*
līne	'rope'	*line*
līnen	'flax'	*linen*
mangian	'trade' (verb)	*-monger* (as in *fishmonger*)
mīl	'mile'	*mile*
mynet	'coin'	*mint* (verb)
pīpe	'musical instrument'	*piper, bagpipes*
strǣt	'road'	*street*
wīn	'wine'	*wine*

We know that these words were absorbed into Germanic dialects before Germanic speakers settled in England because other Germanic languages also contain cognates from very early dates. Since trading often involved basic necessities, some of these Latin words refer to mundane items at the core of the everyday English vocabulary.

The second stage of Latin influence on English is minimal. A very few Latin words came to English through Celtic languages, the most important of which survive in place-names. One is *ceaster*, a form of Latin *castra* 'camp' (not to be confused with English *camp* from Latin *campus* 'field, battle'), which survives in names of (originally) fortified towns in England, like *Lancaster*, *Worcester*, *Chester*, *Manchester*, *Gloucester*, as well as American towns of the same sort (*Lancaster*, Pennsylvania;

The Bayeux Tapestry, created shortly after the Norman Conquest, tells the story of the Battle of Hastings in great detail and informs modern understandings of the event. This is only a small part of the tapestry.

Worchester, Massachusetts; *Westchester*, New York; *Manchester*, New Hampshire). Similar place-name suffixes derive from *wīc* (Latin for *village*), as in *Greenwich* (in both England and Connecticut), and *port* (Latin for *harbor*), as in *Shreveport* (Louisiana) and *Westport* (Connecticut).

The third period of Latin borrowing occurred when the Roman Catholic Church exercised direct influence on English for (primarily) ecclesiastical purposes. The fifth-century Anglo-Saxon invaders were pagans when they landed on the shores of Britain. Subsequently, Saint Columba and others representing the Catholic Church attempted conversion of the English—via Ireland and Northumbria. But the decisive event in the eventual conversion of England to Christianity occurred in 597, when Saint Augustine, at the behest of Pope Gregory, arrived in Kent. Among the Latin words that entered English vocabulary in this period are *abbot, altar, angel, anthem, candle, deacon, disciple, epistle, hymn, martyr, mass, noon, nun, pope, priest, psalm, relic, rule,* and *shrine.* Religion depended on learning, so some educational terms also found their way from Latin into English, such as *gloss, master, notary, school,* and *scribe.* And some nonecclesiastical Latin words found their way in, such as *beet, cook* (noun), *fennel, lentil, pear, radish,* and *oyster.*

The fourth stage of Latin influence on Old English began in the tenth century, during the Benedictine Reform, a theological movement meant to restore monastic life in England. Monastic life had been disrupted by the Danes and Vikings, who had destroyed key centers of English intellectual life, like the monasteries at Jarrow and

Lindisfarne. Unsurprisingly, most of the Latin vocabulary adopted by Old English during the Reform was again ecclesiastical and intellectual, such as *alb* 'white robe', *apostle*, *brief* (verb) 'summarize, instruct', *cell* 'room occupied by a religious (monk, nun, anchorite)', *creed*, *decline* 'itemize forms of a noun or adjective according to grammatical case', *demon*, *history*, *paper*, and *title*. Other learned terms, like those of medicine (as monastic practitioners understood it), were too useful not to borrow: *cancer* and *paralysis*, for instance, entered English during the Reform. And many herbal terms—herbs were fundamental to medicine at the time—likewise found themselves "Englished" from their Latin originals: *cucumber*, *ginger*, and *verbena*, among many others.

Old Norse Borrowing

The other primary foreign influence on Old English was Old Norse, the language introduced by the Danes who settled, more and more permanently, in eastern and northern England. The modern Germanic language closest to Old Norse is Icelandic. If you shop for groceries in Iceland, you might be surprised to find that eggs are called *eggs* in Icelandic. Old English borrowed the Old Norse word *egg*, which gradually obliterated Old English *ay/ey* (which meant 'egg'). The relatively small difference between the forms—a palatal glide *y* in Old English and a velar stop *g* in Old Norse—reflects the close cognate relationship between Old English and Old Norse, both West Germanic languages.

Other differences between Old English and Old Norse exhibit similar phonological alteration. Old Norse *kirk* and Old English *cirice* lived side by side in the Danelaw, both meaning 'church' and closely related as cognates. They differed primarily in that one began and ended with /k/ and the other with /tʃ/. In this case, the Old Norse word did not survive in many varieties of Modern English (it is used in Scots). But most varieties of Modern English contain many other words that we can trace back to Old Norse, including *kid*, *get*, *give*, *skill*, *skin*, and *sky*, as well as the *th-* forms of the third-person pronouns (*they*, *them*, *their*). In cognate words, where Old Norse had /sk/, Old English had /ʃ/, and in Old English, the borrowed word *skirt* and the native Old English word *shirt* referred to the same item of apparel. In the long run, *skirt* specified to draped clothing from the waist down, and *shirt* to draped clothing from the waist up.

Old Norse also contributed new meanings to Old English words. For instance, Old English *gift* referred only to the 'price of a wife'; in the plural it referred to a marriage. In Old Norse, however, the word meant 'gift, present', as it does in Modern English. Old Norse influence generalized the word's meaning.

Native English Word Formation

A typically Germanic way to create new nouns is to take two familiar ones and form a compound. Compounding is still the most productive morphological process in both Modern English and Modern German. Some Old English compounds (like most Modern English ones) are self-explanatory, like *fielleseōocnes* (*fielle* 'falling' + *sēocnes* 'sickness'), which means 'epilepsy'. Old English also employed compounds metaphorically, however, as you can see in *Beowulf* or any other Anglo-Saxon poem. For instance, in *Beowulf*, we are told that Scyld Scēfing crossed the *hronrāde* 'whale-road', rather than merely the sea. The *scop* or singer of poems unlocks his *wordhord* 'word-hoard', rather than his memory of stories or his vocabulary, in order to recite the story of Scyld Scēfing. Such metaphorical compounds are called *kennings*, from Old Norse *kenna* 'know, name'.

The compound noun *fielleseocnes* also features a familiar suffix: Modern English -*ness*. Several other Modern English affixes can be traced back to Old English. Among prefixes, Old English *wið-* has been least durable: only *withstand* among many Old English verbs formed with *wið-* survives, though the Middle English verbs *withdraw* and *withhold* are formed by analogy with Old English models. Old English derivational suffixes, on the other hand, have kept well: -*ful* combines with nouns to generate new nouns, as in *handful*; -*nes* shifts adjectives into nouns, as in *happiness* or *sickness*; -*dom* extends the agent to the area, as in *kingdom;* and -*lic* forms adjectives from nouns, as in Old English *freondlic* 'friendly'—though the reflex of -*lic* (-*ly*) became a homophone with the adverb suffix -*ly* (from Old English -*lice*), and unlike the adverb suffix is no longer productive.

Old English Grammar

Old English grammar differs from Modern English grammar so extensively that speakers of either would find speakers of the other unintelligible.

The Origins of Modern English Noun Inflections

In Modern English, the personal pronouns typically change their form depending on their number (singular or plural) and on their grammatical function in the sentence—specifically, whether they are the subject, object, or possessor. For example:

He/They learned all about Old English grammar. (subject: singular/plural)

The unfamiliarity of Old English grammar surprised him/them. (object: singular/plural)

His/Their performance on the quiz was stellar. (possessor: singular/plural)

Nouns in Modern English change form only to mark number and the possessive:

The quiz/quizzes seemed easy. (subject: singular/plural)

But I bombed the quiz/quizzes. (object: singular/plural)

The quiz's/quizzes' effect on my grade shocked me. (possessor: singular/plural)

Why do Modern English personal pronouns mark the subject/object distinction but Modern English nouns do not? The beginning of an answer is that English nouns used to make this distinction.

Nouns in Old English marked number (singular or plural), **gender** (masculine, feminine, or neuter), and case, all by a system of inflectional endings attached to a noun stem. Number is straightforward enough, and Modern English maintains this distinction. We return to gender in the next section. Case refers to a system in which inflectional endings indicate the grammatical function of the noun. In Modern English, speakers determine a noun's grammatical function primarily by word order. For example, the noun before the verb is typically the subject, and the noun after the verb is typically the direct object. (As we mentioned in Chapter 4, the observation that "The dog bit the man" is not news, but "The man bit the dog" might make the front page.) If there are two nouns directly after the verb, the first noun is the indirect object and the second noun is the direct object: for example, *The instructor gave the class a quiz.*

In Old English, inflectional endings marked grammatical function. So if we take our example sentence, *The instructor gave the class a quiz*, in Old English, the equivalent of instructor, class, and quiz would all take different endings that reflect their role as the subject, indirect object, and direct object, respectively.

Old English had four major cases: nominative, genitive, dative, and accusative. For the most part, nouns in the nominative case are subjects and those in the accusative are direct objects or objects of prepositions. The genitive indicates possession; the dative indicates an indirect object or an object of a preposition. Old English had two major classes of nouns: "strong" nouns, such as *stān* 'stone', *bān* 'bone,' and *wer* 'man'; and "weak" nouns, such as *nama* 'name' and *sunne* 'sun'. One reason these two classes are of interest with respect to the structure of Modern English is that they explain the source of the regular plural ending -*s* and the irregular plural ending -*en*. Let's look at the declension (the list of different forms by case and number) of the masculine strong noun *stān*:

	Singular	Plural
Nominative	*stān*	*stānas*
Genitive	*stānes*	*stāna*
Dative	*stāne*	*stānum*
Accusative	*stān*	*stānas*

The final -*s* in the singular genitive and the final -*s* in the plural nominative and accusative are the ancestors of Modern English possessive -*s* and plural -*s*, respectively. All the other endings eventually dropped away. The Old English weak nouns took a final -*an* to form the plural, and Modern English still retains this feature in *oxen*, *children*, and *brethren*.

The Gender of Things

If English is a Germanic language, and most Germanic languages have grammatical gender, why doesn't English? Well, it used to.

Old English employed **grammatical gender**, much like modern German (and, indeed, Romance languages, like French and Spanish). All nouns carried gender, and the assignment of gender (masculine, feminine, neuter) was semantically arbitrary. By contrast, Modern English employs **natural gender**: inanimate things are typically neuter; animate things are feminine or masculine according to their sex or apparent gender. In Old English, *stān* was masculine and *spēd* 'fortune, luck' feminine, though there's nothing especially feminine about fortune, nothing especially masculine about stones. Old English *wīfmann*, the etymon of *woman*, was masculine: *wīf* 'female, woman' was neuter, and *mann* 'person' was masculine; as a compound, *wīfmann* took the second element's gender. You might think that Old English *scip* 'ship' was feminine, and that the tendency to refer to sailing vessels in Modern English as feminine is an anomalous reflex of the Old English gender. It isn't. *Scip* is neuter. In the seventeenth century, Ben Jonson, who wrote a grammar in addition to his plays, was the first English grammarian to assert that *she* could be used in reference to ships. The origins of this convention are unknown.

The Familiarity of Personal Pronouns

Old English personal pronouns often look familiar to Modern English speakers (despite their less familiar spellings) because Modern English pronouns still mark case to some

TABLE 13.1   **Personal Pronouns in Old English**

	Singular					Plural		
	First Person	Second Person	Third Person			First Person	Second Person	Third Person
			Masculine	Feminine	Neuter			
Nominative	ic	þu	hē	hēo	hit	wē	gē	hīe
Accusative	mē	þē	hine	hie	hit	ūs	ēow	hīe
Genitive	mīn	þīn	his	hiere	his	ūser/ūre	ēower	hiera
Dative	mē	þē	him	hiere	him	ūs	ēow	him

Note: There were multiple variants in different dialects for many of these pronouns. This chart describes primarily the West Saxon most common forms.

extent and because the pronouns, as is typical of closed-class items, have changed less over time than many other words in the lexicon. One big difference is the shift from four cases in Old English to three in Modern English. Historically, the accusative and dative cases, which distinguished between direct and indirect objects, collapsed into one "object" case. See Table 13.1 and Table 13.2.

Old English also used the dual number, a plural restricted to two things. Gradually the dual disappeared and the plural declensions applied to pairs as well as groups of things.

Some changes have occurred in these forms as Old English passed into Middle and Modern English. For example, the aspirated *h* of *hit* has eroded in modern *it.* In some instances, dialectal variants have replaced standard forms: *ūre* was a variant of *ūser* and gives us *our.* The origins of modern *she* remain somewhat mysterious and are a topic of scholarly discussion. The *th-* third-person plural forms are borrowed from Old Norse. The second-person plural form *you* generalized to become both the nominative and object form in the plural and in the singular, replacing *thou/thee.*

The Many Faces of Modifiers

In Modern English, the article *the* and the demonstrative pronoun *that* are invariant—they always and only appear in one form. In Old English, the equivalent of 'the, that' took a different form, depending on the noun's number, gender, and case. (See Table 13.3.) In Modern English, the definite article *the* no longer declines, even for number. The demonstrative pronoun *that* declines only for number, to become *those.*

TABLE 13.2   **Personal Pronouns in Modern English**

	Singular					Plural		
	First Person	Second Person	Third Person			First Person	Second Person	Third Person
			Masculine	Feminine	Neuter			
Nominative	I	you	he	she	it	we	you	they
Objective	me	you	him	her	it	us	you	them
Genitive	mine	yours	his	hers	its	ours	yours	theirs

TABLE 13.3   **Demonstrative Pronoun in Old English**

| | Singular ('the, that') | | | Plural ('the, those') |
	Masculine	Feminine	Neuter	
Nominative	*sē*	*sēo*	*ðæt*	*ðā*
Genitive	*ðæs*	*ðære*	*ðæs*	*ðāra*
Dative	*ðæm*	*ðære*	*ðæm*	*ðǣm*
Accusative	*ðone*	*ðā*	*ðæt*	*ðā*

Adjectives don't decline in Modern English either (except as comparatives and superlatives), but they did in Old English, with a vengeance. Table 13.4 shows the Old English adjective paradigm, illustrated by forms for *gōd* 'good'. As a consequence of grammatical gender, in Old English adjectives had to agree in gender and case with the nouns they modified, much as adjectives in modern Romance languages (French, Italian, Spanish, Portuguese, Rumanian) and in most Germanic languages agree with their nouns: for example, *bon soir*, because 'evening' is masculine in French, but *bonne chance*, because 'luck' is feminine. Whether an adjective appears in "strong" or "weak" form in Old English is based on whether it is in predicative or attributive position, that is, after a linking verb or before a noun (see Chapter 5).

The Origins of Some Modern English Irregular Verbs

There were "strong" and "weak" verbs in Old English, just as there were "strong" and "weak" nouns and adjectives. Strong verbs conjugated for tense by a phonomorphological process called **ablaut**: rather than expressing tense by means of an inflectional suffix, the internal vowel changes to express tense. Modern English still has some strong verbs (e.g., *sing/sang/sung*), but not nearly as many as Old English, and speakers now

TABLE 13.4   **Adjective Declension in Old English**

| | Strong Declension | | | Weak Declension | | |
	Masculine	Feminine	Neuter	Masculine	Feminine	Neuter
SINGULAR						
Nominative	*gōd*	*gōd*	*gōd*	*gōda*	*gōde*	*gōde*
Genitive	*gōdes*	*gōdre*	*gōdes*	*gōdan*	*gōdan*	*gōdan*
Dative	*gōdum*	*gōdre*	*gōdum*	*gōdan*	*gōdan*	*gōdan*
Accusative	*gōdna*	*gōde*	*gōde*	*gōdan*	*gōdan*	*gōde*
PLURAL						
Nominative	*gōde*	*gōda*	*gōd*	*gōdan*		
Genitive	*gōdra*	*gōdra*	*gōdra*	*gōdena/gōdra*		
Dative	*gōdum*	*gōdum*	*gōdum*	*gōdum*		
Accusative	*gōde*	*gōda*	*gōd*	*gōdan*		

view them as irregular verbs rather than as a separate class of regular verbs. In Old English, there were seven subcategories of strong verbs, all of which took different vowel changes. We can see the remnants of these different subcategories in different patterns of vowel changes in Modern English verbs: *swim/swam/swum* versus *drive/drove/driven* versus *run/ran/run* versus *bite/bit/bitten*.

	Ablaut	
Infinitive/Present Tense	*sing*	*drive*
Past Tense	*sang*	*drove*
Past Participle	*sung*	*driven*

The "weak" verbs, which we now call "regular" verbs, conjugated by means of suffixes: the ancestor forms of Modern English final *-ed*, as in *walk, walked, had walked*. Most Modern English verbs now conjugate for tense on the pattern of weak verbs. In fact, many verbs that started out in Old English as strong verbs now conjugate as though they were weak (e.g., *climb*). A handful of verbs, however, have "swum upstream" and changed from historically weak verbs to verbs that undergo ablaut. For example, the past tense of *dig* used to be *digged*, and until quite recently, the only past tense of *dive* was *dived*.

Variation in Word Order

In Modern English, the typical sentence pattern is subject-verb-object (SVO). Old English admitted a broader variety of sentence patterns because the case system marked grammatical function. Old English often used subject-object-verb (SOV) sentence patterns, like other Germanic languages of the period, but it increasingly preferred SVO. In other words, we can already see movement toward Modern English word order during the Old English period.

Let's look at a passage from *Beowulf* to see how case and word order played out in actual texts. The syntax of alliterative poetry, like *Beowulf*, is sometimes more convoluted than prose texts, but it still provides a glimpse of Old English syntax at work. This passage describes the monster Grendel coming into the meadhall, where Beowulf's men are sleeping after the night's feasting. Grendel has just entered the hall, enraged and "intending evil." So *he* in the first line refers to Grendel:

ac hē gefēng hraðe forman sīðe	'and he seized quickly at the first opportunity
slæpendne rinc, slāt unwearnum,	sleeping warrior, slit [him] eagerly,
bāt bānlocan, blod ēdrum dranc,	bit [the/his] bonelocks, blood from veins drank,
synsnædum swealh; sōna hæfde	in chunks swallowed; soon had
unlyfignedes eal gefeormod,	of the living one all consumed,
fēt ond folma. (ll. 740–745)	feet and hands.'

The first two lines demonstrate the SVO word order: *he* (subject) *gefēng* 'seized' (verb) *slæpendne rinc* 'sleeping warrior' (object). In the third line, the object precedes the verb: *blod* 'blood' (object) *dranc* 'drank' (verb).

In this passage and its translation, you can also see the addition of prepositions in Modern English (*at, from, in, of*) where Old English used inflectional endings

(-*an*, -*e*, -*um*, -*es*) to indicate these grammatical relationships. The word *bānlocan* 'bone-locks' is also a good example of an Old English kenning or poetic compound, referring to human joints.

Old English was generally a **paratactic** language: sentences depend on coordination. Take, for example, this sentence from the *Anglo-Saxon Chronicle*:

> Hēr sæt hæþen here on Tenet, and ġenāmon friþ wiþ Cantwarum, and Cantware him feoh ġehēton wiþ þǣm friþe; and under þǣm friþe and þǣm feoh-ġehāte se here hine on niht ūp bestæl, and oferhergode ealle Cent ēasterwearde.

> 'Here, in Tenet, the heathen army settled and made peace with the Kentish folk, and the Kentish folk promised them money for that peace; but, in spite of that peace and the price they paid for it, the army stole up on it and overran all of eastern Kent.'

Spoken Modern English is often paratactic—we often rely on coordination, sometimes in long "run-on" sentences. But written Modern English tends toward the **hypotactic**, readily employing subordination (as we just did in this sentence with the participial phrase *readily employing subordination*) in addition to the paratactic.

Middle English (1066–1476): History of Its Speakers

Middle English is a period of linguistic assimilation and development, during which the language underwent significant phonological, syntactic, and lexical change.

The Norman Conquest

The Norman Conquest of England in 1066 was a critical event for the future development of English. Normandy is the northernmost province of France, directly opposite England across the English Channel. Some 200 years before the Norman conquest of England, Vikings settled in Normandy and ruled it more or less independently of France. Ironically, the Normans were originally a Germanic people, closely related culturally and linguistically to the Angles, Saxons, and Jutes—*Norman* literally means 'person from the North'. After they settled in France, the Normans adopted French. Then they invaded England. With Normans living in and ruling England for over 200 years, the native Germanic language was infused with French vocabulary, though English morphology and syntax changed very little as a direct result of contact between the two languages. French, like Latin, contributes about 25 percent of Modern English words. During these centuries, English was relegated to the language "of the people," not of the court, government, law, or literature.

Language marked relative power. Normans spoke Norman French because they preferred to and could. Anglo-Saxons, now subjugated, weren't inclined to learn French beyond what was necessary to get along, nor were they expected to, unless they wanted to enter the professional class (as administrators, lawyers, diplomats, etc.). French persisted as the first language of the English nobility for centuries, and it was also the language of administration and government. But Norman French, different from Parisian French already, became different still: isolated from continental French, it developed into a dialect known as Anglo-French or Anglo-Norman. A form of French, in other words, was England's prestige language for roughly half of the Middle English period. When written records of English reemerge in the thirteenth century, English looks dramatically different from its Old English form.

All that said, no matter how much foreign vocabulary English has absorbed (and continues to absorb), its syntax and much of its morphology are, and always have been, Germanic. The social boundaries between French and English speakers from 1066 through the thirteenth century kept the languages from influencing each other as much as they might have. And Normans probably never exceeded 2 percent of the population of England. It was not the kind of language contact situation likely to result in a creole. Linguists have found a few features of English syntax that might bear the mark of French influence, but these discoveries do not change the fundamental Germanicness of English.

A Scholar to Know

J. R. R. Tolkien the Philologist

J. R. R. Tolkien (1892–1973) is best known as the author of *The Hobbit* and *The Lord of the Rings*, but for most of his life, he was a professor at the University of Oxford, first the Rawlinson and Bosworth Professor of Anglo-Saxon (1925–1945) and then the Merton Professor of English Language and Literature (1945–1959). He was one of the most important scholars of Old and Middle English language and literature of the twentieth century.

Upon graduating from Oxford, Tolkien spent a year or so as an assistant to Henry Bradley, one of the *Oxford English Dictionary*'s chief editors. After compiling a glossary (1922) to accompany a standard textbook of the day, Kenneth Sisam's *Fourteenth-Century Verse and Prose*, he edited *Sir Gawain and the Green Knight* (a very late fourteenth-century romance) with E. V. Gordon (1925). In 1962, the Early English Text Society published his edition of *Ancrene Wisse* (one of the earliest versions of *Ancrene Riwle*), an early thirteenth-century religious text. He was famous for lectures on *Beowulf* and on the Old English *Exodus*, of which he prepared an edition published after his death.

Tolkien also wrote several seminal articles in his fields of expertise. The most famous is "*Beowulf*: The Monsters and the Critics" (1937), which many scholars would agree is the most important essay ever written about the poem. In it, Tolkien argues that all previous scholars had misunderstood the poem, taking it for an epic when in fact it is a "heroic elegy." The article "Chaucer as Philologist: *The Reeve's Tale*" (1934) attempted to reconstruct the extent to which Chaucer, though an East Anglian, had understood and accurately represented Northern dialect in "The Reeve's Tale." Tolkien's lecture "English and Welsh" (1963) is also considered a philological classic.

Compared to other major scholars of his generation, Tolkien didn't publish much, but everything he did publish was significant. Many of his colleagues were appalled that he spent so much time writing fiction and so little fulfilling his scholarly agenda. But have you ever wondered how Tolkien managed to invent the languages of Middle Earth? No one knew language, or felt it, better than Tolkien.

The Renewal of English

The loss of Normandy to France in 1204 contributed to a consolidation of nationalism on the island of England. In 1258, Henry III promulgated what became known as the *Provisions of Oxford*. These were a response to a movement among English aristocrats to exclude foreigners (namely, French aristocrats) from political influence in England. The *Provisions* were published in both English and French, the first occasion since the Conquest in which English had been used as an official language. The movement was a nationalist one: ironically, most of those who objected to French influence in English affairs were Anglo-French speakers.

From 1258, Anglo-French gradually became less and English more prestigious. A Northern poem (dated ca. 1300) titled *Cursor Mundi* includes these lines, the first record we have of nationalist feeling about the English language during the Middle English period:

Efter haly kyrc[es] state	'After the holy church's state
Þis ilk bok it es translate	This same book is translated
In to Inglis tong to rede	Into the English tongue to read
For þe love of Inglis lede,	For the love of the English people,
Inglis lede of Ingland,	English people of England,
For þe commun at understand.	For the common people to understand.'

In 1362, English was unequivocally reestablished as the national language of England. In that year, Parliament enacted the Statute of Pleading. Before 1362, all arguments in criminal courts were made in Anglo-French, not in English. In the early Middle Ages, an English speaker needed a lawyer not only to argue according to the law, but also to argue in the language of the law: Anglo-French. The Statute of Pleading ensured that English-speaking defendants, if they so requested, could understand the arguments presented in their own cases. In the same year, Parliament heard its first speech in English. Suddenly, English was the language of most of the courts and of politics.

The Emergence of a Standard

There was no standard variety of English when the Statute of Pleading was enacted. By the middle of the fifteenth century, however, a standard had developed. In retrospect, historians can identify several forces pushing toward standardization.

- England was increasingly involved in international trade, which created demand for a standardized language.
- A protracted dynastic war with France, called the Hundred Years War (although it lasted from 1337 through 1453), promoted growing nationalist sentiments. As a result, English was ascending as the language of domestic politics and legal affairs.
- A circle of poets from London and East Anglia, including Chaucer, became preeminent among English writers—overshadowing a concurrent revival of Northern and Western literary traditions. When poets in the fifteenth century proclaimed Chaucer the prince of all English poets, the variety of English in which he had written gained a more widespread, elevated status. (This variety did not, however, become the standard in the end.)

■ The English used by clerks in the Courts of Chancery was regularized and became a sort of "official" English (see Fisher 1996).

Nationalism, commerce, literary culture, and bureaucratic language intersected to produce a late Middle English standard. Unfortunately, there is no chronologically continuous history of the dialect that contributed the most to the emergent standard variety: East Anglian. Of all Old English dialects, East Anglian is the least well attested.

By the end of the fifteenth century, the rising standard had established itself in competition with the enduring regional and local dialects. The standard, primarily a written dialect, did not replace spoken dialects of Middle English. Most of those dialects have survived, in at least a few features, into the twenty-first century, in regional dialects both in Great Britain and in America.

Middle English Dialects

Although the new Middle English standard emerged in the fifteenth century, Middle English was a collection of regional dialects, evolving from the Old English dialects from which they descended. They occupy essentially the same geographic areas.

■ Kentish remained Kentish.

■ West Saxon became the Southern dialect.

■ Northumbrian became the Northern dialect.

■ Mercian became the Midlands dialect, with distinctive varieties in the West and East.

■ Recently, some scholars have granted East Anglian its own space on the map—a fact that becomes especially important in the next section.

As with all geographic variation in all languages, dialect is as local as it is regional, varying from town to town, just as it does in Pennsylvania (see Chapter 12) or anywhere else. Language historians can draw approximate dialect boundaries for Middle English, but they reflect only the broadest generalizations.

Each dialect exhibits features that distinguish it from the others. Many of these are phonological. For instance, the Northern dialect retained the Old English long *ā* (pronounced "ah"), while the other dialects gradually pronounced the same vowel as "oh." So in most dialects, one threw a *stone* and buried a *bone*, while in the North one continued to throw a *stāne* and bury a *bāne*. In the North, what others hooked or netted as *fish* (Old English *fisc*) were *fis*. Across the South (including Kent), and nowhere else, the labiodental fricatives *f* and *v* alternated with respect to other dialects and Modern English, so that a chicken could weigh *vife* pounds, rather than *five*. Similarly, Kentish alternated *s* and *z*. One person's voicing is another's unvoicing. The same is true in the West Midlands, where as a rule voiced *d* in the inflection marking past tense was unvoiced: in the East Midlands, one *cured* an illness, but in the West it was *icuret*.

Middle English dialects varied morphophonologically, too. The present participle took the suffix *-inde* in the South (including Kent), *-ende* in the East and West Midlands, and *-and* in the North. Thus from the Old English verb *wunian* 'dwell, live', the dialects developed in various phonological directions: *wuninde* 'living' in the South, *wuniende* in the Midlands, and *wuniand* in the North. In Southern and East Midlands dialects, weary winter *wolcumeð* the spring, though it *wolcumes* spring in the North, and *wolcumet* spring in the West Midlands. In this case, the Northern form became the standard, and standard Modern English retains -*s* in the third-person singular present tense to this day (e.g., *welcomes*).

Of course, for all sorts of reasons (different foreign influences, different phenomena to name), each dialect also owned peculiar lexical items. For example, the Northern dialect follows Old Norse, with *kirk* and *skirt*, as opposed to the rest of England. Those living along the Welsh border might learn a word or two from the Celtic word-hoard.

Each dialect region produced noteworthy literature that reflects the special features of its variety of Middle English. *Gawain and the Green Knight* belongs to the West Midlands but was written so near the North that it includes a large number of words derived from Old Norse that would have been unusual in the South and Southeast. The mystical religious works of Richard Rolle typify Northern dialect as surely as Michael of Northgate's *Ayenbite of Inwit* ('The Prick of Conscience') is unmistakably Kentish. Many fourteenth-century romances, such as *King Horn, Havelok the Dane*, and *Sir Eglamour*, were written in the East Midlands. *The Owl and the Nightingale* hails from the Southwest, in language not too far from that of the West Saxons (see Exercise 13.2). Here are samples of some of these texts, to give you the flavor of the Middle English dialects.

> The bee has thre kyndis. Ane es þat scho es neuer ydill, and scho es noghte with thaym þat will noghte wyrke, bot castys thaym owte, and puttes thaym awaye. Anothire es þat when scho flyes scho takes erthe in hyr fette, þat scho be noghte lightly ouerheghede in the ayere of wynde. The thyrde es þat scho kepes clene and bryghte hire wyngeȝ. Thus ryghtwyse men þat lufes God are neuer in ydellnes. For owthyre þay ere in trauayle, prayand, or thynkande, or redande, or other good doande; or withtakand ydill mene, and shewand thaym worthy to be put fra þe ryste of heuene, for þay will noghte trauayle here.
>
> —Richard Rolle, *Tretis of the Bee*, Northern, ca. 1440

> And huanne he acsede ate guode wyfman, þo he hedde hise ycleped, hou moche hi hedde him ylete, hi andzuerede þet uerst hi hedde ywrite ine hare testament þet hi him let a þousend abd vyf hondred pond. Ac hi lokede efterward ine hare testament, and hi yzeȝ þe þousend pond defaced of hire write, and zuo ylefde þe guode wyfman þet God wolde þet hi ne zente bote vif hondred.
>
> —Michael of Northgate, *Ayenbite of Inwit*, Kentish, 1340

> A wilde der is ðat is ful of fele wiles:
> Fox is hire to name for hire qweðsipe.
> Husebondes hire haten for hire harm-dedes:
> Ðe coc & te capun ȝe feccheð ofte in ðe tun,
> & te gander & te gos, bi ðe necke & bi ðe nos.
> Haleð is to hire hole: forði man hire hatieð,
> Hatien & hulen boðe men & fules.
>
> —*Physiologus (Bestiary)*, Northeast Midlands, ca. 1300

Þer he watz dispoyled, with spechez of myerþe,
Þe burn of his bruny and of his bryȝt wedez.
Ryche robes ful rad renkkez hym broȝten,
For to charge, and to chaunge, and chose of þe best.
Sone as he on hent, and happed þerinne,
Þat sete on hym semly with saylande skyrtez,
Þe ver by his uisage verayly hit semed
Welneȝ to vche haþel, alle on hews
Lowande and lufly alle his lymmez vnder,
Þat a comloker knyȝt neuer Kryst made
hem þoȝt.

—*Sir Gawain and the Green Knight*, Northwest Midlands, ca. 1400

The Middle English Lexicon

Though it retained its fundamentally Germanic character throughout the Middle Ages, after the Norman Conquest, English vocabulary was profoundly and permanently influenced by French, the language of the conquerors.

French Borrowing

French, of course, contributed richly to Middle English vocabulary. Words of French origin entered every possible register in the lexicon. The Anglo-French aristocracy contributed their own words in government and law. To list only a few of the terms by which the Anglo-French defined the political, legal, social, and economic relations after the Conquest:

accuse	*estate*	*noble*	*servant*
acquit	*evidence*	*oppress*	*sir* (both title and
administer	*felony*	*parliament*	term of respect)
advocate	*fine*	*peasant*	*slave*
attorney	*govern*	*plea*	*squire*
bail	*government*	*pledge*	*subject*
baron	*governor*	*prerogative*	*suit*
constable	*heir*	*prison*	*summons*
convict	*indict*	*property*	*tax*
council	*jury*	*realm*	*tenant*
count (the title)	*liberty*	*rebel*	*traitor*
court (both royal	*madam*	*reign*	*treason*
and legal)	*manor*	*royal*	*verdict*
crown	*mayor*	*sentence*	*warrant*
duke			

A few Old English words survived in this register: *king* and *queen*, *lady* and *lord*, *earl*. The word *law* also continued; it had been borrowed from Old Norse before the Angles, Saxons, and Jutes arrived in England.

The church was a center of power and authority, and after the Conquest, important ecclesiastical positions were generally held by Normans. The terms *religion*, *theology*, *abbess*, *baptism*, *cardinal*, *chaplain*, *clergy*, *confession*, *convent*, *crosier*, *crucifix*, *dean*, *devout*, *faith*, *friar*, *miracle*, *miter*, *parson*, *penance*, *piety*, *prayer*, *preach*, *repent*, *saint*, and *salvation* are only a small subset of the words relevant to religion that English adopted under French influence. Once again, however, Middle English retained some Old English terms of fundamental significance, most notably *church*, not only to designate an official place of *worship* (a native English word), but also to represent both the national and universal organization of Christian *belief* (a native English word).

French words dominated government, law, and religion. But French words also appeared in almost every sphere in English domestic life:

bacon	*cinnamon*	*music*	*sausage*
beef	*cream*	*mustard*	*spaniel*
biscuit	*cushion*	*oyster*	*squirrel*
blanket	*dance*	*paper*	*story*
blue	*dinner*	*pearl*	*sugar*
brown	*herb*	*pork*	*supper*
button	*lamp*	*salad*	*toast*
chair	*mitten*	*salmon*	*vinegar*

French gave us the *air* we breathe, the *debt* we owe, the *marriage* of true minds, the *grief* we suffer, the *pleasure* we feel when studying the *grammar* of a *language*—in other words, the *sum* and *substance* of our everyday lives. Something like 10,000 French words entered English between 1100 and 1500, most of them after 1250. Of these Middle English borrowings, approximately 7,500 survive in Modern English.

Latin Borrowing

Latin contributed words to Middle English, too, but the borrowings were increasingly learned and technical. By the fourteenth century, English scholars were industriously translating important Latin texts. In 1398, John Trevisa completed his translation of the thirteenth-century encyclopedia *De Proprietatibus Rerum*, originally written in Latin by Bartholomæus Anglicus (Bartholomew the Englishman). Trevisa named it *On the Properties of Things*. (Selections from Trevisa's work were reprinted by Stephen Batman in 1582, with the now humorous title, *Batman vppon Bartholomew*. Thus, both Chaucer and Shakespeare may have consulted the same encyclopedia, though in different languages.) The encyclopedia explained planets and stars, animals both real and mythical, the magical properties of gemstones, the operations of the human body, and pretty much everything else, according to the learning of the time. Somewhat later, in the early fifteenth century, someone translated Guy de Chauliac's *Chirurgia magna*, the great medieval medical textbook, from Latin into Middle English. Latin words adapted (sometimes minimally) into Middle English words from translations like these include *allegory*, *index*, *infinite*, *solar*, *ulcer*, and *zenith*.

Sometimes it is difficult to determine whether a word was borrowed into English from Latin or from French. French borrowed many Latin words in the same period as

Middle English, and because French is so closely related to Latin, a French form often so closely approximates its Latin etymon that we can't tell which is responsible for the Middle English result.

Other Borrowing

By the fourteenth century, England engaged extensively in trade with the Low Countries, what is now called the Netherlands, especially Flanders (whose citizens spoke Flemish) and Holland (where people spoke Dutch). England's major export during this period was wool, and the Flemish and Dutch bought the wool and wove it into cloth. Weavers, merchants, and sailors from the Low Countries were constantly in England, sometimes in large numbers, especially in London and other coastal towns. Naturally, many of the words borrowed into English from Flemish and Dutch had to do with the cloth trade in one aspect or another. So we speak of the *nap* 'soft, fuzzy surface' of cloth, unload *freight* from a ship onto a *dock*, and take products to *mart* (in current American English, *-mart* is a very productive combining form). Later on, the Dutch taught the English to drink *gin*, munch on *gherkins*, worship the almighty *dollar*, lower the *boom*, and admire the *landscape* (from which we abstract *-scape*, another familiar combining form in Modern English).

Word Formation Processes

Morphologically, Middle English still tended to form new words by compounding and affixing, but many Old English affixes became much less productive. Among the less productive prefixes, the chief is Old English *for-*, which intensified whatever followed it: *forcleave* means 'cut to pieces', not merely 'break in two'; we all bear sorrow, but when the sorrow is greatest, we must *forbear*. Besides *forbear*, less than a dozen *for*-words survive in Modern English. Either Middle English speakers *forswore* them or decided to *forsake* them, and now they are *forbidden*—but don't be *forlorn*: change is inevitable, not least in language, and it's best to *forgive* and *forget*. Anyway, during Middle English, Latin prefixes grew more and more productive. Try to imagine, for example, how many words we have formed with *dis-* or *re-* since the fourteenth century.

Old English suffixes have fared better. For instance, *-ness* is often cited by language purists as overly productive, since many words formed with it aren't strictly necessary. Old English *-dom* gave us many still useful words, such as *kingdom*, *wisdom*, and *freedom*. In Middle English *-dom* was still productive, as it is in a more limited way today (*fandom*), but few items formed with *-dom* in Middle English have survived. Two that may come to mind—*dukedom* and *thralldom*—certainly aren't everyday words. The suffix *-ship*, used to form abstract nouns, is nearly extinct. A few Old English words formed with it persist and are important elements of our lexicon (*friendship*, *hardship*, *worship*), but none of the words formed with *-ship* in Middle English caught on. Instead, *-ness* usurped its function. You can gauge the extent of their relative productivity (and durability) by taking basic words formed with *-ness* and then consulting the *Middle English Dictionary* to discover whether Middle English formed a *-ship* synonym doomed to failure. Also, in Middle English, Old English suffixes had to contend with interlopers from Latin and French, like *-able/-ible*, *-al*, *-ive*, and *-ous*, all of which are perfect examples of forms so nearly indistinguishable in the two languages that we aren't sure in most cases which exercised its influence.

Middle English Grammar

Given what you have read about the grammar of Old English and what you know about the grammar of Modern English, you know the general direction of many of the phonological, morphological, and syntactic changes during the Middle English period.

The Loss of Inflections and Its Effects

Middle English is characterized by two major trends:

1. English gradually lost inflectional endings representing gender, case, and number. This pattern of morphological change was due partly to phonological change in unstressed syllables of words. First, unstressed syllables lost their terminal consonants; later, they lost the preceding vowels.

2. English gradually developed from synthetic to analytic syntax (i.e., from a case system to grammar that relied on word order), partly as a result of erosion among Old English inflections.

These two grammatical developments fed each other in a circular way. With a heavier reliance on word order, inflectional endings were not needed as much to indicate a word's grammatical function. And as inflectional endings became indistinct or lost, word order became more critical as the way to determine a word's grammatical function.

With the loss of inflectional endings (on both nouns and adjectives) and the rise of invariant *the*, *that*, and *this*, grammatical gender was no longer marked within the noun phrase. Only the personal pronouns (*he*, *she*, *it*) marked gender, and they came to follow natural gender during the Middle English period. Gender in the language came to depend on semantic distinctions about the type of things represented by the noun. There were already seeds of this natural gender agreement system in Old English: for example, the masculine noun *wīfmann* 'woman' was often referred back to with the pronoun *hēo* 'she', not *hē*.

The Inflections That Survive

Most Old English inflectional endings have been lost over the centuries, but a few remain in Modern English. The Middle English period witnesses the generalization of plural *-s*, which originally marked only strong masculine nouns but slowly came to mark the plural for all nouns, including those that had historically been weak and taken plural *-an*. Only three weak plurals survive in Modern English: *children*, *oxen*, and *brethren*. The possessive *-s* also generalized from the strong masculine and neuter nouns to be used for all nouns. Why *-s* for both? We cannot know for certain, but the final *-s* was probably less likely to be phonologically lost in final unstressed syllables than the nasals (/m, n/) and the many inflectional endings that were only vowels with no consonants. Adjectives in Modern English continue to take *-er* and *-est*, historically Old English forms, to mark the comparative and superlative. And the personal pronouns retain case, collapsing the dative and accusative into one "object" case but maintaining distinct forms for subject, object, and possessive (e.g., *I/me/mine*, *she/her/hers*).

The few remaining verb inflections (*-s*, *-ing*, *-ed*, *-en*) can all be traced back to Old English forms. And during the Middle English period, many historically strong verbs began to form the past tense with *-ed* rather than through an internal vowel change. Old English had just over 300 strong verbs, nearly half of which disappeared as strong verbs before the sixteenth century. For example, Old English *helpan* 'help' conjugated *healp/hulpon/holpen*, but today we *help* someone, *helped* someone, and had *helped* someone. By the time Middle English began to absorb French and Latin verbs, the weak pattern was so ascendant that borrowings conformed to it, almost without exception. (Romance languages do not possess, even historically, the strong versus weak distinction.)

Analogy, the process by which the less usual is drawn to resemble the usual, is a powerful linguistic process, of which later sections of this chapter provide further examples. Analogy is potent, both in the historical development of a language and in language acquisition-related processes. You have very likely heard a child insist that he *swimmed across the pool, or that daddy *singed her to sleep with a lullaby. Given the preponderance of weak verbs in English, why would a child ever assume the ablaut (the internal vowel change that expresses tense)? Irregularities must be learned by rote, against the prevailing pattern.

Early Modern English (1476–1776): History of Its Speakers

Although Early Modern English syntax and morphology merely consolidated changes accomplished by the end of the Middle English period, the lexicon expanded and developed dramatically during the Early Modern period. In addition, many social factors of the period contributed to the rise of modern attitudes toward English.

The printing press forever changed written texts by making them quickly, easily, and cheaply replicable and much more standardized.

The Printing Press

In 1476, William Caxton established his printing house in Westminster. The date is often used by historians of English to mark the emergence of Early Modern English from Middle English. Printing contributed to standardization. On a practical level, printers had to invest large sums in the type from which they printed. Each letter printed on a page was the inked impression of a piece of leaden type. Each piece of type was cast in a mold that left the letter raised on one end of a stem. A page-worth of type was placed in a frame on the printing press, the letter ends were inked, and the frame was pressed against the paper that would then become the printed page. Over time, the letter ends broke and otherwise wore away and thus needed to be replaced on a regular basis. How many leaden *e*'s did they need? How many commas and how many apostrophes? Phonology and grammar were suddenly defined in terms of investment, of pounds spent (in type) for pounds earned (in books purchased). That doesn't mean punctuation and spelling were regularized fully in this period. On some pages of Shakespeare's text as printed in the late sixteenth and early seventeenth centuries, we can find *its*, *it's*, and *its'* used interchangeably. It does mean that printed books began to define "correct" English.

The book market played a significant role in the dissemination of the developing standard. When the English Church separated from Rome in 1536, the English people wanted the Bible and other religious works available in print. The Roman Catholic Church still insisted that the only legitimate Bible was the Latin Bible, but English Protestantism required that everyone have access to the Biblical text in English. For religious reasons, people needed to read, so more and more English children, girls and boys, learned to read in school or at home as a matter of religious practice.

In the fourteenth and fifteenth centuries, a merchant class (Chaucer belonged to it) learned to read for commercial purposes. If they could afford manuscripts, they also read literary, historical, and religious texts. By the sixteenth century, England began to develop a bona fide middle class. Its members needed to read for professional purposes, and they also read for pleasure and edification. To meet this demand, Caxton published a version of Aesop's *Fables*, a version of the beast-epic *Reynard the Fox*, and an account of the Trojan Wars, among numerous other books, including the *Promptorium Parvularum*, one of the Latin-English glossaries mentioned in Chapter 2. By the early sixteenth century, the variety of texts available to the reader with some disposable income included poetry, biography, reports of court proceedings, history, prayer books, the lives of saints (Catholic or Protestant), the Bible, political theory, scientific texts, courtesy books (books about how gentlemen or gentlewomen should behave)—nearly every type of text one could imagine reading. By the end of the same century, the numbers and types of texts already exceeded what even the most industrious reader could manage to read in a lifetime.

The mass production of texts went hand in hand with the dramatic expansion of literacy during the period. More texts were available. It became more imperative, regardless of social class, to teach and learn to read. But people cannot easily learn to read if every book is written in a slightly different language. It's easier to teach and (at least in theory) easier to learn how to read if texts conform to certain linguistic standards.

Standardization of English led to regulation. The more that people read, the more they wanted dictionaries to help them read. The more that they wrote, the more they wanted guides to write well, and "well" soon progressed to "correctly." As England became a land of opportunity and aspiration in the sixteenth century, access to the standard dialect meant access to particular professional and social benefits. Readers and writers began to demand "rules" by which they could hoist themselves from one rung of the social ladder to the one above. The details of regulation are summarized in Chapter 2, in the sections about dictionaries and usage books.

Attitudes about English

From the fourteenth century on, English gained social prestige. French had once been the prestige language, but its influence within national affairs passed into history. By the sixteenth century, when English people spoke French, they did so for commercial or diplomatic purposes, as an emblem of class, or as an affectation. Chaucer pokes fun at his Prioress, who spoke only finishing-school Anglo-Norman French, by then regarded as a corrupt dialect compared to the prestigious Parisian French.

Most folk seemed relatively satisfied with the standard dialect that they strove to master—it met their linguistic needs. But learned Englishmen were divided about the status of English among other languages. Some thought that English was crude compared to Latin and the romance languages, especially French and Italian. Even Caxton had questioned the sufficiency of English, and he often apologized for diminishing foreign works by translating them into English for English readers.

For various reasons, England entered the Renaissance later than other European countries. As a result, it found itself short on terminology, compared to other languages. During the Renaissance, every scholarly discipline reorganized and flourished, and knowledge increased exponentially across Europe. The list of figures who transformed the arts and sciences only begins with Leonardo da Vinci, Michelangelo, Copernicus, and the seminal Italian architects, like Brunelleschi, who were also pioneering engineers. Each subject, from architecture to medicine, grammar to mathematics, grew increasingly sophisticated and developed terminology useful in its discourse. Many educated English people, both scholars and amateurs, were interested to learn all there was to know, but strangely found themselves unable to talk about it effectively in English—they lacked the specific vocabulary.

The obvious solution was to borrow foreign words to fill the lexical gaps. English has long borrowed words easily—it is an "opportunistic language" and takes what it needs. But, suddenly, borrowing was seen by some English speakers as problematic. Many public language commentators thought that English was, or ought to be, sufficient unto itself, that it had its own sound and style into which Latin terminology didn't fit comfortably. Others argued that Latin and other foreign words were essential to eloquence, working from the assumption that other languages were naturally more eloquent than English. From these positions, several competing attitudes about the English language developed: (1) there were linguistic nationalists who wanted to keep the English language pure, free from the taint of foreign influence to whatever extent possible; (2) there were rhetoricians who believed a plain, native style was more eloquent than an artificial or excessively Latinate one; (3) there were those who thought borrowing should be restrained, a matter of lexical necessity, not of style; and (4) there were rhetorical sophisticates who welcomed every Latinism, even the most obscure, into English and tried to promote their use. Suddenly, English was a hot topic.

Some English writers in the Early Modern period attempted to use words so obscure as never to be adopted by other writers, let alone everyday speakers of everyday English. If you don't recognize words like *allotheta*, *collachrymation*, *equithorizontal*, or *synnemenon*, don't feel bad—the authors of this book don't recognize them either. They are all terms used once or twice in the sixteenth or early seventeenth century by authors who thought that, when they used them, they captured some meaning precisely, in a way that English words could not. Contemporary detractors called such words "inkhorn terms." Words like these could be written, but they couldn't be used—use implies that someone besides the writers who used them could understand them.

Use of inkhorn terms by some English writers fueled the "Inkhorn Controversy," an argument among English writers about whether English was good enough as a common, native language or whether it could be improved by the introduction of fancy, Latinate words. Thomas Wilson, in the *Arte of Rhetoricke* (1553), advised that "among all other lessons this should first be learned, that wee neuer affect any straunge ynkehorne termes, but speake as is commonly receiued." Wilson sounds like a schoolmaster, but George Gascoigne sounds like a patriot, or English nationalist: "I have rather regarde to make our native language commendable in it selfe, than gay with the feathers of straunge birds."

Gascoigne's nationalism makes sense in historical context. Latin was the language of Renaissance learning, but it was also the language of the Roman church, and Early Modern England was (after 1536) a Protestant state. By the late sixteenth century, many English people were suspicious of Latin and all that it represented, and they weren't merely paranoid—the Spanish Armada of 1588 was an attempt by those who spoke a Romance language (i.e., one derived from Latin) to conquer England and return it to Roman Catholicism. Literary style and politics often mingle: they both construct power, freedom, community, and identity, sometimes separately, sometimes cooperatively.

By the end of the Early Modern period, the dispute had calmed. John Dryden, in the preface to his translation of Virgil's *Aeneid* (1697), sounded the voice of reason: "I trade both with the living and the dead, for the enrichment of our native tongue. We have enough in England to supply our necessity, but if we will have things of magnificence and splendour, we must get them by commerce."

The arguments about borrowing and inkhorn terms weren't the only language controversies in this period. Some observers had noticed that English spelling had little to do with English phonology. How can *breathe*, *green*, and *receive* all sound as though they contain the same vowel yet be spelled in such an apparently arbitrary way? Shouldn't spelling conform to the way that people speak? Early Modern English witnessed the first known attempts to reform English **orthography**, a Latinate term used to refer to spelling.

The earliest spelling reformers were schoolmasters—they tried to help students learn to read, but spelling was always in the way, so they hoped to change spelling to serve education. Among the most prominent were John Hart, whose *The Opening of the Unreasonable writing of our Inglish Toung* (1551) initiated the argument, despite the fact that Hart's own spelling often didn't represent any advance over spelling as historically received. His *Orthographie* (1569) is a classic of the movement and influenced any number of others, including Richard Mulcaster, head of the Merchant Taylor School, who taught the poet Edmund Spenser, among other celebrities of the period. Mulcaster's *First Part of the Elementarie* (1582) extended the tradition, and soon the impetus to "fix" the language manifested itself, not only in tracts on spelling reform, but in dictionaries and usage manuals (see Chapter 2).

The road from Middle to Modern English was paved with change and, importantly, argument about the very nature of a vernacular language. By the end of the period, with the proliferation of rhetorical guides, dictionaries, and grammar books, Early Modern English speakers could praise their tongue as both eloquent and, at least to some extent, regulated.

The Study of English

The Early Modern English period saw the rise of historical interest in the ways in which English had come to be what it was. The sixteenth century gave birth to antiquarianism in England: the collection, preservation, and investigation of Early English documents and literary manuscripts—those few that had survived the dissolution of monasteries when England left the Church of Rome. When the monasteries were abandoned, their libraries were dispersed if they weren't destroyed. Antiquarianism can be described as a movement, since all of the antiquarians knew one another, borrowed one another's manuscripts, and consulted one another about the manuscripts in their own collections. They even formed an Antiquarian Society so they could share materials and argue about their historical, legal, and linguistic values. They sought out facts from the past rather

A Question to Discuss

How Do We Preserve the Evidence of a Language?

After the antiquarian Robert Cotton died, his library was kept intact and, by the eighteenth century, was housed along with the King's Library in Ashburnham House in Westminster, close to the abbey. On October 23, 1731, a fire broke out at Ashburnham House and threatened the library. Most of it was saved, some of it by the librarian, Richard Bentley, who is reported to have run from the house in a nightgown and wig, with books under his arms. For a long time, it was assumed that over 200 of the manuscripts had been lost, though half of those were later restored.

Cotton's prized copy of the Magna Carta was damaged but saved. Two Old English texts were reduced to ash—Asser's *Life of Alfred* and *The Battle of Maldon*, the only surviving example of Anglo-Saxon epic besides *Beowulf*. Luckily, someone had copied *Maldon* only a year or so before the manuscript burned, so we still know the poem, even if certain linguistic details were lost or misrepresented in transcription. An eighth-century book of the gospels from Northumbria, written at the height of Northumbria's linguistic, literary, and political influence, was partially destroyed.

The only manuscript of *Beowulf*, though singed, survived. So did the manuscript that contains *Sir Gawain and the Green Knight* and other examples of Middle English from the Northwest Midlands. It's fair to say that our picture of English literary history, not to mention the history of English language, would look entirely different had these texts

The *Beowulf* manuscript was burned around the edges during the fire at Ashburnham House

not been rescued from the Ashburnham House fire on that October night in 1731.

In the twenty-first century, we worry less than our forbears about unique manuscripts burning in a fire, but that doesn't mean evidence for the history of English in our time is invulnerable. What types of texts are central to the study of current English? Which are vulnerable to loss, and how might we ensure that when you want to write a book about English, all of the relevant materials will be preserved?

than merely retelling the old stories. But in order to use Old and Middle English texts in their research, they needed first to unravel the language.

One of the first antiquarians was William Camden (1551–1623), who wrote a multivolume history of England, drawing upon texts no one before him had ever consulted for historical purposes. Camden was very aware that Elizabethan England was extraordinary, poised to become a great international power. He praised Elizabeth I for leading her nation toward glory in politics, religion, government, law, exploration, and commerce. Sometimes, his work verges on propaganda for the Tudor and Stuart dynasties. But he also recognized that it wasn't all Elizabeth's doing. Who the English were in 1600 somehow depended on who they were in ancient times. It was important to delineate English history from the very beginning, according to Camden, not as myth and story, but as a matter of fact.

Camden had an ally in Sir Robert Cotton (1571–1631), a collector of old books and documents, and the possessor of the greatest library of early English texts in his day. Cotton shared books with Camden while the latter wrote his history and appears to have been a sort of coauthor, though the lines between research associate and collaborator are blurry. Cotton joined the Antiquarian Society in 1590. Other members besides Camden consulted Cotton's collection, including Francis Bacon and Ben Jonson. Cotton's library included 958 manuscript volumes, many of which contained multiple literary works. Cotton owned two of four extant original copies of the Magna Carta, one of them with King John's seal intact. His prize possession was a fifth-century Greek manuscript of Genesis, notable not only for its text, but for its illuminations—it was one of the earliest illustrated manuscripts in existence. The story of Cotton's library is part of the story of many of the medieval manuscripts that we know today, including the *Beowulf* manuscript.

The interest in older English texts led to new publications. William Somner (1598–1669) published an edition of Ælfric's *Dictionarium Saxonicum-Latino-Anglicum* (originally of the eleventh century) in 1659. George Hickes published a grammar of Anglo-Saxon, Gothic, and Icelandic in 1689. Hickes's *Grammar* proved that the older Germanic tongues were just as systematically organized as Latin and Greek, though, at the time, they were held up as superior to English and its cognates. A millennium into the history of English, Early Modern scholars recovered the Old and Middle English origins of English language and literature, the root and branch from which Modern English and its literature blossom to this day.

Early Modern English Lexicon

During the Early Modern period, the English word-hoard increased by some 10,000 words. Many of them were adopted from other languages, including reliable contributors like Latin and French as well as new donors like Spanish and Italian. Although followers of the "native tradition" resisted exotic borrowings, plenty of foreign words found their way into the English lexicon. Indeed, Early Modern English was the first period in which the English could use the word *dictionary* as an English word, though English writers, like Ælfric, had used its Latin etymon centuries before. The alternative *lexicon*, borrowed from Greek, entered a century later, yielding *lexicography* and *lexicographer* alongside *dictionary-maker*, a combination of a Latin borrowing and a native English word.

Greek and Latin Borrowing

The road into English from Greek and Latin took many unexpected turns. Sometimes a word followed the shortest line of entry, as when *emphasis* was adopted directly from

Latin. But *adapt* entered English from Latin through French. The word *parenthesis* (what's included between the marks, not the marks themselves) was borrowed from Greek via Latin, as were *alphabet, euphemism, hyperbole, hypothesis,* and *phrase,* just to name a few. Though *ephemeral* derives from Greek, it made its way into English from French; nonetheless, those who used it recognized it as Greek, so they formed the plural, *ephemera,* according to the Greek pattern.

Many words borrowed during the Early Modern period were terms of art: the specialized terminology of the various academic disciplines and the arts. The words in the previous paragraph were borrowed to serve grammar and rhetoric, disciplines that branched into philology (the study of the development and structure of language), the precursor to linguistics. Other Early Modern borrowings are keywords of modern culture. Perhaps most important is *democracy,* a Greek word borrowed through Latin (though present in Old French). Early Modern Europe didn't include any democracies, but once the word was in the lexicon, people could talk about it, which may be one precondition of achieving it.

Romance Borrowing

Spanish had not significantly influenced English before the sixteenth century, but several indispensable words entered English from Spanish during the Early Modern period. Imagine doing without *banana* or *potato,* and life is certainly more pleasant because of *avocado, barbecue,* and *guitar.* Some speakers would add *tobacco* to the list of pleasures; others may regret the introduction of the plant and the word for it. The word *Negro* (Spanish in origin but probably borrowed into English via Portuguese) has caused more controversy than anyone could have imagined when it entered English in the late sixteenth century. *Creole,* on the other hand, shed most of the vestiges of dysphemism by the twentieth century and serves as an important cultural and linguistic term.

Italian also profoundly affected Early Modern English (and English thenceforth). Consider the following items, all adopted in the sixteenth and seventeenth centuries and all still current in Modern American English:

antic	*broccoli*	*incognito*	*pasta*
artichoke	*carnival*	*lingua franca*	*pistachio*
balcony	*discount* (n)	*lottery*	*tarantula*
ballot	*ghetto*	*macaroni*	*volcano*
bankrupt (n)	*granite*	*motto*	

Italian provided an astonishing number of terms of art: *fresco, gesso, intaglio, miniature, profile* (noun), and *relief* in the visual arts; *cornice, cupola, rotunda,* and *stucco* in architecture; *madrigal, oratorio,* and *trill* in music; and *sonnet* and *stanza* in poetry.

Semantic Change in the Native Lexicon

Borrowing sometimes affected older English words, which specialized, generalized, extended metaphorically, or otherwise underwent semantic change to accommodate new words in the lexicon. A word like *intelligence,* which entered into late Middle English, did not become prominent until the sixteenth century, when it began to compete for semantic space with *wit* (as discussed in Chapter 7). As a result of synonymic pressure, mostly from borrowed terms, *wit* lost all but a few of its original meanings by the end of the seventeenth century. Other words of broad significance in Middle English similarly specialized. *Humour* had originally referred to the fluids supposedly circulating in the human body (*bile*, *blood*, *choler*, and *phlegm*), but that medical sense generalized in Middle English to mean the disposition or character of a person, depending on which fluid was predominant in his or her system (*bilious*, *sanguine*, *choleric*, and *phlegmatic*). By the end of the Early Modern period, after William Harvey had correctly described the human circulatory system, the medical sense of *humour* disappeared; the "psychological" sense was on the wane, and *humour* 'disposition to amuse or be amused' became the dominant, specialized sense.

Some older English words were also revived in the period, and their chic new status could create new words. For example, *hap* 'fortune, chance, luck' had been borrowed into Middle English from Old Norse by the thirteenth century. *Mishap* and *happen* were later Middle English derivations from that word. In the sixteenth century, *hap* received a boost from poetic language. In the 1530s, Thomas Wyatt could write lines like "To mine unhap / For hap away hath rent of all my joy / The very bark and rind." Resurgence of the older term engendered a shift, and Modern English *happy* was born. Poetic usage recuperated many other Middle English words for Early Modern English readers, for instance, *askew*, *astound*, *birthright*, *dit* 'song' (as in *dittie*), *don* 'put on, wear' (as in "Don we now our gay apparel"), *forthright*, *mickle* 'great, much' (now obsolete), and *witless* (derived from the old senses of *wit* and still alive in Modern English).

Affixation

Despite the immense amount of borrowing during Early Modern English, affixation remained the most potent influence in expanding the lexicon of English. Affixation drew on a gamut of prefixes and suffixes. Some were retained from Old English, including:

be-	*-hood*	*mid-*	*-ways*
-dom	*-ing*	*-ness*	*-wise*
-er	*-less*	*-ship*	*-worthy*
for-	*-like*	*-ster*	*-y*
fore-	*-ling*	*un-*	
-ful	*-ly*	*-wards*	

Others were borrowed from Latin and French, among them:

-able	*-cy*	*hyper-*	*non-*
-acy	*de-*	*in-*	*pre-*
-age	*dis-*	*-ity*	*pro-*
-ance/ence	*en-*	*-ive*	*proto-*
-ancy/ence	*-ery*	*mal-*	*re-*
anti-	*-ess*	*-ment*	*semi-*
-ate	*-et*	*mis-*	*sub-*
-ation	*-ette*	*mono-*	*super-*
bi-	*extra-*	*multi-*	*uni-*

The prefixes and suffixes that are most productive today became productive in the Early Modern English period. They may not have originated then, but very active use solidified their role in English morphology.

Early Modern English Grammar

In Early Modern English, the ongoing progression of many grammatical changes under way in Middle English (some even in Old English) proceeded to the point that the language seems more familiar to speakers of Modern English. Such changes include the virtual disappearance of inflectional endings, increasingly analytic sentence structure, the introduction of *do* for questions and negation, the weakening of strong verbs, and the Great Vowel Shift.

Older Grammatical Retentions

Some of what occasionally makes Early Modern English strange to the modern ear is what was retained from Middle English. For instance, Early Modern English could mark the interrogative by placing the verb in the initial position, rather than with an auxiliary verb: the equivalent of "Go you to the movies this afternoon?" as opposed to "Will you go to the movies this afternoon?" The imperative could be expressed with the pronoun, rather than elliptically: the equivalent of "Go you to the movies!" rather than "Go to the movies!" And verbs were used in impersonal sentences more frequently than today. We say, "It bothers me when you make so much noise" and "It pleases me when you are quiet," but not "It likes me not ('I don't like it')" when you listen to the television at that volume" or "It considers me ('I consider it') time to shut the door."

Early Modern English still had both the *thou* and *you* second-person pronouns, which had moved from primarily a singular-plural distinction to an informal-formal distinction (as between French *tu* and *vous*, and Spanish *tu* and *usted*). Shakespeare exploits this distinction for subtle insults and endearments in his plays. The forms are not an innovation of the Early Modern period, however, but relics of Middle English.

Developments in Morphosyntax

There are at least five important morphosyntactic developments in Early Modern English. First, the period is associated with "the rise of periphrastic *do*." Periphrastic *do* is the auxiliary *do* used to form questions and negation (see Chapter 5). Periphrastic *do* first took hold in questions and then in negative declaratives, but in the transitional period there was considerable variation. So Shakespeare could write in his plays "I doubt it not" and "I do not doubt you," as well as "Came he not home tonight" and "Do you not love me?"

Second, the *-s* plural overwhelmed other plural inflections. Although English still retains a few exceptions, like plurals in which the singular form's vowel mutates, such as *mouse/mice* and *foot/feet*, most such nouns were reanalyzed to take the *-s*. Early Modern English reanalyzed plurals such as *shoe/shoon* to *shoe/shoes* and *knee/kneen* to *knee/knees*, until plurals were almost perfectly uniform.

A third important Early Modern morphosyntactic development occurred in verbs, with the replacement of third-person indicative neuter *-eth* with *-s*: *he comes and goes* rather than *cometh and goeth*. By the end of the sixteenth century, the upstart *-s* outnumbered *-eth* approximately two to one, until the latter withered away entirely in fully Modern English.

Language Change at Work

The Invention of *pea*

The singular form *pea* is a sixteenth-century invention. In Middle English, *peasen* was the plural of *peas*, following the *-n* plural paradigm. As unstressed final syllables (especially those with final nasals) gradually eroded, *pease* became the plural form of *peas*, retained today only in the nursery rhyme:

> Pease porridge hot,
> Pease porridge cold,

> Pease porridge in the pot,
> Nine days old.

As final *-e* was lost, *peas* became both the singular and plural form. Because final *-s* typically marks the plural, *peas* was re-analyzed as a root plus a plural inflectional ending. Thus, by analogy, *pea* was invented as the singular of (once singular, now plural) *peas*.

A fourth innovation of fundamental significance was the invention of *its* as the third-person genitive neuter personal pronoun. If you return to the pronoun declension in the section on Old English, you'll see that the historical possessive pronoun was *his*, identical to the third-person masculine genitive. By the sixteenth century, nominative/accusative *hit* had lost its initial aspiration and become Modern English *it*. In order to distinguish among the parallel pronouns, sixteenth-century speakers gradually adopted *its* as possessive *it*.

Finally, written English witnessed the rise of hypotactic structures (sentences with subordinated clauses) instead of paratactic ones (sentences with coordinated clauses). This syntactic development was undoubtedly influenced by Latin grammatical models and notions of eloquence.

The Fate of Final *-e*

Early Modern English phonology is best known for the Great Vowel Shift, but a phonological question of interest to literary scholars is the status of final *-e*. By Early Modern English, the Middle English terminal *-e* was no longer pronounced. "Whan that Aprill with his shoores soote / The droghte of Merche had perced to the roote" ('When April, with its sweet showers, pierces the drought of March to its root'), the opening lines to Chaucer's *Canterbury Tales*, suggest that the final *-e* was mainly poetic even in the late fourteenth century. The *-e* in *droghte* and *Merche* is unambiguously not pronounced. That in *shoores* and *perced* is unambiguously pronounced, but in these cases with the terminal consonant *-s*. The *-e* on *soote* and *roote* is ambiguous. It's likely that Chaucer pronounced them, since he learned English at the end of the period in which they still would have been pronounced, but it's hard to know. Are the decisions to voice or not to voice a matter of poetics, of line length and meter? By the sixteenth century all doubts evaporate: a fully pronounced terminal *-e* was merely a poetic device, not a feature of natural language.

Language Change at Work

The Great Vowel Shift

Sometime beginning in the fourteenth or fifteenth century, a set of English vowels—the historically long vowels which are now mostly described as tense vowels—began to shift toward new pronunciations. Low vowels moved to mid position, mid vowels to high position, and high vowels underwent diphthongization (see the discussion in Chater 3). The vowels with which Chaucer grew up were not the vowels with which folks read his poetry only a couple of centuries later, as illustrated in the diagram below.

Some scholars question whether the Great Vowel Shift was ever a comprehensive phenomenon, and they have a point: *root* to rhyme with *foot*, still a feature of both British and American English (described in Chapter 12), illustrates vowel pronunciations retained from before the supposed shift. Such pronunciations represent Middle English survivals into the Modern English period.

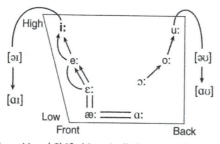

FIGURE 13.3 During the Great Vowel Shift, historically long vowels were raised and the high vowels became diphthongs. Long /æ/ eventually was raised all the way to /e/ and long /ɛ/ to /i/ (except for a few words like *great*, *break*, and *steak*).

Looking Ahead

An unexpected change in the Early Modern English period was the emergence of English as a world language. With the accession in 1603 of James I (James VI of Scotland), English exerted influence on the Scots in the Lowlands, the area closest to England and most interactive with government, law, commerce, and education. In 1707, Scotland and England were united. The English attempted to subjugate Ireland beginning in the sixteenth century. They began to settle North America in the early seventeenth century and islands in the Caribbean soon thereafter. India and other points in the east were introduced to the English people and their language in the eighteenth century. As England became an imperial power, the status of the English language also rose. The standard variety of English became an export of great value. And as the reach of English extended, it confirmed the value of certain varieties of English at home. We see the effects of this global reach in the next chapter.

Suggested Reading

There are several good general histories of English, including A. C. Baugh and Thomas Cable's *A History of the English Language* (5th ed., 2002), N. F. Blake, *A History of the English Language* (1996), and C. M. Millward, *A Biography of the English Language* (2d ed., 1996). The preeminent history is the six-volume *Cambridge History of the English Language*, edited by Richard Hogg, with various volumes appearing at various dates under various editors. The *Oxford English Dictionary*, currently in its second edition (1989), is an indispensable guide to the histories of English words. The best etymological dictionary of English is still W. W. Skeat's *An Etymological Dictionary of the English Language* (4th ed., 1910).

Old English is thoroughly described in A. Campbell's *Old English Grammar* (1959) and conveniently described in *Sweet's Anglo-Saxon Primer*, revised by Norman Davis (9th ed., 1953). Bruce Mitchell and Fred C. Robinson provided the authoritative *Guide to Old English* (1982), though it's not a work for the faint of heart. Most Old English poetic texts are available in G. P. Krapp and E. V. K. Dobbie's six-volume *Anglo-Saxon Poetic Records* (1931–1953). The *Dictionary of Old English* is an ongoing project of the University of Toronto, currently edited by Antonette diPaolo Healey and others. J. R. Clark Hall's *A Concise Anglo-Saxon Dictionary*, revised by H. D. Meritt (4th ed., 1984), is a very useful dictionary in the interim. The best account of Old Norse is still E. V. Gordon's *An Introduction to Old Norse*, as revised by A. R. Taylor (1957).

The *Middle English Dictionary* edited by Hans Kurath, Sherman M. Kuhn, Robert E. Lewis, and others (1952–2001) accounts, exhaustively, for the Middle English lexicon. *An Elementary Middle English Grammar*, by Joseph Wright and Elizabeth Mary Wright, is still an excellent introduction (2d ed., 1928); the material is well expanded and supplemented by J. A. Burrow and Thorlac Turville-Petre in *A Book of Middle English* (1996). Tauno Mustanoja's *A Middle English Syntax*, vol. 1 (1960), is challenging, even for the advanced student. *The Emergence of Standard English* (1996) collects John H. Fisher's important articles on the subject. The Early English Text Society has published a remarkable number of Middle English texts from 1864 to the present. An increasing number are available online through the *Middle English Compendium* (http://ets.umdl.umich.edu/m/mec).

Early Modern English is capably described in Charles Barber's *Early Modern English* (1976). R. F. Jones's *The Triumph of the English Language* (1953) surveys attitudes toward English during the period. E. J. Dobson's two-volume *English Pronunciation 1500–1700* (1957) will daunt even the most professional reader but is nonetheless the authoritative account. Helge Kökeritz's *Shakespeare's Pronunciation* (1953) isn't much more accessible to the lay reader but is a very useful guide to those teaching Shakespeare, if they have the patience to deal with Early Modern English phonology. The most useful and successful recent treatment of this historical period is Terttu Nevalainen's *Introduction to Early Modern English* (2006).

Exercises

Exercise 13.1   Analyzing Early Texts

1. Below you will find versions of the Lord's Prayer from Old English, Middle English, Early Modern English, and Modern English (texts taken from Horobin and Smith 2002, 7). After each passage, we have included questions about what seems familiar and unfamiliar, and what language changes the later passages demonstrate. First, here is the Lord's Prayer in Modern English, as a reference for the other versions.

Modern English (Alternative Service Book)

Our Father in heaven, your name be hallowed; your kingdom come, your will be done, on earth as in heaven. Give us today our daily bread. Forgive us our sins, as we have forgiven those who have sinned against us. And do not bring us to the time of trial, but save us from evil.

Try to read the following passages aloud. The "yogh" (ȝ) sounds sometimes like /j/ and sometimes like /g/. As you read, write down the English words that you recognize.

Old English (West Saxon dialect, late ninth century)

Þū ūre fæder, þe eart on heofonum, sīe þīn nama ȝehālgod. Cume þīn rīce. Sīe þīn willa on eorþan swā swā on heofonum. Syle ūs tōdæȝ ūrne dæȝhwāmlican hlāf. And forȝief ūs ūre ȝyltas swā swā þē forȝiefaþ þǣm þe wið us aȝyltaþ. And ne lǣd þu nū ūs on costnunge, ac ālīes ūs fram yfele.

Questions

a. Given what you have read about case, why do you think the -um inflectional ending is required on heofon?

b. What grammatical role is þu 'thou' playing in the clause And ne lǣd þu nū ūs on costnunge (costnunge 'temptation')?

c. What phrases surprised you by their word order? Try to find at least two.

Middle English (Central Midlands, c. 1380)

Oure fadir, þat art in heuenys, halewid be þi name. Þi kingdom come to. Be þi wile don ase in heuene and in erþe. ȝiue to us þis day oure breed ouer oþer substaunse. And forȝiue to us oure dettes, as and we forȝiuen to oure dettouris. And leede us not into temptaciouns, but delyuere us from yuel.

Questions

a. In which words do you find remnants of the Old English case system? Try to list at least eight.

b. Comparing this text to the Old English version, which of the words new to the Middle English version would you guess are French? Verify your guesses.

Early Modern English (Book of Common Prayer, 1549)

Our Father, which are in heaven, Hallowed be thy Name. Thy kingdom come. Thy will be done, in earth as it is in heaven. Give us this day our daily bread. And forgive us our trespasses. As we forgive them that trespass against us. And lead us not into temptation; But deliver us from evil.

Questions

a. In the first line, what is surprising about the use of *which*? How does it compare to the Middle English version?

b. What about Old English elements? Can you figure out how *þe* is used?

2. Here are the first few sentences of Alfred's translation of Pope Gregory's *Pastoral Care*.

Ælfrǣd cyning hāteþ grētan Wǣrferhþ biscop his wordum lufličě and frēondličě. And ič þē cyðan hāte þæt mē cōm swiðe of on ȝe-mynd hwelče witan ȝēo wǣron ȝeond Angel-cynn, ǣȝðer ȝe god-cundra hāda ȝe weorold-cundra, and hū ȝe-sǣliȝ-liča tīda þā wǣron ȝeond Angel-cynn, and hū þā cyningas þe þone anweald hæfdon þæs folces on þǣm dagum Gode and his ǣreandracum hīer-sumodon, and hū hīe ǣȝðer ȝe hira sibbe ȝe hira sidu ȝe hira an-weald innan-bordes ȝe-hēoldon, and ēac ūt hira eðel ȝe-rǣmdon.

Questions

a. What words do you recognize as Old English forms of Modern English words?

b. Which are the prepositions, and how do they measure up to modern ones?

c. Have Old English prepositional forms changed meaning in the last millennium or so? Explain.

d. Can you identify compounds? List them here.

e. Which nouns seem meaningful to you, and which verbs?

f. To what extent have these terms changed over time, either in meaning or in form?

g. Can you tell what some of the inflections indicate regarding number, gender, and case? Explain.

h. Though it isn't easy, try translating some parts of this passage into Modern English.

3. Here are two passages of early Middle English, one in prose (from the *Ancrene Riwle*) and the other in verse (from *The Owl and the Nightingale*). In what features do they resemble Old English texts? Can you read these more easily than Alfred's translation of Pope Gregory's *Pastoral Care*? If you can, then what has changed?

On oðer half understondeð. ȝe beoð i ierusalem. ȝe beoð iflohe to chirche grið. For nes ower nan þat nere sum chearre godes þeof. Me weiteð ow þat wite ȝe ful ȝeorne wið uten as me deð þeoues þe beoð ibroke to chirche. Haldeð ow feaste inne. nawt te bodi ane. for þat is þe unwurðest. ah ower fif wittes. & te heorte ouer al & al þer sawle lif is.

Ich was in one sumere dale,
in one suþe diȝele hale,
iherde ich holde grete tale
an hule ans one niȝtingale.
Þat plait was stif & starc & strong,
sum wile softe & lud among;
an aiþer aȝ oþer sval,
& let þat vuele mod ut al.
& eiþer seide of oþeres custe
þat alre-worste þat hi wuste:
& hure & hure of oþeres songe
hi holde plaiding suþe stronge.

4. Consider the following passage of Early Modern English. How does it differ from Old English? Middle English? Modern American English? You might list the differences in columns or synthesize your observations into a brief essay.

> there do some faultes remayne therin both because the barbarous and ara-bicke termes which the author dothe chiefly vse, and of the dyuerse and syndry opynyons of moyst notable and well lerned Phisicions alswell in the names as in the natures of herbes and symples, and especially that we be eyther ignorant or destitute of Englyshe names for a great sorte of them, yet I dyd as nigh as I could follow Dioscorides and in such thynges as I could not fynd in hym, I dyd confer Fuchsius, Ruellius, and Dorste-nius together, and folowed the judgement wherein they dyd al or the most part of them agre, and in the Englyshing therof I & al other which intend any such worke are muche beholden to Mayster Wyllyam Turner, who wyth no small dylygence hath in both hys herballes most truly and syncerly set furth the names and natures of dyuerse herbes, vnto whose iudgement and a correccion and all other lerned in the most necessary sci-ence of Physycke, do I submit thys lytle worke.
>
> —Humfrey Llwyd, *The treasuri of helth*, ca. 1550

Exercise 13.2   Borrowing and Native Word Formation

1. Choose one of the listed words adopted into Middle English from French and take it to the dictionaries, especially the *OED*, the *Middle English Dictionary*, and any of a number of good etymological dictionaries. Then write a brief history of the word. When did it enter English? Has its meaning generalized or specialized over time (see Chapter 7)? Has it shifted semantically? If it has, provide informed speculation about why the semantic shifts might have moved in that direction. Has the word shifted into other lexical categories, and when?

2. Choose three affixes listed in the chapter and investigate their historical development. In each case, how does the affix shift the derived word from its stem's lexical category (that is, into what new category is the word derived)? Does the affix have multiple semantic functions? Does its function or meaning change over time? Feel free to consult any and all of the relevant dictionaries.

3. For the following Old English kennings, we have provided the literal meaning of the compound. Take an educated guess at what the word referred to metaphorically.

hwælweg	'whale way'
beadoleoma	'battle light'
bāncofa	'bone house'
sǣhengest	'sea steed'
hēofodgim	'head gem'
vindauga	'wind eye' (from Old Norse)

Exercise 13.3   Nouns and Verbs

1. A few verbs in the history of English have shifted from weak verbs, adding a suffix to form past tense, to strong verbs, forming past tense with an internal vowel change (e.g., *dived/dove*). The past tense of *sneak* has historically been *sneaked.* Why might this verb be shifting to become irregular? (One question to consider: What is the source of the analogy?)

2. Let's imagine that English speakers created a new verb to refer to swimming to stay trim: *twim.* How do you think English speakers would create the past tense and past participle of this verb? Justify your answer.

3. Only three words in English retain the Old English weak noun plural suffix *-en*: *children, oxen, brethren.* Make an argument in each case about whether you think this irregular form will survive for the next 200 years.

Exercise 13.4   Old English in Modern English

Select a passage of about 100 words from a text of your choice (fiction, poetry, periodicals, general nonfiction prose, academic prose, Web text). In order to do this exercise, you will need a good dictionary, like a Merriam-Webster dictionary, an American Heritage dictionary, the *New Oxford American Dictionary*, or the *Oxford English Dictionary*. Any of these will provide sound etymologies for the words in your passage, and etymologies are the focus of this exercise. Now, follow these steps.

Step 1: Determine which words are reflexes of Old English words. List these and determine the proportion of total words that derive from Old English.

Step 2: From what other languages do words in the passage come? Which of these languages are most significant to the history of English?

Step 3: Besides words, which parts of words (inflectional suffixes, derivational prefixes and suffixes) are also Old English in origin. How are they applied? Do Old English affixes cleave only to Old English stems? If so, why do you think that's the case? If not, why, do you suspect, is it not the case?

Step 4: In a summary paragraph or two, describe what types of words in your passage come from Old English. How do you explain the patterns you uncover?

Step 5: In a summary paragraph or two, describe what types of words in your passage come from other languages. How do you explain the patterns you uncover?

Step 6: In a paragraph, speculate about how the *type* of text you've worked on may affect the proportion of native English versus borrowed terms.

Chapter 14

History of English: Modern and Future English

English lives side-by-side with many other languages, not only around the world, but also throughout the United States, as seen here on a trilingual sign for American citizens preparing to vote.

In the year 1564, when William Shakespeare was born, it would have been difficult if not impossible for English speakers in Britain to conceive of English as a world language. First of all, Early Modern English speakers could not have imagined the technological innovations, from the telephone to the personal computer, that have enabled global communication and revolutionized how languages spread and come into contact. In addition, 450 years ago, English was still considered by some influential language authorities to be "rude," "barbaric," and generally unworthy compared to more eloquent languages such as Latin and French, both of which had greater international standing at the time (although "international" was a more geographically limited concept during this period than it is now). The English language was confined to the British Isles, a set of islands in many ways isolated in the Atlantic Ocean off the coast of France—an accurate, although atypical, description of Britain. The political, military, economic, and social forces that propelled English off that island and around the world could not have been predicted.

Where will the English language be 450 years from now? We started this chapter with 1564 as a reminder of how much the world can surprise us beyond our wildest imagination, and how limited our powers of prediction are when it comes to the fate of languages. If there is a global language today, it is English. But the story of English should remind us to think about what the next global language may be. Which language might be propelled around the world from its current location—whether an island or a large part of a continent—due to political, military, economic, or social forces? And no matter what the global status of English is 450 years from now, what will it sound like? We know that all speakers of Modern English sound different from Shakespeare. How different will English speakers sound in the year 2450 from English speakers today? What variety of English will be the standard?

Of course no one, including the authors of this book, *knows* the answers to these questions. But we can certainly speculate sensibly about the future, given what we know about the past and present.

This chapter draws on the linguistic knowledge of Modern English you gained in previous chapters to discuss questions about the future of English. The discussion of Modern English here is brief, and it supplements the earlier chapters. Though they often look back to earlier periods of English, most of the preceding chapters effectively constitute a description of Modern English, from its phonology, morphology, syntax, and semantics, to discourse, style, and variation. Here we explore the social circumstances instrumental to the development of English as we speak it here and now.

Modern English (1776-Present): Social Forces at Work

We can identify several modern social forces that have influenced the shape of Modern English. Certainly no one historical event is responsible for the rise and power of Standard English or for the many varieties of the language encompassed by the label *English*. The rise of Standard English is perhaps the most significant development in the modern period. We began discussion of the standard variety's progress in Chapter 2, and we continue it here, with an eye to the future of the English language around the world.

Prescription and the Standard Variety

Printing changed the character of English permanently—at least until newer media, like the Internet, came along to change it again. Gradually, more people had access to printed texts, of increasingly various kinds. Printed Standard English was increasingly held up as a model for speech, and hopeful purists attempted to close the gap between the way folks actually talked and the way they "ought" to talk, through regulation and prescription.

Over a million copies of various grammars were printed in eighteenth-century England, but these books were not nearly as popular as the usage books that proliferated throughout the nineteenth and twentieth centuries. Beginning in the Modern English period, grammars, usage guides, and dictionaries allowed speakers to refine their English, spoken and written, so that it represented them well in commerce and politics. As Richard W. Bailey notes in *Nineteenth-Century English* (1996, 320), "Writing and reading became more than skills ancillary to real work; they often became the work itself." Aptitude in Standard English gave, and continues to give, speakers a competitive edge in "mainstream" economic and political markets. At the beginning of the twenty-first century, a book like *Eats, Shoots & Leaves* (2003), a prescriptive guide to punctuation, was a best seller both in Britain and in the United States. Accent reduction courses flourish throughout the United States and Britain. The public appetite for guidance on "correct" English remains strong.

The "standard" variety appeals to and alienates different speakers for different reasons. For some, it is the instrument of mobility and social success, and perhaps nothing more: speak your home language at home, but parade the standard to impress others, without whom you cannot succeed. For others, the standard serves as a barrier: if people can't speak and write it, then they don't have access to all of the things that Standard English speakers do. Still others endorse a standard variety of English for what might be considered either logical or aesthetic reasons or both—any language looks better, communicates better, makes better sense, if it is systematically consistent. (Of course, any variety of English is as systematically consistent as the standard one, but each is consistent in its own way, not a way that all will recognize and appreciate.) The standard, too, may serve as common ground for a society, a practical basis for understanding in all public matters, whatever we think of it aesthetically or logically. These views of the standard variety of English, even if implied in its inception, are modern views.

The Media

Despite the pervasiveness of language prescription in Modern English, competing forces, such as commercial speech, have affected the development of Modern English—often not in line with prescriptive forces. For example, in the 1960s, Americans were told that Winston cigarettes "taste good, like a cigarette should." Prescriptive grammars of English agreed that *like* in this sentence ought to have been *as*, but the advertisement was popular, and it may even have reinforced a tendency of speakers to use (or accept) *like* and *as* interchangeably. Advertising language depends on rhetorical "punch" and compression. Compression, in turn, often depends on colloquial discourse. For example, a set of ads in 2007 for Kia's new minivan, the Rondo, took a morphological shortcut very typical of slang to sell these vehicles with words like (huge) *cabinocity*, (seat) *flexology*, and overall *giddyupedness*. All of our experience of conversation indicates that we can make up words on the spot, and that we don't always (even usually) speak in complete, prescriptively grammatical sentences. Natural speech is often elliptical and suggestive instead. Because advertising "befriends" potential buyers and rarely depends on logical argument for commercial results, it talks the purchaser's talk.

As Richard W. Bailey argues, the relationship between advertising and the history of English is more complicated than linguistic critics of "advertising English" admit. True, advertising English historically has not always followed the grammars or usage guides, and it can give status to nonstandard constructions. Alternatively, though, billboards, handbills (what we now call "flyers"), and print advertisements in newspapers demand literacy on the consumer's part. In other words, consumerism, which has driven advertising, has also created a "commercial written English" that sits on a middle ground between the way people speak and the rules of standard written English.

To take another example of influential commercial print, newspapers have had significant consequences for the development of the English language. Although much newspaper text conforms to the prescriptive rules of Standard English, headlines are a linguistic wildcard. E. P. Mitchell, a former editor of the *New York Times*, once said, "The headline is more influential than a hundred chairs of rhetoric in the shaping of future English speech" (qtd. in Mencken 1962, 185). Like advertising, adept headlining requires brevity, partly because the punchy headline captures the newspaper reader's attention, and partly because, given the extra space headlines take by virtue of their size, only a few words will fit into one. A *probe* takes less space than an *investigation*, a *crash* less than a *collision*; *Brits* fits into headlines better than *the British*, *Serbs* better than *Serbians*. New words enter English as headlines clip and backform words, and readers often accept them. Not only do these new words conform to English morphological and morphosyntactic rules as well as their competing forms, but also speakers and readers sometimes seem to prefer them, an insurmountable problem for the prescriptivist trying to block nonstandard forms.

A random selection of headlines from newspapers around the world captures a range of these innovative shortening strategies. For example, the *Sunday Times* (London) opts for a shorter, more informal word than *restrictions*, *limitations*, or even *limits* in this headline—and uses *cheap* over *inexpensive*, as well as omitting the word *telephone*:

"Curbs on Cheap Overseas Calls" (December 16, 2007)

Abbreviations for *government* and for *prime minister* help shorten up these two headlines:

"Sudan: Peace Deal Still on Course, Says Govt" (*Africa News*, May 23, 2006)

"PM Lacks Urgency on Climate Change" (*Toronto Star*, January 9, 2007)

In another article on climate change, the *Globe and Mail* (Canada) opts to use the shorthand *green* to talk about environmental consciousness, as well as the informal phrasal verb *pull for*:

"Pulling for a Green World" (January 4, 2007)

And sports headlines often exploit shortened forms of team's and player's names (e.g., *Cavs* for Cavaliers, *Shaq* for Shaquille O'Neal), as well as punchy, colloquial verbs:

"James Lifts Cavs" (*Gazette* [Montreal], December 23, 2005)

"Big Shaq Shatters Hawks" (*Daily Telegraph*, December 22, 2005)

Commercial concerns have affected Modern English punctuation conventions as well. Early printers and publishers, well into the nineteenth century, relied on lead type, and owning all the required letters to print a page was a significant investment. Printers needed to estimate how many of each letter they needed in their cases, both upper and lower. Dropping final unpronounced *-e* looked like money in the bank. For similar reasons, modern printers also often resisted the practice, typical through the eighteenth century, of capitalizing nouns, since capital (or uppercase) letters take more space than lowercase letters. Should a comma mark each item in a series of three or more items (as in "the bruise was black, blue, and purple") or is it okay to leave out the comma for the last item ("the bruise was black, blue and purple")? Over the course of a book, those commas add up. If printers saved the serial commas, as well as those following adverbial phrases at the beginning of sentences (as in "At the store I paid cash," rather than "At the store, I paid cash"), they would print a somewhat shorter book. Shorter books cost less money to produce. In the period of lead type, they also cost less labor, as there were fewer characters to insert into a line of type.

Electronic technology is changing written English as we write, which we discuss later in this chapter.

Imperialism and War

No social change has influenced the progress of modern English as much as England's imperial grasp on parts of the rest of the world. Wales was annexed to England in the fourteenth century. England subdued Ireland in the sixteenth century, and Scotland was united with England, first when James VI of Scotland also became James I of England (1603), and finally in the Act of Union (1707). In other words, the British Empire was an Early Modern invention, and it rose first in English conquest of other kingdoms within the British Isles. Throughout the eighteenth and nineteenth centuries, however, England colonized or conquered large areas in North America, the Near East, Africa, and Asia, in addition to Australia and New Zealand. U.S. imperialism is often dated back to the end of the nineteenth century and has affected areas of the Pacific such as the Philippines and Guam, parts of the Middle East, and elsewhere. Both Britain and the United States established even more far-reaching trade relationships. As a result, speakers of English came into contact with many languages, each of which contributed to the lexicon of English, if not also to its phonology, syntax, and prosody.

The fact that the United States and Britain were among the victorious nations of both world wars in the twentieth century meant that English often continued to be used in former war zones. And English lost one of its most potent rival languages with the collapse of the Soviet Union in 1989 and the end of the Cold War. Now many speakers in the former eastern bloc countries, as well as in Russia, are learning English in addition to, or rather than, Russian.

The long, strong arm of U.S. political and economic influence twists the arms of speakers around the world. In many countries, people learn English in addition to their native languages. Business worldwide is increasingly conducted in English because it's what Americans speak. Most movies and television shows distributed pretty much everywhere are originally in American English. Local film industries complain that American media flood them out of their own markets, and the fact of American dominance in media, as in so much else, is indisputable. Another way to look at this is to acknowledge the prestige of American culture, and of American English as an aspect of that culture. There's a lot about America and Americans that others like, respect, and finally emulate, including the language. In this regard, America's position among world languages is not unlike that of a prestige dialect among other dialects. Prestige is a characteristic of some dialects and some languages. But prestige is promoted, maintained, and enforced in variously subtle and not quite subtle ways.

Power and prestige have made Modern English both accessible and acquisitive. Lexical expansion is one of its central characteristics—and it works both ways. Words from *adobe* (from Coptic, an Egyptian language) to *zombie* (from Kongo, an African language of the Bantu family) have entered English in the Modern period. And English has entered languages all around the world. The Académie Française tries to stop English borrowings into French, such as *le computer*, but this is just the tip of the iceberg of English borrowing in French and in many other languages. The word *O.K.* might be as close to a "world word" as the world has seen.

In some parts of the globe—for example, in India and Singapore—English has been adopted as a national language alongside indigenous languages. As these international varieties of English develop, they hold the potential to challenge the status of British and American English as the standard for "World English."

Globalization

The word *McDonaldization*, first used in 1974 according to the *OED*, expanded during the 1990s from referring to the spread of an efficient, standardized corporate model to the more general spread of American culture. As the *Daily Telegraph* reported in 1994, "there is much anxious justification of the 'McDonaldisation' of Prague. It's not only a matter of McDonald's (there are two) but of K. Mart." *McDonaldization*, or *coca-colonization* (a humorous derivation from the beverage, cited in 1960), is often linked with globalization, particularly by those who feel more anxious or negative about the phenomenon.

Globalization refers to the expansion of trade and other economic relationships across international borders, the increased movement of labor forces across these same borders, the spread of social and cultural relationships from one point to many around the world, and a heightened "global consciousness," be that about the environment, political and social issues, or anything else. Whatever stance you take on globalization, the fact is that right now, English is the language most often associated with it, from *McDonalds* to *Coke*, from *dollars* to *movies*, from *pop music* to *computers*. The benefits and drawbacks of globalization, from increased global access to technology to the risks to local markets and cultural practices, are much debated and beyond the scope of this discussion. Globalization is not new or static, and it encompasses many diverse cultures and languages. However, for the folks concerned about the spread of one culture at the expense of others, their concern centers on the current spread of Western, if not specifically American culture. Part of that "globalizing" American culture is the English language.

Modern English: Language Change in Progress

Many people assume that the history of English ended, for all intents and purposes, with Shakespeare or Jane Austen or another "older" author whose English we can still understand. Though the English of these authors is sometimes archaic, we still can read it; we assume that all of the changes since "then" have been minor. The history of English is thereby relegated to the times of Chaucer and of Beowulf, where we can see dramatic linguistic differences more clearly. After all, since the eighteenth century, grammar books and dictionaries have attempted to regulate English. Two hundred years and more later, haven't they yet "fixed" the English language?

Language Change at Work

The Debated Origins of O.K.

Should one spell the universal term of assent *O.K.* or *okay*? The distinction looks trivial, but it is actually the center of confusion about the term's origin. *O.K.* (or *OK*) looks like an initialism (or alphabetism—see Chapter 4), while *okay* looks more like a borrowed word than one with an Old English origin. Those who favor the latter spelling (and thus consider *O.K.* a development from *okay*) often expect to find a foreign source for this American word. For instance, some have argued that *okay* is an English form of Caribbean French *Aux Cayes*, a popular rum that when served would elicit cries of approval. Others have suggested an origin in Scots *och aye* 'for sure'. Finnish hasn't had a great influence on American English, but that hasn't stopped Finnish partisans from proposing *oikea* 'correct' as *okay*'s etymon. The Choctaw, a Native American tribe, had little contact with early American settlers, but some have proposed that Choctaw *okeh* 'correct' developed into *okay*. And though we have no documentary evidence that West African languages in the eighteenth century had a term of assent that sounded like *okay*, some have suggested that modern evidence of such West African forms indicates an African American English origin for the word. None of these explanations is sound. *Okay* is a respelling of the original *O.K.* But if *O.K.* is an initialism, what contributes the initials? In a series of articles in the journal *American Speech*, Allen Walker Read identified *O.K.*'s true origin and also dispelled the folklore that surrounds the word.

In 1839, Boston newspapers had taken to using supposedly clever abbreviations in their articles, like *N.G.* 'no go', *G.C.* 'gin cocktail', and *G.T.* 'gone to Texas'. Some of these abbreviations involved humorous misspellings. Thus, *oll korrect* 'all correct' became *O.K.* Within a year, *O.K.* had traveled from Boston to Chicago. In 1840, Martin Van Buren ran for president (and won). Van Buren came from Kinderhook, a village in the Hudson Valley of New York; his supporters affectionately called him "Old Kinderhook," and those who lived in New York City formed the "*O.K.* Club." Within the year, *O.K.* 'Old Kinderhook' intersected with *O.K.* 'oll korrect' in headlines to newspaper articles about Van Buren's candidacy. As a result of the intersections, *O.K.* became a general term of assent within a remarkably short time. And since 1840, *O.K.* as a term of assent has spread, not only throughout the English-speaking world but into many of the world's languages. English borrows freely from other languages. *O.K.* is the term with which we have compensated the world's languages for what we have borrowed.

Whether or not grammars and dictionaries *should* keep the language stable we leave as a question for you to debate among yourselves (would you really want no new words?). The fact is, however, that they *cannot*, no matter what their authors hope. No living language stays fixed in time or in structure. Within any speech community, a language changes from generation to generation, sometimes in minor ways, sometimes in major ones—language changes all the time. Some linguists call it "drift" and others "evolution." One linguist compares language to a lava lamp, constantly in motion but never decaying—or improving for that matter (McWhorter 1998). Although we don't know exactly what will happen to English over the next few centuries, we do know that if "English" is spoken in 2450, it will be different from English today.

It is hard to know exactly how institutionalized prescriptivism, a thoroughly modern tendency, will affect language change—it certainly won't stop it. In the fifteenth century, the rising standard variety depended on new technologies, especially printing, for its success. As more print media developed in the next few centuries, they facilitated regulation and prescription. But, today, prescription competes with the rapid explosion of communication technology, which creates entirely new situations of language expansion and language contact. A page of printed text doesn't much resemble an instant message. Various language technologies allow and even promote different language practices: they enable and limit certain types of discourse. So, what technology giveth, technology also taketh away. That said, let's speculate a bit about some changes that we see already happening and some that we might reasonably expect to see.

Word Formation

Modern English is responsible for several new word formation processes, which continue to expand the vocabulary. These unexpected ways of forming new words constitute significant change, but we are so familiar with them today, so comfortable with the words they produce, that we take them for granted (see Chapter 4). Headlines and advertising promoted shortening, principally clipping and backformation, but shortening went much further, as abbreviations for phrases were lexicalized in acronyms and alphabetisms, such as *snafu* (*situation normal all fucked up*) and *OK*. While there are plenty of acronyms and alphabetisms in mainstream vocabulary, they proliferate in corporate and government jargon. United Parcel Service (or UPS) expects employees to use so many acronyms that they distribute a hefty booklet full of them for employees to study. BTW, if you participate in Internet chat rooms, write a lot of e-mail, IM, or text, you know that acronyms and alphabetisms are significant elements of wired style (the word *IM* alone makes that point!). Though rare until the nineteenth century, acronyms and alphabetisms thrive on the Internet, and some of these words, like *LOL*, *BRB*, and *BFF*, are finding their way into the spoken language. If you think any of these forms sound too awkward for the spoken language, consider whether they are any more awkward than, say, *FYI*.

Other particularly modern types of word formation are infixing, in words such as *absofuckinglutely*, and **interposing**, in fixed phrases such as "Big fucking deal!" (see Chapter 4). Infixing and interposing with lexically meaningful inserts, though not frequent, are increasingly acceptable among American English speakers. For instance, in a list of women celebrities who set a supposedly poor standard for young women, we find the interposing *et Botoxed cetera*; or someone confronts yet another catastrophe with *Oh as usual dear*. Typically such infixing and interposing is humorous and depends heavily on context.

In any given time period, some affixes are hotter than others. As we discussed in Chapter 4, English speakers are currently creating many new adjectives with the suffix *-y*. The suffix *-age* has recently added some new nouns (e.g., *signage*, *drunkage*) to the much longer established set of *-age* words (e.g., *brokerage*, *coverage*, *wreckage*). Because of technological innovations, the prefixes *e-*, *hyper-*, and *cyber-* are spinning a web of new Internet-related words (e.g., *e-ticket*, *e-trade*, *hypertext*, *hyperlink*, *cyberpunk*, *cybersquat*).

Writers using computer-mediated communication and texting make frequent use of rebuses (especially in text-messaging) such as *C U l8er* 'see you later' and *gr8* 'great'.

The Web and texting have also generated all kinds of new words through other word-formation processes such as functional shifts (e.g., *to friend* someone on Facebook), compounds (e.g., *chatroom*), and blends (e.g., *sexting*). You will also see long, unpunctuated sentences. The authors of this book will not venture to guess what technology has in store for us, but we are sure that English will expand and reshape the resources it already has to describe our new world and adapt to it.

Lexical Borrowing

The lexicon most quickly and directly reflects the cultural experience of a language's speakers. We can certainly expect English to continue to borrow words from the languages that English speakers come into contact with. In the United States especially, the influence of Spanish on English may continue to grow, alongside the influence of other languages such as Arabic, Chinese, and various languages from Africa, India, and other parts of Asia, just to name a few.

"Can I borrow your guitar, *mi amigo*?" Spanish has a long history of influence on the English lexicon, particularly that of American English. And while speakers still recognize some words as clearly borrowed (e.g., *amigo*), many of the others, like *guitar*, are fully assimilated into English: *tornado, mesa, mosquito, vigilante, taco, tortilla, coyote, lasso, loco, chili, frijoles, guitar, marijuana, rodeo, corral*, and so much more. Many of these loanwords have been in the language for decades and have become naturalized to the point where speakers can, for example, put them through functional shift, making the nouns *corral* and *lasso* into verbs. Other loanwords are newer, such as *chones* 'underwear'. Some Spanish borrowings are now difficult to recognize as such: for example, the English verb *vamoose* is an adaptation of (and some would say corruption of) Spanish *vamos* 'let us go' that dates back to the nineteenth century. Given the pervasiveness of Spanish-English bilingualism in California, Florida, New York, Texas, and much of the Southwest, we can reasonably expect many more Spanish loans into all varieties of English in the years to come, in addition to the continuing presence of the dialect Chicano English in the United States. And, as immigration patterns into the United States shift, the vocabulary will reflect different patterns of language contact.

Phonological Changes

Subtle sound shifts occur in language on an almost continuous basis. In the history of English, words have lost some initial consonants (e.g., the initial /g/ and /k/ in words such as *gnat* and *knight*) and final consonants (e.g., the final /g/ in the present participle, such as *talking*). Phoneme and allophone distributions can also change: for example, /f/ and /v/ are now two phonemes, whereas in Old English, they were two allophones of /f/ (see Exercise 3.3 in Chapter 3). In Chapter 3, we raised the question of whether /h/ is becoming an endangered phoneme in English. Regionally in the United States, some parts of the South that have traditionally been /r/-less are becoming home to more and more /r/-full speakers.

These examples involve consonants, but sound change even more often affects vowels, perhaps because of the more approximate nature of the target sound. That is, a high vowel is distinct from a mid vowel in relative terms, whereas consonant features such as voicing and manner of articulation create sharper distinctions. In addition, studies of any one speaker's vowels show that his or her production of a given vowel scatters in a clustered pattern on a vowel chart, like shots around a target.

In earlier chapters, we described three major vowel changes happening in the United States right now: the *cot/caught* merger (see Chapter 2); the Northern Cities Vowel Shift (see Chapter 11); and an almost opposite vowel rotation in the Northern California Vowel Shift (see Chapter 12). Other vowel changes are afoot around the country. For example, in Texas and surrounding areas as well as central Ohio, Pittsburgh, and elsewhere, tense/lax vowel pairs are merging before /l/, such that *pool* and *pull* are homophones (or near homophones), as well as pairs such as *filled/field* and *sale/sell*. The fronting of /o/ and /u/ happening in northern California has also been recorded in places like Arizona and Oregon. Utah is witnessing the reversal of the *card/cord* merger (such that *fork* is "fark," *lord* is "lard"), whereas the merger remains relatively healthy (if becoming more stigmatized) in St. Louis.

As we discussed in Chapter 12, American dialects may be diverging from one another, both in pronunciation and grammatical features.

Grammatical Changes

Over the course of its history, English has been changing from a primarily synthetic language—a language highly reliant on inflectional endings to express grammatical function—to a primarily analytic language—a language highly reliant on word order to express grammatical function. As part of this process, almost all inflectional endings on nouns have been lost. Among the few that remain are plural *-s* and possessive *-s*. Will these inflectional endings be lost as well? It is certainly possible, and it has already happened in some dialects of English. In cases where there is a quantifier before the noun that indicates its plurality, the final *-s* is redundant and has already been lost in some dialects in phrases such as *four book* or *many car*. The possessive *-s* could also be interpreted as redundant. Over the past two to three centuries, English has seen an increase in nouns modifying nouns, to create extended strings of nouns in one noun phrase: for example, *textbook cover*, *English class textbook cover*, *English class textbook cover image*. You could add a possessive to these expressions to create, for example, *textbook's cover*. It is understood that the prior noun modifies the subsequent noun, often expressing possession. This relatively new grammatical construction may slowly encroach on the territory of the inflected possessive. In fact, some dialects of English already sometimes employ zero-possessives such as *my friend dad*.

The most systematic remnants of the Old English case system can be found in the personal pronouns, as well as *who/whom*. In these pronouns, we still mark the difference between subject, object, and possessive—or at least most of the time we do. As we discussed in Chapter 2, speakers are struggling with *who* and *whom*, given that the form often appears at the beginning of a sentence and looks like a subject no matter its grammatical function. Many linguists predict that the use of *who* will continue to expand at the expense of *whom*—perhaps to the point where *whom* will be lost. In the electronic version of this chapter, the word-processing program often green-lined (that is, marked as a mistake) historically grammatical uses of *whom*. Such changes in the "standards" by which word-processing programs police our grammar are one step in the wider standard being revised.

It may be harder to predict what will happen with the personal pronouns. Many speakers show variation in the use of subject and object forms, saying, for example, "Me and mom are both Gemini" or "a very personal decision for Michelle and I." (President Obama has been publicly critiqued for that second example.) This kind of variation may well signal a language change in progress. Will it result in an invariable form for each pronoun—so either *I* or *me* for first-person singular, either *they* or *them* in third-person plural, just like the already invariant form *you* for second-person singular and plural? Or will it result in a new pattern, where the subject form appears before the verb and the object form after the verb, no matter its grammatical function? Stay tuned, and watch for clues in the language all around you.

Another process always at work in the language is **grammaticalization**, or the process through which an open-class word becomes a grammatical form. One good historical example is the suffix *-ly*, which began in Old English as a freestanding noun *lic* meaning 'body'. So the Old English form *manly* was a compound meaning 'having the body of a person'. Eventually this type of compound was reanalyzed as a root with a suffix, and the suffix migrated to combine with all sorts of other roots to form adjectives. Today, *-ly* is no longer a productive adjective suffix; the only adjectives formed with *-ly* originated in Old English. The preposition *while* can still express simultaneous action, but it has been bleached of this content in some contexts and now frequently expresses a concession (e.g., "While I agree with your premise, I disagree with your conclusion"). Modern English modal auxiliary verbs such as *will* and *may* used to be full verbs. We still see *will* used this way in a sentence like "I will that to happen," but most of the time it is a grammatical form that marks future tense. Currently, we are witnessing the creation of new modals such as *going to/gonna*, *have to/hafta*, and *supposed to/sposta*. (See pp. 54–55 in Chapter 2 for other grammatical changes happening in Modern English.)

A Question to Discuss

"Hey, You Guys, Is This Grammaticalization?"

The use of the word *guy* has become more and more widespread and varied, especially in American English. It can be used to refer to a male human being (covering a wide age range), as a plural inclusive in the vocative and second person (e.g., "hey, guys" and "you guys"), possibly as a plural inclusive deictic form (e.g., "We want to go to the movies but those guys are being wishy-washy"), and as a quasi-pronoun in reference to an inanimate object (e.g., "this guy over here" referring to a book).

In Modern English at the beginning of the twenty-first century, the use of the plural form *guys* to encompass both male and female human beings seems to be fairly well restricted to forms of address or as a plural marker with the second-person pronoun *you*.

In the phrase *you guys*, we could argue that the form *guys* has been bleached of its semantic content to become just a marker of plurality. If this is the case, is *you guys* becoming grammaticalized as a second-person plural pronoun, parallel to forms like *y'all* and *youse* in other dialects of English?

Along similar lines, we could argue that *guy* has undergone semantic bleaching when it is used as an indefinite or demonstrative phrasal pronoun—that is, when *this guy* or *some guy* is used similarly to *this one*, *this thing*, *someone/somebody*, *something* (Clancy 1999, 288). Is there a difference between saying "this guy" and "this one" when you're referring to the last remaining slice of pizza? "Does anyone else want _____?"

The Status of English in the United States

The United States has no official language. Because English is so widespread in America, the assumed language of government, commerce, education, and media, many people also assume that there is a law or line in the Constitution that makes English the official language of the country. The founding fathers did not stipulate that the new country had an official language, though there were partisans for an American "academy" from a very early date (Read 1935). The status of English in the United States at the beginning of the twenty-first century is not in doubt: about 95 percent of American citizens state that they speak English fluently, and the majority of immigrants seek to learn English as a means of upward mobility if they do not already speak it. However, the debate about whether English should become the official language of the United States has surfaced periodically throughout the history of the country.

In the eighteenth century, the language supposedly threatening the supremacy of English in America was not Spanish but German. In the 1750s, up to one-third of the residents of Pennsylvania were German speakers, a statistic that caused both concern and resentment for some British settlers and government officials. Benjamin Franklin is reported to have said in 1751:

> Why should the Palatine Boors be suffered to swarm into our Settlements, and by herding together establish their Language and Manners to the exclusion of ours? Why should Pennsylvania, founded by the English, become a Colony of Aliens, who will shortly be so numerous as to Germanize us instead of our Anglifying them, and will never adopt our Language or Customs, any more than they can acquire our Complexion? (qtd. in Baron, "Legendary")

Later in life, Franklin actually came to support bilingual education, but his statement here captured a very real concern at the time, one often voiced today in states like California, given the high percentage of Spanish speakers.

Concerns about the presence of "foreign" (i.e., non-English) languages in the United States often surface during times of war and times of high immigration. For example, in 1917, during World War I, twenty-five states banned the teaching of German in schools. There were also efforts to replace some borrowed German words with English ones, using *liberty sandwiches* for *hamburgers* and *liberty cabbage* for *sauerkraut*. In March 2003, after France refused to join the United States in the war in Iraq, the cafeteria in the U.S. House of Representatives replaced *french fries* on the menu with *freedom fries*. (The name was quietly changed back in 2006.)

Serious efforts to change the Constitution to include English as the official language of the country began in 1981, led by Senator S. I. Hayakawa of California. Often referred to as "English Only" amendments, such legislation has met with resistance in Congress and never been passed. In the 1990s, the Language of Government Act (LOGA) passed in the House several times, but it was never voted on in the Senate. The bill proposes to make English the official language of the government (rather than of the nation). It would require that federal employees use English when they conduct official business and that federal ballots appear in English, unless more than 5 percent of the voters are nonnative speakers of English. (The bill allows for exceptions to the English-only policy in federal documents, such as use of the Latin phrase *e pluribus unum*.)

A third alternative, the "English Plus" resolution introduced in the House and Senate, attempts to recognize the important role of English in the United States and guarantee

Language Variation at Work

The Myth of the "German Vote" in 1776

There is a myth in circulation that in 1776 Congress voted on whether German should be considered an official language of the United States. In fact, this vote never took place. In 1795, Congress considered a proposal to print federal laws in both English and German, as the result of a petition by German Americans in Virginia. A motion to adjourn, at one point in the debate, failed by one vote; this vote is often seen as a vote of no confidence in the proposal. About a month later, after further debate, Congress and the president approved a bill that federal statutes would be published only in English. See Dennis Baron's article "The Legendary English-Only Vote of 1795," on his Web site Web of Language, for a full discussion.

It is worth quoting a couple of the statements that Baron reports were made on the House floor during the debate, as they sound strikingly familiar to the current debate about speakers of Spanish and other languages today. Representative Thomas Hartley of Pennsylvania argued, "[It] was perhaps desirable that the Germans should learn English; but if it is our object to give present information, we should do it in the language understood. The Germans who are advanced in years cannot learn our language in a day. It would be generous in the Government to inform those persons." Representative William Murray of Maryland countered, "it had never been the custom in England to translate the laws into Welsh or Gaelic, and yet the great bulk of the Welsh, and some hundred thousands of people in Scotland, did not understand a word of English."

The Continental Congress had printed documents in English, German, and French. During the nineteenth century, some states printed laws in other languages in addition to English, including French, Spanish, and Welsh. But by the end of that century, California had officially banned Spanish language rights and Pennsylvania had made English proficiency a requirement for coal workers.

language rights for speakers of other languages. It proposes increasing investment in language education, including ESL programs and potentially bilingual education programs, and systematizing government services offered to nonnative speakers.

In the meantime, at least twenty-five states have enacted official English statutes or constitutional amendments. For example, Alabama, California, Florida, and Arizona have constitutional amendments adopted by voter initiatives that make English the state's official language; Hawaii passed a constitutional amendment making the state

A Question to Discuss

Official State Languages

Does your state have an official language? How do you feel about having or not having an official language in your state? How do others feel? To answer this last question, you could look for opinions in the press, on Web sites and blogs, or you could even conduct your own survey.

officially bilingual (English and Native Hawaiian). States from the Carolinas to the Dakotas to Iowa and Idaho have statutes that make English the official language, and a few states such as New Mexico and Oregon have passed English Plus resolutions. At the local level, some cities have required signs to be at least half in English, and some have guaranteed bilingual services to ensure access to governmental services. The debates at every level, from the federal government to cities, are sure to continue with ongoing immigration into the United States and the competing demands for a unifying language and the recognition of home languages as part of native cultures and identities.

The courts have been equivocal about the status of English-only laws. Some of the official English constitutional amendments approved in states have been overturned as unconstitutional. For example, in 1988, Arizona amended its constitution to require that all employees of local and state government conduct government business "in English and no other language." Soon thereafter, a state employee, Maria-Kelly Yñiguez, was fired for speaking Spanish to a Spanish-speaking client. She brought suit, and eventually the amendment was found unconstitutional by the Arizona Supreme Court. In 2006, voters in Arizona passed an initiative for a constitutional amendment that made English the official language of the state but with weaker restrictions than the earlier amendment. In 2002 the Equal Employment Opportunity Commission filed a suit on behalf of four Navajo workers at a restaurant in Arizona who were prohibited from speaking Navajo on the job and were fired when they refused to sign an English-only rule. At the same time, in 1995, in a custody suit, a judge ordered a mother in Amarillo, Texas, to speak only English to her child, as speaking only Spanish to her could be considered child abuse and would condemn her "to life as a maid." He later apologized for the comment about maids but held firm on the English-only decision (Baron, Web of Language, see "Spanish Abuse"). In 2000, a Cuban American filed a suit against Provident Life and Accident Insurance Company, which had denied him insurance coverage "in view of [his] inability to speak and understand the English language." Thus, with these many cases, neither the right of citizens to use whatever languages they choose, nor the state's right to establish official languages and exclude others, has yet been clearly established.

Controversy over language laws and their effects takes many forms, from the level of the family to businesses to educational policy and beyond. Here are just three examples:

- In September 2003, in a child custody dispute in Nebraska, a district court judge warned the father, a Mexican American, that if he continued to use the "Hispanic language" with his five-year-old daughter, his visitation rights would be restricted. Supporters of minority language rights argue that the courts have no right to interfere in parent-child relationships this way. Even some supporters of English language rights and the bans on bilingual education were dismayed at the court's decision, as the Nebraska law at issue focused specifically on language teaching in the schools, not at home.

- The California Insurance Code stipulates that no one should be denied coverage on the basis of nationality, race, gender, religion, ancestry, or sexual orientation; it does not say anything specifically about language. To what extent is language assumed under "nationality"?

- Debates about English-only laws often become intertwined with debates about bilingual education. In the past few years, voters in states such as Arizona and California have passed propositions that ban bilingual education. Similar propositions are underway, and under debate, in other states.

We must all grapple with two related questions. To what extent should we see the use of other languages in the United States as a threat to the future of English in this country? To what extent and in what ways should we see the United States as a monolingual or a multilingual country?

When considering these questions, we need to remember this current and historical fact: the United States is not and never has been a monolingual country. Throughout its history, the United States has opened its doors to immigrants, sometimes enormous numbers of them, speaking a wide range of languages. And there have always been citizens (many not recent immigrants) who speak a language other than English. As late as 1990, one could encounter residents of Pennsylvania who spoke Pennsylvania German but no English. They were twentieth-century descendants of the very German settlers about whom Benjamin Franklin complained in 1751. Some who endorse English Only legislation may not realize that German has been spoken in the United States so long and so continuously that Pennsylvania German is considered a dialect of Modern Low German—a uniquely American dialect. Many Native American languages, Spanish, French, and various creoles have even longer histories in North American.

The Status of English Around the World

Many English speakers today assume that English inevitably will remain a global language. When you watch the Olympics, are you surprised when the gold-medalist Swiss skier or Kenyan distance runner can share his or her joy with the television broadcasters in English, no matter what his or her nationality? Or does it seem "natural" that anyone from anywhere would be able to do so? Americans also have the reputation of expecting to be able to use English wherever they travel in the world—an expectation that not all world cultures share. But the current status of English as the world's most commonly spoken second or foreign language is a relatively new occurrence. As early as the 1950s, David Crystal points out in *English as a Global Language* (2003, 28), the idea of English as a world language remained a theoretical but far from inevitable possibility: "Within little more than a generation, we have moved from a situation where a world language was a theoretical possibility to one where it is an evident reality."

If we go back even further in time, the idea of English as a world language would have been close to inconceivable. In the middle of the sixteenth century, as we discussed at the beginning of the chapter, English had yet to compete in any way with the prestige of French or Latin. At that time, no one would have predicted the demise of Latin as the language of learning or French as the language of diplomacy and the court, let alone the rise of lowly English to global status. Look at these quotations about the English language from the sixteenth century:

> The speche of Englande is a base speche to other noble speeches, as Italion Castylion and Frenche, howbeit the speche of Englande of late dayes is amended.
> —Andrew Boorde, *The first boke of the Introduction of knowledge*
> (ca. 1550; qtd. in Barber 1976, 66)

And as for ye Latin or greke tonge, euery thing is so excellently done in them, that none can do better: In the Englysh tonge contrary, euery thinge in a maner so meanly, bothe for the matter and handelynge that no man can do worse.

—Roger Ascham, *Toxophilus* (1545)

Between this time and the beginning of the twenty-first century, the population of native speakers of English has exploded from somewhere between 5 and 7 million people to somewhere closer to 300 million speakers, from speakers isolated on the British Isles to speakers spread around the world. As important, the majority of nonnative speakers no longer live in areas formerly controlled by the British Empire but in countries with no historical political relationship with Britain or the United States (Crystal 2006a). There is no precedent for the kind of global spread of English that we have witnessed over the past few centuries and even more rapidly over the past few decades with technological advances. For instance, English is very much the language of the Internet. But as we look toward the year 2450, it is important to remember that 450 years ago, English would have been a long shot as a global language. So what might seem inconceivable now as a linguistic future may seem inevitable in retrospect by 2450.

As we consider the future of English as a world language, we have no historical precedent to turn to. No language has ever been spoken as widely around the world as English currently is. Skeptics may argue that Latin was once a world language, but in fact, Latin was only a European language. Modern technology, from airplanes to telephones to computers, has allowed rapid if not immediate communication between speakers on different sides of the world, speakers who often do not share a native language, but who do share at least a basic knowledge of English.

The Meaning of a "Global Language"

A "global language" is different from a **lingua franca** or 'common language'. A lingua franca is developed in specific contexts to facilitate communication among speakers who share no common native language. In some trading contexts, that lingua franca will be a pidgin. In other situations, it will be a language with prestige or history or an established presence in that part of the world (e.g., Spanish in South America). And today, in some parts of the world, the lingua franca is also the global language (e.g., much of the communication among countries in Asia today is in English).

As David Crystal (2003) explains, a language takes on a "global" status when it develops a special role that is recognized in every country. There are three general categories for that special role:

1. The language is the first or native language for many if not most speakers in the country.

2. The language is an official language of the country, used for official purposes, as well as in the media and educational system.

3. The language is a priority in the country's educational system.

At the beginning of the twenty-first century, English has taken on all three of these roles in numerous countries around the world. It is hard to quote exact statistics, but in *Globish* (2010, 276), Robert McCrum quotes estimates that 4 billion people (about half the world's population) know or have some acquaintance with English. Probably over 1.5 billion of those people speak competent or fluent English.

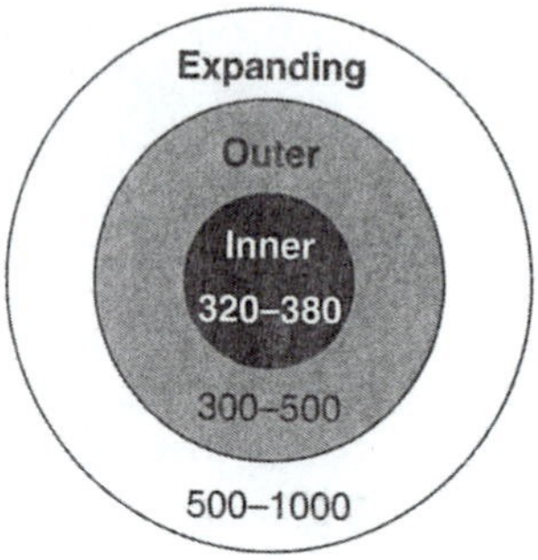

FIGURE 14.1 The three circles of English as described by Braj Kachru categorize countries with English speakers into the inner circle, outer circle, and expanding circle, with L1 speakers of English at the center (numbers represent millions of speakers).

Sources: Adapted from David Graddol, *The Future of English?* © 1997, 2000 by The British Council. Used with permission. Updated numbers from David Crystal, *English as a Global Language* (2003).

The three numbered categories correspond to the three "circles of English," proposed by linguist Braj Kachru (see Figure 14.1). Note that L1 and L2 here refer to speakers, whereas in Chapter 11 L1 and L2 are used to refer to languages in contact.

1. The "inner circle"—countries where the dominant language (and culture) is English: Great Britain, as well as former English-speaking colonies such as the United States, Canada, Australia, New Zealand, and South Africa. Of course, all of these countries have their own national variety of English—a fact to which we return below. Inner-circle speakers, for whom English is a native language, are often referred to as L1 speakers of English.

2. The "outer circle"—countries where English is an official language or an important "second language," used for many governmental and official purposes, often as a legacy of colonialism: countries such as India, Singapore, Sierra Leone, Nigeria, Cameroon, Gambia, Malawi, Zambia, and Zimbabwe. Speakers of English in these countries tend to be L2 speakers of English—it is their second (or additional) language used in specific contexts within their interactions in the country.

3. The "expanding circle"—countries where English takes on a central role as a foreign language taught in the schools, given its international role (but English is not used for official purposes within the country): for example, China, Germany, Russia, and Sweden. For these speakers, often referred to as EFL speakers, English is primarily a way to communicate with speakers from other countries—either native English speakers or speakers of another language who also speak English as a shared international language.

The demographics of the three circles shift constantly. For example, some countries (Sweden, Belgium, the United Arab Emirates, and Nicaragua, to name a few) may be moving from the expanding circle to the outer circle. Other countries, such as Kenya, have renounced the status of English as an official language and are working to support education in native languages.

David Graddol (1997) offers an alternate diagram that does not place "mother tongue" countries in the center and thereby tries to reflect the relative importance of the outer and expanding circles to the future of English (see Figure 14.2). At this point, speakers who use English as a foreign language outnumber those for whom English is a native language, and most statistics indicate that speakers of English as a second language will outnumber native speakers of English within the next decade, if they do not already.

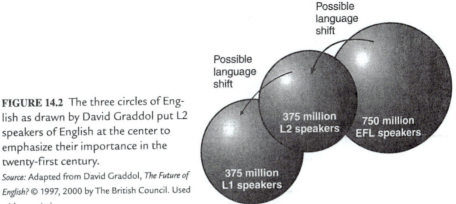

FIGURE 14.2 The three circles of English as drawn by David Graddol put L2 speakers of English at the center to emphasize their importance in the twenty-first century.

Source: Adapted from David Graddol, *The Future of English?* © 1997, 2000 by The British Council. Used with permission.

English as a Global Language

English is a global language for a number of reasons, but not because it is easier to learn than other languages or because it is more logical or more beautiful than other languages. Not only are these things not true of English, but also they are not reasons for any language to become a world language. English is a global language because of British and American colonialism, peaking at the end of the nineteenth century, because of the economic and political power of the United States throughout the twentieth century, and because, for a host of social, political, and economic reasons, English became the language of the industrial and technological revolution, giving it a social prestige that has also made it the language of international communication and entertainment.

Some features of English prove useful, given its current status as a global language. It has borrowed many words from other languages throughout its history, and it assimilates new ones with relative ease. Without grammatical gender or a complicated inflectional system, English can incorporate new words into its grammar as "regular" nouns, verbs, and so on. English also uses the Latin alphabet, which is relatively efficient and has been integral to most modern technological development. (The Chinese ideographic writing system may hinder the Chinese language from becoming more global than it is now, but it may not, and there are also alternative writing systems for Chinese.) But these features of English language are coincidental, rather than causal, to the use of English in countries around the world.

The current predominance of English in many international arenas encompasses more ground than we can cover in this text, but here are a few telling facts and statistics (selected from a more comprehensive list in Crystal 2003, 86–122):

- English is one of the five official languages of the United Nations (the others are French, Russian, Spanish, and Chinese), and one of the two official languages of the Olympics (the other is French). It is also an official or working language of the North Atlantic Treaty Organization (NATO), the European Union, the Organization of African Unity, and the Association of Southeast Asian Nations (ASEAN).
- English is the international language of the sea and of air safety control.
- In most academic fields, between 70 and over 90 percent of academic publications intended for an international audience are in English.

- According to the *Book of Lists* in 1977, the top five newspapers in the world were all in English: the *New York Times*, *Washington Post*, and *Wall Street Journal* from the United States; the *Times* and *Sunday Times* from Britain. Some English-language newspapers like the *International Herald-Tribune* and the *International Guardian* are designed for global circulation.

- In 2002, over 80 percent of all feature films released in theaters were in English, according to the *BFI Film and Television Handbook*.

- In the 1990s, over 95 percent of the top pop music groups or singers sang primarily in English.

- About 80 percent of the world's electronically stored information is in English, including information stored by private and public institutions and information on the Internet.

- In 2001, the United States was the leading tourism earner and spender.

These striking statistics make it obvious why English language teaching (ELT) is a booming industry. You can imagine why a nonnative speaker of English might want to learn the language. But what if we substituted a different language for "English" in all of the statistics above? How about China's Mandarin dialect? How would you react if you felt compelled to learn Mandarin in order to have access to all of this information, or to be able to participate in these conversations and cultural phenomena? The benefits and drawbacks of a global language aside, it puts the burden of learning on those who don't speak the language. Being a native English speaker in today's world automatically gives one many communicative privileges—and often social, economic, and educational privileges as well.

Not all of these statistics will remain stable, and the global status of English will potentially be rivaled by Spanish and Portuguese (which also had histories of linguistic imperialism and are used widely as a lingua franca in South America) and perhaps by Arabic and Chinese. The amount of academic publishing in English seems to be increasing in many fields. At the same time, the percentage of languages other than English on the Internet also seems to be rising. The number of Internet users around the globe is rising at a startling rate: there were about 1 million users in 1990, 40 million in 1995, and 544 million in 2002 (Crystal 2003, 119); statistics for 2010 suggest there are now over 1.5 billion users. Some forecasts predict that only 60 percent of Internet content will be in English within the next decade. The Internet was created in the United States, and the script is based on a Latin alphabet, but programmers are quickly figuring out ways to represent other alphabets on the Web; in 2009, ICANN (the Internet Corporation for Assigned Names and Numbers) decided to allow non-Latin characters in domain names. And the Internet offers speakers of minority languages an inexpensive and easy way to promote and maintain their languages. Bollywood blockbuster hits in Hindi have decisively beaten Hollywood hits in the Indian market. And hip hop has sprung up in Arabic, French, Cantonese, and other languages. Some statistics indicate that the Arabic Al Jazeera channel has as many viewers around the world as the BBC, but English Al Jazeera, launched in 2006, may have more viewers than either.

The question may not be whether any one language will "win" the global-language game, but rather whether other languages can coexist with a global language in such a way that communities can maintain their identities while benefiting from all that knowledge a global language offers.

World Englishes

As English spreads around the world, new varieties of English are born. All over the world, speakers adapt the language, given their other native languages. Each variety changes in slightly different ways over time, and speakers maintain these different varieties as markers of identity. Linguist Tom McArthur (2006) argues that we need to talk about the family of English languages in the same way we refer to the Germanic, Slavic, or Romance languages.

In the inner circle, for example, countries have developed their own distinctive varieties of English over time. British and American English are clearly different not only phonologically but also lexically and grammatically. The same is true of Irish English, Scottish English, Australian English, New Zealand English, and Canadian English. All of these varieties are, for the most part, mutually intelligible, and each serves as the standard for English education in the particular country. Because of settlement patterns, varieties such as Australian and New Zealand English are more closely related than Canadian or American English to British English: Australia, for example, was settled by English speakers as a British penal colony starting at the end of the eighteenth century. Here are a few of the differences within the inner circle:

Phonological Differences among Inner-Circle Varieties of English

- The /w/~/ʍ/ contrast: Irish English and Scottish English maintain this distinction; most varieties of British and American English have lost the distinction.
- Rhoticity: British RP English and Australian and New Zealand English are non-rhotic; /r/ is typically realized as a flap in Scottish English, and as [ɹ] in Irish and North American English.
- Canadian Raising: In Canadian English, the onset of the diphthongs [ɑɪ] and [ɑʊ] is raised to [ʌɪ] and [ʌʊ] before voiceless consonants; thus, words like *sight* and *side*, *bout* and *bowed* have contrastive vowels, which is not true of most varieties of U.S. English. (Or historically the onset never lowered.)
- Scottish English does not maintain the RP distinctions between the vowels /æ/ and /ɑ/ or between /ʊ/ and /u:/.

Grammatical Differences among Inner-Circle Varieties of English

- In Scottish English, the verb *need* can take the past participle as an object, like some varieties of U.S. English (e.g., "My hair needs washed").
- Northern British English allows the construction "Joe gave it me," whereas Northern American, Australian, and New Zealand English do not.
- Welsh English uses negative *too* (as opposed to *either*): "I don't have one too."
- *Do-* substitution works differently in British and North American English such that British English allows "Did you do your homework? Yes, I did do," whereas Northern American English would employ "Yes, I did."

The lexical differences include well-known examples such as *flat* and *biscuit* (British) versus *apartment* and *cookie* (United States) and *goodday* (Australian) versus *hello* (United States/British). Less well-known examples are *to farewell* (New Zealand) and *to barrack for* 'to support' (Australian).

The distinctive variety of English in outer-circle countries is usually influenced by the other native languages spoken in the country. For example, Indian English is a syllable-timed language because native languages like Hindi are syllable-timed (American and British English are stress-timed). Singaporean English uses the pragmatic particle *lah*, which may come from Malay, Hokkien, or Cantonese—other native languages spoken in the country. Many World Englishes do not use forms of *to be* in constructions such as "You (are) terrific," given that many other languages in the world do not require a copula here. And all World Englishes incorporate substantial amounts of loanwords from the other languages spoken in the country.

Let's take Singaporean English as a brief example. Singapore has four official languages: English, Mandarin Chinese, Tamil, and Malay. Despite the government's concerted efforts to promote only Standard (primarily British) English, including the Speak Good English Campaign launched in 2000, the local variety of English, sometimes called Singlish, continues to flourish. Here are a few systematic, grammatical features that distinguish Singaporean English from other varieties of English (Trudgill and Hannah 1994, 136):

Singaporean English

- Some mass nouns are treated as count nouns: for example, *luggages, furnitures.*

- The verb *use to* can indicate habitual activity in the present tense: *I use to go shopping on Mondays* 'I usually go shopping on Mondays'.

- The form *would* is often used for *will*: *We hope you would come tomorrow.*

- Variable tag questions are often replaced by the invariable tag *is it?/isn't it?*: *He is going to buy a car, isn't it?*

- Another tag question is *can or not*: *She wants to go, can or not?* 'Can she go (or not)?'

- The indefinite article is not always used as it is in other varieties: *He is teacher.*

Singaporean English is also full of loanwords from other local languages and it has its own slang ("talking cock" in Singlish), some of which involves calques (loan translations), such as *catch no ball* ('to not understand') from Hokkien *liah boh kiew*, and local idioms: for example, in Singlish, *chiak kantang* (literally 'eat potatoes' from Hokkien *chiak* and Malay *kentang*) means 'to affect a Western accent'. Singlish has a vibrant presence on the Web at talkingcock.com, and it now has its own dictionary, *The Coxford Singlish Dictionary*, derived from the Web site. When the "Save Our Singlish Campaign" was launched by TalkingCock in 2002, founder Colin Goh emphasized that the campaign was not designed to undermine standard varieties. He continued, "Why we're fighting for Singlish, is because it's simply a part of our culture. In fact, it may be the ONLY thing that makes us uniquely Singaporean. It mixes all the various languages, which to me, seems to spread multi-cultural understanding. I thought this was something to be proud of."

In the expanding-circle countries, where the teaching of English takes on a special priority in the educational system, American and British English now compete as the main "target" variety. Historically, British English has long been the primary language of ESL instruction around the world. But the influence of the U.S. economy, government, technology, and entertainment industry has made American English an ever more popular option for English learners in other countries who seek advancement and opportunities through learning English.

The Future of English as a Global Language

The presence of English in outer-circle and expanding-circle countries is not always uncontested. The desire for a shared language (sometimes within the country as well as internationally) and the desire for the opportunities available for speakers of English can compete with the desire to maintain more local identities and, therefore, languages. The debate about the use and status of English in Kenya, for example, has been lively and captures many of the concerns shared by other countries in the expanding (and outer) circle. Kenya was a British colony from 1920 to 1963. English was made the country's official language when it became independent in 1963, but Swahili replaced it as the official language in 1974. In 1986, Ngũgĩ wa Thiong'o wrote:

> We African writers are bound by our calling to do for our languages what Spenser, Milton and Shakespeare did for English; what Pushkin and Tolstoy did for Russian; indeed what all writers in world history have done for their languages by meeting the challenge of creating a literature in them, which process later opens the languages for philosophy, science, technology and all the other areas of human creative endeavors. (qtd. in Bailey 1991, 164–65)

Not all African writers agree, however. Harry Mashabela, a South African, wrote in 1983:

> But learning and using English will not only give us the much-needed unifying chord but will also land us into the exciting world of ideas; it will enable us to keep company with kings in the world of ideas and also make it possible for us to share the experiences of our own brothers in the world: men such as black Americans W. E. Burghardt DuBois, Ralph Ellison, James Baldwin, Richard Wright, Langston Hughes; Chinua Achebe of Nigeria, Ghana's Ayi Kwei Armah. (qtd. in Bailey 1991, 164)

Writer Chinua Achebe has spoken publicly about his mixed feelings toward the perceived "universality" of English as a world language.

Chinua Achebe expressed mixed feelings about English. In 1964 he wrote:

> The price a world language must be prepared to pay is submission to many different kinds of use. The African writer should aim to use English in a way that brings out his message best without altering the language to the extent that its value as a medium of international exchange will be lost. He should aim at fashioning out an English which is at once universal and able to carry his peculiar experience. . . . I feel that the English language will be able to carry the weight of my African experience. But it will have to be a new English, still in full communion with its ancestral home but altered to suit its new African surroundings. (qtd. in Bailey 1991, 170)

Ten years later, however, he stated: "[T]he fatalistic logic of the unassailable position of English in our literature leaves me more cold now than it did when I first spoke about it in the auditorium of the University of Ghana" (qtd. in Bailey 1991, 171). English certainly offers opportunities for wider readership and shared conversation, as well as perhaps unity in countries with multiple local languages, but what gets lost?

This debate raises the important question of whether the use of English as a global language and the maintenance of native languages and multilingualism are truly at odds. In other words, does a global language require or necessarily result in the reduction of local languages? It is certainly a concern: some estimates predict that over the next one hundred years, 50–80 percent of the world's 5,000–6,000 languages will become extinct. But is this the result of the spread of English or of other more local languages? There are clear benefits to having a global language. It facilitates communication in all arenas, including politics, technology, medicine, entertainment. Right now, it opens opportunities for speakers of other languages that might not otherwise be available. There are also clear benefits to maintaining languages other than English. They are fundamental to the world's cultures and these speakers' identities. They capture a perspective on the world and a history that is lost when these languages are lost.

A true global language may well be in our future. Global multilingualism will also probably continue in the future. If English continues to be the global language, what will it look like? It may be American English with many decades of change in it, or it may be another variety of World English that becomes dominant for political, economic, or social reasons. Or perhaps we will develop what Crystal calls the World Standard Spoken English (WSSE), a variety of English separate from all national varieties.

What Happens after Modern English?

The history of English is typically broken down into four major periods with approximate dates: Old English (449–1066), Middle English (1066–1476), Early Modern English (1476–1776), and Modern English (1776–Present). These divisions are, of course, artificial and created in retrospect, to correspond to a specific historical event that was critical to the development of the language: the Norman Conquest, the introduction of the printing press to England, and the Declaration of Independence. Nothing dramatic happened to the language in 1066 or 1476—speakers spoke the same way they had the day before. Only in retrospect can historians frame these moments as turning points for the development of the language. And in some histories of English, the dates are rounded up to century or half-century dates (e.g., 1100, 1500) to deemphasize one specific historical event.

When will Modern English end? And what will it be called? Postmodern English? Late Modern English? New Millennium English?

There is some chance that the end of the twentieth century will be framed, many years from now, as an important transition period in the history of English, given the power of new technologies like the computer and the Internet and the effect of these technologies on English. The printing press, whose introduction to England in 1476 is now used as the artificial divide between Middle English and Early Modern English, revolutionized notions of text and authorship, changed the face of literacy, and allowed for more pervasive standardization of the written language, among many other things. There are many parallels to be drawn between the printing press and the Internet (or even computers more generally). The Internet is currently destabilizing our notion of text and its permanence, as well as our notion of authorship. It has already created an entirely new kind of literacy. It has widened the range and speed of written communication beyond what could be imagined with printed text. And it has the potential to change the standards of written English—whichever world variety of English this standard turns out to be.

Perhaps later historians will decide that the year 2000 makes a neat break between eras, or perhaps the 1970s with the invention of the Internet. It may be described as a moment when the concept of written communication was revolutionized, when English—both spoken and written—spread around the globe along telephone wires and cable lines, and when World Englishes had become world presences to be taken seriously. Later generations will perhaps wonder what it was like to live at this moment in time, to experience this revolution in the language—forgetting that we rarely recognize history when we are experiencing it. We were too busy trying to figure out what that new acronym in an e-mail meant, or how to get that pop-up to disappear from the computer screen, to fully realize the implications of the Internet—the technology that allowed the e-mail to be sent and the pop–up to pop up—for the future direction of the English language.

English and Electronically Mediated Communication

Electronically mediated communication, which includes computer-based tools such as e-mail, IM, and chatting as well as texting, is revolutionizing many aspects of our lives as well as our speech. We can *e-mail* and *text* our friends around the world; we can take classes, find information, and shop *online*, as we *point* and *click* on the *Web sites* of

---

Language Change at Work

Retronymy and Reduplication

Innovations in technology sometimes require us as speakers to be more specific in our references to older items. For example, we now specify *regular mail* or *snail mail* to distinguish that form of mail from *e-mail*. Other examples include: *hard-cover book* once we had *paperbacks*; *landline* or *home phone* once there were *cell phones*; *day game* once most baseball games moved to the evening; *tap water* once there was *bottled water* and *sparkling water*. This process is called *retronymy*: the creation of a new word because the existing term, which could once be used alone, requires modification to be distinguished from a new development.

English speakers have come up with another innovation in word formation for specifying reference, among other functions.

A recent form of reduplication in English (dating back, scholars think, to the 1960s) results in sentences such as: "It's not a *job job*, but it earns me some extra cash." This repetition of a word or phrase can serve at least three different functions:

- For emphasis: "She is *blonde blonde*."
- To identify the prototypical meaning of a word as opposed to less prototypical meanings: "Did you buy a *car car* or an SUV?"
- To specify a stronger or more extreme meaning, sometimes when talking in euphemisms: "Did you get *sick sick*?" (meaning "Did you throw up?"); "Did you *sleep together sleep together* or just sleep together?"

innumerable *dot-coms* and spend hour upon hour *surfing* the *Web*. And as the previous sentence makes clear, electronic communication is also having an impact on the English language—and not just on the lexicon. But when we talk the Internet and texting revolution, it is important to remember that many speakers of English and lots of other languages do not have access to literacy, let alone computers and the Internet; more people (over 4 billion) have access to cell phones, but certainly not all. It does not mean the Internet and texting revolution isn't happening, but it does not affect all speakers at the same time in the same way.

When the American Dialect Society (ADS) held its annual vote for Word of the Year in 2000, the winner was *Y2K*. In addition, the members voted on the Word of the Decade (*web*), Word of the Century (*jazz*), and Word of the Millennium (*she*). The word *web* won the honor of being named Word of the Decade, both because it has become a central term in how we talk about the Internet revolution and because it captured the theme of many Word of the Year votes in the 1990s. *Dot-com* won Most Useful Word and Word Most Likely to Succeed in 2000, beating out *portal* and *e-tail*. The Word of the Year in 1997 was *e-* (ADS is open to considering bound morphemes for the honor in addition to free-standing words). The 1999 Most Creative Word was *multislacking* (the act of having multiple windows open simultaneously so that you can appear to be working when you are, in fact, surfing the Web). And *dot* (as in *dot-com*) won Most Useful Word in 1997. There have been other Web-related winners since 2000: for example, *phish* won Most Useful Word in 2004; *podcast* won Most Useful Word in 2005; *tweet* won Word of the Year in 2009; and the verb *to google* won Word of the Decade for whatever we call the decade from 2000–2009.

One of the oft-voiced concerns about e-mail and texting is that they are undermining all standards for written language. In fact, the Internet and texting have been accused of "ruining" the language. In the banter of e-mail and texting or on the Wall on a Facebook page, for example, writers sometimes abandon capitalization, allow misspellings to stand, employ bizarre abbreviations, write run-on sentences or fragments, and otherwise "wreak havoc" with standard conventions for written prose.

> hey! thinkin of u this am when i saw the nws on tv & blah blah re hotroom yoga the newest health craze, BUT THEN showed random yoga studio w/super sweaty ppl and yr boy he was in the shot. lol. hope your stayin warm ;-) ttyl, j

What is happening here?

Part of what is happening here, in addition to the nonstandard spellings, lack of capitalization, and use of abbreviations, is the mimicry of the spoken language in writing. Given that the speed and directness of much electronic communication resembles a phone conversation more than a letter, users are adapting the language to meet those purposes and this format. If you think about some of the general distinctions between speech and writing discussed in Chapter 2, it becomes clear that electronic communication sits somewhere in between. It often does not involve the typical delay between production and reception that characterizes most written texts. But the recipient is still usually not physically present, so some shared context, as well as the use of gestures and facial expressions, is lost. The easy "deletability" (a non-dictionary-sanctioned word as far as we know—you saw it in edited text here first!) of electronic communication can make it feel less permanent. In fact, though, more of it is stored than many users realize. And some of it—like other written work—is revisable. But the nature of the medium means that we often do not reread or edit before sending, or we are using programs like Instant Messenger (IM), where the messages are transmitted very rapidly in a conversation-like format.

> Julio86 (11:59:47 PM): how r u
> Jenny 1282 (12:00:03 AM): don't abbreviate! it drives me nuts
> Jenny 1282 (12:00:32 AM): i m fine. wat abt u? 4 real. g2g. 2 kewl.
> Julio86 (12:01:24 AM): haha. lol. dont be a weirdo
> Jenny 1282 (12:02:51 AM): okay, okay. I'm doing well—how are you doing?

That said, IM and text users have created new conventions to do things like correct a typo: in the next transmission use * or ^ and type the correct spelling. It is far from editorial chaos out there.

Almost all users of electronic communication are able to control multiple registers of discourse. In other words, they can style-shift from relatively formal electronic communication that resembles a formal letter or memo to very informal communication that could be described almost as "written chatting." These informal contexts are the most interesting to examine because here we see the written language trying to accomplish discourse functions in novel ways. But remember that lots of communication on the Internet, whether Web pages or e-mails, is not vastly different from the very familiar written language of the print world. And as the Internet grows ever more established, there is already a growing body of literature establishing the standard conventions of "netiquette," or how we should communicate properly and effectively in various electronic contexts.

Let's return to the informal e-mail message from "j" above. The informality of a lot of e-mail and texting has encouraged some users to abandon some conventions of written Standard English like capitalization (some will also argue that this speeds the act of typing) as well as conventions of the "letter genre" such as formal greetings, clear paragraph structure, and signatures. Users also worry less about perfect spelling, or using homonyms (e.g., *your* for *you're*)—but if you look again at the message, you will notice that at least half of the words follow standard spelling. It is common for users to represent their spoken pronunciations (e.g., *thinkin*) and to use more of their spoken syntax than adhere to the expectations of written syntax. What does this last point mean? As noted in Chapter 13, the Renaissance witnessed the development of a more syntactically complex prose style as the standard of eloquence, a hypotactic style. Due in large part to the influence of classical texts, various forms of subordination, ellipsis, and other complex clausal constructions came to flourish in written English prose. But we often speak in conjoined clauses and simpler subordinated clauses that constitute, when strung together one after the next, what would be called "run-on" sentences if we wrote them down. And write them down many people do when they are communicating in the less censored world of electronic communication.

Exactly what is happening to punctuation in these informal electronic communications is another interesting phenomenon. There is a widespread notion that punctuation in the written language corresponds to pauses in the spoken language. Although that sometimes is true, and historically it was more true, the set of conventions for proper punctuation is more complicated than a one-to-one correspondence with the timing of speech. For example, most style guides explain the distinction between a semicolon and period as a semantic one (the clauses connected by a semicolon are more closely related in terms of meaning than are clauses separated by a period). Although some commas certainly do correspond to pauses, not all of them do. For example, we are not supposed to put a comma between a subject and a verb in a conjoined construction where some speakers would naturally pause: *She read the long paragraph about punctuation* [PAUSE BUT NO COMMA] *and felt confused.* And we are supposed to use a comma, some say, after an introductory element where many speakers usually would not pause: *Quickly,* [COMMA BUT NOT NECESSARILY A PAUSE] *she returned to the beginning of the paragraph to begin reading it again.*

Conventions for punctuation were in flux for several centuries after printing, and it would not be entirely surprising to see them continue to shift because of forces such as Internet communication. Punctuation, at least theoretically, is designed to aid meaning and clarify potential ambiguity in written texts; it is possible that the demands placed on punctuation by e-mail and other electronic communication will change some of the conventions, at least in electronic registers. Some IM users deploy punctuation and other symbols to mark an action: for example, *banging my head against the wall* (in addition to * . . . *, some use / . . . / or :: . . . ::). If netiquette guides then codify these new conventions, they will not even seem like "bad punctuation."

E-mail, texting, and IM technologies have created a host of new acronyms, many of which are opaque to English speakers who are not regular informal e-mail, text, or IM users. Here are just a few of the more common abbreviations: *b4* 'before'; *bfd* 'big fucking deal'; *brb* 'be right back'; *cu* (*cya*) 'see you'; *cul* 'see you later'; *dk* 'don't know'; *f2f* 'face-to-face'; *imho* 'in my humble opinion'; *jk* 'just kidding'; *lol* 'laughing out loud'; *thx* (*tx*) 'thanks'; *ttyl* 'talk to you later'; *wrt* 'with respect to'.

Critics of IM and texting often overplay the number and opacity of abbreviations in electronic communication, to hype the argument that these new technologies are ruining English. Studies indicate that alphabetisms are much less common than these critics claim; and as David Crystal (2008) points out, the super-long acronyms critics sometimes cite (e.g., *ROTFLMAOWTIME* 'rolling on the floor laughing my ass off with tears in my eyes' and *iydkidkwd* 'if you don't know I don't know who does') appear infrequently in real electronic messages. It is not clever, clear, or time-saving to use abbreviations that your audience does not understand.

Emoticons (another blend inspired by electronic communication, this time of *emoti*onal + *icon*) are those smiling, winking, frowning, and otherwise "expressing" faces that sprinkle electronic messages. Many users think of emoticons as simply a cute device. Although they certainly are cute, they also serve a discourse function: they help create a context, much like a facial expression or a gesture, for a comment that might be ambiguous. In fact, the first emoticons :-) and :-(are believed to have been created in 1982 by computer science professor Scott Fahlman to help disambiguate jokes and non-jokes on an electronic university bulletin board, an innovation that had just come into use. So if you write, "You need to get over it," and you want to indicate that you are teasing rather than giving a command or a piece of serious advice, you might well add ;-) or :-). Abbreviations like *hhok*, *jk*, and *lol* can serve a similar function. They allow electronic communication users to worry less about complete clarity or disambiguation in their syntax, because the emoticons or abbreviations can capture some of the intended meaning. And emoticons aren't just for kids: in a survey of 40,000 Yahoo Messenger instant-message program users, more than half of the respondents over the age of 30 reported using emoticons at least once a day (Williams 2007).

The Web has also had the interesting effect of destabilizing written texts in a way that makes many inhabitants of the print world uncomfortable. Web pages can change

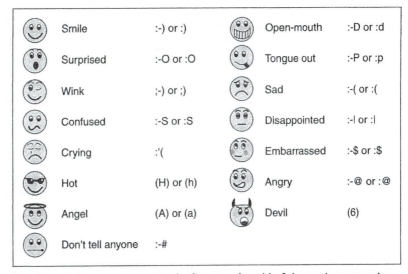

😊	Smile	:-) or :)	😁	Open-mouth	:-D or :d
😮	Surprised	:-O or :O	😛	Tongue out	:-P or :p
😉	Wink	;-) or ;)	☹	Sad	:-(or :(
😕	Confused	:-S or :S	😐	Disappointed	:-I or :I
😢	Crying	:'(	😳	Embarrassed	:-$ or :$
😎	Hot	(H) or (h)	😠	Angry	:-@ or :@
😇	Angel	(A) or (a)	😈	Devil	(6)
🤐	Don't tell anyone	:-#			

Emoticons help create context in the fast-paced world of electronic communication. If there is any ambiguity, a smiley or winky face can identify a joke as a joke.

from day to day in ways that books do not. And authorship, place of publication, and other predictable markers of credibility or authority are often less clear on the Internet.

It is, of course, very hard to know what effect the Internet and texting revolution will have on the future of the English language. Right now, it is allowing English to spread around the world in ways that would have been inconceivable only a few decades ago. It is facilitating electronic conversations among speakers in many countries who may have many different native languages but who often share English as a means of written communication. But other languages also have a foothold on the Internet, and language mixing on the Internet may well affect the future of English. In the shorter term, Internet and text users will probably continue to develop the lexicon and generic conventions that will characterize informal electronic communication. Although we like to think that we are unlimitedly creative, in fact we tend to create and function within genres. In this case, we are adapting the written conventions we know to create a recognizable way to communicate informally in a new written medium.

Electronically mediated communication is changing our notions of "literacy" and how we communicate in ways that we could never have envisioned even 50 years ago. It makes you realize how much could happen in the next 50 years. Or the next 450. What we can be sure of is that English, like all living languages, will continue to change, in both predictable and unpredictable ways. To bring the book full circle, let's return to the variation of *ask* and *aks* that we introduced you to in Chapter 1. *Aks* is the older form; *ask* is now the standard form. Will it remain that way? On an episode of *Futurama* (a cartoon, originally aired on the FOX television network, in which the main character, Frye, has been frozen until the year 3000), Frye has the following conversation, which predicts at least this part of the future of English:

Frye: You've never heard of Christmas? You know, x-m-a-s?

Leela: Oh, you mean "X-mas." You must be using an archaic pronunciation like "ask" instead of "aks."

Now that you know more about how English works, we hope that you will not only notice all the language variation and change around you in everyday written and spoken English, but also think about what it might mean for the future of English.

Suggested Readings

For more information about Modern English, consult the eminently readable *The American Language*, by H. L. Mencken (1962), including *Supplement One* and *Supplement Two*, as well as Richard W. Bailey's *Images of English* (1991) and *Nineteenth-Century English* (1996). Modern English's reliance on words from other languages, not to mention other language systems, is amply described in Allan Metcalf's *The World in So Many Words* (1996). The cutting edge is represented by David Crystal's *Txtng: The Gr8 Db8* (2008) and *Language and the Internet* (2nd ed., 2006), and Naomi Baron's *Alphabet to Email: How Written English Evolved and Where It's Headed* (2000) and *Always On: Language in an Online and Mobile World* (2008). The story of English punctuation is well described in Malcolm Parkes's *Pause and Effect* (1993) and in Geoffrey Nunberg's *The Linguistics of Punctuation* (1990). Together, Allen Walker Read's articles on *O.K.* are a masterwork of language scholarship; they are collected in *Milestones in the History of English in America* (2002).

For a succinct, balanced treatment of English as a world language, turn to David Crystal's *English as a Global Language* (2003). David Graddol provides useful statistics about the role of English around the world in *The Future of English?* (1997), and Richard W. Bailey captures many details of the debate about World English in *Images of English* (1991). The classic treatment of World Englishes is *English as a World Language* (1982) edited by Richard W. Bailey and Manfred Görlach; for more recent linguistic treatments of many World Englishes, including in some cases sound files, we recommend: *The Handbook of World Englishes* (2006), edited by Braj Kachru, Yamuna Kachru, and Cecil Nelson; and *World Englishes: A Handbook of Varieties of English: A Multimedia Reference Tool* (2004), edited by Edgar Schneider and Bernd Kortmann. Dennis Baron's *The English-Only Question: An Official Language for Americans?* (1990) and *Language Loyalties: A Source Book on the Official English Controversy* (1992), edited by James Crawford, provide perspectives on the English Only movement. Baron's article "The Legendary English-Only Vote of 1795" is available at: http://www.pbs.org/speak/seatosea/officialamerican/englishonly.

Exercises
Exercise 14.1   English and the Media

1. Follow the headlines in a major newspaper for a few days. First, list the shortened forms that you find, both abbreviations and more colloquial expressions that may be standing in for longer, more formal terms. Then look at the morphology and syntax of the headlines. In what ways do they stretch, if not break, the rules of Standard English?

2. Find ten examples of print advertisements, billboards, and other forms of advertising and copy down the text. Do you find evidence here for how advertising copy can

stretch, if not break, the rules of Standard English, in terms of both vocabulary and grammar? Explain.

Exercise 14.2   English Punctuation

Examine closely the punctuation in three texts: the two excerpts we provide below and, for the third text, any paragraph(s) of approximately equal length in this textbook. Describe, in detail, the differences in punctuation conventions among the three. Then decide if there are any punctuation conventions from the two earlier texts that you think are preferable to modern conventions and explain why. In both earlier texts, spelling characters have been modernized and abbreviations for *the* and the doubled *n* expanded.

Passage 1

Now this Good-fellow (not
enduring to looke upon a bad face, but his owne, especially
when he is Cup-shot) called aloude to her, Doe you heare
Witch, looke tother waies, I cannot abide a nose of that fa
shion, or else turne your face the wrong side outward, it may
look like raw flesh for flyes to blow maggots in. Stil as the
Witch was ready to reply, hee would crosse her with one
scurvy Jest, & between every Jest drinke to her, yet sweare,
God dam him; she would starve ere she should have a drop
on't, since the pot was sweet hee'd keepe it so, for should but
her lips once looke into the lid on't, her breath's so strong, &
would so stick in the cup; that al the water that runs by Ware
would not wash it out again. At last, the witch got so much
time to cal to him, Doest thou heare good friend (quoth she?)
What sayst thou ill face (quoth he?) Mary I say (quoth she)
that thou throwst in they drink apace, but shall not find it so
easie coming out. Nay, as for the comming out (answerd
the fellow) I throwd it in above, & it schal come out beneath,
& then thou shalt have some of it, if thou wilt, because I am
in hope it will poyson thee.

—From "How the Witch Served a Fellow in an Alehouse," the concluding story
in a pamphlet called *The Most Cruell and Bloody Murder* (1606)

Passage 2

Thus the pronunciation of our language, tho' the most important and difficult part of grammar, is *left* to parents and nurses—to ignorance and caprice—to custom, accident or nothing—Nay to something worse, to coxcombs, who have a large share in directing the *polite taste* of pronunciation, which of course is as vicious as that of any other class of people. And while this is the case, every person will claim a right to pronounce most agreably to his own fancy, and the language will be exposed to perpetual fluctuation.

This consideration gave rise to the following little system, which is designed to introduce uniformity and accuracy of pronunciation into common schools. It cost me much labour to form a plan that should be both *simple* and *accurate*.

The one here adopted seems to unite these two articles; at least so far as to prevent any material errours. A more accurate method might have been invented; but it must have been too complicated to be useful. The rules for ascertaining a just pronunciation are so simple and concise, that I flatter myself they fall within the comprehension of the most indifferent capacity. Some may possibly be too indolent to study them; and others, from a principle of self-sufficiency, may affect to despise them. The former will be modest enough neither to approve nor condemn what they deem beneath their attention; and I would inform the latter that after I had devoted nine years to the acquisition of knowledge, three or four of which were spent in studying languages, and about the same period in teaching the English, I was astonished to find myself a stranger to its principal beauties and most obvious faults. Those therefore who disdain this attempt to improve our language and assist the instructors of youth, must be either much more or much less acquainted with the language than I am. The criticisms of those who know more, will be received with gratitude; the censure or ridicule of those who know less, will be inexcusable.

—From Noah Webster's *A Grammatical Institute of the English Language* (1783)

Exercise 14.3   English and the Internet

1. Print out an IM (Instant Messenger) conversation, either from your own experience or from someone you know who IMs. Look back at the material in Chapter 8 about the structure of conversation. Then describe how the turn-taking and the turns themselves in the IM conversation resemble spoken conversation and how they differ. What do you think accounts for the differences and for the similarities?

2. Create a list of ten etiquette rules for IM. Then compare your list with your classmates' lists. How many of the rules do you share? What are the implications for critics' claim that IM (and texting) are "wreaking havoc" on the English language?

3. Find a blog that you think is doing interesting things with the English language as it is written down. Provide three examples of language that stretches conventions or surprises you in each of the following categories: words, meanings of words and phrases, morphology (e.g., prefixes and suffixes), and syntactic patterns. How do these examples resemble or differ from spoken American English?

4. The Internet opens new venues for the promotion of minority languages, dying languages, dead languages, artificial languages, and more. Choose a language that you are interested in that falls into one of these categories (e.g., Manx, Cornish, Latin, Esperanto, Klingon) and explore the resources that are now available for that language on the Web. Describe your findings and speculate about their implications for the vitality of this language.

Exercise 14.4   World English(es)

Here is the scenario: This textbook is being revised for a fourth edition and the editors are debating whether the subsection in this chapter currently titled "World Englishes" would be more appropriately titled "World English," given the material in the chapter on English as a global language. The editors have e-mailed you, as a user of the book, to get your informed opinion about which would be a more appropriate title. Compose a response that provides detailed justification of why you think one title is more appropriate than the other.

Glossary

ablaut Change in vowel sound that indicates tense in English "strong verbs," as in *sing*, *sang*, *sung*.

abstract Short introductory summary of what happened or an overview statement that captures the interest of a NARRATIVE. See also CODA, COMPLICATING ACTION, EVALUATION, ORIENTATION, and RESOLUTION.

accent Systematic phonological variation among DIALECTS.

accentual-syllabic meter Patterned distribution of stress and SYLLABLES into poetic feet; according to traditional poetics, most English poetry employs accentual-syllabic meter. See also FOOT, METER, PURE ACCENTUAL METER, PURE SYLLABIC METER, RHYTHM, and SCANSION.

acoustic phonetics Study of sound in language focused on how sound is transmitted. See also ARTICULATORY PHONETICS and AUDITORY PHONETICS.

acrolect CREOLE that closely resembles its LEXIFIER LANGUAGE, that is, exhibits relatively few creole features. See also BASILECT and MESOLECT.

acronym Result of a word-formative process in which the initial sounds of a phrase or compound name make a word, as in *scuba* from *s*(elf)-*c*(ontained) *u*(nderwater) *b*(reathing) *a*(pparatus); the process by which such words are made is **acronymy**.

adjacency pairs In DISCOURSE, UTTERANCES (like questions, requests, or invitations) that require a response together with the response: "I'm going to the movies. Do you want to go with?" "Yeah." The invitation and its response are adjacent (that is, immediately next to each other) in the conversation.

adjectival Any CONSTITUENT that modifies a NOUN or noun phrase. See also ADVERBIAL and NOMINAL.

adjective Word that modifies (limits, qualifies, or specifies) a NOUN; also, a LEXICAL CATEGORY that includes such words. See also ADJECTIVAL.

adverb Word that modifies (limits, qualifies, or specifies) either a VERB or an ADJECTIVE or another ADVERB; also, a LEXICAL CATEGORY including such words. A CLAUSE with an adverb or adverbial phrase at its head is called an **adverbial clause**. See also ADVERBIAL, DISCOURSE ADVERB, MANNER ADVERB, SENTENCE ADVERB, and TEMPORAL ADVERB.

adverbial Any CONSTITUENT that functions as any kind of ADVERB, including DISCOURSE or SENTENCE ADVERBS. See also ADJECTIVAL and NOMINAL.

affix BOUND MORPHEME that precedes a base (a PREFIX, such as *pre-*, *suf-*, or *in-*), follows a base (a SUFFIX, such as *-s* to form plurals or *-y* to form adjectives from nouns, verbs, or other adjectives), or is inserted into a base or MATRIX (an INFIX, such as *-freaking-* in *unfreakingbelievable*). The process of forming a word with an affix is called **affixing** or **affixation**.

affricate Speech sound composed of a STOP followed by a FRICATIVE, for instance, the initial sound in *chatter*. See also NASAL and OBSTRUENT.

agglutinative language A language in which words are formed from various linguistic elements, often representing different LEXICAL CATEGORIES, so that individual words approximate what, in English, would be considered a sentence. See also ANALYTIC LANGUAGE and SYNTHETIC LANGUAGE.

alliteration   Repetition of sounds or groups of sounds (usually, but not always, word-initial sounds) in successive words, as in the phrases "coordinating conjunction" and "past participle." See also ASSONANCE and CONSONANCE.

allomorph   Any variant of a MORPHEME; for instance, the morpheme [PLURAL] is realized in English as several allomorphs: *-s* (as in dog*s*), *-es* (as in hors*es*), *-en* (as in ox*en*), and zero-plural, when the plural form is the same as the singular (as in *deer*).

allophone   Any variant of a PHONEME; for instance, *perhaps* realizes two allophones of the phoneme /p/, one aspirated (the initial one), the other not.

alphabetism   Word formed from the first letters of words in a phrase or compound name, as in *FBI* for *F*(ederal) *B*(ureau of) *I*(nvestigation) or *ACLU* for *A*(merican) *C*(ivil) *L*(iberties) *U*(nion); also, the word-formative process that results in such a word. Also called INITIALISM.

alternation   Switching between grammatical structures of two languages. See also CODE-SWITCHING, CONGRUENT LEXICALIZATION, and INSERTION.

alveolar ridge   Tissue above the upper teeth where the tongue rests to produce certain sounds, such as [z]. A sound thus produced is called an **alveolar**.

amelioration   Semantic process by which a word means something "better" than it had at an earlier stage of its history; for instance, *knight* once simply meant 'boy, servant', but now indicates someone of a relatively high social rank. See also DYSPHEMISM, EUPHEMISM, PEJORATION, and REAPPROPRIATION.

analogical mapping   Projection of meaning from one semantic domain into another, as when the term *virus* extends from human disease to computer malfunction; analogical mapping operates in many SEMANTIC SHIFTS.

analogy   Linguistic process by which the less usual is drawn to resemble the usual; for instance, in the sixteenth century, *pea* was invented as a singular form to replace historical singular *peas*, because, generally, English plurals are formed with the suffix *-s*.

analytic language   A language in which word order, rather than inflection, mostly indicates grammatical functions in a sentence, and in which auxiliary words (PREPOSITIONS, AUXILIARY VERBS, etc.) partially or wholly replace inflections. See also AGGLUTINATIVE LANGUAGE and SYNTHETIC LANGUAGE.

anaphora   Repetition of a word or phrase within a sentence or, especially, among lines of a poem.

anaphoric reference   Within NARRATIVE, reference to something previously indicated; in "Let me tell you about fish. They lead boring lives," *They* refers to the *fish* mentioned in the previous sentence. See also CATAPHORIC REFERENCE, COMPARATIVE REFERENCE, DEMONSTRATIVE REFERENCE, ENDOPHORIC REFERENCE, EXOPHORIC REFERENCE, and PERSONAL REFERENCE.

anticipation   Verbal slip in which a later sound accidentally also occurs earlier than it should in a word or phrase, as in *wish a brush* for *with a brush*. See also MALAPROPISM, PRESERVATION, and SPOONERISM.

antonyms   Pair of words each member of which means the opposite of the other, such as *good* and *evil*. The semantic relationship of such words is **antonymy**. See also COMPLEMENTARY ANTONYMS, CONVERSENESS, GRADABLE ANTONYMS, and NONGRADABLE ANTONYMS.

aphasia   Partial or total inability either to convey ideas in language or to understand language, as a result of damage to the brain, whether from injury or disease.

applied linguistics   A branch of linguistics that applies linguistic theory to real-world problems, in areas such as language policy, education, and speech pathology.

approximant   Sound made by restricting but not blocking the vocal tract, such as /r/ or /j/. See also BUNCHED /r/, GLIDE, LATERAL LIQUID, LIQUID, and RETROFLEX LIQUID.

articulator   Organ a speaker employs to produce and distinguish certain speech sounds; those a speaker moves, like tongue and lips, are called **active articulators**, whereas those a speaker cannot move, like the hard and soft PALATES, are called **passive articulators**.

articulatory phonetics   Study of sound in language focused on how speakers produce it. See also ACOUSTIC PHONETICS and AUDITORY PHONETICS.

aspect   Category of VERB meaning that indicates whether, for instance, an action is in progress or completed, momentary or habitual, etc. See also MOOD and TENSE.

assertive   ILLOCUTIONARY ACT that represents a state of affairs, characterized, for instance, by stating, claiming, insisting, suggesting, etc. Assertives are also called REPRESENTATIVES. See also COMMISSIVE, DECLARATION, DIRECTIVE, EXPRESSIVE, and VERDICTIVE.

assimilation   Phonological process in which a sound changes to resemble a nearby sound, as when *in-* 'not' becomes *im-* in *impossible*.

assonance   ALLITERATION in which the repeated sound is a VOWEL. See also CONSONANCE.

attributive   ADJECTIVE or NOUN that describes a quality or characteristic of a noun and modifies that noun directly, as opposed to a PREDICATIVE. *Attributive* is also used as an adjective, as in the phrase *attributive noun*.

auditory phonetics   Study of sound in language focused on how people perceive it. See also ACOUSTIC PHONETICS and ARTICULATORY PHONETICS.

auxiliary verb   VERB used in combination with another verb to indicate TENSE, MOOD, or ASPECT of that other verb; in English, *will, may*, etc., are auxiliary verbs. See also DEONTIC MODAL AUXILIARY, EPISTEMIC MODAL AUXILIARY, and MODAL AUXILIARY.

back-channeling   In conversation, any indication that a participant is paying attention; backchanneling may be verbal ("yeah" or "uh-huh" or "mmm") or nonverbal (as in head nodding). See also MINIMAL RESPONSE.

backformation   Word derived by loss of a supposed (but unhistorical) prefix or suffix from another word; for instance, the verb *backform* is a backformation of *backformation*, as are the verbs *burgle* from *burglar* and *edit* from *editor*. *Backformation* is the name of the wordformative process, as well as the derived form. See also INNOVATIVE CLIPPING.

backness   DISTINCTIVE FEATURE of VOWELS realized when the tongue is placed toward the back of the mouth. See also BACK VOWEL, FRONTNESS, HEIGHT, LAXNESS, and TENSENESS.

back vowel   VOWEL sound produced when the tongue is placed toward the back of the mouth, such as the vowels in *put* and *bought*. See also CENTRAL VOWEL and FRONT VOWEL.

bare infinitive   NONFINITE form of a VERB that serves as the base for inflectional development or expresses the core meaning of a verb, without concern for NUMBER or PERSON. See also INFINITIVE.

basilect   CREOLE strongly marked against its LEXIFIER LANGUAGE, that is, one with extensive creole features. See also ACROLECT and MESOLECT.

blend   Word that combines two or more words, at least one of which is CLIPPED; for instance, *smog* is a blend of *sm*(oke) and (f)*og*. The relevant word-formative process is **blending**.

borrowing   1: Word adopted, adapted, or literally translated from another language. 2: The word-formative process that produces such a word. See also CALQUE and LOAN TRANSLATION. 3: Process in which dialectal vocabulary is enriched by contact languages. See also COINING, LANGUAGE CONTACT, NATURALLY OCCURING INTERNAL LANGUAGE CHANGE, RETENTION, SOCIAL FACTOR, and STRUCTURAL INFLUENCE.

bound morpheme   MORPHEME used only when attached to a morpheme that can be used independently; AFFIXES are bound morphemes. See also FREE MORPHEME.

branch   In a PHRASE, CLAUSE, or SENTENCE structure TREE, the line drawn from one CONSTITUENT level to another, in order to indicate syntactic hierarchy. See also NODE.

Broca's aphasia   APHASIA caused by damage to BROCA'S AREA, because of which a speaker finds it difficult, if not impossible, to form comprehensible sentences. See also WERNICKE'S APHASIA.

Broca's area   Area in the CORTEX at the LEFT HEMISPHERE of the brain partly responsible for language production. See also WERNICKE'S AREA.

bunched /r/   ALLOPHONE of /r/ produced when the tongue is tense and placed toward the roof of the mouth. See also APPROXIMANT, GLIDE, LATERAL LIQUID, LIQUID, and RETROFLEX LIQUID.

caesura   Pause inserted into the metrical structure of a line of poetry.

calque   Word translated literally when borrowed from one language into another, such as *cover* 'table setting' from French *couvert*. See also LOAN TRANSLATION.

case   Quality of a NOUN, PRONOUN, ADJECTIVE, PARTICIPLE, or DETERMINER that indicates syntactic FUNCTION; for instance, a noun may take the SUBJECT, DIRECT OBJECT, INDIRECT OBJECT, or possessive case, depending on how it is used in a sentence (if you have studied a classical language, you may be familiar with older terms for these cases, such as *nominative*, *accusative*, *dative*, and *genitive*).

cataphoric reference   Within NARRATIVE, reference to something subsequently indicated; in "It's a boring life. Fish need useful employment or, at least, hobbies to occupy their spare time," *It* refers to a fish's life of spare time. See also ANAPHORIC REFERENCE, COMPARATIVE REFERENCE, DEMONSTRATIVE REFERENCE, ENDOPHORIC REFERENCE, EXOPHORIC REFERENCE, and PERSONAL REFERENCE.

CDA   ALPHABETISM for CRITICAL DISCOURSE ANALYSIS.

central vowel   Most common VOWEL in English, formed in the center of the mouth, as in *but* and the first syllable of *about*; IPA represents the central vowel differently when it appears in stressed syllables and unstressed syllables—in stressed syllables it is indicated by a ʌ (wedge) and in unstressed syllables by a ə (schwa). See also BACK VOWEL and FRONT VOWEL.

change from above   Development of language above the level of consciousness, that is, as a result of deliberate choices on the parts of speakers. See also CHANGE FROM BELOW.

change from below   Development of language below the level of consciousness, that is, when speakers are unaware of their own speech and its place in language change. See also CHANGE FROM ABOVE.

clause   Syntactic structure composed of a subject and a predicate. See also COMPLEX SENTENCE, COMPOUND SENTENCE, MAIN CLAUSE, SENTENCE, and SUBORDINATE CLAUSE.

clipping   Word shortened from a larger one, generally at its primary morphemic boundary, such as *taxi* from *taxicab*. Also the word-formative process that produces such a word. See also BACKFORMATION, FORECLIPPING, HINDCLIPPING, and INNOVATIVE CLIPPING.

clitic   Reduced form of a word (usually an AUXILIARY VERB in an unstressed position) that attaches to another, as in contractions like *I'll* and *what's*, so that the combination is pronounced as one word, even though both elements retain independent syntactic functions. See also ENCLITIC and PROCLITIC.

closed morphological class   LEXICAL CATEGORY in which new items rarely develop, such as CONJUNCTION, DETERMINER, and PREPOSITION. See also OPEN MORPHOLOGICAL CLASS.

coda   1: In PHONOLOGY, the optional, final PHONEME in a SYLLABLE; in *cot*, /t/ is the coda. See also NUCLEUS and ONSET. 2: In a NARRATIVE, a final summary or comment that may provide a moral or lesson or connect the narrative to the context in which it's told. See also ABSTRACT, COMPLICATING ACTION, EVALUATION, ORIENTATION, and RESOLUTION.

code-switching   Movement from one language to another (for instance, from Spanish to English) or from one variety of a language to another (for instance, from African American English to Standard English) depending on the social or linguistic situation. Also called **code-mixing**. See also STYLE-SHIFTING.

cognate   Word from one language that shares an ETYMON with a word from another language; for instance, English *fish* and French *pêche* are cognates, as they share an Indo-European etymon. It may be helpful to think of an etymon as a "parent" (or great-great-grandparent) word, a REFLEX as a "child" (or great-great-grandchild) word, and cognates as "cousin" words.

cohesion   Property of NARRATIVE in which a set of linguistic features (for instance, REFERENCE, ELLIPSIS, and CONJUNCTION, among others) connects sentences into a larger linguistic structure. See also SUBSTITUTION and LEXICAL COHESION.

coining   1: Word creation. 2: Process in which speakers enrich dialectal vocabulary by creating new words. See also BORROWING, LANGUAGE CONTACT, NATURALLY OCCURING INTERNAL LANGUAGE CHANGE, RETENTION, SOCIAL FACTOR, and STRUCTURAL INFLUENCE.

collocation   Arrangement of words into a PHRASE; combination of words that commonly co-occur as a phrase; such words are called **collocates**, and **collocate** is the related verb form.

combining form   BOUND MORPHEME abstracted from a word (like *-holic* from *alcoholic* or *-scape* from *landscape*) or shifted from FREE MORPHEME to bound status (like *-free* from *free*) that functions as a SUFFIX.

comma splice   Attempt to connect two INDEPENDENT CLAUSES with a comma but without a COORDINATING CONJUNCTION, generally perceived as a grammatical error.

commissive   ILLOCUTIONARY ACT that requires the speaker (the performer of the act) to do something, such as promise, threaten, intend, or refrain. See also ASSERTIVE, DECLARATION, DIRECTIVE, EXPRESSIVE, REPRESENTATIVE, and VERDICTIVE.

communicative competence   Ability, whether innate or learned, to communicate with language in conversation with other speakers.

community of practice   Group of speakers who share speech practices because they engage in a common enterprise. See also SPEECH COMMUNITY.

comparative adjective   Form of an adjective indicating that one item possesses a quality to a greater degree than another; for instance, grass can be *green*, but it can be even *greener* on the other side of the fence.

comparative reference   Use of COMPARATIVE ADJECTIVES, SUPERLATIVE ADJECTIVES, or other words that compare (such as *same*, *likewise*, *other*, or *such*) in order to promote COHESION in a NARRATIVE.

complement   PHRASE or CLAUSE that follows a VERB to complete a verb phrase.

complementary antonyms   Words with absolutely opposite meanings, such as *alive* and *dead* (either you're alive or you're dead), and no relative or intermediary ones, such as *half-alive* or *undead* (except in a fictional context). Complementary antonyms are also called NONGRADABLE ANTONYMS; by contrast, *old* and *young* are GRADABLE ANTONYMS. See also ANTONYMS and CONVERSENESS.

complementary distribution   Systematic organization of ALLOPHONES such that no two allophones of the same PHONEME occur in exactly the same environment.

complementizer   SUBORDINATE CONJUNCTION that serves as the head of a SUBORDINATE CLAUSE that functions as a NOMINAL. See also COMPLEMENTIZER CLAUSE.

complementizer clause   DEPENDENT CLAUSE that serves as a noun phrase, typically introduced by *that* or *wh-* words; in "We know what a complementizer clause is," *what a complementizer clause is* is the complementizer clause.

complex sentence   SENTENCE with one or more SUBORDINATE CLAUSES embedded within or appended to the MAIN CLAUSE. See also COMPOUND SENTENCE.

complicating action   Moment(s) in the ordering of a NARRATIVE when "something happens" or the situation changes. See also ABSTRACT, CODA, EVALUATION, ORIENTATION, and RESOLUTION.

compositionality   In SEMANTICS, the view that sentence meaning depends not only on the meanings of a sentence's parts, but also on how those parts are put together.

compound   Word in which two or more FREE MORPHEMES combine (without significant modification) into a single lexical item, for instance, when *blue* and *bird* combine to form *bluebird*. The word-formative process that produces such words is called **compounding**.

compound sentence   SENTENCE with two or more INDEPENDENT CLAUSES. See also CLAUSE and COMPLEX SENTENCE.

congruent lexicalization   Switching between lexical inventories of two language varieties that share grammatical structure. See also ALTERNATION, CODE-SWITCHING, and INSERTION.

conjugation   Process of distinguishing forms of a VERB that indicate TENSE, MOOD, voice (active or passive), ASPECT, person (first, second, or third), and NUMBER. The verb form is **conjugate**. See also DECLENSION.

conjunction   1: Word used to connect words, PHRASES, CLAUSES, or SENTENCES. 2: In NARRATIVE, use of ADVERBIALS, CONJUNCTIONS, or PREPOSITIONS to promote COHESION among sentences.

connotative meaning Lexical meaning that depends on linguistic and cognitive associations on the parts of speakers and hearers, rather than on relationship of a word to nonlinguistic things in the world. Also called **connotation**. See also DENOTATIVE MEANING.

consonance ALLITERATION in which the repeated sound is a CONSONANT. See also ASSONANCE.

consonant Speech sound produced by partial or total obstruction of air flow by one or more speech organs, like the tongue, lips, teeth, etc. See also DISTINCTIVE FEATURES and VOWEL.

constative speech act UTTERANCE that can be evaluated in terms of its TRUTH CONDITIONS. See also DIRECT SPEECH ACT, ILLOCUTIONARY ACT, INDIRECT SPEECH ACT, LOCUTIONARY ACT, PERLOCUTIONARY ACT, PRAGMATICS, SPEECH ACT, and SPEECH ACT THEORY.

constituency test Method for determining whether a linguistic unit is, in fact, a CONSTITUENT of some larger syntactic structure. See also COORDINATION TEST, MOVEMENT TEST, STAND ALONE TEST, and SUBSTITUTION TEST.

constituent Any component that functions as part of a larger linguistic structure; for instance, a DETERMINER or DET (for instance, *the*) and NOUN or N (for instance, *cat*) are constituents of the NOUN PHRASE or NP (*the cat*).

conversational floor Metaphorical area occupied by a person speaking in conversation, on which participants in the conversation take TURNS. See also EYE CONTACT, GESTURE, INTONATION, QUESTION, SILENCE, TURN, and TURN-TAKING VIOLATION.

conversational implicature Meaning that can be deduced from an utterance without its being explicitly stated; for instance, "Anne just pulled into the driveway" implies "Prepare to meet her at the door."

converseness Distinguishing property of a class of NONGRADABLE ANTONYMS that have dependent meanings, such as *sister/brother*, *parent/child*, and, proverbially, *apples/oranges*, though the latter are not actually **converse**. See also ANTONYMS, COMPLEMENTARY ANTONYMS, and GRADABLE ANTONYMS.

Cooperative Principle In conversation, the principle that participants will cooperate with one another, especially that they will observe the conversational maxims defined by H. P. Grice, namely the MAXIMS OF MANNER, MAXIMS OF QUALITY, MAXIMS OF QUANTITY, and MAXIMS OF RELATION.

coordinating conjunction CONJUNCTION used to indicate that the words, phrases, or clauses it connects are functionally equal.

Coordination Test CONSTITUENCY TEST in which one balances a linguistic unit with a coordinate unit (a unit of the same hierarchical value) in order to determine whether the original unit is a CONSTITUENT. See also MOVEMENT TEST, STAND ALONE TEST, and SUBSTITUTION TEST.

corpus Any collection of texts from which linguistic information can be extracted, but especially those collections designed and developed specifically for that purpose. The plural form of *corpus* is **corpora**.

corpus callosum Tissue that connects the brain's LEFT and RIGHT HEMISPHERES and allows them to communicate.

corpus linguistics Branch of linguistics concerned with the design, development, and use of CORPORA to study language.

correlative conjunction CONJUNCTION that expresses the equality or alternative value of elements within a syntactic structure; in "A correlative conjunction expresses either the equality of elements within a syntactic structure or their alternative value," *either* and *or* are correlative conjunctions that express alternative value.

cortex Layer of gray matter that covers the hemispheres of the brain.

countable nouns NOUNS that can be counted; for instance, *noun* is a countable noun ("There are one hundred nouns on this page") but *linguistics* is not (*"There are one hundred linguistics in this book"). See also NONCOUNTABLE NOUNS.

covert prestige Value that a nonstandard variety of a language carries within a speech community. See also OVERT PRESTIGE.

creole   Full-fledged language developed from a PIDGIN that has become the natural language of a SPEECH COMMUNITY once children are born into it and develop the pidgin in the expected course of language acquisition. See also ACROLECT, BASILECT, and MESOLECT.

Critical Age Hypothesis   Position taken in theories of language acquisition that language learning is most fully realized before a speaker reaches puberty.

critical discourse analysis   Systematic study of features within a DISCOURSE in relation to the sociopolitical context in which the discourse occurs; also called **CDA**. See also STYLISTICS.

DA   ALPHABETISM for DISCOURSE ANALYSIS.

dangling participle   PARTICIPLE used (some would say illogically or ungrammatically) without an antecedent subject, such as "Crumbling in his hand, he ate the cookie."

declaration   ILLOCUTIONARY ACT that brings about the state of affairs to which it refers, such as blessing, firing, sentencing, or bidding. See also ASSERTIVE, COMMISSIVE, DIRECTIVE, EXPRESSIVE, REPRESENTATIVE, and VERDICTIVE.

declension   INFLECTION of NOUNS, PRONOUNS, and ADJECTIVES according to categories like CASE, NUMBER, and GENDER. The verb form is **decline**. *Declension* is to *decline* as CONJUGATION is to CONJUGATE.

deep dyslexia   DYSLEXIA in which language users substitute SYNONYMS or words phonologically similar to those intended. See PHONOLOGICAL DYSLEXIA and SURFACE DYSLEXIA.

defining vocabulary   Lexicon from which definitions in a dictionary or glossary are written; most dictionaries ensure that all words used in their definitions are also defined in the same dictionaries, whereas glossaries like this one do not make a similar assurance that all words used in them are defined in them.

deixis   Reference to personal, temporal, or locational features of the circumstance in which an utterance is made, by means of adverbs (*here, there, now, then*) and pronouns (*this* and *that*) whose meaning is relative to the circumstance. See also ENDOPHORIC REFERENCE, EXOPHORIC REFERENCE, PERSONAL DEIXIS, SPATIAL DEIXIS, and TEMPORAL DEIXIS.

deletion   PHONOLOGICAL process in which speech sounds disappear from words, for instance, as when the vowel in the second syllable of *laboratory* is lost in pronunciation of the word.

demonstrative pronoun   PRONOUN that specifies a person or thing, for instance, *this* in *this guy* or *this apple*. Such pronouns are also called **demonstratives**.

demonstrative reference   Within NARRATIVE, reference, whether ENDOPHORIC (either ANAPHORIC or CATAPHORIC) or EXOPHORIC, by means of a DEMONSTRATIVE PRONOUN. See also COMPARATIVE REFERENCE and PERSONAL REFERENCE.

denotative meaning   Lexical meaning that depends on the relationship of a word to nonlinguistic things, rather than on linguistic and cognitive associations on the parts of speakers and hearers. Also called **denotation**. See also CONNOTATIVE MEANING.

density   In SOCIAL NETWORK THEORY, the measure of how many of the people that one person knows and interacts with also know and interact with one another. See also MULTIPLEXITY.

deontic modal auxiliary   AUXILIARY VERB used to indicate the necessity or inevitability of an action or state, to imply an AGENT'S obligation to act as a PREDICATE specifies, or to indicate permission; for instance, "Necessity *must* be indicated by means of a deontic modal auxiliary," "Deontic modal auxiliaries *must* be used to indicate inevitability," "You *must* employ a deontic modal auxiliary if you want to convey obligation," and "You *might should* employ a deontic modal auxiliary in this sentence, if you like" all illustrate deontic modal auxiliaries. Also see EPISTEMIC MODAL AUXILIARY for clarification.

dependent clause   CLAUSE that cannot function as a SENTENCE, but that must be attached to or embedded in an INDEPENDENT CLAUSE; also called a SUBORDINATE CLAUSE.

derivational morpheme   MORPHEME, whether a BOUND MORPHEME (COMBINING FORM, INFIX, PREFIX, or SUFFIX) or a FREE MORPHEME, that contributes to formation of a new word. See also INFLECTIONAL MORPHEME.

description   Telling of how things are, were, or will be, as distinct from NARRATIVE. See also EXPOSITION and PERSUASION.

descriptive rule   Statement of what regularly actually occurs in a language or languages generally, as opposed to what supposedly *should* occur. See also PRESCRIPTIVE RULE.

descriptivist   Person inclined to describe language as it is, has been, or will be, rather than to regulate language according to what he or she believes it *should* be; as an adjective, typical of such a person's attitude toward language. See also PRESCRIPTIVIST.

determiner   Word that co-occurs with a NOUN to express certain qualities of that noun; for instance, *a* in *a noun* indicates that we mean 'any noun from among all nouns,' whereas *the* in *the noun* indicates that we mean 'noun previously selected from among all nouns for purposes of this sentence.'

diachronic   Historical or concerned with history; language develops **diachronically**. See also SYNCHRONIC.

diacritics   PHONETIC marks that indicate a value not expressed in the accompanying phonetic symbol or letter, as when [ë] represents a centralized vowel or the sound of the letter *e* is distinguished in *résumé* and *crèche*. See also INTERNATIONAL PHONETIC ALPHABET.

dialect   Variety of a language, whether regional or social, systematically different from other varieties of the same language in structural (i.e., morphological, syntactic) or lexical features. See also ACCENT.

dialectology   Study of variation in a particular language or language family. See also SOCIOLINGUISTICS and VARIATIONIST SOCIOLINGUISTICS.

diction   Choice of words in speech or writing.

diphthong   VOWEL that begins at one PLACE OF ARTICULATION and ends at another, as in *right*.

directive   ILLOCUTIONARY ACT designed to get the person addressed to do something, such as asking, ordering, and challenging. See also ASSERTIVE, COMMISSIVE, DECLARATION, EXPRESSIVE, REPRESENTATIVE, and VERDICTIVE.

direct object   Recipient of a verb's action; in the sentence "I wrote a letter to my best friend," *letter* is the direct object. See also INDIRECT OBJECT.

direct speech   Unmodified UTTERANCE, as opposed to indirect or reported speech; "Do you know what direct speech is?" is direct speech, whereas "Michael asked whether you know what direct speech is" is INDIRECT SPEECH.

direct speech act   SPEECH ACT in which a LOCUTIONARY ACT corresponds exactly to an ILLOCUTIONARY ACT. See also CONSTATIVE SPEECH ACT, INDIRECT SPEECH ACT, PERFORMATIVE SPEECH ACT, PERLOCUTIONARY ACT, PRAGMATICS, and SPEECH ACT THEORY.

discourse   Continuous speech, whether spoken or written, larger than a SENTENCE.

discourse adverb   ADVERB that modifies a sentence or longer segment of DISCOURSE, rather than a specific VERB; in "Hopefully, I'll always use adverbs grammatically," *hopefully* is a discourse adverb, and some consider it ungrammatical English usage; also called a SENTENCE ADVERB.

discourse analysis   Systematic study of DISCOURSE; also called DA. See also CRITICAL DISCOURSE ANALYSIS and STYLISTICS.

discourse markers   Lexical items, for instance, *I mean* and *well*, used to segment discourse into smaller, sequential units.

displacement   Human cognitive ability, reflected in LINGUISTIC COMPETENCE, that allows projection forward and backward in time, as well as for abstract ideas.

distinctive features   Characteristics of speech sounds that distinguish them from one another, namely, MANNER OF ARTICULATION, PLACE OF ARTICULATION, and VOICING in the case of CONSONANTS, and HEIGHT, BACKNESS or FRONTNESS, and TENSENESS or LAXNESS in the case of VOWELS.

ditransitive verb   VERB that appears with two OBJECTS, as in "We give you lots of examples"; the essential property of such verbs is **ditransitivity**. See also INTRANSITIVE VERB, OBJECT-PREDICATIVE VERB, and TRANSITIVE VERB.

dyslexia   Learning disorder in which recognizing and comprehending written words is relatively difficult.

dysphemism   Word or expression with negative CONNOTATIONS, used in place of a neutral term; for instance, in "Anne is easygoing, but Michael is lax," *lax* is a dysphemism for 'lacking rigor, strictness, or firmness.' Also, the semantic process by which such words are formed. See also AMELIORATION, EUPHEMISM, PEJORATION, and REAPPROPRIATION.

eggcorn   Phonetic reinterpretation of a word, such as *eggcorn* for *acorn*, so that the new form makes some kind of sense. See also FOLK ETYMOLOGY and REANALYSIS.

elaboration   Re-presenting or clarifying material for purposes of narrative COHESION, by means of certain CONJUNCTIONS; for instance, *for instance* is a narrative conjunction that introduces elaboration. See also ENHANCEMENT and EXTENSION.

ellipsis   1: Omission of a word or phrase necessary to complete a syntactic structure in the abstract but unnecessary in speech; for instance, in "I'm going to the movies. Do you want to go with?" the OBJECT *me* is omitted from the second sentence. "Do you want to go with?" is **elliptical**—it is an **ellipsis** (omission of *me*) and also represents the syntactic process called **ellipsis**. 2: In NARRATIVE, use of ellipsis to promote COHESION by connecting the points at which information is omitted and supplied.

emoticon   Symbol that communicates emotional response in Internet DISCOURSE, such as the ubiquitous smiley face :-).

enclitic   CLITIC that attaches to the word preceding it. See also PROCLITIC.

endophoric reference   Dependence of one NOUN or PRONOUN within a text to another preceding it (called ANAPHORIC REFERENCE) or following it (called CATAPHORIC REFERENCE) within the same text. See also EXOPHORIC REFERENCE.

enhancement   Indication of cause, manner, space, or time by means of certain narrative CONJUNCTIONS, such as *meanwhile* and *because*, in order to promote COHESION. See also ELABORATION and EXTENSION.

enjambment   Extension of a clause across two or more lines of poetry, as in the fifth stanza of Lewis Carroll's "Jabberwocky":

> One, two! One two! And through and through
> The vorpal blade went snicker-snack!
> He left it dead, and with its head
> He went galumphing back.

entailment   Logical relationship between a statement and the conditions on which it is true. Whereas "Not everyone did well on this quiz" might mean that any number taking the quiz performed less than well, it only **entails** that one person did not perform well; whereas the same statement may imply that some students did poorly (it might function as a EUPHEMISM), it only says that at least one person did less than *well*, whatever *well* means. See also IMPLICATURE.

epiglottis   Cartilage that covers the opening between the VOCAL CORDS and the LARYNX.

epistemic modal auxiliary   AUXILIARY VERB used to indicate that the proposition underlying a statement is simply the case or is believed to be the case; for instance, in "Dinner must be ready now," *must* functions as an epistemic modal auxiliary. See also DEONTIC MODAL AUXILIARY.

etymology   1: History of a word. 2: Study of word history.

etymon   Historical word from which a more recent form was derived, whether in the same or a different language. For instance, Old English *ācsian* is the etymon for Modern English *ask*. It may be helpful to think of an etymon as a "parent" (or great-great-grandparent) word, a REFLEX as a "child" (or great-great-grandchild) word, and COGNATES as "cousin" words.

euphemism   Word or expression with positive CONNOTATIONS used in place of a neutral term; for instance, in "Anne is easygoing, but Michael is lax," *easygoing* is a euphemism for 'lacking rigor, strictness, or firmness.' Also, the semantic process by which such words are formed. See also AMELIORATION, DYSPHEMISM, and PEJORATION.

evaluation   Comments throughout a NARRATIVE that address why it is interesting. See also ABSTRACT, CODA, COMPLICATING ACTION, ORIENTATION, and RESOLUTION.

exophoric reference   Reference to something in a text's context or situation; for instance, "Did you see that?" refers to something in the speaker's environment, rather than to something identified previously in the text by means of a NOUN or PRONOUN. See also DEIXIS and ENDOPHORIC REFERENCE.

exposition   Explanation of how things are, were, or will be, as distinct from NARRATIVE. See also DESCRIPTION and PERSUASION.

expressive   ILLOCUTIONARY ACT that expresses a speaker's mental state, such as apologizing, congratulating, or welcoming. See also ASSERTIVE, COMMISSIVE, DECLARATION, DIRECTIVE, REPRESENTATIVE, and VERDICTIVE.

extension   Material added or qualified by means of narrative CONJUNCTIONS, such as *also*, *yet*, and *on the other hand*, in order to promote COHESION. See also ELABORATION and ENHANCEMENT.

eye contact   Nonverbal means by which one indicates willingness to turn the CONVERSATIONAL FLOOR over to another participant. See also GESTURE, INTONATION, QUESTION, SILENCE, TURN, and TURN-TAKING VIOLATION.

eye rhymes   Words that look as though they would RHYME exactly, but do not, such as *move* and *glove*.

face   Conversational persona responsible for POLITENESS toward others and receiving others' politeness. See also FACE-THREATENING ACT, NEGATIVE FACE, NEGATIVE POLITENESS, POLITENESS, POSITIVE FACE, and POSITIVE POLITENESS.

face-threatening act   Any utterance that challenges the level of POLITENESS in conversation. Also called FTA. See also FACE, NEGATIVE FACE, NEGATIVE POLITENESS, POSITIVE FACE, and POSITIVE POLITENESS.

felicity conditions   Criteria on which SPEECH ACTS and ILLOCUTIONARY ACTS are judged more or less successful, that is, to have achieved their purposes.

finite verb   VERB form that indicates TENSE. See also NONFINITE VERB.

flap   CONSONANT sound produced by single, rapid contact between two organs of articulation. In American English, it is best represented by the medial consonant sound in *butter* (the [t] is not produced like that in *cat*); in British English, it is best represented by the [r] in *worry*.

folk etymology   1: Word-formative process in which a new word emerges from popular mis-understanding of its form or meaning, as when *plantar wart* (from Latin *planta* 'sole'), a wart on the sole of one's foot, becomes *planter's wart*, presumably because the wart is caused by farm or field work. 2: Commonsense explanation of a word's origin or development other than the word's actual ETYMOLOGY. See also EGGCORN and REANALYSIS.

foot   Metrical unit in poetry composed of a certain number of SYLLABLES arranged in a certain pattern of stress. See also ACCENTUAL-SYLLABIC METER, METER, RHYTHM, and SCANSION.

fore-clipping   Word shortened from a larger one by loss of its initial element, as in *plane* from *aeroplane*. Also the word-formative process that produces such a word. See also BACKFORMATION, CLIPPING, HIND-CLIPPING, and INNOVATIVE CLIPPING.

form   Grammatical class or lexical category of a word. See also FUNCTION.

formant   Frequency regions of the sound spectrum of relative intensity that determine the character of a VOWEL Sound.

free morpheme   MORPHEME that functions without modification as a word. See also BOUND MORPHEME.

fricative   Speech sound, such as /f/, produced when ARTICULATORS are brought so close together that friction is created as air passes through the mouth. See also AFFRICATE, NASAL, OBSTRUENT, and STOP.

front vowel   VOWEL sound, like that in *beat*, *bait*, and *bat*, formed when the tongue is placed forward in the mouth. See also BACK VOWEL and CENTRAL VOWEL.

frontal lobe   Part of the brain toward the front of each cerebral hemisphere; the frontal lobe of the LEFT HEMISPHERE contains centers important to LINGUISTIC COMPETENCE and speech production, including BROCA'S AREA. See also OCCIPITAL LOBE, PARIETAL LOBE, and TEMPORAL LOBE.

frontness   DISTINCTIVE FEATURE of VOWELS realized when the tongue is placed toward the front of the mouth. See also BACKNESS, FRONT VOWEL, HEIGHT, LAXNESS, and TENSENESS.

FTA   ALPHABETISM of FACE-THREATENING ACT. See also FACE, NEGATIVE FACE, NEGATIVE POLITENESS, POLITENESS, POSITIVE FACE, and POSITIVE POLITENESS.

function   Role of a word in a PHRASE or CLAUSE. See also FORM.

functional shift   Word-formative process in which a word historically belonging to one LEXICAL CATEGORY begins to function in another, as when the verb *swim* functions as the noun *swim*— "Did you have a good swim?" See also SEMANTIC SHIFT.

gender   Grammatical category that depends on the contrasts among masculine/feminine/neuter, used to classify NOUNS, PRONOUNS, and ADJECTIVES. See also GRAMMATICAL GENDER and NATURAL GENDER.

generalization   Process of semantic change in which a word with a specific meaning develops one or more related senses and so becomes a word of more general significance; for instance, in the fourteenth century, *ceiling* meant, narrowly, 'wooden lining of roof or walls of a room' but later came to mean the upper limit of a room and, even later, any upper limit (e.g., *price ceiling*). See also AMELIORATION, DYSPHEMISM, EUPHEMISM, HYPONYMY, MERONYMY, PEJORATION, POLYSEMY, SPECIALIZATION, and SYNONYMY.

genre   Category of texts that share certain formal characteristics and textual functions (such as sonnet, novel of manners, and even résumé) and serve to shape audience response. See also REGISTER.

gerund   VERB form constructed with the suffix *-ing* that functions as a NOUN, as in "*Reading* is fundamental!"

gesture   Meaningful nonverbal supplements to conversation. See also CONVERSATIONAL FLOOR, EYE CONTACT, INTONATION, QUESTION, SILENCE, TURN, and TURN-TAKING VIOLATION.

glide   Speech sound produced by transition from one speech sound to another, such as /w/ and /j/. See also APPROXIMANT, BUNCHED /R/, LATERAL LIQUID, LIQUID, and RETROFLEX LIQUID.

glottal stop   Speech sound produced in the LARYNX, when the **glottis**, or opening between the VOCAL CORDS, is closed and then audibly released. See also EPIGLOTTIS and STOP.

gradable antonyms   ANTONYMS that are conceptually opposite, but not absolutely so; *long* and *short* are opposites, but some short things are nearly as long as some long things. See also ANTONYMS, COMPLEMENTARY ANTONYMS, CONVERSENESS, and NONGRADABLE ANTONYMS.

grammar   Structure and rules governing a language at the levels of PHONOLOGY, MORPHOLOGY, SYNTAX, and SEMANTICS and arguably DISCOURSE. Features of a language that conform to such rules, and are therefore comprehensible to other native speakers of the language, are characterized as **grammatical**.

grammatical gender   GENDER marked to associate words within a sentence as syntactically related, without reference to gender of real-world persons or things. See also NATURAL GENDER.

grammaticalization   Process in which an open-class word becomes a grammatical form, as when Old English *lic* 'body' later functions as the adjective suffix *-ly*, as in *manly*.

hard palate   Front surface of the roof of the mouth, leading forward to the ALVEOLAR RIDGE and back to the SOFT PALATE.

height   DISTINCTIVE FEATURE of VOWELS determined by the relative position (high, low, or mid) of the tongue when producing the sound. See also BACKNESS, FRONTNESS, LAXNESS, and TENSENESS.

hind-clipping   Word shortened from a larger one by loss of its final element, as in *jet* from *jetpropelled plane*. Also the word-formative process that produces such a word. See also BACKFORMATION, CLIPPING, FORE-CLIPPING, and INNOVATIVE CLIPPING.

historical linguistics   Branch of LINGUISTICS focused on the development of language over time, also called DIACHRONIC linguistics.

homographs   Words spelled identically, though of distinct origin and different meanings, and perhaps pronounced differently, such as *wind* 'moving air' and *wind* 'coil; turn; wrap.' See also HOMONYMS and HOMOPHONES.

homonyms   Words of different meanings that take the same form, such as *cleave* 'join' and *cleave* 'divide, separate, sunder.' See also HOMOGRAPHS and HOMOPHONES.

homophones   Words of different meanings and distinct origins pronounced (more or less) the same, such as *witch* and *which*. See also HOMOGRAPHS and HOMONYMS.

hypercorrection   Linguistic form, structure, or pronunciation that a speaker supposes to be correct (or formal) in a variety that he or she does not control fully, thus, usually a result of STYLE-SHIFTING; for instance, "They gave a wonderful gift to Janie and I" is a hypercorrection of "They gave a wonderful gift to Janie and me." Also, use of such a form, structure, or pronunciation.

hypernym   Word of more general meaning than others defined in relation to it; for instance, *vehicle* is a hypernym for *car*, *bus*, *bicycle*, *motorcycle*, etc. Also called a SUPERORDINATE. See also HYPONYM.

hyponym   Word semantically subordinate to a HYPERNYM or SUPERORDINATE and semantically parallel to other words subordinate to the same term; for instance, *car*, *bus*, *bicycle*, and *motorcycle* are all hyponyms under *vehicle*; their semantic relationship to one another, as well as to their hypernym, is called **hyponymy**.

hypotactic   SYNTAX or STYLE characterized by subordination. See also PARATACTIC.

idiom   Expression whose meaning cannot be derived directly from the elements of which it is composed; for instance, *My dogs are barkin'* 'My feet hurt' is an idiom; such statements are **idiomatic** and are a sort of "discourse metaphor." See also METAPHOR and METAPHORICAL EXTENSION.

illocutionary act   In SPEECH ACT THEORY, intended or conventional meaning that can accompany a LOCUTIONARY ACT within the compass of an UTTERANCE. See also CONSTATIVE SPEECH ACT, DIRECT SPEECH ACT, INDIRECT SPEECH ACT, LOCUTIONARY ACT, PRAGMATICS, PERFORMATIVE SPEECH ACT, and PERLOCUTIONARY ACT.

implicature   Meaning implied in addition to the truth-conditional meaning of a proposition. See also ENTAILMENT.

indefinite pronoun   PRONOUN, like *all*, *anything*, *everyone*, *no one*, *something*, or *whatever*, that represents an unknown or unspecified element in a CLAUSE.

independent clause   CLAUSE that is a complete SENTENCE. See also DEPENDENT CLAUSE.

indexical meaning   Meaning within DISCOURSE that depends on context outside the discourse, including social circumstances and the construction or maintenance of social identities, etc. Speech is thus **indexed** to context, and speakers **index** their discourse to phenomena outside it.

indirect object   To or for whom a verb's action is done; in the sentence, "I wrote my best friend a letter," *best friend* is the indirect object. See also DIRECT OBJECT.

indirect speech   Within a NARRATIVE, speech of one reported by another. See also DIRECT SPEECH.

indirect speech act   SPEECH ACT in which a LOCUTIONARY ACT does not directly correspond to an ILLOCUTIONARY ACT. See also CONSTATIVE SPEECH ACT, DIRECT SPEECH ACT, PERFORMAIVE SPEECH ACT, PERLOCUTIONARY SPEECH ACT, PRAGMATICS, and SPEECH ACT THEORY.

infinitive   NONFINITE form of a VERB that serves as the base for inflectional development or expresses the core meaning of the verb, without concern for NUMBER or PERSON; in late Middle and Modern English, the infinitive is often marked with the PARTICLE *to*; in "We prefer to mark infinitives with *to*," the phrase *to mark* is the infinitive.

infix   1: AFFIX inserted into a word at an appropriate morphophonemic boundary; also called an INSERT, such as *-ma-* in *edumacation*. 2: Word-formative process involving such affixing. 3: Word resulting from that process, such as *edumacation*. Usage is unsettled, and some linguists and language scholars prefer **infixing** for senses 2 and 3.

inflectional morpheme   MORPHEME that indicates something about a word's grammatical function, such as NUMBER or TENSE; in English, such morphemes are generally (but not always) realized in a suffix—for instance, plurals are usually marked with a suffix like *-s* (*dogs*) or *-en* (*oxen*), though the plural morpheme in *deer* is not. See also DERIVATIONAL MORPHEME and ZERO MORPHEME.

initialism   Word formed from the first letters of words in a phrase or compound name, as in *FBI* for *F*(ederal) *B*(ureau of) *I*(nvestigation) or *ACLU* for *A*(merican) *C*(ivil) *L*(iberties) *U*(nion); also, the word-formative process that results in such a word. Also called ALPHABETISM.

innovative clipping   Word shortened from a larger one at a point other than a morphemic boundary, as in *nuke* from *nuclear weapon*. Also the word-formative process that produces such a word. See also BACKFORMATION, CLIPPING, FORE-CLIPPING, and HIND-CLIPPING.

insert   In INFIXING and INTERPOSING, the BOUND MORPHEME, word, or phrase that interrupts the MATRIX; for instance, in *edumacation*, *-ma-* is the insert, whereas in *guaranfuckinteed*, *-fuckin-* is the insert.

insertion   Phonological process in which a sound is added to a word, as in the /k/ in some pronunciations of *length* or /r/ in some pronunciations of *wash*.

International Phonetic Alphabet   Set of symbols and DIACRITICS designed by the International Phonetic Association to represent phonemes of the world's languages, as well as their realization in speech. Also called **IPA**.

interposing   Word-formative process involving insertion of a word or words into a fixed or idiomatic phrase, as in "No fucking way!" (*fucking* inserted into the idiomatic phrase *No way!*). See also INFIX, INSERT, and MATRIX.

interrogative pronoun   Set of *wh-* PRONOUNS, such as *who*, *what*, and *which*, that represent unknown elements in sentences that are questions.

interruption   Attempt by one party to take the CONVERSATIONAL FLOOR from the speaker who occupies it. See also OVERLAP and TURN-TAKING VIOLATION.

intonation   1: Change in PITCH that indicates something about sentence meaning; for instance, in Standard American English, rising intonation usually indicates that a sentence is a question. 2: Change in PITCH that may indicate a participant's desire to relinquish or retain the CONVERSATIONAL FLOOR. See also EYE CONTACT, GESTURE, INTONATION, QUESTION, SILENCE, TURN, and TURN-TAKING VIOLATION.

intransitive verb   VERB that either does not require or cannot take a DIRECT OBJECT; the essential property of such verbs is **intransitivity**. See also DITRANSITIVE VERB, OBJECT-PREDICATIVE VERB, and TRANSITIVE VERB.

isogloss   Line that separates an area that uses one lexical item, grammatical construction, or pronunciation from another area on a dialect map; a DIALECT boundary.

language contact   Process in which speakers enrich dialectal vocabulary by adopting items from a contact language. See also BORROWING, COINING, NATURALLY OCCURING INTERNAL LANGUAGE CHANGE, RETENTION, SOCIAL FACTOR, and STRUCTURAL INFLUENCE.

langue   Underlying, abstract system of language; relationships of linguistic signs to one another both in the lexicon and in syntax of a language. See also *PAROLE*.

larynx   Muscular, cartilaginous part of the respiratory tract that contains the VOCAL CORDS.

lateral liquid   The PHONEME /l/, so called because, in its production, air passes along the sides of the tongue. See also APPROXIMANT, BUNCHED /r/, GLIDE, LIQUID, and RETROFLEX LIQUID.

lateralization   Distribution of a function, such as speech, to the RIGHT or LEFT HEMISPHERE of the brain.

laxness   DISTINCTIVE FEATURE of VOWELS indicating the relatively loose (central) or tense (peripheral) position of the tongue. Also called TENSENESS. See also BACKNESS, FRONTNESS, HEIGHT, and LAX VOWEL.

left hemisphere   Part of the brain the FRONTAL LOBE of which contains centers important to LINGUISTIC COMPETENCE and speech production, including BROCA'S AREA and WERNICKE'S AREA.

lexical category   Grammatical function of a word, such as NOUN, PREPOSITION, CONJUNCTION, ADVERB, etc.

lexical cohesion   COHESION achieved by repetition of words, COLLOCATIONS, or SYNONYMS across sentences.

lexical field   Set of words that, on some conceptual basis, belong together; for instance, *annual*, *journal*, *magazine*, *monthly*, *newspaper*, *periodical*, *quarterly*, and *weekly* all belong to the same lexical field.

lexical gap   Blank space in a LEXICON, such that a concept lacks a word in a particular language to represent it.

lexical prototype semantics   Theory of meaning in which IMAGE SCHEMAS at least partially represent lexical development.

lexicography   1: Art and craft of writing dictionaries. 2: Writing about the LEXICON, whether in dictionaries or elsewhere.

lexicon   Collection of a language's MORPHEMES, whether in a speaker's mind or in a book; the vocabulary of a language, broadly conceived.

lexifier language   Language from which the bulk of a CREOLE vocabulary comes. See also ACROLECT, BASILECT, MESOLECT, and PIDGIN.

lingua franca   Common language developed or adopted in specific contexts to facilitate communications among speakers who do not share a common language.

linguistic competence   Innate human ability to acquire and use language, given certain biological and developmental constraints. See also LINGUISTIC PERFORMANCE.

linguistic determinism   System in which linguistic categories establish the parameters of cognition. See also LINGUISTIC RELATIVITY.

linguistic market   Social arena in which the value of one's speech depends on the linguistic variety in which it is encoded. See also COMMUNITY OF PRACTICE, SOCIOLINGUISTICS, SPEECH COMMUNITY, and VARIATIONIST SOCIOLINGUISTICS.

linguistic performance   A speaker's utterances in a given language, as opposed to his or her innate LINGUISTIC COMPETENCE.

linguistic relativity   System in which cognition varies or develops according to linguistic variation. See also LINGUISTIC DETERMINISM.

linguistic sign   Linguistic entity that joins SIGNIFIER and SIGNIFIED in one linguistic representation.

linguistics   Study of language in any or all of its aspects.

linking verb   VERB, such as *be* or *seem*, that more or less identifies the SUBJECT and PREDICATE of a sentence as the same.

liquid   CONSONANT produced when ARTICULATORS are in proximity to each other but do not impede airflow, such as /l/ and /r/. See also APPROXIMANT, BUNCHED /r/, GLIDE, LATERAL LIQUID, and RETROFLEX LIQUID.

loan translation   Word simultaneously BORROWED and translated from an etymological language; for instance, American English *groundhog* is a loan translation of Dutch *aardvark*. See also CALQUE.

localization   Distribution of mental tasks to specific sites in the brain; for instance, speech production and language centers are located in the FRONTAL LOBE of the left hemisphere. Also called MODULARITY OF MIND. See also BROCA'S AREA and WERNICKE'S AREA.

locutionary act   In SPEECH ACT THEORY, the sounds and words that compose the supposedly referential meaning of an UTTERANCE. See also CONSTATIVE SPEECH ACT, DIRECT SPEECH ACT, ILLOCUTIONARY ACT, INDIRECT SPEECH ACT, PERFORMATIVE SPEECH ACT, PERLOCUTIONARY ACT, PRAGMATICS, and SPEECH ACT THEORY.

main clause   INDEPENDENT CLAUSE in which a DEPENDENT CLAUSE is embedded.

malapropism   Verbal slip in which a similar word is substituted for an intended one, as when Mrs. Malaprop (the character from Richard Sheridan's play *The Rivals* [1775], who gave the slip its name) says that someone "is the very pineapple of politeness," when she means *pinnacle*. Usually, malapropism occurs when the speaker tries to use an unfamiliar word in an effort to seem especially intelligent or sophisticated. See also ANTICIPATION, PRESERVATION, and SPOONERISM.

manner adverb   ADVERB that describes how an action or state occurs, such as *softly* or *swiftly*. See also DISCOURSE ADVERB, SENTENCE ADVERB, and TEMPORAL ADVERB.

manner of articulation   DISTINCTIVE FEATURE that describes proximity of ARTICULATORS and the accompanying effect on airflow in production of a speech sound. See also PLACE OF ARTICULATION and VOICING.

marginal auxiliary   VERBS, like *dare* and *need*, that behave somewhat like AUXILIARY VERBS. See also MODAL AUXILIARY.

matrix   Lexical base on which either an INFIXING or INTERPOSING is made. See also AFFIX, INFIX, INSERT, and INTERPOSING.

maxims of manner   Components of the COOPERATIVE PRINCIPLE, literally, "Avoid obscurity of expression; avoid ambiguity" and "Be brief; be orderly." See also MAXIMS OF QUALITY, MAXIMS OF QUANTITY, and MAXIMS OF RELATION.

maxims of quality   Components of the COOPERATIVE PRINCIPLE, literally, "Do not say what you believe to be false"; "Do not say that for which you lack adequate evidence." See also MAXIMS OF MANNER, MAXIMS OF QUANTITY, and MAXIMS OF RELATION.

maxims of quantity   Components of the COOPERATIVE PRINCIPLE, literally, "Make your contributions as informative as required"; "Do not make your contribution more informative than is required." See also MAXIMS OF MANNER, MAXIMS OF QUALITY, MAXIMS OF RELATION.

maxims of relation   Components of the COOPERATIVE PRINCIPLE, literally, "Be relevant." See also MAXIMS OF MANNER, MAXIMS OF QUALITY, and MAXIMS OF QUANTITY.

McGurk Effect   Name for the discovery (by Harry McGurk and John McDonald) that what we see can affect what we think we hear.

meronym   Lexical item that participates in a whole/part relationship, such as *whiskers*, *ears*, *tail*, and *cat*. The lexical relationship is called **meronymy**. See also HYPONYM.

mesolect   CREOLE historically and developmentally between its acrolectal and basilectal stages. See also ACROLECT, BASILECT, and LEXIFIER LANGUAGE.

metaphor   Figurative language in which a word or phrase that designates one thing is applied to another, as a form of comparison. For instance, these lines from Shakespeare's *Macbeth* are chock full of metaphors:

> Life's but a walking shadow, a poor player,
> That struts and frets his hour upon the stage,
> And then is heard no more; it is a tale
> Told by an idiot, full of sound and fury,
> Signifying nothing.

Life is not, in fact, a walking shadow, a poor player, or an idiot's tale, but metaphor compares two dissimilar things in order to draw out their similarities.

metaphorical extension   SEMANTIC SHIFT in which a word takes on a metaphorical sense, as when *virus* in the biological/medical sense is applied to antagonistic, invasive computer programs. See also IDIOM and METAPHOR.

metathesis   Phonological process in which sounds switch places in the phonemic structure of a word, as when Old/Middle English *bridde* becomes Middle/Modern English *bird* or *aks* becomes *ask*.

meter   Patterned arrangement of words in poetry, for instance, according to stress, number of syllables, or vowel length, etc., or some combination of these. See also ACCENTUAL-SYLLABIC METER, PURE ACCENTUAL METER, PURE SYLLABIC METER, RHYTHM, and SCANSION.

mimetic   Imitative, in some sense, whether ONOMATOPOEIA or some broader imitative effect of literary speech.

minimal pair   Words distinguished by only one DISTINCTIVE FEATURE of one sound, as in *pat* and *bat*.

minimal response   In conversation, any indication that a participant is paying attention; backchanneling may be verbal ("yeah" or "uh-huh" or "mmm") or nonverbal (as in head nodding). See also BACK-CHANNELING.

misplaced participle   Participial phrase placed next to a constituent that it does not modify, for instance, in "Dangling from the beginning of her sentence, Alisse misplaced her participle." See also DANGLING PARTICIPLE.

modal auxiliary   VERB used in combination with another verb to indicate MODALITY of that other verb; in English, *can*, *may*, and *must*, etc., are MODAL AUXILIARIES, also called **modals**. See also AUXILIARY VERB, DEONTIC MODAL AUXILIARY, and EPISTEMIC MODAL AUXILIARY.

modality   Conditionality, necessity, possibility, etc., that qualify a VERB, expressed by various means, whether in the verb, a MODAL AUXILIARY, certain CONJUNCTIONS, sentence structure, or in a combination of these. See also MOOD.

modularity of the mind   Distribution of mental tasks to specific sites in the brain; for instance, speech production and language centers are located in the FRONTAL LOBE of the LEFT HEMISPHERE. Also called LOCALIZATION. See also BROCA'S AREA and WERNICKE'S AREA.

mood   GRAMMATICAL expression of conditionality, necessity, possibility in a VERB by various means. In English, moods include the indicative ("I love grammar"), the interrogative ("Have you studied grammar?"), the imperative ("Read grammar!"), and the conditional ("If you study grammar, then you will have a happy life"). See also ASPECT, MODALITY, and TENSE.

morpheme   Smallest meaningful unit of language; independently meaningful part of a word. The adjective form of *morpheme* is **morphemic**. See also ALLOMORPH, BOUND MORPHEME, and FREE MORPHEME.

morphology   Study of word forms and the processes by which words are formed.

morphology tree   Diagrammatic representation of a word's hierarchical MORPHEMIC structure.

Movement Test   CONSTITUENCY TEST in which one moves a supposed CONSTITUENT to different syntactic positions in order to determine whether it is, in fact, a constituent. See also COORDINATION TEST, STAND ALONE TEST, and SUBSTITUTION TEST.

multiplexity   Number of capacities in which members of a social network know one another. See also DENSITY and SOCIAL NETWORK THEORY.

narrative   Story or structured account of events, as distinguished from DESCRIPTION, EXPOSITION, and PERSUASION.

nasal   STOP produced when air flows from the lungs through the nose, such as [m], [n], and [ŋ], the final sounds in *sum*, *sin*, and *sting*. See also AFFRICATE, FRICATIVE, and OBSTRUENT.

natural class   Set of sounds that share features in such a way as to include all sounds in the set and to exclude all others; for instance, /p, b/ is the natural class of bilabial oral stops.

natural gender   GENDER marked grammatically to reflect the gender of real-world persons or things. See also GRAMMATICAL GENDER.

naturally occurring internal language change   Process in which the dialectal vocabulary is enriched by the sorts of change and variation that occur within any SPEECH COMMUNITY. See also BORROWING, COINAGE, LANGUAGE CONTACT, RETENTION, SOCIAL FACTOR, and STRUCTURAL INFLUENCE.

negation   Contradiction expressed within a sentence of at least part of that sentence's meaning; in terms of SYNTAX accomplished by use of *not*: "Negation is what I'm trying to express here" does not exhibit negation, whereas "Negation is not what I'm trying to express here" does.

negative face   Desire to be unimpeded in one's actions which, in part, determines conversational POLITENESS. See also FACE, FACE-THREATENING ACT, FTA, NEGATIVE POLITENESS, POLITENESS, POSITIVE FACE, and POSITIVE POLITENESS.

negative politeness   Respecting another's NEGATIVE FACE, especially by using markers of deference, apology, etc. See also FACE, FACE-THREATENING ACT, FTA, POLITENESS, POSITIVE FACE, and POSITIVE POLITENESS.

node   In a PHRASE, CLAUSE, or SENTENCE structure TREE, the point at which one CONSTITUENT level is distinguished from another, in order to indicate syntactic hierarchy. See also BRANCH.

nominal   Any CONSTITUENT that functions as a NOUN. See also ADJECTIVAL and ADVERBIAL.

nonce word   Word created for a specific purpose in a specific context.

nonfinite verb   VERB form, such as the INFINITIVE or the PARTICIPLE, that does not express TENSE. See also FINITE VERB.

nongradable antonyms   Terms representing absolute opposites, such as *alive* and *dead*, that cannot be considered in comparative terms, as "more" or "less" what they are; also called COMPLEMENTARY ANTONYMS. See also ANTONYMS, CONVERSENESS, and GRADABLE ANTONYMS.

nonrestrictive clause   CLAUSE that provides additional information about a NOUN or noun phrase but does not specify or restrict the referent, for instance, "One of the earliest English grammars was written in Latin, which is pretty amusing when you think about it." See also RESTRICTIVE RELATIVE CLAUSE.

noun   Word that represents a person, place, thing, quality, action, concept, idea, etc., and that functions as SUBJECT or OBJECT in a SENTENCE; also, a LEXICAL CATEGORY including such words. See also NOMINAL and PRONOUN.

nucleus   VOWEL required as the central PHONEME of a SYLLABLE; for instance, /o/ is the nucleus of *boat*. See also CODA and ONSET.

number   Grammatical indication that a NOUN, PRONOUN, ADJECTIVE, or VERB is singular, dual, or plural.

object   NOUN, noun phrase, or PRONOUN that receives the action of a VERB or is governed by a PREPOSITION in a prepositional phrase; also the CASE in which such a word functions. See also DIRECT OBJECT, INDIRECT OBJECT, and SUBJECT.

object-predicative verb   VERB that connects an object-predicative to an OBJECT, as in "We called them silly." See also DITRANSITIVE VERB, INTRANSITIVE VERB, and TRANSITIVE VERB.

objectivism   Theory of the relationship between language and thought in which people have access to an external or nonmental reality regardless of language. See also LINGUISTIC DETERMINISM and LINGUISTIC RELATIVISM.

Observer's Paradox   Reluctance of folks to speak naturally in the presence of observers when observers need them to speak naturally.

obstruent   Speech sound, such as an AFFRICATE, FRICATIVE, or oral STOP, produced with obstruction of air flow in the mouth. See also NASAL.

occipital lobe   Area toward the lower rear of the LEFT HEMISPHERE responsible for, among other things, vision. See also FRONTAL LOBE, PARIETAL LOBE, and TEMPORAL LOBE.

offglide   Speech sound produced when a VOWEL moves into a GLIDE, as (repeatedly) in "How now, brown cow?" See also ONGLIDE.

onglide   Speech sound produced when a GLIDE moves into a VOWEL, as in some pronunciations of *Tuesday*. See also OFFGLIDE.

onomatopoeia   Creation or use of words with sounds that imitate those associated with the things to which they refer, such as *buzz* and *gasp!*

onset   Optional, initial PHONEME in a SYLLABLE; for instance, /k/ in *cot* is an onset. See also CODA and NUCLEUS.

open morphological class   LEXICAL CATEGORY to which new items can be added, such as ADJECTIVE, NOUN, and VERB. See also CLOSED MORPHOLOGICAL CLASS.

oral sound   Speech sound, such as an AFFRICATE, FRICATIVE, or STOP, produced by funneling air through the mouth.

orientation   Background information that clarifies setting and characters of a NARRATIVE. See also ABSTRACT, CODA, COMPLICATING ACTION, EVALUATION, and RESOLUTION.

overlap   Concurrent speech by two or more participants in a conversation, when one mistakenly believes that the participant who holds the CONVERSATIONAL FLOOR has relinquished it and thus takes a TURN. See also INTERRUPTION and TURN-TAKING VIOLATION.

overt prestige   Value that a variety of a language carries within a speech community. See also COVERT PRESTIGE.

paratactic   SYNTAX or STYLE characterized by coordination. See also HYPOTACTIC.

parentese   Version of language that adults (including nonparents) use when talking to young children.

parietal lobe   Area in the upper rear of the LEFT HEMISPHERE of the brain responsible for, among other things, sense of touch. See also FRONTAL LOBE, OCCIPITAL LOBE, and TEMPORAL LOBE.

parole   Actual speech, as opposed to *LANGUE*.

parse   Analyze a SENTENCE into component parts.

part of speech   LEXICAL CATEGORY to which a word belongs and according to which it functions grammatically.

particle   Word with the FORM of a PREPOSITION or ADVERB, such as the infinitive marker *to*, that does not FUNCTION as a preposition or adverb.

passive construction   Results of TRANSFORMATION in which a SENTENCE'S DIRECT OBJECT becomes the grammatical SUBJECT and the AGENT NOUN or noun PHRASE moves to the end of the sentence; or, you might say that the object is moved to the position of the grammatical subject—if you want to use a passive construction.

past participle   PARTICIPLE derived from a bare infinitive form of a VERB by addition of *-ed/ -en* or an internal vowel change, as in "The definitions *provided* in this glossary did not fall from the sky."

past tense   TENSE that indicates an action that has already occurred or a state that has already been the case.

pejoration   Semantic process in which a term of neutral significance takes on a negative meaning. See also AMELIORATION, DYSPHEMISM, and EUPHEMISM.

perceptual dialectology   Study of how speakers perceive variation. See also DIALECTOLOGY, SOCIOLINGUISTICS, and VARIATIONIST SOCIOLINGUISTICS.

perfect aspect   ASPECT that indicates completed action, formed by *have* + PAST PARTICIPLE.

performative speech act   Utterance that explicitly states or entails the action that it performs, as in "I now pronounce you husband and wife"—the words and the act are one and the same. See also DIRECT SPEECH ACT, ILLOCUTIONARY ACT, INDIRECT SPEECH ACT, LOCUTIONARY ACT, PERLOCUTIONARY ACT, PRAGMATICS, SPEECH ACT, and SPEECH ACT THEORY.

periphrastic do   Auxiliary *do* that substitutes for verbal inflection, as when "I did look it up in the glossary" replaces "I looked it up in the glossary."

perlocutionary act   In SPEECH ACT THEORY, the effect achieved by an UTTERANCE on a hearer. See also CONSTATIVE SPEECH ACT, DIRECT SPEECH ACT, ILLOCUTIONARY ACT, INDIRECT SPEECH ACT, LOCUTIONARY ACT, PERFORMATIVE SPEECH ACT, PRAGMATICS, and SPEECH ACT.

personal deixis   Reference to a person who figures directly in the circumstance in which an UTTERANCE is made, usually by means of a PERSONAL PRONOUN. See also DEIXIS, SPATIAL DEIXIS, and TEMPORAL DEIXIS.

personal pronoun   Word that indicates grammatical person, NUMBER, and CASE of a person or thing, in place of a common NOUN or name; also the LEXICAL CATEGORY to which such a word belongs. See also PRONOUN.

persuasion   Argument for how things were, are, or ought to be, as distinct from NARRATIVE. See also DESCRIPTION and EXPOSITION.

phoneme   Distinctive sound of a language. See also ALLOPHONE and DISTINCTIVE FEATURES.

phonetics   Description and classification of sounds and the study of their production and perception. See also ACOUSTIC PHONETICS, ARTICULATORY PHONETICS, AUDITORY PHONETICS, and PHONOLOGY.

phonological dyslexia   DYSLEXIA in which speakers struggle to read unfamiliar or nonsense words aloud. See also DEEP DYSLEXIA and SURFACE DYSLEXIA.

phonology   Study of sound systems and sound change, usually within a particular language or family of languages. See also PHONETICS.

phonotactic constraint   Rules for what sounds or sequences of sound can occur in the ONSET or CODA of a SYLLABLE in a particular language.

phrasal verb   VERB formed from two or more words, such as *bail out*, *freak out*, and *pass out*.

phrase   Any meaningful sequence of words below the level of the CLAUSE.

phrase structure rule   Rule that generates allowable CONSTITUENTS within sentence TREES.

pidgin   Highly simplified communicative system that arises when adult speakers who share no common language need to communicate with each other. See also CREOLE.

pitch   Rate of repetition or vibration of the VOCAL CORDS in the production of speech sounds.

place of articulation   DISTINCTIVE FEATURE that indicates the location of ARTICULATORS in the production of speech sounds. See also MANNER OF ARTICULATION and VOICING.

politeness   Ways in which speakers adapt (or do not adapt) to the needs and wants of other participants in conversation. See also FACE, FACE-THREATENING ACT, FTA, NEGATIVE FACE, NEGATIVE POLITENESS, POSITIVE FACE, and POSITIVE POLITENESS.

polysemy   General semantic process by which a single word develops many meanings; also, a quality such words express; the adjective form is **polysemous**. See also AMELIORATION, DYSPHEMISM, EUPHEMISM, GENERALIZATION, HYPONYMY, MERONYMY, PEJORATION, and SYNONYMY.

positive face   Desire to be approved of or liked by other participants in conversation; in part, determines conversational POLITENESS. See also FACE, FACE-THREATENING ACT, FTA, NEGATIVE FACE, NEGATIVE POLITENESS, and POSITIVE POLITENESS.

positive politeness   Enhancing the POSITIVE FACE of others in conversation, for instance, by means of compliments and other markers of friendliness. See also FACE, FACE-THREATENING ACT, FTA, NEGATIVE FACE, NEGATIVE POLITENESS, and POLITENESS.

pragmatics   Study of how we communicate in language, with emphasis on SPEECH ACT THEORY; an approach to DISCOURSE ANALYSIS. See also CONSTATIVE SPEECH ACT, DIRECT SPEECH ACT, ILLOCUTIONARY ACT, INDIRECT SPEECH ACT, LOCUTIONARY ACT, PERFORMATIVE SPEECH ACT, PERLOCUTIONARY ACT, SPEECH ACT, and SPEECH ACT THEORY.

predicate   VERB and elements governed by a verb in a CLAUSE or SENTENCE; also called a PREDICATIVE, which serves as the adjective form, as well. See also ATTRIBUTIVE.

predicative   Noun or adjective phrase in the verb COMPLEMENT that modifies a SUBJECT or OBJECT. See also ATTRIBUTIVE.

prefix   AFFIX attached to the front of a word, in English usually a DERIVATIONAL MORPHEME.

prefixing   1: Word-formative process involving a PREFIX. 2: Word resulting from that process.

preposition   Word, such as *at*, *by*, *from*, and *with*, that indicates the relation of a NOUN, PRONOUN, NOUN PHRASE, or NOMINAL to another NOUN, VERB, or ADJECTIVE, especially relations of location, direction, duration, manner, etc.; also, the LEXICAL CATEGORY of such a word.

prescriptive rule   Statement of what supposedly *should* occur in a language or languages, rather than what has occurred or does occur. See also DESCRIPTIVE RULE.

prescriptivist   Person inclined to regulate language as he or she believes it *should* be, rather than describe what it is, has been, or will be; as an adjective, typical of such a person's attitude toward language. See also DESCRIPTIVIST.

present participle   PARTICIPLE derived from a bare infinitive form of a VERB by addition of the suffix *-ing*, as in "Glossary entries aren't *falling* out of the sky."

preservation   Verbal slip in which an earlier sound is also accidentally retained in a later position in a word or phrase, as in *big bilch* for *big belch*. See also ANTICIPATION, MALAPROPISM, and SPOONERISM.

presupposition   Assumption that makes the truth of a proposition or UTTERANCE possible, as when the assumption of a "king of France" allows us to consider the truth of the claim that "The present king of France is bald."

priming   Mental activation of a word's lexical associations and COLLOCATES.

proclitic   CLITIC that attaches to the word following it. See also ENCLITIC.

progressive aspect   ASPECT that indicates continuing action, formed by the appropriate form of *be*+the PRESENT PARTICIPLE.

projection rules   System that guides words into appropriate syntactic roles. See also THEMATIC ROLES.

pronoun   Word that within a syntactic structure stands in for a NOUN or noun phrase. See also DEMONSTRATIVE PRONOUN, INDEFINITE PRONOUN, INTERROGATIVE PRONOUN, PERSONAL PRONOUN, REFLEXIVE PRONOUN, and RELATIVE PRONOUN.

prosody   1: Distribution of INTONATION and stress. 2: Systematic arrangement of intonation and stress in poetry. See also ACCENTUAL-SYLLABIC METER, METER, PURE ACCENTUAL METER, PURE SYLLABIC METER, RHYTHM, and SCANSION.

proto-language   Language of which there is no written evidence, but which can be reconstructed from the evidence of related written languages, according to systematic rules of historical sound change and word formation; for instance, proto-Indo-European, Germanic, and Italic are proto-languages of particular importance to the development of English.

prototype   Mental "best examples" of things that allow speakers to structure linguistic categories and create meaningful semantic relationships.

psycholinguistics   Study of the relationships among language, mind, and the brain, including processes of language acquisition; also called "cognitive linguistics."

pure accentual meter   Patterned distribution of stress among SYLLABLES in a poetic line. See also ACCENTUAL-SYLLABIC METER, METER, PURE SYLLABIC METER, RHYTHM, and SCANSION.

pure syllabic meter   Pattern of SYLLABLES per line of poetry, as in haiku. See also ACCENTUAL-SYLLABIC METER, METER, PURE ACCENTUAL METER, RHYTHM, and SCANSION.

question   In conversation, a means of taking TURNS, often by constructing ADJACENCY PAIRS. See also CONVERSATIONAL FLOOR, EYE CONTACT, GESTURE, INTONATION, SILENCE, TURN, and TURN-TAKING VIOLATION.

reanalysis   Word-formative process that redistributes PHONEMES to create new MORPHEMES, as when a *napron* becomes an *apron*. See also EGGCORN and FOLK ETYMOLOGY.

reappropriation   Process of claiming or reclaiming a historically derogatory term by a community that has been oppressed or stigmatized by that term. See also AMELIORATION, DYSPHEMISM, EUPHEMISM, and PEJORATION.

recursion   Capacity of language to embed an infinite number of elements into its grammatical structure.

reduplication   Word-formative process in which MORPHEMES (or rhymes of morphemes) are repeated, such as *boo boo, hanky-panky,* or *car car,* as in "Did you buy a car car or an SUV?"

reflex   Word derived from an older form, whether in the same or a different language, called an ETYMON. For instance, Modern English *ask* is a reflex of Old English *ācsian*. It may be helpful to think of an etymon as a "parent" (or great-great-grandparent) word, a REFLEX as a "child" (or great-great-grandchild) word, and COGNATES as "cousin" words.

reflexive pronoun   PRONOUN that represents an entity identical to a subject, such as *herself, himself, itself, myself, themselves, yourself,* and *yourselves*.

register   Text type that exhibits characteristics that distinguish it from other text types; for instance, personal letters constitute a register distinct from résumés, etc. See also GENRE.

relative clause   DEPENDENT CLAUSE typically introduced by a RELATIVE PRONOUN that functions as an ADJECTIVAL.

relative pronoun   PRONOUN used to introduce a RELATIVE CLAUSE, such as *that, which, who, whom,* and *whose*.

relevance   Assumption, given the COOPERATIVE PRINCIPLE, that speakers' contributions to conversation will have an optimal bearing on the matter at hand.

repair   Attempt to restore cooperation or POLITENESS to a conversation when either has broken down. See also COOPERATIVE PRINCIPLE.

representative   ILLOCUTIONARY ACT that represents a state of affairs, characterized, for instance, by stating, claiming, insisting, suggesting, etc. Representatives are also called ASSERTIVES. See also COMMISSIVE, DECLARATION, DIRECTIVE, EXPRESSIVE, and VERDICTIVE.

resolution   Closing material about what finally happens in a NARRATIVE. See also ABSTRACT, CODA, COMPLICATING ACTION, EVALUATION, and ORIENTATION.

restrictive relative clause   Clause that specifies the referent of the noun or noun phrase it modifies. See also NONRESTRICTIVE CLAUSE.

retention   Process in which speakers establish dialectal vocabulary by bringing dialects/languages with them at emigration/migration. See also BORROWING, COINING, LANGUAGE CONTACT, NATURALLY OCCURING INTERNAL LANGUAGE CHANGE, SOCIAL FACTOR, and STRUCTURAL INFLUENCE.

retroflex liquid   Speech sound produced when the tongue is curled up toward the top of the mouth and air is funneled over it. See also APPROXIMANT, BUNCHED /R/, GLIDE, LATERAL LIQUID, and LIQUID.

retronymy   Word-formative process that creates words or phrases (*snail mail* or *regular mail*) to augment or replace words once used alone (*mail*), in order to distinguish them from new words or phrases (*e-mail* or *express mail*) for new developments.

rhyme   Correspondence of word-final sounds generally, but especially among poetic lines or parts of those lines. See also EYE RHYMES.

rhythm   Arrangement of stress in natural speech. See also METER and SCANSION.

right hemisphere   Side of the brain responsible for interpreting spatial relationships, jokes, and irony. See also LEFT HEMISPHERE.

run-on sentence   Complex or compound SENTENCE ill-formed because it lacks hierarchical markers, such as CONJUNCTIONS.

scansion   Symbolic representation of METER. See also ACCENTUAL-SYLLABIC METER, METER, PURE ACCENTUAL METER, PURE SYLLABIC METER, and RHYTHM.

semantics   Systematic study of meaning in language, especially word and sentence meaning.

sentence   Syntactic unit that includes at least one SUBJECT and one PREDICATE but may be composed of one or more INDEPENDENT CLAUSES, as well as SUBORDINATE or DEPENDENT CLAUSES.

sentence adverb   Adverb that modifies a sentence or longer segment of DISCOURSE, rather than a specific verb; in "Hopefully, I'll always use adverbs grammatically," *hopefully* is a sentence adverb, and some consider it ungrammatical English usage; also called a DISCOURSE ADVERB.

sentence fragment   Sentence ill-formed because it lacks either a SUBJECT or PREDICATE, or because it proposes a SUBORDINATE as an INDEPENDENT CLAUSE.

sibilant   Speech sounds that "hiss" rather than "hum." See also SONORANTS.

signified   Concept that a SIGNIFIER represents; one essential component of a LINGUISTIC SIGN.

signifier   Any meaningful string of sounds, that is, a linguistic form; one essential component of a LINGUISTIC SIGN.

silence   Pause that allows someone else to take the CONVERSATIONAL FLOOR. See also EYE CONTACT, GESTURE, INTONATION, QUESTION, SILENCE, TURN, and TURN-TAKING VIOLATION.

social factor   Process in which speakers enrich dialectal vocabulary by adopting (usually below the level of consciousness) features of speech marked for their social significance. See also BORROWING, COINING, LANGUAGE CONTACT, NATURALLY OCCURRING INTERNAL LANGUAGE CHANGE, RETENTION, and STRUCTURAL INFLUENCE.

social network theory   Theory of SPEECH COMMUNITIES that focuses on the network of interpersonal relationships within such a community. See also COMMUNITY OF PRACTICE, LINGUISTIC MARKET, and VARIATIONIST SOCIOLINGUSITICS.

sociolinguistics   Study of language in use, especially in terms of variation. See also DIALECTOLOGY and VARIATIONIST SOCIOLINGUISTICS.

soft palate   Rear surface of the roof of the mouth, leading forward to the HARD PALATE and back toward the LARYNX; also called the VELUM. See also PALATE.

sonorant   Any speech sound that includes "humming" or VOICING. See also OBSTRUENT and ORAL SOUND.

spatial deixis   Reference to a location that figures directly in the circumstance in which an UTTERANCE is made, usually by means of an ADVERB. See also DEIXIS, PERSONAL DEIXIS, and TEMPORAL DEIXIS.

specialization   Process of semantic change in which a word with a general meaning becomes a word of more specific meaning; for instance, by the eighteenth century, *wit* meant, narrowly, 'clever speech; faculty of clever speech; person with the faculty of clever speech,' even though, in Old English, *wit* had referred to nearly any intellectual or mental ability. See also AMELIORATION, DYSPHEMISM, EUPHEMISM, GENERALIZATION, HYPONYMY, MERONYMY, PEJORATION, POLYSEMY, and SYNONYMY.

spectrogram   Image of a sound wave. See also ACOUSTIC PHONETICS and AUDITORY PHONETICS.

speech act theory   Approach to language that conceives of language as performing actions; any instance of language that does so is called a **speech act**. See also CONSTATIVE SPEECH ACT, DIRECT SPEECH ACT, ILLOCUTIONARY ACT, INDIRECT SPEECH ACT, LOCUTIONARY ACT, PERFORMATIVE SPEECH ACT, PERLOCUTIONARY ACT, and PRAGMATICS.

speech community   Group of speakers who share linguistic norms and ideologies. See also COMMUNITY OF PRACTICE, LINGUISTIC MARKET, and SOCIAL NETWORK THEORY.

Spoonerism   Exchange of (usually initial) sounds in a series of two or more words, such as "Let me sew you to your sheet," usually to humorous effect. See also ANTICIPATION, MALAPROPISM, and PRESERVATION.

Stand Alone Test   CONSTITUENCY TEST in which a supposed CONSTITUENT, standing alone, adequately answers a question. See also COORDINATION TEST, MOVEMENT TEST, and SUBSTITUTION TEST.

stop   Speech sound produced, in part, by complete obstruction of airflow. See also AFFRICATE, FRICATIVE, NASAL, and OBSTRUENT.

structural influence   Phonology, morphology, or syntax of a language variety that is affected by a contact language. See also BORROWING, COINING, LANGUAGE CONTACT, NATURALLY OCCURING INTERNAL LANGUAGE CHANGE, RETENTION, and SOCIAL FACTOR.

style   1: Use of supposedly "good" or "correct" English. 2: Specific type of speech, for instance, formal speech or colloquial speech, academic speech or gossip, etc.

style-shift   Movement from one STYLE to another in any type of DISCOURSE. See also CODESWITCHING, CRITICAL DISCOURSE ANALYSIS, DISCOURSE ANALYSIS, and STYLISTICS.

stylistics   Study of language as used in artificial contexts, such as literature, judicial and political speech, etc.; study of language as art or craft. See also CRITICAL DISCOURSE ANALYSIS and DISCOURSE ANALYSIS.

subject   NOUN, noun phrase, or PRONOUN that acts through a VERB or is described in a PREDICATE; also the CASE in which such a word functions. See also DIRECT OBJECT, INDIRECT OBJECT, and OBJECT.

subjunctive mood   MOOD that expresses types of conditional meaning, especially command, hypothesis, or wish.

subordinate clause   CLAUSE that cannot function as a SENTENCE, but that must be attached to or embedded in an INDEPENDENT CLAUSE; also called a DEPENDENT CLAUSE.

subordinating conjunction   CONJUNCTION, such as *although*, *because*, *if*, *unless*, that connects a MAIN CLAUSE and a DEPENDENT or SUBORDINATE CLAUSE.

substitution   In NARRATIVE, partial replacement of ELLIPSIS to promote COHESION by connecting the points at which information is omitted and supplied.

Substitution Test   CONSTITUENCY TEST in which one replaces the CONSTITUENT in question with a single word that should serve the same syntactic FUNCTION. See also COORDINATION TEST, MOVEMENT TEST, and STAND ALONE TEST.

suffix   AFFIX attached to the end of a word, sometimes a DERIVATIONAL, sometimes an INFLECTIONAL MORPHEME.

suffixing   1: Word-formative process involving a SUFFIX. 2: Word resulting from that process.

superlative adjective   Form of an ADJECTIVE indicating that one item possesses a quality to the greatest possible degree; for instance, grass can be *green*, but it is *greenest* in a baseball infield when you listen to a game on the radio and have to visualize that green field in the mind.

superordinate   Word of more general meaning than others defined in relation to it; for instance, *vehicle* is a superordinate for *car*, *bus*, *bicycle*, *motorcycle*, etc. Also called a HYPERNYM. See also HYPONYM.

suppletion   Partial merger of two VERBS, so that some forms derive from one verb and some from the other, as with *go* (from Old English *gan*) and *went* (from Old English *wendan*).

surface dyslexia   DYSLEXIA in which speakers have trouble reading words with irregular spellings. See also DEEP DYSLEXIA and PHONOLOGICAL DYSLEXIA.

syllabic consonant   CONSONANT that participates in or constitutes the NUCLEUS of a SYLLABLE.

syllable   Unit of speech consisting of uninterrupted sound, composed of one or more phonemes, which generally includes a vowel NUCLEUS and may include a consonant ONSET or CODA or both. See also PHONOTACTIC CONSTRAINT and SYLLABIC CONSONANT.

Sylvian fissure   Division between the FRONTAL and TEMPORAL LOBES of the LEFT HEMISPHERE of the brain.

synchronic   Concerned with the present state of affairs; language can be considered **synchronically**. See also DIACHRONIC.

synonym   Word very close in meaning to another; word that shares a DENOTATIVE MEANING, but not CONNOTATIVE MEANING, with another; the lexical relationship among such terms is **synonymy**. See also GENERALIZATION, HYPONYMY, MERONYMY, and POLYSEMY.

syntax   Systematic ways in which words combine to create well-formed PHRASES, CLAUSES, and SENTENCES.

synthetic language   Language in which inflection, rather than word order, mostly indicates grammatical functions in a sentence. See also AGGLUTINATIVE LANGUAGE and ANALYTIC LANGUAGE.

tag question   YES-NO QUESTION added to the end of a declarative SENTENCE that repeats the AUXILIARY VERB and PRONOUN (or introduces a pronoun for a NOUN or NOMINAL in the sentence) in inverse positions, such as "We have finally reached the end of this definition, haven't we?"

temporal adverb   ADVERB that describes when an action or state occurs, such as *now* or *soon*. See also DISCOURSE ADVERB, MANNER ADVERB, and SENTENCE ADVERB.

temporal deixis   Reference to a time or period of time that figures directly in the circumstance in which an UTTERANCE is made, usually by means of an ADVERB. See also DEIXIS, PERSONAL DEIXIS, and SPATIAL DEIXIS.

temporal lobe   Part of the brain toward the lower front of each cerebral hemisphere; the CORTEX at the temporal lobe of the LEFT HEMISPHERE contains centers important to speech production, including WERNICKE'S AREA. See also FRONTAL LOBE, OCCIPITAL LOBE, and PARIETAL LOBE.

tense   GRAMMATICAL indication, in the form of a VERB or a verb phrase, of time at which an event or state occurs. See also ASPECT and MOOD.

tenseness   DISTINCTIVE FEATURE of VOWELS indicating the relatively loose (central) or tense (peripheral) position of the tongue. Also called LAXNESS. See also BACKNESS, FRONTNESS, HEIGHT, LAX VOWEL, and TENSE VOWEL.

tone   PITCH of a word that changes the meaning of the word. See also INTONATION.

trachea   The "windpipe" through which air flows from the lungs to the LARYNX.

transformation   Syntactic processes that generate "surface" realizations from "underlying" sentences, as in the passive transformation "The definition was written by Michael" generated from "Michael wrote the definition."

transitive verb   VERB that requires a DIRECT OBJECT; the essential property of such verbs is **transitivity**. See also DITRANSITIVE VERB, INTRANSITIVE VERB, and OBJECT-COMPLEMENT VERB.

tree   Analytic tool used to expose the hierarchical structure of words, phrases, clauses, and sentences. See also BRANCH and NODE.

truth conditions   What must be true for an UTTERANCE or SENTENCE to be true.

turn   Basic unit of conversation. See also CONVERSATIONAL FLOOR, EYE CONTACT, GESTURE, INTO-NATION, QUESTION, SILENCE, and TURN-TAKING VIOLATION.

turn-taking violation   Attempt to take or reluctance to give up the CONVERSATIONAL FLOOR once a TURN is indicated, for instance by INTERRUPTION or OVERLAP.

uncountable nouns   NOUNS that represent things or concepts that cannot be counted, such as *stuff* and *water*, sometimes called "mass nouns."

Universal Grammar   According to Noam Chomsky, who conceived it, the "system of princi-ples, conditions, rules that are elements or properties of all human languages" (1975, 29).

utterance   Realization of a given unit of speech on a specific occasion in a specific context; the basic unit of DISCOURSE.

variationist sociolinguistics   Study of distributional patterns of linguistic variables within SPEECH COMMUNITIES. See also COMMUNITY OF PRACTICE, DIALECTOLOGY, LINGUISTIC MAR-KET, LINGUISTIC NETWORK THEORY, and SOCIOLINGUSTICS.

velum   Rear surface of the roof of the mouth, leading forward to the HARD PALATE and back toward the LARYNX; also called the SOFT PALATE. See also PALATE.

verb   Word that represents action, existence, relation, or state of being; also the LEXICAL CATE-GORY to which such words belong.

verdictive   ILLOCUTIONARY ACT that judges, assesses, or ranks. See also ASSERTIVE, COMMISSIVE, DECLARATION, DIRECTIVE, EXPRESSIVE, and REPRESENTATIVE.

vocal cords   Elastic muscles that stretch over the LARYNX.

voicing   DISTINCTIVE FEATURE that describes the extent to which the vocal cords are pulled back ("voiceless" or "unvoiced") or vibrate ("voiced"). See also MANNER OF ARTICULATION and PLACE OF ARTICULATION.

vowel   Speech sound characterized by unimpeded airflow and produced by shape of the oral cav-ity and the tongue's shape and position. See also CONSONANT and DISTINCTIVE FEATURES.

Wernicke's aphasia   APHASIA caused by damage to WERNICKE'S AREA, because of which a speaker finds it difficult to understand speech. See also BROCA'S APHASIA.

Wernicke's area   Area in the CORTEX at THE TEMPORAL LOBE of the LEFT HEMISPHERE of the brain partly responsible for language production. See also BROCA'S AREA.

***wh-* question**   Question formed by movement of PRONOUN beginning with *wh-* from the end of a question ("You moved which pronoun?") to the front ("Which pronoun did you move?") with reattribution of TENSE to the AUXILIARY.

yes-no question   Question formed by rearrangement of CONSTITUENTS within a declarative sen-tence into a question that elicits either "Yes" or "No," as when "This is a well-formed yes-no question" becomes "Is this a well-formed yes-no question?" The answer is "Yes."

Bibliography

Ackerman, Jennifer. 2004. Untangling the Brain: The Search for the Causes and Cures of Dyslexia. *Yale Alumni Magazine* (January/February): 47–55.

Adams, Michael. 2000. Lexical Doppelgängers. *Journal of English Linguistics* 28: 295–310.

Adams, Michael. 2009. *Slang: The People's Poetry*. New York: Oxford University Press.

Adams, Michael P., and Newton A. Perrin. 1995. *Unless* 'in case' in Berks County, Pennsylvania. *American Speech* 70 (4): 441–42.

Aitchison, Jean. 2001. *Language Change: Progress or Decay?* 3d ed. Cambridge: Cambridge University Press.

Algeo, John. 2001. External History. In *The Cambridge History of the English Language*. Vol. 6, *English in North America*, edited by J. Algeo, 1–58. Cambridge: Cambridge University Press.

Algeo, John, and Adele S. Algeo, eds. 1991. *Fifty Years Among the New Words: A Dictionary of Neologisms 1941–1991*. Cambridge: Cambridge University Press.

Allan, Keith. 2001. *Natural Language Semantics*. Malden, MA: Blackwell.

Alim, H. Samy. 2003. On Some Serious Next Millennium Rap Ishhh: Pharoahe Monch, Hip Hop Poetics, and the Internal Rhymes of Internal Affairs. *Journal of English Linguistics* 31: 60–84.

Allende, Isabel. 2003. *My Invented Country: A Nostalgic Journey through Chile*. Trans. Margaret Sayers Peden. New York: HarperCollins.

Altmann, Gerry. 1997. *The Ascent of Babel: An Exploration of Language, Mind, and Understanding*. Oxford: Oxford University Press.

American College Dictionary. 1947. Ed. Clarence L. Barnhart and others. New York: Random House.

American Heritage Dictionary of the English Language. 1969. Ed. William Morris and others. Boston: Houghton Mifflin.

American Heritage Dictionary of the English Language. 2000. 4th ed. Ed. Joseph P. Pickett and others. Boston: Houghton Mifflin.

Ammer, Christine. 1997. *American Heritage Dictionary of Idioms*. Boston: Houghton Mifflin.

Anthony, Louise M., and Norbert Hornstein, eds. 2003. *Chomsky and His Critics*. Malden, MA: Blackwell.

Atwood, E. Bagby. 1953. *A Survey of Verb Forms in the Eastern United States*. Ann Arbor: University of Michigan Press.

Atwood, E. Bagby. 1962. *The Regional Vocabulary of Texas*. Austin: University of Texas Press.

Attridge, Derek. 1982. *The Rhythms of English Poetry*. London: Longman.

Austin, J. L. 1962. *How to Do Things with Words*. Cambridge, MA: Harvard University Press.

Bailey, Nathan. 1721. *An Universal Etymological English Dictionary*. London: E. Bell, J. Darby, A. Bettesworth, and others.

Bailey, Richard W. 1991. *Images of English*. Ann Arbor: University of Michigan Press.

Bailey, Richard W. 1996. *Nineteenth-Century English*. Ann Arbor: University of Michigan Press.

Bailey, Richard W. 2006. Talking about Split Infinitives. *Michigan Today News-E* (June). http://www.umich.edu/NewsE/06_06/words.html.

Bailey, Richard W., and Manfred Görlach, eds. 1982. *English as a World Language*. Ann Arbor: University of Michigan Press.

Barber, Charles. 1976. *Early Modern English*. London: Andre Deutsch.

Baron, Dennis. 1990. *The English-Only Question: An Official Language for Americans?* New Haven: Yale University Press.

Baron, Dennis. Essays on Language, Reading, Writing, and Technology. http://www.english .illinois.edu/-people-/faculty/debaron/essayset.html.

Baron, Naomi. 2000. *Alphabet to Email: How Written English Evolved and Where It's Headed.* New York: Routledge.

Baron, Naomi. 2008. *Always On: Language in an Online and Mobile World.* New York: Oxford University Press.

Barrett, Rusty. 1997. The "Homo-genius" Speech Community. In *Queerly Phrased: Language, Gender, and Sexuality,* edited by A. Livia and K. Hall, 181–201. New York: Oxford University Press.

Barton, Ellen. 1993. Evidentials, Argumentation, and Epistemological Stance. *College English* 55: 745–69.

Battistella, Edwin. 2005. *Bad Language.* New York: Oxford University Press.

Bauer, Laurie. 1988. *Introducing Linguistic Morphology.* Edinburgh: Edinburgh University Press.

Baugh, Albert C., and Thomas Cable. 2002. *A History of the English Language.* 5th ed. Upper Saddle River, NJ: Prentice Hall.

Baugh, John. 1999. *Out of the Mouths of Slaves: African American Language and Educational Malpractice.* Austin: University of Texas Press.

Baugh, John. 2000. *Beyond Ebonics: Linguistic Pride and Racial Prejudice.* New York: Oxford University Press.

Bawarshi, Anis. 2003. *Genre and the Invention of the Writer: Reconsidering the Place of Invention in Composition.* Logan, UT: Utah State University Press.

Beebe, Leslie M. 1995. Polite Fictions: Instrumental Rudeness as Pragmatic Competence. *Georgetown University Roundtable on Languages and Linguistics*: 154–68.

Bex, Tony, and Richard J. Watts, eds. 1999. *Standard English: The Widening Debate.* London: Routledge.

Biber, Douglas, Susan Conrad, and Randi Reppen. 1998. *Corpus Linguistics: Investigating Language Structure and Use.* Cambridge: Cambridge University Press.

Biber, Douglas, Stig Johansson, Geoffrey Leech, Susan Conrad, and Edward Finegan. 1999. *The Longman Grammar of Spoken and Written English.* Harlow, UK: Longman.

Blake, Norman F. 1996. *A History of the English Language.* New York: New York University Press.

Bloom, Paul. 2000. *How Children Learn the Meanings of Words.* Cambridge, MA: MIT Press.

Bloomfield, Leonard. 1933. *Language.* New York: Holt, Rinehart and Winston.

Blount, Thomas. 1969 [1656]. *Glossographia: or, A Dictionary Interpreting all such Hard Words . . . as are now used in our refined English Tongue.* English Linguistics 1500–1800: A Collection of Facsimile Reprints 153, edited by R. C. Alston. Menston, UK: Scolar Press.

Boroditsky, Lera. 2009. How Does Our Language Shape the Way We Think? In *What's Next? Dispatches on the Future of Science,* edited by Max Brockman, 116–29. New York: Vintage Books.

Boylan, James. 2004. Review of *Eats, Shoots & Leaves: The Zero Tolerance Approach to Punctuation. Columbia Journalism Review* (May/June), http://cjrarchives.org/issues/2004/3/boylan-books.asp.

Bradford, Richard. 1994. *Roman Jakobson: Life, Language, Art.* London: Routledge.

Bradley, Mary O. 2008. Country Rife with Sloppy English. *Ann Arbor News* (March 12), A1, A12.

Brewer, Charlotte. 2007. *Treasure-House of the Language: The Living OED.* New Haven: Yale University Press.

Bright, William. 2004. *Native American Placenames of the United States.* Norman, OK: University of Oklahoma Press.

Bronowski, Jacob. 1977. *A Sense of the Future: Essays in Natural Philosophy.* Cambridge: MIT Press.

Brown, Penelope. 1980. How and Why Are Women More Polite. In *Women and Language in Literature and Society,* edited by Sally McConnell-Ginet, Ruth Borker, and Nelly Furman, 111–36. New York: Praeger.

Brown, Penelope, and Stephen C. Levinson. 1987. *Politeness: Some Universals in Language Usage*. Cambridge: Cambridge University Press.

Bryson, Bill. 1990. *The Mother Tongue: English and How It Got That Way*. New York: W. Morrow.

Bucholtz, Mary. 1999. You da Man: Narrating the Racial Other in the Production of White Masculinity. *Journal of Sociolinguistics* 3 (4): 443–460.

Bucholtz, Mary, Nancy Bermudez, Victor Fung, Lisa Edwards, and Rosalva Vargas. 2007. Hella Nor Cal or Totally So Cal? The Perceptual Dialectology of California. *Journal of English Linguistics* 35 (4): 325–52.

Bullokar, William. 1966 [1580]. *Short Introduction or Guiding to Print, Write, and Reade Inglish Speech*. Facsimile. Ed. B. Danielsson and R. C. Alston. Leeds, UK: University of Leeds, School of English.

Burchfield, R. W. 1996. *The New Fowler's Modern English Usage*. 3d. ed. Oxford: Clarendon Press.

Burrow, J. A., and Thorlac Turville-Petre. 1996. *A Book of Middle English*. Cambridge, MA: Blackwell.

Bybee, Joan L. 1985. *Morphology: A Study of the Relation Between Meaning and Form*. Amsterdam: John Benjamins.

Cameron, Deborah. 1995. *Verbal Hygiene*. London: Routledge.

Cameron, Deborah. 1997. Performing Gender Identity: Young Men's Talk and the Construction of Heterosexual Masculinity. In *Language and Masculinity*, edited by Sally Johnson and Ulrike Hanna Meinhof, 47–64. Oxford, UK: Blackwell.

Cameron, Deborah, and Don Kulick. 2003. *Language and Sexuality*. Cambridge: Cambridge University Press.

Campbell, Alistair. 1959. *Old English Grammar*. Oxford: Clarendon Press.

Campbell, George. 1776. *The Philosophy of Rhetoric*. 2 vols. London: W. Strahan and T. Cadell.

Canada, Mark. Homepage. http://www.uncp.edu/home/Canada/work/markport/language/aspects/spg2003/05syntax.htm.

Carey, Susan. 1978. The Child as Word Learner. In *Linguistic Theory and Psychological Reality*, edited by J. Bresnan, G. Miller, and M. Halle, 264–93. Cambridge, MA: MIT Press.

Carnie, Andrew. 2002. *Syntax: A Generative Introduction*. Oxford: Blackwell.

Carroll, David. 1999. *Psychology of Language*. 3d ed. Pacific Grove, CA: Brooks/Cole.

Carroll, Lewis. 2003 [1871]. *Alice's Adventures in Wonderland and Through the Looking-Glass: And What She Found There*. Ed. Hugh Haughton. Harmondsworth, UK: Penguin.

Carver, Craig. 1987. *American Regional Dialects: A Word Geography*. Ann Arbor: University of Michigan Press.

Catford, J. C. 1977. *Fundamental Problems in Phonetics*. Bloomington: Indiana University Press.

Catford, J. C. 1988. *A Practical Introduction in Phonetics*. Oxford: Oxford University Press.

Cattell, Ray. 2000. *Children's Language: Consensus and Controversy*. London; New York: Cassell.

Cawdrey, Robert. 1966 [1604]. *A Table Alphabeticall of Hard Usual English Words*. Gainesville, FL: Scholars' Facsimiles and Reprints. http://www.library.utoronto.ca/utel/ret/cawdrey/cawdrey0.html.

Chambers, J. K. 1995. *Sociolinguistic Theory: Linguistic Variation and Its Social Significance*. Oxford: Blackwell.

Chomsky, Noam. 1955. Transformational Analysis. Ph.D. diss., University of Pennsylvania.

Chomsky, Noam. 1957. *Syntactic Structures*. The Hague: Mouton.

Chomsky, Noam. 1965. *Aspects of the Theory of Syntax*. Cambridge, MA: MIT Press.

Chomsky, Noam. 1966. *Cartesian Linguistics: A Chapter in the History of Rationalist Thought*. New York: Harper and Row.

Chomsky, Noam. 1968. *Language and Mind*. New York: Harcourt Brace and World.

Chomsky, Noam. 1975. *The Logical Structure of Linguistic Theory*. New York: Plenum.

Chomsky, Noam. 1980. *Rules and Representations*. Oxford: Blackwell.

Chomsky, Noam. 1981. *Lectures on Government and Binding*. Dordrecht: Foris.

Chomsky, Noam. 1995. *The Minimalist Program*. Cambridge, MA: MIT Press.

Chun, Elaine W. 2001. The Construction of White, Black, and Korean American Identities through African American Vernacular English. *Journal of Linguistic Anthropology* 11 (1): 52–64.

Clanchy, M. T. 1993. *From Memory to Written Record: England 1066–1307*. 2d ed. Oxford, UK; Cambridge, MA: Blackwell.

Clancy, Steven J. 1999. The Ascent of *guy. American Speech* 74 (3): 282–97.

Clark, Eve. 1988 [1981]. Lexical Innovations: How Children Learn to Create New Words. In *Child Language: A Reader*, edited by Margery B. Franklin and Sybil S. Barten, 118–29. New York: Oxford University Press.

Clark, Eve V. 1998. Morphology in Language Acquisition. In *The Handbook of Morphology*, edited by A. Spencer and A. M. Zwicky, 374–89. Oxford: Blackwell.

Clark, John, and Colin Yallop. 1995. *An Introduction to Phonetics and Phonology*. 2d ed. Oxford: Blackwell.

Clyne, M. G. 1987. Constraints on Code-switching: How Universal Are They? *Linguistics* 25: 739–64.

Coates, Jennifer. 1996. *Women Talk: Conversation between Women Friends*. Oxford: Blackwell.

Coates, Jennifer, ed. 1998. *Language and Gender: A Reader*. Oxford: Blackwell.

Cockeram, Henry. 1968 [1623]. *The English Dictionarie: or, an Interpreter of Hard English Words*. English Linguistics 1500–1800: A Collection of Facsimile Reprints 124, edited by R. C. Alston. Menston, UK: Scolar Press.

Cook, Vivian J., and Mark Newson. 1996. *Chomsky's Universal Grammar: An Introduction*. 2d ed. Oxford: Blackwell.

Crawford, James, ed. 1992. *Language Loyalties: A Source Book on the Official English Controversy*. Chicago: Chicago University Press.

Crawford, James. 1999. *Bilingual Education: History, Politics, Theory and Practice*. 4th ed. Los Angeles, CA: Bilingual Educational Services.

Cruse, D. A. 1986. *Lexical Semantics*. Cambridge: Cambridge University Press.

Crystal, David. 1997. *The Cambridge Encyclopedia of the English Language*. 2d ed. Cambridge: Cambridge University Press.

Crystal, David. 2001. *Language and the Internet*. New York: Cambridge University Press.

Crystal, David. 2003. *English as a Global Language*. 2d ed. New York: Cambridge University Press.

Crystal, David. 2006a. Into the Twenty-first Century. In *The Oxford History of English*, edited by Lynda Mugglestone, 394–413. Oxford: Oxford University Press.

Crystal, David. 2006b. *Language and the Internet*. 2d ed. New York: Cambridge University Press.

Crystal, David. 2008. *Txtng: The Gr8 Deb8*. Oxford: Oxford University Press.

Dailey-O'Cain, Jennifer. 2000. The Sociolinguistic Distribution of and Attitudes toward Focuser "Like" and Quotative "Like." *Journal of Sociolinguistics* 4 (1): 60–80.

D'Arcy, Alexandra. 2007. *Like* and Language Ideology: Disentangling Fact from Fiction. *American Speech* 82 (4): 386–419.

Davis, Norman. 1953. *Sweet's Anglo-Saxon Primer*. Oxford: Oxford University Press.

Dehaene, Stanislas, Véronique Izard, Pierre Pica, and Elizabeth Spelke. 2006. Core Knowledge of Geometry in an Amazonian Indigene Group. *Science* 311 (January 20): 381–84.

Dictionary of American Regional English. 1985–. Ed. Frederic G. Cassidy, Joan Houston Hall, and others. Cambridge, MA: Belknap Press of Harvard University Press.

Dilworth, Thomas. 1967 [1751]. *A New Guide to the English Tongue*. English Linguistics 1500–1800: A Collection of Facsimile Reprints 4, edited by R. C. Alston. Menston, UK: Scolar Press.

diPaolo Healey, Antonette, and others, eds. Ongoing Project. *Dictionary of Old English*. Toronto: Toronto University Press. http://www.doe.utoronto.ca/.

Dixon, R. M. W. 1991. *A New Approach to English Grammar, on Semantic Principles*. Oxford: Clarendon.

Dobson, E. J. 1957. *English Pronunciation, 1500–1700*. 2 vols. Oxford: Clarendon Press.

Earley, Tony. 1998. The Quare Gene. *New Yorker* (September 21): 80–85.

Eckert, Penelope. 2000. *Linguistic Variation as Social Practice: The Linguistic Construction of Identity in Belten High*. Malden, MA: Blackwell.

Eckert, Penelope. 2004. California Vowels. http://www.stanford.edu/eckert/vowels.html.

Eckert, Penelope, and Sally McConnell-Ginet. 1992. Think Practically and Look Locally: Language and Gender as Community-Based Practice. *Annual Review of Anthropology* 21: 461–90.

Eckert, Penelope, and Sally McConnell-Ginet. 2003. *Language and Gender*. Cambridge: Cambridge University Press.

Eggcorn Database. Maintained by Chris Waigl. http://eggcorns.lascribe.net.

Eliason, Norman. 1956. *Tarheel Talk: An Historical Study of the English Language in North Carolina to 1860*. Chapel Hill: University of North Carolina Press.

Erard, Michael. 2007. *Um . . . : Slips, Stumbles, and Verbal Blunders, and What They Mean*. New York: Pantheon.

Everett, Daniel L. 2005. Cultural Constraints on Grammar and Cognition in Pirahã: Another Look at the Design Features of Human Language. *Current Anthropology* 46 (4): 621–46.

Fahnestock, Jeanne, and Marie Secor. 1991. The Rhetoric of Literary Criticism. In *Textual Dynamics of the Professions: Historical and Contemporary Studies of Writing in Professional Communities*, edited by C. Bazerman and J. Parades, 76–96. Madison: University of Wisconsin Press.

Fillmore, Charles J. 1997. *Lectures on Deixis*. Stanford: CSLI Publications.

Finegan, Edward. 1980. *Attitudes toward English Usage: The History of a War of Words*. New York: Teachers College Press.

Finegan, Edward. 2008. *Language: Its Structure and Use*. 5th ed. Boston: Thomson Wadsworth.

Finegan, Edward, and John R. Rickford, eds. 2004. *Language in the USA: Themes for the Twenty-first Century*. Cambridge: Cambridge University Press.

Fisher, John. H. 1996. *The Emergence of Standard English*. Lexington: University Press of Kentucky.

Fishman, Pamela. 1983 [1978]. Interaction: The Work Women Do. In *Language, Gender, and Society*, edited by B. Thorne, C. Kramarae, and N. Henley, 89–102. Rowley, MA: Newbury House.

Fitch, W. Tecumseh, Marc D. Hauser, and Noam Chomsky. 2005. The Evolution of the Language Faculty: Clarifications and Implications. *Cognition* 97: 179–210.

Follett, Wilson. 1966. *Modern American Usage: A Guide*. New York: Hill and Wang.

Foster, Don. 1989. *Elegy by W. S.: A Study in Attribution*. Newark: University of Delaware Press.

Foster, Don. 2000. *Author Unknown: Tales of a Literary Detective*. New York: Henry Holt.

Fought, Carmen. 2003. *Chicano English in Context*. New York: Palgrave Macmillan.

Fowler, H. W. 1926. *A Dictionary of Modern English Usage*. Oxford: Oxford University Press.

Fox, Margalit. 1999. Dialects: The Good, the Bad and the Ugly—They're All Myths. *New York Times Sunday Magazine* (September 12).

Freeman, Jan. 2009. *Ambrose Bierce's* Write It Right: *The Celebrated Cynic's Language Peeves Deciphered, Appraised and Annotated for 21st-Century Readers*. New York: Walker & Co.

Fries, Charles Carpenter. 1952. *The Structure of English*. New York: Harcourt, Brace, and Company.

Fromkin, Victoria, Robert Rodman, and Nina Hyams. 2007. *An Introduction to Language*. 8th ed. Boston, MA: Thomson Wadsworth.

Fry, D. B. 1979. *The Physics of Speech*. Cambridge: Cambridge University Press.

Funk and Wagnalls Standard College Dictionary. 1977. 2d ed. Ed. Sidney I. Landau and others. New York: Funk and Wagnalls.

Fussell, Paul. 1979. *Poetic Meter and Poetic Form*. Rev. ed. New York: McGraw-Hill.

Garner, Bryan. 1998. *A Dictionary of Modern American Usage*. New York: Oxford University Press.

Giegerich, Heinz J. 1992. *English Phonology: An Introduction*. Cambridge: Cambridge University Press.

Gill, Jerry. 1997. *If a Chimpanzee Could Talk and Other Reflections on Language Acquisition*. Tucson: University of Arizona Press.

Gilman, E. Ward, ed. 1994. *Merriam-Webster's Dictionary of English Usage*. Springfield, MA: Merriam-Webster.

Goldin-Meadow, Susan, H. Nusbaum, S. D. Kelly, and S. Wagner. 2001. Explaining Math: Gesturing Lightens the Load. *Psychological Science* 12: 516–22.

Gopnik, Alison. 2003. The Theory Theory or an Alternative to the Innateness Hypothesis. In *Chomsky and His Critics*, edited by L. M. Antony and N. Hornstein, 238–54. Oxford: Blackwell.

Gopnik, Alison, Andrew N. Meltzoff, and Patricia K. Kuhl. 1999. *The Scientist in the Crib: What Early Learning Tells Us about the Mind*. New York: HarperCollins.

Gordon, E. V. 1957. *An Introduction to Old Norse*. Revised by R. Taylor. Oxford: Clarendon Press.

Gordon, Matthew. 2001. *Small-Town Values and Big-City Vowels: A Study of the Northern Cities Chain Shift in Michigan*. (Publication of the American Dialect Society 84.) Durham, NC: Duke University Press.

Gordon, Matthew. 2006. Straight Talking from the Heartland (Midwest). In *American Voices: How Dialects Differ from Coast to Coast*, edited by Walt Wolfram and Ben Ward, 106–11. Malden, MA: Blackwell.

Graddol, David. 1997. *The Future of English?* London: British Council.

Gray, John. 1993. *Men Are from Mars, Women Are from Venus*. New York: HarperCollins.

Greaves, Paul. 1969 [1594]. *Grammatica Anglica*. English Linguistics 1500–1800: A Collection of Facsimile Reprints 169, edited by R. C. Alston. Menston, UK: Scolar Press.

Green, Lisa. 2002. *African American English: A Linguistic Introduction*. Cambridge: Cambridge University Press.

Greenbaum, Sidney. 1996. *Oxford English Grammar*. London: Oxford University Press.

Grice, H. Paul. 1989. *Studies in the Way of Words*. Cambridge, MA: Harvard University Press.

Gumperz, John J. 2001. Interactional Sociolinguistics: A Personal Perspective. In *The Handbook of Discourse Analysis*, edited by D. Schiffrin, D. Tannen, and H. E. Hamilton, 215–28. Malden, MA: Blackwell.

Gumperz, John J., and Eduardo Hernandez-Chavez. 1971. Cognitive Aspects of Bilingual Communication. In *Language Use and Social Changes*, edited by W. H. Whitely, 111–25. London: Oxford University Press.

Gumperz, John J., and Stephen C. Levinson, eds. 1996. *Rethinking Linguistic Relativity*. Cambridge: Cambridge University Press.

Hall, J. R. Clark. 1984. *A Concise Anglo-Saxon Dictionary*. 4th ed. Revised by H. D. Meritt. Toronto: University of Toronto Press.

Halliday, M. A. K. 1985. *An Introduction to Functional Grammar*. London: Arnold.

Halliday, M. A. K., and Raqaiya Hasan. 1976. *Cohesion in English*. London: Longman.

Harris, Randy Allen. 1993. *The Linguistics Wars*. New York: Oxford University Press.

Harris, Zelig. 1942. Morpheme Alternants in Linguistic Analysis. *Language* 18: 169–180.

Hauser, Marc D., Noam Chomsky, and W. Tecumseh Fitch. 2002. The Faculty of Language: What Is It, Who Has It, and How Did It Evolve? *Science* 298: 1569–79.

Heaney, Seamus. 2000. *Beowulf: A New Verse Translation*. New York: Farrar, Straus, and Giroux.

Hespos, Susan J., and Elizabeth S. Spelke. 2004. Conceptual Precursors to Language. *Nature* 430 (July 22): 453–56.

Hitchings, Henry. 2005. *Defining the World: The Extraordinary Story of Dr. Johnson's Dictionary*. New York: Farrar, Straus and Giroux.

Hogg, Richard, general editor. *Cambridge History of the English Language*. 6 vols. Cambridge: Cambridge University Press.

Holmes, Janet. 1995. What a Lovely Tie! Compliments and Positive Politeness Strategies. In *Women, Men and Politeness*, edited by J. Holmes, 115–53. London: Longman.

Holmes, Janet, and Miriam Meyerhoff, eds. 2003. *The Handbook of Language and Gender*. Malden, MA: Blackwell.

Hopper, Paul. 2007. Linguistics and Micro-rhetoric: A Twenty-first Century Encounter. *Journal of English Linguistics* 35 (3): 236–52.

Huddleston, Rodney, and Geoffrey K. Pullum. 2002. *Cambridge Grammar of the English Language*. Cambridge: Cambridge University Press.

Hughes, Geoffrey. 1991. *Swearing: A Social History of Foul Language, Oaths and Profanity in English*. Oxford: Basil Blackwell.

Humboldt, Wilhelm von. 1999 [1836]. *On Language*. Trans. Peter Heath. Cambridge: Cambridge University Press.

Humphries, Tom, Carol Padden, and Terrence J. O'Rourke. 1994. *A Basic Course in American Sign Language*. 2d ed. Illustrated by Frank A. Paul. Silver Spring, MD: T. J. Publishers.

Hyland, Ken. 2005. Stance and Engagement: A Model of Interaction in Academic Discourse. *Discourse Studies* 7 (2): 173–92.

International Dictionary of the English Language. 1890. Ed. Noah Porter. Springfield, MA: G. and C. Merriam.

International Dyslexia Association. http://www.interdys.org/.

Jackendoff, Ray. 1990. *Semantic Structures*. Cambridge, MA: MIT Press.

Jackendoff, Ray. 2002. *Foundations of Language: Brain, Meaning, Grammar, Evolution*. Oxford: Oxford University Press.

Jackendoff, Ray, and Steven Pinker. 2005. The Nature of the Language Faculty and Its Implications for Evolution of Language (Reply to Fitch, Hauser, and Chomsky). *Cognition* 97: 211–25.

Jakobson, Roman. 1987a. Linguistics and Poetics. In *Language in Literature*, edited by K. Pomorska and S. Rudy, 62–94. Cambridge, MA: MIT Press.

Jakobson, Roman. 1987b. Two Aspects of Language and Two Types of Aphasic Disturbances. In *Language in Literature*, edited by K. Pomorska and S. Rudy, 95–119. Cambridge, MA: MIT Press.

Johnson, Samuel. 1755. *Dictionary of the English Language*. London: Dodsley, Hitch, Mellar, Longman, and Knapton.

Johnstone, Barbara. 2000. *Qualitative Methods in Sociolinguistics*. New York: Oxford University Press.

Johnstone, Barbara. 2002. *Discourse Analysis*. Malden, MA: Blackwell.

Jones, Richard Foster. 1953. *The Triumph of the English Language*. Stanford, CA: Stanford University Press.

Jucker, Andreas H. 1997. The Discourse Marker *well* in the History of English. *English Language and Linguistics* 1 (1): 91–110.

Kachru, Braj, Yamuna Kachru, and Cecil Nelson, eds. 2006. *The Handbook of World Englishes*. Malden/Oxford/Carlton: Blackwell.

Kalcik, Susan. 1975. ". . . like Ann's gynecologist or the time I was almost raped": Personal Narratives in Women's Rap Groups. *Journal of American Folklore* 88: 3–11.

Kenneally, Christine. 2007. *The First Word: The Search for the Origins of Language*. New York: Viking.

Kennedy, Randall. 2002. *Nigger: The Strange Career of a Troublesome Word*. New York: Pantheon.

Kersey, John. 1702. *A New English Dictionary*. London: Henry Bonwicke and Robert Knaplock.

Kiesling, Scott. 2004. *Dude*. *American Speech* 79 (3): 281–305.

Kittay, Eva. 1987. *Metaphor: Its Cognitive Force and Linguistic Structure*. Oxford: Clarendon.

Klammer, Thomas P., Muriel Schultz, and Angela Volpe. 2004. *Analyzing English Grammar*. 4th ed. New York: Pearson Longman.

Kökeritz, Helge. 1953. *Shakespeare's Pronunciation*. New Haven: Yale University Press.

Krapp, George P., and Eliott V. K. Dobbie, eds. 1931–1953. *Anglo-Saxon Poetic Records*. 6 vols. New York: Columbia University Press.

Kulick, Don. 2000. Gay and Lesbian Language. *Annual Review of Anthropology* 29: 243–85.

Kurath, Hans. 1949. *A Word Geography of the Eastern United States*. Ann Arbor: University of Michigan Press.

Kurath, Hans, and others. 1939–1943. *Linguistic Atlas of New England (LANE)*. 3 vols. in 6 parts. Providence, RI: Brown University.

Labov, William. 1972. *Sociolinguistic Patterns*. Philadelphia: University of Pennsylvania Press.

Labov, William. 1994. *Principles of Linguistic Change*. Vol. 1, *Internal Factors*. Oxford: Blackwell.

Labov, William. 2001. *Principles of Linguistic Change*. Vol. 2, *Social Factors*. Oxford: Blackwell.

Labov, William, Sharon Ash, and Charles Boberg. 2005. *The Atlas of North American English: Phonetics, Phonology, and Sound Change*. Berlin: Mouton de Gruyter.

Labov, William, and Joshua Waletzky. 1967. Narrative Analysis: Oral Versions of Personal Experience. In *Essays on the Verbal and Visual Arts*, edited by J. Helm, 12–44. Seattle: University of Washington Press.

Ladefoged, Peter. 1999. *Handbook of the International Phonetic Association: A Guide to the Use of the International Phonetic Alphabet*. Cambridge: Cambridge University Press.

Ladefoged, Peter. 2001a. *A Course in Phonetics*. 4th ed. Boston: Heinle and Heinle.

Ladefoged, Peter. 2001b. *Vowels and Consonants: An Introduction to the Sounds of Languages*. Malden, MA: Blackwell.

Lakoff, George. 1987. *Women, Fire, and Dangerous Things: What Categories Reveal about the Mind*. Chicago: University of Chicago Press.

Lakoff, George, and Mark Johnson. 1980. *Metaphors We Live By*. Chicago: University of Chicago Press.

Lakoff, Robin. 1975. *Language and Woman's Place*. New York: Octagon Books.

Lakoff, Robin. 1990. *Talking Power: The Politics of Language in Our Lives*. New York: Basic Books.

Lakoff, Robin. 2000. *The Language War*. Berkeley: University of California Press.

Lakoff, Robin, with Mary Bucholtz, ed. 2004. *Language and Woman's Place: Text and Commentaries*. Oxford: Oxford University Press.

Landau, Sidney I. 2001. *Dictionaries: The Art and Craft of Lexicography*. 2nd ed. Cambridge: Cambridge University Press.

Lanham, Richard A. 1991. *A Handlist of Rhetorical Terms*. 2d ed. Berkeley: University of California Press.

Lee, Jamie Shinhee. 2007. *I'm the illest fucka*: An Analysis of African American English in South Korean Hip Hop. *English Today* 23 (2): 54–60.

Lewis, C. S. 1960. *Studies in Words*. Cambridge: Cambridge University Press.

Lighter, J. E., ed. 1994– . *Random House Historical Dictionary of American Slang*. New York: Random House.

Linguistic Atlas of the Middle and South Atlantic States (LAMSAS). http://hyde.park.uga.edu/lamsas/.

Lippi-Green, Rosina. 1997. *English with an Accent: Language, Ideology, and Discrimination in the United States*. London: Routledge.

Lowth, Robert. 1762. *Short Introduction to English Grammar*. London.

Lust, Barbara C., and Claire Foley. 2004. *First Language Acquisition: The Essential Readings*. Malden, MA: Blackwell.

Lyons, John. 1977. *Semantics*. 2 vols. Cambridge: Cambridge University Press.

Macaulay, Ronald. 1994. *The Social Art: Language and Its Uses*. New York: Oxford University Press.

Mallinson, Christine, Becky Childs, Bridget Anderson, and Neal Hutcheson. 2006. If These Hills Could Talk (Smoky Mountains). In *American Voices*, edited by Walt Wolfram and Ben Ward, 22–28. Malden, MA: Blackwell.

Martel, Yann. 2001. *Life of Pi*. New York: Harcourt.

Matthews, P. H. 1974. *Morphology: An Introduction to the Theory of Word-Structure*. Cambridge: Cambridge University Press.

McArthur, Tom, ed. 1992. *Oxford Companion to the English Language*. Oxford: Oxford University Press.

McArthur, Tom. 2006. English World-wide in the Twentieth Century. In *The Oxford History of English*, edited by Lynda Mugglestone, 360–93. Oxford: Oxford University Press.

McCrum, Robert. 2010. *Globish: How the English Language Became the World's Language*. New York: W. W. Norton & Company.

McCrum, Robert, William Cran, and Robert MacNeil. 1986. *The Story of English*. New York: Penguin.

McEnery, Tony, and Andrew Wilson. 1996. *Corpus Linguistics*. Edinburgh: Edinburgh University Press.

McGurk, Harry, and John MacDonald. 1976. Hearing Lips and Seeing Voices. *Nature* 264: 746–48.

McKean, Erin. 2007. On Language: Corpus. *New York Times Sunday Magazine* (July 29): 14.

McMahon, April. 1994. *Understanding Language Change*. Cambridge: Cambridge University Press.

McMahon, April. 2002. *English Phonology*. Oxford: Oxford University Press.

McMillan, James B. 1980. Infixing and Interposing in English. *American Speech* 55: 163–83.

McMorris, Jenny. 2001. *The Warden of English: The Life of H. W. Fowler*. Oxford: Oxford University Press.

McWhorter, John. 1998. *Word on the Street: Debunking the Myth of a "Pure" Standard English*. Cambridge, MA: Perseus.

Mehler, Jacques, and Emmanuel Dupoux. 1994. *What Infants Know: The New Cognitive Science of Early Development*. Trans. Patsy Southgate. Cambridge, MA: Blackwell.

Mencken, H. L. 1962. *The American Language*. New York: Knopf.

Mendoza-Denton, Norma. 1995. Pregnant Pauses: Silence and Authority in the Anita Hill–Clarence Thomas Hearings. In *Gender Articulated: Language and the Socially Constructed Self*, edited by K. Hall and M. Bucholtz, 51–66. New York: London: Routledge.

Metcalf, Allan. 1999. *The World in So Many Words*. Boston: Houghton Mifflin.

Metcalf, Allan. 2000. *How We Talk: American Regional English Today*. Boston: Houghton Mifflin.

Metcalf, Allan. 2002. *Predicting New Words: The Secrets of Their Success*. Boston: Houghton Mifflin.

Metcalf, Allan A., and David K. Barnhart. 1997. *America in So Many Words*. Boston: Houghton Mifflin.

Meyer, Charles. 2002. *English Corpus Linguistics*. Cambridge: Cambridge University Press.

Middle English Dictionary. 1952–2001. Ed. Hans Kurath, Sherman M. Kuhn, Robert E. Lewis, and others. Ann Arbor: University of Michigan Press.

Miller, Hillis J. 2001. *Speech Acts in Literature*. Stanford: Stanford University Press.

Mills, Sara. 1995. *Feminist Stylistics*. London: Routledge.

Millward, C. M. 1996. *Biography of the English Language*. 2d ed. New York: Harcourt Brace Jovanovich.

Milroy, Lesley, and Matthew Gordon. 2003. *Sociolinguistics: Methods and Interpretation*. Malden, MA: Blackwell.

Mitchell, Bruce, and Fred C. Robinson. 1982. *Guide to Old English: Revised with Texts and Glossary*. Toronto: University of Toronto Press.

Montgomery, Michael, and Joseph S. Hall, eds. 2004. *Dictionary of Smoky Mountain English*. Knoxville: University of Tennessee Press.

Morenberg, Max. 1997. *Doing Grammar*. 2d ed. New York: Oxford University Press.

Morton, Herbert C. 1994. *The Story of Webster's Third: Philip Gove's Controversial Dictionary and Its Critics*. Cambridge: Cambridge University Press.

Mufwene, Salikoko. 2001. *The Ecology of Language Evolution*. Cambridge: Cambridge University Press.

Mufwene, Salikoko S., John R. Rickford, Guy Bailey, and John Baugh, eds. 1998. *African American English: Structure, History, and Use*. London: Routledge.

Mugglestone, Lynda. 2005. *Lost for Words: The Hidden History of the Oxford English Dictionary*. New Haven: Yale University Press.

Mülhaüsler, Peter. 1986. *Pidgin and Creole Linguistics*. Oxford: Blackwell.

Murray, K. M. Elisabeth. 1977. *Caught in the Web of Words: James Murray and the* Oxford English Dictionary. New Haven: Yale University Press.

Mustonoja, Tauno. 1960. *A Middle English Syntax*. Vol. 1. Helsinki: Société Néophilologique.

Muysken, Peter. 2000. *Bilingual Speech: A Typology of Code-Mixing*. Cambridge: Cambridge University Press.

Myers, Greg. 1989. The Pragmatics of Politeness in Scientific Articles. *Applied Linguistics* 10 (1): 1–35.

Myers-Scotton, Carol. 1993. *Duelling Languages: Grammatical Structure in Codeswitching*. Oxford: Oxford University Press.

Myers-Scotton, Carol. 2002. *Contact Linguistics: Bilingual Encounters and Grammatical Outcomes*. Oxford: Oxford University Press.

Nagle, Traci. 2007. The Productivity of Full Reduplication in Dialects of Modern English. Paper presented at Studies in the History of the English Language 5. Athens, Georgia.

Nevalainen, Terttu. 1999. Early Modern English Lexis and Semantics. In *Cambridge History of the English Language*. Vol. 3, *1476–1776*, edited by Roger Lass, 332–458. Cambridge: Cambridge University Press.

Nichols, Patricia. 1982. Black Women in the Rural South: Conservative and Innovative. In *American Minority Women in Sociolinguistic Perspective*, edited by B. L. Dubois and I. Crouch, 45–54. The Hague: Mouton.

Ninio, Anat, and Jerome Bruner. 1988 [1978]. The Achievement and Antecedents of Labeling. In *Child Language: A Reader*, edited by Margery B. Franklin and Sybil S. Barten, 36–49. New York: Oxford University Press.

Nunberg, Geoffrey. 1990. *The Linguistics of Punctuation*. Stanford, CA: Center for the Study of Language and Information.

O'Barr, William, and B. Atkins. 1980. Women's Language or Powerless Language? In *Women and Language in Literature and Society*, edited by S. McConnell-Ginet, R. Borker, and N. Furman, 93–109. New York: Praeger.

O'Connor, Patricia T. 1996. *Woe Is I: The Grammarphobe's Guide to Better English in Plain English*. New York: Putnam.

Official Scrabble Players Dictionary. 1996. 3d ed. Springfield, MA: Merriam-Webster.

Oxford American Desk Dictionary. 1998. Ed. Frank Abate. New York: Oxford University Press.

Oxford English Dictionary. 1989. 2d ed. Oxford: Clarendon Press. http://dictionary.oed.com/entrance.dtl/.

Özçalişkan, Seyda, and Susan Goldin-Meadow. 2005. Gesture Is at the Cutting Edge of Early Language Development. *Cognition* 96: B101–B113.

Parkes, Malcolm. 1993. *Pause and Effect: An Introduction to the History of Punctuation in the West*. Berkeley: University of California Press.

Pederson, Lee. 2001. Dialects. In *The Cambridge History of the English Language*. Vol. 6, *English in North America*, edited by J. Algeo, 253–90. Cambridge: Cambridge University Press.

Pei, Mario. 1967. *The Story of the English Language*. Rev. ed. Philadelphia: Lippincott.

Pei, Mario, and Frank Gaynor. 1954. *Dictionary of Linguistics*. New York: Philosophical Library.

Perales-Escudero, Moisés D. 2011. To Split or To Not Split: The Split Infinitive Past and Present. *Journal of English Linguistics* 39.

Perry, Theresa, and Lisa Delpit. 1998. *The Real Ebonics Debate: Power, Language, and the Education of African-American Children*. Boston: Beacon Press.

Pfaff, Carol W. 1979. Constraints on Language Mixing: Intrasentential Code-switching and Borrowing in Spanish/English. *Language* 55 (2) 291–318.

Pieces of Mind. Hosted by Alan Alda. 60 min. *Scientific American Frontiers* 7, 1997. Videocassette.

Pinker, Steven. 1994. *The Language Instinct*. New York: W. Morrow.

Pinker, Steven. 1995a. Language Acquisition. In *Language: An Invitation to Cognitive Science*, Vol. 1, 2d ed., edited by L. R. Gleitman and M. Liberman, 135–82. Cambridge, MA: MIT Press.

Pinker, Steven. 1995b. Why the Child Holded the Baby Rabbits: A Case Study in Language Acquisition. In *Language: An Invitation to Cognitive Science*, Vol. 1, 2d ed., edited by L. R. Gleitman and M. Liberman, 107–33. Cambridge, MA: MIT Press.

Pinker, Steven, and Ray Jackendoff. 2005. The Faculty of Language: What's Special about It? *Cognition* 95: 201–36.

Pop vs. Soda Controversy. http://www.popvssoda.com.

Poplack, Shana. 1980. Sometimes I'll Start a Sentence in Spanish Y TERMINO EN ESPAÑOL: Toward a Typology of Code-switching. *Linguistics* 18: 581–618.

Poplack, Shana. 1981. Syntactic Structure and Social Function in Code-switching. In *Latino Language and Communicative Behavior*, edited by R. P. Duran, 169–84. Norwood, NJ: Ablex.

Pratt, Mary Louise. 1977. *Toward a Speech Act Theory of Literary Discourse*. Bloomington: Indiana University Press.

Preminger, Alex, and T. V. F. Brogan, eds., and Frank J. Warnke, O. B. Hardison Jr., and Earl Miner, associate eds. 1993. *The New Princeton Encyclopedia of Poetry and Poetics*. Princeton, NJ: Princeton University Press.

Preston, Dennis. 2000. Some Plain Facts about Americans and Their Language. *American Speech* 75 (4): 398–401.

Preston, Dennis. 2003. Presidential Address: Where Are the Dialects of American English at Anyhow? *American Speech* 78 (3): 235–54.

Preston, Dennis, and Gregory C. Robinson. 2005. Dialect Perception and Attitudes to Variation. In *Clinical Sociolinguistics*, edited by M. J. Ball, 133–49. Oxford: Blackwell.

Priestley, Joseph. 1969 [1761]. *Rudiments of English Grammar*. English Linguistics 1500–1800: A Collection of Facsimile Reprints 210, edited by R. C. Alston. Menston, UK: Scolar Press.

Queen, Robin M. 1997. "I Don't Speak Spritch": Locating Lesbian Language. In *Queerly Phrased: Language, Gender, and Sexuality*, edited by A. Livia and K. Hall, 233–56. New York: Oxford University Press.

Quine, W. V. O. 1969. *Ontological Relativity and Other Essays*. New York: Columbia University Press.

Quirk, Randolph, and Sidney Greenbaum. 1990. *A Student's Grammar of the English Language*. London: Longman.

Quirk, Randolph, Sidney Greenbaum, Geoffrey Leech, and Jan Svartvik. 1985. *A Comprehensive Grammar of the English Language*. London: Longman.

Random House Dictionary of the English Language. 1966. Ed. Jess Stein, Laurence Urdang, and others. New York: Random House.

Read, Allen Walker. 1935. The Membership of Proposed American Academies. *American Literature* 7: 145–65.

Read, Allen Walker. 2002. *Milestones in the History of English in America*. Ed. R. W. Bailey. Durham, NC : Published for the American Dialect Society by Duke University Press.

Rhodes, Hillary. 2007. Musical Grammar Tips: Word Gal and Music Guy Weigh in on Songs That Are Grammatically Challenged. *Jackson Citizen Patriot* (January 21): D1–2.

Rickford, John R., Isabelle Buchstaller, Thomas Wasow, and Arnold Zwicky. 2007. Intensive and Quotative *all*: Something Old, Something New. *American Speech* 82 (1): 3–31.

Rickford, John R., and F. McNair-Knox. 1994. Addressee- and Topic-Influenced Style Shift: A Quantitative Sociolinguistic Study. In *Sociolinguistic Perspectives on Register*, edited by D. Biber and E. Finegan, 235–76. New York: Oxford University Press.

Rickford, John R., and Russell J. Rickford. 2000. *Spoken Soul: The Story of Black English*. New York: Wiley.

Robins, R. H. 1997. *A Short History of Linguistics*. 4th ed. New York: Longman.

Rodale, J. I. 1947. *The Synonym Finder*. Emmaus, PA: Rodale Press.

Roget, Peter Mark. 1852. *Thesaurus of English Words and Phrases*. Essex: Longman.

Romaine, Suzanne. 1988. *Pidgin and Creole Languages*. London: Longman.

Romaine, Suzanne. 2001. Contact with Other Languages. In *The Cambridge History of the English Language*. Vol. 6, *English in North America*, edited by J. Algeo, 154–83. Cambridge: Cambridge University Press.

Rothstein, Edward. 2000. Is a Word's Definition in the Mind of the User? *New York Times* (November 25).

Rubin, Donald L. 1992. Nonlanguage Factors Affecting Undergraduates' Judgements of Non-native English-Speaking Teaching Assistants. *Research in Higher Education* 33 (4): 511–31.

Saeed, John I. 2003. *Semantics*. 2d ed. Malden, MA: Blackwell.

Safire, William. 2003. On Language: Miffy Prometheus. *New York Times Sunday Magazine* (July 6).

Safire, William. 2006. On Language: Incorrections. *New York Times Sunday Magazine* (December 10): 24.

Sandler, Wendy, Irit Meir, Carol Padden, and Mark Aronoff. 2005. The Emergence of Grammar: Systematic Structure in a New Language. *Proceedings of the National Academy of Sciences* 102 (7): 2661–65.

Sapir, Edward. 1921. *Language: An Introduction to the Study of Speech*. New York: Harcourt.

Sapir, Edward. 1929. The Status of Linguistics as a Science. *Language* 5: 207–14.

Saussure, Ferdinand, de. 1983. *Course in General Linguistics*. Ed. Charles Bally and Albert Sechehaye, with the collaboration of Albert Riedlinger. Translated and annotated by Roy Harris. London: Duckworth.

Saussure, Ferdinand, de. 2006. *Writings in General Linguistics*, translated and further edited by Carol Sanders and Matthew Pires from the French edition by Simon Bouquet and Rudolf Engler. New York: Oxford University Press.

Savage-Rumbaugh, Sue, Stuart G. Shanker, and Talbot J. Taylor. 1998. *Apes, Language, and the Human Mind*. New York: Oxford University Press.

Sawin, Patricia E. 1999. Gender, Context and the Narrative Construction of Identity: Rethinking Models of "Women's Narrative." In *Reinventing Identities*: *The Gendered Self in Discourse*, edited by M. Bucholtz, A. C. Liang, and L. Sutton, 241–58. Oxford: Oxford University Press.

Schane, Sanford. Homepage for Linguistics 105: Law and Language. http://ling.ucsd.edu/courses/ling105/illoc.htm.

Schiffrin, Deborah. 1994. *Approaches to Discourse*. Oxford: Blackwell.

Schiffrin, Deborah, Deborah Tannen, and Heidi E. Hamilton, eds. 2001. *The Handbook of Discourse Analysis*. Malden, MA: Blackwell.

Schilling-Estes, Natalie. 1998. Self-conscious Speech on Ocracoke English. *Language in Society* 27 (1): 53–83.

Schneider, Edgar, and Bernd Kortmann, eds. 2004. *A Handbook of Varieties of English: A Multimedia Reference Tool*. New York: Mouton de Gruyter.

Scragg, D. G. 1974. *A History of English Spelling*. New York: Barnes and Noble.

Searle, John. 1969. *Speech Acts: An Essay in the Philosophy of Language*. London: Cambridge University Press.

Secret of the Wild Child. Written, produced, and directed by Jane Garmon. 60 min. Boston: WGBH, 1994. Videocassette.

Sedaris, David. 1997. *Naked.* Boston: Little, Brown.

Sheidlower, Jesse. 2009. *The F-Word.* 3d ed. New York: Oxford University Press.

Skeat, Walter W. 1910. *An Etymological Dictionary of the English Language.* New ed. Oxford: Clarendon Press.

Sledd, James. 1965. On Not Teaching English Usage. *English Journal* 54: 698–703.

Sledd, James H., and Wilma R. Ebbitt, eds. 1962. *Dictionaries and That Dictionary.* Chicago: Scott Foresman.

Smith, Adam. 1776. *An Inquiry into the Nature and Causes of the Wealth of Nations.* London: W. Strahan and T. Cadell.

Smitherman, Geneva. 1977. *Talkin and Testifyin: The Language of Black America.* Boston: Houghton Mifflin.

Smitherman, Geneva. 1991. "What Is Africa to Me?": Language, Ideology, and African American. *American Speech* 66 (2): 115–32.

Smitherman, Geneva. 1998. Ebonics, *King*, and Oakland: Some Folk Don't Believe Fat Meat Is Greasy. *Journal of English Linguistics* 26 (2): 97–107.

Smitherman, Geneva. 2000a. *Black Talk: Words and Phrases from the Hood to the Amen Corner.* Rev. ed. Boston: Houghton Mifflin.

Smitherman, Geneva. 2000b. *Talkin That Talk: Language, Culture, and Education in African America.* London: Routledge.

Spark, Muriel. 1962. *A Muriel Spark Trio.* Philadelphia: Lippincott.

Stainton, Robert J. 2004. The Pragmatics of Non-sentences. In *The Handbook of Pragmatics*, edited by Laurance R. Horn and Gregory Ward, 266–87. Malden, MA: Blackwell.

Stockwell, Robert, and Donka Minkova. 2001. *English Words: History and Structure.* Cambridge: Cambridge University Press.

Stotko, Elaine M., and Margaret Troyer. 2007. A New Gender-Neutral Pronoun in Baltimore, Maryland: A Preliminary Study. *American Speech* 82 (3): 262–79.

Strawson, P. F. 1965. On Referring. In *Classics of Analytical Philosophy*, edited by A. R. Ammerman, 315–34. New York: McGraw-Hill.

Swift, Jonathan. 1969 [1712]. *A Proposal for Correcting, Improving and Ascertaining the English Tongue.* English Linguistics 1500–1800: A Collection of Facsimile Reprints 213, edited by R. C. Alston. Menston, UK: Scolar Press.

Takekuro, Makiko. 2000. Longitudinal Analysis of Japanese Women's Language Use. Paper presented at the MLA Annual Convention, Washington, DC, December.

Talmy, Leonard. 2000. *Toward a Cognitive Semantics.* 2 vols. Cambridge, MA: MIT Press.

Tannen, Deborah. 1986. *That's Not What I Meant!: How Conversational Style Makes or Breaks Your Relations with Others.* New York: Morrow.

Tao, Hongyin. 2007. A Corpus-based Investigation of *Absolutely* and Related Phenomena in Spoken American English. *Journal of English Linguistics* 35 (1): 5–29.

TELSUR Project, University of Pennsylvania. http://www.ling.upenn.edu/phono_atlas/home.html.

Thomason, Sarah Grey, and Terrence Kaufman. 1988. *Language Contact, Creolization, and Genetic Linguistics.* Berkeley: University of California Press.

Timm, Lenora A. 1975. Spanish-English Code-switching: El Porqué [sic] and How-Not-To. *Romance Philology* 28: 473–487.

Tolkien, J. R. R. 1934. Chaucer as Philologist. *Transactions of the Philological Society*: 1–70.

Tolkien, J. R. R. 1937. *Beowulf: The Monsters and the Critics.* London: H. Milford.

Tolkien, J. R. R. 1963. English and Welsh. In *Angles and Britons: O'Donnell Lectures*, 1–41. Cardiff: University of Cardiff Press.

Toolan, Michael. 1996. *Language in Literature: An Introduction to Stylistics.* London: Arnold.

Trager, George L., and Henry Lee Smith. 1951. *An Outline of English Structure*. Studies in Linguistics, Occasional Papers no. 3. Norman, OK: Battenburg Press.

Trott, Kate, Sushie Dobbinson, and Patrick Griffiths, eds. 2004. *The Child Language Reader*. London: Routledge.

Trudgill, Peter. 1983. *On Dialect: Social and Geographical Perspectives*. Oxford: Blackwell.

Trudgill, Peter, and Jean Hannah. 1994. *International English: A Guide to Varieties of Standard English*. London: E. Arnold.

Truss, Lynne. 2003. *Eats, Shoots & Leaves: A Zero Tolerance Approach to Punctuation*. New York: Gotham.

Underhill, Robert. 1988. Like Is, Like, Focus. *American Speech* 63: 234–46.

van Dijk, Teun A, ed. 1997. *Discourse as Structure and Process*. 2 volumes. London: SAGE.

Vargha-Khadem, Faraneh, Lucinda J. Carr, Elizabeth Isaacs, Edward Brett, Christopher Adams, and Mortimer Mishkin. 1997. Onset of Speech after Left Hemispherectomy in a Nine-Year-Old Boy. *Brain* 120: 159–82.

Wallace, David Foster. 2001. Tense Present: Democracy, English, and the Wars over Usage. *Harper's Magazine* (April): 39–58.

Ward, William. 1967 [1765]. *An Essay on Grammar*. English Linguistics 1500–1800: A Collection of Facsimile Reprints 15, edited by R. C. Alston. Menston, UK: Scolar Press.

Wardhaugh, Ronald. 1999. *Proper English: Myths and Misunderstandings about Language*. Malden, MA: Blackwell.

Wardhaugh, Ronald. 1995. *Understanding English Grammar: A Linguistic Approach*. Oxford: Blackwell.

Wassink, Alicia Beckford. 2005. "My Teacher Says . . .": Mastery of English and the Creole Learner. In *Language in the Schools: Integrating Linguistic Knowledge into K–12 Teaching*, edited by A. Lobeck and K. Denham, 55–70. Mahwah, NJ: Lawrence Erlbaum.

Wassink, Alicia Beckford, and Judy Dyer. 2004. Language Ideology and the Transmission of Phonological Change: Changing Indexicality in Two Situations of Language Contact. *Journal of English Linguistics* 32 (1): 3–30.

Webster, Noah. 1828. *An American Dictionary of the English Language*. New York: S. Converse.

Webster, Noah. 1789. *Dissertations on the English Language*. Boston.

Webster's New International Dictionary of the English Language. 1934. 2nd ed, unabridged. Ed. W. A. Neilson, Thomas A. Knott, and others. Springfield, MA: G. and C. Merriam.

Webster's Third New International Dictionary of the English Language. 1961. Ed. Philip B. Gove and others. Springfield, MA: G. and C. Merriam.

Wei, Li. 2002. "What do you want me to say?": On the Conversation Analysis Approach to Bilingual Interaction. *Language in Society* 31: 159–80.

West, Candace, and Don H. Zimmerman. 1998 [1977]. Women's Place in Everyday Talk. In *Language and Gender: A Reader*, edited by J. Coates, 165–75. Oxford: Blackwell.

Wetzel, Patricia. 1988. Are "Powerless" Communication Strategies the Japanese Norm? *Language in Society* 17 (4): 555–64.

Whitman, Walt. 1969 [1885]. Slang in America. In *The English Language: Essays by Linguists and Men of Letters, 1858–1964*, edited by W. F. Bolton and D. Crystal, 54–58. Cambridge: Cambridge University Press.

Whorf, Benjamin. 1956. Grammatical Categories. In *Language, Thought, and Reality*, edited by J. B. Carroll, 87–101. Cambridge: MIT Press.

Wierzbicka, Anna. 1992. *Semantics, Culture, and Cognition: Universal Concepts in Culture-Specific Configurations*. New York: Oxford University Press.

Williams, Alex. 2007. (-: Just Between You and Me ;-). *New York Times* (July 29), http://www.nytimes.com/2007/07/29/fashion/29emoticon.html.

Williams, Edwin. 1994. *Thematic Structure in Syntax*. Cambridge, MA: The MIT Press.

Williams, Joseph M. 1997. *Style: Ten Lessons in Clarity and Grace.* 5th ed. New York: Addison-Wesley.

Winchester, Simon. 1998. *The Professor and the Madman: A Tale of Murder, Insanity, and the Making of the* Oxford English Dictionary. New York: HarperCollins.

Winchester, Simon. 2003. *The Meaning of Everything: The Story of the* Oxford English Dictionary. Oxford: Oxford University Press.

Wolford, Tanya, and Keelan Evans. 2007. Puerto Ricans' Use of AAE and the Emergence of an Urban English Dialect. Paper presented at the Annual Meeting of the Linguistic Society of America. Anaheim, California.

Wolfram, Walt. 1969. *A Sociolinguistic Description of Detroit Negro Speech.* Washington, DC: Center for Applied Linguistics.

Wolfram, Walt. 1991. *Dialects and American English.* Englewood Cliffs, NJ: Prentice Hall.

Wolfram, Walt, and Donna Christian. 1976. *Appalachian Speech.* Arlington, VA: Center for Applied Linguistics.

Wolfram, Walt, and Natalie Schilling-Estes. 1998. *American English: Dialects and Variation.* [2d ed, 2005.] Malden, MA: Blackwell.

Worcester, Joseph. 1860. *A Comprehensive Dictionary of the English Language.* Boston: Swan, Brewer, and Tileston.

Wright, Joseph, and Elizabeth Mary Wright. 1928. *An Elementary Middle English Grammar.* 2nd ed. London: Oxford University Press.

Wright, Laura, ed. 2000. *The Development of Standard English, 1300–1800: Theories, Descriptions, Conflicts.* Cambridge: Cambridge University Press.

Wu, Siew Mei. 2007. The use of Engagement Resources in High- and Low-Rated Undergraduate Geography Essays. *Journal of English for Academic Purposes* 6: 254–71.

Zwicky, Arnold M., and Geoffrey K. Pullum. 1983. Cliticization vs. Inflection: English *N'T. Language* 59: 502–13.

Credits

Chapter 1, page 1: Reproduced by permission of The Huntington Library, San Marino, California; **Chapter 1, page 9:** Keystone/Getty Images; **Chapter 1, page 16:** Courtesy Great Ape Trust of Iowa; **Chapter 1, page 18:** Savage-Rumbaugh, Sue, Stuart G. Shanker, and Talbot J. Taylor; **Chapter 1, page 19:** D. Robert and Lorri Franz/Corbis; **Chapter 1, page 24:** Aitchison, Jean. 2001. *Language Change: Progress or Decay? 3E.* Cambridge: Cambridge University Press; **Chapter 1, page 25:** Wallace, David Foster. 2001. "Tense Present: Democracy, English, and the Wars over Usage," *Harper's Magazine* (April): 39–58; **Chapter 2, page 31:** Colleen Harrington/zefa/Corbis; **Chapter 2, page 33:** Safire, William. December 10, 2006. "On Language." *The New York Times Magazine*; **Chapter 2, page 48:** "Ain't" entry from *Merriam-Webster's Collegiate Dictionary,* 11th Ed. Copyright © 2003 by G & C, Merriam: Springfield, MA. Reprinted with permission; **Chapter 2, page 51:** Fowler, H.W. 1926. *A Dictionary of Modern English Usage.* Oxford: Oxford University Press; **Chapter 2, pages 51–52:** Follett, Wilson. 1966. *Modern American Usage: A Guide.* New York: Hill and Wang; **Chapter 2, page 56:** Table from "A Corpus-Based Investigation of Absolutely and Related Phenomena in Spoken American English" by Hongyin Tao, from *Journal of English Linguistics,* March 2007 35.1. Copyright © 2007 by SAGE PUBLICATIONS INC. JOURNALS. Reproduced with permission of SAGE PUBLICATIONS INC. JOURNALS in the format Presentation via Copyright Clearance Center; **Chapter 2, page 58:** Courtesy of Dennis Preston; **Chapter 3, page 62:** J Group Photo; **Chapter 3, Figure 3.1, page 66:** "Different Parts of the Vocal Tract Are Involved in the Production of Different Sounds," from *Speech Physiology, Speech Perception, and Acoustic Phonetics* by Philip Lieberman and S.E. Blumstein. Copyright © 1988 by Cambridge University Press. Reprinted with the permission of Cambridge University Press; **Chapter 3, Figure 3.2, page 76:** "Cot and Caught Dialectic Map of U.S." from the *Atlas of North American English* by William Labov, Sharon Ash, and Charles Boberg. Copyright © 2005 by Walter de Gruyter GmbH & Co. KG D-10785 Berlin. Reprinted with permission; **Chapter 3, Figure 3.3, page 76:** "Pin and Pen Dialectic Map of U.S." from the *Atlas of North American English* by William Labov, Sharon Ash, and Charles Boberg. Copyright © 2005 by Walter de Gruyter GmbH & Co. KG D-10785 Berlin. Reprinted with permission; **Chapter 3, page 78:** *Left:* Darrell Gulin/Corbis; *Right:* Steve Kaufman/Corbis; **Chapter 4, page 98:** Rob Colvin/Getty Images; **Chapter 4, page 115:** Metcalf, Allan. 2002. *Predicting New Words: The Secrets of Their Success.* Boston: Houghton Mifflin; **Chapter 4, page 117:** Table regarding "New Words, 1941–1991 (% by types)," from *Fifty Years Among the New Words: A Dictionary of Neologisms* by John Algeo and Adele S. Algeo. Copyright © 1991 by Cambridge University Press. Reprinted with the permission of Cambridge University Press; **Chapter 4, page 120:** Sledd, James, 1965 "On Not Teaching English Usage"; **Chapter 4, pages 125–127:** Words and definitions taken from 2002–2009 "Words of the Year," from American Dialect Society, http://americandilect.org/index.php/amerdial/catergories/C178/. Copyright © 2002–2009 by the American Dialect Society. All rights reserved; **Chapter 5, page 128:** © 1986 Watterson. Dist. by UNIVERSAL PRESS SYNDICATE. Reprinted with permission. All rights reserved; **Chapter 5, page 145:** Fotostock; **Chapter 5, Table 5.5, page 149:** Pgs. 213–216, adapted from *Oxford English Grammar* edited by Sidney Greenbaum. Copyright © 1996 by Oxford University Press. Reprinted with permission; **Chapter 6, page 163:** Dale C. Spartas/Corbis; **Chapter 6, page 167:** Jeff Titcomb/Alamy; **Chapter 6, Table 6.1, page 173:** Phrase and Clause Functions adapted from material by Mark Canada and University of North Carolina at Pembroke, from http://www.uncp.edu/home/canada/work/markport/language/aspects/

spg2003/05syntax.htm; **Chapter 6, page 182:** Garner, Bryan. 1998. *A Dictionary of Modern American Usage.* New York: Oxford University Press; **Chapter 6, page 196:** Dennis Galante/Corbis; **Chapter 6, page 200:** Green, Lisa. 2002. *African American English: A Linguistic Introduction.* Cambridge: Cambridge University Press; **Chapter 7, page 202:** Mary Evans Picture Library; **Chapter 7, page 210:** Strawson, P.F. 1965. On Referring. In *Classical Analytical Philosophy,* edited by A. R. Ammerman, 315–334. New York: McGraw-Hill; **Chapter 7, page 211:** Quine, W.V.O. 1969. *Ontological Relativity and Other Essays.* New York: Columbia University Press; **Chapter 7, page 217:** left to right: Roy Morsch/Corbis; Corbis; Roy Morsch/Corbis; **Chapter 7, pages 219–220:** *The American Heritage Dictionary of the English Language,* 2000; **Chapter 7, pages 228–229:** Sapir, Edward. "The Status of Linguistics as a Science." *Language* 5: 207–214; **Chapter 7, page 229:** Gill, Jerry, 1997. *If a Chimpanzee Could Talk and Other Reflections on Language Acquisition.* Tucson: University of Arizona Press; **Chapter 7, page 230:** *The American Heritage Dictionary of the English Language,* 2000; **Chapter 7, pages 231 and 232:** Smitherman, Geneva. 1991. " 'What Is Africa to Me?': Language, Ideology, and *African American*." *American Speech* 66 (2): 115–32; **Chapter 7, page 232:** Cameron, Deborah. 1995. *Verbal Hygiene.* London: Routledge; **Chapter 8, page 236:** Chuck Savage/Corbis; **Chapter 8, page 239:** Department of Philosophy, University of California at Berkeley; **Chapter 8, Table 8.1, page 240:** "Illocutionary Acts," adapted from material by Sanford Schane, from *Homepage for Linguistics 105: Law and Language*; http://ling.ucsd.edu.edu/courses/ling105/illoc.htm. Reprinted with permission of the author; **Chapter 8, page 250:** Courtesy of Robin Lakoff; **Chapter 8, page 253:** Allende, Isabel. 2003. *My Invented Country: A Nostalgic Journey through Chile.* Trans. Margaret Sayers Peden. New York: Harper-Collins; **Chapter 8, page 261:** left to right: Michael Jang/Getty Images; Ewing Galloway/Index Stock; **Chapter 8, pages 261–262:** Eckert, Penelope. 2002. *Linguistic Variation as Social Practice: The Linguistic Construction of Identity in Belten High.* Malden, MA: Blackwell; **Chapter 8, page 265:** Tannen, Deborah. 1986. *That's Not What I Meant!: How Conversational Style Makes or Breaks Your Relations with Others.* New York: William Morrow & Co; **Chapter 8, page 273:** Excerpt from *Language and Gender: A Reader* by Jennifer Coates. Copyright © 1989 by Jennifer Coates. Reproduced with permission of Blackwell Publishing Ltd.; **Chapter 9, page 274:** Archives Charmet/The Bridgeman Art Library International; **Chapter 9, page 283:** Sedaris, David. 1997. *Naked.* Boston: Little, Brown & Co.; **Chapter 9, page 294:** Foster, Dan. 2000. *Author Unknown: Tales of a Literary Detective.* New York: Henry Holt & Co.; **Chapter 9, pages 295–296:** "anyone lived in a pretty how town." Copyright © 1940, 1968, 1991 by the Trustees for E.E. Cummings Trust, from *Complete Poems: 1904–1962* by E.E. Cummings, edited by George J. Firmage. Used by permission of Liveright Publishing Corporation; **Chapter 9, page 298:** Jakobsen, Roman. 1987. *Linguistics and Poetics. In Language and Literature,* edited by K. Pomorska and S. Rudy, 62–94. Cambridge, MA: MIT Press; **Chapter 9, page 299:** Courtesy MIT Museum; **Chapter 9, page 301:** "On a Tree Fallen Across the Road" from *The Poetry of Robert Frost* edited by Edward Connery Lathem. Copyright 1923, 1969 by Henry Holt and Company. Copyright 1951 by Robert Frost. Reprinted by permission of Henry Holt and Company, LLC; **Chapter 9, pages 306–307:** Tannen, Deborah. 1986. *That's Not What I Meant!: How Conversational Style Makes or Breaks Your Relations with Others.* New York: William Morrow & Co.; **Chapter 10, page 309:** Leslie Carver/UC San Diego Developmental Cognitive and Social Neuroscience Lab; **Chapter 10, Figure 10.1, page 314:** From *The Human Body: An Illustrated Guide to Its Structure, Function, and Disorders.* Ed. Charles Clayman (New York: Dorling Kindersley, 1995), p. 66. Reprinted by permission; **Chapter 10, page 317:** Mr. Potato Head ® & © 2005 Hasbro, Inc.; **Chapter 10, page 320:** A.N. Meltzoff & M.K. Moore, "Imitation of facial and manual gestures by human neonates." *Science,* 1977, 198, 75–78; **Chapter 10, Table 10.1, page 324:** Table 28 "Constituent Combinations That Occur and Constituents That Are Omitted from the Main Verb Paradigm," p. 205 reprinted by permission of the publisher from *A First Language: The Early Stages* by Roger Brown, Cambridge, Mass.: Harvard University Press. Copyright © 1973 by the President and Fellows of Harvard College; **Chapter 10, Table 10.2, page 325:** Table: "Acquisition of Words and Word Meanings for Children," from *How Children Learn the Meaning of Words* by Paul Bloom. Copyright © 2000 by Massachusetts Insititute of Technology, by permission of The MIT Press; **Chapter 10, page 325:**

Altmann, Gerry. 1997. *The Ascent of Babel: An Exploration of Language, Mind, and Understanding.* Oxford: Oxford University Press; **Chapter 10, page 327:** Altmann, Gerry. 1997. *The Ascent of Babel: An Exploration of Language, Mind, and Understanding.* Oxford: Oxford University Press; **Chapter 10, page 328:** Gopnik, Alison, Andrew N. Meltzoff, and Patricia K. Kuhl. 1999. *The Scientist in the Crib: What Early Learning Tells Us about the Mind.* New York: Harper Collins; **Chapter 10, page 331:** Courtesy Ann Senghas/Columbia University; **Chapter 10, page 335:** Carroll, David. 1999. *Psychology of Language,* 3rd ed. Pacific Grove, CA: Brooks/Cole; **Chapter 10, page 338:** International Dyslexia Association; **Chapter 10, page 338:** Altmann, Gerry. 1997. *The Ascent of Babel: An Exploration of Language, Mind, and Understanding.* Oxford: Oxford University Press; **Chapter 10, page 339:** Interview for the Academy of Achievement, 1994; **Chapter 10, page 343:** Clark, Eve. 1998. Morphology in Language Acquisition. In *The Handbook of Morphology,* edited by A. Spencer and A.M. Swicky, 374–389. Oxford: Blackwell; **Chapter 10, page 343:** Pinker, *Child Language: A Reader,* 1998; **Chapter 11, page 346:** J Group Photo; **Chapter 11, Figure 11.1, page 352:** "The Northeast New England to New York City" from the *Atlas of North American English* by William Labov, Sharon Ash, and Charles Boberg. Copyright © 2005 by Walter de Gruyter GmbH & Co. KG D-10785 Berlin. Reprinted with permission; **Chapter 11, Figure 11.2, page 353:** Figure 1 "The DARE Map of the United States," Volume 1, page xxiv reprinted by permission of the publisher from *Dictionary of American Regional English, Volume I: A–C,* edited by Frederic G. Cassidy, Cambridge, Mass.: The Belknap Press of Harvard University Press. Copyright © 1985 by the President and Fellows of Harvard College; **Chapter 11, Figure 11.3, page 353:** Map entry for "Dropped Egg," reprinted by permission of the publisher from *Dictionary of American Regional English, Volume II: D–H,* edited by Frederic G. Cassidy, Cambridge, Mass.: The Belknap Press of Harvard University Press. Copyright © 1991 by the President and Fellows of Harvard College; **Chapter 11, Figure 11.4, page 354:** "Whippletree," from *A Word Geography of the Eastern United States* by Hans Kurath. Copyright © 1950 by The University of Michigan Press. Reprinted with permission; **Chapter 11, Figure 11.5, page 355:** Map courtesy of Gregory Plumb and East Central University, Department of Cartography & Geography; **Chapter 11, page 356:** Department of Linguistics, University of Pennsylvania; **Chapter 11, page 357:** Labov, William. 1982. Objectivity and Commitment in Linguistic Science. *Language in Society* 11: 165–201; **Chapter 11, Figure 11.7, page 364:** Figure from page 296 from *Language and Gender* by Penelope Eckert and Sally McConnell-Ginet. Copyright © 2003 by Cambridge University Press. Reprinted with the permission of Cambridge University Press; **Chapter 11, page 368:** Wassink, Alicia Beckford. " 'My Teacher Says . . .': Mastery of English and the Creole Learner." In *Language in the Schools: Integrating Linguistic Knowledge into K–12 Teaching,* edited by A. Lobeck and K. Denham. Mahwah, NJ: Lawrence Erlbaum; **Chapter 11, Figure 11.8, page 369:** Courtesy of Dennis Preston; **Chapter 11, Figure 11.9, page 369:** Courtesy of Dennis Preston; **Chapter 11, Figure 11.10, page 370:** Courtesy of Dennis Preston; **Chapter 12, page 377:** Fox/Photofest; **Chapter 12, Figure 12.2, page 395:** "The Major Dialect Areas of American English" from the *Atlas of North American English* by William Labov, Sharon Ash, and Charles Boberg. Copyright © 2005 by Walter de Gruyter GmbH & Co. KG D-10785 Berlin. Reprinted with permission; **Chapter 12, Figure 12.4, page 401:** "The Northern California Vowel Shift" by Penelope Eckert. Copyright © 2004 by Penelope Eckert. Reprinted with permission of the author; **Chapter 12, page 412:** Courtesy Michigan State University; **Chapter 13, page 417:** Chris Collins/zefa/Corbis; **Chapter 13, page 421:** South West Images Scotland/Alamy; **Chapter 13, page 424:** Giraudon/Art Resource, NY; **Chapter 13, page 432:** Bettmann/Corbis; **Chapter 13, page 440:** Bettmann/Corbis; **Chapter 13, page 444:** HIP/Art Resource, NY; **Chapter 14, page 456:** Tim Boyle/Getty Images; **Chapter 14, page 465:** *The Daily Telegraph,* 1994; **Chapter 14, Figure 14.1, page 472:** "The Three Circles of English," from *The Future of English?* adapted by David Graddol. Copyright © 1997, 2000 by The British Council. Reprinted with permission; **Chapter 14, Figure 14.2, page 473:** Adapted from David Graddol, *The Future of English?* © 1997, 2000 by The British Council. Used with permission; **Chapter 14, page 476:** Goh, Colin. April 2002. "Save Our Singlish Campaign"; **Chapter 14, page 477:** Kathy McLaughlin/The Image Works; **Chapter 14, page 477:** Bailey, Richard W. 1991. *Images of English.* Ann Arbor: University of Michigan Press.

Index